PSYCHOANALYTIC

PIONEERS

PSYCHOANALYTIC PIONEERS

EDITED BY

FRANZ ALEXANDER

SAMUEL EISENSTEIN

&

MARTIN GROTJAHN

BASIC BOOKS, INC.

PUBLISHERS

NEW YORK LONDON

Library of Congress Catalog Card Number: 66–11692
Manufactured in the United States of America
DESIGNED BY VINCENT TORRE

Preface

The history of psychoanalysis has recently received profound attention. Most historical work has centered around the life, the personality, and the achievement of Sigmund Freud, culminating in Ernest Jones's monumental biography of the man. Other research has reconstructed the development of centers of psychoanalysis, for example, The Berlin Institute or those in Chicago, New York, and Boston. *The Minutes of the Vienna Psychoanalytic Society*, recently published, vividly describe the life of that Society and the men around Freud in the early days. These minutes have given insight into the atmosphere out of which psychoanalysis grew. However, biographies of the great men in psychoanalysis are practically nonexistent: information has been limited to brief obituaries in the professional journals, and analytic autobiographies are rare and fragmentary.

Under these circumstances, writing a history of the pioneers in psychoanalysis and a description of pioneering in the psychoanalytic movement was a temptation and a challenge, especially a history that would present a genetic picture of psychoanalysis during its development. The history of the men and women who have made psychoanalysis what it is today ought to be written *now*, we felt, although much of the correspondence between Freud and his early followers still awaits publication and is bound to have immediate and important impact on any such study. Freud and Ferenczi's correspondence, containing more than two thousand letters, has been read by a few trusted friends. Freud's correspondence with Karl Abraham—almost 360 letters—has been published by Basic Books, Inc. The unique correspondence among Freud, Ferenczi, and Georg Groddeck is extant, but it has been studied incompletely. The letters exchanged between Freud and Ludwig Binswanger and between Freud and Oskar Pfister have recently been published. Many other letters of the untiring, letter-writing Freud are being collected by the Sigmund Freud Archives and are not available at this time.

The editors decided, however, not to delay publication of this book any further, despite the unavailability of important historical source material. Right now, we still have living contact with the early times, be it directly or indirectly, through many of the authors who have contributed to this book. We stand at an advantageous distance from these early times for seeing the growth of psychoanalysis and the contributions to it by the pioneers; we are close enough to get first-hand impressions and reports, and far enough away to avoid the danger of uncritical hero worship or partisanship. Many of the early pioneers are portrayed here by their former students, who themselves have reached eminence in our field. It is significant for the spirit of pioneering that those who first contributed to our knowledge were also inspired teachers and continued to keep a spirit of scientific inquiry alive in our ranks.

These essays are not limited to historical descriptions of psychoanalytic pioneers and their contributions. We also give some evaluation of their contributions to the evolution of psychoanalytic thought. We have tried to describe those who developed psychoanalysis as a science, as a method of investigation, as a technique of treatment, and as an organization.

Psychoanalysis was created by Freud and his early followers. A pioneer in psychoanalysis is a person who, having recognized the truth and importance of Freud's teachings, devoted his life to the advance and spread of our knowledge through research and teaching. We have dealt with the great teachers and clinicians in psychoanalysis.

We are aware of the incompleteness and deficiencies of this book. Some may look in vain for their personal friends or may differ with the evaluation given by the many different authors included. Our work will not be futile if such controversial profiles should inspire further investigation.

Some omissions will be obvious to all. These are due to our inability to obtain adequate biographies or to other circumstances beyond the editors' control. They neither constitute intentional omissions nor imply negative evaluation.

The pioneers are presented according to their appearance on the psychoanalytic stage. A chronological order could not always be followed because of inaccurate historical reporting, and the editors have preferred a meaningful rather than a strictly historical order.

Some pioneering efforts in the field of psychoanalysis have not been the sole responsibility of a single man, but have rested instead on the shoulders of several men working together. We have attempted to describe such movements according to countries. This volume treats such groups in England and the United States only. Material for various other countries has been collected, but must await later publication.

Pioneering is not a privilege restricted to early times. Scientists must continue to pioneer, or science will die. The main purpose of this book is to describe the history of psychoanalysis through the lives and works of its teachers, thinkers, and clinicians. Their example will keep the spirit of adventure, of conquest, and of creation alive in the present generation of psychoanalysts. This book is a study in creativity and the atmosphere from which analytic creativity has emerged and flourished. Alienation from this spirit, which would lead to conformity, mass organization, and administrative bureaucracy, could happen even to analytic groups and institutes, which should instead serve progress and freedom.

This book about pioneering in the past is dedicated to the pioneers of the future.

The editors wish to thank Mrs. Frances Mazerov for her loyal and efficient work in preparing their manuscript for the publishers.

FRANZ ALEXANDER
SAMUEL EISENSTEIN
MARTIN GROTJAHN

On March 8, 1964, a short time after our last editorial meeting, Franz Alexander died in his home in Palm Springs, at the age of 73. This book was almost completed, and several other projects were well on their way; he had left his desk as though he were planning to return soon.

For more than four years, the three editors had worked together on this project about psychoanalytic pioneers, and the memories of these editorial meetings with him are unforgettable. This book was close to his heart, for he liked to search out memories that spanned the early pioneering days of Berlin through the Chicago period and, finally, Los Angeles.

He was a pioneer throughout his entire life, and as such we will remember him.

SAMUEL EISENSTEIN
MARTIN GROTJAHN

Los Angeles
October 1965

The Authors

FRANZ ALEXANDER, M.D. Formerly Training Analyst, Southern California Psychoanalytic Institute; Director of Psychiatry, Mt. Sinai Hospital, Los Angeles. Deceased.

PHILIP L. BECKER, M.D. Instructor in Extension Division, Southern California Psychoanalytic Institute; member of Clinic Committee, Southern California Psychoanalytic Institute.

MARIE H. BRIEHL, Supervising Analyst in Child Analysis, Southern California Psychoanalytic Institute; Psychoanalytic Consultant, Department of Child Psychiatry, Cedars-Sinai Hospitals, Los Angeles, and Pacific Oaks College, Pasadena, California.

WALTER BRIEHL, M.D. Fellow, American Psychiatric Association; Attending Psychiatrist, Cedars-Sinai Hospitals, Los Angeles, California.

SAMUEL EISENSTEIN, M.D. Training Analyst, Southern California Psychoanalytic Institute; Associate Clinical Professor of Psychiatry, University of Southern California, Los Angeles.

RUDOLF EKSTEIN, Ph.D. Training Analyst, Los Angeles Institute for Psychoanalysis; Director, Project on Childhood Psychosis, Reiss-Davis Clinic for Child Guidance, Los Angeles.

GLENN W. FLAGG, M.D. Formerly Chief of Psychiatric Research, Division of Psychiatry, Cedars-Sinai Hospitals, Los Angeles; Assistant Clinical Professor of Psychiatry, University of Southern California, Los Angeles. Deceased.

ADOLF FRIEDEMANN, M.D. Hon. Professor, University of Freiburg i/Br. Germany; Superintendent of the Mental Hygiene Institute, Biel, Switzerland.

EDWARD GLOVER, M.D., LL.D. Hon. Consulting Physician, Portman Clinic for the Treatment of Delinquency, London; Lecturer on Dynamic Psychology, Maudsley Hospital, University of London.

RALPH R. GREENSON, M.D. Training Analyst, Los Angeles Institute for Psychoanalysis; Clinical Professor of Psychiatry, University of California, Los Angeles.

MARTIN GROTJAHN, M.D. Training Analyst, Southern California Psychoanalytic Institute; Clinical Professor of Psychiatry, University of Southern California, Los Angeles.

HANS A. ILLING, Ph.D. Staff member, The Hacker Clinic, Beverly Hills and Lynwood; California Parole Outpatient Clinic, Los Angeles.

RUTH JAFFE, M.D. Clinical Director, Shalvata Hospital, Magdiel-Ramataim, Israel; Training Analyst, Institute of Psychoanalysis of Israel.

WESTON LA BARRE, Ph.D. Professor of Anthropology, Duke University; Clinical Professor, Department of Psychiatry, University of North Carolina Medical School, Chapel Hill.

BARBARA LANTOS, M.D. Formerly member of the British Psycho-Analytic Society. Deceased.

NOLAN D. C. LEWIS, M.D. Formerly Professor of Psychiatry, College of Physicians and Surgeons, Columbia University; Director, New York Psychiatric Institute.

JOHN ARNOLD LINDON, M.D. Assistant Clinical Professor of Psychiatry, University of Southern California, Los Angeles; President, Psychiatric Research Foundation.

RUDOLPH M. LOEWENSTEIN, M.D. Training Analyst, New York Psychoanalytic Institute; Instructor, New York Psychoanalytic Institute.

SANDOR LORAND, M.D. Honorary President, Psychoanalytic Association of New York; Professor of Clinical Psychiatry, State University of New York Downstate Medical Center.

JOHN A. P. MILLET, M.D. Professor of Psychiatry, New York School of Psychiatry; Past President, Academy of Psychoanalysis.

FRITZ MOELLENHOFF, M.D. Staff member, Chicago Institute for Psychoanalysis; Training Analyst, Chicago Institute for Psychoanalysis.

GEORGE J. MOHR, M.D. Formerly Director, Child Study Center, Mt. Sinai Hospital, Los Angeles, California; Training Analyst, Southern California Psychoanalytic Institute. Deceased.

JOSEPH M. NATTERSON, M.D. Training Analyst, Southern California Psychoanalytic Institute; Assistant Clinical Professor, Psychiatry, University of Southern California, Los Angeles.

JOHN S. PECK, M.D. Assistant Clinical Professor of Psychiatry, University of Southern California, Los Angeles; Fellow, American Psychiatric Association.

SYDNEY L. POMER, M.D. Faculty, Southern California Psychoanalytic Institute; Contributing Editor, Annual Survey of Psychoanalysis.

EUGENE PUMPIAN-MINDLIN, M.D. Professor of Psychiatry and Vice Chairman of the Department of Psychiatry, Neurology and Behavioral Sciences, University of Oklahoma; Training Analyst, Southern California Psychoanalytic Institute.

LUCILLE B. RITVO, M.A. History of Science and Medicine, Yale University.

SAMUEL RITVO, M.D. Associate Clinical Professor of Psychiatry, Yale University Child Study Center and Department of Psychiatry, Yale University School of Medicine; Training Analyst, New York Psychoanalytic Institute and Western New England Institute for Psychoanalysis.

MAY E. ROMM, M.D. Training Analyst, Southern California Psychoanalytic Institute; Senior Psychiatrist, Cedars-Sinai Hospitals, Los Angeles.

SHELDON T. SELESNICK, M.D. Faculty, Southern California Psychoanalytic Institute; Coordinator of Psychiatric Research, Cedars-Sinai Hospitals, Los Angeles, California.

JACOB SPANJAARD, M.D. Training Analyst, Dutch Psycho-Analytical Society; member, Dutch Psycho-Analytical Society.

CLAUDE STEIN-MONOD Licencié ès Lettres de l'Université de Genève.

LILLA VESZY-WAGNER, Ph.D. Member of the British Psycho-Analytical Society.

CHARLES WILLIAM WAHL, M.D. Associate Professor and Chief, Division of Psychosomatic Medicine, Department of Psychiatry, University of California, Los Angeles; Consultant in Psychiatry, Sepulveda Veteran's Hospital, Camarillo State Hospital and Metropolitan State Hospital.

EDOARDO WEISS, M.D. Emeritus Staff Member, Chicago Institute for Psychoanalysis; Former Visiting Professor in Psychiatry, Marquette University, Milwaukee, Wisconsin.

ISIDORE ZIFERSTEIN, M.D. Faculty, Southern California Psychoanalytic Institute; Associate Clinical Professor of Psychiatry, University of Southern California, Los Angeles.

HANS ZULLIGER Dr. phil. h.c., University of Bern, Switzerland; Dr. med. h.c. University of Heidelberg.

Contents

Preface v
The Authors ix

KARL ABRAHAM
The First German Psychoanalyst
MARTIN GROTJAHN 1

SÁNDOR FERENCZI
Pioneer of Pioneers
SANDOR LORAND 14

OTTO RANK
The Myth of the Birth of the Hero
SAMUEL EISENSTEIN 36

MAX EITINGON
The Organization of Psychoanalytic Training
SYDNEY L. POMER 51

CARL GUSTAV JUNG
Contributions to Psychoanalysis
SHELDON T. SELESNICK 63

ALFRED ADLER
The Psychology of the Inferiority Complex
SHELDON T. SELESNICK 78

PSYCHOANALYTIC PIONEERS

ERNEST JONES
The Biography of Freud
LILLA VESZY-WAGNER 87

PAUL FEDERN
The Theory of the Psychosis
EDOARDO WEISS 142

EDWARD HITSCHMANN
Psychoanalysis of Great Men
PHILIP L. BECKER 160

OSKAR PFISTER
Psychoanalysis and Faith
HANS ZULLIGER 169

HANNS SACHS
The Creative Unconscious
FRITZ MOELLENHOFF 180

MOSHE WOOLF
Pioneering in Russia and Israel
RUTH JAFFE 200

ABRAHAM ARDEN BRILL
First American Translator of Freud
MAY E. ROMM 210

SMITH ELY JELLIFFE
Psychosomatic Medicine in America
NOLAN D. C. LEWIS 224

VICTOR TAUSK
The Influencing Machine
MARTIN GROTJAHN
HANS A. ILLING 235

SANDOR RADO
The Adaptational Theory
FRANZ ALEXANDER 240

THEODOR REIK
Masochism in Modern Man
JOSEPH M. NATTERSON 249

ELLA FREEMAN SHARPE
The Search for Empathy
CHARLES WILLIAM WAHL 265

GÉZA RÓHEIM
Psychoanalysis and Anthropology
WESTON LA BARRE 272

HELENE DEUTSCH
The Maturation of Woman
MARIE H. BRIEHL 282

FELIX DEUTSCH
Psychoanalysis and Internal Medicine
GLENN W. FLAGG 299

GEORG GRODDECK
The Untamed Analyst
MARTIN GROTJAHN 308

AUGUST STÄRCKE
The Sources of Castration Anxiety
JACOB SPANJAARD 321

HEINRICH MENG
Psychoanalysis and Mental Hygiene
ADOLF FRIEDEMANN 333

HANS ZULLIGER
Psychoanalysis and Education
ADOLF FRIEDEMANN 342

AUGUST AICHHORN
Friend of the Wayward Youth
GEORGE J. MOHR 348

MELANIE KLEIN
Her View of the Unconscious
JOHN ARNOLD LINDON 360

PSYCHOANALYTIC PIONEERS

ERNST SIMMEL
Psychoanalytic Pioneering in California
JOHN S. PECK 373

FRANZ ALEXANDER
The Western Mind in Transition
MARTIN GROTJAHN 384

MARIE BONAPARTE
The Problem of Female Sexuality
CLAUDE STEIN-MONOD 399

SIEGFRIED BERNFELD
Sisyphus or the Boundaries of Education
RUDOLF EKSTEIN 415

WILHELM REICH
Character Analysis
WALTER BRIEHL 430

OTTO FENICHEL
The Encyclopedia of Psychoanalysis
RALPH R. GREENSON 439

KAREN HORNEY
The Cultural Emphasis
JOSEPH M. NATTERSON 450

PAUL FERDINAND SCHILDER
Psychoanalysis and Psychiatry
ISIDORE ZIFERSTEIN 457

HEINZ HARTMANN
Psychology of the Ego
RUDOLPH M. LOEWENSTEIN 469

ERNST KRIS
Twentieth-Century Uomo Universale
SAMUEL RITVO
LUCILLE B. RITVO 484

EDWARD GLOVER
Theory of Technique
CHARLES WILLIAM WAHL 501

KATE FRIEDLÄNDER
Prevention of Juvenile Delinquency
BARBARA LANTOS 508

ANNA FREUD AND ERIK H. ERIKSON
Contributions to the Theory and Practice of Psychoanalysis and Psychotherapy
EUGENE PUMPIAN-MINDLIN 519

PSYCHOANALYSIS IN ENGLAND
EDWARD GLOVER 534

PSYCHOANALYSIS IN THE UNITED STATES
JOHN A. P. MILLET 546

Name Index 597

Subject Index 605

PSYCHOANALYTIC PIONEERS

Karl Abraham

1877–1925

THE FIRST GERMAN PSYCHOANALYST

*

MARTIN GROTJAHN

§ His Life

Karl Abraham was born in Bremen, Germany, on May 3, 1877. He died forty-eight eventful years later, in Berlin, on Christmas Day, 1925. Karl was the second of two sons born into an old and well-established Jewish family. Originally, his absorbing interest was the study of language, and for a long time languages remained his great love. Besides his mother tongue, he spoke fluent English, Spanish, and Italian, and he could make himself well understood in Danish, Dutch, and French. He once surprised the Psychoanalytic Congress in the Hague in 1920 by addressing his colleagues in perfect Latin. He also knew Greek extremely well and read Greek drama during his final illness. As a linguist, he wrote with an exquisite style—clear, uncomplicated, and factual.

It is important for the history of psychoanalysis that the first German psychoanalyst, as Sigmund Freud called him, took six years of intensive psychiatric training in mental hospitals. After finishing his medical studies in 1901, his first post was as physician in the State Hospital at Dalldorf, near Berlin, where he worked for four years.

Abraham then applied for an appointment as psychiatrist at Burghölzli, Bleuler's psychiatric clinic at Zurich. After some years, a vacancy made it possible for Abraham to be appointed there, and he worked for three years with C. G. Jung and his group.

Abraham married soon after his arrival in Switzerland, in 1906. His widow, now living in London, remembers their marriage as happy, tranquil, perfect. She shared her husband's interest in languages and helped him with his analytic writings. Their daughter Hilda was born in Zurich. Hilda Abraham, M.D., became an outstanding analyst and is now a senior member of the London Psychoanalytic Society and the editor and translator of her father's collected works. She is preparing for publication the original German and an English translation of the correspondence between Abraham and Freud, which consists of approximately 360 letters.

Abraham's son was born in Berlin in 1912. Forced to change his profession after his emigration from Berlin to London, he joined the British army, distinguished himself during the war in India, and now lives in London.

The first meeting between Karl Abraham and Sigmund Freud took place in November 1907; from then on the two men met regularly, until their last meeting in August 1924. Almost from the beginning, Sigmund Freud and Karl Abraham were close friends, and Abraham belonged to the small group of trusted members of the inner circle called "The Committee of the Seven Rings." Besides Sigmund Freud and Karl Abraham, the ring was worn by Sándor Ferenczi, Ernest Jones, Hanns Sachs, Otto Rank, and Max Eitingon. All these men, who were born between 1873 and 1885, became acquainted with Freud in the heroic years of isolation before 1910.

In December 1907, Abraham settled in Berlin, becoming the first German physician with a private psychoanalytic practice. He organized gatherings in his home and showed an optimistic interest in gaining a hearing from his medical colleagues and the Berlin medical societies. He would have liked to become professor of psychoanalysis at the University of Berlin under Karl Bonhoeffer, who was professor of psychiatry at the time. Although Bonhoeffer was not totally antagonistic to psychoanalysis (as Jones has claimed), he was cautious and conservative and opposed the formation of a pocket-sized department of psychoanalysis within the university. Abraham founded the Berlin Psychoanalytic Society and Institute early in 1910. The sister society in Vienna was founded in April of the same year. Both societies remained outside the university.

It was Abraham's custom to read all his papers personally to the society in Berlin. In one year he addressed his local society twelve times and he was to address them many more times during the fifteen years in which he presided over the group.

Abraham analyzed many colleagues, for example, Karen Horney, Theodor Reik, Hans Liebermann, Helene Deutsch, Edward and James Glover, Sandor Rado, Ernst Simmel and Felix Boehm. He also continued the analysis of Melanie Klein, who had started training with Ferenczi. When he found that the time and effort devoted to training analysis made it too difficult for him to continue his therapeutic work, which interested him equally, he was instrumental in bringing Hanns Sachs to Berlin to take over the bulk of the training analyses. By this time, experience had shown that the interests of an analytic group are best served if all aspects of analytic training are not handled by one and the same person.

When World War I broke out, Abraham opened a psychiatric unit that served as a clearing house for psychiatric cases on the Eastern front, where he spent four years. During this period, he had a severe attack of dysentery, which he never quite managed to throw off and which drained much of his strength. He also contracted chronic bronchitis, for which Wilhelm Fliess treated him. Abraham found Fliess to be truly interested in the progress of psychoanalysis. He always maintained that Fliess sent him the most suitable cases for analysis, and his trust in Wilhelm Fliess as a capable diagnostician endured to Abraham's last illness.

In May 1925, Abraham inhaled a small foreign body and developed bronchopneumonia. From that time he remained ill; after several severe relapses followed by generalized septicemia, he died on Christmas Day 1925, from a subphrenic abscess. During his prolonged illness, his many friends tried to help him. At Freud's instigation, and stimulated by his own friendship, Felix Deutsch made the journey from Vienna to Berlin several times.

§ His Scientific Work

According to today's standards, Karl Abraham was not a prolific writer: a collection of his complete works would fill a volume of approximately 800 pages. Following good German tradition, some of his early work consists of collected reviews designed to keep him and his students abreast of progress in the early analytic literature.

Abraham's psychiatric training is noticeable in all his writings. As a rule, he remained clinically oriented, and he denied himself what he called "the narcissistic indulgence of theoretical speculations." His relationship to objects under his observation was almost tender, and it was his greatest delight to report observations, connect them, and interpret them with a minimum of theoretical construction. He was a pioneer in the study of libido development, character formation, schizophrenia, manic-depressive psychosis, alcoholism, and drug addiction. Such borderline fields as anthropology, history, and mythology are frequently represented in his writings. As early as 1909, he wrote a paper about the influence of incestuous fixation on the choice of a mate. He was aware of the special psychological position of grandparents in the Continental family, and of the shift of authority from the father to the grandparents (or even to more remote forbears) as the basis for ancestral culture, which he described in 1913.

Karl Abraham sometimes behaved as if the study of orality were his personal and private domain. He established our knowledge of levels of development as they are related to character formation and to the different forms of insanity. He divided character development into three stages: the oral stage (which he subdivided into the passive sucking phase and the active, sadistic, biting phase); the two anal-sadistic phases (culminating in mastery through toilet training); and the genital stage of libido development (beginning with the partial-love, or phallic, phase and developing into the maturity of the adult). The mark of maturity is the ability to overcome ambivalence. This leads to a better capacity to discharge great quantities of excitement, making reaction formations unnecessary and increasing the ability for sublimations.

It is difficult to decide to what extent Abraham expressed the collective thinking of the analytic group of his era, how greatly his views were influenced by his friendship with Freud, and which of his concepts were original and pioneering. His studies of manic-depressive psychoses go hand in hand with Freud's contributions (Jones, 1953, Vol. II, pp. 329–331) to the understanding of grief and mourning: he paralleled, confirmed, and deepened Freud's work on mourning and melancholia. Psychotic despair is always the result of a loss, the renunciation of a (sexual) goal or love object. Abraham related schizophrenia to regression from a traumatic situation to an early narcissistic, infantile fixation, and he related melancholia to a similar regression to early oral levels. The depressive patient seems to say: "I cannot love because of my hate. Because I hate I am hated, and so I am depressed—but I have the right to hate back." The sense of guilt and sin develops out of this repressed hate and the return of the repressed, early, oral sadism so familiar to Abraham from his study of the oral character.

Depression centers around a conflict concerning ambivalence; this conflict is more intensive than in compulsive neurosis. The quanta of coexisting love and hate seem almost equal. Depressive patients cannot love in the proper sense of the word: either they simultaneously develop love and hate, or, more frequently, they show paralysis and inhibition of all feelings. According to Abraham, all depression leads back to a loss of someone's love and is patterned after mourning, such as follows the death of a beloved person. The loss activates in the patient long-forgotten wishes to kill people whom he consciously loved but unconsciously hated. The hostile orientation paralyzes the faculty to love. The depressive feeling, "I am hated," is a projection of the inner perception, "I hate." The depressive patient loves himself no more than he loves an external object. His superego is rigid, cold, unforgiving, hateful, and destructive, an attitude that originates from sadistic trends turned against one's self. The depressive fear of poverty is an expression of the patient's realization that he is incapable of loving. The depressive inability to eat is explained by the oral relationship between receiving love and eating food. Since the depressive patient regresses to oral, ambivalent narcissism, he will try to destroy his introjected objects in order to establish the object-free state of early, primary narcissism. The patient's superego treats his ego as the patient unconsciously wishes to treat the object that was lost.

Freud found that depressive self-reproach is an accusation directed against the introjected object. Abraham added that many complaints appear to come from the introjected object, repeating accusations originally made by the real object, which has now been turned against the self.

Because of his psychiatric training, Abraham believed in the existence of constitutional factors that might predispose to early fixations. Regression to this early fixation is caused by repeated, severe, narcissistic insults in childhood.

It appeared to Abraham that the manic episode is a triumph re-enacted between the patient's ego and his superego. The conflict leading to the manic episode must have been extreme, and the release sudden, to account for the intensity of the manic experience of well-being. Even so, it is not difficult to recognize the despair of the patient behind his manic-like defenses.

Abraham assumed an anal, sadistic fixation for the obsessional neuroses and an oral fixation for melancholia. The melancholic abandons his relationship to the object and to reality, whereas the obsessional neurotic retains this relationship, trying to master it with his magic, mystical ritual.

Abraham recognized the primal depression of infants as a precursor of later melancholia. Many years later, Melanie Klein continued where Abraham (once her analyst) had left off. She developed her system of thought from the model of early, infantile mother relationships dominated by envy, guilt, and gratitude. Further confirmation of Abraham's early views may be found in René Spitz's research on hospitalism of motherless orphans. Abraham had postulated direct and indirect relationships between oral frustration in early infancy and schizophrenia. Spitz demonstrated these clinically.

Abraham's next step was the analytic investigation of drug addiction, which he related closely to depression and compulsion. The addict clings to his drug with the same despair the depressive feels concerning the loss of his love object. Abraham remained unaware of the homosexual basis of jealousy-paranoia, which he described largely as a displacement and projection of guilt. Sigmund Freud, during the analysis of Schreber's paranoid delusions, interpreted jealousy as a defense against homosexuality.

Abraham's experience as an army psychiatrist in World War I stimulated him to report his experiences, together with Ernst Simmel, Sándor Ferenczi, and Ernest Jones, and to publish the first analytic essays about war neuroses. Sigmund Freud wrote the introduction for this valuable volume, which, more than twenty years later during World War II, gave a new generation of army psychiatrists a first start in their understanding. In his appraisal of Freud's paper, "Thoughts for the Times on War and Death," Abraham pointed out similarities between war and totem festivals. In both situations, the whole community combines to do things absolutely forbidden to the individual, and common action provides necessary sanction for the murderous orgy. The short book on war neuroses is of great importance in the history of psychoanalysis for it shows the efficiency of analytic treatment in traumatic emergency situations.

In addition to his great and important works about character development and the psychodynamics of psychoses, Karl Abraham wrote many short communications. Some of his observations concern the influence of grandparents on infantile fantasy, others, the reactions of children to the primal scene experience. Abraham's remarks on the importance of names has become a classic. His investigation of foot and corset fetishism gave impetus to the study of perversions.

These studies were made at a time when great inhibitions against such observations had to be overcome. Abraham opened doors to new fields that are no longer so tightly closed by guilt and taboo. He joined Freud in revealing secrets that had been carefully kept by collective taboos. He did not participate in the collective conspiracy of silence, but had the courage to look about him and see what was to be seen, to report his findings, and then to advance, together with a few friends of equal courage and adventurous spirit.

Abraham's numerous short papers, which are delightful to read, impressively document his joy in making clinical observations and expressing his realism, as well as his alertness, optimism, and pioneering spirit regarding the unconscious. His analysis of premature ejaculation in relationship to orality ("spilling the milk before it reaches the lips") gives testimony to his keen insight. Ejaculatio praecox was analyzed by him as leading back to a hostile feminine identification—a sadistic orientation usually covered by passivity, but incorporating the intention of soiling and injuring the female partner. Ejaculatio praecox is a use of the genital apparatus for pregenital aims. This important concept was first described by Abraham. He used the same mechanism to understand the tic. Patients with tics belong to the anal character type and have a narcissistic make-up; nevertheless, their tics represent a pregenital conversion.

Abraham also distinguished two variations of penis envy in women:

the wish fulfilling and the vindictive. From this it was a short step to an analysis of female homosexuality, according to the slogan, "I do not need any man; I can be a man myself."

He gave a striking interpretation of the symbol of the forked road (the *via bifurcata*) where Oedipus met his father and slew him. The road symbolizes the mother's genitals, where no son should meet his father. The number three can be interpreted as a symbol for the male genitals, but also for the triad of father, mother, and child. On deeper levels, the number three represents the oral, anal, and urogenital orifices. In a most original way of thinking, Abraham demonstrated that the fairy tales show knowledge of such symbolic connections, for instance, the story of the father who gave one of his sons a table that produced any food imaginable, the second, an ass that produced gold, and the third, a cudgel that thrashed any adversary. The third son is thus endowed with the gift of unlimited aggressive potency: he alone has obtained the father's final recognition.

Abraham's study of the Prometheus myth, which appeared in 1909, is the heart of a great book, *Dreams and Myths*. Here he joined forces with his friends Otto Rank and Theodor Reik in correlating dreams and myths. Myths are relics from the early prehistoric mental life of groups or tribes, whereas dreams constitute the myths of the individual person. Dreams resemble myths in egocentricity, censorship, condensation, displacement, secondary elaboration, and wish fulfillment. There is a possible symbolic sexual implication in the production of fire by man. As the boring rod kindles the fire in the wooden disc, so human life is kindled in the womb. In this sense the Prometheus myth can be seen as the Greek equivalent of the biblical story of Adam and Eve. In its oldest layers, the myth represents the identification of man with fire and of man's origin with the origin of fire. The Fire God is also the Man God who procreates man and fire.

In his description and interpretation of the cult of the Great Mother, Abraham was apt to refer to the clinical applications. In myths and in dreams, the lonely house in a garden, in a wood, or in a "lost valley"—where one feels one has lived in former times—represents the mother. Similarly, the mother is represented by the secret room, the narrow portal in which one would like to take refuge from danger.

Abraham's studies in art and history, are laid down in his book on the Italian-born painter of the Swiss Alps, Segantini, and in his study of

Amenhotep IV. Here Abraham came close to anticipating Freud's later concept of the death instinct.

Each of Abraham's works shows an awe-inspiring, detailed knowledge of the literature. He was an expert in each field of his study, as well as in psychoanalysis—a combination that makes his pioneering studies stand up through the years.

§ The Man

Karl Abraham was a realistically optimistic man with good, sober judgment and with quiet, unswerving confidence both in himself and in psychoanalysis. He was a "knower of man," possessing understanding of more than man's unconscious. Today, we should probably classify him as a moderate but incurable optimist of great maturity, with a well-developed sense of humor and tireless kindness. He had the good fortune to be drawn to Freud at the right moment in history and at the right time in his own personal life. His genius lay in recognizing this constellation and living by it.

People with life-accepting optimism are known for their "good luck"—actually the fruit of hard, skillful, intuitive, albeit unconscious, arrangements. From the beginning, Abraham had a deep insight into the possibilities of psychoanalysis as a method for investigating the unconscious and discovering new dimensions of human experience. He considered himself a scientist, rather than an adventurer or a leader of men. Because of their similarity in background and training, Abraham joined Freud in a consistently biological outlook. Freud referred to him as the first true psychoanalyst in Germany (as distinguished from Austria).

Abraham's sensitive social conscience did not permit him an ivory-tower existence. He became an active member of the psychoanalytic movement: he founded the Berlin Institute and Society, which became the center of the international analytic movement and served as the model for institutes all over the world. Since he did not look upon himself as a born leader, he found it strange that, as he grew in understanding and stature, he was called upon to lead. As had his biblical namesake, he accepted his fate. He retained his modesty, charm, youth, and buoyancy, and—despite war between nations and factional strife within the psychoanalytic movement—retained his sanguine optimism and hopeful outlook. According to Abraham, the sign of maturity is the overcoming of primary narcissism and ambivalence. His life typified this postambivalent character.

All of Abraham's friends agree that he possessed great personal charm. At heart, he was a clinical observer and a listener, interpreting sparingly and only after giving much thought to factual evidence. His greatest satisfaction was in explaining clinical findings and establishing connections between seemingly unrelated events.

He had little personal ambition. What Jones has called his "odd desire to become a docent at the University of Berlin" can be explained as the wish to have psychoanalysis represented in at least one university. He was apparently fairly devoid of hateful emotions, hence he was almost blind to the strength of hostility in those around him. Ernest Jones relates that he often saw Abraham cheerfully reasoning with someone who was glowering with anger and resentment—ignoring the emotion, and full of hope that quiet exposition would settle the controversy. Abraham could fight, but he could not hate; consequently he did not provoke hatred. He had opponents and rivals, but hardly any enemies.

Often in the history of the psychoanalytic movement, Karl Abraham proved a better "knower of men" than Freud or any other analyst. This was especially notable when Abraham had to rescue the analytic movement from domination by C. G. Jung or, later, from the influence of Otto Rank. The controversy between Abraham and Jung started when Abraham presented an analysis of schizophrenia, which he traced back to an early fixation point and regression to autoeroticism. Because he considered their work mystical rather than scientific, he did not mention the work of either Bleuler or Jung. Freud tried in his warm paternal way to keep his followers together. He wanted Abraham to make a friendly move toward Jung. In a letter dated May 1908 (Jones, 1953, Vol. II, p. 46), he wrote, "It would greatly please me and would show that all of us are able to gain from psychoanalysis, practical advantages for the conduct of our own life." Freud considered Abraham as the closer friend and the one who ought to make the gesture of conciliation, since Jung was "a Christian" and the son of a pastor, who "can only find his way to me against great inner resistances. . . . We Jews have an easier time, having no mystical element." Freud tried hard to pair Abraham's keenness and Jung's enthusiasm, but he did not succeed.

Freud did not always appreciate Abraham's superior appraisal of people and his "level-headedness," as Jones called it. Freud tried to interfere in favor of Jung and to influence Abraham by various means. He felt that Abraham should ". . . develop a little masochism and be prepared to endure a certain amount of injustice. . . . After all our Aryan comrades are quite indispensable to us; otherwise psychoanalysis would fall victim to anti-Semitism" (Jones, 1953, Vol. II, p. 50). Time showed Freud to be wrong and Abraham right. Finally, in 1914, Jung resigned from his post as editor of the *Psychoanalytic Year Book*, and Abraham was appointed his successor. Freud could say only, "I have been warned against contradicting you in the judgment of the [Swiss] people."

During World War I, Sigmund Freud went through a period of national enthusiasm, hoping perhaps to overcome his feeling of national, racial, and professional isolation. He was joined in this emotional upheaval by Ferenczi, but Abraham never faltered in his realistic appraisal of the situation. Finally, Freud recognized this in a letter to Abraham: "My alternation of courage and resignation takes shelter in your even temperament and your indestructible sense of vitality" (Jones, 1953, Vol. II, p. 196).

After World War I, Abraham had hoped that the International Psychoanalytic Congress of 1920 would take place in Paris. He could not understand that passionate feelings against Germany existed in France and England.

Around 1922, the break between Freud and Otto Rank seemed unavoidable. As the secretary of the International Association, Abraham was instrumental in the ousting of Rank from the association. He had watched Rank's personal and scientific development carefully, and he detected in Rank's last book, *The Trauma of Birth*, unmistakable signs of a scientific regression resembling that of Jung twelve years earlier. Perhaps Abraham's psychiatric training allowed him to see more clearly than anyone else, with the possible exception of Jones, that Rank was suffering from a psychotic-depressive episode and could no longer be tolerated as a responsible member of the association. At times Abraham almost assumed the attitude of an analyst toward Freud, who did not always want to admit a painful truth (Jones, 1953, Vol. III, p. 54).

The last letters between Abraham and Freud reveal an odd disagreement: Samuel Goldwyn wanted to make a movie showing famous love stories in history and had apparently offered one hundred thousand dollars to Freud as consultant. Naturally, Freud was indignant, as was Jones, and Abraham was naturally looking for a compromise. When, in the ensuing argument, Abraham pointed out that his judgment had frequently proved right, Freud answered with pique: "You are not necessarily always right. But should you turn out to be right this time too, nothing would prevent me from once again admitting it" (H. Abraham & E. Freud, 1966).

In 1926 when Freud reached seventy years of age, he wrote the obituary for his friend who had died so young. As he so often was in personal matters, Freud was brief in expressing his sorrow, not only there, but in an earlier letter to Jones:

> I applied to him Horace's line: *Integer vitae scelerisque purus* (he whose life is blameless and free of guilt). I have always found exaggerations on the occasion of death particularly distasteful, and I have been careful to avoid them; but in citing this quotation, I feel I have been sincere.
>
> Who would have thought when we met that time in the Harz Mountains that he would be the first to leave this unreasonable life! We must continue to work and stand together. As a human being, no one can replace this loss, but for psychoanalysis no one is allowed to be irreplaceable. I shall soon pass on, others not till much later, but our work, compared to whose importance we are all insignificant, must continue (Freud, 1960, No. 216).

REFERENCES

Abraham, Hilda, & E. Freud (Eds.) *A psychoanalytic dialogue: The letters of Sigmund Freud and Karl Abraham, 1907–1926*. New York: Basic Books, 1966.

Freud, E. L. (Ed.) *The selected letters of Sigmund Freud*. New York: Basic Books, 1960.

Jones, E. *Life and work of Sigmund Freud*. New York: Basic Books, 1953. 3 vols.

BIBLIOGRAPHY

Eitingon, M. In memoriam, Karl Abraham. *Int. Z. Psychoanal.*, 1926, **12**, 195–197.

Fenichel, O. *Outline of clinical psychoanalysis*. New York: Norton, 1939.

Fenichel, O. *The psychoanalytic theory of neuroses*. New York: Norton, 1945.

Freud, S. Obituary for Karl Abraham. *Int. J. Psycho-anal.*, 1926, 7, 1.

Grinstein, A. Bibliography of Karl Abraham's works. In *Index of psychoanalytic writings*. Vol. 1. New York: International Universities Press, 1960.

Jones, E. In memoriam, Karl Abraham. *Int. Z. Psychoanal.*, 1926, **12**, 131–183.
Rado, S. In memoriam, Karl Abraham. *Int. Z. Psychoanal.*, 1926, **12**, 203–208.
Reik, T. In memoriam, Karl Abraham. *Int. Z. Psychoanal.*, 1926, **12**, 209–214.
Sachs, H. In memoriam, Karl Abraham. *Int. Z. Psychoanal.*, 1926, **12**, 198–202.
Woolf, M. In memoriam, Karl Abraham. *Int. Z. Psychoanal.*, 1926, **12**, 215–218.

Sándor Ferenczi

1873–1933

PIONEER OF PIONEERS

*

SANDOR LORAND

Arma virumque cano . . .

He was called the "romantic" among psychoanalysts. He was deemed an *enfant terrible* by his colleagues. Freud called him "my dear son."

From 1908, when he met Freud for the first time, almost until his death, Sándor Ferenczi played a heroic part—second only to that of Freud—in building psychoanalysis into a branch of science. Freud had described Ferenczi's theoretical and clinical contributions as "pure gold." He was a pioneer of the heroic period of psychoanalysis—an inspiring teacher and a man beloved by everyone. Yet, "He who had so many friends all over the world, died almost entirely isolated, escaping only by a hair's breadth a fatal break with Freud, his friend and master, whom he had loved so loyally and so devotedly" (Balint, 1949).

Ferenczi was born in 1873, in Miskolc, a city of about 60,000 inhabitants, not far from Budapest. As a young man, his father had migrated to Hungary from Krakow; his mother was also of Polish origin. The elder Ferenczi ran a bookstore and a lending library, the largest in the county, which had been started by an American citizen who had returned to the United States. He had also established an artists' bureau through which guest artists and lecturers were engaged.

There were eleven children in the family, seven boys and four girls; Sándor was the fifth son. He was especially close to a sister ten years younger than himself. All the children grew up in the bookstore, which was their second nursery. Ferenczi's greatest pleasure throughout his life was reading.

A person of varied interests from his youth on, Ferenczi was a keen observer of nature and was especially fond of birds. He kept a feeding station on the grounds of his villa, where he loved to sit during his free time, watching and listening to them.

After his father's death, when Sándor was fifteen, the family became an even more closely knit unit. Sándor was very much attached to all the members of his family, especially his oldest brother, a fine musician. Music was always heard in the Ferenczi house.

As a youth, he wrote poetry. At twenty-four he penned sentimental poems to his mother. His sister recalls that his poetry was romantic and in the style of Heine.

After completing the Gymnasium, Ferenczi went to Vienna to study medicine. As a medical student he became interested in psychic phenomena. He tried hypnosis—at first with his sisters, who were not good subjects, and later with a seventeen-year-old clerk in the bookstore.

Upon receiving his medical degree in 1894, he served as a military physician in the army for one year. His interest soon turned to nervous and mental diseases, along with the study of neurotic difficulties and their treatment.

In 1900, when he opened his own office for the practice of neurology and psychiatry, he was chief neurologist for the Elizabeth Poorhouse. Five years later he was appointed psychiatric expert to the Royal Court of Justice in Budapest.

He was a prolific writer, contributing many papers on neurologic and psychiatric problems. When the analytic phase of his career began in 1907, he had already published about thirty papers in Hungarian and German medical journals.

Ferenczi first met Freud in 1908, after he had written to him and been invited to visit. From then on they were close friends, a friendship lasting nearly to the end of Ferenczi's life. He underwent his personal analysis with Freud, and they spent many summers together.

Ferenczi was a devoted, enthusiastic supporter of the psychoanalytic movement, following Freud on the arduous road of establishing psychoanalysis as a science and a new therapy. In the development of psychoanalytic theory, Ferenczi gave a strong impetus to the practical application of Freud's findings. In 1908, he gave a series of lectures, "Popular Lectures on Psychoanalysis," before the Budapest Medical

Association. An inspiring lecturer, he communicated his thoughts dramatically, with clear, graphic examples to illuminate difficult psychological problems. His intuitiveness, original thinking, and enthusiasm endeared him to Freud. In 1909 Freud asked Ferenczi to accompany him to Clark University in the United States. There, they walked together every morning before Freud's lectures, and Ferenczi suggested to him the topic of the day (Freud, 1933).

From the beginning of his psychoanalytic practice in 1908, Ferenczi was recognized as an outstanding therapist; his clinical publications and lectures on psychoanalysis attracted great attention.

Quite early in his life, Ferenczi became a central figure in the psychoanalytic movement. His psychological acumen and insight into problems of psychopathology and the speed with which he could appraise and handle them made him a rare and outstanding contributor to psychoanalysis and the advancement of its techniques. In his work and research, he always attempted to illuminate difficult problems in order to understand them theoretically and deal with them practically. In the record of those early years of analytic practice, we see in his publications diverse and original ideas concerning different types of neurotic difficulty and the various approaches to their clinical appraisal and technical management. Ferenczi provided a steady flow of clinical and theoretical contributions to psychoanalysis, touching on every phase and topic in psychoanalytic research and therapy.

In 1908, he wrote "The Effect on Women of Premature Ejaculation in Man" and a paper on the analytic interpretation and treatment of psychosexual impotence in man. These problems had interested him since his work in the prostitution ward of the Budapest Hospital.

In his 1911 paper, "Nosology of Male Homosexuality," he described for the first time the fundamental difference between active and passive homosexuals. He expressed the opinion that passive types, being satisfied with their role, do not seek treatment, whereas active types are more aware of their disturbance and try to change. The passive, "subject homoerotic," whose aggression is inhibited, assumes feminine attitudes and wants to be loved by men. Active types are typical obsessive neurotics whose homosexuality is a compulsion: the "object homoerotics," they are very aggressive and are the ones who are disturbed by their problems. In this paper, Ferenczi opened the way for further investigation of the manifold syndromes of homosexuality. In 1911 he also wrote an essay, "On the Part Played by Homosexuality in the

Pathogenesis of Paranoia," pointing out the important fact that "the paranoiac mechanisms are directed only against the homosexual choice of object" and describing the important role of anal eroticism in paranoia.

In his classic original essay, "Stages in the Development of the Sense of Reality," Ferenczi systematically described children's megalomanic views of their own omnipotence. In the light of mental mechanisms and psychopathological phenomena uncovered in the analysis of adults as well as the observation of infantile behavior, he depicted—in chronological order—four stages in the development of the sense of reality: (1) the period of unconditional omnipotence; (2) the period of magic-hallucinatory omnipotence; (3) the period of omnipotence through magic gestures; and (4) the period of magic thoughts and magic words. This pioneering work, his discoveries and description of ego regression, was later described and confirmed by many analysts. Ferenczi described the feeling of omnipotence in neuroses as a projection that one must obey like a slave. The magic is a fantastic attempt to restore the mortified narcissism through the fiction of self-sufficiency in every respect. Magical thinking in neurosis, then, is a narcissistic wish either to eliminate the disturbing reality principle or to so change it that it will not cause disturbance. This classic essay is of basic importance in the study and understanding of magical thinking and its role in human conduct. It is also an important contribution to ego psychology.

Ferenczi's constant alertness to, and keen observation of, the patient during the analytic session—his awareness of the bodily movements, positions, gesticulations, modulation of voice, and the like—were inexhaustible sources of information on repression and unconscious processes. To him they were as significant as free associations and verbalizations and had to be understood and interpreted. Ferenczi was also the first to observe and interpret dizziness at the close of the analytic hour, or the patient's tendency to fall asleep during the therapeutic session.

In addition to expanding Freud's technical papers, checking Freud's findings, and indicating new applications and approaches thereto, Ferenczi's short works of this period also extended and consolidated Freud's basic contributions. The originality and clarity of Ferenczi's thinking and the sharpness of his observations are well illustrated in these *Short Communications*, which are gems on technique.

In "Transitory Symptom-Formation," Ferenczi described the symptom as a resistance of the ego to the emerging unconscious drives and tendencies mobilized by analysis. These drives then seek an outlet through new symptoms, providing the opportunity to observe and study symptoms *in statu nascendi.*

In 1914, Ferenczi was called to military service as chief medical officer to a squad of hussars in a small town garrison, where Freud visited him. In this "exile," as Ferenczi called it, he spent his leisure hours translating Freud's *Three Essays on the Theory of Sexuality* into Hungarian. It was almost inevitable, Ferenczi wrote, that he should have elaborated in his mind certain ideas suggested by this work of Freud. His ideas evolved around a fuller elucidation of the act of coitus, conceived in the *Three Essays* as a terminal phase in the total course of sexual development, but not dealt with in detail from the standpoint of its evolution and development. When Freud visited him at his military station, Ferenczi expounded his ideas on ontogenetic and phylogenetic theory. In 1919, he repeated this theory before Freud and a small group of friends, who urged him to publish it. The resultant book, *Thalassa: A Theory of Genitality*, appeared in 1924, and was translated into English ten years later (Ferenczi, 1933–1934). (*Thalassa* is the Greek work meaning "sea.") It is considered a masterpiece by many analysts.

Here, Ferenczi continued Freud's ideas, correlating biology with psychology. The knowledge derived from earlier investigations with animals and data from embryology helped him explain the "status of the psyche during coitus and in sleep." In this work of creative intuition, the richness of thought and imagination so characteristic of all his scientific work is brilliantly displayed. In tracing the genital drives back to the tendency of thalassal regression, he created a new scientific method, which he named "bioanalysis." According to bioanalysis, the sexual drive, which aims at depositing the spermatozoa in the womb, also participates in the act of returning to the uterus. Here the uterus symbolizes the sea, from which all life originates.

Freud considered this work, which he described as a "biological rather than a psychoanalytic study," to be Ferenczi's "most brilliant achievement and richest in thoughts." It is, he continued "an application to the biology of sexual process—and beyond this to organic life in general—of the points of view and insights that psychoanalysis had coordinated; it is perhaps the boldest application in analysis ever attempted . . . on reading those essays one felt that one understood numerous singularities of sexual life which one had never previously been able to survey in their connection, and one felt enriched by suggestions which promised far-reaching vistas over the wide fields of biology."

In the first issue of the *International Journal of Psycho-Analysis*, 1920, Jones reported on a "striking new departure in technique—Ferenczi's active therapy." However, Ferenczi said he was only following Freud's lead: he developed his active technique on the basis of Freud's statements at the Budapest Congress in 1918, wherein Freud had suggested the use of active measures in certain cases of phobias, for instance, when therapy can advance only if the patient is induced to face his phobia or anxiety. Freud also had suggested active measures in cases of obsessional neurosis.

Ferenczi's first essay on active therapy aroused enthusiasm: everyone wanted to hear more about it. However, when he did publish further reports about his active innovations, many analysts were taken aback: these views were too new and too bold. Ferenczi based his conclusions on refined clinical material derived from years of analytic work carried on in the classical manner.

Individual analysts were trying new procedures that were not counter to the classical analytic principles. Most felt a need to make analysis more adequate, to achieve better therapeutic results; therefore, the interest in technique became universal among analysts.

When, in 1924, Federn and I discussed Ferenczi's technique of active interference, Federn claimed that experimentation in new technical methods was common, although nobody talked about it. He himself and his colleagues in Vienna had tried various methods for furthering analysis in cases that had reached a standstill. Federn also mentioned this fact in his Ferenczi Memorial (1933).

The central idea of Ferenczi's active technique, as he described it, is to request the patient—in addition to using free association—to act or behave in a certain way, in the hope of increasing tension, thereby mobilizing unconscious material. He also attempted to help the patient fight certain habits and give up the subjective advantages of the primary and secondary gains from his neurosis. Ferenczi did not advocate handling all patients in this way: he always emphasized that the technique could be used only with some patients and only under certain conditions. He cautioned against "haphazard, wild" activity. As he pointed out, active therapy is simply a means to an end, and the exaggeration of active measures may create strong resistance in the patient, endangering analysis. Thus, Ferenczi himself considered active therapy a mere detail in the over-all endeavor to remove the patient's resistance.

In 1921, in his essay on the development of active therapy, he called attention to the fact that, on closer inspection, the employment of active therapy was not really new. Interpretation itself is an active interference with the patient's psychic activity "because it turns the thoughts in a given direction and facilitates the appearance of ideas that otherwise would have been prevented by the resistance from becoming conscious."

Among the younger analysts, Ferenczi's name is associated mainly with his work in active technique and allied concepts, in which activity includes "prohibitions," "commands," and "active interference." It is true that at the beginning Ferenczi used prohibitions and commands; however, his work on activity represents only a small fraction of his contribution to psychoanalytic thought.

The Development of Psychoanalysis, written by Ferenczi and Rank in 1924, was reviewed in great detail by Franz Alexander (1925). He pointed out that the book—a synthesis and survey of the fundamental problems of psychoanalytic therapy from systemic, critical, and historical viewpoints—filled a great general need.

In the critical and historical sections, Ferenczi and Rank specified the errors that might result from Ferenczi's analytic technique and indicated how to avoid them. *The Development of Psychoanalysis* also provides a comprehensive survey of the abundant but previously unsummarized material acquired in the preceding years of psychoanlytic investigation. In his review, Alexander commented: "The rich store of the experience acquired during an investigation carried on for thirty years needs to be worked through into general theoretical principles, in order to open up new paths for further research."

By 1925, Ferenczi had discarded commands and prohibitions in favor of positive and negative suggestions. In "Contraindications to the Active Psychoanalytic Technique," published in 1926, he stated that he was always ready to retreat if there were no responses to a suggestion. He reiterated that active technique is only an auxiliary and pedagogic supplement to real analysis, and can never take the place of analysis. In discussing contraindications to activity, he presented evidence of his past mistakes, describing instances in which the results of active measures had been disappointing. He emphasized the difficulties that arise from "putting forward certain injunctions and prohibitions which are far too strong." Again he warned against being too emphatic or forceful: such an attitude on the part of the therapist may duplicate for the patient the child–parent situation and be experienced as a sadistic attack.

Among Ferenczi's essays on the problems connected with active technique, the two most important are "Contraindications to the Active Psychoanalytic Technique," and "Elasticity of Psychoanalytic Technique." In these communications he carefully reviewed the problems involved in the active techniques he had previously promulgated.

In *Further Contributions to the Theory and Technique of Psychoanalysis*, Ferenczi referred to various aspects of psychoanalytic therapy and the types of difficulty encountered in psychoanalytic practice. This multifaceted volume contains clinical observations and original notes concerning technical management of the patient. It is outstanding in its richness of thought and fantasy in science and research and for the clarification of the fundamental relationship between technical proceedings and theoretical deduction; it constitutes an illuminating record of Ferenczi's contributions to the early development of psychoanalysis. He himself considered the most vital contributions in this volume to be the clinical observations on the psychopathology of hysteria, the pathoneuroses, and tics, along with his further elaboration and attempt to systematize the active technique.

The contributions on hysteria, phenomena of materialization, erogeneity of body organs, and pathoneurosis have opened the way to an understanding and explanation of the mental processes in bodily symptoms and have spurred further consideration of psychogenic influences in organic diseases.

All the contributions, especially "Psychoanalysis of Sexual Habits," widen and deepen our knowledge of infantile development. Clinical observation of patients' attitudes enabled Ferenczi to describe the formation of *sphincter morale*, which in turn led him to outline the development of the physiological forerunner of the ego ideal or superego. With this he pointed to the assumption of the pregenital development of the superego.

The current revived interest in ego psychology—which has given us deeper insight into the pathology of character neuroses, perversions, schizophrenic regression, and moral masochism, and which has furthered evaluation and therapeutic management of these cases—was foreshadowed by Ferenczi's work.

Innovations or modifications in our therapeutic armamentarium may be necessary in treating borderline cases or cases with ego weakness. Ferenczi described such cases as "dried-up difficult cases whom nobody wanted to work with." He remarked, "I became a specialist in peculiarly difficult cases with which I go on for many years." In attempting to achieve better results with them, he experimented with new procedures that he felt might prove effective. When results proved him wrong, he lost no time in reporting his errors.

Ferenczi has indelibly influenced the fundamentals of psychoanalytic technique. In "Recent Advances in Psychoanalysis," which appeared in 1920, Jones attempted for the first time to describe Ferenczi's active technique, "the importance of which, however, cannot yet be estimated because it is relatively at the beginning." In a detailed review of *Further Contributions to the Theory and Technique of Psychoanalysis,* Glover states: "Whatever the *ultimate verdict* [italics mine] on his active therapeutic devices, whether they come to be incorporated wholly or partly into a standardized psychoanalytic technique, I venture to think that his original papers on this subject will, in the long run, be valued more for their clinical illustrative material than for the technical conclusions they embody" (1927). Early and later doubters of "activity" are numerous: direct methods are used, but they are called by some other name.

Some analysts have elaborated upon his technique. In a symposium on neurotic acting out held by the San Francisco Psychoanalytic Society in 1941, Fenichel brought up the problem of active therapy. He cautioned that prohibition should be avoided as long as possible or should be given in a way that avoids appearing castrative. Fenichel believed that at best prohibition can be combined with analytic interpretation—that the analyst should show the patient why prohibition is necessary. As he said, "You can prohibit in a way that looks more like advice or suggestions." This is in line with Ferenczi's shift from prohibition and interference to suggestion.

To Ferenczi, the use of free association was an active measure. In a recent paper, Tarachow (1962) refers to interpretation as a deprivation which ". . . is designed to rob the patient of something—his fantasies, his defenses, his gratifications." He also points up the analyst's *demand* for free association as a demand that the patient surrender "his hard-won defenses against painful ideas and affects."

Numerous papers have been written in the last few years about procedures in psychoanalytic therapy in which technical variations are suggested, but with the qualification that these suggestions are not "active measures." These suggestions consist of various types of manipulation and emphasize the "humanness" of the analyst, giving "love" to the patient and so forth. Some refer to activity by the term "parameters." We read about "formative activity of the analyst," which means helping the patient to establish a reorientation of his personality and a readaptation to his outside world. All these "new" methods can legitimately be classified as activity, and all were described and utilized at some point by Ferenczi. In many instances their origins have been forgotten.

In continuing to probe for success with the "dried up" cases, who came to him from all over the world as their last hope, Ferenczi experimented with adjusting the atmosphere of the analytic situation to the patient's needs. He believed that the analyst must give love to these very difficult patients in order to help them resolve their pathological difficulties by reaching their pretraumatic experiences. He therefore assumed and played certain roles in the transference relationship which were designed to influence the emotional and mental processes of the patient. He described this approach in his essay, "The Principle of Relaxation and Neocatharsis," in which he tried to show how the analyst can consciously attempt to ease the atmosphere in the analytic situation. His thesis is that indirect contact with the patient through interpretation is insufficient in these very disturbed cases and that, in addition, a more direct approach to the childish, infantile part of the patient is necessary.

Because of their controversial nature and their departure from classical procedure, "The Principle of Relaxation and Neocatharsis" and two later papers, "Child Analysis in the Analysis of the Adult" and "Confusion of Tongues between Adults and the Child," which appeared between 1931 and 1933, created a wide gap between Ferenczi and many of his colleagues. The latter two papers deal primarily with the problems and technical handling of early psychic trauma; however, they contain some thoughts pointing to the importance of the earliest object relationships and their impact on personality development. They also contain ideas about more extensive and deeper functions of ego, mechanism of defense, and so forth, all of which presently occupy psychoanalytic thinking and have already produced a number of controversial theories.

It was Ferenczi who first emphasized the great importance to healthy infant development of sufficient, loving body contact with the mother, as well as the dangers of too intense stimulation of the baby by adults.

There was no limit to Ferenczi's interest in psychological problems. When resting from his clinical work and consideration of the theoretical or technical problems of psychoanalysis, he wrote about sociological problems, or concerning art, literature, or the like, in such essays as "Philosophy and Psychoanalysis," "Goethe—of the Reality Value of the Poet's Fantasy," "Psychology of Mechanics," and many others. Space does not permit enumeration of all his contributions and comments upon them, although each is deserving of such recognition.

Of all Freud's disciples, Ferenczi made the greatest number of original contributions to psychoanalysis. Not only was he an excellent teacher who, as Freud said, "made us all his pupils," but he was also an outstanding organizer. In Freud's "On the History of the Psychoanalytic Movement," we read: "Hungary, so near geographically to Austria, and so far from it scientifically, has produced only one collaborator, S. Ferenczi, but one that indeed outweighs a whole society" (1961). In 1910 at the Nürnberg Congress, Ferenczi, acting on Freud's suggestion, proposed organizing the International Psychoanalytic Association. He attended all subsequent meetings and was a most colorful figure who captivated everyone by his warmth and charm. Ferenczi radiated a quality of joyousness that drew everyone to him. When he spoke at meetings there was barely sufficient standing room. This was also true when Ferenczi lectured at the University of Budapest where, from 1919, he was Professor of Psychoanalysis.[1] There was never enough space in the auditorium to accommodate all who wished to attend his lectures.

In his organizational work, Ferenczi showed enthusiasm, determination, and perseverance concerning courses of action that he believed advantageous for the advancement of psychoanalysis. One such decision brought about the creation of the *International Journal of Psycho-Analysis,* the first volume of which appeared in 1920. Ferenczi had been aware of the growing interest in psychoanalysis in America and England and had realized that the German-language journals could not fill the needs of the English-speaking analysts. "I decided that the most satisfactory method would be to have a distinct journal in the English language," he reported. He did not wait until the next Congress to dis-

[1] The first university professorship in psychoanalysis.

cuss the new venture, but set the project in motion at once, with Jones as the editor.

In September 1918, in Budapest, the Fifth International Psycho-Analytic Congress was held. This was the first congress attended by representatives of the Austrian, Hungarian, and German governments. Impressed with the results of psychoanalytic treatment, these governments planned to establish psychoanalytic clinics for the treatment of war neuroses.

In 1919 Ferenczi married. While courting his wife he had written her a great many poems. Thus far, his family has refused to permit their publication. Mrs. Ferenczi was a highly cultured, charming woman, and their life together was a happy one. There were no children from their union, but Mrs. Ferenczi's two daughters by a former marriage lived with them. After Ferenczi's death in 1933, Mrs. Ferenczi remained in Budapest until 1946. She then moved to Switzerland, where she died three years later.

In 1926, the New School for Social Research, in New York City, invited Ferenczi to give a lecture course in psychoanalysis. He arrived in New York in the Fall of that year, accompanied by his wife. They remained for eight months. The time he spent here was important in furthering the development of psychoanalysis in America. His lectures contributed to the growth of psychiatry and psychoanalytic thought in the medical world and introduced psychoanalysis to the general public. His visit also gave a strong impetus to the investigation in the United States of the problems of teaching analysis and training analysts.

Never before had such a comprehensive discussion of psychoanalysis been presented to the lay public or to professionals in the United States. Throughout the Fall and Winter of 1926–1927, Ferenczi presented a weekly ninety-minute lecture as part of a general course, "Selected Chapters in the Theory and Practice of Psychoanalysis." Designed primarily to meet the requirements of intelligent laymen and students of psychology and psychoanalysis, lecture topics included: "Suggestion and Psychoanalysis," "Development of the Ego and the Instincts," "Ego and the Personality," "Freudian Metapsychology," "The Technique of Psychoanalysis," "Main Forms of Neurosis and Psychoanalysis," and "Character and Its Possible Changes through Psychoanalysis." Concurrent courses were presented by Frankwood Williams, who lectured on mental hygiene, and J. B. Watson, whose subject was behaviorism and psychoanalysis.

I should here like to discuss, not only errors in Jones's report—in his biography of Freud (Vol. 3, 1957)—of Ferenczi's 1926 trip to America, but also Oberndorf's glaring omissions regarding important aspects of Ferenczi's visit to New York. I shall preface my description of this event by introducing some personal history, which explains how I happened to be in New York at that time and in a position to observe closely the events of Ferenczi's trip.

When I came to the United States, I had known Ferenczi for five years. We had met in 1920, in Kosice, Czechoslovakia, where I had been living for a year during my affiliation with the city hospital. I had written him regarding his theory of hypnotic suggestion, in connection with a research project on painless delivery under hypnosis. After an exchange of letters, I invited him—in the name of the Medical Society of Kosice, which consisted of approximately 150 physicians—to spend some time with us as a guest lecturer. Graciously he accepted, and in the Fall of 1921 he spent two days in Kosice, presenting one lecture before the Medical Society and another to a general audience. At the time, Ferenczi mentioned that being in Kosice near the Tatra Mountains had brought back happy memories of his youth, when he had spent weeks climbing them with his brother and sister. Later, he spent vacations with Freud in the same Tatra Mountains.

During our discussion of my therapeutic work with shell-shocked soldiers during the war and the satisfactory results I had obtained with hypnosis, Ferenczi suggested that I try a personal analysis. "You may like to do analysis," he said. "If not, it may interest you and help in your work." In the Spring of 1923, I went to Budapest and started my analysis with Ferenczi, finishing in June, 1924. A year later I emigrated to America.

Although the New York Psychoanalytic Society had no official contact with Ferenczi throughout his stay in the United States, upon his arrival in New York in the Fall of 1926, A. A. Brill gave a private dinner for him and Mrs. Ferenczi, which was attended by some of the New York analysts.

Ferenczi's visit was mentioned briefly by Oberndorf in his *History of Psychoanalysis in America* (1953). He mentioned Ferenczi's classes at the New School and his lecture, "Gulliver's Fantasies," in December, 1926, before the New York Society of Clinical Psychiatry. But Oberndorf neglected to mention the highly stimulating lecture Ferenczi gave before the American Psychoanalytic Association's Christmas meeting in New York. Ferenczi had been invited by the American Psychoanalytic Association, whose members included both the New York analysts and analysts from various cities throughout the United States. For reasons to be disclosed further on, Oberndorf did not want to connect Ferenczi's name with official psychoanalytic societies or movements in the United States.

At the time, Oberndorf was the secretary of the American Psychoanalytic Association and Adolf Stern was president. Both were members of the New York Psychoanalytic Society, and both attended the Christmas meeting, at which Ferenczi was invited "to give a short résumé of the most important practical and theoretical problems" occupying the attention of analysts at the time. Members of the American Psychoanalytic Association, and those of the New York Society in particular, were troubled about problems of didactic analysis. There was open disagreement about evaluation of the voluminous psychoanalytic literature and what should be considered fundamental (Oberndorf, 1953).

In his discussion, "Present-Day Problems in Psychoanalysis," Ferenczi emphasized the practical significance of developments in the field of ego psychology. And, for the first time, he mentioned the need for postgraduate instruction in psychoanalysis. As usual, Ferenczi was enthusiastic, inspiring, and charming in his lecture. After his talk, a long discussion ensued, primarily among Harry Stack Sullivan, I. Coriat (from Boston), and H. W. Frink.

Despite its importance, Oberndorf omits mention of this meeting in his history, although a report of it appears in the *International Journal of Psycho-Analysis* of 1927 above Oberndorf's signature as secretary of the American Psychoanalytic Association. Also omitted from Oberndorf's history are the seminars on technique that Ferenczi gave privately to members of the American Psychoanalytic Association and of the New York Society.[2] Further, Oberndorf does not state that some analysts from New York and elsewhere regularly attended Ferenczi's lectures at the New School.

[2] I was reminded by a colleague and member of the New York Society, Dr. Emanuel Klein, who did secretarial work for Dr. Dorian Feigenbaum (founder of *The Psychoanalytic Quarterly*), that he had arranged for those technical seminars many months before Ferenczi's arrival in America, and that they were well attended by both New York analysts and members of The American Psychoanalytic Association.

The attitude toward Ferenczi shared by Oberndorf and the other members of the New York Society grew out of their anger with him for his support of lay analysis. In his history, Oberndorf has written at great length about the discussion of the question of lay analysis at the New York Society meeting in November 1926 and the subsequent adoption of a resolution—supported by a large majority of the members—expressing opposition to the practice of therapeutic analysis by lay persons.

Oberndorf also mentioned the firm stand the representatives of the American Society took against lay analysis when the question first came up at the International Congress in Bad Homburg in 1925. He described the disagreement as a clash between the Americans and *all* the Europeans, none of whom disagreed with Freud's position that persons from disciplines other than medicine can become thoroughly competent psychoanalysts. Indeed, the European psychoanalysts had ample proof of the validity of their position. Ferenczi firmly believed that educators should be analyzed in order to truly understand the children whose minds and characters they attempt to mold; he had no objections to an educator becoming a qualified therapist. That Ferenczi emphatically expressed his agreement with Freud, some of the New Yorkers (and particularly Oberndorf) neither forgot nor forgave.

When Ferenczi arrived in New York only one year after the Bad Homburg Congress, resentment was strong in the hearts of some members. Oberndorf was always vehement about Ferenczi's acceptance of lay analysis. (I am reminded here of Anna Freud's correction of a speaker who referred to the graduates of the Hampstead Therapy Course and Clinic as "lay analysts," by stating that they were "professional" and not "lay" people.)

This irksome problem was alone responsible for the New York Society's official nonrecognition of Ferenczi and for the behavior of some of its members toward him, including Oberndorf's incomplete history. I was then working with Oberndorf and five other analysts on the staff of the Mental Health Clinic of Mount Sinai Hospital, and we discussed the matter. Oberndorf answered my criticism of the Society's discourteous behavior by saying, "When in Rome do as the Romans do." [3] I could not help thinking to myself that in the past Ferenczi had traveled regularly from Budapest to Vienna to further the training of several of

[3] That is, "When in New York, do not refer patients to lay analysts or accept nonmedical persons for training analyses."

the very men who now were ignoring him. Disrespect and discourtesy to a famous teacher—moreover to someone who was Freud's direct representative and close associate—were inconceivable to me. To observe it was an extraordinary experience. Particularly puzzling was the fact that the Society's official position on lay analysis was privately disregarded by some of its members. Blumgart and Brill, among others, referred children to nonmedical analysts. Two child therapists who worked with me in the Mental Hygiene Clinic of Mount Sinai Hospital were not physicians, but had had psychoanalytic training.

Plainly, Jones was misinformed about the New York scene: in his biography of Freud, he reported that the New York Society analysts were offended because Ferenczi had not communicated with them about his coming, but that nevertheless they received him in a friendly manner. He also stated: "They invited him to address the winter meeting of the American Psychoanalytic Association." Jones has confused the New York Society with the American Psychoanalytic Association. Their attitudes were quite different; whereas the American Association invited Ferenczi to speak, the New York Society did not communicate with him at all, although its members were aware of Ferenczi's acceptance of the American Association's invitation and, had they so wished, they had had ample opportunity to get in touch with him before he left the Continent.

Jones also wrote: "Relations became more and more strained as the months went by until he [Ferenczi] was almost completely ostracized by his colleagues." The attendance of some New York analysts at his lectures and the friendly relations existing between him and many New York analysts indicate that only the official relationship—promoted by a hard core of determined individuals—was cold and distant: there was no question of ostracism.

Jones claimed that, while in New York, Ferenczi "trained eight or nine lay people"; this he gave as a second reason for the unfriendly attitude toward Ferenczi. During his stay, Ferenczi did have an analytic practice, consisting not only of former American patients who had originally been in analysis with him in Europe and who took advantage of his presence in America for additional analysis, but also of some physicians who were interested in being analyzed, and of a few educators. They all were analytic patients, and Ferenczi certainly did not set up a training program for them, as Jones has implied. But it is certainly true that Ferenczi never would have refused to analyze someone because that person planned to be a therapist at some future time. He analyzed anyone who wished to undergo analysis.

Ferenczi left New York in the Spring of 1927. I did not see him again until the Oxford Congress in 1929, when the question of lay analysis came to a peaceful settlement between American and European groups. At the insistence of the Americans, the European analysts agreed not to accept American physicians or lay persons for training in Europe unless the American Educational Committee gave its endorsement, which, of course, they never would give for a lay person.

In the Summer of 1931, I visited Ferenczi in Budapest. He lived in a charming villa on the right bank of the Danube. He was then revising the most recent phases of his theory and technique. He told me he was changing some of his methods because he had not achieved the anticipated results. Freud had been highly critical of some of Ferenczi's experiments in technique, with the result that, although they continued to correspond, their relationship had become strained. Ferenczi expressed the hope that, now that Freud had been proved correct and the most radical of Ferenczi's experiments in technique had been proved mistaken, his closeness with Freud might be reestablished.

He corresponded with Freud about these changes. In a letter written in October 1931, he stated: "I will certainly not deny that subjective factors do influence, often very considerably, both the form and the content of what I produce. In the past this has at times led to exaggerations. Eventually, however, I believe I succeeded in understanding where and how much I had gone too far." And, further on in the same communication: "My latest views are only in process of formulation. I should be most grateful if you would write me in more detail about those points which seem incapable of 'leading to any desirable goal' " (Ferenczi, 1949).

During my visit with Ferenczi, we also discussed *Psychoanalysis Today*, a book I was editing (which just appeared in 1933) and the contributors thereto. Ferenczi's contribution to the volume (1944), "Freud's Influence on Medicine," was prepared especially for the book and was his last published paper. At that time he appeared in excellent health without the slightest indication of mental or physical fatigue. We sat in the garden of his villa, and I answered many of his questions about America, analysis, books, and people.

The psychoanalytic movement in Hungary was begun by Ferenczi, and it revolved around him throughout the years. In 1913, he founded the Hungarian Psychoanalytic Society. The first members were Stefan Hollós, chief psychiatrist and director of the Royal State Hospital for the Insane, at Nagyszeben; Hugo Ignotus, the outstanding literary critic; L. Levy, an internist who later became director of the Jewish Hospital in Budapest and who was Ferenczi's lifelong friend as well as his physician; and Sandor Rado. Ferenczi was the president of the Society, a position he held until his death. The first secretary was Rado. Although World War I paralyzed the Society's activities, its membership grew rapidly after the war. It became very active and publications by its members on various psychoanalytic topics appeared frequently. The psychoanalytic clinic of the Society was established in Budapest in 1930.

Attending a meeting of the Society was an unforgettable experience. In the early twenties, these meetings were held at Ferenczi's home or at the home of Mrs. Vilma Kovács, one of the training and supervising analysts in Budapest. The wives of the members were also invited. Everyone sat in a circle. After the presentation of the topic, Ferenczi asked each individual present for spontaneous responses. A discussion ensued during which Ferenczi, in his friendly manner, encouraged anyone who hesitated. When the discussion slackened, Ferenczi would take over. His spontaneity, imagination, and creative elaboration on aspects of the problems presented inspired everyone. He created great eagerness and enthusiasm in his audience.

Ferenczi liked the spirited world of the artists, musicians, and writers who formed the cultural elite of Hungary, and he always associated with them. Before his marriage, he lived in the Hotel Royal, a favored residence of the literary group, and spent his evenings at the permanent roundtable reserved for artists and writers. They were a prominent and gay group, with whom Ferenczi formed lifelong attachments. He enjoyed going to small restaurants with his friends, where they dined and listened to gypsy music, sipping vintage Tokay wines.

That some of the young writers of that avant-garde circle were influenced by Ferenczi and psychoanalysis is reflected in their writings. Ferenczi, in turn, contributed a few articles on art and literature to *Nyugat* (West), the literary review.

Despite the brevity of this biography of Ferenczi, I feel it my duty to help to set the record straight concerning Ferenczi's terminal illness and the false impressions of it created by Jones in the second and third volumes of the Freud biography. As is amply demonstrated in this great biography, Jones was critical of nearly all the early associates of Freud. For some reason—which I shall not attempt to interpret—he wanted to believe, and to prove to others, that Ferenczi, who had been the closest to Freud, suffered from a latent psychosis.

Jones made his first public reference to this belief in the eulogy he delivered after Ferenczi's death (Jones, 1933), before the British Psychoanalytic Society in June 1933. He said then that mental regression was apparent in Ferenczi's later writings; that ". . . Ferenczi showed unmistakable signs of mental regression in his attitude towards fundamental problems of psychoanalysis." In other words, Jones diagnosed as mental regression Ferenczi's experimental departures, in the late twenties, from classical psychoanalytic technique, although there is not a shred of evidence that Ferenczi ever suffered from personality impairment or mental illness, except during the last weeks of his life, when his spinal cord and, perhaps, his brain were attacked in the terminal phase of pernicious anemia. Any neurological textbook description of pernicious anemia makes clear that, in its terminal phases, symptoms of confusional delusions, phobias, or manic-depressive symptoms may occur (Wilson & Bruce, 1936). Although originally a neurologist, Jones failed to verify the neurologic pathology and therefore inferred that Ferenczi must have had a latent psychosis. Michael Balint and others who were in contact with Ferenczi until his death have said that, until the very last week, he remained completely clear-minded and alert, although painfully feeble and incapacitated.

Unquestionably, Ferenczi had many neurotic problems, among them hypochondria,[4] which made it difficult to determine exactly when the pernicious anemia started. In a personal communication, Balint has informed me that Ferenczi was apparently still all right at the Wiesbaden Congress in 1932. From that Congress he went to Biarritz, where the first symptoms appeared. Eventually he had difficulty walking and, possibly because of the increasing ataxia and paralysis, needed support from his wife. It was then that the true nature of his anemia was dis-

[4] Ferenczi had an inordinate need to be liked, which he succeeded in gratifying through his great charm. He possessed a childlike quality that probably helped him to identify with and understand young children. Unresolved problems of frustrated parenthood may have provided the impetus for some of the more radical experiments in "activity" and role-playing with patients.

covered, together with the neurological complications of combined lateral sclerosis.

He worked with his patients until Christmas of 1932. In the following February or March, he became so weak that he retired to bed, from which he never arose. Balint described how painful it was to watch Ferenczi's paretic movements. At first, only the lower limbs were affected and then gradually his hands, as well. Balint continued to see him every week. The Sunday before his death, Ferenczi had become so weak and his hands had been so much affected that he could hardly hold a glass. The immediate cause of death was paralysis of the respiratory center.

It is entirely possible that during the last week of his life Ferenczi suffered from delusions as a result of the anemia. Jones's thesis is that the "dark side" of Ferenczi was always lurking in the background, and that toward the end of his life Ferenczi developed psychotic manifestations which caused him to turn away from Freud's doctrines. The facts disprove Jones's diagnosis.

In the Freud biography (1957, Vol. III), Jones stated that Ferenczi withdrew from Freud in the autumn of 1929. To the contrary, as the "Ten Letters to Freud" (Ferenczi, 1949) prove, Freud and Ferenczi corresponded until Ferenczi's death. Ferenczi's letters show the dignity, courtesy, and affection with which he responded to Freud's openly expressed criticism. Had there been a break, it is highly unlikely that the Viennese Psychoanalytic Society would have invited Ferenczi to speak in honor of Freud's seventy-fifth birthday. On that occasion, in May 1931, Ferenczi read his paper, "Child Analysis in the Analysis of Adults."

Jones believed that Ferenczi was intriguing against him. He cited instances in the Freud biography of Ferenczi's talking behind his back, and accused Ferenczi of lying to Freud, and the like. One need only scan the pages to see how much subjective, negative feeling toward Ferenczi Jones harbored. In personal discussions with me more than twenty years after Ferenczi's death, Jones frequently expressed irritation and criticism of Ferenczi. Obviously this personal bias disturbed his scientific attitude: because of this, Jones failed to check on the accuracy of reports about Ferenczi's health, relationships, and behavior.

Ferenczi's "Confusion of Tongues between Adults and the Child," and the notes and fragments published posthumously in the last volume of his collected papers, are proof of the clarity of his mind and the richness of his ideas at the time they were written, shortly before his death.

He was a master in the technique of healing and, first and foremost, he was a physician interested in helping the suffering. He put his heart into his work and he worked ceaselessly. His radiant personality, his warmth, and his spirit, kept him surrounded by friends. But these friends began to look askance at him and became distant and strained, as did Freud, when he began to experiment with radical innovations, in the late twenties.

Although one seldom hears Ferenczi's name today, and references to his papers are rare in the latest literature, Ferenczi's controversial papers, written more than thirty years ago, deal with topics around which analytic research centers today. As fresh and illuminating today as when they were first written, his writings are an inspiration to all who read them. During Ferenczi's lifetime many of his most original and valuable contributions were so generally accepted as axiomatic that they were frequently attributed to Freud.

Among contributors to psychoanalysis, no one, with the exception of Freud himself, has contributed so many valuable and original ideas or done as much as Ferenczi has to develop psychoanalysis and bring it to the status that it enjoys today.

REFERENCES

Alexander, F. Review of *Entwicklungsziele der Psychoanalyse* by S. Ferenczi and O. Rank. *Int. J. Psycho-Anal.*, 1925, 6, 484–496.

Balint, M. Sándor Ferenczi obituary, 1933. *Int. J. Psycho-Anal.*, 1949, **30**, 215–219.

Federn, P. Sándor Ferenczi obituary. *Int. J. Psycho-Anal.*, 1933, **14**, 467–485.

Ferenczi, S. Thalassa: a theory of genitality. (Bunker, H. A., Jr. Trans.). *Psychoanal. Quart.*, 1933–1934, **2–3**.

Ferenczi, S. Freud's influence on medicine. In Lorand, S. (Ed.), *Psychoanalysis today*. New York: International Universities Press, 1944.

Ferenczi, S. Ten letters to Freud. (Riviere, Joan Trans.). *Int. J. Psycho-Anal.*, 1949, **30**, 243–245.

Freud, S. Sándor Ferenczi obituary. *Int. J. Psycho-Anal.*, 1933, **14**, 297–299.

Freud, S. On the history of the psychoanalytic movement (1914). *Collected papers.* Vol. I. New York. Basic Books, 1959. Pp. 257–359.

Glover, E. Review of *Further contributions to the theory and technique of psycho-analysis* by S. Ferenczi. *Int. J. Psycho-Anal.*, 1927, 8, 417–421.

Jones, E. Sándor Ferenczi obituary. *Int. J. Psycho-Anal.*, 1933, **14**, 463–466.
Jones, E. *Life and work of Sigmund Freud*. Vol. 3. New York: Basic Books, 1957.
Lorand, S. Sándor Ferenczi obituary. *J. nerv. ment. Dis.*, 1934, **79**, 372–374.
Oberndorf, C. *A history of psychoanalysis in America*. New York: Grune & Stratton, 1953.
Tarachow, S. Interpretation and reality in psychotherapy. *Int. J. Psycho-Anal.*, 1962, **43**, 377–387.
Wilson, S. A. K., & Bruce, A. N. *Neurology*. Vol. II. Baltimore: Wm. Wood, 1940.

Otto Rank

1884–1939

THE MYTH OF THE BIRTH OF THE HERO

*

SAMUEL EISENSTEIN

Otto Rank joined the original circle around in Freud in 1906, and, until 1924, he was one of the most creative and loyal men among the original pioneers. The year 1924, when his book *The Trauma of Birth* appeared, marked the beginnings of Rank's separation from psychoanalysis. To the end of his life in 1939, Otto Rank worked to create a new psychology, a work that took him far afield from psychoanalysis. However, he continues to be one of the most important figures in the history of psychoanalysis.

§ The Man

Rank was born in Vienna in 1884. Born Otto Rosenfeld, he assumed the name of Rank in 1901. He was one of three children, with a brother three years his senior and a sister who died a few months after birth. According to diaries discovered after his death (Taft, 1958), life within the Rosenfeld family was unpleasant and painful. His alcoholic father had a violent temper and could not support the family; Otto's gentle mother assumed the responsibility. When Otto was sixteen, he and his brother, whom Otto liked very much, decided to discontinue relationship with their father. Although they continued to live in the same house, they ceased conversing with him. In his diary he wrote: "We finally fell out with him and did not greet him any more." No word was spoken in their home because, he wrote, "If a voice ever became loud, it became very loud; it screamed, for everyone had deep rage inside."

The lack of a father or other strong individual in his environment while he was growing up caused pain and sadness to young Rank, who could only borrow ego ideals from literature, philosophy, and art and try to mold himself after these imaginary heroes. Beginning in his high school days, he read Darwin, Ibsen, Wedekind, Dostoevski, Schopenhauer, Weininger, and others with great interest. They were a great source of insight and inspiration to this young man. Schopenhauer in particular became an admired and respected image: his pessimistic philosophy fitted well into the sadness and disappointment of Rank's life.

Rank, endowed with high intelligence, had from early adolescence felt a strong creative surge within himself. He worked hard—reading, writing, and dreaming of himself as a great man. He was curious about the character of the great men he read about and endowed some with qualities they did not have. For example, he compared Nietzsche with Jesus; he felt shattered when he discovered that Nietzsche had died of syphilis. Although he liked Otto Weininger's *Sex and Character*, he disagreed with Weininger's antifeminine views. At one time he contemplated writing a biography of Napoleon. (Freud as a youth had also admired great men—although for reasons different than Rank's—and he, too, had greatly admired Napoleon.) In his search for an ideal man, Rank became deeply interested in the artist, the artist's psychology, and the psychology of creativity generally. In the psychology he developed, the artist is considered the ideal man, the nonneurotic man.

He attended a technical school, contemplating becoming a mechanic, but because of physical weakness and (apparently) an old rheumatic condition, took an office job. The theater became an outlet for his deprived and lonely life. Suicide is often mentioned in his diaries, but these depressed periods alternated with active periods showing "an intense desire for life, joy, and creativity." Of Nietzsche, he said: "I bathed, as it were, in Nietzsche's spirit and got a charmed, weatherproof skin that should protect me in the meantime from external attacks." At another time he wrote: "I have an aversion to every contact with people—I mean, to every physical contact. It costs me an effort to extend my hand to anyone, and if I must do it, I first put on gloves. I couldn't kiss anyone." Despite these troubled feelings, his creativity was already apparent. He wrote constantly, claiming to have completed three novels, fragments of which were found by his biographer Jessie Taft (1958). His most important creation from this period, probably written in 1903 or 1904, is *The Artist* (*Der Kuenstler*) (1907), a study of the creative powers and psychology of the artist.

He first came across Freud's work in 1904, at the age of twenty. After reading some of Freud's writings, according to Taft (1958), he went through almost a religious and ecstatic revelation. "Now I see everything clearly," he said, "The world process is no longer a riddle." Adler suggested a personal meeting with Freud, and Rank took along the manuscript of *The Artist*. Especially in the light of his poor relationship with his own father and the deprived life he had led as a child, it must have meant a great deal to Rank to have been immediately accepted by Freud. Here was a kind, well-known and strong father image who readily accepted and helped him in many ways. Schopenhauer, Nietzsche, and other ideal images faded. He had finally met the man of whom he had dreamed from early childhood. Of this first encounter, Freud wrote:

> One day a young man who had passed through the technical training school introduced himself with a manuscript which showed very unusual comprehension. We induced him to go through the gymnasium and the university and to devote himself to the non-medical side of psychoanalytic investigation. The little society acquired in him a zealous and dependable secretary, and I gained in Otto Rank a faithful helper and co-worker (Freud, 1959, Vol. I, p. 307).

§ The Psychoanalytic Period: 1906–1924

After their first encounter, a close relationship developed between Freud and Rank which was at times stronger than the relationships Freud had developed with the other pioneers around him. Freud was impressed by Rank's talents, enthusiasm, and creativity. Freud included Rank in his social activities, helped him financially, and on one occasion provided him with money for a much-needed vacation. This contact with Freud helped Rank's maturation. He worked hard and read intensively; he took to psychoanalysis as if it were something he had been seeking all his life.

Psychoanalysis provided Rank with the technique for analyzing the lives of the renowned artists and philosophers who had stimulated his fantasy in the early years of his life. That first book, *The Artist*, was prepared before he met Freud, but now the two men discussed it at length, and Rank made use of Freud's criticisms and suggestions.

In *The Artist* (*Der Kuenstler*, 1907), Rank states that the psychic conflict in the "normal" individual is unconscious and finds expression through dreams or other psychic acts. The artist however does not find enough outlet through his dreams, but utilizes his creative fantasies to express his ungratified wishes. In doing this, the artist offers the public, whose needs for art are parallel to his but not so intense, the opportunity for gaining esthetic pleasure and at the same time work through its own psychic conflict. Through his work of art the artist requires less psychic energy to repress conflict than the "normal" individual. But some economy of psychic energy is also afforded the public who otherwise would have to rely entirely on dreams and other outlets.

As for the neurotic, both he and the artist are on the lookout for an opportunity to discharge psychic conflict, but the artist has the advantage that he can channel his fantasies into artistic creations. In this way he can avoid serious illness and still retain his hold on reality.

The artist employs his creative gifts in modifying or altering what is unacceptable in the unconscious and offers the end result of his elaboration as a work of beauty and art. He offers the public the freedom he is trying to achieve for himself. In Tragedy, the highest form of poetry, the spectator identifies with the actors and through them with the poet, and in this way he abreacts his affects. The viewer works at his own psychic conflict, but while he can fall back on his esthetic enjoyment he leaves the suffering to the fantasy image of the hero on the stage. Beyond a certain limit art cannot go, the artist himself stands in front of his creation as in front of a miracle. He does not understand it anymore than the dreamer his dreams or the neurotic his symptoms.

The psychic conflict finds it outlet, says Rank, through neurosis, perversion, or a third outcome, sublimation. It is in this last solution that one finds one of the sources of artistic creativity.

Rank was an active member of the Wednesday evening meetings in Freud's home, where he was always seated at Freud's left hand.[1] From

[1] In a conversation with Lou Andreas-Salomé (1964), Freud remarked about Rank, "Why don't we have such a lovely person six times instead of only once in our Society?"

1906 to 1915, he was the secretary of the Vienna Psychoanalytic Society and kept the records of the meetings. Through Rank's lucidity and writing ability, the minutes of the Society, not always clear before his time, were edited in intelligible form (Nunberg & Federn, 1962). Jones reports that Rank possessed a great facility for interpreting unconscious material, especially that related to literary and poetic work. His knowledge of mythological literature was exceptional. Before the outbreak of World War I, he had planned a personal analysis and apparently had gone to England for this purpose, but his analysis was delayed by the start of the war.[2] He wrote and published many papers, some of them classics on psychoanalysis. He wrote on narcissism, symbolism, and the folkloristic parallel to infantile sexual theories, and made many contributions to dream analysis.

His second book was *The Myth of the Birth of the Hero* (1909), to which Freud contributed the part on the "family romance." Rank discussed myths as products of man's wishes and fantasies. He traced the myth back to the pregenital complexes of childhood, and interpreted the miraculous and supernatural meanings of myths by attributing human motives to them. He demonstrated that in mythology the hero begins his career in conflict with the older generation and, consequently, becomes a rebel, a renovator, and a revolutionary. Originally, every revolutionary is a disobedient son—a rebel against his father. Rank found support for this thesis particularly in the Greek myths, where the sons of the gods must first remove the father before they can take his place. The castration of the father is the strongest expression of revolt against the father and is at the same time proof of this myth's sexual origin. Rank suggests that "myths are created by adults by means of retrograde childhood phantasies, the hero being credited with the myth-maker's personal infantile history." This process in the life of the hero is the same as is found in the unconscious of persons who have gone through their own infantile revolt against the father. In the birth myth, the infantile rebellion against the father is provoked by the hostile behavior of the father; this justifies the son's rebellion. The projection mechanism used in the myth requires the characterization of the myth as a paranoid structure. This explains why the hero so frequently starts life persecuted by the father, who has him cast off a mountain or

[2] In 1918, when Herman Nunberg suggested at the Budapest Congress that analysts should have personal analyses before treating patients, Rank and Tausk vigorously opposed the suggestion (Nunberg & Federn, 1962).

abandoned in a basket on the waters. *The Myth of the Birth of the Hero* is Rank's greatest contribution to applied psychoanalysis.

Rank was the first lay analyst to treat patients. At about this time, he and Hanns Sachs became close friends—a friendship that lasted until Rank turned his back on psychoanalysis. Sachs and Rank exchanged views about papers they were planning to write, sometimes showing each other their manuscripts. A good deal of their work at this time bears the sign of their discussions. After the Vienna Society was formed and Rank had become its secretary, on their way home from meetings Rank and Sachs would accompany Freud on long walks through the streets of Vienna. Freud communicated many of his thoughts to the two men and listened to their views and criticisms. He spoke freely, coloring his conversation with his famous witty anecdotes and expressions. Either alone or with Sachs, Rank was invited to Freud's home almost weekly; after supper they worked on publications of the psychoanalytic movement (Sachs, 1944).

In 1912, Rank received his doctoral degree from the University of Vienna, and shortly thereafter he published *The Incest Motif in Poetry and Saga* (1912). Rank elaborated on the frequency with which writers and poets have chosen incest as their main theme and the manner in which this Oedipus complex has been modified and embellished to make it morally and artistically acceptable. The book contains a series of stimulating Oedipal analyses. Thus again Rank shows how the artist derives unconscious gratification for his forbidden wishes through his artistic creations.

In 1912, Rank and Sachs started the journal *Imago*. Rank also edited, together with Ferenczi and Jones, the *Internationale Zeitschrift für Psychoanalyse*, from its beginnings in 1913, and he was the sole editor from 1921 to 1924. After he became secretary of the Vienna Society, he often acted as private secretary to Freud. As Jones says, "Rank was always willing; he never complained of any burden put upon him and was a man of all work turning himself to any task" (Vol. II, 1955). Shortly after the inception of *Imago*, he published "Nakedness in Saga and Poetry" (1913), which was based on a paper he had read at the Third International Congress on Psychoanalysis in 1911. In this paper Rank reviews the idea of "looking" and the consequent punishment of blindness for gazing at erotic nakedness from mythological writings to modern literature and offers its psychoanalytic connections. He considers the blindness of Oedipus for having gazed at his mother and offers as psychoanalytical evidence how the mother is the first object of the child's peeping desire. The mythological change of the lower half of a woman's body into a serpent or a fish he attributes to repression of the original desire, the desired part having become disgusting, bestial, or repulsive. Rank discussed the various forms the repression of nakedness assumes as it proceeds from pleasure and gratification of exhibitionistic impulses toward shame and guilt feelings.

The same year, he also published another book, which Sachs co-authored, *The Significance of Psychoanalysis for the Mental Sciences* (1913). In this volume, Rank and Sachs produced an introduction to the nonmedical applications of psychoanalysis. They indicated the most important fields to which psychoanalysis has brought light, and from which psychoanalysis has gained important confirmation of its findings. In 1914, Rank contributed the section on dreams in literature and mythology to Freud's *The Interpretation of Dreams* (Fourth Edition).

The strength of Rank's creativity is astounding. In addition, that year he published the *Doppelgänger* (1914). In "The Double," Rank after reviewing the writings of E. T. Hoffmann, Goethe, R. L. Stevenson, Oscar Wilde, and Dostoevski in which the "double" has been dealt with, traces the association that the "double" has with reflections in the mirror; with shadows, ghosts, or guardian spirits; with belief in the soul; and with fear of death. Rank thinks that since primitive man the "double" has been a narcissistic protection against the destruction of the ego; and "energetic denial of the power of death." The "immortal soul" was very likely the first "double" of the body. The narcissistic omnipotence was challenged by the idea of death and compelled man to attribute some of this omnipotence and wish for immortality to spirits and ultimately to the soul. The soul having been since earliest time considered a reduplication of the body. With this solution the thought of death is made tolerable by conceiving of another existence in the "double" form.

With the start of World War I in 1914, Rank entered the army, becoming editor of the official paper of the Austrian Army. In Poland where he was stationed, he met his future wife, Beata, who came to Vienna after the war. Following his discharge from the army and his return to Vienna, Rank seemed a different man from his prewar self. The hard-working, enthusiastic, and somewhat compliant man had given place to a more determined and tougher individual. As Jones reported it: "In stalked a wiry, tough man with a masterful air, whose first act was to deposit on the table a huge revolver. I asked him what he wanted with it, and he nonchalantly replied, 'It is for any eventuality' " (Vol. III, 1957).

Rank continued to work with the same energy he had displayed before the war, now as the director of the International Psychoanalytic Publishing House in Vienna. However, the war experience and his marriage had made definite changes in him. A certain antagonism developed between him and Abraham, and also Jones. Lilla Veszy-Wagner says that "Otto Rank constantly poured into Freud's ears stories of how impossible Jones was as a colleague, particularly when Rank and Jones were jointly engaged in editing the International Journal. He accused Jones of poor control over his moods and passions and of unjust susceptibilities—in fact, of personal interference in every step of the editing process" (Alexander, Eisenstein, & Grotjahn, 1966).

In 1923, Rank became friendly with Ferenczi; together they published *The Development of Psychoanalysis* (1924). In this book, one detects for the first time a change in Rank's views about psychoanalysis: it presages his departure from psychoanalysis. Some of the thoughts expressed therein have been further developed by other psychoanalytic writers; some findings have become part of today's psychoanalytic thought. The authors stressed the importance of the mother to the infant, and "acting out" is mentioned for the first time in psychoanalytic literature. Rank and Ferenczi expressed the view that the analysis of the acting out of the unconscious material should become the primary aim of the therapy, the theoretical reconstruction of the patient's past and development being secondary aspects of the analysis. In his review of the book, Franz Alexander (1925) expressed the concern about it that prevailed at the time in Vienna and Berlin. Alexander mentioned that the acting-out factor had already been indicated by Freud years before in the term "the experience factor." He concurred with the authors' insistence that repetition and recollection in treatment are most important in the recovery of the patient. However, he objected to their crediting analysis of the acting out with being the "ultimate method for the cure of the neurosis." "It is too bad," Alexander stated, "that the book was published before the authors had been able to take full advantage of the material in *The Ego and the Id* and other important theoretical papers which Freud had published shortly before."

Rank and Ferenczi deserve credit for underscoring the importance of transference in psychoanalytic therapy; but in claiming that this is the most important dynamic factor in therapy, they tended to disregard the importance of the recollection of repressed material. The authors advocated considerable activity on the part of the therapist, but they did not indicate how this should be undertaken. They also mentioned setting an end to the analysis[3]; however they failed to explain how this should be connected to the patient's ability to give up the transference. Abreaction as an important psychoanalytic technique was also stressed, but they placed insufficient significance on the working through of the repressed material.

In "Don Juan" (1922) Rank studies the Don Juan legend in tradition and literature culminating with Mozart's *Don Giovanni.* Rank noticed the motive of guilt and punishment that pervades the Don Juan stories. He confirmed this through psychoanalytic findings that stress the guilt and punishment rooted in the Oedipus complex.

The numerous women sought by Don Juan represent the mother to whom he is unconsciously attached, while the injured and betrayed men represent the father. By means of repression and displacement the individual attached to the mother becomes faithless and a cynical despiser of women. Don Juan becomes in the literature and in the unconscious the striving, struggling man, whose faithlessness is due to his search for an ideal woman.

Rank attributes Mozart's treatment of Don Juan to Mozart's loss of his father and that of his best friend at the time he was working on the opera *Don Giovanni.* The overture to the opera was feverishly composed in one night as by one "possessed."

Two years after this paper, without warning to Freud or anyone else associated with him, Rank published *The Trauma of Birth* (1924). For one of Freud's group to publish a book without discussing it with at least some other member was most unusual. It was especially unexpected that Rank should have published such a book without first speaking with Sachs, for Sachs and Rank were accustomed to exchange views about material they intended to publish, and together had written *The Significance of Psychoanalysis for the Mental Sciences.* Sachs and Rank had spent the summer vacation together at the very time Rank was writing the book.

[3] Freud himself in a case treated in 1910 used "end setting": he considered it a "blackmailing device" effective in some cases, "provided that one hits the right time at which to employ it." "Analysis, Terminable and Interminable," first published in 1937 (1959, Vol. V, 317f.).

In *The Trauma of Birth,* Rank constructed a new approach to the genesis of mental development, based on the separation anxiety every baby experiences when he is born. Rank interpreted this experience, which he called "primal anxiety," as the most important element for the future development of the individual, and also as the source of neurosis. Sachs, in his review of the book (1925), objected that Rank had not provided clinical material to back his new views, and claimed that most of his material was based on "interesting analogies" or "striking agreements in obviously forced inferences." Rank introduced technical innovations, claiming that his discoveries had convinced him of their importance, but he gave few details about these innovations. The "pathologic drama" of birth is stressed continuously; it is resolved in therapy. The importance of the Oedipus complex is minimized and the hatred and fear of the father is considered as secondary to the trauma of birth. The fixation on the mother is due to biological factors, that is, the freedom from pain she affords, memory of which is recorded at the deepest levels of the unconscious and reproduced in analysis. The relationship to the father not only is of secondary importance but is purely in the nature of fantasy. Because the relationship is not based on intrauterine experience, it belongs to a far later period than the trauma of birth and to a "higher mental stratum." All things that happen to the individual after separation from the mother are simply expressions of the primal anxiety. This experience is both prior to and subsequent to all individual development, and common to all persons. Rank compared the analytic experience to the "gradual passing into a state almost free from reality." He likened the position on the couch in the analytic situation with the intrauterine position, and completely disregarded the demands of the analytic situation. To Rank (Sachs, 1925), masochism represented the "transformation of the pain suffered at birth into pleasurable sensations." In *The Trauma of Birth,* Rank tried to bring psychoanalytic views into line with his own views. He recommended revealing the primal trauma to the patient from the start of therapy. The fact that such a trauma is repressed did not bother Rank. His technique started with the birth trauma and followed through later life experiences until it terminated in the immediate conflicts that had brought the patient into analysis.

Freud's initial reaction to *The Trauma of Birth* was one of tolerance and an attempt at understanding. He is said to have told Ferenczi: "I don't know whether 66 percent or 33 percent of it is true, but in any case it is the most important progress since the discovery of psychoanalysis." Rank later claimed that Freud had told him that "Anyone else would have used such a discovery to make himself independent" (J. Jones, 1960). To members of the inner circle, Freud wrote, "Some instinct must be associated with birth trauma which aims at restoring the previous existence. One might call it the instinctual need for happiness." In the beginning, Ernest Jones was favorably impressed by the publication. In "Psychoanalysis and Anthropology," read before the Royal Anthropological Institute in 1924, he stated: "The importance of birth on primitive man's belief is one that would meet with extensive support from psychoanalysis and is quite along the lines of a recent important study by Otto Rank."

Nevertheless, Rank's views met with strong opposition from Abraham and the others. Abraham referred to the work as "scientific regression." Freud had difficulty in recognizing the beginnings of deviation in his pupils, and it must have been particularly difficult for him to suspect such a deviation in Rank, of whom he was so fond. The book was dedicated to Freud, and Rank apparently was startled by the animosity it stirred up (Karpf, 1953).

There seem to have been definite reasons for Freud's willingness to accept *The Trauma of Birth* as an important contribution to psychoanalysis. In a footnote to *The Interpretation of Dreams* (Second Edition), published in 1909, Freud noted that "the act of birth is the first experience of anxiety, and thus the source and prototype of the affect of anxiety." In the same year, in remarks before the Vienna Psychoanalytic Society, he said that children begin their experience of anxiety in the act of birth itself. He made no further mention of this concept until the end of *The Ego and the Id*, when he referred to the birth act as "the first great anxiety state." In a footnote, written in 1923, to "Phobia in a Five-Year-Old Boy," he noted: "Rank's view of the effects of the trauma of birth seems to throw special light on the predisposition to anxiety-hysteria which is so strong in childhood."

Since Freud had first mentioned the concept in 1909, re-emphasizing it as he worked on *The Ego and the Id* in 1923, it is very likely that Rank first heard of it from Freud and constructed about it an entirely new theory that repudiated the Oedipus complex and postulated radical new changes in theory and technique.

Freud was willing to accept the concept of birth trauma, but he was definitely startled by Rank's attempts to weave a new psychoanalytic theory and technique around it. In a letter to Rank he said, "You overlook the danger, to which some have already succumbed, namely, of projecting into science as a theory that which moves in oneself, that has really no value as a conquest" (Taft, 1958).

Rank's extreme views and the controversy that followed stimulated Freud to review once more the problem of anxiety. In his 1926 paper, "Inhibitions, Symptoms and Anxiety," he refuted for the first time Rank's hypothesis concerning birth trauma.

In "Analysis, Terminable and Interminable," which first appeared in 1937, Freud expressed definitive views on the trauma of birth:

> Otto Rank made a particularly determined attempt to shorten analysis. He assumed that the cardinal source of neurosis was the experience of birth, on the grounds of its involving a possibility that the infant's "primal fixation" to the mother might not be surmounted but persist in the form of "primal repression." His hope was that, if this primal trauma were overcome by analysis, the whole neurosis would clear up, so that this one small piece of analytic work, for which a few months should suffice, would do away with the necessity for all the rest. Rank's argument was certainly bold and ingenious, but it did not stand the test of critical examination. Moreover, it was a child of its time, conceived under the stress of the contrast between the postwar misery of Europe and the "prosperity" of America, and designed to accelerate the tempo of analytic therapy to suit the rush of American life (Freud, 1959, Vol. V).

Had Rank continued within the framework of psychoanalysis, his idea about birth anxiety would probably have found some acceptance in psychoanalytic circles. The importance of the mother in modern psychoanalytic theory may have had a pioneer in Rank with his concepts of "primal fixation," "primal regression," and "primal anxiety." The modern concepts of "good and bad mother," "primal love" and "return to womb fantasies," and "fusion with the mother" may owe their origins in part to Rank. His idea of "end setting" is now employed in specific cases, and "separation anxiety" in analysis is a successor to Rank's "primal anxiety." Shortening the therapeutic process and working on dependency in analysis are also used in specific cases; the "active therapy" postulated by Rank and Ferenczi has followers today both within and outside of the psychoanalytic field—particularly in work with borderline and psychotic cases.

At first, Rank had no wish to separate himself from the psychoanalytic movement; surprised by the controversy his book had aroused, however, he decided to leave for Paris and wait there for things to quiet down. When he returned in 1926, he realized how far away from his friends and psychoanalysis he had strayed. His new views also seem to have caused considerable stress in his marriage; his wife Beata continued to work within the classical psychoanalytic framework. On his return, Rank met with Freud in what he later called "analytic conferences." Following these meetings, he addressed a letter to the members of the inner circle, apologizing for his behavior, in which he said: "From a state which I now recognize as neurotic, I have suddenly returned to myself." He attributed his actions during the past year to neurotic conflicts.

Rank made several trips to the United States, where he was treated coldly in psychoanalytic circles. Although Freud gave him letters of introduction to A. A. Brill and other analysts in New York, his lecturing about his new views did not make for a favorable climate during his trip. He was particularly pained by his encounter with Ferenczi in Pennsylvania Station, when, according to Rank, Ferenczi pretended not to see him. Jessie Taft (1958, p. XVI) quoted Rank as having said, "He was my best friend, and he refused to speak to me."

On his return from the United States, Rank published three volumes, *Psychoanalytic Technique,* the last of which appeared in 1931, in which he developed his birth trauma theories in greater detail. This marked the beginning of his new psychological views. Ferenczi, who reviewed the first volume (1927), said that Rank should have titled the work "The Rank Technique for the Treatment of Neurosis." Volume I contains some traces of Rank's former psychoanalytic thoughts, but in the second and third volumes he completely rejected psychoanalytic views, taking off on his own. Ferenczi compared Rank's technique with that of "wild analysts who neglect the historical backgrounds of the patient's personality and start off straight away upon a chase for infantile traumas." Ferenczi wrote that he had tried Rank's technique but abandoned it when he found that patients willingly accept interpretation about birth trauma and mother transference but then use this as a defense against castration anxiety.

Freud made several attempts to bring Rank back within the psychoanalytic family, before he realized how hopeless this was. He later attributed the beginning of Rank's separation to 1923, when Freud's malignant disease was first diagnosed. At the time, even Freud was unaware of the diagnosis, but Rank had learned of it from Freud's physicians. Later, Freud is said to have maintained that the knowledge of his illness had a fateful effect on Rank. According to Jessie Taft (1958), Rank's attachment to Freud was perhaps his deepest relationship, except for that with his mother. Despite Freud's warm feelings for Rank, according to Sachs (1944), when Freud realized that all his efforts to reach an agreement with Rank were futile and that Rank was firm in his decision to estrange himself both from him and from psychoanalysis, Freud considered the separation final, saying, "Now that I have forgiven him everything I am finished with him."

Between 1926 and 1935, Rank lived in Paris, commuting frequently to the United States. In 1935 he moved permanently to New York, where he worked with doctors and patients, and continued to develop his theories, which are not germane to this book.

Rank's struggles are best described in one of his writings about the artist:

> The artist usually shows himself in the choice of some recognized master as the ideal pattern. In doing so, he becomes a representative of an ideology and at first his individuality vanishes until later, at the height of his achievement, he strives once more to liberate his personality, now a mature personality, from the bounds of an ideology which he has himself accepted and helped to form (1932, pp. 371–372).

In 1939, Rank divorced his wife and two months later married his secretary. Soon after his second marriage he died of an infection. Freud had died in London a month before Rank's death.

As if he had been a character in *The Myth of the Birth of the Hero*, Rank started as an obedient son, but was unable to mature and grow at his father's side. He had to rebel and, in so doing, he attempted to destroy what he himself had helped shape.

REFERENCES

Alexander, F. Review of *The development of psychoanalysis* by O. Rank and S. Ferenczi. *Internat. J. Psycho-Anal.*, 1925, 6, 484–495.

Alexander, F., S. Eisenstein, M. Grotjahn. *Psychoanalytic pioneers.* New York: Basic Books, 1966.

Ferenczi, S. Review of *Psychoanalytic technique* by O. Rank. *Internat. J. Psycho-Anal.*, 1927, 8, 93–100.

Freud, S. *The collected papers of Sigmund Freud.* New York: Basic Books, 1959. 5 vols.

Jones, E. *The life and works of Sig-*

mund Freud. New York: Basic Books, 1957. 3 vols.

Jones, J. Otto Rank: a forgotten heresy. *Commentary*, September, 1960, 219–229.

Karpf, F. B. *The psychology and psychotherapy of Otto Rank*. New York: Philosophical Library, 1953.

Leavy, S. A. (Trans.) *The Freud journal of Lou Andreas-Salomé*. New York: Basic Books, 1964.

Nunberg, H., & E. Federn (Eds.). *Minutes of the Vienna Society*. Vol. I. New York: International Universities Press, 1962.

Rank, O. *Art and the artist*. (English transl. Charles Francis Atkinson) New York: Alfred A. Knopf, 1932.

Rank, O. *Der Kuenstler*. Vienna: Heller, 1907.

Rank, O. *The myth of the birth of the hero*. Leipzig, Vienna: Deuticke, 1909.

Rank, O. *The incest motif in poetry and saga*. Leipzig and Vienna: Deuticke, 1912.

Rank, O. Nakedness in saga and poetry. *Psychol. Rev.*, 1917, 4, 444.

Rank, O. *Der Doppelgänger*. *Imago*, 1914, 3, 97–164.

Rank, O. Don Juan. *Psychol. Rev.*, 1926, 13, 480–484.

Rank, O. *The trauma of birth*. Leipzig: Inter. Psycho. Verlag, 1924.

Rank, O. *Will therapy*. (Taft, J. Trans.) New York: Knopf, 1936.

Rank, O., & S. Ferenczi. *The development of psychoanalysis*. Leipzig & Vienna: Zurich International Press, 1924.

Rank, O., & H. Sachs. *The significance of psychoanalysis for the mental sciences*. Wiesbaden: Bergmann, 1913.

Sachs, H. Review of *The trauma of birth* by O. Rank. *Int. J. Psycho-Anal.*, 1925, 6, 499–508.

Sachs, H. *Freud, master and friend*. Cambridge: Harvard University Press, 1944.

Taft, Jessie. *Otto Rank*. New York: Julian Press, 1958.

Max Eitingon

1881–1943

THE ORGANIZATION OF PSYCHOANALYTIC TRAINING

*

SIDNEY L. POMER

"You were the first to come to the lonely one," Sigmund Freud was to write to Max Eitingon on several occasions (E. L. Freud, 1960). It was indeed a new beginning in the history of the psychoanalytic movement when this scholarly and cultured young man of twenty-six came from Switzerland as a visitor to a meeting of the Vienna Psychoanalytic Society on the evening of January 23, 1907. This was Max Eitingon, the first to come from a foreign country to study psychoanalysis at its source.

He was at this period working as a voluntary assistant at Bleuler's psychiatric clinic, the Burghölzli, in Zurich. His purpose in Vienna was twofold: he had brought a severely disturbed patient (later found unsuitable for analysis) about whom he had already written Freud. He came also at Bleuler's behest to discover what a psychiatrist might learn from psychoanalysis. He stayed to attend two meetings of the Society as a guest, asking interested and perceptive questions; afterward he spent several evenings on long walks with Freud.

These visits undoubtedly began a personal analysis, for such was the pattern of his teacher. Of Eitingon's early visits with Freud, Jones says, "This was indeed the first training analysis!" He added that it must have been something of an athletic endeavor, winding even younger men. "I remember the swift pace and the rapid spate of speech on such walks. Walking fast used to stimulate the flow of Freud's thoughts, but it was at times breathtaking for a companion who would have preferred to digest them (Vol. II, 1957). The impact of the master on the student at this first acquaintance must have been considerable, for Eitingon's personal devotion came to know no bounds, and he was second to none in his hero-worship and total dedication to Freud (Eitingon, 1950).

Max Eitingon was born on June 26, 1881, at Mohilev in Russia. He was the son of a very wealthy, orthodox Jewish family (Gumbel, 1950). When he was twelve, his family moved to Leipzig, Germany, where he went to school. Possibly because of a speech impediment, a stammer that afflicted him through life, he left school before matriculation. Later, at Marburg, he began his medical studies and pursued philosophy under the neo-Kantian, Hermann Cohen (Jones, Vol. III, 1957).

It was in 1909 that Eitingon received his medical degree. It must have been much on his mind, for Freud is recorded by Erich Gumbel [1] as having said wryly to the young man just prior to this time, "I will make you a Doctor of Psychoanalysis!"

Upon attaining his medical doctorate, Eitingon moved to Berlin, to join his friend Abraham, where he was to remain until his departure for Palestine more than twenty years later, during the rise of Hitler. Many years before, his father had bought land in Israel, possibly as a future haven.

In Berlin, he seems to have played an unusual role. For one thing, he was the only psychoanalyst in the world of that time with independent means. In thus escaping the need to plunge immediately into practice, he was in a sense freed for his real role in the psychoanalytic movement—that of initiator, teacher, administrator, reporter[2] and, thanks to a generous nature, quite often financial backer. Fortunately, he was in the position to be of enormous financial assistance to the movement. In his complete devotion to Freud, he was of invaluable material aid in countless undertakings (Jones, Vol. III, 1957).

[1] E. Gumbel, personal communication. 1964.

[2] Jones claimed he published little and made no scientific contributions to the movement. Actually, he is the author of several reports on the Berlin Institute and the International Association, which exhibit fluency, deep thought, and great power of expression—indications that he could write but evidently chose not to publish extensively, since his scientific publications are few.

The onset of World War I found Eitingon entering the service of Austria as a captain in the Medical Corps. By 1917, he began to be known for his work with war neuroses. "Excellent practical work performed by Abraham, Eitingon and Ferenczi," reports Jones, "had made an impression, if not on the general medical public, at least on the high-ranking Army medical officers, and there was talk of erecting psychoanalytical clinics at various centers for the treatment of war neuroses" (Vol. III, 1957).

At the end of the war, Eitingon was using every resource to aid Freud and his family in stricken Austria. Once he sent gifts of food and cigars, to which Freud responded in a letter dated December 2, 1919: "You send us quantities of material for life [food] and work [cigars] . . . and even with all this you still aren't satisfied. Your last precious gift, by the way, met with an accident about which Mathilde didn't want me to tell you."

It was in this same year that a signal honor came to Eitingon: he was added to the small inner circle at the heart of the psychoanalytic movement. With von Freund failing, "Freud suggested," says Jones, "that Eitingon be invited to join our private Committee. We at once agreed, and Abraham was commissioned to procure Eitingon's consent" (Vol. III, 1957). Eitingon accepted. From Freud's letter confirming the appointment, he learned the true extent of Freud's regard for him: "The secret of the Committee is that it has taken from me my most burdensome care for the future, so that I can calmly follow my path to the end" (E. L. Freud, 1960).

Freud was referring here to a problem we can best understand from another letter:

> The care that weighs me down about the future I can best convey to you genetically. It comes from a time when psychoanalysis depends on me alone, and when I was so uneasy about what the human rabble would make out of it when I was no longer alive. In 1912, when we saw an example of these possibilities, the Committee was formed and took on the task of continuation along the right lines. Since then I have felt more light-hearted and carefree about how long my life will last (E. L. Freud, 1960).

This was the group in which Freud now included Eitingon.

The following year, 1920, Eitingon began to emerge from his long years of study and preparation to play an infinitely more active role in the movement as he, with Abraham and Simmel, first founded and then headed the Berlin Polyclinic. Then, as always, Eitingon was shy, modest and quietly reserved. He was by nature kind, warm-hearted, and always ready to help those in need. His generous deeds were done in silence and were learned of indirectly or not at all. Though Jones hazards the opinion that Freud's friendship with Eitingon ". . . cannot lead one to suppose he thought especially highly of his intellectual abilities . . ." [3] the man is on record as a connoisseur in many fields of art, the owner of a large library and a gifted linguist. In addition to Russian and German, he read Polish, French, English, and Hebrew. His home was in exquisite taste; and his wife Mira, who matched him in elegance and artistry, joined Eitingon in many of his intellectual pursuits.

This, then, was the man who made one of the most important contributions to psychoanalysis in providing, anonymously, the means to found the Polyclinic in Berlin. "My friend," Freud later wrote, "who created the Berlin Psychoanalytic Polyclinic and has hitherto supported it out of his own resources" (1961). On February 14, 1920, the clinic was opened with the twofold purpose of offering treatment to the economically deprived as well as to provide an opportunity to establish a practical and theoretical curriculum for the teaching of psychoanalysis.

Its aim, Freud wrote in 1930—prefacing a ten-year report on the institution—was not only to make help available to those in need but to provide a center at which analysis could be taught theoretically, and training and supervision offered, with the final goal of perfecting knowledge of neurotic illness and therapeutic techniques by applying them and testing them under fresh conditions. It was a sorry note, Freud added, that the dedicated and self-sacrificing men who originated and ran the institution waited in vain for assistance from the state or interest from the University. Of Eitingon's selfless contribution, Freud said in the same context: "Anyone who in whatever sense has a share in psychoanalysis will unite in thanking him."

It was indeed the case that Eitingon, Simmel, and Abraham, as well as their colleagues, saw the Polyclinic as a hopeful center for psychoanalytic education. From this it seems likely that, in the creation of the clinic, Eitingon's strongest impetus was an utterance by Nunberg at the Budapest Congress in 1918. As Eitingon wrote years later: ". . . it was Nunberg who declared that no one could any longer learn to practice psychoanalysis without having been analyzed himself. As these words

[3] Jones himself confutes this by recording many instances of Freud's sending original drafts to Eitingon for critical appraisal.

left his lips, we realized their momentous character, and that what Nunberg desiderated would immediately become a universal ideal and very soon a reality" (1937).

Eitingon "often tried to formalize good practice into rules," as has been noted by Lewin and Ross.

It must have been the continued contemplation of this goal that led to a new name for the Polyclinic in 1924. To emphasize the greater development of its role in the training of analysts, the Polyclinic was rechristened the "Institute." [4] From the beginning, Eitingon played a central role in the Institute (aided greatly by Abraham and Simmel); and although he did not himself lecture, he conducted a seminar on technique, supervised courses of study, and handled the administration of the Institute.[5]

An extension of the role in the Institute played by this self-effacing man came about in 1925 at the Congress in Bad Homburg when, as Secretary, he proposed that the Berlin system of training candidates, which gradually was being followed in other centers, should be made universal and standardized under the aegis of an International Training Commission. This proposal was accepted, and Eitingon appointed its president, a position he retained to his death in 1943.

As Anna Freud noted in an article on control analysis, the major contribution by Eitingon was his work in the gradual development and formalization of the training program for psychoanalytic candidates as it is known today. Balint saw the International Training Commission as Eitingon's favorite creation.

Eitingon was bringing into actual practice what he felt were Freud's deepest wishes for the progress of psychoanalysis. The early foundations of the training system were laid in Budapest in 1918, when three

[4] Balint, in his paper on the psychoanalytic training system (1947), quotes Eitingon's report on the Berlin Polyclinic in June, 1922: "We are all firmly convinced that henceforth no one who has not been analyzed must aspire to the rank of practising analyst. It follows that the analysis of a student himself is an essential part of the curriculum and takes place at the Poliklinik in the second half of the training period, after a time of intensive theoretical preparation by lectures and courses of instruction."

[5] The history of supervised practical work began with the numerous letters written by Freud in answer to colleagues asking his opinion on psychoanalytic cases. Eitingon states that he regularized and systematized his own correspondence as Freud did, so that the letters of both of them constituted actual supervision. *Kontrol* analysis of this sort became a regular feature of psychoanalytic clinics and was imported to this country around 1930, when European influence was most deeply felt. The American Educational Committees are also modeled on Eitingon's.

events took place: First, and most important, was Freud's warning that the time had come when analysis must prepare for the coming demand by the masses for psychotherapy. The second was Anton von Freund's offer to put a considerable sum of money in the service of Freud's idea. And, of course, the third event was Nunberg's assertion, always remembered by Eitingon, "No one should henceforth be allowed to analyze who has not himself been analyzed previously." The Training Commission thus was an extension of the implications of these remarks. Eitingon's position as its president was the work nearest his heart. "His name will live in the history of psychoanalysis most of all for the ardor with which he first initiated and then developed the high standards of training that were his life's ideal," was Jones's encomium.

Not all his endeavors afforded Eitingon so much gratification as the foregoing. The Verlag, for instance, was destined to be a constant problem. Conceived of and founded by Freud in 1919, the Verlag was a publishing firm for psychoanalytic material. By its very nature, it gave Freud independent control of all its projects. It had unending financial problems. As early as 1921, it was threatened with collapse. Freud called Eitingon in, as a director, to shore up its quaking condition. This he did both with his own funds and his endeavors. Eitingon proved deft at seeking funds for the Verlag, once even securing a donation of $5,000 from a sympathetic brother-in-law in New York. At another time of financial crisis, Freud plunged back all royalties; but this was not enough, and Eitingon had to seek more donations. In spite of these difficulties, Eitingon and Freud opposed the sale of the Verlag's stock and good will to a commercial firm. "Once we give it away," Eitingon said, "we shall never get it back." Much later, in 1931, Freud unwillingly consented to the collection of a fund to assist the Verlag, but he placed on Eitingon the restriction that no analyst or patient be asked to subscribe.

In 1925, at the time of the creation of the Training Commission at the Bad Homburg Congress, Abraham was president of the International Association, and Eitingon its secretary. Many Americans were present at the Congress, and it was becoming increasingly clear that serious differences over the problem of lay analysis were arising between them and the European groups.

The Training Commission, with Eitingon as its head, looked for a hopeful solution to the problem. Unfortunately, Abraham died shortly thereafter, and Eitingon took over as interim president until the Congress at Innsbruck in 1927. He then offered to resign, asking Freud whom he would recommend for the post.[6] Freud answered he would prefer that Eitingon himself remain. Jones added his persuasions, and Eitingon continued in the post. This gave rise to future trouble when, holding two important presidencies simultaneously, Eitingon took the view that the Commission had the right to impose the same standards and rules of admission everywhere—a position that many analysts, including the Americans, resisted. The schism thus created was exacerbated by Eitingon's apparent firm advocacy of lay analysis. As a result he was unfairly regarded in some quarters as both fanatical and dictatorial.

As president of the International Association he opposed the acceptance of Ferenczi's American lay group in the Association. Later, at a preliminary meeting of the Training Commission, he presented a resolution stressing the desirability of candidates' acquiring medical qualifications. Actions such as these led Freud to communicate with Ferenczi thus: "You are right when you say that Eitingon has not his heart in the matter [of lay analysis]; he has forced himself into a friendly attitude out of consideration to Anna and me. As usual, he was here for my birthday, and I used the opportunity to paint to him the gloomy future of analysis if it does not succeed in creating an abode for itself outside of medicine" (E. L. Freud, 1960).

At this time, Freud ruefully described his position as that of Commander-in-Chief without any army (E. L. Freud, 1960).

But Eitingon was to be swept up in problems more overwhelming. The onset of the Depression in the United States in 1928 had gravely affected his fortunes. The American family business from which he had drawn much of his income began to fail, and before long he was poor for the first time in his life. One result was that he could no longer finance the Berlin Institute; he appealed to the members of the Society to contribute what they could. The help that came was not enough, and Freud, himself, solicited backing for the Institute. Eitingon was for the first time faced with the need to earn his own living: he had but a single patient and small prospect of more (E. L. Freud, 1960).

The circumstances of this usually fortunate man underwent a further bitter change. At a time in 1932 when he had already resolved not to seek re-election as president of the International Association, he suffered a cerebral thrombosis. This occurred just when the usual diffi-

[6] He was to chair, in all, three congresses.

culties of the Verlag had resulted in a decision by Freud and Eitingon to call a meeting of its creditors and ask for a moratorium. With paresis of the left arm, there was no doubt that Eitingon would have to relinquish his post in the International Association.[7]

Hard on the heels of this came new problems set in motion by the rise of Hitler in Germany. In January of the year immediately following his illness, Eitingon went to Freud in Vienna to discuss the future of the Berlin Institute, which was in danger, along with every other institute in Germany. Freud encouraged him to hold on as long as possible. Correspondence between the two on this subject continued until April of that year. Then, at a time when Eitingon and his wife were vacationing in Mentone, the new government passed a decree forbidding any foreigner to function in the Central Executive Committee of any German medical society. Since at this time Eitingon was a Polish national, he had to resign his post at the Institute. Thereafter he was so caught up in the press of his affairs that for the first time he missed his annual birthday visit with Freud, who was seventy-seven.[8]

He made up for the visit later, and by September of that year—it was 1933—he had decided to settle in Palestine and had made a preliminary trip there.

Eitingon had long promised himself he would one day found a psychoanalytic institution in Jerusalem. He began his activities on this first visit there by organizing the Palestinian Psychoanalytic Society, which still flourishes. He returned to Berlin to prepare for his final removal, and though England and America both beckoned him, Israel remained his choice. "It now appears," he had said to Idelson at the beginning of the Hitler movement, "that it is time to go to Israel." This was thus a plan long cherished and, on the final day of 1934, he realized it. He left Germany for Israel, settling there permanently.

Characteristically, he helped many colleagues out of Europe during the time that he was laying his own plans. Even earlier in that year he

[7] A reversal of the usual circumstances between Freud and Eitingon came about as a result of this illness. With a stay in bed stretching ahead of the stricken man, Freud offered to lend him $1,000 (E. L. Freud, 1960).

[8] The birthday visits were not necessarily welcomed by Freud, and when, three years later, Eitingon again missed the visit, sending congratulations instead, Freud, eighty, replied testily: "Nearly all of those who have congratulated me on my birthday this year will wait in vain for thanks or acknowledgment. I will educate them by this technique not to do it again next time, but I must make an exception of you . . ." (E. L. Freud, 1960).

had appeared at the Lucerne Congress to suggest a resolution enabling the Central Executive Committee to grant "direct membership" in the International Association to those who had had to leave their own countries and, hence, association with their own societies. Although this applied at the time only to former members of the German Society, the suggestion was resented in the United States as foreign interference with American institutions (Jones, Vol. III, 1957). Consequently, in 1938, the American Psychoanalytic Association announced the withdrawal of this kind of free-floating membership from analysts settling in the U.S. This had been one of three conditions laid down by the American Society as requisite to its reassociation with the International group.[9]

The advent of World War II altered everything, leaving in its wake so little of the psychoanalytic movement on the continent of Europe that the United States—with a majority of the world's analysts—not only lost its former apprehension of the International Association, but has since most cordially cooperated with it (Jones, Vol. III, 1957).

For Eitingon, the move to Israel was more than a wartime necessity: it was a natural consequence of his lifelong interest in Zionism. In him was deeply ingrained the devotion to those related to him, the reverence for tradition, and the genuine piety characteristic of the old patriarchal Jewish family.[10] Every cultural Jewish activity drew him. The Bezalel Art Institute enjoyed his support, and he dedicated himself to the furtherance of the Hebrew University in Palestine. According to Gumbel, it was a fulfillment of his most profound aspirations that he could settle in Jerusalem and introduce psychoanalysis there.

In Israel, Eitingon devoted himself to founding an institute and furthering the psychoanalytic movement. It is almost incredible that, despite his age and recent illness, he should have brought to his work in Israel the zeal which had been his in youth.

There were problems, however. In correspondence reported by Rosenbaum (1954), the hopes and desires of Freud and Eitingon to estab-

[9] The other two: that the International Training Commission be abandoned as a superfluous institution which interfered with internal affairs in the U.S.; and, second, that the International Association should meet for scientific purposes only and should be deprived of all its administrative functions (Jones, Vol. III, 1957).

[10] Jones suggests this as a possible explanation of Eitingon's failure to make scientific contributions to the field, saying it seemed as though he had a Biblical attitude toward Freud's writings that rendered him inaccessible to any innovations from other sources, including, presumably, his own thinking.

lish an institute of psychoanalysis at the Hebrew University were not fulfilled. The University's President, J. L. Magnes, responded to Eitingon's overtures by saying, "It is premature to introduce . . . psychoanalysis before a Chair in Psychology has been established." Nonetheless, the attempt to do so was historic: it was the first effort to introduce psychoanalysis into a university. Undeterred by failure, Eitingon went on to establish, as before, a private institute.

This was his gift to Israel: an institute furnished with a library—his own property—brought from the Berlin Institute. He headed the Hebrew Institute as he had the other, filling the post of director for the remaining years of his life. He laid the groundwork for a very active and well-trained psychoanalytic group. To all this endeavor he made his contribution by his unique, rich and enthusiastic personality.

Eitingon attended the Paris Congress in 1938, and at that time noted the beginning of the cardiac condition that was to claim him five years later. There is no doubt that he was well aware of the implication of his symptoms, but he refused to take care of himself—choosing instead to cross the Channel to visit Freud, who was then eighty-two and near the end of his life. It was the last visit between the pair so long associated, and after Freud's death in 1939, Eitingon himself began to fail. As Dreyfuss (1950) has noted, Eitingon was ill on the occasion of his sixtieth birthday, in honor of which his friends had put together a little pamphlet about him.

At some time in the two years remaining him, he murmured to a friend, "I am not curious," implying within the context of the conversation that he did not yearn for knowledge, that there was, in short, nothing new under the sun. He was driven, rather, by a motive other than curiosity, and he expressed it in his motto. Under the painting of a flame by the Florentine, Giambattista Moroni, Eitingon had had engraved the words: *Et quid volo, nisi ut ardeat* (I only want it to keep burning). He died on July 30, 1943, and is interred on Mount Scopus outside the borders of Jerusalem in Jordan.

His wife Mira did not survive him by many years. A volume dedicated to him, *Max Eitingon, in Memoriam,* composed of articles by friends and colleagues (Dreyfuss, 1950), was in preparation, but unfortunately she died before its pages could be shown her. It contains an account of Eitingon's thirty-six years of dedication to the field of psychoanalysis. Among the encomiums are those of Gumbel, who found

Eitingon's four main characteristics to be warmth, sympathetic understanding, respect for other people, and patience. Writing of him elsewhere,[11] Gumbel has amplified:

> He was an aristocrat of the mind, noble and, with all the great achievements to his credit, immensely modest. . . . Deeply cultured, he excelled in the knowledge and enjoyment of literature, art, music and philosophy. He had a rare understanding of the human psyche, unconscious and conscious, and he was as devoted to his patients as he was to his pupils and friends. He was . . . the most faithful friend of Freud's and never shrank from the greatest sacrifice—even to his own detriment—for the great name and his cause. . . .

Others in the memorial volume are Ellen Simon, one of his last students, who said she had found him warm and sincere, and felt she was in the hands of a virtuoso of an analyst. Anna Freud noted that Eitingon had been a training analyst, supervising analyst, and teacher for more than thirty years in the field of psychoanalysis.

By no means did all the praise for this man come after his death. What must have been to him the most gratifying commendation of all came from the hand of Freud himself, in one of the 250 letters he wrote to Eitingon in the course of their association. It is dated 1922:

> You are aware of the role you have played in my life and that of my family. I know I was not in a hurry to assign it to you. For many years, I was aware of your efforts to come closer to me, and I kept you at bay. Only after you had expressed in such affectionate terms the desire to belong to my family—in the closer sense—did I surrender to the easy, trusting ways of my earlier years, accepted you and ever since have allowed you to render me every kind of service, imposed on you every kind of task. . . . Today I confess that in the beginning I did not appreciate your sacrifices as highly as I did later after recognizing that—burdened with a loving and loved wife who isn't too fond of sharing you with others, and tied to a family who fundamentally has little sympathy for your endeavors—you actually overtaxed your strength in making the offer. But do not conclude from this remark that I am ready to release you. Your sacrifices have become all the more valuable to me . . . so I suggest that we continue our relationship, which has developed from friendship to sonship, until the end of my days. Since you were the first to come to the lonely man, you may as well stay with him to the last . . . (Dreyfuss, 1950).

[11] E. Gumbel, personal communication. 1964.

Later he wrote, on the occasion of Eitingon's fiftieth birthday:

We are all so built that criticism and reproaches commonly clamor for expression, while feelings of contentedness and tenderness think they have to hide themselves in embarrassment. I do not often tell you, but I never forget what you have done for us all these years . . . (Dreyfuss, 1950).

This was Max Eitingon.

REFERENCES

Balint, M. On the psychoanalytic training system. *Int. J. Psycho-Anal.*, 1947, **29**, 163–173.

Dreyfuss, D. K. In memoriam. In M. Wulff (Ed.), *Max Eitingon, in memoriam.* Jerusalem: Israel Psychoanal. Soc., 1950. Pp. 16–22.

Eitingon, M. Concluding remarks on the question of lay analysis. *Int. J. Psycho-Anal.*, 1927, 8, 399–401.

Eitingon, M. Report of Marienbad Congress. *Int. J. Psycho-Anal.*, 1937, 18, 351.

Eitingon, M. In the dawn of psychoanalysis. In M. Wulff (Ed.), *Max Eitingon, in memoriam.* Jerusalem: Israel Psychoanalytic Soc., 1950.

Freud, E. L. *Letters of Sigmund Freud.* New York: Basic Books, 1960.

Freud, S. Preface to Report on the Berlin Psychoanalytic Polyclinic (March 1920 to June 1922), by Max Eitingon. In *The complete psychological works of Sigmund Freud* (Standard Ed.), Vol. 19. London: Hogarth Press, 1956–.

Gumbel, E. In memoriam. In M. Wulff (Ed.), *Max Eitingon, in memoriam.* Jerusalem: Israel Psychoanal. Soc., 1950. Pp. 22–29.

Jones, E. *The life and work of Sigmund Freud.* Vols. 2, 3. New York: Basic Books, 1957.

Nunberg, H., & E. Federn (Eds.), *Minutes of the Vienna Psychoanalytic Society.* New York: International Universities Press, 1962.

Rosenbaum, Milton. Freud-Eitingon-Magnes correspondence, *J. Amer. psychoanal. Assn.*, 1954, **2**, 311–317.

My thanks to Emanuel M. Honig, M.D., for his translation from the Hebrew of selections in the bibliography, and to my wife, Kato van Leeuwen, M.D., for her invaluable assistance in the preparation of this manuscript—S. L. P.

Carl Gustav Jung

1875–1961

CONTRIBUTIONS TO PSYCHOANALYSIS

*

SHELDON T. SELESNICK

Jung's paternal grandfather and great-grandfather were physicians of great renown, and his father—a parson of the Reformed Church who was greatly interested in Oriental and classical studies—had married the daughter of his Hebrew professor. The maternal grandfather was the head of the Basel clergy.

Carl Gustav was born in 1875 in the Swiss village of Kesswil. An only child until he was nine, Jung was lonely and withdrawn. Having been instructed in Latin by his father from the age of six, Jung was far ahead of his contemporaries by the time he entered the *Gymnasium* at Basel. At nineteen, the young bibliophile acquired a first edition of a book by Erasmus in which he came across the phrase *Vocatus atque non vocatus deus aderit* ("Invoked or not invoked the god will be present"). These words, which were inscribed on his bookplate, he later had carved into the stone lintel over the door of his house (Bennet, 1961, p. 146).

Jung entered the University of Basel in 1895, first studying natural science, later, medicine. While a student, he chanced on some books dealing with spiritualism, mesmerism, and similar topics. He became engrossed in the subject and in the following years attended a number of spiritualist séances. Jung was at the same time interested in the study of philosophy, especially the writings of Kant and Schopenhauer. Just before his final examinations, Jung happened to read the introduction to Krafft-Ebing's textbook of psychiatry and "suddenly understood the connection between psychology or philosophy and medical science." He then and there decided to specialize in psychiatry.

In 1900 Jung went to the Burghölzli in Zurich, which was then under the direction of Eugen Bleuler. Here Jung found case material that permitted him to round out former observations made during occult séances, which he then presented in his first book, *On the Psychology and Pathology of So-Called Occult Phenomena* (Vol. 1, 1961, pp. 3–88). In this book, the inaugural dissertation for his medical degree, he wrote "the split of personality in a spiritualist medium is traced to tendencies during infancy, and at the roots of the fantasy systems delusionary sexual wishes were discovered." The thesis includes several references to Freud's *Interpretation of Dreams* and to Breuer's and Freud's *Studies in Hysteria.*

In this same early work, Jung referred to the phenomenon of word associations. He was to devote much of his research to this subject during the years immediately following: the results are contained in *Studies in Word Association.* As the subtitle states, these are "contributions to experimental psychopathology." He recognized that the word-association experiment permits a more efficient detection of characteristic disturbances due to emotionally laden ideas. Freud evaluated these studies favorably, saying that they made it "possible to arrive at rapid experimental confirmation of psycho-analytic observations" and that "the first bridge linking up experimental psychology with psycho-analysis had been built" (1959, p. 311).

At the Burghölzli, Jung had ample opportunity to apply his association tests to subjects with dementia praecox. After three years of investigation, he presented his findings in *The Psychology of Dementia Praecox,* completed in 1906 (1936), which Jones acknowledged "made history in psychiatry." Another devotee of Freud, A. A. Brill, wrote an introduction to the English translation of this work, in which he stated that, along with Freud's studies, this book "forms the cornerstone of modern interpretive psychiatry." In the first quarter of the book, Jung gives one of the most comprehensive surveys of the theoretical literature on dementia praecox. He based his own position on a synthesis of the concepts of many contributors, especially Kraepelin, Janet, and Bleuler, but maintained that he was most indebted to "the ingenious conceptions of Freud" (1936, p. iii), who, ". . . in his works on hysteria, compulsion neurosis, and dreams . . . has, after all, given all the essentials" (1936, p. 33).

In 1900, Bleuler had recommended to Jung that he review Freud's *Interpretation of Dreams*, which Jung concluded is a "masterpiece." Subsequently, Jung read Freud's other works, and in his book on dementia praecox he cited Freud's two papers on the defense neuropsychosis. In the 1894 paper, Freud had reported the case of a girl forsaken by her lover, whose ego rejected the idea that "he is not here" by enlisting the mechanism of hallucinating his voice. In this hallucinatory psychosis, as in hysteria and obsessive-compulsive disorders, the symptoms result from attempts to defend against (repress) unacceptable ideas, and in this sense they are defense neuropsychoses. In the 1896 paper, Freud used a case of paranoia (dementia praecox) to demonstrate that, as in hysteria and obsessions, the emotionally unacceptable experience or idea is partially admitted to consciousness in the compromise symptom formation, which represents a return of the repressed.

In his book on dementia praecox, Jung stated that a repressed idea is linked with affect; in the association experiments, he had called this combination a "complex." Affect is defined in the usage of Bleuler as a feeling tone, mood, or emotion and is considered a "driving force" that seeks conscious expression.

It is not only the force of the complexes striving toward consciousness that results in the return of the repressed. Jung was familiar with Janet's concept that consciousness itself may be weakened (*abaissement du niveau mental*), as in hypnosis, and that unconscious processes could thereby emerge into awareness. Yet, there may be strong complexes or weakened conscious perceptions in both hysteria and dementia praecox. According to the thought current at the time (under the influence of Kraepelin), dementia praecox was considered to be irreversible, whereas it was thought that hysteria might abate. Consequently Jung wrote that the results "produced by the hysterogenic complex are reparable," but the effects of the dementia praecox complex are "more or less" irreparable.

Kraepelin had postulated that brain injury due to an unknown metabolite (autotoxin) accounted for the irreversible character of dementia praecox and concluded that this toxin is the basic cause of the illness. Bleuler also believed that some organic condition (either a toxin, infection, or "glial proliferation") is the underlying determinant in this disorder. In *The Psychology of Dementia Praecox*, Jung acknowledged that Kraepelin and Bleuler might be correct, but proposed that the toxin could be produced by the dementia praecox complex rather than by somatic processes; he further suggested that the hysterogenic complex does not release a toxin.

Thus, Jung not only integrated the theories then current but earned the distinction of being the first to offer a tentative psychosomatic model for dementia praecox in which the brain became the target organ. The complex with its powerful affect (Bleuler and Jung) produces a toxin (Kraepelin's toxin is somatic; Jung's is a psychotoxin) that injures the brain, paralyzing psychic functioning (Janet's *abaissement*) so that the complex is released from the unconscious and results in the characteristic symptoms of dementia praecox (Freud's "return of the repressed").

The proposal formulated by Jung in 1906 carried a vital impact since, on such a basis, dementia praecox could be understood within a psychoanalytic framework. By 1914 he went further, stating that "the practicing analyst knows cases where patients on the borderline of dementia praecox could still be brought back to normal life" (Jung, 1953, Vol. III, p. 156). At that time, even Freud was not so optimistic; in the same year, he had considered such patients "inaccessible to the influence of psychoanalysis" because they had withdrawn their interests from people.

In *The Psychology of Dementia Praecox*, Jung, as a respected Swiss psychiatrist, drew world-wide attention to Freud's fundamental theories. He deplored Freud's being a "still too little appreciated investigator" and countered the critics of Freud's radical concepts with the statement, "So far as I know no real refutation of Freud's views has yet been made."

Just before putting the finishing touches on the book, in April 1906 Jung initiated a correspondence with Freud. At the end of February 1907, he journeyed to Vienna, accompanied by his wife and Ludwig Binswanger, who was then a volunteer physician at the Burghölzli (Binswanger, 1957, p. 2). The first meeting of Jung and Freud lasted for thirteen uninterrupted hours. As Jung later recalled: "It was a *tour d'horizon*." He found Freud and his circle "impressive" and at the same time "peculiar."

Freud was grateful to the Zurich group for their efforts to gain recognition for psychoanalysis. He was eager to establish psychoanalysis on a broader basis than could be provided by the Viennese intellectuals.

He considered Switzerland the hub of international scientific activity, whereas he felt that Vienna not only lay outside the great centers of Western European culture but was subject to strong prejudices. In a letter to Abraham in the spring of 1908, Freud wrote: "It was only his [Jung's] emergence on the scene that has removed from psychoanalysis the danger of becoming a Jewish national affair." Moreover, beyond the consideration of bringing respectability to psychoanalysis, Freud regarded Jung as "a truly original mind." He saw in him "the Joshua destined to explore the promised land of psychiatry which Freud, like Moses, was only permitted to view from afar."

Even so, Freud did not mention Jung's first visit either in *The History of the Psychoanalytic Movement* or in his autobiography. A possible explanation of this curious omission is suggested in Binswanger's report (1957): "The day after our arrival Freud questioned Jung and me about our dreams. I do not recall Jung's dream, but I do recall Freud's interpretation of it, namely, that Jung wished to dethrone him and take his place." This fear of being displaced by Jung again became apparent in an episode that occurred when both were in Bremen in 1909. Jung had wanted to make an excursion to see some relics of anthropological interest, whereupon Freud became irritated and concluded that Jung's interest in dead bodies indicated a wish for Freud's death!

Freud's ambivalent feelings toward Jung were paralleled by Jung's tendency to vacillate between whole-hearted espousal of Freud's theories and cautious reservations. Soon after their first meeting, Jung wrote to Freud, pleading with him to use some word other than "sexual"—a suggestion Freud firmly rejected. Later that same year, at the First International Congress of Psychiatry and Neurology in Amsterdam, Jung read a paper, "The Freudian Theory of Hysteria." It was presumedly a defense of psychoanalysis; in actuality it became almost an apology for Freud's ideas, or at least for his use of such terms as "infantile sexuality" and "libido." Considering their later differences, Jung's remarks in that paper about Freud's sexual symbolism are interesting: "There are uncommonly far-reaching and significant analogies between the Freudian symbolisms and the symbols of poetic fantasy in individuals and in whole nations. The Freudian symbol and its interpretation is therefore nothing unheard of; it is merely something unusual for us psychiatrists."

During the next few years, Jung wrote a number of papers that follow precisely the lines of Freudian analysis. The most clear-cut statements are found in "The Significance of the Father in the Destiny of the Individual," first published in 1909 (1956, Vol. IV, pp. 301–323). The following passage, which appeared in the original work, was deleted in later editions: "It will be asked, wherein lies the magic power of the parents to bind their children to themselves, often for the whole of their lives? The psychoanalyst knows that it is nothing but sexuality on both sides." It may be seen that during this period Jung carried the Freudian position to an extreme, as in the following passage, also omitted from later editions: "If we now survey all the far-reaching possibilities of the infantile constellation, we are obliged to say that *in essence our life's fate is identical with the fate of our sexuality*." At the same time there are glimmerings of Jung's later concept of opposing tendencies: ". . . the conscious expression of the father-constellation, like every expression of an unconscious complex when it appears in consciousness, acquires its Janus face, its positive and its negative components."

There is no doubt that Jung made a considerable contribution to the psychoanalytic movement during this period. A few months after his first visit to Freud, he founded the Freud Society in Zurich and later organized the First International Psychoanalytical Congress, in Salzburg, in 1908. At this meeting, the first periodical exclusively devoted to psychoanalysis, the *Jahrbuch für psychoanalytische und psychopathologische Forschungen,* was founded, with Bleuler and Freud as directors and Jung as editor. In 1909, Jung gave up his post as chief physician at the Burghölzli, to devote himself to psychoanalytic practice and activities. The International Psychoanalytical Association was founded in 1910 during the Congress at Nuremberg, and, over the angry protests of the Viennese group, Jung was elected president. According to Freud, the selection of Jung was based on his "exceptional talents, the contributions he had already made to psychoanalysis, his independent position and the impression of assured energy which his personality conveyed" (Freud, 1953, p. 43).

Jung was now ready to embark on another project: to extend psychoanalytic principles to subjects that had fascinated him for years, namely, the material gathered from myths, legends, fables, stories from the classics, and poetic fantasies.

After more than a year of research, Jung published his findings in the first half of Volume 3 of the *Jahrbuch,* under the title *Wandlungen und Symbole der Libido, Part I* (1911). Even Ferenczi, in a pungent critique of this work, admitted that Jung's knowledge of classical literature and myths was remarkable. In *Wandlungen I,* Jung quoted a vast number of sources, to draw a "parallel" between the fantasies of the ancients, as expressed in myths and legends, and the "similar thinking of children" (Jung, 1916b, p. 27). He also set out to demonstrate the "connection between dream psychology and myth psychology." Rank, Riklin, Abraham, and Jones had come to similar conclusions. Jung arrived at the unique position that the mind "possesses . . . historical strata" containing "archaic mental products" that become manifest in psychosis when there is "strong" regression. He argued that, since symbols used throughout the ages are similar, they are "typical" and cannot belong to one individual alone. In this sequence of ideas we can detect the germination of the later concept of the collective unconscious.

Freud was always pleased when psychoanalytic writers delved into mythological material. He was impressed with *Wandlungen I,* and a few months after it appeared he wrote: "Jung had excellent grounds for his assertion that the mythopoeic forces of mankind are not extinct but that to this very day they give rise in the neuroses to the same psychological products as in the remotest past ages" (S. Freud, 1911). Freud even interpreted a statement by Schreber to imply that he had "rediscovered the mythological method of expressing his filial relation to the sun." In concluding this postscript, Freud concurred with Jung's position that dreams and neurotic fantasies are similar not only to the thinking of the child, but also to the primitive mentality as revealed in ethnologic research. There is no hint that Freud deemed it necessary to take issue with Jung's earliest formulations of the archaic unconscious. In the following year, Jung became more explicit, first in *Wandlungen II* (Jung, 1912), and again in the Fordham Lectures, in his assumption of a collective unconscious. Only then—in *Totem and Taboo,* published in 1913[1]—did Freud indicate his points of disagreement with this theory of Jung's.

In the same section of the *Jahrbuch* in which *Wandlungen I* ap-

[1] In the first three parts of *Totem and Taboo* (written between September 1911 and January 1913), Freud seemed to follow a line of thought very similar to Jung's ideas. However, in the fourth part, "The Infantile Recurrence of Totemism" (written in the spring of 1913), he took sharp issue with Jung's interpretation. Here Freud described a *parallel,* or *analogy* between the psychology of primitives, children, and neurotics. In contrast, Jung assumed a *continuity* of archaic material gathered into a collective unconscious.

peared, Freud dealt with the mechanisms of paranoid delusion by examining the memoirs of Daniel Paul Schreber, a psychotic who had been president of the Court of Appeals of Saxony. Jones, evidently reluctant to give credit to Jung, asserted that Freud had "come across" the Schreber diary. However, Freud had carefully read Jung's *Dementia Praecox,* which contains six distinct references to Schreber's autobiographical notes. Since Freud had little opportunity to study psychotic patients, it is probably true, as Jung claimed, that it was he who had called Freud's attention to Schreber's autobiography. Attempting to understand Schreber's "end of the world" fantasy, Freud used the explanation that Schreber's "internal" turmoil was projected outward so that he felt the world was collapsing. Schreber, Freud continued, was unable to maintain his ties to the external world because he had withdrawn his libido from the real world of things and people. But Freud himself was not fully satisfied with this explanation, for it did not clarify the effect on the ego instincts. In the absence of a "well-grounded theory of instincts," he considered two different hypotheses: It must be assumed either that the sexual libido coincides with "interest in general," or that a disturbance in the distribution of the sexual libido exerts a disruptive effect on the ego.

In *Wandlungen II* (1912), Jung quoted verbatim the crucial passage from Freud's paper, suggesting the alternate hypothesis, and gave emphasis to the first choice, that is, libido coinciding with "interest in general," by adding his own italics. Jung seized this opportunity to criticize the psychoanalytic libido theory in order to divest it of its sexual connotations. He argued that the psychotic had withdrawn from the external world not his sexual interests alone but all his general interests. Although Jung had defended Freud's position on sexuality for a number of years, he had never totally accepted the sexual theories. In fact, before he ever met Freud, he had written in the preface to *Dementia Praecox* that he could not ascribe such importance to Freud's concepts of infantile sexual trauma, nor could he agree to placing sexuality itself so pre-eminently in the foreground.

Jung was now interpreting libido in a way that Freud had not intended. Freud had indicated that libido was not to be understood in the restricted sense of genital love as known by adults. When Freud had first proposed his dualistic instinct theory in 1906 (ego instincts or self-preservative instincts versus sexual instincts), the term "libido" was synonymous with gaining pleasurable gratification. Freud's view of the libido, although broader than Jung had inferred, was not so broad as the one proposed by Jung in *Wandlungen II,* which eliminated the sexual connotation.

Although schizophrenia always remained Jung's chief clinical interest, he was no longer able to maintain that the illness is distinguished from the transference neuroses (hysteria and obsessive-compulsive states) because of a hypothetical toxin. In *Wandlungen II,* Jung was correct in noting that Freud had not differentiated neurosis from psychosis in the Schreber analysis, and that withdrawal of libido is presumed to occur in both. Freud, concerned with the mechanisms of paranoia, had not yet given his attention to the differences in libido attachment characteristic of these disorders. In 1913, Jung argued further that, if the sexual libido were merely withdrawn onto the ego, the result would be, not dementia praecox, but the psychology of an ascetic whose "whole endeavor is to *exterminate* [italics mine] every trace of sexual interest." After these arguments in *Wandlungen II,* Jung stated:

> The sexuality of the unconscious is not what it seems to be; *it is merely a symbol* . . . a step forward to every goal of life—but expressed in the unreal sexual language of the unconscious and in the thought-form of an earlier stage; a resurrection . . . of earlier modes of adaptation (Jung, 1916b, p. 146).

It took Freud over a year to respond to Jung's arguments in *Wandlungen II,* for he was now obliged to revise his libido theory to meet this challenge. Obviously he was not going to stand by and watch while his libido concept was entirely abandoned, since he saw in it the only basis for an understanding of mental aberrations. Yet, he must have realized the pertinence of Jung's contention that the libido theory—as conceived at that time—did not suffice to distinguish neuroses from psychoses. The answer came in *On Narcissism,* in 1914. On the very second page, Freud made the distinction: the psychotic affixes his withdrawn libido to his own ego, whereby he returns to a state of infantile self-love (narcissism); the neurotic, who retains a mental image of objects from the external world, attaches his libido to this image. Thus, the neurotic does not break off his "erotic relations to persons and things," whereas the psychotic loses his tie to reality by regressing to the state of narcissism. Furthermore, Freud refuted the hermit argument that Jung had used as a decisive link in his chain of reasoning. The anchorite, according to Freud, seemingly "tries to erase every trace of sexual interest" in human beings, when actually he has "sublimated it to a heightened interest in the divine, in nature, or in the animal kingdom, without his libido having undergone introversion to his fantasies or retrogression to his ego."

This libido controversy had an important impact on psychoanalytic theory. In *On Narcissism,* Freud replaced the conflict between ego instincts and sexual instincts with the new dualism of ego-libido (narcissism or self-love) versus object-libido (love of others). On the basis of the new concept, the esssential issue became whether the sexual instincts turn to the self or to the outer world. At the same time, Freud postulated that parts of the ego instincts were nonlibidinous, thus leaving the door open for the final revisions of his libido theory, which he was to develop in *Beyond the Pleasure Principle* and in *The Ego and the Id,* during the early 1920s.

The very problem that brought Jung and Freud together in the first place, namely, the psychic mechanism underlying dementia praecox, subsequently led to serious differences regarding the libido theory and, ultimately, to the severing of their collaboration. Compared with this fundamental disagreement, other issues—the understanding of myths, the interpretation of symbols and dreams, and the like—were of secondary importance. Interlinked with this theoretical controversy were certain personal tensions that presaged the final break.

During the American lecture tour of 1909, several episodes occurred which, Jung felt, reflected a cooling off in Freud's attitude toward him. During a session of mutual analysis, for example, Freud declined to communicate associations on one of his dreams, saying that to do so would cause him to lose his authority. Jung interpreted this lack of frankness as indicating a loss of Freud's confidence in him, as well as a weakness in Freud himself. In retrospect, Jung was convinced that, from then on, their personal relationship had begun to suffer.

However, there is no evidence that Freud's feelings for Jung had changed at that time. In the early months of 1911, he still considered Jung his "Crown Prince" and staunchly maintained, "When the empire I founded is orphaned, no one but Jung must inherit the whole thing" (Binswanger, 1957, p. 31). Later that year, Freud became irritated with Jung because the time Jung devoted to research and to a second trip to America seemed to interfere with the duties of his office; besides, Jung had become tardy in answering Freud's letters. Other minor details, together with Jung's minimizing the sex theory in his Fordham lectures, were the "first signs" that prompted Freud to "withdraw his libido" from Jung, as he wrote to Binswanger on July 29, 1912.

Their correspondence soon became impersonal, restricted to business matters. Jung and Freud met for the last time at the International Congress in Munich, September 1913, where Jung was re-elected president of the International Psychoanalytic Association. At this meeting, Jung read a paper, "A Contribution to the Study of Psychological Types" (1916a, pp. 287–298), in which he attempted to estabish a correlation between nosological types and the direction of libidinal flow. In dementia praecox, the subject has withdrawn his general interest from the world—a mechanism designated by Jung as "introversion"—and exhibits an apathetic response to his environment. The hysteric, in contrast, has an abnormally intense level of affective investment in the external world—"extroversion"—and presents a picture of "exaggerated emotivity." These two opposite directions of libidinal flow are assumed to be psychic mechanisms encountered in normal persons as well as in mental patients.

One month after the Munich Congress, Jung resigned as editor of the *Jahrbuch* and, in April 1914, he resigned as president of the Association. In July 1914, after the appearance of *The History of the Psychoanalytic Movement*, in which Freud demonstrated the incompatibility of his views and those of Adler and Jung, the entire Zurich group withdrew from the International Association.

After his parting from Freud and the psychoanalytic movement, Jung "had to establish his own values, to gain a new orientation, to be himself." During the remaining forty-eight years of his life, there followed an impressive literary output of some 100 books, articles, reviews, and other publications. Jung traveled far and wide to study primitive civilizations—the Pueblo Indians in Arizona and New Mexico, the Elgonyi in British East Africa. He went to the Sudan, Egypt, and India. He read papers at many international congresses, and in 1937 he delivered the Terry Lectures at Yale, taking as his subject the relationship between psychology and religion. He resumed teaching in 1933, giving weekly lectures at the Eidgenössische Technische Hochschule in Zurich, where he received the title of professor two years later. In 1944, the University of Basel—his alma mater—created for him a chair in medical psychology; however, he resigned therefrom after a short time for reasons of health.

In his later work, although he recognized the importance of Freud's causal approach, Jung considered it reductive and felt that mental life could be better understood by adding a teleological perspective. The psyche has a future as well as a past; the study of the mind should reveal not only whence a man has come but also the direction of his future. Jung maintained that because the causal view is finite it portends fatalism. The teleological position holds out hope that man need not be victimized by his past. The symbol that represents unconscious thoughts and feelings can transform psychic energy (libido) into positive and constructive values. As they are revealed in psychoanalysis, dreams, myths, and religions are the means for coping with conflicts through wish fulfillment. However, in addition they contain hints for a prospective resolution of the neurotic dilemma. To Jung, dream interpretation restricted to revealing variations of the Oedipal theme—which, incidentally, is not the sole approach of psychoanalysis—misses the mark by not recognizing the creative futurity of the dream. As Bennet has shown, Jung was repeatedly inspired by dreams, or influenced by them to change the direction of his life—almost as though the dreams had oracular portent. Hopeful prognostications based on dreams may reassure the subject, but this is the province of the oneiromancer rather than the clinician.

In later writings, Jung suggested techniques of psychotherapy that may be clinically validated. The method of "active imagination" advocated by the school of analytic psychology, for instance, is occasionally used by therapists from other disciplines.

Exploring the individual's potential and attempting to help a patient toward "self-realization," or evaluating neurotic behavior patterns by taking into consideration present-day stress situations, are techniques not confined to the Jungian school alone; they are utilized by all conscientious psychotherapists.

The concept of the collective unconscious has remained speculative. Jung divided the unconscious mind into the "personal unconscious" (similar to Freud's unconscious + preconscious) and the "collective unconscious," which is "the mighty deposit of ancestral experience accumulated over millions of years, the echo of prehistoric happenings to which each century adds" (Jung, 1956, Vol. VIII, p. 376). According to Jung, the collective unconscious contains "primordial images" or "archetypes" which represent modes of thinking that have developed over the centuries. However, that people of different centuries have used similar symbols does not prove that a specific symbol has been inherited from ancestral forebears. Man is qualitatively distinguished from other animals by being a symbolizing creature, and his basic drives and desires have not varied greatly throughout the ages. Nor is there an infinite number of symbols by which man can represent these urges. In any event, it is impossible to trace the archetypes to their origin. As Jung himself jocularly remarked, he "wasn't there when the first archetypes were laid down."

By adopting the same terms as were used in Freud's psychoanalysis, while investing them with different meaning in his own discipline, Jung clouded the connotation of general psychoanalytic concepts. For example, it would have served to clarify matters had Jung invented another term for "libido." The same applies to "introversion." It was Jung who introduced the term in 1910, giving it the meaning of withdrawal of sexual libido from the external world. This connotation was continued by Freud, whereas Jung's deviation in the libido theory after 1911 led ultimately to a new meaning for introversion, as describing a specific psychological type rather than a pathological process. A useful term coined by Jung that has survived and is still employed by both schools is "complex."

Jung's later contributions and concepts became increasingly vague. In his classic history of psychology, Brett has stated that "much of Jung's later work . . . is so mysterious as to be almost undiscussable." It is precisely this elusive style that has enabled racists to use Jung's "racial unconscious" for their own purposes—a misinterpretation to which Jung did not subscribe, but which at times he did not refute.

Jung has been accused of anti-Semitism, but Bennet (1961, pp. 56–62) and Harms present arguments that such charges were unfounded. More recently, F. Alexander and S. T. Selesnick (in press) and Erich Fromm (1963) have taken the position that Jung was neither anti-Semitic nor anti-Nazi, but instead that he opportunistically took advantage of situations to promote his own interests. The 1933 Deutsche Allgemeine ärtzliche Gesellschaft für Psychotherapie was organized by Hitler's appointee, Dr. M. H. Göring, a relative of the Nazi Hermann Göring. Jung took over the presidency of the organization and became the editor of its official journal, the *Zentralblatt für Psychotherapie*. However, in an early edition of this journal, Jung wrote:

> The Jews have this peculiarity in common with women: Being physically the weaker they must aim at the chinks in their opponent's armor. . . . They also owe to the experience of ancient culture the ability to live con-

sciously in a benevolent, friendly and tolerant neighborhood with their own defects [Untugenden], while we are still too young to have no illusions about ourselves. . . . The Jew, as relatively a nomad, never has produced and presumably never will produce a culture of his own since all his instincts and gifts require a more or less civilized host-people for their development. . . . The Aryan unconscious has a higher potential than the Jewish (Jung, 1934).

During a decade of decisive importance for the later development of psychoanalysis, Jung made many significant contributions. His word-association experiments confirmed Freud's hypothesis of repression, which proved to be the cornerstone of psychoanalytic theory. In turn, Jung applied the knowledge he gained from Freud to dementia praecox and never wavered in his conviction that the illness could be treated by psychological means. By stressing the connection between the physiologic and psychological aspects of the disease, he was able to construct the first psychosomatic model for dementia praecox. Jung was instrumental in bringing Freud's writings to the attention of the scientific world and later played an important part in organizing the psychoanalytic movement. According to Jung, it was he who suggested to Freud that all psychoanalysts should go through a training analysis. Jung's application of psychoanalytic theory to the understanding of myths and their relationship to dreams and neuroses rekindled Freud's interest in anthropology, eventuating in *Totem and Taboo.* Jung's most vital contribution, however, was in pointing out that Freud had failed to distinguish between neurotic and psychotic phenomena in the Schreber case. Faced with the necessity of solving this problem, Freud was spurred on to revise his libido theory: the resulting new understanding of narcissism suggested the nonlibidinal nature of parts of the ego instincts and paved the way for his final dualistic concept of the life instinct versus the death instinct. Thus, in his own fashion, Freud eventually broadened his concept of libido by combining it with the life instinct.

Although this process of cross-fertilization was productive for both sides insofar as Jung's own development was concerned, Freud's theories had their major impact in the years before the two men had met personally. In spite of his attraction to psychoanalysis and his transitory defense of its fundamental principles, Jung was never to stray from the path he indicated in his earliest work in 1902. The seeds of the collective unconscious were apparent even in this first dissertation. And from

1913 on, his abundant writings, elaborating those theories that today typify Jungian thought, reveal little or nothing of Freudian influence.

REFERENCES

Alexander, F., & S. T. Selesnick. *History of psychiatry*. New York: Harper & Row, in press.

Bennet, E. A. *C. G. Jung*. London: Barrie & Rockliff, 1961.

Binswanger, L. *Sigmund Freud: reminiscences of a friendship*. New York: Grune & Stratton, 1957.

Freud, S. Postscript to the Schreber case. *Jb. Psychoanal. Psychopath. Forsch.*, 1911, 3 (2nd half), 588–590.

Freud, S. On the history of the psychoanalytic movement. In *Collected papers. . . .* Vol. I. New York: Basic Books, 1959. Pp. 287–359.

Fromm, E., C. G. Jung: Prophet of the unconscious. *Sci. Amer.*, September 1963, 288.

Jung, C. G. Wandlungen und Symbole der Libido, I. *Jb. Psychoanal. Psychopath. Forsch.*, 1911, 3, 120–227. (English edition: *Psychology of the unconscious: a study of the transformations and symbolisms of the libido.* [Hinkle, Beatrice M. Trans.] New York: Moffat, Yard, 1916.)

Jung, C. G. Wandlungen und Symbole der Libido, II. *Jb. Psychoanal. Psychopath. Forsch.*, 1912, 4, 162–464. (*Psychology of the unconscious: a study of the transformations and symbolisms of the libido.* [Hinkle, Beatrice M. Trans.] New York: Moffat, Yard, 1916.)

Jung, C. G. *Collected papers on analytical psychology*. London: Baillière, Tindall & Cox, 1916. (a)

Jung, C. G. *Psychology of the unconscious*. New York: Moffat, Yard, 1916. (b)

Jung, C. G. Zur gegenwärtigen Lage der Psychotherapie. *Zbl. Psychother.*, 1934, 7, 1–16.

Jung, C. G. The psychology of dementia praecox. *Nerv. ment. Dis. Monogr.*, 1936, No. 3.

Jung, C. G. *Collected works. . . .* New York: Pantheon Books, 1956–. 18 vols.

Alfred Adler

1870–1937

THE PSYCHOLOGY OF THE INFERIORITY COMPLEX

*

SHELDON T. SELESNICK

In the fall of 1902, Kahane, Reitler, Stekel, and Alfred Adler met with Freud to set up the Wednesday evening discussion group that was to become the first psychoanalytic society.

Alfred Adler was thirty-two when he joined the Viennese group. He was thoroughly familiar with the cultural climate of Vienna and no stranger to controversy. Born in a suburb of Vienna, he spent his youth in the environs of Vienna and attended its university, from which he received his medical degree in 1895. His knowledge of the history of psychology and of German philosophy, his ability to quote the Bible, Shakespeare, and Greek tragedies, and his eloquent speaking ability accounted for his holding the center of attention in groups.

Adler had a strong affinity for anyone who advocated social reform, and he found himself greatly attracted to Raissa Timofeyewna Epstein, who had come from Russia to study at the University of Vienna. Raissa was a vibrant intellectual, politically active and socially aware. She and Adler were married two years after his graduation from medical school.

Influenced by the lectures of Krafft-Ebing, Adler then undertook the study of neurology, wherein he hoped to combine his social interests and his medical background. Because he had been giving considerable thought to the role of organic disease as well as social conditions in the psychic lives of his patients, he welcomed the opportunity to participate in Freud's study group, which promised something new and stimulating to psychological thought. In 1907, after joining Freud's group Adler published his first major publication (Adler, 1917).

From personal experience, Adler knew the meaning of somatic defect. Because of rickets he had not walked until he was four, and once said, "For me any sort of movement was a strain and effort." Soon after he could move about—even though clumsily—he developed a serious case of pneumonia. While still uncertain on his feet, he was involved in several street accidents. Nevertheless, he did not resign himself to a life of infirmity. After frequent contacts with physicians, Adler resolved to become a doctor. While longing for the days when he could join the other boys in athletics, he spent his time reading works of the great classical writers and pursued his botanical and biological interests by cultivating flowers and collecting pigeons. Both Adler's intense gregariousness later in life and his interest in the psychological effects of organ inferiority may be traced to his personal organic defect. In his 1907 work, Adler stressed that the failure to adapt to organic weakness leads to emotional disturbances.

Adler's concepts concerning organ inferiority are further elaborations of the principle of the great French physiologist, Claude Bernard (1813–1878), who taught that an organ attempts to maintain constancy within its internal environment, a concept later amplified in W. B. Cannon's principle of homeostasis. In the same year as Adler's publication, in France Pierre Janet proposed similar ideas in his "Sentiment d' Incompletitude" (Sentiments of Incompleteness). Freud had respect for some of Pierre Janet's views and considered Adler's contribution on the inferiority of organs a "valuable work"; he expected that eventually Adler would extend his work to "the biological foundations of instinctual processes."

In 1908, Adler did turn his interests to instincts, but not as Freud had anticipated (Adler, 1908). In 1906, Freud had proposed that the basis for neurosis is conflict between the ego instincts (the self-preservative drives) and the sexual instincts. Adler was searching for a principle that would unify psychological and biological phenomena and still fall within the framework of an acceptable instinct theory. The aggressive drive was introduced by Adler as a unitary instinct principle in which the primary drives, whatever they might be, lose their autonomy and find themselves subordinated to this one drive. The aggressive instinct, then, is the biological anlage or source of psychic energy utilized when individuals overcome their organic inferiorities through compensation. If there is a "confluence of drives,"[1] for example, if the sexual and aggressive drives occur together, aggression is always subordinated to the sexual drive. Adler proposed that drives can be converted into their opposites: for example, that the instinct of voyeurism could be turned into exhibitionistic behavior. Furthermore, he suggested that a drive can be turned against one's self. Freud later adopted these two principles in regard to instincts, calling the former "reaction formation" and the latter "turning" of the instinct "upon the subject." Later, Anna Freud, in *The Ego and Mechanisms of Defence*, listed these mechanisms as two basic ego defenses.

At this point, Adler was not aware that he was dealing with unconscious defensive functions of the ego. Nor, in his 1908 paper, did he attempt to create another dualistic instinct theory. Instead, he was searching for a basic and "higher principle of motivation." Even though the aggressive drive as conceived by Adler is constitutionally and biologically derived, Freud could not include it in his instinct theory. In the case of "Little Hans," Freud considered that the boy's hostile and aggressive feelings were manifestations of "aggressive propensities," which seems "a most striking confirmation of Adler's views." Nevertheless, Freud believed that all instincts have the "power of becoming aggressive." He could see no reason at the time to include the aggressive instinct in his duality concept, or even to give it a place of pre-eminence—as Adler had proposed. In 1920, and again in 1923, Freud had placed the aggressive instinct within the death instinct, which was considered antagonistic to the life instinct. By this time, Adler himself was no longer concerned with instincts; he considered that the aggressive drive was really a mode of striving by which one adapts to arduous life tasks. Freed of the necessity to reason in terms of instincts, Adler had sarcastically remarked that he was glad to have made a present to Freud of the aggressive drive. Adler was never to ask for the return of this gift.

It was not this paper on the aggressive instinct that initiated the break with Freud, but rather Adler's work during the years 1910 and 1911. In 1910, Adler began to write for the first time about "feelings of inferior-

[1] Freud borrowed the phrase "confluence of drives," acknowledging Adler as the source.

ity." He thus laid the cornerstone for his theory that the child *feels* weak and insignificant in his relationship to adults. Biological stresses and the outcome of instinctual strivings were now relegated to insignificant roles as compared to how individuals react to feelings of inferiority, and the crucial reaction was that of the "masculine protest." The masculine position in our culture is one of strength; the feminine is one of weakness. Each of us has a feeling of weakness (femininity) and a masculine tendency to overcome it; from this point of view, we are psychologically "hermaphrodites." Some thirteen years previously, Freud had had a similar notion but had dismissed it because he felt it could not be validated. Nevertheless, Freud never disavowed his somewhat similar concept of bisexuality. Freud's concept of bisexuality—rooted in instinct and to be taken literally—differs from Adler's concept of hermaphroditism, which considers sex metaphorically.

Adler was now proposing that sexuality be considered in its symbolic sense. According to his beliefs, women in our culture have a tendency to become neurotic, not because they covet the penis, but because they envy the pre-eminence of man in contemporary culture. To women, then, the penis symbolizes the overexalted position of men in society. Should they wish to become men, renouncing their femininity, they suffer from such neurotic symptoms as painful menses, painful intercourse, or even homosexuality—all expressive of masculine protest reactions. Men who try to become excessively masculine (for example, performing as daredevils, or presenting a picture of the romantic masculine lover, the typical Don Juan) are not reacting to anxiety over fear of castration but are overcompensating for their feelings of inadequacy as men. Adler considered that dreams constantly demonstrate the masculine protest reaction.

It was now evident that Adler had broken with Freud's sexual theories, and by 1911 he became bold in his criticisms of them. The Oedipal situation was understood not as the striving of the boy to achieve sexual pleasure with his mother, but as a symbolic battle. Feeling weak and defenseless, the son uses overcompensation to achieve superiority over father and dominance over mother.

In 1910, Freud attempted to reconcile the gap between himself and the Adlerians, who resented Freud's favoritism toward Jung. He named Adler president of the Viennese Analytic Society and appointed Adler and Stekel co-editors of the *Zentralblatt für Psychoanalyse*.

These measures proved temporary; a heated polemic was brewing and no lid could contain the roiling steam. Freud acknowledged that Adler had made "useful contributions to the psychology of the ego." However, psychoanalysts had not yet fully resolved the problem of instinct theory and, at this time, were theoretically unequipped to deal with the defenses of the ego. Furthermore, Adler had not made clear how the masculine protest differs from repression. Instead of holding that the masculine protest occurs in the process of repressing feminine traits, Adler confused the issue by reversing the relative importance of these factors, viewing repression as "only a small segment of the effects of the masculine protest." [2] It was equally unclear whether neurotic symptoms evolved because of the lack of the use of overcompensation or with the failure of that mechanism. Moreover, neurotic symptoms all appeared to have as their goal the purpose of dominating someone in the environment. To the Freudians, this was not a prime cause of symptoms, but it coincided with what they considered to be pleasurable secondary gains of illness. Adler's system, which dismissed repression and replaced causality with teleology, had relegated the libido to a no man's land. The establishment of one ego mechanism as a mainstay led to its condemnation as an oversimplification. Freud had regarded Adler as a "remarkable intellect," who he hoped would help to develop psychoanalytic theory. Freud's disappointment was bitter when he realized that the time for reconciliation had passed. In his own words: "There is room enough on God's earth, and anybody who can is fully entitled to cut any capers he likes on it without interference; but it is not a good thing for people who no longer understand one another and no longer agree to remain under the same roof together."

Adler rejected Freud's insistence on adherence to basic doctrine. He considered that Freud's was the rule of an autocrat. Freud, he believed, was behaving as the typical, insecure, threatened eldest son, who must domineer tyrannically in order to protect himself against "dethronement." Bottome (1957) [3] remarks that Adler considered Freud "an eldest brother." It is significant that Adler himself said, "My eldest brother was the only one with whom I did not get along well. . . ." Alfred felt that his mother—a simple, good-natured, self-sacrificing woman—showed her preference for this elder son. Alfred's father, a

[2] These are Adler's words as recorded by the secretary of the meeting of February 1911, in which Freud and Adler presented their differences. Translation is by K. M. Colby.

[3] Phyllis Bottome was asked by Adler to write his biography; he supplied her with notes about his life and attitudes. Her book is most uncritical of Adler.

sharp-witted grain merchant, highly respected in the community, was more tender to Alfred and held high expectations for him. Relationships between his parents and between Alfred and his two younger sisters and his two younger brothers were harmonious. Nevertheless, Alfred regarded his childhood as unhappy because of his sentiments toward his older brother. If Alfred could not tolerate being in the shade of his eldest brother, it is not surprising that he remarked to Freud that it was no pleasure being in Freud's shadow.

Adler had abandoned the Jewish orthodoxy of his ancestors because he believed that it engendered parochial isolationism. If Adler believed Judaism to be constraining, Freud's group was even more restricting for him. By 1911, Adler felt he was no longer a member of an open discussion group: together with nine of the thirty-five members of the Viennese Psychoanalytic Society, he resigned from that organization to found the Society for *Free* Psychoanalysis. With this caption they exhibited their contempt for the alleged insular policies of the Freudian circle.

In his autobiography, Freud refers to many intelligent men who made contributions to psychoanalysis and "who have worked with me for some fifteen years in loyal collaboration and for the most part in uninterrupted friendship." The disagreements that many of these workers had with Freud are recorded in the autobiography. It is unreasonable, nevertheless, to assume that Adler's sole motivation was to usurp an older brother's authority: this entirely negates Adler's intelligent system of thought and disregards his genuine dissatisfaction with the libido theory. Furthermore, it is contradictory to the testimony of many men and women who worked with Adler and considered him least of all a power-seeking person.

The official break between Adler and Freud did not end their acrid feud. Adler had not been analyzed by Freud and later prided himself on not having been Freud's pupil. Freud later referred to Adler as a "Pigmy," saying, "I made a Pigmy great." In turn, Adler countered that even a "Pigmy" perched on the shoulders of a "great giant" could see farther than his supporter. When Freud heard of this statement, he chided that this might be true of a Pigmy but not of a louse in the giant's hair.

In 1912, the Adlerian group adopted the name, The Society for Individual Psychology. Freed of a biological orientation, Adler's interest turned to social philosophy in order to redefine his system in terms of the individual. He became impressed with the writings of Vaihinger, the idealistic positivist, who in 1911 had published *The Philosophy of the "As If."* In one of Adler's most important works, *The Neurotic Constitution* (completed in 1912 and published several years later), he showed that man deludes himself by accepting fictions that become his final goals. The neurotic's character traits, his symptoms, and even his dreams can be understood as means by which individuals strive for power over their fellow men, to reach fictitious goals of completion. Because of earlier life experiences we have come to feel incomplete, imperfect. We are unaware that we have constructed plans of life (later called "styles of life") designed to pursue fictional goals of superiority by driving ourselves into positions of power over others. As Adler noted, Nietzsche expressed the view that goals of this sort are pursued with a "will to power." The greater the feelings of inferiority, the stronger is the need to control and overpower others.

During World War I, Adler served for four years in the Austrian army medical corps. Although his wife and his socialist friends believed that war is caused by economic tensions, for Adler this was not the full explanation. The ideal of peace, Adler thought, could be accessible only when man surrenders his self-centered orientation, which seeks to overcome feelings of insignificance. Even during the horrors of war, Adler had seen remarkable examples of man's unselfish duty to his fellow beings. From those days onward, Adler began to emphasize the importance of *Gemeinschaftsgefühl*—only through good-will, not with a "will to power," could man find his full potential.

Adler acknowledged that throughout the years individual psychology has been changing into a "psychology of values." More than ever, Adler felt an urgency to incorporate a social message into his works. Education of children is essential for the perpetuation of the social values of the community. The school system of Vienna sought Adler's advice, and, in 1919, he founded the first child guidance clinic connected with the Viennese school system. There were more than thirty clinics at the time they were closed by the Fascists.

Adler was keenly interested in his children's academic life and encouraged them in their studies.[4] His belief in the importance of edu-

[4] Adler's son, Kurt, and one daughter, Alexandra, have become active as teachers in New York in the field of psychiatry. Another daughter, Vali, who held a doctorate in economics and taught social science, was a political prisoner of Stalin and died in a Russian prison. Nelly, who lives in America, had been a successful actress and student of drama in Vienna.

cation was responsible for his waiting until the twelfth hour—when Hitler had become more than a threat—before bringing his family to the United States. He had wanted his children to complete their preliminary education in their native country.

From 1926 to 1934, Adler frequently visited the United States on exhausting lecture tours under the auspices of departments of medicine and psychology of universities, child guidance clinics, church groups, and parent-teacher associations. Although Adler suffered from myocarditis and was taking cardiac medication, he journeyed from America to Scotland to lecture. Prior to his departure for Scotland, he had told a student, "We have been given hearts not to keep them preserved as they are, but to wear them out while engaged in meaningful work." On a May morning in 1937, while rushing to his audience, he collapsed and died on an Aberdeen street.

To Adler's way of thinking, having the patient recline on the couch while the therapist sits behind him is not conducive to promoting parity. Adler preferred to face the patient and engage in free discussion, not in free association. Sessions were fewer per week and the length of treatment was comparatively shorter than in analysis. According to Adler, the task of the therapist is to interpret whenever it becomes apparent how the patient deceives himself in regard to his life style. Because of the interest, warmth, and activity of the therapist, the patient's feelings of being attacked or criticized are minimized. Adler regarded the dream as evidence of the patient's attitude toward something in the present—as a symbolic rehearsal of an act that the patient must soon perform in real life and an indication of his personal attitude toward the act. Although acknowledged to exist, the unconscious recedes into the background as the patient and therapist discuss the manner in which early life experiences have led to the patient's feelings of inadequacy and resulted in his characteristic life plan. Adler did not consider that a person had redirected his life style until he had established social interests.

Despite shortcomings, Adler deserves a place in the history of psychoanalysis because he heralded the arrival of important trends. In his early book, he emphasized two basic principles of psychosomatic medicine: first, that there is within the organism a basic organ vulnerability; and second, the importance of the individual's inner image in regard to his defective functioning. In 1908, Adler stressed the importance of aggression, which today is considered one of the major human attributes with which clinicians must deal. Adler proposed that the ego defends itself; he emphasized one mechanism—overcompensation—and suggested the mechanisms of reaction formation and the turning of aggression onto oneself. These proposals were in advance of the systematic explorations of ego psychology in the 1930's and 1940's.

Even though Adler minimized intrapsychic phenomena by overemphasizing social factors, it must be recalled that in his days the importance of the social milieu was not sufficiently appreciated by psychiatrists. The growth of the cultural schools in the last two decades testifies to the fact that an increasing number of psychoanalysts deem it necessary to relate our social institutions to the individual patient's problems.

The "idealized image" of Karen Horney, by which the individual creates a false picture of himself, is strikingly similar to Adler's concept of the "fictional goal."[5] Harry Stack Sullivan's stress on the "self-esteem system" of the individual is reminiscent of Adler's "feelings of adequacy." If not influenced directly by Adler, the cultural schools were at least spearheaded by his direction toward reshaping psychiatric thought from a biological to a social orientation. Although the Adlerians do not underscore the transference and countertransference, Adler was one of the first to consider the relationship between the doctor and patient as a meaningful experience by which an individual overcomes many of his earliest problems.

Finally, genuine credit must be given to Adler for the widespread influence he has had on teachers, counselors, and educators. The inferiority complex, masculine protest, the value of social investment—these are all practical concepts that have aided professionals in dealing with human problems.

REFERENCES

Adler, A. Der Aggressionstreib im Leben und in der Neurose. *Forteschritte der Medizin,* 26, 1908, 577–584.

Adler, A. *Study of organ inferiority and its psychical compensation: a contribution to clinical medicine.* New York: Nervous & Mental Diseases, 1917.

Bottome, Phyllis. *Alfred Adler: a portrait from life.* (3rd ed.) New York: Vanguard Press, 1957.

[5] Karen Horney admitted that Adler had influenced her thinking. Ruth Munroe regards Horney as the "Adler of our decades."

Ernest Jones

1879–1958

THE BIOGRAPHY OF FREUD

*

LILLA VESZY-WAGNER

§ Life and Personality

Ernest Jones was a Welshman, the only son of fairly well-to-do parents. He decided on a medical career at an early date, a choice prompted by childhood feelings of awe and admiration toward doctors who came to the house to deliver his two sisters and later by a matter-of-fact, skeptical nature that directed him toward the sciences. His interest in medicine was furthered by his basic good will and an unquenchable thirst for knowledge—the outcome and sublimation of his infantile curiosity. He was an excellent student and won first class honors in both medicine and obstetric medicine (both first place and gold medal in the latter); he passed his later examinations with marks of 100 per cent. Nevertheless, his interest in the unconscious parts of the mind, especially in the sexual instincts—a subject taboo in the nineties—soon forced him to relinquish ambitions for a successful medical career in London and (combined with the prompting of an adventurous spirit) to spend years as a voluntary exile in Canada. After his return to England, he not only built a sound psychoanalytic career for himself, but through his numerous publications he created and steadily advanced the theory of psychoanalysis, a focal body politic for psychoanalytic research, and an organization for the steadily increasing number of researchers in Britain.

He was one of Freud's closest friends: the earliest in time, he remained Freud's most faithful supporter throughout life. His paper before the American Therapeutic Congress in 1909 was the first presentation on psychoanalysis ever given at a medical congress. During his lifetime he knew closely and was befriended by many of the prominent analysts and such luminaries of psychology and allied sciences as did not fight the psychoanalytic approach.

Jones once told me that in the later chapters of his autobiography he intended to report on the circumstances, difficulties, and fortunes of the British Psycho-Analytical Society's beginnings. Indeed, these are inseparable from his name. It was impossible to deal with this matter as extensively in the Freud biography as Jones would have liked, inasmuch as this subject is of only peripheral interest to Freud's story. (In Freud's biography, Jones had confined his report to the fact that the Society was founded in 1913 and that at the time it had nine members, including only four practicing psychoanalysts.[1])

I shall postpone discussion of Jones's personal development toward psychoanalysis: the subject is intimately related to both his *oeuvre* and to his relationship to Freud, and these questions must be considered separately. We have here first to fathom the meanings of those personality traits that have lead to this amazing career and its results.

Especially in his youth, Jones certainly must have had the dashing and intrepid character of a crusader. The shrewd acumen of the propagandist coupled with an admirable tenacity and capacity for hard work made him an excellent missionary for the "movement."[2] From the standpoint of the "cause," it was by no means ironic grandiloquence nor an overstatement when Freud wrote to Jones, "You have, as it were, conquered America in no more than two years." Proof of this is the swift and steady mushrooming of an unparalleled number of new psychoanalytic associations, centers, and publications from these early and stirring times onward.

Jones was an ambitious man. As a youth he could scarcely wait to start his career, and as a man his stupendous capacity for work drew powerful energies from his ardent desire to assert himself. At first he

[1] As I was not associated with Jones nor with the London Society at the time, I shall leave this topic to some psychoanalyst with more definitive information.

[2] Jones intensely disliked the term "movement." In his view, it was a concept transforming the "cause" (Freud's term) into something partaking of the nature of a religious movement.

rushed headlong into life and was full of unbridled ambitions to arrive at the top. Because of the extra years of training this would involve—in order to speed up his entrance into medical school—he renounced plans to enter Cambridge University. At twenty-one, he was already a physician. Nevertheless, after abandoning many of his early impatient attitudes, he reaped the fruits of his moderation: in later years, life rewarded him with wisdom and increased dignity.

He certainly was a hard worker. Whether this was because of his ambition or because he simply had to—he mentions both—is hard to decide. I am inclined to think that neither of these was the decisive factor, that the driving factors were his zest for life and his blessed ability to regard work as fun. I doubt that his ambition alone could have triumphed so decisively over physical frailty. Early life had made him delicate; he had a tendency to giddiness and, as a child, had suffered from nightmares. Despite this, his son Mervyn described him as sturdy later in life, and Jones himself admitted to "enough resilience."

Although he obviously had to work rather hard at times—especially after his university years—he was nonetheless fairly well-off throughout his life. Of course, the ambitious young man wanted to earn his own living. Here, the disappointments set in, and he felt that he had to work hard for everything he acquired. He found life a less easy affair than he had once thought: more depended on the chance of circumstances and relations with other persons than he cared to think. Jones does not mention that he may have been spoiled by an overly permissive father and the cushioning effect of early life in a prosperous family willing to spend generously for the well-being of an only son.

In addition, he felt humiliated—and legitimately so—when he was reduced to applying unsuccessfully for positions at second- or third-rate children's hospitals or hospitals for the treatment of nervous diseases and by the increasing coldness with which he was received as time went on. He soon awoke to the fact that knowledge and industry are not enough and that he must look out for the interests of his career as well. This proved not so difficult after all: while attending scientific meetings as the reporter for a medical periodical, he came to know most of the consultants.

As a splendid although retarded reaction formation, he developed a shrewd economic sense and financial ability of which he was rather proud in his later years. He invested his earnings and his inheritance well; this was fortunate, because as a result he never was forced to become a "grasping" doctor. The fees he asked were handsome but, considering his status, never disproportionate.

To understand his role, we must consider two divergent traits in Jones's character which, seemingly irreconcilable, he nevertheless managed to coalesce into a well-balanced personality. On the one hand was his militant, sometimes belligerent character; on the other, his warm-hearted and kindly disposition. Perhaps his recourse to the sober, impassive scientific attitude and his strict, intellectual impartiality kept these conflicting emotional bents under control. Yet, his attitude never became inhumane. A radiating, genuine sympathy for man and his plight, and the heartfelt worship of truth—a feature that brought him nearest to Freud—prevented the light of reason cast on reality from becoming too cold. Jones has said about Freud: "One might wonder if his pronounced independence had not in part been developed as a reaction to some early propensities." Jones felt that for Freud the reaction was against Freud's credulity and suggestibility. One wonders whether Jones did not know this so well because of an inner similarity of character. There was always in Jones a struggle for independence, and I suspect that his often charming amiability coupled with an optimistic approach, which I think was lacking in Freud, must have set for him many traps in life.

D. W. Winnicott remarked in his funeral speech (1958) that there was "a sharp edge to Jones's wit that seems to have no counterpart in Freud." Wit certainly seems to have done its best to diminish the sharpness and sublimate some remnants of the adolescent aggressiveness, which he not only admitted but sometimes deplored.

We do not know about his possible preschool aggressiveness, but it is likely that Ernest Jones, although generally a good brother, occasionally bullied his younger siblings. Being a frail child he must have resented bullying at school. With unusual bitterness he remarked (1959) that he had learned there about the "depths of cruelty and of obscenity to which human beings can descend." This may explain the ensuing dichotomy: although an outwardly merry and friendly boy, he became, inwardly, overearnest for his age. Jones's impetuosity and ambition soon combined, and he attacked work with a near frenzy. His amazing working powers must have originated in part from his innate gifts of intelligence, interest, and concentration and in part from this successful sublimation.

Whereas Mervyn Jones has stressed his father's essential sturdiness and unusually strong and tenacious constitution, W. H. Gillespie has emphasized the contrast between Jones's burning energy and his physical frailness (Funeral Speeches, 1958). In his autobiography, Jones himself draws attention to his delicacy during childhood. However, there is no contradiction here: the frailty remained and sometimes prevailed, but the burning energy always won out—perhaps often without any conscious awareness of the effort. To quote from Jones's own writings: "When I was a small boy, I startled my mother by telling her I knew what quality I most longed to possess, . . . 'energy.' . . . That was a childhood wish the fairies granted me in full measure" (1959).

As his son remarks, Jones was fitted for anything but inactivity. He was a zestful traveler. Never exhausted, he sometimes treated ten to eleven patients a day, and even in old age could not resign himself to treating less than two a day. Although he was already ill, following an invitation to the United States, he prepared his *Four Centenary Addresses* on Freud in 1956 and participated in, and was honorary president at, his last International Psycho-Analytical Congress in Paris, in 1957.

During the early stages of his fight on behalf of psychoanalysis, Jones did not command or attract the adherence, confidence, and sympathy to which his unselfish work on behalf of the "cause" entitled him: his critics attribute this to his "intolerance."

It is difficult to assess to what extent Jones was liked or disliked by his fellow analysts. Winnicott has alluded to a certain hostility toward Jones. We do not know, for instance, what Jung thought of Jones. In his autobiography, Jones expressed himself about Jung with a certain reserve, although he deplored that Jung had "degenerated into mystical obscurantism." Jones claimed that he could not really understand what had happened to Jung, who had once possessed an apparently lucid insight into the depths of the mind and then lost it again—probably for good.

At least unconsciously, Jones must have had hopes that he might replace Jung in Freud's affection after Jung's withdrawal. Strangely enough, this did not take place: rather, it strengthened Freud's mistrust (always imperceptibly present) in non-Jews as friends and temporarily made Freud more susceptible to Jones's detractors among his circle, although it did not effectively cool the deeply anchored friendship between the two men. In later years, Freud naturally could not remain unaffected by Jones's upright and courageous help and by the practical support Jones provided to Freud and a number of other analysts in their escape from Nazi Germany and her satellites. As a result, their friendship became deeper and possibly even more genuine than heretofore. The awkward formality that had sometimes crept into Freud's correspondence with Jones disappeared entirely.

In later years, Jones actively helped many analysts of Jewish extraction, yet for a long time they regarded him with superficially rationalized and basically irrational suspicion, which made even Freud falter for a time. The pretext was that Jones was authoritarian and intolerant: he may have seemed so because of his exacting strictness or formalism in certain questions, or—as he himself thought possible—because of his disregard for the sensibilities of other persons. But an additional factor was the unformulated but intense suspiciousness within Freud's circle (following the defection of Jung, Adler, and Stekel) that such an original and forceful personality—furthermore, a non-Jew—might easily be tempted to break away and found yet another "new school."

Otto Rank constantly poured into Freud's ears stories of how impossible Jones was as a colleague, particularly when Rank and Jones were jointly engaged in editing the *International Journal.* He accused Jones of poor control over his moods and passions and of unjust susceptibilities—in fact, of personal interference in every step of the editing process.

Ferenczi, too, was antagonistic to Jones, although Jones first learned of this when, in the preparation of the Freud biography, he read Ferenczi's correspondence with Freud. Ferenczi's letters expressed both suspicion and derogation of Jones's activities. A letter dated August 6, 1912, reads: "You must keep Jones constantly under your eye and cut off his line of retreat" (Jones, 1957, Vol. II, p. 153). Ferenczi was convinced that Jones was an unscrupulous and dangerous person who was trying to unite the Anglo-Saxon world under his own scepter, that in order to promote his own ambitions Jones had conspired with Brill to promote lay analysis. Jones, on the contrary, meant only to reconcile the views of the Americans (who were unalterably opposed to lay analysis) with those of Freud, hoping thereby to prevent the split. The relationship of Ferenczi and Jones was ambivalent throughout. The tensions might have resulted from Jones's training analysis with Ferenczi or, as Jones believed, solely from Ferenczi's neurotic suspiciousness and vanity. Jones had supplanted Ferenczi as president of the International Association after World War I, and he felt that Ferenczi bore him an irrational grudge thereafter. It is my impression that Jones attributed Freud's tentative interest toward telepathy to Ferenczi's detrimental influence and could never forgive him for this.

Jones himself was to some degree aware of his intolerance, which he attributed in part to reasons of an emotional nature and in part to an addiction to "honesty in thought." It was because of the latter that he could not approve of Jung and despised Pierre Janet. Jones could be very cutting when he believed that analysts had become renegades out of mean motivation or had behaved reprehensively from a professional point of view. He was also sarcastic toward persons who had turned against Freud or psychoanalysis because of dishonesty or similar character defects. His temperament sometimes carried him so far in these matters that he had to consult his solicitor as to whether he could allow his statements to appear in print without laying himself open to charges of libel. In these cases, he showed no mercy for the dead.

As a young doctor, Jones's insistence on the highest work standards made him unpopular with the nurses and his colleagues. In retrospect, Jones remarked that he had had a rather obsessive insistence on doing things in what he had conceived to be the way, with an impatience for sloppiness, at the risk of provoking the sensibilities of others.

Beside this nevertheless laudable side of his character, which in spite of his mellowing he never gave up entirely, there was another side—his intransigence—that he admitted, and later even deplored. Almost until his old age he was often irreconcilable when he ought not have been, and not for the sake of lofty ideals alone. This trait he attributed in part to the influence of Wilfrid Trotter's "iconoclastic wit," although he did not deny that his own chief failing in those days was an unduly critical attitude toward the shortcomings of others. In a way, he regarded this as a late outcome or remnant of what he termed "having a tongue" during his years as a student, when he "was so filled with righteousness" that he could not restrain it. Others, he felt, might put it in harsher terms—opinionated, tactless, conceited, or inconsiderate.

Later, a slow character change came over him: his initial attitude of intolerance was replaced by a remarkably conciliatory, mediative comportment. As he says in his autobiography, he had revived a capacity for tact that in his school days had softened roughness but had subsequently lain dormant. This continued to develop and, many years later, Freud was to say laughingly that Jones's diplomatic abilities might lead to his "being taken over by the League of Nations." By the time of the first psychoanalytic congress in Salzburg, Jones had acquired a mild reputation for tactfulness and settling disputes. Because he was not from Central Europe, he had a somewhat privileged position with Freud, who often discussed with Jones difficulties that it would not have been expedient for Freud to discuss with the members of his immediate circle.

As Mervyn Jones has remarked, Jones's tact and firmness were largely responsible for the favorable outcome when, with Edward Glover, he defended the interests of psychoanalysis before the special committee of the British Medical Association between 1926 and 1929. Jones was one of the subcommittee of three members who drew up the report. He was uniquely qualified by his standing, his diplomatic skill, and his first-hand knowledge of professional conditions on the Continent, in Britain, and in the United States for his position as chief administrator of the International Psycho-Analytic Association.

Although accused by each side of being an advocate for the other, Jones believed that within the "committee" around Freud he functioned as a mediator between East and West: he looked back with satisfaction on having in the long run prevented the split that several times appeared imminent. He expressed the same views to me with respect to the dissension in the British Society between the groups centered about Melanie Klein and Anna Freud.

He also felt he was in a mediating position when—in controversy with those anthropologists who did not embrace Freud's ideas—he gave a conciliatory and persuasive paper on psychoanalysis and anthropology before the Royal Anthropological Institute in 1924.

He interpreted his role—as he did many activities in his later life, even to the site for his country house—as arising from his unconscious desire to unite his parents, for whose imagined separation he must have felt guilty. His international affiliations and his adherence to both the Welsh and English roots of his upbringing he attributed to the same desire to unite the "parent" countries. When Freud proposed to separate psychoanalysis from medicine, Jones claims that the same tendency made him oppose the plan, since it would lead to the impoverishment of both.

It could well be that after his youth had passed, Jones felt that he would be ill-advised to launch himself again and again into eternal fights, as befits only the very young or, on the other hand, to submit to bullying. Yet, in answer to the question as to why and how this change of character had come about, Jones could not have been—and was not—satisfied with the shallow explanation that age alone had mellowed him. In his autobiography, he offers two explanations.

First, he felt that his early successes had initially created an "omnipotence complex": these years, he said, had a certain dreamlike quality—coming, as they did, after earlier years of burning self-criticism, with its sense of guilt—that necessarily put a considerable strain on his mental balance and harmony. Concerning this we must remark that, although Jones himself does not say so, his apparent victory as an adolescent over the seemingly weak father, which preceded his scholarly success, had more to do with his later sense of guilt than did his failures.

Too, the tragic death of his first wife caused life to lose most of its savor, and the acuteness of his loss had the effect of bringing out all the gentleness and kindliness in his nature. There was, in addition, an inborn gentleness in his character: we should not forget that early in childhood he had already overcome his jealousy of his younger sister, whom he rocked and sang to sleep. In the moving words of his son Mervyn, at Jones's funeral, Jones was a "wise and trusted counsellor, tolerant and understanding listener." As his research assistant, I often experienced this personally: he always thanked me for the trouble I had taken, and his praise was lavish. In his oration at Jones's funeral, W. H. Gillespie indicated that Jones had remained a generous giver even after his retirement.

Jones very seldom drew attention to his own person although, understandably, he had to deal often enough with his role in the psychoanalytic movement, especially in his Freud biography. In a letter to me dated February 14, 1955, he wrote: "I am finding Volume III much heavier going than the others, partly because of being personally involved in somewhat unpleasant ways."

In later years Jones affected a melancholy assessment of the "deterioration" of his faculties: "My memory is failing fast," he wrote me in a letter dated October 3, 1955, when, in fact, it was some trifling data he could not recall. At the same time he could remember amazing clusters of relevant materials in all fields better than a younger man might, and secretly he was proud of his good memory. Although he kept his lucid, concise style to his ripe old age, he did not trust it more than before.

When I asked him a question (for the scope and general aim of a query), he wrote: "Your question discloses how ill-defined are my thoughts," which, of course, was not so.

He was always probing his intellectual gifts with cautious scrutiny and a preliminary self-criticism. Obviously, he did not suppose himself to be a prodigy and must have hinted at more than financial difficulties when he claimed that he had had to work hard for everything he had acquired.

It is ironic that his early failures in obtaining an appropriate medical post can be traced back to a banal incident: he was made to resign because he spent a night away from the hospital without the committee's permission (he had received the surgeon's permission)—surely a disproportionate punishment, when one considers the dire consequences.

Ernest Jones had a very full life. He married twice and had four children, three of whom survived; he lived to see several of his grandchildren. He was able to devote the greater part of his life to intellectual pursuits, and, during his professional career, he reached the highest positions in the psychoanalytic movement.

In the preface to *Free Associations,* he states as his motive for writing the autobiography "gratitude for life . . . to those to whom I owe it"; but with this gratitude was also included real thankfulness for the spiritual stimulation he received from Freud's works and ideas. It is hard to imagine a more integrated enjoyment of self-importance and gratitude to those who have not attempted to crush this.

Like Freud, Jones was a favorite child and, because he had no serious guilt feelings, had no intrapsychic need to quash his more or less innocent "megalomanic" daydreams. Thus he daydreamed later in life that in the future the analyst or medical psychologist—like the priest of ancient times—might serve as a source of practical wisdom and a stabilizing influence in the chaotic world, whom the community would consult before embarking on any important social or political enterprise. Although indeed too ambitious, in his old age this daydream became true at least in part, if we consider Jones's personal influence within the psychoanalytic movement.

In his autobiography, Jones mentioned the solemn self-importance that he had felt on his birthdays as a small child because of the blasts of his father's factory hooters at midnight on New Year's Day: he had mistaken these for birthday tributes. The joyous solemnity did not vanish with the years. He thoroughly enjoyed the celebration of his fiftieth birthday and saw no reason why he should not, after the seventieth or seventy-fifth, similarly enjoy his eightieth. Unfortunately he died about a year before his eightieth anniversary, which he had genuinely anticipated.

In the third volume of his Freud biography, Jones mentioned that Freud did not want celebrations on Freud's eightieth birthday. In contradicting his friend, Jones also expressed his personal attitude to this question—perhaps a healthier and pleasanter one than that of the great Exile—with the remark that such a celebration presents the desire to express one's pleasure at the coexistence of someone one loves, which can be done more decidedly on a selected occasion than in everyday life. In his centenary address, "Our Attitude toward Greatness," he returned to the topic: "Surely the commemoration of a birthday is a purely friendly gesture. . . . With an old person . . . is there never an undercurrent of feeling that he has had a good run and really now might well retire from the world?" Yet perhaps he was not quite fair in his annoyance at Freud's attitude—disregarding the old man's possible bitterness about his exiled state and long-standing, painful illness, as well as his open-eyed knowledge of a slow extinction. Mercifully, providence spared Jones that at least. Hence the difference in the attitudes of these two personages, in many respects so similar.

In retrospect, Jones's attitude toward his parents was friendly. As an analyst he could not avoid mentioning and analyzing at least some of the details of his childhood. But he did this sparingly, with the normal reticence of a person who is not an exhibitionist. He had some serious, conscientious doubts, which he discussed with me, about certain details that he might omit from his autobiography and others that he felt he must include.

He spoke freely of his own *pavor nocturnus* and wolf-phobia and mentioned his interest in inventing ciphers, which he interpreted as a derivative from the secretiveness that so often heralds the approach of puberty, combined with an always strong instinct of curiosity. He mentioned his poor head for heights and tendency to giddiness, yet here he did not suspect psychological causation and did not comment analytically on two matters connected therewith: his dislike for waltzing, and his desire to conquer his acrophobia by amateur climbing, in consequence of which he brought himself "into the danger of death" near the Zermatt in Switzerland in 1901.

Jones made a point of mentioning little girls and later ladies in his life—an engagement dissolved, a near involvement in a duel because of a young lady in Brussels, a lasting friendship with Loe, and others—as if he wished to convince the reader that the description of his sex and love life has been left incomplete not only because he did not feel inclined to masochism or exhibitionism, but because the details are for the most part not very interesting.

There is comparatively little reticence about his relationship with his father, who emerges as a rather permissive and even doting parent. Thomas Jones allowed young Ernest free access to his steel works and took the youth on expensive foreign holidays; however, because Ernest resented his father's tutelage, his father permitted him to finish the second foreign tour by himself.

Jones seems to have gone through his Oedipal conflict with his father successfully, but his violent atheism may have been at least partly the by-product of this struggle. Originally a Baptist, the elder Jones later became an Anglican and finally an atheist himself. (Ernest's mother deplored the trend.) The reason given is that Anglicanism is more tolerant, less strict, more mundane, and less serious. A great number of examples in "Rationalisation in Everyday Life," published in 1908, concern reasons given by religious persons as to why they believe in their creeds: among these, he mentions the person who is highly offended if one bluntly says that he believes in baptism simply because his father did.

Jones mentioned in his autobiography both his mother's demise and his mourning for her, but his relationship to her is described as little as possible. Almost flippantly he remarks that as a small boy, on the occasion of his sister's birth, he felt that doctors were "superior to his father's misdeeds" and that this is why he wanted to become a doctor. Ernest felt that his father's anglicizing tendencies were for him like "desecrating the mother":[3] nevertheless, he did not learn to speak Welsh and later became enthusiastic about the purity of the English language.

There is little direct mention of the mother's influence on the child, except in the best Victorian tradition and, later, within a negation: "My mother's influence over me did not continue much beyond the age

[3] This is reflected in his thought about one's country as a "virginal island" (in "The Island of Ireland," published in 1922).

of eight, and it made no direct contribution to my intellectual development."

One aspect here is worth noting, inasmuch as it points to a second possible source of Jones's atheism, namely, the influence of his nanny[4] on young Ernest's mental development. By projection, Jones seems to have attributed his night terrors to his nanny, who had frightened him with superstitious tales. Jones was very sympathetic toward Freud's similar experiences with his nanny, although he refused to believe that these experiences could have had a lasting influence on Freud, as some researchers have assumed. Jones knew from his personal experience that the young child interprets threats as applying to his personal life in the near future, and Freud's contact with his nanny had ceased at two and one-half years of age. To the end of his life, Jones staunchly maintained that neither his personal aversion to religion and superstition nor his atheism could be interpreted psychoanalytically, because they originated from rational sources. Nevertheless, both Freud's and Jones's early childhood disillusionment with the "omniscience" of the uneducated nurse collapsed, instead of fading away as had their belief in the omniscience of parents, who had backgrounds and sociointellectual ability similar to that of their children. This had in fact contributed largely to their having become combative atheists, attacking religious creeds as unconscious representatives of an early witchlike, wicked, and cruel mother figure, and their having turned to enlightenment, truth, and science as to corresponding benevolent father figures. The nurse inspired Jones with a dread of the "burning fire," and the *Pen-y-ceffyl* (The Welsh nightmare figure) inspired him with skepticism of his nurse. Hence his *écrasez l'infâme* attitude.

§ Principles and Views

An indefatigable writer, Jones always was full of new plans and ideas; he enjoyed them immensely, even in old age. An interesting parapraxis is contained in his letter to me of February 14, 1955, in which he acquainted me with his plan to revise his Freud biography: "After that comes the selecting and editing of some volumes of his correspondence, and then a medical book on his final illness. After 86 (originally typed

[4] Melanie Klein would have said, "of the 'bad mother.' "

76; corrected to 96 in handwriting, then re-corrected to 86), I may take a year off to reflect on [the completion of the biography]."

Since he loved to work, he expected others to come up to his exacting standards. I knew him only as an old man, but I found him very easy and agreeable to work with. Whether this was because of his inborn courtesy, or his confidence in the persons he chose to work with him, I cannot say. He accepted suggestions he believed had merit and rejected others, but always with marked consideration—never in a scornful or angry way. Only once in our relationship did I experience even a hint of impatience. Up to the end he was very punctilious: he worked methodically, and his attitude as to the verification of his sources was scholarly. In fact, he sometimes asked me to recheck references that he himself had verified. Up to a late age, he did his own research, with the aid of a typist-secretary and of Mrs. Jones, herself a college graduate. Only when it became progressively more cumbersome for him to visit libraries did he employ a research assistant.

A spaciously built quadripartite desk accommodated all the implements he required, and he had a simple and well-devised system for the management of the huge material for the Freud biography. Files with the titles of intended chapters were kept in special drawers, arranged according to their numbers; and a formidable-looking (although really simple) nest of wire baskets held in alphabetical order letters and other material pertaining to persons to whom he planned to refer.

Throughout his life he had the widest range of interests, along with a special gift for utilizing whatever he had read, studied, or experienced in life for research, and later for the purposes of psychoanalytic investigation. He had the talent to benefit from both the things he enjoyed and those he pursued out of a sense of duty.

Jones owed his lucid, concise style to a period spent when a young man as reporter for a medical periodical. His patience and didactic abilities were developed during long years as tutor in a university correspondence college—for ten years he had the largest coaching practice in the country—and by giving evening lectures for the London City Council on hygiene and first aid.

He owed his broad outlook to his penchant for catholic reading. Jones was a voracious but by no means omnivorous or indiscriminate reader, with a strict method to his extracurricular reading. Even works unrelated or only remotely connected to the subject under study somehow turned out to be germane. Bordering topics always fertilized his mind and guided him to new interests and directions: for example, when dealing with war neuroses he was not content to read only the relevant material; he went on to study the history of the European countries involved in the war, the theory of war, and war strategy. The topic of strategy attracted him particularly because of his interest in chess. No reader of Jones's writings would second his belief that he would have achieved more in life had he not been fascinated by so large a variety of its aspects.

Although Winnicott (Funeral Speeches, 1958) mentions eighty of Jones's publications, other sources mention 233 original contributions—not counting translations, abstracts, and reviews. Only a medical person could deal appropriately with his medical (mostly neurologic) publications. Suffice it to point out that his early training in neurology provided a sound basis for his psychoanalytic work.

Jones started medical research in neurology in 1901 and was lecturer in neurology in the London School of Clinical Medicine. He was soon attracted to psychiatry, but—despite his interest in the unconscious—his keen and all-around interest prevented him from becoming a mere physician of the mind. At the time alienists were held in great contempt in England, and psychopathology—what we now call "medical psychology"—was entirely the prerogative of the organic neurologist and in an even more abysmal state of ignorance than the study of insanity.

Jones's development toward psychoanalysis started in 1906, when he was making tests on normal and defective children. He noted the frequency of guilt reactions in the association tests, and became aware of the unconscious sources of infantile guilt. In treating a ten-year-old girl, he uncovered a sexual basis for the hysterical paralysis of her left arm; this attracted his interest to functional mental disorders and the workings of the unconscious. He soon found that a bowing acquaintance with the unconscious is a very different matter from a direct apprehension of its workings; he realized that he must cooperate wholeheartedly with others having the same aim.

This attitude prevented him from being adversely influenced by persons who were incompletely analyzed—by Otto Gross, his first instructor in the technique of psychoanalysis, who suffered from an unmistakable form of insanity, and by Ferenczi, with whom he had a didactic analysis in 1913 (Jones was the first among analysts who underwent this experience) and who in later years showed some signs of a paranoid trend.

Although Jones had become acquainted with Freud's name and the work of the Nancy School in 1898, he was to conduct his first analysis in 1906 and to make Freud's personal acquaintance in 1908. From the time of their meeting, he spent thirty uninterrupted years in and for the psychoanalytic movement. Apart from the great impact of Freud's personality on him, Jones gave the following reasons for his choice of a destination: on the grounds of his personal experiences, he had no doubts of the presence of sexual life in children, and of repression, the problem of which "even yet is not completely solved." On the basis of his anthropological knowledge, he appreciated the role of symbolism in the unconscious mind.

Jones felt that Freud was the first person to take a scientific interest in mental processes. He was perhaps most impressed with Freud's invention of the "free association" method of investigation: the idea of flawless continuity behind it at once appealed to him as an intelligible example of law and order in an apparent chaos, an illustration of determinism reigning in the sphere where it is most often denied—a most impressive extension of scientific law.

Jones was simply staggered to discover to what depths men of scientific standing could descend, once their unconscious minds were stirred up by the new teachings. He has told of the time in 1911, when his paper, "The Pathology of Morbid Anxiety," met with violent opposition from the floor. During the banquet that followed, "bawdy jokes were the order of the day," and Jones related that he had pointed out the identity of symbolism in these remarks with those he had described in his paper. Then, he said, Professor Vogt turned to him with an astonished air, saying, "But this is not science; you must not mix the two things up."

As Jones was well aware, the psychology of pioneers is peculiarly difficult: truths painfully won are apt to be defended with great tenacity. Therefore, the overcoming of certain unconscious processes or inner conflicts with respect to a problem is of a challenging or defying order that may lead to dogmatism.

Every pioneer must overcome not only personal internal resistances but external opposition or prejudice. "By means of the mechanisms of denial, of discounting, of accepting with lip service only, of reinterpretation in more innocent terms . . . the disturbed outer world sooner or later [comes] once more to a position of rest, feeling it [has] satisfactorily digested these new discoveries, but really reducing them in this fashion to harmlessness" (Jones, 1959). However, some of the pioneers were prepared to shoulder the responsibility—to do all in their power to combine insight into the astonishing discoveries with the balance appropriate to scientific investigators. Jones found that Abraham of Berlin shared this attitude with him to the full, Ferenczi to a large extent, and Putnam in his special way.

This reason also underlay Jones's special emphasis on popularizing psychoanalysis in the vein of Freud's "On Psychoanalysis" and "The Claims of Psychoanalysis to Scientific Interest." Psychoanalysis owes an immense debt to Jones: it is mainly because of his patient and painstaking endeavors that psychoanalysis broke through the hostile defences of other professions and was able to occupy its rightful place among medicine and the sciences. As S. Hampshire affirms: "The name of Ernest Jones will always be associated with the free crossing of academic boundaries" (1962).

The clarity of Jones's formulations is admirable. In "The Relationship between Dreams and Psychoneurotic Symptoms," he noted the identity between the latent content of many dreams and the latent content of many neurotic symptoms from which the patient suffers. He suggested in "Psycho-Analysis and Psychotherapy" that the pathology in the psychoneuroses is a defect in assimilation. His paper "Jealousy" lists many of man's needs: security (from fear), certainty (against doubt), peace of mind (from the tremblings of unconscious guilt), potency, and freedom. In an undated article titled "Psychology in Modern Life," he referred to man as an unpsychological animal—because forces come up against the uncovering of the unconscious, man has a deep aversion to self-knowledge. Freud's great lesson has been in teaching us to face new truths and to hold truth above all considerations ("The Future of Psychoanalysis"), and in one of Jones's most interesting articles, "Psycho-Analysis and Biology," he characterized Freud as "the Darwin of the mind."

Jones intended to deal with the polemic side of his life and career in his autobiography. He felt that references to his own life should be sparse in his biography of Freud: this was less reticence than a sense of proportion and tact. Nevertheless, Jones felt that he would have done himself a disservice had he omitted some mention of his own views. Also, he had to touch on these points at least perfunctorily in the biography because of their correlation with Freud's person. Unfortunately, the proposed later chapters of Jones's autobiography, in which he would have put his role in the movement into a proper and apposite light, were never written.

Jones published few case histories. Perhaps he felt that behind the primary importance of purely theoretical, albeit technical, papers, the subsidiary, popularizing papers took temporary precedence. Although a medical man himself, he felt that case histories can occupy only a tertiary position, especially at that juncture of the expansion of psychoanalytic knowledge.

Jones devoted a paper to the case history of a person who, under quite different circumstances, exhibited the simulated stupidity of Hamlet. In part, the simulated stupidity was a deliberate ruse, a defense against certain unfavourable circumstances; in part, it was occasioned by hostility toward parent figures whom the patient wanted to offend yet, at the same time, to lull into the false belief that they could speak freely before the child about (sexual) matters that they preferred not to convey to the child, as the child was apparently too stupid to understand: "By this means children can view and overhear private things which they are not supposed to." These findings Jones utilized in his book on Hamlet.

Jones held originality in high esteem and was keenly interested in the psychology of creative work. One of the most difficult tasks in appraising Jones's lifework is the assessment of his own originality and the determination of which ideas the science of psychoanalysis owes exclusively to him. His work is overshadowed by his own emphasis on Freud's doctrines and on the overwhelming personality of the originator of psychoanalysis. In view of Jones's otherwise strong personality (by no means devoid of the original leader's legitimate vanity or the born leader's ambitions), this confronts us with the psychological *non sequitur*. Lesser thinkers than he could strongly emphasize the authorship of new ideas—whether given to deflection from Freud's ideas and leadership, or under his wing. The psychoanalytic reader associates certain ideas with each of Freud's followers[5] of the first or second generation. However, in considering Jones, one must first range over a fairly large field without being able clearly to ascertain which of the ideas propounded originated with Jones, and which are only popularizations of Freud's teachings, albeit more succinct and more self-evident than the original.

In his personal relationship with Freud, Jones was outspoken though

[5] Jones abhorred the term "disciple" because he felt it smacked of religion.

respectful, but he never committed to writing such details of possible disagreements as were unnecessary from the theoretical point of view.[6] Most of Jones's ideas were accepted by Freud, but Jones rarely received credit for the ideas and apparently was too proud to stress his own importance, which therefore has never been fully appreciated by the psychoanalytic movement. Perhaps this is one reason why Jones's biography of Freud has been almost unanimously acclaimed as the culmination of his literary career, whereas his scientific contributions have been sorely neglected.

Although several among the first generation of Freud's followers have set up closely knit "schools," Jones had only a few personal followers and adherents among those whom he taught. A free spirit himself, he never imposed doctrines on his students, and thus there was never any strong group tie among them. On the other hand, many of his ideas have been appropriated by all and sundry—sometimes with acknowledgment and sometimes without—and rapidly have become not only psychoanalytic truisms, but commonplaces for all educated men and women of our century. Although some of Jones's ideas have been absorbed into newer and theoretically more detailed studies, almost none of his original ideas have been taken up for further development except, perhaps, those on symbols and symbolism, to which H. Segal has linked her new and valuable concept of symbolic equations. Nevertheless, few if any of Jones's ideas ever have been refuted.

Why did Jones's ideas never express those latent, popular vogues in psychoanalytic interest that tend to attract new followers? Irreverent critics may venture the opinion that perhaps his ideas were less first-rate than had been assumed. I should disbelieve this: a serious revival of interest in Jones's ideas and their values is timely, if not overdue.

Jones's essays are distinguished examples of scholarly work. He was meticulous and used as many relevant references as necessary—without, however, encumbering his work with a flood of references. In addition to his exact, albeit intense, style, one of Jones's greatest assets was his almost aesthetic sense of proportion.

Unfortunately, Jones never attempted to build a systematic structure

[6] "The inception of *Totem and Taboo*" is a good example. In a letter to Ferenczi, Freud said that he had reverted from his original high estimate of the work and was critical of it. Jones suggests that Freud had, in his imagination, lived through the experiences he had described; that his elation represented the excitement of killing and eating the father; and that Freud's doubts were only the reaction to this.

within which to place his contributions. Both his *Papers on Psycho-Analysis* and his *Essays in Applied Psycho-Analysis* appeared in loosely knit units throughout numerous editions; each edition added some new essays, dropped some previous ones. It seems that this unfinished appearance of clusters of ideas, as if they were in turmoil, sprang from two opposing tendencies: Jones's bent on orderliness and precision bordering on perfectionism, in contrast to his impetuosity, impatience, and vacillation as to firm self-appraisal.

Once his duty to Freud's memory had been fulfilled, Jones felt that his first obligation was not to bring systematic order to his own writings but to finish his autobiography. Not long before his death Jones told his wife that a new edition of his *Papers* was now expedient. Perhaps he still had so much to say and to write that he felt the cornerstones of the edifice were not yet assembled and therefore architectural plans would have been premature. Jones may have still felt too young to fulfill that eminent task of the elderly, to revise and overhaul his own lifework. Both assumptions seem contradicted by his having started his autobiography but such contradictions in human behavior only prove the conflictual nature of some of its ambitions. Jones's very exterior reflected something of this: although very youthful, even boyish, in appearance, and swift in his movements until his late seventies, at the same time he had the rare dignity of a patriarch, even before the last year of his life when he decided to grow a beard.

A multitude of sparkling new ideas are interspersed throughout Jones's papers: this wealth has never been exploited to its full value. They demonstrate the extraordinary riches of his creative spirit, yet his haste to leave each idea once newer ideas attracted his fancy. Jones felt that these riches could be developed later, but that time never came. It was as if he were afraid of never attaining a ripe old age, and thus had to use the time available expeditiously in giving birth to as many ideational progeny as possible. Elaboration of the ideas could wait.

Not unlike Freud, Jones was interested in an immense number of topics in addition to his psychiatric interests. And neither man shared the narrow views of some colleagues who would have liked to limit the psychoanalyst's interests to clinical cases and topics of therapeutic technic.

Jones's most prominent original monographs are *Hamlet and Oedipus* and *On the Nightmare*. His writing on Hamlet constitutes one of the best examples of the amalgamation of Freud's teachings and Jones's original research. Reviewing the whole tremendous bulk of Shakespearean literary criticism and mentioning only sources of psychological value to the understanding of both Shakespeare's personality and that of Hamlet, Jones based his own reasoning on Freud's views of Hamlet's Oedipus complex (passing over Freud's tentative theories—with which he disagreed—as to Shakespeare's identity), added a few exceptionally interesting points, and drew a similarly interesting conclusion. Since Jones did not lay emphasis on his personal contributions, one is apt to miss some of his important additions, for example, that Hamlet's courtship of Ophelia originates in an unconscious desire to play her off against his mother—incidentally, a powerful motive in bisexual (or latently homosexual) males, which makes them appear as pseudoheterosexuals; he feels that she is sent to lure him on and then, as his mother has done, to betray him. This could contribute materially to the study of some paranoid traits.

There is also much thought-provoking material in Jones's views about Polonius. Perhaps one of Jones's shorter essays, "The God Complex," stems from his meditation on Polonius. In another essay, on grandfathers, he quotes Polonius. Jones may be correct in his estimate of Hamlet's attitude toward Polonius, that the absence of family tie enables him to indulge his hostility toward his father to a relatively unrestrained extent.

A further interesting point concerns Hamlet's "simulated madness" and the caution of a man who must keep his secret. Another essay, "Simulated Foolishness in Hysteria," deals with feigned stupidity. In addition, Jones dealt amply with the literature on the "dull hero," also in folklore; no other author seems to have been interested in that aspect of the problem.

No one has pursued further Jones's conclusions as to why Shakespeare wrote *Hamlet* and what prompted him to deal with the hesitant hero. Jones contends that the all-important respect in which Shakespeare changed the story is the vacillation and hesitancy he introduced into Hamlet's task. Freud believed that this was due to intrapsychic (Oedipal) conflicts. Jones suggests that, when Shakespeare introduced his beloved friend of the *Sonnets* to his mistress of the *Sonnets*, they became disloyal to him, that when the double betrayal by his friend and his mistress broke over him he was unable to deal with it by any action, and he responded by creating *Hamlet*.

Jones's other extensive work, a book of 350 pages, is *On the Night-*

mare (1909). Its central thesis is that the nightmare is an expression of conflict over an incestuous desire. He believed that the repression of the feminine masochistic component of the sexual instinct is apt to engender the typical nightmare. Another paper on the same subject is his "Beliefs Concerning the Nightmare."

We might assume, also on the grounds of Jones's autobiography, that when he was a child suffering from nightmares, his nurse did her best to intimidate the child. Jones managed to turn even this to the advantage of his creative intellect. As regards the nightmare, he concluded that the intensity of the fear is proportionate to the guilt of the repressed incestuous wishes that are striving for imaginary gratification, the physical counterpart of which is an orgasm. If the wish were not in a state of repression, there would be no fear and the result would be a simple erotic dream. Jones suggested that what are now called neurotic or psychotic patients are in large measure the descendants of old witches, lycanthropes, and the like, together with the people who believed in their existence.

Part II of *On the Nightmare* deals with connections between the nightmare and certain medieval superstitions. One chapter is devoted to the devil. Jones equated fantasies of suckling milk or blood with fellatio fantasies—not, as Melanie Klein later did, the other way around; however, he too refers to the source that influenced her thoughts on the subject, Karl Abraham's "Traum und Mythus."

Part III of *On the Nightmare* is devoted to the role in infantile sexuality of fantasies about the horse. The folklore of the horse is indicative of the phallic stage of development. Observed as potently urinating, it either is admired or regarded as a fiend in equine disguise. Attitudes of overadulation and contempt for the creature alternate, depending on whether it is used to symbolize the male or female genitals. Jones noted that the steed in question is born ugly, misshapen and deformed, and only later becomes noble and handsome; this whole theme relates to the attaining of virility or overcoming the fear of castration. The sun-horse gods represent the infantile-sadistic conception of coitus, together with the assault on the female's penis, so closely associated with the maternal genitalia. The sexual or tormenting power of the night-fiend resides in his evil eye—a thought from which inferences could be drawn to the scopophilic instinct.[7] The symbolism of theft is mentioned also: it means castration if it refers to the penis, and has homo-

[7] Jones objected to use of the term scop*to*philic on linguistic grounds.

sexual connotations if it refers to treasure (meaning feces) or woman.

Problems of art, the study of creativity, the psychoanalytic concept of sublimation, and the psychology of symbolism occupied an extensive place in his writings. An enthusiastic play-goer from early youth, Jones liked to think back on the plays he had seen and was a keen observer and an authentic judge of the arts.

He noted that intellectual appreciation is heightened by understanding and comprises an important part of the higher forms of aesthetic appreciation: thus, he was not afraid that under too scrutinizing a gaze beauty might vanish. In each work his interest was aroused by a special psychoanalytic problem, for he had a delicate sensitivity to psychological problems behind works of art that personally moved him. It seems that in *Hamlet and Oedipus* he was attracted by the impression it made on him of, "not as Goethe depicted . . . a gentle soul crushed beneath a colossal task, but one of a strong man tortured by some mysterious inhibition" (1923). He felt, and rightly, that the cause for Hamlet's vacillation had not yet been fathomed, and at that time could not accept the abulic interpretations of some literary critics.

Another paper, "On Dying Together," deals with Heinrich von Kleist's suicide—it compares his poetry, on the one hand, with necrophilia, coprophilia, sadism, and birth fantasy, on the other. The same topic is also illustrated by a case report, "An Unusual Case of 'Dying Together.' "

From the standpoint of a critical appreciation of the arts, "The Influence of Andrea del Sarto's Wife on His Art" may be less than satisfactory, but it does reveal the personal psychoanalytic factors that made del Sarto an eminent painter. Yet, the result—the *oeuvre* of the artist—remains somewhat neglected. One gets the impression that, as an experiment, Jones had deliberately tried to dissociate the two subjects, thereby producing a brilliant essay on latent homosexuality.

Jones had valuable ideas about the tragedy and other forms of art. In "What is Psycho-Analysis?" he notes that "the attribute of certainty and if possible, perfection, the justness of the formal relationship that evokes aesthetic feeling—all this provides a refined kind of security—allaying conscious tension. Tragedy . . . has to do with the conviction of inevitability." He had a high appreciation of the aesthetic value of the sense of order therein. Jones also wrote two additional papers, "The Artistic Form and the Unconscious" and "Psycho-Analysis and the Artist."

Jones was already interested in the psychology of genius by 1910: in the opening sentence of *Hamlet and Oedipus*, he noted that psychologists had as yet devoted little attention to the analytic study of individual genius and artistic creativeness and wondered about the author's unawareness of the ultimate sources of his creation. However, he did not again take up the problem in his writings until late in life, when he considered "The Nature of Genius" in the first of his centenary addresses. Dealing with Freud's greatness in that paper, he was more interested in the creative genius of the scientist than that of the artist—always maintaining, nevertheless, the essential identity of character of the endowment in both. In his essay on del Sarto, he insisted upon the importance of the *internal battle* for all artistic creation—later extending the assertion to all creative endeavors.

He had the greatest admiration for creativity: it was perhaps what he esteemed most in genius—especially in Freud. Jones had a certain contempt for mere self-criticism, which he regarded as a negative quality —being able to decide what is wrong, but not necessarily what is right. Since he was himself endowed with originality, his appraisal of persons with genius never became sycophantic; on the contrary, he esteemed those who resembled him in this respect and, although he never acknowledged it openly, he had an aristocratic sense for distinguishing the creative from the noncreative. This drew his attention to the importance of intuition. He felt that psychology cannot yet explain what underlies the flair of intuition that guides the observer to follow up something his feelings tell him is important. Failure of this critical faculty, according to Jones, is most often caused by interference from another idea or emotion associated with the theme.

The phenomenon of "genius" as he had observed it in Freud always puzzled and attracted him. This was reflected also in his second centenary address, "Our Attitude toward Greatness." Previously, he had dealt with the problem in his essay on a minor genius, the chess-player Morphy. Jones defined genius as the capacity to apply unusual gifts with intense, even if only temporary, concentration—this dependent, in turn, on a special capacity for discovering conditions under which the unconscious guilt can be held in complete abeyance. He had less consideration for the distortions of the genius—the prodigy who is liable to suffer breakdowns and whose objectives are futile. Although Jones indulged in chess as a pastime, he regarded such genius as Morphy's to be uncreative. He believed that creative geniuses possess a sense of the really significant; that they not only have the power of concentration but look at things in an essentially new way; and that, finally, at the successful moment, a remarkable degree of integration must have been achieved between the ego, the superego, and the id. In addition, the genius possesses a particular skepticism: he must have refused to acquiesce in certain previously accepted conclusions, to take something for granted; yet, he must have a kind of naïveté or credulity. In "Sigmund Freud, the Man and His Achievements," Jones reminds us that simplicity always seems to accompany true greatness.

How may significant originality be described? Certainly, it must embody more than occasional flashes of insight. Similarly, a mere tendency to doubt and to ignore conventional opinion cannot of itself lead to orginality in any significant sense. Jones wondered whether Freud's pronounced independence of thought had not in part been developed as a reaction to early credulity or suggestibility. He regarded creative thinking as almost a prerogative of the male sex, for he believed that this was their substitute for the gift of bodily creation bestowed on women.

In "Our Attitude toward Greatness," Jones showed a parallel to the ambivalence of the son toward his father. He reported a general resistance toward greatness, terror creating angry hostility; this results in opposition and all of the various attitudes the son might display. Misapprehensions would then arise from mental confusion.

Only persons who can sublimate successfully may become great men. In connection with Morphy's breakdown, Jones remarked that the process of sublimation has, ultimately, a defensive function; that its breakdown signifies the cessation of this defensive function. Jones contended that the most brilliant sublimations stem from the successful overcoming of the anal-erotic stage. Thus, in "The Madonna's Conception through the Ear," he said:

> When we remember how extensively these repressed . . . tendencies contribute, in their sublimated forms, to every variety of artistic activity . . . it becomes evident that in the artist's striving for beauty the fundamental part played by these primitive infantile interests . . . is not to be ignored: the reaction against them lies behind the striving. . . . We cannot but be impressed by the ingenuity and fine feeling with which an idea so repellent to the adult mind has been transformed into a conception not merely tolerable, but lofty in its grandeur (1923, p. 13).

And, in "The Value of Sublimating Processes for Education and Re-education," he wrote of the necessity of sublimation of infantile tendencies because they form not only the basis of erotic desire but also the basis for many nonsexual interests. "War and Sublimation" deals with the value of established sublimation in these crises.

Jones believed, however, that symbol formation is incapable of sublimation. He noted that with the metaphor the feeling is oversublimated, whereas with the symbol it is undersublimated. From Freud's *Interpretation of Dreams* onward, the topic of symbol formation has attracted almost all of Freud's followers. Jones suggested that a committee of Abraham, Stekel, Maeder, and himself prepare a collective study of symbolism for presentation to the 1910 Congress. Unfortunately, this was not done, and Jones was forced to tackle the task singlehandedly—under the restrictions imposed by a one-man approach. A most accomplished paper, "The Theory of Symbolism," resulted. Even now it is hard to measure the impact of this paper on the future development of psychoanalysis. Jones's paper decisively separated the theoretical outlook of the psychoanalytic school from attempts at explaining symbolism by Silberer and Maeder, and from the Jungian school, which, through its treatment of the phenomenon of symbolism, gradually became more and more addicted to obscure mysticism, divorcing itself from the more scientific research into these more mysterious mental phenomena.

In opposition to Jung's views, Jones held that symbolism must be re-created afresh out of individual material, and that the stereotypy of seemingly collective archetypical symbols is due to the uniformity of the human mind. Always, the more essential idea is symbolized by the less essential one: they are linked by internal or external association. The symbolized is the more sensorial (usually visual) and concrete, whereas the symbol is relatively more abstract and complex. Although the number of ideas that can be symbolized is few, there are, comparatively, many symbols. As Jones was aware, it is more pleasant to remember the features of a new idea if it resembles an old, familiar one. Fatigue promotes symbol formation, which is one of the more primitive functions of the mind: there are similarities between its working and that of the "wit." Here Jones dealt also with the problem of the secret. True symbolism is distinguished from other forms of indirect representation—the simile or the metaphor—by the suppression of the *as* or the *or*. Symbolism arises in its most typical form when inhibition is at its maximum. When the meaning of the symbol is disclosed, the conscious attitude is one of surprise, incredulity, and often repugnance. In "What Is Psycho-Analysis?" Jones defined the symbol as a pure substitute for an unconscious idea.

As I already have noted, Jones also contributed his share to the detection of symbolic meanings. In *On the Nightmare,* he mentioned the symbolism of theft—penis, treasure, woman, and so forth. He wrote a paper on snake-symbolism in dreams; and, in "The Madonna's Conception through the Ear," he described the ear as a symbol for the anus and the vagina. In his essay on the meaning of the foreskin, "The Mantle Symbol," Jones corrected (tactfully and convincingly) Freud's statements on that subject. Interesting remarks on the "timorous bridegroom" are to be found in his "Individual and Society." "Cold, Disease, and Birth" uncovers the importance of precursors of the castration complex—that the castration complex proper originates in the fear of removal of the feces, identified with the penis (Freud later endorsed this view). It may appear strange to us—a generation to whom this appears self-evident—that in 1948 Jones needed to remind us that the body-inside is a "sack" concept, or that in the young child's spontaneous fantasy the abdomen is merely a bag of undifferentiated contents.

The symbolic idea of the *messenger* (as propounded in the essay on the Madonna), who represents one or more aspects of the main personality and the notion of which is based on perfection, could have been developed into a study of a most important feature in male homosexuality—the need for a "deputy," bridge, or buffer between oneself and the object—that would pertain also to the problem of isolation as a defense: both originate in fear of contact, its anal and tactile implications, and the like.

In his indication of the anal-erotic meaning of traveling, Jones has provided another fruitful subject for future investigation. In "On Dying Together," he mentioned that "movement" is a synonym for defecation, and "motion" for feces. Jones may have been planning to write about traveling phobia, but he dropped the idea, perhaps out of consideration for Freud (who was subject to this fear), or because he was waiting for Freud himself to deal with the topic. His private papers include a short typescript on Freud's early travels that bears the handwritten note, "Not to be printed." Had Jones written on traveling, he might have shed light on states of fugue, on the group enjoyment of processions and pageants, and on other problems with which Michael

Balint has dealt. Jones has devoted a few interesting lines to the meaning of homesickness: when excessive, this is due to overattachment and rooted in unconscious wishes. This, too, is an analytic commonplace today, but it was not so self-evident in 1912, when propounded in "The Symbolic Significance of Salt in Folklore and Superstition."

The last-mentioned paper, an exemplary instance of orthodox anthropological dissertation, introduces Jones's folkloristic and anthropological interests. His unique stylistic ability renders the tortuous and adventurous career of the hero, salt, not only very readable but almost breathtakingly enjoyable. The same applies to his motif research in the Hamlet story. In "A Case of Obsessional Neurosis" Jones mentioned the prominence in mythology and folklore of the motif of a child who springs from a corpse or out of a grave. "The Significance of Christmas" deals with yet another motif, and "Psychoanalysis and Folklore" with the entire domain. He also dealt with the "doubling process" in literature and saga, especially with respect to the grandfather figure, whom he regarded as the duplication of the father image.

Except for Géza Róheim, Jones was perhaps the only analyst to follow closely Freud's lead along anthropological lines while remaining strictly scientific, even when fascinated by his topics. He never permitted his fantasy to extend into mystical or otherwise unfounded speculation.

"The Madonna's Conception through the Ear" is Jones's most accomplished publication. He had some misgivings about it, that it might offend the Church and the devout. Yet, perhaps an impish, unconscious wish to offend them contributed to the brilliant and ruthless pursuit of the topic to its well-documented and logical conclusions. He related the symbolic meanings of wind—breath, sound, and flatus—to sexual activities, just as, in his essay on salt, he connected all those multifarious symbolic implications relevant to the sexual significance of urine and semen. Jones has also reminded us that in symbolic language the flower signifies a child (an unconscious equivalent of the female genitalia). This idea was not new; it had already appeared in Freud's dream interpretations. We see, here, how difficult it is to separate Jones's contributions from those of Freud: in a way, they fuse. Jones never attempted positively to dissociate them from the contributions of his "introjected subject" (Glover, 1958).

"A Psycho-Analytical Study of the Holy Ghost Concept" led Jones even further into the domain of religion and its psychological purport.

This essay shows definite traces of Jones's Protestant upbringing. He starts by explaining how the mother or goddess has been replaced by the mysterious figure of the Holy Ghost, and that the unpardonable sin against the Holy Ghost is equivalent to the defilement of the Holy Mother and an attempted castration of the father. According to Jones, the Protestant solution of the Oedipus complex is the replacement of the mother by the Woman, whereas the Catholic solution consists in a change from the masculine to the feminine attitude. It appears that Jones's aversion to the Church and to Christianity—his mother had wanted him to become a minister—also goes back to his fear of and distaste for homosexuality: he spoke of the extensive part played by sublimated homosexuality throughout the Christian religion, and of the hermaphroditic ideal offered to the world as Christianity. Both essays reduce the concept of the Holy Ghost to the archaic image of a powerful, concrete phallus that expels the wind, from which Jones drew the conclusion that the belief in gaseous impregnation represents a reaction to an unusually intense castration fantasy. Yet, he himself was puzzled by the contrast, and also pointed out "why this most repellent of sexual phantasies should lend itself better than any other to the conveyance of the most exalted and spiritual ideas of which the mind is capable."

Jones's antireligious ideas are distributed among many of his writings. In his view, Christianity is a sublimation of, and a defense against, Oedipal wishes. His militant atheism equated religiosity and the established Churches with the acceptance of superstition. In "Rationalisation in Everyday Life," he adduces many examples of rationalization in religious thinking, basing his tenets relating to these matters on anthropological and mythological material, and on certain mental phenomena of the anal stage.

Emotionally, his atheism had four main sources. I have mentioned one already, the reaction to the unwholesome influence of his nanny—the "bad" mother. For some reason his longings for the virginal "good" mother (and anger against the intruding father) were not fully sublimated in these angry essays against the idolatry of the virginal mothers, who have conceived in such funny, revolting, or abstruse ways. He was able to mitigate them only vaguely by his geographical contemplations (that is, middle position between the parents) or in such nostalgic articles as "The Island of Ireland."

The entire social, emotional, and intellectual climate in medical and scientific circles in the late 1890s and early 1900s provided a second source for Jones's atheism. A third and more controversial source was Jones's lifelong association with Freud, most of whose ideas he shared. This does not imply a simple or unambiguous "taking over" of Freud's position; that would not have been in Jones's character.

A fourth source Jones himself acknowledged in his *Free Associations*, namely, his childhood conflict with his father. Although Jones had intellectual knowledge of this, emotionally he does not seem to have fathomed its full extent. He attributed his (apparently incongruous) sublimation of his Oedipal hatred to a desire to reunite the parents.

It is true that Jones's atheism was to some extent fomented by his conviction that there are noxious, latent homosexual and masochistic elements in Christianity. Nevertheless, the idea of "God" was also repugnant to him because it evoked for him the picture of an honorable Victorian father in a Judaic disguise. This often unpleasant father figure, so common in the established churches, obviously affected his distaste for religion, although he abhorred even more the mother figure of the superstitious adorations. In theory, Jones felt himself to be impartial toward religion, and he distinguished between superstition and religion, which he described as one of the means of helping mankind to cope with the burden of guilt and fear. In fact, he usually overlooked this distinction.

A telling sentence in "The God Complex" shows Jones's undigested Oedipal wrath. This essay deals with a certain type of classical (unpleasant) father figure in society—the person who considers himself divine and a fountainhead of authority, the questioning of which is sacrilege. In "The God Complex," Jones suggested that as a rule such father figures are atheists: they cannot suffer the existence of any other God. Here again one may wonder whether, or to what extent, Jones's own atheism stemmed from a powerful defense against possible similar wishes in himsself, and whether his father's and Freud's atheism are not implied and censored in the essay, together with the atheism of some other scientists—mayhap implying that Jones's own atheism owed its origin to purer, more sublimated and rational sources. In Freud's interest in the occult, Jones seemed to sense a spirit of heresy to the commonly (and mutually) held atheistic creed.

§ Freud and the Freud Biography

Jones distrusted every form of adoration. In "The Nature of Auto-Suggestion," he deals with its primarily narcissistic roots, pointing out that adoration, devotion, and general overestimation are much more a matter of narcissistic identification than of object love. Perhaps this is the reason that Jones severely checked every trace in himself of such emotions toward father figures—even in relation to Freud.

He tried to keep his feelings toward Freud unadulterated, permitting himself only those of friendship and intellectual admiration. By keeping his Celtic enthusiasm under strict control he succeeded in striking a balance in his attitudes toward Freud: cautious but narcissistic identification with the founder of psychoanalysis, yet the ability to criticize (albeit reverently and in a constructive way) on the rare occasions when they disagreed. Jones was careful not to permit himself any demonstration that might suggest a "cult" for psychoanalysis. He attempted to guard himself both against critics who display a "dithyrambic identification" with geniuses, permitting themselves to praise their own glory under guise of adoration, and against critics who labor to find direct or indirect ways of disparaging men of genius and their achievements. Jones found it particularly hard to forgive reviewers who described Freud as either "a very disagreeable man" or "an opinionated, irascible, tyrannical" father, difficult to live with, quarrelsome, and intolerant. Jones saw in Freud a combination of strong emotion, strong self-control, and tenacious reserve.

To Jones, Freud's having made a statement was sufficient reason for investigating the matter with especially careful attention; however, his respect for probity made his judgment dependent on evidential data alone. This is diametrically opposed to the attitude he described with strident criticism in "The God Complex," wherein he contrasted the correct analytic attitude with that of the traditional or academic psychologists of Jones's time, those evidently "bad" father figures who (according to the subtitle of the essay) have "the belief that one is God." In "The God Complex" Jones spoke about the flood and curves of statistics that threaten to suffocate the science of psychology. He spoke of psychologists who often display a striking ignorance of the human mind and—because they lack creative powers—often attempt to make up for their deficiencies by invention of "objective" methods that make them independent of intuition.

More specifically, this essay deals with the infantile, narcissistic impotence-fantasy in the grown-up, particularly with the elderly man occupying or close to a father's position. Jones shows brilliant psychological acumen but unmistakable animosity in his Hamlet studies. Two further essays are devoted to the same topic: "The Significance of the Grandfather for the Fate of the Individual," and "The Phantasy of the Reversal of Generations." Polonius is a prying busybody, a senile nonentity concealed behind a show of fussy pomposity in which profound ignorance of life is thinly disguised by a would-be worldly-wise air; he represents a near-homosexual figure with obnoxious elderly attitudes. In "The God Complex" Jones pointed to this person's exceptional curiosity (one wonders how far a projection) and somewhat maliciously remarked that such an individual seems to show some interest in psychology and tends to become a professional psychologist or psychiatrist. This childish curiosity is matched by an equally childish secrecy —about his name, age, profession, house, and privacy—despite his apparent narcissism and exhibitionism, that is, vanity. It was Jones's observation that nothing offends such a man as does the suggestion that he resembles someone else; that he shows extreme tolerance or intolerance, according to whose will infringes, his or the others'. The degree to which Jones represents father figures behind the grandfather façade is revealed in his remark about this type's desire to be loved and to attain immortality. As Jones noted, such persons show a fear and jealousy of younger rivals, although a desire to protect may be manifested if a person acknowledges his helpless position and appeals to him "as the weak to the strong" in a masochistic way.

It did not escape Jones's eye that these figures show no inhibition (a trait also pertaining to the childish personality). I believe that King Lear's cantankerousness (as analyzed by Ella F. Sharpe) escaped his special interest in part because Lear was confronted by daughters rather than sons. Jones assures us through various mythological references that the tyrannical father's (grandfather's) hostility toward a daughter really is directed against the innocent grandson—which seems to prove that in Jones's mind it is also the male offspring's hostility toward the primal father that, for obvious reasons of mitigation, becomes displaced to the figure of the grandfather.

There was an almost Promethean revolt in Jones against persons (in society, private life, or in the battle of old versus new tendencies in the realm of scientific progress) who "cannot suffer the existence of any other God." We do not know whom Jones had most in mind in this respect: wicked father-figures among the older generation of psychiatrists who opposed Freud and psychoanalysis, some deviant analysts perhaps, Pierre Janet, or possibly a compound image. Jones called attention to this figure's low personal standard of honor in the matter of probity and truthfulness, although he conceded that such a person could become a successful lecturer and after-dinner speaker. Such a person, Jones said, is a bad citizen, although he may have a theoretical interest in social reform; his ideal is to be "the man behind the throne." As a thinker, this type of individual is disinclined to accept new knowledge: his way of accepting new ideas is to modify them and then give them out as entirely his own, maintaining that the difference between his version and that of the discoverer is vitally important. Whenever the modifications are considerable, they weaken the original idea. A second way is to devalue the new idea—so describing it as to stress its links with older ideas, claiming always to have been familiar with it. These persons feel that their time is always correct and valuable and lay particular stress on punctuality; they have pride in their excellent memories and in their abilities to predict the weather.

When writing Freud's biography, Jones carefully checked whether (and how many) of these bugbears were still alive. I had expressed doubts about the death of one individual, and in a letter to me dated December 13, 1954, Jones could scarcely conceal his pique when he wrote: "I don't care when he died so long as I can be sure he is thoroughly dead now, since I am libelling him severely."

Jones himself shared one or two of the characteristics he denounced in "The God Complex." Not only was he, too, an atheist, but he was also punctual, proud of his memory, and an excellent after-dinner speaker.

Because the subjective ethos of Jones's biography can be understood only through some passages of "The God Complex," it is best discussed at this point. Jones despised not only those who attacked rather than criticized Freud, but also those who rejected him under the guise of acceptance (much of so-called acceptance is really a subtle form of rejection). He pointed out the shallowness of so much that passes as acceptance of Freud's ideas, and the superficiality with which they are treated. It is difficult to ascertain how far his resentment was due to personal experiences in connection with his own teachings and to what extent he saw it in connection with Freud's teachings.

The majority of his critics regard Jones's biography of Freud as his *chef-d'oeuvre*. Unquestionably, it is a *chef-d'oeuvre*—one of the masterpieces in biography, the crowning of Jones's literary career—and certainly the best among the works on Sigmund Freud. Yet, for all its greatness, I prefer to think that, had Jones systematized his own teaching, one would remember him less as Freud's biographer than as a great and original thinker.

Although the biography earned him the greatest praise, it also earned him the most spiteful criticism. Erich Fromm and others have accused Jones of idolatry, of idolizing Freud, thus giving a false picture of the founder of psychoanalysis. Fromm rebuked Jones for his "unanalytic approach" and for a psychological naïveté ill-befitting a psychoanalyst.

Jones himself accepted Freud's greatness wholeheartedly. In 1910, he had already acclaimed Freud as "the Darwin of the mind," and he stated in 1918 that Freud's greatest lesson to us has been to face new truth, and to hold truth above all other considerations.

As the sole survivor of the small circle of co-workers in constant intimate contact with Freud, Jones felt it incumbent on him to undertake to write his biography—to bring this double offering to his friend and to the history of the psychoanalytic cause. He felt sufficiently free from undue subjectivity to venture into such a work. He believed that the story of Freud's life and work would at the same time provide an early history of the movement, historically still unexplored to the full extent of its impact on our whole cultural outlook. The task was performed partly out of duty and piety, but it also afforded Jones great delight in recalling the well-fought battles in which he had joined with his leader and comrade-in-arms. In preparing Freud's biography he relived his own youth, just as he did in the narratives of his own autobiography. In a way, he regarded the Freud biography as a part of his autobiography. He felt a great obligation to Freud and—much as he had wished to complete his autobiography—planned to complete the revised edition of the Freud biography before he took up his own narrative again.

In writing the biography, he emphasized the positive side, that is, what he believed most essential. The wonderful balance in the biography is a reflection of Jones's flair for choosing the essential in a collection of material.

The subjective side constituted a major problem to his conscience. Jones was animated by a great affection for Freud's personality and was sure of Freud's friendship. Therefore, he had to guard against tainting his work by unsavory hero-worship or uncritical filial revolt—both attitudes he abhorred. In retrospect, we may say that he succeeded remarkably well in both respects.

One of the most tantalizing points in the appraisal of Jones's lifework is the deeper psychological problem of his friendship with, and the nature of his adherence to, Freud. Freud himself seldom referred to this friendship. After their first encounter, he mentioned to Jung that he found Jones "very clever." He praised Jones for his Salzburg paper, "Rationalisation," and in his address on Jones's fiftieth birthday, he employed the customary laudatory but somewhat pale remarks that befit such occasions: he emphasized the good qualities of being "zealous, energetic, valiant, and devoted to the cause." Contrast this with what Jones had to say of Freud: that he was not only "easy and pleasant to work with" but "a warm-hearted friend, a delightful companion with a rich sense of humour covering his underlying seriousness." Admittedly, Jones wrote these lines at a mellower age; nevertheless, the difference is overwhelming.

Persons who knew Jones must feel that the emotional characteristics he attributed to and cherished most in Freud were present in himself to a very large extent. He seems to have valued most in Freud the qualities which, despite their different upbringing, he also possessed, for example, intellectual courage and optimism. As Jones noted, Freud was not a pessimist; he never saw Freud depressed. The two men were akin not only in their intellectual pursuits and reactions but also to some extent in character—even to the slightly tyrannical, authoritarian slant that Jones so hotly denied was present in Freud. Both had been favorites as children, and both were subjected to the unwholesome influence of uneducated nannies. Of course, there were also differences.

Freud was the harder, cooler, perhaps even the more callous of the two. With ill-concealed bitterness Jones recalled that, when his first child had died, he would have preferred to receive some words of consoling wisdom; Freud suggested, in a letter of condolence, that he undertake a piece of research on Shakespeare. Obviously, Freud had the best of intentions, but the bereaved father resented the apparently inappropriate remark. He could not know how far this issued from ill-advised reserve or from Freud's aversion to writing such letters. From some of Freud's recently published letters, and his beautiful memoir, "Transience," we can see that he was neither unfeeling nor heartless.

Jones knew that he must keep his mercurial enthusiasm for Freud under control. It constituted a problem for him throughout life, and one might wonder whether he was really so confident as he pretended that his hero-worshiping propensities had been worked through before he encountered Freud. Jones admitted that his romantic idea of building an especially close inner group of trustworthy analysts, who would serve somewhat as a bodyguard to Freud, was derived from boyhood reading of Charlemagne and his paladins. Jones had no illusions about the reserved nature of Freud's friendship: he felt in a somewhat privileged position, because Freud would relieve his mind by discussing with Jones various problems that it would have been inexpedient to discuss with members of his inner circle.

Not without bitterness, Jones commented on Freud's assessment of Jung's personality. Freud was not, he said, a connoisseur of men: he overestimated or underestimated people on the simple criterion of his personal liking or disliking for them. I have already mentioned Freud's attitude in connection with Jones's rivals and the temporary estrangement it produced between the two men.

In addition to Jones's positive attitude, a slightly negative one revealed itself in his slips of the pen—many of which he reported in "Psychology of Everyday Life." There was an intrepid simplicity with which Jones was by no means loath to illustrate his didactic essays—especially this one—with examples from his personal life. In this he also emulated Freud, who did the same in his *Interpretation of Dreams* and his *Psychopathology of Everyday Life*, with the difference that Jones may have displayed a little more candor when owning up to his examples. The most amusing anecdote concerns his posting a letter. It is significant that Jones committed quite a few revealing parapraxes in connection with Freud (the essay includes only a select few). In the German manner, Freud signed his letters and papers with his surname only, using no initials. Jones had informed him that in Britain only titled persons are entitled to use this form of signature. Imagine his chagrin when he found that he had by the slip of a pen signed a paper with the sole appellation "Ernest." Shortly thereafter, in a letter to a friend, Jones wrote, "Dear Freud," rather than "Dear Fred." He was doubly embarrassed, because he felt obliged to recognize his conceited wish to be "on terms of sufficient equality with Professor Freud to allow such a familiar mode of address." Was the slip a giving in to, or an unconscious equating of this aristocrat of the spirit with, "royalty?"

Without entirely denying this, Jones energetically set about correcting views circulated by his adversaries that Freud was himself a neurotic. Because a psychoanalytically oriented biography must stress unconscious motivations that—directly or indirectly, decisively or fundamentally, in a good or bad sense—have modified the person's attitude to any given problem, he mentioned (without placing undue emphasis on them) one or two traits that he felt to be characteristic. The psychoanalytic commonplace that neurotic and even psychotic traits can be discovered in the otherwise healthy person's mind makes it unremarkable that such traits are also discernible to a modest extent in some psychoanalysts, Freud included. To the best of Jones's knowledge, he had not omitted these from his biography of Freud, although he often had pondered whether the inclusion of one detail or another was necessitated by this self-imposed condition. He did not want to violate by unkindliness the memory of his friendship with that great man, but neither did he wish his duty as an independent investigator, biographer, and analyst to be overshadowed by too delicate concerns about secrecy.

Certainly, his delicacy prevailed in matters concerning Freud's private life, the surviving members of Freud's family, and certain aspects of Freud's Jewishness. He was adamant as to the strict observance of his rule not to involve personal matters implicating survivors, as he told me (during the preparatory stages of the Freud biography) when I asked why he omitted deeper analysis of special questions referring to Freud's emotional relationships with his mother, sisters, wife, and daughters. He felt that the material he gave *sapienti sat.* A later biographer may (or may not) attach greater importance to them than he did; but because Jones was senior among Freud's first-generation adherents, he felt these matters were of minor importance, as compared to facts which it was imperative that posterity should learn from an authoritative source. In a way, I regretted this—especially that he was averse to dealing with Freud's exalted ideas about truth (and also about *Ananke*) which, in my eyes, were connected with his earlier idealization of his mother. This, like the nanny's influence, Jones vehemently denied.

Jones also dealt only half-heartedly with psychological motivations underlying Freud's undeniably astounding lack of musical interest and discrimination—conspicuous for its rarity in Viennese middle-class society, especially among persons of Jewish extraction.

In my view, the secret of the Freud biography's success is Jones's deep understanding of Freud—not only of his theoretical and practical approaches, but of the underlying emotions. Jones noted that Freud's reaction was more balanced than that of the majority of his followers. It was marked by dignity throughout. To quote Jones: "I dimly sensed some slightly feminine aspect in his manner and movements, which was perhaps why I developed something of a helping or even protective attitude towards him, rather than the more characteristic filial one of many analysts" (1957, Vol. 2, p. 43).

Both Jones and Freud deprecated any contributions that could be called solicitous or importunate. Both liked to illustrate their didactic essays with examples from their personal lives, although perhaps Jones felt freer when it came to owning up to the personal origins of the examples. They had many common interests: Jones seemed to have had an emotional need to stress these similarities. Their association was always pregnant with meaning, as well as promise for the further propagation of ideas. One cannot help wondering how far Jones himself was aware of the unconscious significance of his and Freud's ideational intercourse, and to what extent Jones's hesitancy to refer unambiguously to differences between his and Freud's contributions to the birth of an idea was related to Jones's unconsciously attributing the alternating paternal and maternal role at one time to Freud and another to himself. Generally, Jones was reticent about drawing attention to himself in this respect.

Jones had a gift for paying tribute to Freud's genius, even if he opposed one or another of Freud's tenets. He noted with regret that there were matters on which he had to disagree with Freud: telepathy, the precise attitude toward lay analysis, and his own support of Melanie Klein's work (1957 Vol. 3, p. 129). He failed to mention three other matters, the first anxiety theory, the female Oedipus complex, and the death instinct.

In "Fear, Guilt and Hate," Jones reminded us that for many years he had expressed the view that Freud's formula of the conversion of repressed libido into anxiety is untenable on both psychological and biological grounds, and that Freud recently had withdrawn it. Concerning supporters of all Freud's opinions on the development of female sexuality, he remarked: "We seem to be compelled here to be *plus royalist que le roi*" ("The Phallic Phase"); and in summing up his own views—almost diametrically opposed to Freud's—he cautiously concluded: "This view seems to me more in accord with the ascertainable facts" ("Early Female Sexuality").

A further point of theoretical disagreement concerned Freud's theory of the death instinct: Jones admitted that in rare cases of melancholia death wishes may result in suicide; however, he held that this is no proof that death wishes arise from a primary wish for self-destruction on the part of the body. Nevertheless, he did not accept the view held by some that Freud had "invented" the death instinct out of personal pride, in order to "justify" his own death. When I drew his attention to Freud's failure to include the fear of cancer—so ubiquitous in neurotics and psychotics—in his almost complete list of phobias and fears, Jones dismissed the suggestion. He did concede that in forming an opinion about the validity of Freud's theory of a death instinct, we are justified in taking into account possible subjective sources.

From this statement, it is clear that Jones could not have sided as entirely with Melanie Klein's theories (based on the death instinct) as Freud had assumed when he complained strongly about a "public campaign" that Jones was supposed to be conducting in England against his daughter Anna and perhaps, therefore, against himself. The only basis for this charge, according to Jones, was his publication in the *Journal* of a detailed report of a discussion on child analysis, at which Anna Freud and Melanie Klein were at variance.

There was a remarkable affinity between Freud and Jones in their attitudes toward death. As W. H. Gillespie said: "The significance of death was one of the major subjects on which [Jones] took issue with Freud. Jones held that it required more courage as well as a greater sense of reality to admit that death is simply the end of the individual's life than to believe that death is the fulfillment of a basic inner urge." Even so, in their basic, courageous attitude toward the phenomenon of death, the two men were remarkably similar.

In the controversy about lay analysis, Freud had reproached Jones for not supporting his sponsorship of equality between medical and nonmedical analysts, in opposition to the views of the American colleagues: he was convinced that, if Jones had not joined forces with the Americans, they would have withdrawn their objections. Jones believed that Freud had considered him as much an opponent as if he had altogether opposed lay analysis, thereby misunderstanding Jones's "reconciling aims." As Jones said, "The history of my country had taught us that force is not the most successful method to employ with Americans." (Jones, 1957, Vol. III, p. 295). "[Freud] would never admit . . . that the opposition of American analysts to lay analysis was to a considerable extent a part of the struggle of various learned professions in America to secure respect and recognition for expert knowledge and the training needed to acquire it" (Jones, 1957, Vol. III, p. 297). Eventually, Freud recognized Jones's true intent in the matter.

Jones was rather worried about Freud's interest in telepathy. He was skeptical of evidence in support of clairvoyance and like studies, and believed that Freud had been unduly influenced by Fliess, Ferenczi, and Jung. He did not conceal his suspicion that Freud's views were less scientific than Freud would have had him believe. In a circular, Jones expressed his view that these phenomena are of subjective origin and involve ideas of which those who allegedly experience them are ashamed, and which therefore are in a state of repression. All the same, he tried to understand (and excuse) Freud's interest, on the grounds that the idea of a possible "kernel of truth" in telepathy may have fascinated Freud. Jones suggested that Freud's mentality led him to take a special interest in things that are not as they seem—that he seemed to wish that a certain part of reality could be changed. By way of reply—also in a circular—Freud adopted a rather amused attitude about the whole controversy, saying: "Our friend Jones seems to me too unhappy about the sensation that my conversion to telepathy has made in English periodicals." An exchange of letters on the subject also occurred between Freud and Jones, and Jones has left an unfinished manuscript on "Belief and the Occult"—perhaps undeveloped because of concern for Freud.

To sum up, the autobiographical value of the Freud biography is unique. It contains many trenchant and often impulsive remarks that we may regard as spontaneous but not deliberate references to Jones's own emotions, of which even he, the analyst, was not always aware. Far from being a shortcoming of his work, these make the biography even more vivid and personal in the silent dialogue with the reader, and extremely attractive. They also prevent Jones's studies from becoming dry and mummified, even after a considerable lapse of time. Far from growing subjective, his pugnacious, often charming, often wise and conciliatory nature becomes even more endearing, and his purely, and puritanically objective, observations more colorful through this by no means incongruous and never unbecoming admixture.

§ Social and Political Views

Just as the Freud biography—this most accomplished among Jones's works—is in a way autobiographical, so also in a paradoxical way are the papers he never completed. "Belief in the Occult" seems to be the last among these; a book on which he and Trotter collaborated, the *Maladies of Civilisation,* based on Trotter's "herd instinct" and Karl Pearson's "racial survival value of altruism," is the first. Although Jones regretted very much the abandonment of the former, Trotter had withdrawn from the effort.

Jones regretted even more that he had not completed his projected "Napoleon's Orient Complex." Prior to World War I, he had spent two years collecting material for this study, but unfortunately his notes were lost. He had planned to stress the importance of Joseph in Napoleon's life. He mentioned the reason for his not completing the study of Napoleon in a note attached to his comparatively meager essay, "The Case of Louis Bonaparte, King of Holland." In the Freud biography he related that Freud had spoken to Jekels of Jones's plan, and that Jekels had published his own version shortly thereafter—and the "cream" was gone. Whether it was too strenuous a work—like that on civilization—pushed aside for the sake of more immediate or more important tasks, or a disillusionment because of Freud's indiscretion and lack of interest, we do not know. He could not seriously have considered Jekels as a rival; yet, as he closed up like a clam when queried about this, it would seem that Freud's attitude had been most important.

Finally, I should like to mention *Moses,* which would have been an expansion of his "Birth and Death of Moses." He both loved and hated the topic, but he was afraid that Jewish clerical circles would accuse him of anti-Semitism. At first he was all enthusiasm: "I am hot on the trail of Moses," he wrote to me on October 7, 1956. But soon he felt overwhelmed by the material—"the mire of this Moses affair," he wrote on October 21, 1956; and then, on February 5, 1957, "We have let ourselves in for more than we bargained for over this wretched Moses." These alternate in the correspondence with references to "little Moses" and "our friend Moses."

Most of Jones's unfinished works are in the realm of applied psychology, more specifically, with a social or political interest in addition to the psychological. He always had a keen interest in these subjects, but apparently felt on less firm ground with them. As a rather young man he had shown an acute interest in political and public affairs and for a time held Liberal sympathies, feeling "hatred for oppression, impatience with conservatism." Although he had a positive social sense, he accepted social and economic differences as they existed in society.

Jones's interest in these matters stemmed from three roots. The first was his divided loyalty to the Welsh and the English, which spurred his interest in the differences between national groups. This was connected also with his gift for languages: he read and spoke several, and was a member of the University of London Board of Studies for Comparative Philology. As a born Welshman, he made a special point of cultivating a perfect English style. He admired Freud as a master of the German prose, stressing his originality, elegance, and dignity. Many of these characteristics also distinguished Jones, in his use of the English language. Jones felt that much of the original flavor is lost in translations, for example, that "repression" is not an absolutely appropriate translation of "Verdrängung."

Jones's linguistic interest was first aroused when he worked on phonetics, making records of tests on normal and defective children. "A Linguistic Factor in English Characterology" deals with English prudishness, which originates in the horror of self-display but degenerates from propriety. A short discourse on obscene words (which preceded R. Graves's similar study by approximately two decades) points out the emotional difference between the Anglo-Saxon and the Norman-French usages and their shades of meaning. As Jones suggested, the existence of this double stratum of words enables us to indulge in fastidiousness to a degree not open to any other nation and is responsible for the outstanding English character of propriety.

"The Psychology of Constitutional Monarchy" pays tribute to Jones's patriotic feelings. This essay notes that growing up signifies that the early sense of dependence on the parent, both real and imaginary, is replaced by a proper independence and self-reliance *without* any need for violent repudiation and destruction; that parricide is replaced by an attitude of friendliness combined with a preparedness to oppose if need be. Whatever its deficiencies may be, the success of the constitutional monarchy is due essentially to the respects in which this advance has been achieved, that even as princesses cannot be abolished from fairy tales without starting a riot in the nursery, so it is impossible to abolish the idea of kingship in one form or another from the hearts of men. The mysterious identification of king and people reaches deep into the unconscious mythology, and people's secret daydreams are finally gratified in august stateliness and ceremonial pomp. In "What is Psycho-Analysis?" Jones proposed that interest in the Royal Family proceeds from an unconscious identification between it and the individual's own family, that the one is simply the glorification of the other along the lines of childish fairy tales and fancies.

"The Psychology of Quislingism," written in 1940, sums up Jones's views on patriotism, which he managed to reconcile with his humanitarian views and with the broader internationalism of the intellectual elite. Jones believed that the key to the understanding of Quislingism and related phenomena is the realization that they are based on a peculiar inability to face or even to recognize an enemy, that is, one whose interests run diametrically counter to one's own. For mental integrity and the practical issue, it is of utmost importance that an individual be able to recognize and face such a situation when it does arise; Quislingism implies a denial of the aggressiveness of the enemy. Jones mentioned two types of Quisling, the dissatisfied and the insecure, and stated that "the cardinal attribute of . . . the formidable father imago is his [the Quisling's] reaction to it . . . denying the person's serious aggressivity behind the irresistibility . . . the denial of danger, and therefore . . . the repression of fear." He gives as the second attribute the admiration of irresistibility and the attempt to convert the imago of the evil father into that of a good one, originating in the identification of sadism with sexual potency. These are homosexual solutions: the fear is both sexualized and moralized. Persons who deal with problems of juvenile delinquency should give serious study to this short but illuminating paper.

In the 1938 paper, "How Can Civilization Be Saved?" Jones contended that analysts investigating the psychology of a nation should pay attention to its wishes, anxieties and defenses. Although he wrote small contributions about other nations, Jones confined his longer essays to psychoanalytic studies of the Irish, the Welsh, and the Jews.

His short paper, "The Island of Ireland," describes a "magic island" that symbolically represents the womb, and includes a nice diversion about the uterine conception of death. There is an ambivalence in wishful thought whereby one's native land possesses matronly characteristics without the presence of a husband—is a mother but remains a virginal island. Perhaps some of Jones's unconscious thoughts about the mother have been sublimated into his interest in countries.

His "The Inferiority Complex of the Welsh" is an even more personal affair. Jones was proud to be Welsh and regretted that he could not speak the language. Although he disliked the parochial, even petty, nature of their interests, he delighted in the Welsh quickness of response and ready reaction to friendliness and helpfulness (which he possessed to a full extent). They afforded him a pleasant relief from the tortuous and circumlocutory social contacts of the English.

His membership in a minority group, the Welsh, along with certain friendships and family relationships, brought him close to a similar psychological understanding of the plights of the Jewish people. As he was wont to say, "Coming myself from an oppressed race, it was easy for me to identify myself with the Jewish outlook, which years of intimacy enabled me to absorb to a high degree." Because misfortune and suffering often evoke a sense of inferiority, he felt that the Welsh and Jews have much in common. His "Psychology of the Jewish Question" shows the other side of the coin, the psychology of racial prejudice.

As a young man, Jones worked in a hospital in the Jewish quarter of London's East End; thus he came to know Jews early in life. His unusual capacity for adaptation and sympathetic understanding led to his being admitted to their intimacy on practically equal terms. He found them personally interesting—alive, witty and alert. His Gaelic mind, "a little impatient of Anglo-Saxon complacency and slowness of imagination, responded gratefully to these qualities," and he enjoyed Jewish society. He tried not to be influenced by his own philo-Semitism or by the tremendous literature of Jewish self-justification, already gigantic before Hitler's appearance on the historic scene. He did not try to gloss over factors by which the Jews themselves contribute to anti-Semitism, although he found psychological excuses for these. Thus, he spoke more of their aversion to physical violence than of the alleged lack of patriotism of which their enemies accuse them. He did not omit mention of their sharp practices or pushing ways, but he regarded these as the manner in which persons would react "whose manliness has been impaired." As other analysts have, he also stressed the role of circumcision in this respect and traced anti-Semitism back to castration fear and anal factors. He also made mention of the Hittite nose, Zionism, and other factors. He had great admiration for the moral eminence of some of their great men, noting that moral teachers are often feared, seldom liked. Anti-Semitism, Jones said, is a sign of weakness rather than strength; tolerance betokens self-confidence and sanity.

A second source of Jones's philo-Semitism was his close personal friendship with Freud, who felt no religious affiliation to Judaism despite his strong racial identification with the Jewish people. Until Hitler's advent, Freud's allegiance was to the Germans. This was a link between Jones and Freud, for it was similar to Jones's Welsh-English compromise. In conformity with the prevalent Jewish view, Jones became convinced that Freud could not have accomplished his work without certain traits inherited from his Jewish ancestry—shrewdness, a skeptical attitude toward illusion and deception, and determined courage. Jones felt that the opposition to psychoanalysis was doubtless heightened by anti-Semitic prejudice.

When, thanks to Jones's persistence and ingenuity, fifty German or Austrian analysts found refuge in England—either permanently, or on their way to America—this was a fulfillment of his humanitarianism, his personal philo-Semitism, and his feelings of obligation to the "cause."

A second root of Jones's social interest was his fascination with group psychology. In "The Relation of Abnormal Psychology to Social Psychology," he dealt with the consistent correlation of subject matters concerning the group and the individual. He acclaimed Trotter's "herd instinct" and Freud's *Totem and Taboo*, and fought a long-standing battle against anthropologists with opposing views. Although otherwise not unappreciative of Karen Horney's views on kindred questions (especially those concerning factors in feminine development), he opposed the arguments she and Malinowski raised against the ubiquity of the Oedipus complex, and concerning a possible matriarchy prior to patriarchy. Freud's *Civilisation and Its Discontents* also left a deep impression on Jones's fertile mind. One of his publications in the field of group psychology is "The Individual and Society," which deals with relevant problems of the ego. He also collaborated on *Social Aspects of Psychoanalysis* (1924).

"How Can Civilisation Be Saved?" begins with the premise that it would be queer indeed if, as many sociologists believe, human nature is totally different in the mass from what it is in the individual. He suggests that the psychoanalytic approach is equally applicable to different political sides and tendencies; that the tremendous effects of the press, wireless, and other means of propoganda are possible because they are "well aimed at a body of highly-charged emotion . . . already present in a latent form in the victims."

In a companion piece, "Evolution and Revolution," Jones distinguished between revolutionary changes in the strict sense, and evolutionary changes in which former and now displaced conditions are permitted to survive or are transformed in such a fashion that their essential elements persist, even if in a new guise. From here he proceeded with a psychoanalytic explanation of how and why the destructive changes might occur. Ideas of danger are visualized by the unconscious ego as concrete evil objects derived from distorted pictures of persons or bodily parts of persons, principally the parents.

Like all progressive thinkers of the postwar years and the between-war period, Jones was troubled that civilization seems unable to eliminate wars from the progress of history. As did Freud, he also ventured to solve this problem. In "Psychopathology and International Tension," Jones distinguished between "aggressive" and "quarrel" wars, and noted that the history of mankind is a struggle between the desire for freedom, self-confidence, and self-defense, on the one hand, and the craving for protection and help from stronger beings, on the other. At cyclic periods in history, one or the other of these opposing tendencies gains the upper hand.

The central theme of "War and Individual Psychology" is that historically a periodic outburst of warlike impulses is followed by a revulsion against war. If repression is carried too far, the energies in question revert to their unconscious sources and sublimation is no longer possible. The essay raises the question whether the science of psychology can ever show us how to abolish war.

A third essay on the same subject is entitled, "War and Sublimation." In people living beyond their psychological means, as during war, when the real test comes their false acquisitions fall away, just as the parvenu loses his veneer of good manners. An inexplicable change seems to come over them, but this change is only in their external behavior: their real nature remains what it always was. It was Jones's opinion that a civilized man should be able to kill when necessary, but never to murder.

"The Concept of a Normal Mind" contains a few trenchant remarks on pacifism. Jones had analyzed several conscientious objectors; each had come to recognize the neurotic basis of his attitude. Also, he had analyzed many ex-combatants; of these, none had at the end adopted the attitude of the conscientious objector. Did this, he wondered, suggest that it was time to rethink our psychological evaluations of certain brands of pacifism?

A fourth, illuminative article, "Psychology and War Conditions," intended primarily as a guide to practical selection for defense (military) purposes, deals also with individual attitudes toward the blitz, psychotic-like mechanisms dominating the effective part of whole nations, mass movements, and the Nazi paranoid mechanism. Jones also wrote an article, "War Shock," and was attacked by one of *The Times* leaders for his paper on the psychology of warlike impulses.

Jones had offered his services in World War I, but was found unfit for military service. He also failed to get an appointment at a hospital specializing in war neuroses. In World War II, the Minister of Information proposed to make use of Jones's psychological knowledge but was replaced before the appointment was made. Jones was bitter when he had to accept a post as "salvage officer," saying, "I have laboured faithfully for 40 years, and what is the pitiful outcome? In a lethal war in which psychological factors played a central part, the only 'psychologists' engaged by our Government to advise them were advertising agents."

His brilliant study, "The Problem of Paul Morphy: a Contribution to the Psychoanalysis of Chess," owes its origins to Jones's interest in the problems of war and strife. No one was better fitted for the elucidation of chess and the chess player's psychology. He was an ardent devotee of the game, which he recognized as a play-substitute for the art of war. In chess symbolism, the most potent assistance in attacking the father is offered by the mother (the queen).

Jones contended that Morphy, the American chess prodigy, owed his successes to a remarkable combination of capacity and confidence. Why, then, had Morphy experienced his breakdown? In addition to the superficial explanation that as a grown-up Morphy had become aware that a mere chess player is inacceptable as either a lawyer or lover, Jones attributed Morphy's breakdown and the accompanying paranoia to an inability to stand up under too great success, explaining that to castrate the father in a dream is a very different matter from doing this in reality: the real situation provokes the unconscious guilt in full force, and the penalty may be mental collapse. Morphy's aim of dealing with this repressed hostility toward his father—and fear of his father's hostility toward him—had miscarried by converting this into a friendly homosexual encounter. Mental stability can exist only so long as there is guiltlessness, and what had appeared as an innocent and laudable expression of the personality was now shown to be actuated by the most childish and ignoble of wishes—the unconscious impulse to commit a sexual assault upon and utterly maim the father.

We can find a third root for Jones's interest in social matters in his tendency to find correlations between thoughts and reality, and between thoughts and actions. His ideas about social and political psychology bear the mark of his uncompromising concern—matched only by Freud's—about man's duty, especially the scientist's duty, to serve truth and nothing but the truth. He was merciless in questions of scientific honesty and morality. Being a whole man himself, he had nothing but disdain for those who were not whole; and he had no qualms about exposing them. He fought against the Jungian approach in the British (then "London") Psycho-Analytical Society because he could not tolerate ambiguity. (As a result, the Jungians were finally excluded from the Society.) This was so much a principle for Jones that he pursued it down to the minutest matters. He also had condemnatory words against the spurious supporters of psychoanalysis, for he believed that when an analyst loses insight he previously had, the recurring wave of resistance that has caused the loss is apt to display itself in the form of pseudoscientific explanations of the data before him and to be dignified with the name of "new theory."

Jones was extremely interested in the borderline between the sound and unsound, and also in the difference between the normal and the abnormal mind. The so-called normal, he believed, are simply those who deal with the deep disharmonies that lie at the center of human nature by various inner defenses such as deadening, inhibiting, and so on. Although he gave no definition of normal in "The Concept of a Normal Mind," a diagnosis is derived from assessment of the nature of a person's relations with his fellows, the relations between his individual and social interests, his mental efficiency, and his subjective feeling of happiness. This latter Jones regarded as a combination of capacity for self-enjoyment with self-content. He mercilessly debunked false illusions of "conciliatoriness," "excessive friendliness," or "unselfishness," and only in the end suggested that the nearest attainable criterion of normality is fearlessness. In "Love and Morality" he was perhaps more explicit: a well-balanced mind is also fairly moral, but he regarded the substitution of morality for love with the psychiatrist's customary suspicion. In "The Genesis of the Super-Ego," he pointed out the pseudo-moral feeling of "oughtness."

Because of Jones's interest in the psychological foundations of ethics, he was also concerned with education. His "Psycho-Analysis and Education" was followed by "The Value of Sublimating Processes for Education and Re-education," in which he gave the first and still valid formulation of sublimation (based on Freud's teachings). He described sublimation as "concerned with the various infantile tendencies that later on form the basis of erotic desire[8] as well as many other [non-sexual] interests." [9]

§ Direct Contributions to Psychoanalysis

Almost all Jones's essays are studded with examples of the personal psychological wisdom with which his analytic techniques and methodological researches are imbued. "The Theory of Symbolism" contains a wealth of apposite remarks on the method and value of scientific research. The same paper passes judgment on failure to discriminate because of lack of interest—in a sense, on all generalization. But this harsh indictment is softened in a later publication (1918) wherein he stated that "the great criterion of the importance of scientific generalization is its fertility."

As Jones reverently said in "What Is Psycho-Analysis?" no scientific man could feel that gaining knowledge weakens his sense of wonder at the universe. As illusions born of ignorance are dispelled, humility before the unknown increases. In a practical paper excelling in clarity and brevity, "The Criteria of Success in Treatment," he set forth the rule that the main symptom is the last to disappear.

[8] Also in "The Nature of Desire" (1922).

[9] Jones also wrote "Some Questions of General Ethics Arising in Relation to Psychotherapy" (1910), and "The Nature of Morality" (1955).

In "The Individual and Society," Jones dealt with the concepts of ego and self, regarding the latter as the conscious part of the former. The ego he defined as that part of our primary nature whose activity does not generate fear. In "Sigmund Freud, the Man and His Achievements," he wrote of the importance a strong ego plays in bringing about psychic integrity.

I have already mentioned Jones's epoch-making papers on symbolism, sublimation, and rationalization. Rationalization occurs whenever an individual considers a given process as being too obvious to permit of any investigation into its origin and shows resistance to such an investigation. When this occurs we are right in suspecting that the actual origin is concealed from the individual—almost certainly because of its inacceptable nature. Jones pointed to the blind acceptance of the suggestive influence of our environment, fortified by the most elaborate evasions and rationalizations.

Jones also tried his hand on "The Nature of Auto-Suggestion." He saw twin factors of suggestion in an "intense self-absorption" and in "the concentration on the idea of an external person." He distinguished between heterosuggestion and autosuggestion on the basis that in the former it is the idea of the parent; in the latter, the self. The individual's primal narcissism is distributed in his real ego, in the parents' ego, and in the ideal ego, and is only later transformed into true object love.

Jones's views on pleasure are scattered among his many writings. Perhaps the most characteristic can be found in "Psycho-Analysis and Biology," wherein he explained that data of the pleasure-pain series should not be subordinated to the utility principle. This is one of the extremely subtle ways in which puritanical motives can discredit the importance of pleasure.

Parallel to this attitude of revolt against the principles that entrammel pleasure went Jones's deep concern and sympathy as to pain. Remarkable passages on suffering and pain are included in "Psycho-Analysis and Modern Medicine" and in Jones's autobiography. He believed that the secrets of the human soul can be apprehended and understood only in connection with suffering—through being able to suffer oneself and thus entering into contact with the suffering of others. He had already held this view before getting acquainted with the Nancy school and with Freud's teachings: it seems to have stemmed from his deep and violent mourning for his first wife. I have been unable to trace the subjective origins of another of Jones's beliefs: that undue complaining to one person often means that unconsciously the sufferer is ascribing his troubles to that other person's agency, and is in fact begging him to desist. However, one of his last communications—a rather short one on pain—unfortunately owed its origin to the subjective experience of acute bodily pain during treatment for the illness which a year later proved fatal. After returning from the hospital, he wrote to me: "Back from the Gestapo. . . ."

Next comes the problem of fear. In "The Psychopathology of Anxiety," he wrote of a "fear instinct," which in neurotic conflicts has been stimulated to activity as a protection against the threatening libido. We do not know whether he seriously included fear among the instincts: he did not elaborate further on the idea. In "Fear, Guilt and Hate," he conclusively aligned his views about anxiety with Freud's later (rather than earlier) ones. This preoccupation with fear gave rise to one of Jones's most original ideas concerning *aphanisis*. The theory evolved partly from his opposition to Freud's doctrine of the ubiquitous and all-pervading castration fear, which Jones could not envisage in its narrowest sense. Even as he believed that a deeper prehistory lay behind castration fear proper (which makes it easier to understand the phenomenon through the contemplation of its precursors), in the same vein he believed that a deeper, more essential and comprehensive fear must underlie it: fear of the loss of the ability to experience pleasure. "Love and Morality" ascribes the obsessional and hysterical types of revolt against morality to this dread, and suggests the use of the Greek word *aphanisis* to indicate the total and permanent extinction of the opportunity and capacity for sexual enjoyment. (See also "The Early Development of Female Sexuality.") Jones suggested that guilt, and with it the superego, is, as it were, artificially built up for the purpose of protecting the child from the stress of privation, that is, from ungratified libido, thereby warding off the dread of *aphanisis* that always goes with this. For the girl, the privation of not being allowed to share the possession of the father's penis is an unendurable situation tantamount to the fundamental dread of *aphanisis*. In other works, *aphanisis* is described as "the equivalent of dread of frustration" or as "the total exhaustion of the libido." Newer theories that stress the paramount importance of separation anxiety in the later development of the child owe much to Jones's theory of *aphanisis*.

This brings us to the theory of guilt. In "Fear, Guilt and Hate," Jones stated that the total annihilation of the capacity for direct or indirect sexual gratification, arising in a primary traumatic situation of danger, is already inherent in the simple situation of libidinal privation. The social aspects of guilt also interested Jones. In "What Is Psycho-Analysis?" he remarked that the present generation is suffering from a much heavier burden of an unconscious sense of guilt than the preceding generation.

Jones's paper, "Anal-Erotic Character Traits," published in 1918, preceded some findings in Freud's later-published "Die Disposition zur Zwangsneurose." Jones's findings in this area were fully endorsed by Freud, especially those in which he attributed paramount importance in the genesis of hatred to the earlier educational interference with the anal-erotic activities. Jones included among these traits the tendency to be occupied with the reverse side of various things and situations; also, the importance attributed to one's last will and testament—the association is doubtless the sense of value and the prominence of the idea of something left behind.

In "Hate and Anal Erotism," similar ideas prevail. The child feels that he is loved when the person obeys his commands. Hate is preceded by an earlier, undifferentiated state in which pain, annoyance, and perhaps anger are experienced when the infant finds that any of his wishes are not being immediately gratified. In paranoia, hate arises in connection with persons whom the patient has tried to love. These ideas are further elaborated in "Fear, Guilt and Hate": here Jones pointed out that the sense of guilt is the most concealed among all traits, that manifestations of the hate impulse can cover both anxiety and guilt, and that hate is one of the commonest covers for guilt. A patient may have succeeded so extensively in expressing unconscious guilt conflicts in terms of conscious fear and may be so completely convinced that his difficulties arise from fear and nothing else that in certain cases it may take years of analysis to bring the underlying guilt to consciousness. Human consciousness tolerates either fear or hatred more readily than a sense of guilt; a feeling of general unworthiness is the most that the majority of persons can achieve in this direction.

Apparently, Jones exhibited less bias than Freud in his views of the social, sexual, and individual roles of the female sex. Even though in some cases he incurred the displeasure of Freud thereby, he did not hesitate to express his views. "Psycho-Analysis and Biology" is devoted to the question of sex differences: generalizations on the topic are the surest invitations to subjectivity—men tend to stress sex differences, women to minimize them. Jones suggested that far more bisexuality exists in the deeper layers of the mind than is generally supposed and that hereditary variation occurs in several erotogenic zones.

Jones's most important papers in this field are "The Early Development of Female Sexuality" and "The Phallic Phase," which developed out of the turmoil created among psychoanalysts, especially female psychoanalysts, on the publication of Freud's views on female sexuality. Much of the turmoil ended after Jones expressed a possible solution or compromise between the controversial views, although it did not cause a complete reconciliation between the two camps. In the former paper, he declared that there is "a healthy suspicion that men analysts have been led to adopt an unduly phallo-centric view of the problems in question"; in the latter paper, that "masculine primacy of the female infant may well be kept in suspense until we know more about the sexuality of this very early stage." A third essay, "Early Female Sexuality," sums up his views about the problem.

Jones noted that in girls the differentiation of anus and vagina takes place at an earlier age than is generally supposed.[10] Jones commented that "penis envy soon sets in, and apparently always" (which seems a somewhat cautious formulation), "no woman escapes the early penis envy stage but . . . what we meet clinically as penis envy in neuroses is only in small part derived from this source." We must distinguish between pre-Oedipal and post-Oedipal penis envy, between autoerotic and alloerotic penis envy. Jones held that initially the attitude toward the penis is purely positive, a desire to suck the penis for a nipple (fellatio), in which formulation it could not pass for the adoption of a theory of primary penis envy. He emphasized the privation resulting from continual disappointment at never being allowed to share the penis with the father, which reactivates the girl's early wish to possess a penis of her own. This privation, primarily an unendurable situation, is tantamount to the fundamental dread of *aphanisis*. According to Jones, in the mouth-anus-vagina stage the girl identifies with the mother, but either the father or the vagina must be renounced. In normal girls the phallic stage is but a mild form of the father-penis identification of the female homosexual and, like it, is of an essentially secondary and defensive nature.

In "The Phallic Phase," Jones cautiously expressed "the doubt that

[10] This doctrine has been more fully developed in Judith Kestenberg's latest studies.

Freud does not attach enough significance to the girl's concern about her external organs, at the expense of her terrible fears about the inside of her body." In "Early Female Sexuality," he summed up the situation: at all events one can hardly sustain any longer the view that the vaginal attitude does not develop before puberty. As the vagina is the seat of the deepest anxieties, an extensive displacement outward takes place. He regarded the deuterophallic phase as essentially a defense against the already existing Oedipus complex. In girls the masculinity stage is a defense against a still earlier repressed femininity, rather than —as Freud thought—a primary and normal stage of female development.

Jones's ideas about homosexuality are deep and fundamental. In *Hamlet and Oedipus*, and even more in his essay, "The Death of Hamlet's Father," he gives a clue to the connection between procrastination and homosexuality. Shakespeare wrote *Hamlet* partly as a successful abreaction of the emotions aroused by the painful situation depicted in his *Sonnets*, the betrayal by both his beloved young noble and his mistress. Jones mentioned in this essay that the ear is an unconscious equivalent for the anus, but he did not go on to explain how for the homosexual the ear must become a vaginal organ, just as it becomes in sublimation an organ for the enjoyment of music and hence an equivalent for the anus. As early as 1923 he drew attention in *Hamlet and Oedipus* to the fallacy of the popular belief that (with Ferenczi's support) had distinguished between active and passive homosexuality, stating that these do not represent two different inborn types, a view now almost generally accepted.

Other valuable views on latent homosexuality are contained in his paper, "The Influence of Andrea del Sarto's Wife on His Art," which describes the role of a tolerable marriage in the life of a latent homosexual. As Jones noted, del Sarto's love had to serve the purpose of damming both repressed hate and homosexuality. His wife could demand anything of him and treat him howsoever she pleased, for without her he was lost. She forced the internal battle to be fought out in all the current details of everyday life and allowed him no opportunity to gather strength and inspiration that could be applied to higher aims.

"The Psychology of Quislingism," which touches on homosexuality indirectly, shows that the psychological roots of treachery lie in a latent homosexual attachment to the aggressive father image, the fear of which is both sexualized and moralized. The essay on Paul Morphy suggests that Morphy wanted to convert his hostility toward his father into a friendly homosexual encounter, but that his homosexual friendliness to men had broken down, and the antagonism underlying it lay exposed.

In closing, we must mention Jones's tentative ideas about projection. He did not follow up certain lines of his paper on Heinrich von Kleist, which is still the best discussion on necrophilia. This perversion is traced back to the unresisting condition of the object, which can endure without limit and is forever loyal. Although Jones related this to the coprophilic tendency, he did not connect it with the omnipotent wish to project one's own infantile helplessness into the object. Yet, he must have had precisely this in mind, for it cannot be a mere coincidence that another, astonishing interpretation of projection is mentioned, that "sexual projecting is closely associated with passing flatus" (into the female cloaca). This is very close to the concept of projection in Melanie Klein's teachings, wherein the self tries to rid itself of bad parts or particles by depositing them into the object.

Jones had a long, fruitful, and accomplished life. Still, we feel a sense of regret that he, who has bequeathed to us such a wealth of knowledge, did not live to complete the edifice of his teaching and to expand the insight that illuminated his life's work. As his heirs, we will try to continue on the path from which he was forced to step aside.

REFERENCES

Glover, E. Obituary, Ernest Jones. *Brit. med. J.*, 1958, 5058, 464–465.

Hampshire, S. Disposition and memory. *Int. J. Psycho-Anal.*, 1962, 43, 59–68.

Jones, E. Some questions of general ethics arising in relation to psychotherapy. *Dominion med. Monthly*, 1910, 35, 17–22.

Jones, E. Introduction. *Papers on psychoanalysis.* New York: Wood, 1918.

Jones, E. The nature of desire. *J. Neurol., Psychopath.*, 1923, 3 (12), 338–341.

Jones, E. *Essays in applied psycho-analysis.* London: International Psycho-Analytic Press, 1923.

Jones, E. *Social aspects of psychoanalysis.* London: Williams & Norgate, 1924.

Jones, E. *On the nightmare.* London: Hogarth, 1931.

Jones, E. The nature of morality. *Observer*, 1955.

Jones, E. *The life and work of Sigmund Freud.* New York: Basic Books, 1957. 3 vols.

Jones, E. Funeral speeches. *Int. J. Psycho-Anal.*, 1958, 39, 298–310.

Jones, E. *Free associations: memoirs of a psycho-analyst.* London: Hogarth Press, 1959.

Paul Federn

1871–1950

THE THEORY OF THE PSYCHOSIS

*

EDOARDO WEISS

Paul Federn was thirty-seven years old, and still practicing internal medicine in addition to psychoanalysis, when I first met him in 1909. I had recently come to Vienna to study medicine at the university. Since I had already decided that I wished to be a psychiatrist, I called on Professor Freud to ask him how I could learn to understand myself better, as well as how to become an analyst. From among the few analysts of that time, Freud recommended Dr. Paul Federn and gave me a reference to him. On the last day of February in 1909, I telephoned Federn for an appointment, and, on March 1, I began my personal analysis with him.

He was a slender man—bald-headed, with a full black beard, expressive gray eyes and an extremely gentle manner. His sensitivity to the needs and feelings of others and his unusual ability to create an atmosphere of understanding soon gave me a feeling of closeness that persisted in my later friendship with him until his death. On the wall to the right of the analytic couch, as I remember, hung an oil painting of Freud as I had seen him a few months before—beardless, with a trimmed mustache and penetrating eyes. Because this portrait drew too much of my attention during analytic sessions, it was soon replaced by a less interesting picture.

Another trait of Federn's that impressed me early in my analysis was the breadth of his scientific and literary background. He knew by heart many passages and verses from the great writers and poets, and he had an extraordinary talent for illustrating a significant point by these quotations, which often threw the right light on the particular problem under investigation. In Federn, scientific understanding of mental phenomena was combined with emotional understanding.

In the course of my analysis, and particularly in later association with him as a colleague and friend, I came to know Federn's personality, special talents, and abilities and to hold a deep respect for his scientific contributions as a pioneer in psychoanalysis. For more than forty years we maintained a close relationship and exchanged opinions through voluminous correspondence and occasional meetings. If, then, this brief biography seems less than a strictly objective historical sketch, I hope that it may gain in being the more personal story of a man who considered me his friend. Excepting a few brief vignettes from my memory, all the facts of Federn's life presented here—both personal and professional—are documented either in letters in my possession or in other correspondence and records that his son, Ernst Federn, kindly put at my disposal.

Federn's grandfather, Bunzlfedern, was a famous rabbi of Prague and, like all the Federns, a liberal thinker. His father Salomon Federn, who lived from 1832 to 1920, was a distinguished Viennese physician whose patients included not only the famous Rokitansky but also the staff of *Die Wiener Kredit Anstalt,* the most important bank of Middle Europe. His prominent practice was, in fact, so well known that a verse was made about it: "Das Glueck tritt ein, wo die Federns sein" ("Fortune enters where the Federns are"). In liberal circles in Vienna, also, Federn was one of the leading names. Paul's mother, the former Ernestine Spitzer, was an outstanding beauty of an old Jewish merchant family. For many years, Ernestine Federn was active in the movement for women's emancipation.

Paul Federn was born on October 13, 1871, in Vienna. He was his parents' third child and third son. He had two younger sisters and a younger brother. His mother was disappointed that of all her children only Paul could be considered good-looking. His beard gave him a deceptive look of strength and even fierceness, for actually he was a melancholy, romantic, and exceedingly mild man.

In his youth, Federn was subject to depressive moods that caused concern among his many friends. During his military service in the cavalry of the Austrian Army, he was an ardent soldier. Afterward, he continued to be an enthusiastic horseman. Under instructions of his dominating father, who prescribed a career for each of his sons, Paul studied medicine, although he would have preferred to be a biologist. He was graduated from the Medical School of the University of Vienna in 1895 and subsequently spent seven years in internships and residency at the *Allgemeines Krankenhaus* (General Hospital) in Vienna. Federn established his own practice as a specialist in internal medicine in 1902. His personality suited the role of physician well, and he became an outstanding internist. His only publication from this time is a paper, "Zur Reform des aertzlichen Spitaldienstes," issued in 1901.

From his very early days, Federn was an admirer of German culture, discipline, and order. In this he was very idealistic and—as I sometimes tried without success to point out to him—almost fanatically one-sided. Although he respected my preference for Italian culture and the men of genius whom Italy had produced, in Federn's opinion no other cultural group or way of life could compare with the German. In our discussions it was clear that his enthusiasm was focused on the Germans' great contributions in philosophy, literature, arts, and science and that he recognized only the positive sides of German discipline and order and ignored or was blind to the weaknesses and abuses in their system and character.

As a young man Federn was a great success with the ladies. He first met his wife, Wilma Bauer, when she was only twelve years old. Her family were close friends of the famous internist, Herman Nothnagel, who was Federn's teacher in internal medicine and his mentor. Federn was courting Wilma's older sister at the time, but the little girl fell in love with him. She was chronically ill with a heart ailment even then, as she was all her life. In 1905, when Wilma was twenty-one and he was thirty-three, they were married. A daughter Annie was born to them in December 1905, a son Walter, in July 1910, and another son, Ernst, in August 1914.

Federn's wife was a Protestant, and their children were raised in that faith. Many times throughout the years he pondered whether he, too, should become a Protestant. I remember that once, early in my analysis, Federn told me that for developing love of other people, it is important to acquaint children with the history of Jesus' suffering.

Wilma Bauer Federn was a poet and a playwright. While she was still a young girl, her work was noticed by the Viennese poet, I. I. David, who was interested in publishing some of her poems. However, Federn insisted that all her poems belonged to him, and she gave them to him in written contract. (This eccentricity was characteristic of the Federn family as a whole.) Freud was very much impressed with her psychoanalytic plays, but he advised her that—in 1915—they could not be produced because of public resistance to the concepts they embodied.

As I remember it, Federn's office was located in the apartment where he lived with his family, at Riemergasse number one. One day during the first months of my analysis, when he opened the door of the waiting room to me, he was holding his three-year-old daughter Annie in his arms and introduced us with pride before taking her to her mother. Sometimes it was his wife who answered my ring at the door.

As far as his place in the history of psychoanalysis is concerned, we may distinguish four periods of professional activity. The first, from 1904 to 1914, was the period of the early pioneers.

When he was thirty years old, Federn read Freud's *Interpretation of Dreams,* and he remained forever fascinated by it. His teacher, Herman Nothnagel, gave him an introduction to Freud in 1902. From that time, Federn was an ardent and unceasing admirer; Freud became his idol. There is no evidence that he underwent any kind of analysis with Freud, but Federn considered himself to have been trained by Freud and to have analyzed himself under Freud's guidance. Following his meeting with Freud, Federn's melancholic phases decreased markedly and were evidenced only by sharp changes of mood and by the persistent idea that he would end his life in suicide if ever he felt that he could no longer master it.

In 1904, when he joined Freud's inner circle, Federn was the fourth physician to become an adherent of psychoanalysis—preceded only by Adler, Stekel, and Reitler. He was a regular participant at the original Wednesday Psychological Society, which met each week at Freud's home. In 1908, the group was organized into the Vienna Psychoanalytic Society. Federn's first office in the group was that of comptroller. The records show that Freud referred to Federn many times as the one who best understood the essence of an issue under discussion. His absence from the meetings was so rare that on one occasion Freud wrote him, "It is unheard of that you missed the meeting yesterday!"

At these meetings of Freud and his adherents, serious consideration was given to topics that met only derision from the official clinicians, for example, infant sexuality, interpretation of dreams, the unconscious, and the essential role of sexuality in neurosis. The importance of Freud's discoveries at this time was only recognized by a small, slowly increasing group of academically educated people.

Federn's loyalty to groups in whose ideas he believed, and to their leading exponents, was unshakable. His strong positive father-transference to Freud was an important factor in all his attitudes toward psychoanalysis—not only in his adherence to Freud's views but also in regard to his own diverging ideas, which Federn was very late in recognizing as such. He admired Freud as a man and as a scientist, and considered him an outstanding genius. In spite of the evidence that Freud accepted him more as a colleague than as a pupil, Federn took on the role of disciple. He saw himself as "Apostle Paul" to Freud.

Regarding Federn's scientific contributions during this early period, a statement which he himself made many years later seems appropriate: "My work in psychoanalysis was the first that seemed to me worth publishing. My studies combined the viewpoints of biology and psychology. I was interested above all in the theory of instinct, especially the explanation of sadism and masochism, and in the expression of instinctive forces in dreams." [1] At this time his publications included a contribution in 1912 to a collective work on the problem of masturbation, papers in 1913 on libido displacement and *pavor nocturnus,* and, most important, his papers on sadism and masochism of 1913 and 1914. In these last, and also in his contributions to dream analysis in 1914, his approach to these problems included for the first time an ego-psychological point of view.

After I became a member of the society in 1913, I often sat with Federn at the meetings. After each meeting Freud wished to continue discussion at the *Café Bauer*. A group of us would walk there with him—Federn, Tausk, Rank, Sachs, Steiner, and others. Freud confided to us theories and convictions that he did not make public. I remember, for example, his telling us that he was convinced of the existence of telepathy. But, he said, he had decided not to publish his views nor to speak of them generally because to do so might result in further prejudice against psychoanalysis.

Federn, too, showed a dynamic orientation toward telepathy. This is particularly evident in his report, "The Undirected Function of the

[1] Excerpted from Federn's petition, September 7, 1946, in application for a medical license in New York.

Central Nervous System: A Question Put to Physiology by Psychology" (1937). Through his accurate examination of the mental activity in the analytic process, he came to the conclusion that stimuli from one part of the brain to another (correlated to the mental systems) cannot occur through conducting fibers, but must occur through distance by means of waves or other processes. We might express this idea nowadays as "by remote control." From this report of Federn's, one can understand also that through this remote control some stimuli from one brain can excite another brain, a phenomenon which we now term "extrasensory perception."

In Spring 1914, Federn came to the United States to treat a patient who later became a prominent American political leader. The New York psychoanalysts, including C. P. Oberndorf, Smith Ely Jelliffe, Dorian Feigenbaum, and many others, were deeply impressed with him. Some account of Federn's impact at that time is recorded in Oberndorf's *History of Psychoanalysis in America.*

Federn started for home late in July, in order to be in time for the birth of his third child. While he was on his way, war declared between Austria and Serbia immediately involved most of Europe.

Federn served as an army doctor in the war years. In view of his loyalties, his idealism, and his admiration for the German way of life, it is not surprising that Federn was a convinced patriot, confident of victory for the Central Powers. Jones's report that Federn believed in England's victory as early as 1914 is incorrect. Once during the course of the war, I remember vividly that Federn and I discussed the situation in warm disagreement. At that time I felt strongly identified with Italy through my native Trieste, but his patriotism for the Central Powers was unwavering.

Federn put all his gold into Austrian War Bonds, on the advice of his economist brother Walter, who argued that if Austria should lose the war everything was lost, the world would no longer make sense, and possession of gold would be meaningless. From that time on, with the exception of a few years in his later life in New York, Federn was never financially well off. His financial worries were increased further by the fact that he had little money sense and was sometimes careless with it. On one occasion, having just received payment for a month's consultations, he carried this substantial sum to a concert by Yvette Guilbert and was victim of a pickpocket. There is some irony in this incident, although it is doubtful that he appreciated it at the time: in his youth he himself used to pick pockets very expertly—as a parlor trick for the amusement of his friends at parties. (For the later teacher of Aichhorn this talent is not without significance.)

As an analyst he was not strict in exacting payment from his patients and sometimes treated them without fees. Freud disagreed with this practice, but his disapproval did not change Federn's casual attitude toward bill-collecting. Federn's lack of feeling for money seems to have been due to a deep sense of guilt for having been born into a wealthy family. At the same time, contrarily, he always maintained that money indicated will power, and he admired people for having amassed great wealth.

During the years from 1914 to 1924, which we may call the second period in his professional activity, Federn spent much of his time in didactic analyses. Besides being one of the leading training analysts in Vienna, he was also chairman of the Education Committee of the Vienna Society. It is noteworthy that the great majority of his students from this period later attained distinction for their own achievements.

During this period, Federn was developing ideas on social psychology closely parallel to those of Freud. His major work in this field, *Zur Psychologie der Revolution: Die vaterlose Gesellschaft* ("Psychology of Revolution: The Fatherless Society"), was published in 1919.

Federn also reported in 1920 on his study of inhibition dreams, "Zur Frage des Hemmungstraumes." He presented his conclusion that inhibition in a dream is a counterwish, mostly from conscience. Mental inhibition, he observed, is sensed as bodily inhibition, as when a dreamer finds himself unable to follow his dreaming inclination to run or to lift his arm. On the other hand, when the dreamer's movements are hindered by *external* objects in the dream (a crowd, cramped quarters, and so on), this indicates a feeling of physical inhibition; for example, in one case Federn presented, the dreamer had suffered a transitory paralysis due to a slight stroke.

Among his other publications at this time were papers in 1914 on the pain-pleasure and reality principles, in 1919 on falling asleep and lulling to sleep, and in 1923 on melancholia. His interest in the phenomenon of delinquency also took form during this period.

At heart Federn was a reformer with a great sense of social responsibility. This may be seen as a reflection of his father's influence, which had been strong in Federn's early years. He often took stands on social issues and was active in many movements designed to improve standards of medical and social welfare, in the fields of sex education, maternal health, pedagogy, and family guidance. With his sister, he was instrumental in founding the Settlement Verein, the only private nonsectarian agency in Vienna modeled after the English system, and for a while he served as physician there. Later, in collaboration with his close friend, Dr. Heinrich Meng, he contributed to and edited (1924) *Das Ärtzlich Volksbuch* ("The People's Medical Book") and (1926) *Das Psychoanalytische Volksbuch* ("The People's Book of Psychoanalysis").

Politically Federn was a Social Democrat. Although he was the only member of his family to endorse this political party, all the Federns shared the same pro-German sentiments, that is, anti-Hapsburg and anti-Catholic. In Vienna at the turn of the century, it should be noted, German nationalism was an evidence of liberalism. The newly formed Austrian Democratic party, also favored a democratic federation of German states, and the *Anschluss* was an important part of their program. How different this nationalism was from the Nazism to which Federn and his family were later subjected! Federn's political interest in democratic socialism dates from his early days when, through his parents, he became acquainted with the Ecksteins, another prominent Jewish family in Vienna. Fritz Eckstein was a lifelong friend of Freud's and a member of his card party. Eckstein's daughter, Therese Eckstein Schlesinger, also an adherent of Freud's, was one of the founders and leaders of the Austrian Social Democrats. Later, as a member of the Austrian Parliament, she exerted political influence for psychoanalysis whenever she was called on to do so. Federn became a member of the Social Democratic party in 1918. He was elected to public office as district councilman, and also was active in the Society of Social Democratic Physicians.

In 1924, after Freud was struck with cancer, he named Federn his personal deputy, and in the same year he was elected vice-president of the Vienna Psychoanalytic Society. All who called upon Freud were then automatically referred to Federn, who presented to Freud only those cases of particular clinical interest. Two years later he became coeditor of the *Internationale Zeitschrift für Psychoanalyse* as well. He continued in these capacities as Freud's substitute—the third phase of his professional life—and also as teacher at the Psychoanalytic Institute in Vienna and a member of the Viennese Section of the International Board of Mental Hygiene, until 1938, when he came to the United States. The society was dissolved in the same year.

As acting president of the Psychoanalytic Society, Federn was in a powerful position. Since Freud trusted him completely and Anna Freud, as second vice-president from 1931, never disputed the decisions made by her father and Federn, the society was in effect dominated by the ideas of these three. As a result, admission to the meetings was granted at that time to a number of people who had extraordinary minds even though they had no medical degrees.

Also in his role as Freud's deputy, Federn frequently represented him on public occasions, as, for example, at the unveiling of a plaque on October 25, 1931, at Freud's birthplace in Freiberg. (This is reported incorrectly by Jones.) In honor of Freud's seventieth birthday, Federn delivered the commemorating address over the Austrian Broadcasting System. This was the first official recognition of Freud in Vienna.

On the occasion of Federn's sixtieth birthday five years later, in 1936, Freud wrote him a letter of congratulations and appreciation: "Permit me to congratulate you without publicity on your sixtieth birthday, and on this occasion I thank you for all the support you have given me in very good sentiment and indefatigable zeal. Affectionately, Sigm. Freud" (translation from the original letter in German). In celebration of this birthday, Federn and his wife took a brief vacation in Venice. I was disappointed that their plans did not include a visit to Rome, where I had recently come from Trieste to embark on new activity.

Personal disagreements were few between Freud and Federn. When they did occur, disagreements centered mainly around evaluation of people, that is, colleagues and friends. Far more than Freud, Federn was inclined to be lenient toward unorthodox thinking, especially when such thinking was compensated by enthusiasm for his idol. He was easily deceived by people—even gullible. He saw every human being as a mother's child whose feelings must be understood and respected and, given any evidence of suffering, he felt immediately compelled to help. Most people responded with gratitude and devotion, but there were those who took advantage of him; and on the rare occasions when he felt that he had been duped or deceived, his wrath was formidable in so mild a man. Federn also was very unforgiving toward any who betrayed Freud: he called Adler a Judas and severed his former close friendships with Adlerians. Many years later, when one of these former friends experienced the tragedy of mental illness in a member of his family, Federn relaxed his stand in order to help the patient, but the old close friendship was never re-established. He was also severe toward some analysts who discredited psychoanalysis and was instrumental in getting them to leave the society.

Federn's own personal integrity was absolute. Although he and Freud were influenced by different ideologies in the development of their thinking, for both of them honesty was axiomatic. This attitude was, in fact, a part of Federn's culture—a residue of the historical code of chivalry that some patrician families had acquired from the old aristocracy. In Federn, the sense of chivalry, not quite identical with being a gentleman, sometimes took on the romantic, unrealistic character of Don Quixote.

Federn maintained a good working relationship with the medical school and faculty of the University of Vienna. More conciliatory in his approach than Freud, he was an effective liaison man to Wagner-Jauregg and Pötzl. He was also useful to the clinicians because of his readiness to treat severely psychotic patients. As Wagner-Jauregg would say, "Your daughter is incurable, but perhaps Dr. Federn can help her." If he did so—and he was not infrequently successful in these cases—credit was given to his psychiatric and medical skills rather than to psychoanalysis.

It was during this period that Federn developed his early phenomenological concepts of the ego and the psychoanalytic approach to the treatment of psychoses. Gradually his concepts departed from those of Freud, who maintained a negative attitude toward psychotic and psychopathic patients. In Federn's view, psychotic and psychopathic egos are weak egos, and as such they can be helped by psychotherapy. Many patients who would have been rejected by Freud were accepted for treatment by Federn, and he exerted unusual effort toward their cure. In one instance, as I remember and as he afterward reported in one of his publications, he took a schizophrenic woman, an artist, into his home during the course of her treatment.

In spite of this difference in their professional attitudes, Federn remained loyal to Freud and accepted his concepts without mental reservation, apparently unaware that his own findings were sometimes at variance with Freud's. On occasion, when I commented to him about this divergence, he insisted that I was wrong and explained that all his own expositions had already been implied by Freud's statements. This attitude is clearly expressed in the preface to a book Federn intended to write on "The Theory of Instinct and Its Relation to the Experience of Pain and Pleasure." Translation from the original manuscript in German follows:

If we attempt to give an explanation by means of theoretically derived primary instincts, we must recognize and also tell our readers that we utilize the Freudian view and that we go beyond the mere results of our own observations. We do this heuristically and in good conscience: Freud called his instinct theory a speculation:—This means for Freud a day-dreaming along exact scientific lines. In all areas of human knowledge we have such confidence in the tool "Freud" that we apply the poet's words to him: "Your dreaming I respect more than what the others think." (Footnote: Grillparzer: Libussa, 1, 144) I am convinced that *all* theories of Freud must contain new truth, because he was as he was. I know myself confirmed when I find an observation, a conclusion and a theory already in Freud. Whenever I departed from Freud, or whenever I was in opposition to him I have always waited 10–20 years and have tested my conclusions anew. Also, in this book I follow only Freud's insights and methods and merely add new knowledge to it.

During this third phase of his professional activity, Federn published a series of articles in which he brought the essential findings and concepts of Freud closer to the understanding of all educated people interested in mental hygiene and the prevention of mental illness. Among these, his contributions to *Das Psychoanalytische Volksbuch* (1926), previously mentioned, are particularly noteworthy. In 1931, he also became co-editor of *Zeitschrift für Psychoanalytische Pädagogik*.

However, Federn's most original findings, which led him to therapeutically important conclusions, were in the field of ego psychology and the psychoses. Few analysts realized that his new concepts were not theoretical formulations but were, rather, the result of a meticulous exploration and exact description of inner experiences and modes of behavior of both diseased and healthy individuals, himself included. This introspective approach, a phenomenological one, was the basis for his studies in 1926 on the variation in ego feeling. In Federn's opinion, feelings of estrangement and depersonalization are due to a deficient ego cathexis, rather than to a deficient object cathexis. His conclusions were at variance with the concepts of all other psychoanalysts who had tried to explain the dynamics of these feelings.

Even though his formulations regarding the ego and its functions were divergent from Freud's in some respects, Federn's efforts were still constantly directed toward proving the correctness of Freud's teachings. In 1920, when Freud came to the conclusion that a death instinct must exist in all living beings, Federn could not accept this idea immediately. But he soon found himself convinced by clinical evidence rather than by speculation, and from then on he supported Freud's view. In his articles, "Narcissism in the Structure of the Ego" in 1927 and "The Ego as Subject and Object of Narcissism" in 1929, he adhered to the new dualism of instincts, libido and destructive cathexis derived from the death instinct. In "The Reality of the Death Instinct" of 1930, he reported that he found in certain self-destructive manifestations of severely melancholic patients an inescapable evidence of the existence of the death instinct. But Federn never abandoned his earlier belief in separate self-preservative (ego) instincts and sexual instincts powered by libido. It was his opinion, as he often told me, that at least three basic cathexes must exist: self-preservative, libidinal, and destructive cathexis (which he later called "mortido").

Initially Federn's writings on ego psychology were not much appreciated by his colleagues, and within the psychoanalytic group he experienced a scientific isolation that was in a way analogous to Freud's isolation from his medical colleagues when he first began his psychoanalytic explorations. For Federn—the dreamer and the romantic—far less realistic than Freud, this was a very painful experience. When, after 1930, some psychoanalysts who had attended his seminars published articles and books on ego psychology without mentioning him, he suffered great disappointment.

The fact was, however, as Federn himself admitted to me more than once, that in his publications he did not express himself clearly regarding his own difficult and original findings. This lack of clarity was due, at least in part, to his unshakable loyalty to Freud, which led him always to direct his communications toward corroborating Freud's concepts. Even though I had been analyzed by Federn and was familiar with the vagaries of his exposition, I could not always follow his writings in every detail. It was only after lengthy discussions with him, often by correspondence, that I became well acquainted with his ideas and was able to recognize their scientific and therapeutic value.

Particularly in "The Ego Feeling in Dreams" of 1932, Federn revealed his increasing understanding of the "ego phenomenon," as he used to call the manifestations of the ego. He equated "ego" with "ego feeling" and studied the different "ego stages" and "ego states." He came to the conclusion that, like the schizophrenic ego, the dreaming ego is a weakly cathected ego and that, from a strict structural point of view, it is not overcathected, as the term "narcissistic" ego implies.

In his study and treatment of psychotic patients, he elaborated on specific psychotherapeutic methods that were quite different in some respects from those used in the classic psychoanalytic treatment of neuroses. In recognizing the importance of a corrective mother figure for the treatment of defective egos, he came to the realization that the participation of a woman therapist (a properly trained nurse or social worker) is indispensable in the psychotherapeutic treatment of psychotic patients. Gertrud Schwing, the Swiss nurse whom he trained, became well known in this capacity. Federn introduced her to Poetzl, head of the Vienna University Psychiatric Clinic where insulin treatment was first tested. Her experiences there were later published in Switzerland, *Ein Weg zur Seele des Geisteskranken,* in 1940; a translation, *A Way to the Soul of the Mentally Ill,* appeared some years later (1954). Through Federn's efforts Gertrud Schwing was accepted for control analysis by Grete Bibring and Anna Freud, and on the basis of her diploma as a registered nurse she became a member of the Vienna Psychoanalytic Society. This precedent has not yet been followed by any other psychoanalytic society.

Although he was skeptical of shock treatment, Federn was one of the very early clinicians to try chemical cure for schizophrenia. It was characteristic of him that, in his approach to the problems of mental disease, he was never satisfied to limit himself to the theories and techniques of psychoanalysis. Until his death, Federn remained actively interested in the study of other disciplines that might explain or cure mental disorders.

In 1933, Federn published "The Analysis of Psychotics: On Technique," which included a report on the case of the schizophrenic woman painter mentioned earlier. In the following year, he came to a descriptive, a phenomenological (that is, subjectively descriptive) and a metapsychological definition of the ego, which was not based on Freud's ego concept. This was reported in "The Awakening of the Ego in Dreams: I. Orthriogenesis; II. Postulates to Serve as Basis for an Ego-psychology" (1934). Another important paper, in 1936, concerned the distinction between healthy and diseased narcissism. Federn's concepts of the flexible bodily and mental ego boundaries are the basis for understanding the phenomena of hallucinations and delusions, as well as feeling of derealization (estrangement) and depersonalization. He found that these phenomena are due not to a failure in "reality testing" but to a weakening or disappearance of ego cathexis at the ego boundaries. "Reality testing," he observed, is a function quite different from the "sense of reality," which is a function of the ego boundaries. He also clarified the ego involvement in specific neurotic diseases.

In his personal copies of Freud's books (*Problems of Anxiety*, *The Schreber Case*, and many others), and also in Anna Freud's volume on ego defenses, Federn made numerous marginal notations that have never been published. These comments, frequently in disagreement with the texts, are now being examined with interest by Federn's students. In a recent publication, I mentioned his notes regarding the Schreber case. A longer paper was presented in New York at the winter meetings of the America Psychoanalytic Association in 1960–1961 by Dr. I. Peter Glauber. It was titled "Federn's Annotations of Freud's Theory of Anxiety" (1963).

During the fourth period of his professional activity, until his death in 1950, Federn lived in the United States. In September 1938, he left Vienna for New York. Although war had not yet been declared, his younger son Ernst had already been arrested by the Gestapo and was forced to remain behind. In February 1939, I came to the United States and, during my first month in New York, again had an opportunity to renew my friendship with Federn. In frequent meetings we discussed psychoanalytic matters as well as our personal concerns.

Freud's death in September 1939, was deeply upsetting to Federn. However, it became evident that afterward he felt more freedom in expressing his own divergent concepts. From 1940 on, the dynamics of the psychoses became increasingly clearer to him: he did not consider them to be the result of excessive narcissism but recognized them as "ego diseases." In his elaborate therapeutic procedures for the treatment of psychotic patients, he took into account the economic impairment of various ego functions. His papers in 1943 on analysis of the psychoses, avoidable errors in treatment, and transference, in 1949 on the principles of psychotherapy in latent schizophrenia, and on the mental hygiene of the ego and the psychotic ego—all were more lucid than his previous publications on these subjects. His analysis of a dream under general anesthesia, published in 1944, reported his own experience during a dental operation and brought new light to the understanding of the dream phenomenon and the dreaming ego.

In 1946, Federn's lawyer discovered a New York law that admitted to medical practice without examination those physicians who had obtained their doctorates at recognized foreign universities prior to 1914, and Federn was finally granted a license to practice medicine. Only then was he admitted to full membership in the New York Psychoanalytic Society and its training institute.

As training analyst, Federn found himself in some disagreement with the New York Institute. His views regarding the damage done by too rigid a system of supervision and training analysis may be seen as prophetic. He warned particularly that a system which permits the analyst to pass judgment on the candidate is detrimental to the training, the trainee, and the training analyst.

In November 1946, only a few weeks after receiving his New York license, Federn underwent cystoscopic examination, which disclosed a tumor of the bladder. Postoperative radium treatments followed. At the year's end he wrote to me that two events had made him very happy: first, he believed that the tumor had been benign and, second, he had at last obtained his license to practice in New York. The truth was, however, that a diagnosis of cancer had been made, but Federn was not told at that time because persons close to him were reluctant to spoil either his pleasure in his new medical status or his anticipation of the return of his son Ernst, recently released from a concentration camp in Europe.

Perhaps the height of Federn's professional life in the United States was his invitation to present his concepts at the Winter Veteran's Hospital in Topeka, Kansas, in June 1949. His report on the mental hygiene of the ego and of the psychotic ego (Weiss, 1952) made a lasting impression on the group. According to those who saw him there, he himself was an awe-inspiring figure, talking extemporaneously to a large audience because an eye injury prevented him from reading the text he had prepared.

On his way home, Federn stopped in Chicago. He was in excellent spirits when I met him at the train—clearly pleased with the response of the psychiatrists in Topeka. Later, at a dinner I gave in his honor—the guests were other analysts and mutual friends—I remember that he was even more than usually conversational and entertaining.

When he returned to New York, he was told for the first time that he had cancer of the bladder. After consultation with a number of specialists, he decided on immediate surgery and for the first time entered the hospital. "Krebs musst heraus" ("Cancer, out with it"), he said to his cousin, pathologist Paul Klemperer. The initial step of what was to have been a two-step operation was a failure. Federn suffered physically and emotionally. Except for the earlier bladder surgery in November 1946, this was his first surgery and, at the age of seventy-eight, he was a difficult patient. His wife, who had been chronically ill all her life with a congenital heart disease, collapsed at the news. Gradually Federn regained some of his strength and returned to his work, but his wife did not recover. She died on December 15, 1949.

My last meeting with Federn was at Christmastime of that year. Knowing that he had only a little longer to live, he told me then that he would end his own life before his time was up. Much as I wanted to encourage him, I felt helpless to do so. From our conversation, it was clear that for him the world seemed very much impoverished without his wife, and without Freud. Still, he expressed himself as satisfied that he completed his own work. "Don't grieve when I am gone," he told me, "for I have already put down in writing what I had to say in the field of ego psychology."

From January until the end of April 1950, Federn continued his professional activities on a limited scale. He saw five patients a day—interestingly, the same number of patients seen by Freud after Freud, too, was stricken with cancer—and also conducted a seminar in his home. In a letter that I received from him on April 13, Federn mentioned his seminar and, more remarkable, for the first time he acknowledged the importance of the divergence between his concepts and Freud's: "Dadurch, dass ich in meinem Seminar (Moderne Yeshivah) 'Das Ich und das Es' commentiere, muss ich mir alle Gegensätze zwischen Freud und meiner Ichpsychologie klar stellen. Sie sind wesentlicher als ich stets annahm" ("Since I have to comment in my Seminar [Modern Yeshivah] on 'The Ego and the Id,' I have to make clear to myself all contradictions between Freud's and my ego psychology. They are more essential than I ever assumed").

During these last months, Federn went to the Psychoanalytic Institute only once, on that occasion merely to indicate to his colleagues that despite his illness he had regained his professional interests and activity. When Anna Freud visited New York for the first time in April, he sent his son Ernst to the lecture at the Institute in his place. However, he was pleased when she called on him at his home late one evening in the company of Drs. Schur and Hoffer. At that time he spoke to her of money which he still owed to Freud from their Vienna days. Anna Freud assured Federn that her father had never mentioned any debt. As for herself, she said, she felt that her debt to Federn far exceeded any obligation on his part. Later she wrote to his son that Federn had seemed like a man who had something very important yet to be finished.

Federn died on May 4, 1950. On that date he was to have undergone another operation, to which he apparently had agreed. The fact was, however, he had learned that there was little expectation of his regaining full working capacity. On the pretext of preparing for surgery, he put his personal affairs in order and arranged for his patients to be transferred to other psychotherapists. At his request, a former patient drove Federn to his bank, supposedly to remove from the vault some jewelry which he wished to give his daughter. The truth was, however, he went there to get a gun with two bullets, which he had kept in his safe for some time. At home he joked about suicide with the family's faithful housekeeper, Mrs. Frieda Bobach, discussing the various methods and expressing a preference for shooting. Frieda responded, in the same vein, that it would be hard to shoot oneself without a gun. "You are right," Federn said, laughing. "Where would I get a gun?"

On May 3, he saw his patients for the last time, in order to explain the arrangements for their transfer. That evening he was cheerful and apparently confident when his physicians and his attorney assembled with his sons at his home. His last will was signed, and he apparently was in the best of spirits when he bid them all goodnight. At three o'clock the next morning, seated in the analytic chair in his office, he shot himself. His son Walter heard the shot. On his desk Federn had left a note, warning that one bullet remained in the gun. In the words of his son Ernst, "He was, until his last breath, more concerned about others than about himself."

In his will, Federn expressed the "hope and desire" that I collect into one volume his papers on ego psychology and the psychoses. I complied wholeheartedly, not merely from a feeling of personal obligation, but because I believe in the significance of Federn's contributions to psychoanalytic theory and therapeutic technique. It was and is my conviction that his findings in the field of ego psychology are of paramount practical importance and constitute a basis for further far-reaching exploration, both in theory and in therapy. The posthumous volume that I edited, *Ego Psychology and Psychoses*, includes a number of previously unpublished papers and the first English translations of two contributions to the theory of narcissism, as well as articles reprinted from various British and American journals.

REFERENCES

Alexander, F., P. Federn, & H. Meng. (Eds.) *Das psychoanalytische Volksbuch*. Stuttgart: Hippokrates, 1926.

Federn, P. Zur Psychologie der Revolution: die vaterlose Gesellschaft. In *Der Aufsteig, neue Zeit- und Streitschriften*. Nos. 12–13. Vienna: Anzengruber, 1919.

Federn, P. Zur Frage des Hemmungstraumes. *Int. Z. ärzt. Psychoanal.*, 1920, 6, 73–75.

Federn, P. Narcissism in the structure of the ego. *Int. J. Psychoanal.*, 1928, 9, 401–419.

Federn, P. Das Ich als Subjekt und Objekt im Narzissmus. *Int. Z. Psychoanal.*, 1929, **15**, 393–425.

Federn, P. Reality of the death instinct, especially in melancholia. *Psychoanal. Rev.*, 1932, **19**, 129–151.

Federn, P. The ego feeling in dreams. *Psychoanal. Quart.*, 1932, **1**, 511–542.

Federn, P. The awakening of the ego in dreams: I. Orthriogenesis; II. Postulates to serve as a basis for an ego-psychology. *Int. J. Psychoanal.*, 1934, **15**, 296–301.

Federn, P. The undirected function of the central nervous system. *Int. J. Psychoanal.*, 1938, **19**, 173–198.

Glauber, I. P. Federn's annotations of Freud's theory of anxiety. *Amer. J. Psychoanal.*, 1936, **11**, 84–96.

Meng, H. *Das ärztliche Volksbuch*. Stuttgart: 1924.

Schwing, Gertrud. *A way to the soul of the mentally ill.* (English ed. R. Ekstein & B. H. Hall.) New York: International Universities Press, 1954.

Weiss, E. (Ed.) *Ego psychology and the psychoses.* New York: Basic Books, 1952.

Edward Hitschmann

1871–1957

PSYCHOANALYSIS OF GREAT MEN

*

PHILIP L. BECKER

Edward Hitschmann was born and educated in Vienna. He had two brothers, one the director of a bank in Vienna, and the other a lawyer. Although his father was a banker, Hitschmann pursued the profession of his grandfather, a physician, and graduated from the University of Vienna Medical School in 1895. He practiced internal medicine until 1905, when he became interested in psychoanalysis and became a member of the Vienna Psychoanalytic Society.

At the age of forty-two, Hitschmann married a gifted young concert singer; whom he had known for about twelve years. In addition to her singing, Hedwig Hitschmann gave voice lessons and later became an excellent speech therapist.

A daughter, Margaret, was born in 1913, in the first year of their marriage. Now assistant professor of psychiatry at the University of Colorado Medical Center, Dr. Margaret Hitschmann is married to Dr. Sydney Margolin, professor of psychiatry.

Paul Federn introduced Hitschmann to Freud and the psychoanalytic group in 1905. At the early meetings of the Vienna Psychoanalytic Society, he made original contributions, reviewed books, and made sharp critical remarks on other presentations. With Hitschmann's death in 1957, one of the last original pioneers passed away.

In the early days, Hitschmann was less profoundly convinced than some of the others of the incestuous roots of neurosis. When Otto Rank read his paper, "The Incest Motive in Literature," Hitschmann stated that love between relatives need not always have incestuous roots but can be nonsexual. Incest should not be regarded as significant but rather as a component phenomenon of sexual needs. The libido pursues gratification through the path of least resistance; the son's sexual attraction to his mother exists because she represents the first woman within reach. Intercourse with a servant girl might have occurred instead, if she fulfilled the condition of the vagina which was present. (At this point, Heller, the first publisher of the *Imago*, interrupted and asked why, then, incest was considered contrary to the laws of nature.)

When he reviewed Bleuler's book, *Affectivity, Suggestibility, and Paranoia*, Hitschmann stated that the mechanism of paranoia is clear, but the processes leading to paranoia remained to be explored. This was accomplished five years later by Freud in the analysis of Dr. Schreber's paranoia.

In 1907, Hitschmann was already interested in "pathographies," as Moebius termed biographies written from the medical point of view with particular attention to psychic anomalies.

The meetings of the Vienna Society during 1906 and 1908 were marked by Hitschmann's biting witticisms and play on words; his wit and the puns he delighted in were particularly evident in his criticisms of Wittels' essays on women.

In 1907, Hitschmann noted that, according to Freud's writings, sexual trauma was no longer to be considered of paramount importance in the etiology of the neuroses. Nevertheless, Hitschmann was convinced that sexual enlightenment was necessary and proposed that it be given in three stages: when children begin to ask about their origin; somewhat later, more specific information; and at puberty, on sexual intercourse.

Hitschmann was interested in the sexual anesthesia of women, which he attributed to four factors: unsuccessful repression of sexual experiences, constitutional weakness of the genital zone, excessive masturbation of the clitoris, and a preponderance of homosexual inclination.

In cooperation with Hirschfield in 1908, he prepared a questionnaire dealing with statistics concerning the sex life of healthy and ill people. It was in connection with this questionnaire that the group around Freud first introduced itself to the public as the Psychoanalytic Society.

In the following year, Hitschmann wrote the first definitive and organized text on Freud's theories, *Freud's Theories of the Neuroses* (1909). This volume received Freud's approval and commendation. Hitschmann hoped to enlighten therapists who were antagonistic or indifferent to psychoanalysis.

In 1912, Hitschmann became interested in the psychoanalytic study of various outstanding literary personalities. Freud believed that *medical studies* of the morbid conditions that affect various famous personalities are of little value in throwing light either on their personalities or on their works; however, he considered that *psychoanalytic studies* of their minds from the earliest beginnings would throw light both on their motivations and on the inner meaning of their works. Of the early psychoanalytic studies by Sadger, Stekel, and Hitschmann, Freud approved only of the studies by Hitschmann. Hitschmann's analytic biographies will long retain an honored position.

Hitschmann shared with Freud an interest and admiration in Goethe's life and works. Perhaps an unconscious identification with Freud stimulated him to write analytic biographies as Freud had done with the lives of Leonardo da Vinci, Dostoevski, and Moses. Hitschmann found many joys in writing analytic biography, including the intellectual sense of satisfaction that is achieved by knowing more than others and the gratification of gaining insight into the life of a great man.

As a result of his biographical studies, Hitschmann felt that creation is experienced in two phases: the first is the moment of inspiration—the moment, probably, of narcissistic acknowledgment of something which had unconsciously been in preparation for a long time; the second phase is that of elaboration. Some subjects of Hitschmann's biographies had been stimulated to creation by traumatic experiences in their childhood. All, however, had been excessive daydreamers in their childhood and had often been rebuked and punished for this. Nevertheless, it was not the daydreaming alone that made the subjects of his biographies creative; the giving up of daydreaming, along with the attached guilt feelings, harnessed the creative powers.

From his work with patients, Hitschmann gained a general impression of the significance of the father for the fate of an individual. He found that the father always is the most important person, the decisive factor for the destiny of the son—not only the main influence, but also the source of life and inspiration.

Included among the subjects of Hitschmann's psychoanalytic studies are Gottfried Keller, Knut Hamsun, Selma Lagerlöf, Max Dauthenday, Emanuel Swedenborg, Johannes Brahms, Franz Schubert, Franz Werfel, William James, Johann Eckermann, Samuel Johnson, and James Boswell.

Freud once suggested that the curriculum at a psychoanalytic institute should include such subjects as history of civilization, mythology, psychology of religion, and literature. To this, Hitschmann would have added the science of biography.

Hitschmann first became interested in Schopenhauer when Hitschmann's grandfather, a homeopathic physician, gave him two volumes of Schopenhauer's works with the remark, "I do not like the work of a man who hated women." In his essay, "Psychoanalysis of a Philosopher" (1913), Hitschmann was able to show why Schopenhauer had developed into a philosopher and had formulated the principles of his particular philosophical system. Although most of Schopenhauer's predecessors had considered man a rational being, Schopenhauer developed the theory of the will as a blind, driving force in the individual and in the world. He recognized the unconscious in the psychoanalytic sense. In his essay, Hitschmann correlated Schopenhauer's various impulses and defenses with Schopenhauer's philosophy: Schopenhauer's asceticism and saintliness were a reaction against his sensuality; his ethics of compassion were a reaction against his malicious and cruel nature. Schopenhauer's hostility to women and disparagement of sex were due to the hatred of his mother, a feeling derived from his unconscious longing for his mother. From his study of Schopenhauer and Schopenhauer's philosophy, Hitschmann drew the conclusion that ultimately all philosophy is self-contemplation.

In 1912, Hitschmann's paper, "Swedenborg's Paranoia," was published in *Zentralblatt für Psychoanalyse*. He described Swedenborg as an excellent and practical worker in the field of natural science, who in the fifth decade of his life had renounced science and devoted himself to supernatural phenomena and had recorded these revelations in a hundred volumes. Hitschmann concluded that Swedenborg suffered from religious paranoia, and attributed Swedenborg's attacks of hallucination to homosexual gratifications. He attributed Swedenborg's insanity to a fulfillment of infantile narcissistic megalomania, namely, to become a son who surpasses his father, a kind of son of God, a redeemer and reformer of Christendom.

Hitschmann founded the Vienna Psychoanalytic Clinic in 1922 and was its Director until 1938, when the Clinic was dissolved, upon the Nazi invasion of Austria. During its existence, the Clinic provided free and low-fee help to patients of limited means.

In 1934, together with Dr. Edmund Bergler, Hitschmann published *Frigidity in Women: Its Characteristics and Treatment,* which was designed to demonstrate to nonpsychoanalytic physicians the psychic nature of frigidity in women and the value of psychoanalysis in treatment of this pathological inhibition. In the monograph, Bergler and Hitschmann describe the development of female sexuality and state that, as a result of their experience, they are led to conclude that not only the boy but the girl as well has a castration complex.

"Psychoanalytic Comments about the Personality of Goethe" (1932) was intended to appraise the importance of Goethe's father, to solve the riddle of Goethe's love life, and to shed some light on the poet's development. Hitschmann attributed the incentive for Goethe's writings to Goethe's narcissism and his desire to mature. For countless human beings, such a genius as Goethe represents a father image, to whom they transfer the feelings of admiration, gratitude, and respect that they once had for their real fathers.

In the following year, Hitschmann published "Johann Peter Eckermann," the psychoanalytic study of a man whose talks with Goethe resulted in the *Conversations with Goethe in the Last Years of His Life.* Hitschmann described Eckermann as inhibited and devoid of any aggressiveness. Eckermann fulfilled himself not with women, but in his dreams, in his poetry, and in his Goethe. This was a sublimated relationship with an exalted father image that provided his life with meaning.

Hitschmann's essay, "Johannes Brahms and Women" (1933), treats the enigma of why Brahms resisted marriage. He had wanted marriage and felt that his life was incomplete without wife and child. Yet Brahms brought into his relationship with women a love for his mother which excluded sexuality. Brahms suffered from a castration complex in that he doubted his own masculinity and felt that he would be unable to satisfy the higher "female" being—particularly in the lasting union of matrimony. Brahms even may have welcomed suffering as an incentive for creativeness, which then became a love substitute.

Hitschmann fled from the Nazis in Vienna to London, in 1938. He practiced psychoanalysis in London for two years before migrating in

1940 to Boston, where he became a member of the faculty and a training psychoanalyst at the Boston Psychoanalytic Institute.

Two years after Freud's death, Hitschmann wrote "Freud in Life and Death," which appeared in the *American Imago*. He described Freud, his personality and appearance, and attempted a psychoanalytic explanation of the cancer of Freud's mouth.

In his study of Samuel Johnson, Hitschmann emphasized the importance of Johnson's strong oral and anal aggressive drives. Johnson's orality contributed to his composition of poetry. He had developed an extremely strict and aggressive superego. A life-long struggle between instincts and conscience had resulted in a compulsion neurosis, with tics and depression. Nevertheless, a strong ego was able to build up the façade of a higher type of man—of a moralist, a man of letters, and an erudite conversationalist. Johnson's character verifies the psychoanalytic formula that character traits are continuations of the original instincts, their sublimation, or reactions against them.

In "New Varieties of Religious Experience," which appeared in 1947, Hitschmann quoted William James as having said that religion does not come from God but differs according to individuals. In his discussion, Hitschmann stated that the two supports of the religious person's belief in God are the memory image of the overrated father of his childhood, and his lasting need for protection. The ambivalence toward the father determines the relation of mankind to its deities. Originally, the Devil and God were one and the same, a single figure containing diametrically opposed characteristics; the figure later was split into two. The repressed Oedipus complex, Hitschmann stated, sublimates itself in myths and religion. Franz Werfel is mentioned as proof of Freud's principle that the religious *Weltanschauung* is determined by our childhood. He had an archaic hatred of his father, with the resultant fear of punishment by God-Father. This fear of death was his basis for religious conversion. In another case cited, a counterconversion occurred, wherein a girl broke with God when she had the impression of a husband violently assaulting his wife; this negated the formerly loved father. Hitschmann suggested that Jung, when he broke with psychoanalysis, may have undergone regression, and that Albert Schweitzer's becoming a doctor and his sojourn in Africa were due to an unconscious guilt feeling that originated in his early years and was revived by regression. According to Hitschmann, Gandhi's life proves that, through repression and reaction formation, a very aggressive boy can develop into an ascetic and pious man. Gandhi's masochism contributed to his fanaticism, purity, charity, and asceticism. Noncooperation and obedience were substitutes for violence, and the prayers, the fasting, and the self-ordained silences were compulsive means to expiate his sins. Hitschmann concluded that the religious *Weltanschauung* is determined by the situation that existed in childhood.

In "Boswell: The Biographer's Character" (1948), Hitschmann wrote that Boswell sought in Johnson a father who would not be cold and dignified but would show warmth, who would be admonishing but forgiving. Boswell was a psychopathic personality, with intact intelligence, defective superego, self-destructive tendencies, social maladaptation, and a weak ego.

In "The History of the Aggression-Impulse," published in *Samiksa* (1947), Hitschmann contrasted the scientific caliber of Freud with that of Adler. While a follower of Freud, Adler described sadism and masochism as a union of two originally separated impulses, the sexual and aggressive impulses. According to Hitschmann, Adler had become a one-sided pedagogue, overvaluing organ inferiority. He never returned to the problem of the aggression impulse. "As a hen, Adler found a corn, and the blind hen dropped the corn again."

"Franz Schubert's Grief and Love" (1915) was translated into English in 1950. The analysis of *My Dream* provided some understanding of Schubert's rich emotionality, perceptivity, and understanding of pain, joy, love, and hate. As Hitschmann has emphasized, understanding Schubert's inner motivation has nothing to do with the question of the origin of his musical gift, which is unsolvable. The composer was unable to find inner freedom or happy love because of his rebellion against a powerful father; therefore, he remained passive and effeminate all his life. A union of sensual and pure love remained impossible for him. "Eternally incomprehensible longing" remained the lot of Schubert, who died unmarried at thirty-one.

"Freud's Conception of Love" (1952) was read as the A. A. Brill Memorial Lecture in New York on November 12, 1950; subsequently it was read in 1951 at the Seventeenth International Psychoanalytic Congress in Amsterdam. Hitschmann recalled Freud's assumption that the suckling of the child at the mother's breast is the model of every love relationship and that the finding of a love object actually is a refinding. Bertram Lewin had confirmed Freud's thesis by interpreting elation as the reliving of early infantile bliss at the mother's breasts. In his presentation, Hitschmann also cited Theodor Reik, who felt that Freud's view of love was incorrect—that, in its essential nature, love is an emotional reaction-formation to envy, possessiveness, and hostility. Reik, who furnished a new concept of love, termed his systematization "neo-psychoanalysis."

In his lifetime, Hitschmann wrote 109 scientific articles on internal medicine, psychopathology, and psychoanalysis, including his psychoanalytic biographies. He is credited with initiating the science of psychoanalytic biography, and it is in this field that he has made his outstanding contributions. Hitschmann did not intend these essays to be definitive answers to questions of the personalities of the men described and their works, but as beginnings and stimulation for others. Nine of his analytic biographies and essays are included in the book, *Great Men* (1956).

Hitschmann was a faithful and loyal follower of Freud. This loyalty extended from their first meeting in 1905 until Hitschmann's death in 1957. Hitschmann had a great appreciation of Freud and his discoveries and, to quote Goethe whom they both admired, "anybody who appreciates me is my equal." Hitschmann often wondered what would have happened to him had he not gone to hear Freud's lecture at the encouragement of his friend, Federn.

A proud physician and an experienced internist, Hitschmann accepted nonmedical persons as colleagues in the analytic field. For a short time, he had been Freud's personal physician, but for some reason a change of doctors was made—without any difficulties. There was no friction between the two men, and the change was made long before the development of Freud's cancer.

Hitschmann's personal analysis had consisted of several months of analysis with Freud. In his analytic cases, Hitschmann saw patients five and six times each week and put a great deal of effort into detailed dream analysis. He felt that extensive psychoanalytic experience was necessary to do effective psychotherapy; without this experience, psychotherapy was "guessing around." In 1945, he wrote that the fight to establish psychoanalysis in the United States was won. To someone who once asked him why he became angry when anyone expressed belief in religion, he replied, "The irrational makes me angry."

Hitschmann died suddenly following a spontaneous pneumothorax, on July 31, 1957, while vacationing at Gloucester, Massachusetts. On the morning of the day he died, he commented, "Today I feel as well as if I were sixty." At the time of his death, he had been practicing psychoanalysis eighteen years longer than Freud and, of course, longer than anyone else.

REFERENCES

Hitschmann, E. Swedenborg's paranoia. *Zbl. Psychoanal.*, 1912, 3, 32–36.

Hitschmann, E. Schopenhauer, an attempted psychoanalysis of a philosopher. *Imago*, 1913, 2, 101–174.

Hitschmann, E. *Freud's theories of the neuroses* (1909). New York: Moffat, Yard, 1917.

Hitschmann, E. Franz Schubert's grief and love. *Amer. Imago*, 1950, 7, 67–75.

Hitschmann, E. Psychoanalytic comments about the personality of Goethe. *Imago*, 1932, 18, 42–66.

Hitschmann, E. Johann Peter Eckermann. *Psychoanal. Bewegung*, 1933, 5, 392–415.

Hitschmann, E. Johannes Brahms and women. *Amer. Imago*, 1949, 6, 69–96.

Hitschmann, E. Freud in life and death. *Amer. Imago*, 1941, 2, 127–133.

Hitschmann, E. The history of the aggression impulse. *Samiksa*, 1947, 1, 137–141. (a)

Hitschmann, E. New varieties of religious experience. In W. James & S. Freud (Eds.), *Psychoanalysis and the social sciences*. Vol. I. New York: International Universities Press, 1947. (b)

Hitschmann, E. Boswell, the biographer's character. *Psychoanal. Quart.*, 1948, 17, 212–225.

Hitschmann, E. Freud's conception of love. *Int. J. Psychoanal.*, 1952, 33, 421–428.

Hitschmann, E. *Great men*. New York: International Universities Press, 1956.

Hitschmann, E., & E. Bergler. *Die Geschechtskälte der Frau: Ihr Wesen und ihre Behandlung*. Vienna: Ars Medici, 1934.

Oskar Pfister

1873–1956

PSYCHOANALYSIS AND FAITH

*

HANS ZULLIGER

§ Contribution to Psychoanalysis

Oskar Pfister was the first educator to recognize the importance of psychoanalysis for education; he fitted psychoanalysis into his busy schedule of activities as teacher and pastor.

During the first decade of the twentieth century, long before other educators had introduced Freud's teachings into the technique and theory of education, Pfister tried to win friends for his psychoanalytic approach. In a number of publications and in his lectures for teachers, he summarized the information he had gathered in his pastoral activities —especially from his relationships with adolescents.

He was seeking, not to influence others or to make a name for himself, but rather to do his duty as a Christian and as an advocate of that doctrine. In all his works and in his life he was driven by a Christian eros, as was obvious to everyone who knew him. Pfister was a fighter for everything he considered right, good, and true and lived according to his Christian ethos, which demanded love for one's neighbor. In spite of all resistance and hostility, he advocated his ideas for psychoanalytic pastoral care and education until he aroused interest among his theological colleagues, government authorities, and the great army of teachers and educators. Soon a group of disciples gathered about him. His publications were translated into many languages, and he was invited to speak abroad.

Together with E. Bleuler (from Burghölzli in Zurich), he was a cofounder of the first Swiss Society for Psychoanalysis, which closed its doors in 1914 when the other founding fathers turned away from Freud. Pfister remained loyal to Freud because of his firm belief in Freud's discoveries of infantile sexuality and concerning the Oedipus and castration complexes. As he said, "For a number of years, I was alone in Zurich with my opinion." Then he collected new friends around him and, in February 1919, together with Emil Oberholzer, he founded a new society. Oberholzer became the president of the new Swiss Society for Psychoanalysis, which was and remains affiliated with the International Psychoanalytic Association. Soon this group, which became world-famous, was joined by several well-known persons, including Hermann Rorschach, developer of the Rorschach Psychodiagnostic Plates (Ink Blots). Hans Behn-Eschenburg, who developed a variation of the Rorschach plates, also became a member.

Membership in the Swiss Society for Psychoanalysis was open not only to physicians but to lay persons, especially to pastors and teachers. All had been analyzed and were eager to apply analytic principles in their work. The inclusion of lay members within the Swiss Society provoked discussion throughout the world as to the advisability of lay analysis, and prompted Sigmund Freud to write his paper, "The Question of Lay Analysis." The controversy prompted Emil Oberholzer to found a second Swiss psychoanalytic society, the Swiss Medical Society for Psychoanalysis, which limited its membership to physicians. Nevertheless, Oberholzer invited two prominent laymen, Oskar Pfister and Hans Zulliger, to join the Society as extraordinary members without voting rights. Both refused, as they did not want to become second-class members.

If, at that time, Pfister had forsaken the Swiss Society for Psychoanalysis in favor of Oberholzer's new group, the older psychoanalytic society might have foundered as the earlier society had in 1914. However, Pfister remained steadfast and loyal to Freud, and eventually most members who had shifted their allegiance to the all-medical group returned. Thus it was the Swiss Medical Society for Psychoanalysis that closed, whereas the Swiss Society for Psychoanalysis thrived under the presidency of Philipp Sarasin.

Pfister made two important contributions to psychoanalysis: he founded psychoanalytic education, from which child analysis later developed; and three times he carried Freud's standard to Switzerland, taking care that the ideal of the great Viennese scientist remained alive and untarnished.

§ My Encounter with Pfister

In the year 1911, I visited the Teachers' Seminary at Berne. The Director, Ernst Schneider, was a disciple of Freud and one of Pfister's students. He told us about the success of his friend, the Pastor in Zurich.

He inspired those of us who were beginning to teach, and I remember asking myself whether Pfister's experience with adolescents could not be applied to younger children, especially to students in the public schools.

In 1912, I decided to follow Pfister's example and apply psychoanalysis to children twelve or thirteen years of age, within the regular public school system. Again following Pfister's example, I prepared myself for this task by going through an analysis and by reading and rereading Freud's works. As psychoanalysis was under heavy attack in Switzerland at this time, I had to proceed with caution. Working alone, I succeeded in freeing individual boys and girls in my class from their inhibitions to learning, from reactive hostility and aggression, and lack of relationships, from bed-wetting and guilt feelings because of masturbation, and from impulsive stealing, and similar symptoms. I had "beginner's luck."

Around 1920, two factors influenced me to report on my experience. In the first place, I felt that my work would gain from the criticism of experts. Second, Director Schneider had been asked to abandon his analytic teaching, and I wanted to illustrate through case histories the benefits that could be expected if psychoanalysis were applied to educational problems. I believed that my reports of Schneider's work would not only justify his use of psychoanalytic principles, but also demonstrate the usefulness of psychoanalysis for the teacher and the student. I hoped that my slim volume, *Psychoanalytic Experience within the Public Schools,* which was published in 1921, would aid in Schneider's vindication.

My publisher asked Pfister, Oberholzer (in Zurich), Piaget (in Geneva), and Claparède (in Geneva) to evaluate my manuscript. They had just published several books, *Schriften zur Seelenkunde und Erzie-*

hungskunst ("Writings in Psychology and Education"); they had edited four small volumes, two written by Pfister.

Pfister and Oberholzer invited me to read from the manuscript at a meeting of the Swiss Society for Psychoanalysis. Following my presentation, Pfister, the first discussant, was paternal and encouraging; and Oberholzer commented that I had observed directly many situations that psychoanalysts working with adults can reconstruct only from their patients' associations. I had seen in the children what grown-ups recall and talk about from their childhood. My presentation afforded everybody an opportunity to discuss the differences between actual experience and fantasies elaborated later.

When I next saw Pfister, he invited me to give a second lecture. This received the same approval as the first, and Pfister and Oberholzer invited me to join their Society. Pfister became my paternal friend.

After the publication in 1923 of my second volume, *From the Unconscious Mental Life of Our Youth*, many parents of young children —some of preschool age—consulted me.

Pfister also made it possible for me to participate in the Congress of the International Psychoanalytic Association and, in Berlin, he introduced me to Freud. As it happened, this was the last Congress in which Freud took part. I saw Freud only twice again, when I traveled to Vienna to attend and conduct lectures. Freud showed his friendliness in many ways: he invited me to visit him in his home and to attend extension courses for teachers, and he arranged for me to lecture in Stuttgart together with Heinrich Meng. Freud and I remained friends until his death, although he never agreed with my view that psychoanalytic education is more of a collective and social institution than a matter of individual treatment. I became more convinced of this as I gained in age and experience: if a child was so sick that he required individual psychoanalysis, I referred him to child analysts. I always have differentiated between psychoanalytic education and child analysis.

§ Pfister's Development

Oskar Pfister was born in a suburb of Zurich on February 23, 1873. His father was later to become a liberal preacher; and although Oskar's mother was strict and Puritanical, she was an understanding wife. She and her husband collaborated happily in trying to raise their four sons, of whom Oskar was the youngest, in a devoted, God-fearing manner.

Faced with the sick and the dying in his parish, Oskar's father had decided that he must become a physician to the body as well as a healer of the soul. He was especially moved when he visited children suffering from diphtheria, for he felt that, if he had been a physician, he might have saved their lives. The elder Pfister died before he finished his medical studies. Perhaps he had undertaken too much work and died of exhaustion.

Oskar was only three years of age when his father died, and the newly widowed Mrs. Pfister moved with her four sons to the Moravian Brotherhood Community at Konigsfeld, in the Black Forest Region of Baden. Here Mrs. Pfister devoted her life to her fatherless children.

In their new Black Forest home, little Oskar had an experience that exerted a great influence on his later life. One of his friends in kindergarten dropped off to sleep during the lesson and was cruelly beaten by the woman teacher. As Oskar stated, "I have been unable to forget the hurt expression of the sick child, as he vomited over the dress of the disciplinarian teacher. When, a few days later, we chanted our songs of grief and mourning at the open grave of my little friend, I wanted to push the teacher away from my friend's wax-pale face." At that time young Oskar gave thought to becoming a teacher and educator: he would be a far different, more human sort of teacher.

In 1880, Mrs. Pfister moved her family back to their home in Zurich, Switzerland. There, Oskar attended the public school and had an encounter with another unworthy teacher, a confirmed alcoholic, whose sole teaching method was to beat his pupils. This sadist paid especial attention to two feeble-minded girls, whom he beat cruelly every day in the belief that in this way he could teach them to read. As is usual under these circumstances, the majority of the pupils enjoyed these scenes: they fed on reactive sadism. Oskar felt deep pity for the two persecuted little victims. He was terribly upset with the teacher, despite the fact that the teacher was well inclined toward Oskar because he was an intelligent pupil. The boy was happy when, at the close of his tenth year, he was transferred to the class of a fine and sensitive teacher whom Pfister has called "a benefactor and spiritual quartermaster." He felt an intensive love for this man, and he "would have walked through fire for him." Without noticing it, the young teacher awakened in Oskar the tendency to be critical. In his autobiography, Pfister wrote:

> He had invited us to pray in all difficulties, because then help would come. So I tried it. Once when I did not learn a poem by heart because of trouble in my family, I was very calm—totally convinced that nothing would happen to me when it was my turn to recite the poem. As the time for my recitation drew closer and closer, with unshaken confidence I expected a miracle to happen. When it did not occur, I felt a terrifying confusion; but I was reassured by the teacher, who took part of the guilt upon himself and spoke to me in a most understanding manner.

Pfister began to doubt the Christian belief in miracles, but he never doubted the grace of God. More important for Pfister—and this became clearer every day—a devoted Christian must continue to think and to question.

As Pfister became older and more mature, his conviction of the supremacy of human thinking deepened. Later, after he had passed his college entrance examinations in Zurich, he frequently attended psychology lectures at the University in Basel, where he was studying theology and philosophy. Although Pfister had grown up in the spirit of orthodox dogmatism, he could not accept it: he felt himself so opposed to the orthodox beliefs that he almost abandoned the study of theology. As a young student, he devoted his study to a sharp, deep-going critique of the Bible. He was annoyed when a conservative professor tried to ridicule his studies. Nevertheless, he also rejected the idea of seeking a scientific, historical explanation for Biblical accounts of such miracles as the changing of water into blood, or the transformation of Moses' staff into a snake and again into a staff before the Egyptian Pharaoh.

After eight semesters he passed his examination in theology and, following additional studies in Berlin, he also earned his Doctor of Philosophy. For his dissertation he chose a problem in religious philosophy and psychology: *Die Genesis der Religionsphilosophie A. E. Biedermanns* ("The Origin of the Religious Philosophy of A. E. Biedermanns") (1898).

He then accepted the position as a village pastor in Wald near Zurich. As he said:

> I loved to preach from the pulpit. I loved the pastoral care of the sick and the suffering, of the lost and of the poor. Most of all, I loved teaching religion. I never had the slightest difficulty keeping order among the 400 children between the ages of 12 and 16 years who came from seven different school districts. They came from many mountains to my school. The

most effective method of discipline was a lively way of teaching, which described religion as salvation, as a source of joy and support in times of danger.

The influence of Pfister's personality was apparent during one's first encounter with him. He radiated a quality that brought people to pour out confidences to him, with no conscious attempts or intentions on his part to seek such confidences. Instantaneously, one felt his integrity, his wisdom, his kindness, his reassuring empathy, and his inner peace.

After he had identified himself with the teachings of Sigmund Freud, he showed in addition a penetrating psychological understanding.

In 1897, Pfister married Erica Wunderli. Their son later became a psychiatrist, director of the State Hospital at Realta in Graubünden, and is today in private practice in Zurich.

After Pfister had worked for five years as a pastor in the village of Wald, he moved his family into the city of Zurich where, in 1902, he was elected Pastor of the Prediger Church, and the family moved into a new parish house. At this time was started an ever-deepening relationship with Sigmund Freud, whom Pfister visited for the first time in 1908.

Although Pfister had by then acquired the working tools of academic psychology, these did not provide him with adequate training as pastor and healer of the soul. He sought a way to satisfy the needs of the children in his parish. Pfister hoped to offer them more than temporary or momentary aid: he was struggling for an active Christian orientation, and his highest requirement was the demand for love of Jesus Christ. Psychoanalysis became not only his personal way of life but the technical tool he might use to realize his Christian orientation. How he did this, he described in his first work, *The Psychoanalytic Method* (1917). In his introduction to this volume, Freud wrote:

> Let us hope that the application of psychoanalysis to the service of education will quickly fulfil the hopes which educators and doctors may rightly attach to it. A book such as this of Pfister's, which seeks to acquaint educators with analysis, will then be able to count on the gratitude of later generations.

To Freud's comments, Meng added the following:

> The new psychology awakened in him the clarity of thought and sensitive empathy which enabled him to learn the long-forgotten language of demons and gods in the unconscious, and which simultaneously made it pos-

sible to bring to life the meaning and the language of the Bible without dogma and in the service of pastoral work . . . He was by nature a fighter, which was necessary to serve his ideas, which caused fierce resistance when he tried to realize them. In the same degree to which he defended Freud and to which he identified himself with his work, he developed hostility to his colleagues, pastors, psychologists, physicians, and parents. For instance, he developed such controversy with William Stern, who at that time was a leader of psychology in Germany. . . .

Between Pfister and Freud a lifelong and deeply fulfilling friendship developed. This is all the more remarkable because at that time numerous disappointments had made Freud cautious, and he was wary lest he again be disappointed. The friendship between the two men was very productive of scientific work. In their meetings and in an animated correspondence of approximately 120 letters, Pfister and Freud discussed the then current problems of psychoanalysis, which included such topics as neurosis, hysteria, compulsion, phobia, obsession, anxiety and guilt, superego, ethos, mass psychology, anthropology, war and peace, communism and revolution, capitalism, and questions of faith and religion. In addition to the correspondence between Pfister and Freud, approximately 300 publications of varying length and importance bear testimony to Pfister's scientific activities.

Oskar Pfister held his position as pastor for thirty-seven years. In this period he experienced all the vicissitudes of human life—its joys and sorrows, in war and peace. His wife died in 1929, and a year later he was married for the second time to a widow, Martha Zuppinger-Urner, with whom he lived happily until his death on August 6, 1956.

In 1908, he was offered the position of professor of theology at the University of Zurich and, somewhat later, a professorship of philosophy at the University of Riga. As he wished to remain loyal to his pastoral and psychoanalytic activities within his parish, he did not accept either of these posts. The Department of Theology at the University of Geneva conferred an honorary doctorate upon him on May 23, 1934.

By 1939, Pfister had retired and moved with his family into their new home in Witikon. Despite his retirement, he continued to write and published his second most important work, *Christianity and Fear* (*Das Christentum und die Angst*) (1944).

§ Pfister through the Eyes of Sigmund Freud

The correspondence between Freud and Pfister started in January 1909 and continued throughout their lives. The friendship between the two men was very close, and Pfister never participated in the disagreements among Freud's followers. As it would be interesting to know Freud's views concerning Pfister and his method of employing psychoanalysis in his pastoral duties, I include here quotations from several letters, which show the high esteem in which Freud held Pfister and his work.

On January 18, 1909, Freud wrote for the first time:

I cannot content myself with just thanking you for sending me your paper *Wahnvorstellung und Schülerselbstmord* ["Delusion and Student Suicide"]; I must also express my satisfaction that our psychiatric work has been taken up by a minister of religion who has access to the minds of so many young and healthy individuals. Half in jest, but really quite seriously, we often complain that psycho-analysis requires a state of normality for its application and that the organised abnormalities of mental life impose a limitation on it, with the result that the optimum conditions for it exist where it is not needed—*i.e.*, among the healthy. Now it seems to me that this optimum exists in the conditions in which you work (Meng & Freud, 1963, p. 15).

On February 9, 1909, he wrote that:

They do not suspect that success with them comes about in your case primarily by the same route as it does with us, by way of erotic transference to yourself. But you are in the fortunate position of being able to lead them to God and bringing about what in this one respect was the happy state of earlier times when religious faith stifled the neuroses (p. 16).

In itself psycho-analysis is neither religious nor non-religious, but an impartial tool which both priest and layman can use in the service of the sufferer (p. 17).

October 4, 1909:

A letter from you is one of the best possible things that could be waiting for one on one's return. But do not believe that I believe everything or even a large part of the delightful things that you say to me and about me, *i.e.*, I believe them of you but not of me. I do not deny that it does me good to hear that sort of thing, but after a while I recall my own self-knowledge and become a good deal more modest. What remains behind is the belief that you honestly mean what you say, and the pleasure given by your kind and enthusiastic nature. What I should like would be to win over more such people as yourself . . . (p. 29).

November 21, 1926:

Of all the applications of psycho-analysis the only one that is really flourishing is that initiated by you in the field of education. It gives me great pleasure that my daughter is beginning to do good work in that field (p. 106).

During this friendship, which lasted from January 1909 to the death of the founder of psychoanalysis, Freud retained his high opinion of Pfister. Such exemplary friendship and loyalty deserves to be remembered. Freud may have valued Pfister's friendship even more than he did Pfister's scientific findings and contributions to psychoanalysis.

From their first meeting in 1908 until Freud's death, Freud and Pfister remained good friends. Such friends are as necessary to the scientist as his disciples and students are, for no one is as alone as the scientist. And, among scientists, Freud's position was especially unique and lonely in that he had to defend himself against both inner and outer aggressions. Oskar Pfister participated in the inner and outer struggles of his friend in Vienna: his participation was open, honest, and courageous, as his correspondence with Freud and his numerous controversial pamphlets bear witness. We must not underestimate the interpersonal relationship between Pfister and Freud, or consider it less important than the scientific co-operation and teamwork between the two.

The remaining contribution of Pfister to the scientific achievements of psychoanalysis is his "The Domain of Pedanalysis" (1917), the practical application of a modified psychoanalytic technique in the education and therapy of children.

Contemporary students of psychoanalysis can scarcely realize the importance at the time of the application of Freudian psychoanalysis to education. Two benefits resulted: education received a new orientation, later termed "psychoanalytic education"; and Pfister's "The Domain of Pedanalysis" developed into child analysis.

It is the aim of this profile to establish the place of Oskar Pfister as a pioneer in this development.

REFERENCES

Meng, H., & E. L. Freud. (Eds.) *Sigmund Freud, psychoanalysis and faith: dialogues with the Reverend Oskar Pfister*. New York: Basic Books, 1963.

Pfister, O. *The psychoanalytic method.* (Trans. C. R. Payne.) New York: Moffat, Yard, 1917.

Pfister, O. *Christianity and fear*. (Trans. W. H. Johnston.) New York: Macmillan, 1948.

Pfister, O. *Die Genesis der Religionsphilosophie A. E. Biedermanns*. Zurich: Frick, 1898.

Translated and adapted from the German by Martin Grotjahn.

Hanns Sachs

1881–1947

THE CREATIVE UNCONSCIOUS

*

FRITZ MOELLENHOFF

Hanns Sachs was born in Vienna, Austria, on January 10, 1881. His ancestry included rabbis who lived in the Sudeten country, and his father was a lawyer who had moved to Vienna. With his two older sisters and an older brother, Otto, Hanns Sachs grew up in an atmosphere pervaded by the artistic and literary interests of practically every member of the family. Otto died when Hanns was sixteen years old. In 1899, Sachs graduated from high school (the Gymnasium), where he had been a very good student, and studied law. He passed the Bar in 1904 and started a law practice. That same year he read Freud's *Interpretation of Dreams.*

Sachs was married to—as Ernest Jones described her—"an attractive, highly cultured lady." Why the marriage did not last, neither Jones nor I knew, as Sachs always showed reserve in matters past and personal. However, he rescued his former wife, who lived in Vienna when Hitler occupied it in 1938, and brought her—among a dozen or more of his relatives and friends—to the United States.

In 1909, the most important event in his life occurred, according to Sachs. He joined Freud and his group. In 1910, he was called into its *Vorstand* (Executive Board) and became one of the six men who for many years worked in closest co-operation with Freud. In 1912, together with Rank, he became co-editor of the *Imago*, in which post he continued for twenty years.

Pulmonary tuberculosis that started with hemoptysis during the Fifth International Psychoanalytic Congress in Budapest in 1918 forced him to interrupt his work. He went into the mountains of Switzerland where, after about two years, he fully recovered. At that time he decided to abandon his law practice entirely. He wrote to Freud about his decision and opened a psychoanalytic practice in Zurich. In 1920, he was invited to become a training analyst at the Psychoanalytic Institute in Berlin, founded by Abraham and Eitingon.

Between 1923 and 1929, Berlin was a center of blossoming experiments in art, literature, theater, and music—short-lived but most stimulating. These twelve years in Berlin were a serene and fulfilled period of Sachs's life, as is best reflected in Eitingon's short speech in honor of Sachs's fiftieth birthday: Eitingon wished him good, long years "au jardin d'Epicure." I do not know how Sachs received his friend's remark—with skeptical amusement, I should imagine. Early in 1932, he recognized that his "garden" was threatened by a brewing storm (Hitler and his brown shirts). He accepted an invitation from the Boston Psychoanalytic Society, and left Berlin for Boston. Soon after he arrived, he bought the former home of a sea captain at 168 Marlborough Street, with all its old-fashioned furniture, marine paintings and prints, and leather-bound books. This new home fitted Sachs well (his Berlin apartment, the study excepted, had had few individual traits). For some years an English butler and his wife served him. Sachs occasionally poked fun at the butler, whose formal behavior and expectations amused him, despite the fact that the butler's service contented him. Sachs possessed a marked sense for form and its aesthetically and socially varied aspects.

Soon new friends surrounded him; his adaptation to the new country and its culture resulted in a strong and grateful attachment. Sachs's work remained almost the same as in Berlin—training analyses, and lectures that he gave, not only at the Boston Institute, but also at colleges and hospitals. He received one of the few nonmedical appointments as instructor at the Harvard Medical School.

When, in March 1938, Hitler occupied Austria, Sachs had to face the terribly exhausting task of rescuing his sisters, their families and several friends. He did this with unending energy and patience. Although he was successful in saving his relatives, his success could not protect him from experiencing more and more deeply the European catastrophe—the fate of the Jews, of many friends, and of men he admired. Elements of melancholic skepticism in Sachs, formerly well hidden under an urbane witty cover, dominated him more and more. As Ann and Merrill Moore put it, "One could recognize a pervasive sadness creeping over his personality like a fog" (1954). His loneliness was mitigated by the residence of his sister Olga and her son Max in his household from 1938 on. They lovingly provided for Sachs's comfort.

Illness came with anginal attacks and an abdominal operation in 1945. He worked and wrote until January 10, 1947, when he died on the morning of his sixty-sixth birthday.

§ The Man

To draw the portrait of a man of Sachs's complexity requires the pen of an artist. Of necessity I must limit myself to throwing some incidental light on his personality as it revealed itself to me in the course of our relationship, which started when he was my analyst and continued during a friendship of many years' duration. In my attempt to sketch this portrait, sixteen years after I saw him last, I have been helped by what others have said and written about him and—last but not least—by the many letters I received from him.

An event comes to my mind that took place in 1936, when Sachs visited us at Black Mountain College. In accordance with college custom, Sachs was asked to give a lecture; he readily agreed, choosing as the topic of his speech, "The Analytic Approach to Shakespeare's Macbeth." Investigations of this nature had been for many years the core of Sachs's interest. The lecture was brilliant and was for days a topic of conversation among students and faculty alike. However, it is not the lecture or the college's reaction on which I should like to focus, but the brief conversation I had with Sachs before introducing him to the audience. To my question as to how he would like to be introduced, he replied: "Do not say anything but that I have worked with Professor Freud." It was a terse request, and I followed it literally. I knew that he most definitely wanted it this way—that in his work and while giving a lecture, he was the disciple of Freud.

This brief episode permits me to elucidate one facet of his personality: the terse request might seem to indicate that Sachs was a somewhat abrupt man, averse to using more words than was absolutely necessary or to geniality of any kind. In truth, he was the opposite of the abrupt man. Chatting with Sachs was as enjoyable as it was stimulating. He was a storehouse of stories, particularly of Jewish anecdotes and quotations from European literature. Most of his stories were from the English, French, Russian, or German; they were innumerable, witty, and profound, told with a playful elegance characteristic of his Viennese origin.

To the Viennese also, as the world knows, belongs a discriminating palate, and so it was also a pleasure to dine with Sachs and to see him sip from a glass filled with a St. Emilion or a Chablis. *Le Jardin d'Epicure*—I again refer to Eitingon's friendly remark—would not be a garden without women. They, too, belonged to his life. During a certain period, Sachs might have impressed many people as being a successful cross between a scholar and—for want of a better word—*bon vivant* (this term comes close to the German word "Lebenskünstler"), though in one of his books, *Masks of Love and Life*, Sachs professed never to have seen a person who successfully combined the two. Nevertheless, Freud often teased Sachs about his persistent optimism. This quality is not only a matter of temperament, but includes one's attitude toward his fellow human beings. Something in Sachs reminded me of the French novelist Stendhal, who in his diaries once said: "What is the goal of a man of the world? To generate serenity and to comfort his fellow human beings." [1]

In my outline of Sachs's life, I mention the change beginning in 1938 and becoming more marked after the start of World War II, when he isolated himself more and more. Sachs knew that he had changed. In one of his letters he sarcastically reflected on narcissism as an existential technique. Two of Sachs's attitudes remained unchanged: one was, as it were, inborn—a love of literature, of its creations and creators, that is, reading. He often said: "I am a reading addict." What had been a challenging and most pleasurable fulfillment from the beginning also served later as a comfort. At a time when he was tortured by SOS cables from relatives and friends threatened by deportation, he wrote: "My refuge is as always reading, especially English literature and biographies of the

[1] Sachs occasionally read Stendhal, whom he mentioned on page 73 in his small 1920 treatise, "Psychoanalytic Prescriptions for Love-Making." It seems possible that Stendhal's famous *On Love* had, among other causes, inspired Sachs to write his spirited essay, wherein woman's superiority in *rebus amoris* is unequivocally expressed. This again reminds us of Stendhal.

18th century, Robinson Crusoe included." Although Sachs was addicted to reading, I have never seen a more discriminating, subtle, and productive addict.

The second attitude that remained unchanged has already been mentioned: his attitude toward Freud. Sachs remained the undeviant disciple. His devotion was enviable. We might also envy Sachs's experience when he first read and then met Freud.

We have a very vivid account of how this occurred in Sachs's book, *Freud, Master and Friend* (1944), which also reveals much of the personality of its author. The spark of an artist is apparent in Sachs's writings, particularly in the style. Certain sentences in the book made me go back and try to imagine how profoundly Sachs must have been dazzled as an adolescent by the impressions aesthetic beauty and its radiations caused in him. The daydream to become a writer was there. Such a dream can be a companion throughout life—blessing, disturbing, or amusing, according to the intensity of the artistic spark. However, Sachs had been directed by his father and uncles to walk the traditional path, to become a lawyer.

Sachs was twenty-four years old when he read Freud's *Interpretation of Dreams*. The book struck him forcibly, and I wonder whether his occupation with it did not immediately become more than a hobby, as one of his friends, Felix Deutsch (1947), believed it to be. I presume that the detours ended then, and Sachs's exclusive career began. "He must have intuitively recognized that dreams border the realm where the creations of the poet grow, and though a dream may look clumsy and crude it is related to poetry" (Moore & Moore, 1954).

It was not only literary writings, poetry, and novels that held Sachs in their grip; his admiration for Dostoevski and study of the great Russian's life had led him into the fields of psychiatry and psychopathology that satisfied his "youthful longings for the sensational and exotic." His letter of September 18, 1943, expressed how deeply involved he had become in his thoughts and reminiscences about his master: "My book, memories about Freud, is still a strict secret which probably it will remain after its publication also. [This was very typical of Sachs.] I have revised it three times but I am not yet contented with it. Of course, this does not prevent me from doing it with gusto, even with passion."

Freud, Master and Friend is a small book of 189 pages but, in the words of one reviewer, Gosselin (1946), it clearly shows the austere and heroic proportions of Freud's personality. Homage is paid to the master and his work, and the details of his life—calmly and inconspicuously regulated as it was—are described with a tender lightness. According to Sachs, nightly walks with Freud were as unforgettable as the scientific discussions in the study together with other colleagues. The second chapter contains a masterly picture of the social and moral atmosphere of Vienna during the first two decades of the twentieth century.

I know that in the United States some voices accused Sachs of idealizing, even idolizing Freud. The constellation of master and disciple, for centuries an accepted, almost classical, concept in Europe, might have sounded foreign to American ears (Gosselin). Sachs himself said (1944, p. 110) that his description would give the impression of hero worship and *furor biographicus,* as Freud used to say. Sachs calmly asked himself the question: "Am I more independent, less under his influence now, several years after his death, than I was in his lifetime? I do not think so nor do I wish it, even if it would help my purpose which I doubt" (p. 12). There was in Sachs awe of the genius and gratefulness to the man who had led him into the exclusive path on which he could use what he had of longing, talent, and ardor to know.

In *Freud, Master and Friend* (1944, p. 14), Sachs has made a "confession": "I have reason to think that Freud did not find in me some of those qualities which he valued most highly. In the bond between us something was missing—the something that leads to spontaneous intimacy between characters of similar type and tone." The confession ends with: "I have no wish to appear here as a shining example of self-humiliation and repentance." When I read the manuscript this paragraph struck me as being too modest, almost masochistic. When I expressed this feeling, Sachs said simply: "It was this way."

Much later I found that in his obituary of Hanns Sachs, Ernest Jones (1946) briefly touched on this relationship and on Freud's coolness toward Sachs. Freud expected four qualities from the ring-bearers: duty, responsibility, obligation, and devotion. Sachs excelled in devotion, Jones wrote, but the other qualities were not strong, or at least not active enough. I cannot agree with Jones's evaluation. In my opinion Sachs had all the qualities required as a teacher of psychoanalysis. The ease with which he taught may have deceived his co-workers.

In his book (1944), Sachs called the experience with Freud's *Interpretation of Dreams* a stupendous revelation.

The years of listening to Freud's lectures on Saturday evenings in the auditorium of the Psychiatric Clinic in Vienna "became the pivot around which my private universe revolved." There were also seminars and discussions, for example, on the right method of interpretation of works of literature. It was a new learning experience for Sachs, and in many respects the beginning of an intensive identification with his teacher. If one can measure these processes, I should say that the intensity of the identification grew with time.

He began a friendship with Otto Rank, who had met Freud in 1906 and who "was then and remained for a long time Freud's right-hand man." Sachs called this friendship the first thread of his personal relation with Freud. Sachs's translation of Kipling's "Barrackroom Ballads" had been published and provided the final impetus toward establishing personal contact with Freud. No doubt their empathy was immediate despite the difference in age—Freud was fifty-four, Sachs twenty-nine—and despite the "gulf that separates the genius from ordinary minds" they had in common a community of deep interests and a mobility of expressive forces, plus a ready admiration in Sachs and a sympathetic interest in Freud. From this time onward, Sachs's path was clear and unmistakable. His mode of working has been lucidly described by Eitingon on the occasion of Sachs's fiftieth birthday. "One of his prominent qualities," Eitingon wrote, "appears to be that he does not like routine, but he is one of our strongest workers; he works so easily and effortlessly as if he would not prefer anything else to it" (1931).

The same relaxed elegance was apparent in his lectures. Nevertheless, as seen from within, the picture was quite different: there were the long, hard struggles, the preparation, and the absorption in work.

After his first visit with Freud, Sachs became a member of the group. Four of the men around Freud were physicians. Sachs, a practicing lawyer, had never been attracted to medicine, and he consistently disputed whether or not analysis could and should remain independent of medicine. However, because of his drive to know and to see, he went on regular visits and rounds to a State Hospital near Berlin for a period of six weeks. It was strenuous, he told me, but very rewarding.

In the Viennese group, he adapted easily to the fact that he and his friend Rank were laymen. At that time, the role of psychoanalysis in medicine was of peripheral interest, and psychoanalysis was fighting for the right to exist as an independent science. Sachs, whose temperament and nature forced him to live with the motto: "the pen is mightier than the sword," knew that the printed and spoken word would serve him as weapons. It characterizes his spirit that during the Psychoanalytic Congress in Weimar in 1911, Sachs, together with Ernest Jones (1957, Vol. 2, p. 86), called on Mrs. Elizabeth Förster-Nietzsche to tell her about the Congress, and to comment on the similarity between some of Freud's ideas and those of her famous brother. I only repeat myself when I mention here Jones's letter to Freud (Jones, 1957, Vol. 3, p. 105) in which he praised a course of lectures Sachs gave in London in 1924. Everyone who heard Sachs was enchanted by the polished ease and the clarity of his delivery.

In comparing Sachs's role with that of the other members of the group, we see that Sachs was not a flag-bearer such as Ferenczi, Abraham, and Jones, who actively founded psychoanalytic groups in Budapest, Berlin, and London and reached and influenced their medical colleagues.

The question remains whether Sachs was not a more solitary walker in life than he had appeared to most of his friends, despite his free movements within the group, his influence on its members, and his friendship. When necessary he became a foe. In October 1911, he suggested a clean break with Adler (Jones, 1957, Vol. 2, p. 134); and in 1924, after a long struggle and strong attempts to repair the deep dissensions, he broke with his closest friend, Rank. What happened in 1927 during the Innsbruck Congress may confirm what I have already said about Sachs's solitary path. It was then decided to change the structure of the famous committee, which had functioned very privately, to change it into a group consisting of "officials" of the International Psychoanalytic Association (Jones, 1957, Vol. 3, p. 135).

Sachs dropped out, I suppose with not too heavy a heart: administrative, organizational (political) activities never had attracted him, although he probably felt the narcissistic injury when he was excluded from the committee. At that time he had been in Berlin for almost seven years and was, as Loewenstein has said, "one of a small group of analysts who had to learn by trial and error the intricacies of the unknown field of training analysis" (1947). Sachs fulfilled this task willingly, admirably, and with a remarkable evenness (so his analysands felt).

He practiced in a small apartment in Berlin. The analysand was advised to wait in the dining room. The door opened, and Sachs—with a measured smile—shook hands; his facial expression suggested something like, "I expected you to come, let's work together." The couch was placed in such a way that the analysand faced a portrait bust of Freud standing on a high wooden pedestal. Sachs did not say much during the hour. When he spoke, the sentences were concise and short. He loved to put interpretations, whenever possible, into quotations from poets and writers. If charm can have an impact or impact a charm, this was the case—at least with me. No doubt the "mirror concept" pervaded the hour—the objectified distance between analyst and analysand—the few exceptions occurring when Sachs interpreted his own slips of the tongue or of action, a surprise for the novice with his magic expectations of the analyst's infallibility.

During the last eight years of Sachs's life, events no longer permitted him to breathe freely. The loss of Europe, as it were—the loss of many relatives and friends—was coupled with the loss of Freud, whom he had visited for the last time in July 1939, shortly before Freud's death. The contents of a letter written on June 3, 1943, seemed sarcastic and embittered: "I live, as always, as a psychoanalytic hermit, with the motto: 'Nobody tells me anything.'" Often he had to endure this mood of isolation. In February 1944, three years before his death, when he awaited a manuscript that had been sent to a publisher, he wrote, "in the meantime I cannot start with any larger work because I have to keep myself free for the revision."

What did the hermit do? Throughout his life Sachs was very fond of translating, as he himself mentioned in the foreword to his book about Freud. A translation of Kipling's "Barrackroom Ballads" had been his first publication, which he had hopefully brought to Freud.[2] For someone who has strongly cathexed work and language, translating is an intellectual and aesthetic or stylistic exercise. Translating involves communication with the people into whose language one translates, and the gift of something that may give pleasure. So, while Sachs awaited word from his publisher, he again spent his time in translation, which in itself was not unusual. However, his comments in his letter, and the material he chose to translate, clearly showed the man, his inner freedom and measured being. The letter continues: "Therefore I have chosen something very sublime, something undirtied by any earthly purposeful-

[2] The ballads are peculiarly realistic, unsophisticated, direct expressions of feelings, frustrations, hopes of the English colonial soldiers. They are like folk songs —slangy, sarcastic and sentimental, genuine and, occasionally, profound. Suffering and duty are stressed.

ness. I shall translate Goethe's *Sprüche in Reimen* ("Short Maxims in Rhymes"), always a special favorite of mine.[3] This work—if this is work, and somehow I doubt it—can be taken up and interrupted momentarily."

Sachs was waiting; he was not sure whether the publisher would accept his book, but he was free enough to transcend earthly purposefulness, knowing that he would be rewarded—as he had so often been rewarded—by experiencing the beauty of art and its universal sound, to which he had listened all his life. His life had to change much: the man of the world, the *bon vivant,* had said adieu to that world long ago; Sachs had to watch his health very carefully. The letter quoted above ends with a remark about his condition: "The state of my health is unchanged. It is right that I make an effort to cope with the new situation *comme philosoph.* I mostly succeed but not always." But the letter does not really end there. Below his signature, in a postscript as it were, he put down one of the maxims he had translated and for which he chose as a heading, "Goethe about the superego."

> There is a universum, too, within.
> Therefore all nations are in that akin
> That every man what seems to him the best,
> As god, or even as his god addressed,
> Heaven and earth to hand him over strove
> Whom he felt bound to fear and tried to love.

A paragraph in Sachs's book about his master and friend belongs here. It is in the chapter, "All I Know about Him": "He (Freud) took life as a task that had been set, as a duty imposed on anyone of us by the past of which we are the product. This inheritance is always with us in the form of our superego—invisible, intangible, and yet the most indubitable reality that shapes our life" (1944). There was a detachment in Sachs, an unjustly chosen isolation sometimes bordering misanthropy; but, as I tried to show through his letter, his moral and aesthetic fibers were alive throughout, as they were at the beginning. He remained the untiring, responsible, and creative interpreter.

[3] See also Chapter 15, *Masks of Love and Life* (Sachs, 1948).

§ Sachs's Work

Throughout his life, Sachs was an indefatigable editor, as the many volumes of the *Imago* attest; and from 1939 until 1947, it was the *American Imago* to which he devoted his strength and discrimination. Despite his free and helpful comments on submitted manuscripts, his benevolence never prevented him from putting first the *Imago* and its proper functioning. The author had to be punctual, for instance. In one of his letters, he wrote: "There is only one answer appropriate for an editor who is asked when a manuscript should be delivered: the day before yesterday."

In Berlin, in 1925, he made a brief excursion into the movies. Together with Abraham, he was the advisor to Pabst, the director of "The Secrets of the Soul." Sachs kept in touch with Pabst, because the artist in him knew how helpful, sometimes indispensable, visual means are for the understanding of psychic processes. In a brief paper, "Notes about the Psychology of the Movie," (1925) he shows how much we can learn while "only looking."

In 1936, the Berlin Psychoanalytic Institute published a review of its activities during the preceding ten years. It mentions the wide range of Sachs's teaching. What has already been said about his lectures and speeches mainly describes their formal aspects; the lecturer has been stressed, but, beyond the lecturer, there was in Sachs the teacher who made his pupils feel how deeply he had experienced, and pupils who understood what Sachs taught and how constantly alive and communicable his knowledge was. During Sachs's dream seminar in Berlin, for instance, the listener was captivated by his forcible but ever flexible intention to unfold Freud's ideas and to illustrate them by examples. A good teacher creates an atmosphere filled with the unverbalized entreaty that his pupils experience what he feels. This Sachs was able to do, whether teaching in seminars, small discussion groups, or lectures. He lectured in order to reach and to teach the public, and a large number of his brief contributions could be brought under the heading: look here and learn something about what you see around you, about your fellow human beings, about yourself.

In one of these contributions, the former lawyer spoke about the death penalty, the rationale of which he doubted, as the punishment lies only in the fear of death. The basis of the death penalty, Sachs believed, is sociological—a group phenomenon, a common sadistic wish, a common act, a common guilt and its sanctification.

The work of the training analyst belongs in the realm of teaching. Sachs wrote a brief note in a humorous vein for the 1936 review, in which he compared training analysts with the novitiate of the Catholic Church. The candidate must learn to carry his psychoanalytic spectacles more or less continuously and to endure his work, which makes him face so many "abysmal" matters without being himself perturbed. The training analysis is in itself a branch of psychoanalysis. "How can one select the right candidates, judge character disposition, blind spots, education and life activities, and how can one know when to terminate a training analysis?" Fifteen years after he had been appointed a training analyst (in company with Freud, Ferenczi, Abraham, Rank, Eitingon, Rado, and Reik) he rewrote these notes (1947). In a letter dated August 3, 1946, from West Campton, New Hampshire, where Sachs spent his summer vacation, he wrote, "I live here even more quietly than usually. Conversations with some old ladies do not attract me. Yesterday I finished a little article about my experiences as a training analyst. As soon as it has been typewritten, I shall send it for your criticism."

That "little article" was published and has become a guidepost when a psychoanalytic institute is concerned with the problems of selection. "Our question is," Sachs wrote, "whom one should select as a candidate, and how one should do this." His answer is: a trial analysis. He decidedly warns against the applicant with a constricted, and hence deprived, ego that functions well in life and work but is narcissistically too tightly barricaded and too well adapted. Also, as a matter of course, he warns against the psychopathic character, the addict, and the full-fledged pervert. Every candidate should have a lively interest in literature and art. One has to watch what there is of *furor sanandi* (Freud) that can lead the carrier to become a renegade. Although there are no fundamental differences between a training analysis and the treatment of a patient, one might give more detailed information to the candidate. The training analysis should contain some discussion about the attitudes and reactions expected from the trainee, and attempt to correct the trainee's mistaken notions. Firmly established in the candidate should be the attitude that the termination does not mark the end of the analysis but its beginning. "The training analyst has to resist optimistic illusions about his success, since, altogether, he is the extremely short-sighted leader of the blind." The majority of Sachs's analysands had been training candidates, but there also was, as he put it, "a steady trickle of neurotic patients on his list."

Sachs reflected about his therapeutic experiences in the article "Psychotherapy and the Pursuit of Happiness" (1941), which reads like an extract of his many years of therapeutic work. The patient's expectations, needs and demands can be recognized, and temptations for the therapist to fulfill them are many. The therapist is not safe, his narcissistic self-assurance is easily mobilized, his way of living can become the model for his patients, his ability to give love is there, but is "by no means inexhaustible." At the end of this article he says, "We are bound to admit that we are just beginners, or 'pioneers,' to use a softer term"; and in the last paragraph: "We must never forget that we meet our patient's real ultimate wishes empty-handed; with great luck, we can set his feet on the right way." A mood of resignation seems to pervade this article, but I think its conclusions stem from the author's feeling of responsibility. Sachs believed that he had to warn against the danger of an optimistic faith that comes from our ever-present narcissistic needs.

Thus far, I have concerned myself with Sachs as the editor, the teacher, and the therapist. It is not surprising to find that his main written work comprises the application of psychoanalysis to literature, art, and the knowledge of man. He was an aesthete, and he looked at the world contemplatively. In the strict sense, he was not a psychoanalytic theoretician, although he did write some metapsychological papers.

"On the Genesis of the Perversions," which is still widely quoted (although it never was translated into English), appeared in 1923. Based on clinical material, the paper discusses the ego-syntonicity of the perversions, their neighborhood to addiction, and their competition with the genital primacy. According to Sachs, "Dreamwork achieves easily what the perversion performs laboriously."

"Metapsychological Points of View in Technique and Theory," written in 1925, explores the manner in which technique and theory are related and how much service technique can render to theory. The "Ego and the Id" is quoted frequently and he mentions Ferenczi's concept of an active technique—which at that time was eagerly discussed in its importance for overcoming resistance, and is still accepted. Sachs called the term "active" misleading. At that time there was already a full awareness of how significant a role the analyst's personality plays in treatment, as is indicated by the sentence: "Unperturbed by the idiosyncracies and difficulties in the personality of the analyst, both in his ego and in his superego, the patient should adopt the analyst's ideal of the analysis itself."

Formation of the superego in women is the topic of another metapsychological paper written in 1928 (Sachs, 1929). The girl frustrated by her father takes an orally regressive step and introjects him. A woman's superego is based on the idea of renunciation, on leaning toward self-denial. Oral regression during the Oedipal phase is responsible for the subtle difference between the female and male superego, as Sachs concluded from his observations of transference reactions and resistances.

The first of Sach's publications was "Dream Interpretation and Knowledge of Man," in which he discussed two of his own dreams. Seven brief contributions to the psychology of dreams followed, among them an interpretation of one of Bismarck's dreams, and a study of the representations of anal stimuli that begin to wake the sleeper. We find brief notes and remarks on behavior and acting out during treatment, and on slips of action. In one note Sachs showed that a slip can serve also as a means of calming oneself.

I wonder where to place the article "Prospects of Psychoanalysis," written in 1939. In it Sachs pointed out that psychoanalysis, "a one man's job," has been brought under the sheltering roof of an organization—that "the extraordinary spreading of psychoanalysis in many directions could be dangerous, could water it down." He encouraged himself and his readers by comparing Freud's doctrine to Moses' teaching, which went through many changes and transformations but "later, core and essence re-appeared." Was it the teacher's conscience that made him write this article?

A great enthusiasm pervades his first larger publication written in cooperation with Otto Rank, *The Significance of Psychoanalysis for the Mental Sciences* (1915b), which remains a cornerstone in the literature of applied psychoanalysis. This monograph is search, research, and a program in the best sense. After an introductory chapter about Freud's doctrine, the unlimited importance of the unconscious for the understanding of the origin and development of civilized life, myth and religion, art and philosophy, and ethics and law is emphasized, as exemplified by much historical and anthropological material, and by saga and fairy tales of different countries and cultures. As one might expect from both authors, artists are accorded a very high place in human society and endeavor. The artists' psychology is dynamically examined; they are called "leaders in the struggle for the taming and ennobling of the instincts hostile to culture." "The artist and his inner kingdom" is another condensed expression of the authors' admiration and awe.

From then on, Sachs's main endeavor was directed toward the psychoanalytic illumination of works of literature and art, toward the possibilities of understanding the creative process and the creative personality.

A study of Schiller's *Geisterseher* (Sachs, 1915a) followed the programmatic essay. The *Geisterseher* is an unfinished novel from which the German poet and playwright abruptly turned away, and which has a particular place in his life. Sachs, recounting the determining historical and personal events, shows that, at that time, the poet was not able to solve his stormy inner conflicts by writing the story, whereupon the creative process became inhibited. Schiller had to turn to historical and philosophical studies in order to weather the internal turbulence. Sachs demonstrated minutely and clearly how, at a later date, Schiller could again use his unconscious motives with freedom and intensity in the dramatic compositions to which Schiller's genius was particularly suited. Sachs tells us how the reciprocal effects of inhibited and propelling unconscious needs and attitudes can lift the barrier that blocks an undisturbed sublimation.

In his book, *The Creative Unconscious* (1942), Sachs compiled what he had thought and written in his search for the understanding of the fundamental problems of aesthetics. As the title demonstrates, for Sachs the unconscious remained the source of creativity. The daydream is a starting point: the daydream that is the property of the daydreamer and is never told; the shared daydream; and, third, the poet's daydream, which, after a long struggle and hard work, becomes his creation. The first chapter of the book is an amalgamation of clinical observations and an ever-expanding attempt at understanding the creative process, the personality of great writers. How these writers—possessed and absorbed as they are—succeed in resigning and repenting here, and tirelessly building there, is investigated. Sachs shows where the transitions are from the asocial daydream to the artistic creation, which is designed to bind people together. The socializing aspects of art led Sachs into a brief essay about personal and impersonal art. The Ravenna mosaics were for Sachs examples of impersonal art, wherein the creator's individuality can no longer be recognized—"his name may be known but his psychic physiognomy is lost." In the sphere of early religious art, the superego asks for a complete resignation from the expression of individual tendency and characteristics; after this has been achieved, an almost depersonalized devotion can create an "enduring harmony."

Creativity in a very different area is contemplated in Chapter 4 of "The Delay of the Machine Age" (1933). It poses the question why the man of antiquity—although enough mathematicians and engineers were around—did not arrive at inventions of machines as we have them and suffer from them today. Sachs concluded that men of antiquity could not get away from their body-egos and their "naïve" narcissism, which protected them from the troubles modern man has to face. This brief survey can only hint at the richness of the historical, sociological, and psychological examples and historical parallels. Again here Sachs has demonstrated so well which factors, external and internal, inhibit or unfold human creativity.

In Part III of "The Delay of the Machine Age," Sachs turned to the age-old aesthetic question: What is beauty? He based his answer on Freud's "Beyond the Pleasure Principle." The essentially philosophical nature of Freud's essay must have attracted Sachs deeply. Although the basis is admittedly a theoretical speculation and could therefore lead to an abstraction alienating the reader, there is so much immediate empathy with the essence of beauty and man's experience of it, there are so many profound contemplations about man's taste, aesthetic needs, and creations, that one never tires of reading it. Man's relations to the beauty of nature—when does beauty unite human beings, when does it isolate them, and the principles involved, static (the death instinct) and dynamic—are discussed and illustrated. Experiencing beauty is never connected with anxiety but always with sadness, or what borders on sadness. Many a reader will consider this a very personal reaction.

Some friends and critics of Sachs, including Freud, thought that he was at his best in his published studies of Shakespeare. The completeness of the literary research that went into each of his essays was a *conditio sine qua non* for Sachs. What one sees so well is the perfectly balanced combination of the researcher, who wants to know and has the objective means for this, and the loving connoisseur, whose tender and cautious hand unfolds the hidden connections between the creation and the artist's unconscious needs and conflicts, certain events in his life, and certain phases in his development. By writing *The Tempest*, the aging Shakespeare liberated himself from the guilt about having left his daughter, when she was a small girl. *The Tempest* is believed to be Shakespeare's last play, after which he planned to retire from his life at Court, from his renown. In his studies of Shakespeare, Sachs's purpose was to "comprehend a single trait in Shakespeare's mind in his latter years." A modest formulation, it became much more than that.

Shakespeare's *Measure for Measure*—called the least attractive of his comedies by the scholars of Shakespeare and therefore possibly most attractive to Sachs—is another subject of Sachs's analytic literary research. Since it concerns a judge and justice, the attraction might have had some bearing on Sachs's past. What is measured is the unconscious in judge and criminal and, in an inconspicuous way, clinical knowledge and methods are used to show the result. "What happens to justice if the austere judge could commit . . . would commit . . . has unconsciously committed the same crime for which he condemns the offender?" Under the guise of a comedy, the double-faced justice, "the identity of the man who judges and the man who is judged" are revealed. Literary comparisions concern Sophocles, Kleist, and Dostoevski.

The ever-present questions, "How much can we know of a human being? How clearly can a human being know himself?" produced three books. In a foreword to the second, Anna Freud stated: "For Hanns Sachs, more than for most authors in the same field, psychoanalytic psychology meant, above all, the means to inquire into the daily behavior of human beings, into their relations with each other and with their chosen love objects, as well as into their attitude toward the inevitable problems of life and death."

Historical figures are good objects from which to learn about the human heart and its passions. Sachs the scholar needed perspectives and wanted to prove their usefulness. That Sachs chose the Roman Emperor Caligula as an object for study—*Caligula* (1931)—might have been determined by the very interesting pathological character of this young man; however, the choice of Caligula may also have been Sachs's reaction to the political atmosphere in which he lived at that time (Hitler and his cohorts were already very much in the foreground). Indeed what Sachs tells us about the ways in which Caligula tried to engender and to keep his popularity often reminds us of the modern dictator's machinations; Chapter X even describes the negotiations between the Emperor and the envoys of the large Jewish community of Alexandria, Egypt. In the frame of the turbulent cultural and political period, the personality of the Emperor is analyzed, and we are shown his fragmented ego living in borrowed roles, his infantile and counterphobic attitudes, and, finally, his massive self-destructive drives. In the last chapter, a brief survey makes clear how productive psychoanalytic thinking can be if applied to historical events as well as to personalities. Sachs's last book, to which I shall come later, contains a brief sketch of Julius Caesar's personality and a chapter about the Apostle Paul. It was the latter to whose life Sachs devoted much time and energy during the years 1943 and 1947. In one of his letters, he mentioned that he intended to consult with two clergymen about Apostle Paul.

In 1936, a booklet of 122 pages appeared, entitled, *Notes about the Knowledge of Human Beings* (not translated into English). One could call it a psychoanalytic, philosophical treatise. "The ego in the familiar intercourse with itself," "The family with and without love," and "About good fortune—without giving any postal address" are the headings of three chapters. In the last chapter, Sachs has conjured up the figure of a universal teacher.

> He who would be able to instruct man how to fantasy, to teach each one which type is healthiest for him, where the too much and the too little is hidden, how to suppress a dangerous part and supplant it—might bring us closer to happiness than the greatest technical achievements. Alas, we wait for this teacher in vain; our fantasy life cannot be altered and cut, like an ill-fitting garment, for it is the expression of our essential, deepest nature. Each fresh disappointment is grafted on a previous frustration, and from it blossoms a fantasy, in which in spite of all repressions the thwarted wish is granted—in a daydream or, if it is photophobic, in a dream. As long as we are at variance with our wishes, as long as we cannot do without suffering and self-punishment, no soul-engineer will be able to devise a plan which prescribes to our fantasy its course and regulates its channel!

A benign and smiling irony pervades the book; the examples are light, the contemplations, though skeptical, are never discouraging. The illusions—which bring about human wishes and from which human beings suffer—are not removed, but the "teacher" takes his pupils to a more distant point from which they are able to look at their illusions more calmly and confidently.

About ten years later Sachs broadened and deepened the theme. In a letter of January 15, 1945, he wrote, ". . . besides I'm working whenever possible on my book, and I shall soon finish the second revision. How many revisions still will come, of course I cannot say; but I know that it won't be received as favorably as its predecessors. . . . Because I never was fond of friendly reviews I shall ignore all this." For this book he had chosen the title, *The People of a Strange Planet,* and the initials P.S.P. recur frequently. However, A. A. Roback, who edited the material (published in 1948 after Sachs's death) gave it the title, *Masks of Love and Life.*

In the sixteen chapters we find a restatement of much that Sachs had written earlier, albeit formulated more distinctly and showing new facets and ideas. Personal experiences and reactions recognizable to people who knew him are inconspicuously woven throughout, giving the texture of thoughts a peculiar aliveness. The chapters teach us again about the illusions, frailties, and aberrations of the human soul and body. A brief light is thrown on some great men of history: Napoleon's "attitude to life is hemmed in by his one-sided, inexorable monomanic ambition, which binds as closely as any inhibition." Caesar—psychologically almost unique—"has given the world the only example of a life and death in perfect freedom, as far as fate ever permitted such fulfillment to anyone of the P.S.P."

I noticed an occasional dissonance in this book. I could feel a dilemma that affects its structural coherence, and I commented on this to Sachs in a letter. In March 1946, Sachs answered me: "My intention was to write something multi-colored and unsystematic, to let myself—in a measured way—go into free associations, hoping that the unified basic outlook would pervade the whole book. Evidently my intention has failed, but I do not believe that I still shall be able to revise it thoroughly." Sachs showed resignation, but we find it is eased by the serenity contained in the final paragraph of this last book: "It [our life] is shown to us in the light of growing self-detachment as through a thinning mist—not only as to what it was, or ought to have been, or might have been, but also as what it was bound to be, because we were just this sort of a human creature."

REFERENCES

Deutsch, F. Obituary of Hanns Sachs, 1881–1947. *Amer. Imago,* 1947, 4 (2), 3–11.

Eitingon, M. Hanns Sachs 50 Jahre. *Int. Z. Psychoanal.,* 1931, 17, 158–159.

Gosselin, R. Review of *Freud, master*

and friend. Psychoanal. Quart., 1946, **15**, 104–106.

Jones, E. Obituary of Hanns Sachs. *Int. J. Psycho-Anal.*, 1946, **27**, 168–169.

Jones, E. The life and work of Sigmund Freud. New York: Basic Books, 1957. 3 vols.

Loewenstein, R. M. In memoriam, Hanns Sachs. *Psychoanal. Quart.*, 1947, **16**, 151–156.

Moore, Ann Leslie, & M. Moore. Notes on re-reading of Hanns Sachs's last book. *Amer. Imago*, 1954, **11**, (1), 3–9.

Sachs, H. *Ars Amandi Psychoanalytica, oder Psychoanalytische Liebersregeln.* Berlin: Reuss & Pollak, 1920.

Sachs, H. Gemeinsame Tagträume. *Int. Psychoanal. Verlag*, 1924.

Sachs, H. Zur Psychologie des Films. *Psychoanal. Bewegung*, 1925, **1**, 122.

Sachs, H. One of the motive factors in the formation of the super-ego in women. *Int. J. Psychoanal.*, 1929, **10**, 39–40.

Sachs, H. *Caligula.* (Trans. H. Senger.) London: Elin Matthews & Marott, 1931.

Sachs, H. The delay of the machine age. (Trans. M. G. Powers.) *Psychoanal. Quart.*, 1933, **2**, 404–424.

Sachs, H. Psychotherapy and the pursuit of happiness. *Amer. Imago*, 1941, **2**, 356–364.

Sachs, H. *The creative unconscious, studies in the psychoanalysis of art.* Cambridge, Mass.: Science-Art Publications, 1942, 1951.

Sachs, H. *Freud, master and friend.* Boston: Harvard University Press, 1944.

Sachs, H. Observation of a training analyst. *Psychoanal. Quart.*, 1947, **16**, 157–168.

Sachs, H. *Mask of love and life, the philosophical basis of psychoanalysis.* Cambridge, Mass.: Science-Art Publications, 1948.

Sachs, H., & O. Rank. The significance of psychoanalysis for the mental sciences. *Nerv. ment. Dis. Mongr.*, 1915, No. 23.

Moshe Woolf

b. 1878

PIONEERING IN RUSSIA AND ISRAEL

*

RUTH JAFFE

Moshe Woolf[1] was born in Odessa, Russia, on October 5, 1878. He studied medicine in Berlin; his teachers in psychiatry were Mendel and Jolly. After his final examinations, he entered the newly opened laboratory of the Charité, the University Hospital in Berlin, where he worked as Ziehen's first assistant. In 1907, he began work at Mendel's psychiatric sanatorium, where he read *Studies on Hysteria*—his first and unexpected encounter with the young psychoanalytic movement. The book was a revelation to him. He later read *The Psychopathology of Everyday Life*, and found in the bulletin of the Berlin Neuropsychiatric Society the report on a case of kleptomania presented with a psychoanalytic orientation by Otto Juliusburger. Woolf decided to get in touch with Juliusburger, who at that time was working in the sanatorium of Berlin-Lankwitz, and, in 1908, he became Juliusburger's assistant. When Karl Abraham returned from Zurich and also started working at the sanatorium in 1908, he became Woolf's teacher, introducing him to psychoanalysis proper.

In 1911, Woolf returned to Russia as Russia's only trained analyst, remaining until 1927. During those years, his many widespread and diverse activities eventually resulted in the acknowledgment and devel-

[1] Spelled *Wulff* in his German publications.

opment of psychoanalysis. In 1914, he went to Moscow, where he worked for some years in a private sanatorium. He later worked at the Psychiatric Neurological Institute, chiefly in the outpatient clinic, to which he brought his analytically orientated approach. In 1920, he went to a military psychiatric hospital.

After the revolution, Woolf joined a large psychiatric outpatient clinic: there, too, he opened a special department for psychoanalytic treatment and trained two doctors in psychoanalysis. He became *Dozent* and the first psychoanalyst at the Second Medical Clinic of the University of Moscow. To his already full program, he added work at the psychoanalytically oriented children's home of Zermakow,[2] where he was then living. This institution had four groups, each consisting of five children between one and five years of age. Some of Woolf's later papers on child psychology are based on his observations at the children's home (1926; 1929; 1949). Although he lived in Russia, Woolf had become a member of the Vienna Psychoanalytical Society in 1912. In 1927, he left Russia for political reasons. He and his wife returned to Berlin and went to live in the Tegelsee sanatorium—the famous psychoanalytic institution under Simmel's direction—where Woolf worked until 1930.

In 1933, Woolf left Berlin, once more for political reasons, migrating to Palestine (today, Israel). Max Eitingon, who arrived in Palestine the same year, together with Woolf and Schalith, founded the Psychoanalytic Society of Palestine, in 1934.

After Eitingon's death, Woolf became president of the Israeli society —a position he held for ten years. Since that time, he has been its honorary president. He has trained a generation of pupils, some full-fledged psychoanalysts and some psychiatrists who sought training useful for their psychiatric and psychotherapeutic activities. Today, most of the directors of the public mental institutions, psychiatric departments, and outpatient clinics of the Tel-Aviv district, and elsewhere, are psychiatrists trained by Woolf. To this day, he conducts a regular seminar for his pupils.

Apart from teaching psychoanalytic practice, Woolf has done much to further the acceptance of analysis in Israel—especially in educational circles. For years he lectured to teachers, including kindergarten teachers, on child psychology. These lectures finally found their expression in a Hebrew publication, *Nefesh Hayeled* ("The Mind of the Child")

[2] Vera Schmidt has written a book about this home.

(1946b), which is used as a standard textbook for psychologists and teachers. Especially important is his strong and lasting influence on *kibbutz* education, mitigating and permeating its socialist ideology with analytic thought and application. This was achieved by his influence on S. Golan, himself a pupil of Woolf and head of the central educational committee of the *kibbutz* movement, *Hashomer Hatzair*.

Woolf's earliest publication on children is "Contributions to Infantile Sexuality" (1912). As a result of this paper, he was admitted to membership in the Vienna Psychoanalytic Society. His observations and interpretations were then so new and original that the paper was compulsory reading for analytic candidates. Most interesting are the cases of four children, three of them described in detail, who suffered from frequent short attacks of what appeared to be petit mal, which Woolf considered to be hysterical. Each attack consisted of a very short loss of consciousness, accompanied by a frozen, blank, upward stare of the eyes and a quiver or convulsive movement of the mouth. All the children were sexually overstimulated, and each had experienced an unexpected and sudden prohibition of his sexual activity by a parent. The resulting struggle against masturbation expressed itself in a substitute—the attack—which is likened to orgasm, with momentary clouding of consciousness, convulsions, and a blank expression. When a change in their environment led to a lessening of sexual excitability, the children improved.

"Fantasy and Reality in the Mental Life of the Infant" (1934) is based on a lecture Woolf delivered to an educational board of the Communist party in Moscow which, for ideological reasons, was planning to forbid the reading of fairy tales and to permit only factual books. As a result of Woolf's lecture, fairy tales were not banned. Woolf's starting point is the observation that the little child does not differentiate between fantasy and reality. Fairy tales deal with the same complexes that fill the mind of the child. He can always turn from frustrating reality to wish-fulfilling fantasy by way of his narcissistic feeling of omnipotence and identification with the hero, which serves as a catharsis. The child's transition from fantasy to reality must be gradual and slow; sudden devaluation of his fantasy world is dangerous. According to Woolf, gruesome tales do not provoke fear: only fearful children nourish their fears by such tales.

"Fetishism and Object Choice in Early Childhood" (1946a) is one of Woolf's most important contributions to psychoanalysis. In this paper, he analyzed the significance of the fetish for the child throughout the phases of his development. On the basis of his findings, Woolf formulated a theory about the transition from infantile narcissism to the first genuine libidinal cathexis of an outside object. This explanation provides the missing link in the theory of primary object choice in childhood. After analyzing cases reported by Friedjung and Sterba, plus three instances he himself had observed, Woolf came to the following conclusions: in the oral phase, the fetish represents, as a partial object, the mother's breast and her body. This substitution is rendered possible by the odor, the warmth, and the tactile sensations the fetish provides for the child. As early as the anal phase, the fetish acquires the attributes of an object.

The significance of the fetish in the phallic phase is highlighted by an illustrative case: a fifteen-month-old boy used a bib as his fetish, smelling it and sucking his thumb, until he fell asleep. When he was two-and-a-half years old, the fetish was lost. He reacted with manifestations of mourning, stopped sucking, and again started bedwetting. At three years and eleven months, he chose another fetish, one of his mother's handkerchiefs that, because of its odors, reminded him of her. Bedwetting stopped. He would smell the handkerchief and sometimes put it into the trousers of his pajamas, pressing it against his genitals, so "that it might not get lost." The first fetish belongs to the oral phase; the second one, to the phallic. The boy identified the new fetish with his phallus, pressing it against his organ as an expression of fear of possible loss, and thereby transferred to the fetish part of the narcissistic libido with which his phallus was cathected, converting it to object libido. Consequently, the fear of losing the phallus (castration anxiety) was transformed into the fear of losing the object. Since the fetish represented the mother, there was, then, the following chain of identifications: phallus-fetish-mother.

These findings suggest that the first genuine libidinal tie to an outside object develops through an identification of this object with the individual's own phallus. "This perhaps explains why it is that rejection on the part of the love-object is felt as a very severe narcissistic injury and is experienced by many neurotics directly as castration." The parallel process in the girl is less understood. Woolf concluded that, for the small child in the oral phase, the fetish represents a substitute for the mother's breast and body; for the adult fetishist, it represents a substitute for the fantasized missing phallus of the mother. In infantile fetishism, the process of development into complete autoerotism after weaning is apparently disturbed by a tenacious adherence to the maternal breast. This is also probably an important etiological factor in adult fetishism.

Among Woolf's many papers on clinical aspects of the neuroses, one of the most important and oft-cited is "An Interesting Oral Symptom Complex and Its Relation to Addiction" (1932). Here, Woolf has described five patients, one man and four women, suffering from a circumscribed symptom-complex that consisted of craving for food, dull depression and apathy, disgust concerning their own bodies, neglect of outer appearances, disorderly surroundings, and excessive need for sleep. This symptom-complex appeared with great uniformity and a certain periodicity. After its disappearance, a short period of fasting tended to occur, accompanied by euphoria and a feeling of inner cleanliness. Rather than a typical neurosis, this seems to be a symptom complex of pathological phenomena consisting of certain changes in important biological functions likely to appear in different types of neurosis. The craving for food was an expression not of a compulsion but of addiction, of "drivenness." Consequently, a feeling of tension, rather than anxiety, appeared when the patients tried to suppress the drive to eat.

Case five may serve as an example: Because of disappointment in her father, a woman, had from her thirteenth year, developed platonic relationships with men, frequently changing the object of these relationships. As a token of love, she asked for sweets. At sixteen, she married, on the condition that she would not have to submit to intercourse. When, after waiting three months, the husband forced intercourse, she reacted with disgust and once more began to have relations with other men, without actual intercourse. In the presence of a lover, she would be seized by an uncontrollable ravenous hunger and have to leave the room, in order to eat secretly. After satiation, she would lose all interest in the lover. Her eating appears to be a sexual perversion, the food taking on the unconscious meaning of the penis. These periods of greedy eating were interrupted (as they were also for the other four patients) by short periods of fasting, during which she had no need for lovers.

Woolf concluded that the superego reacts with disgust and despair to the oral drive. First, disgust for the dirty food, which represents a dirty penis, appears; then, disgust spreads to the patient's own dirty body, because an identification of the body with the introjected penis has taken place. This identification leads to a deepening of the depression. However, this symptom complex does not belong to melancholia, despite certain similarities. Rather, in food addiction, a regression takes place whereby the patient tries, through introjection, to rebuild the object relations on the primitive oral level. The melancholic, on the other hand, wants to destroy the hated object, but reacts with refusal to eat, thus giving way to the pressure of the superego. In the state of fasting and euphoria, the ego submits to the superego, whereas, in the state of mania, the ego frees itself from the supergo. The counterpart of food addiction appears to be *anorexia nervosa.*

Another important clearly formulated, but less known paper is "Concerning the Hysterical Attack" (1933). It is of interest that the rigid and orthodox editors of the *Zeitschrift,* refused at the time to publish the paper on the grounds that it deviated from Freud's acknowledged opinion on the subject. They accepted the paper for publication only after they were convinced that, following a lively discussion between the two men, Freud had asked Woolf to write the paper. According to Freud the hysterical attack represents a pantomimed fantasy enacted by the motor system. Woolf found that real events are equally represented in the attack. After having dealt with aspects of the psychic content of the hysterical attack, he tries to come to a genetic understanding of the form of the attack. He arrives at the conclusion that the attack expresses a deep regression of the mental processes to the earliest and most primitive form of thinking, which is interpreted as organic thinking: it relies on kinaesthetic sensations and experiences. This organic thinking expresses itself in motor language and is part of the normal way of reaction in earliest childhood, before the system consciousness has learned to control motility. However, the enacting of old fantasies and events in the hysterical attack is not confined to the motor system, but comprises the sensory system as well. Old sensory perceptions may be revived hallucinatorically and are apt to be transformed—together with recent perceptions—into illusions. This medley of hallucinations, illusions, and actual perceptions, which appear together in the hysterical attack, corresponds to a very early developmental stage of the perceptive functions in which inner stimuli are not yet differentiated from outer ones.

In "A Case of Male Homosexuality" (1941), Woolf described what had been an unknown psychic constellation, which may determine later homosexuality. This case is of an impotent married man, who had formerly indulged in masturbation, accompanied by homosexual fantasies. From his earliest childhood, the patient's mother had been sick, and she had died when he was four years old. He had then slept with his father, whose erect penis he had occasionally touched while the father slept. When the father remarried, the boy repressed his love for the father and turned instead to his new step-sister. She betrayed their sex play to his father, who punished him and threatened him accordingly. Consequently, he turned away from the step-sister, too, and, at the age of eight, seduced a boy of his own age into mutual masturbation. During this activity, he had fantasies of adults engaged in intercourse, identifying himself with the female partner. In this case, the first love object was the father, rather than the mother. Disappointed by the father's second marriage, the boy attempted heterosexual sex play with his step-sister. Frustrated and intimidated, he returned to the original homosexual phase in which he had identified, as a motherless boy, with the mother in relation to the father. Until publication of "A Case of Male Homosexuality," the known determinants of homosexuality had included early fixation to the mother, narcissism, castration anxiety, and early seduction. Here, mother fixation and narcissism are absent. Castration is accepted; therefore the patient is free of anxiety. In contradistinction to prior cases in the literature, the case presented by Woolf contained two formerly unrecognized elements—an early homosexual tie to the father and fear of the father.

In "On Castration Anxiety" (1955) Woolf discussed, and modified, Freud's thoughts on the subject. According to Freud, castration anxiety is reality anxiety because of the high value the little boy attributes to his genitals in the phallic stage. Later, in "Inhibitions, Symptoms and Anxiety," Freud referred to castration anxiety as separation anxiety. Fear of loss of love and separation anxiety are primary forces in repressing erotic impulses toward the mother. To safeguard the positive relationship to the mother, she is relinquished as a sexual object. Freud says that "If masturbation is continued, punishment will take the form of the loss or castration of the organ." "In this way, fear of separation from the mother can change into castration anxiety, even in those cases where castration has not been threatened." Woolf adds that "Castration anxiety is therefore separation anxiety displaced onto the penis, whence it now appears very like a neurotic symptom, with the structure of a phobia" (1927; 1951). If so, Freud's statement that the Oedipus complex succumbs to the threat of castration can no longer be upheld. Instead, Freud's earlier assumption, that the ontogenetic and phylogenetic influences on the emotional development of the child bring about the inevitable decay of the Oedipus complex, is probably correct. Freud did not acknowledge castration anxiety in girls, since there is no threat of castration; but if castration anxiety is a phobic symptom, as Woolf considers it, it can also occur in girls. According to Woolf's belief, it develops in girls through the displacement of the separation anxiety onto a new psychic contact—the imagined loss of the penis. Woolf's example is the case of a twenty-three-month-old girl: When separated from her mother she cries, "The dog has bitten off my wee-wee." As long as the mother is present, the lack of her wee-wee does not worry her. "This girl has developed a castration phobia." In the phallic stage, separation anxiety can be transferred from the mother to the father and to men in general. This can bring about fear of menstruation, defloration, orgasm, and giving birth, or heightened muscular tension of the abdomen, with ensuing constipation.

In "On the Psychology of Suicide" (1958), Woolf has discussed what brings about the destruction of the instinct of self-preservation, and how self-hate triumphs over healthy narcissism. Woolf analyzed examples from the literature and from his own clinical cases and arrived at the following conclusions: (1) An individual's wish to kill a beloved person with whom his ego has become identified, because that person has disappointed him, may lead to suicide, since his hatred toward that person has been transferred to his own ego. Suicide then replaces the murder of the object. (2) The normal reaction toward the loss of the object (mourning, which subsides gradually) does not take place in suicide, because the loss of the object leads to deep narcissistic mortification, with impairment of ego feeling, impoverishment of the ego, and inner emptiness, together with self-contempt and self-hatred. (3) Similarly, a strong narcissistic disappointment with one's own ego may lead to suicide as a result of self-contempt and self-hatred.

All of Woolf's clinical papers contain a great deal of rich material.

Other papers deal with cultural, sociological and anthropological topics. Outstanding amongst them is a highly interesting paper on "Prohibitions against the Simultaneous Consumption of Milk and Flesh in the Orthodox Jewish Law" (1945). Here Woolf gives analytic interpretations of the ritual laws applying to food as well as Passover laws, tracing them back to early historic and prehistoric times.

His scientific work is always based on clinical material. He is an empiricist like his teacher, Abraham.

Because Woolf did not live in Vienna, his contact with Freud was limited to occasional personal encounters and to a correspondence chiefly about the development and recognition of the psychoanalytic movement in Russia and translations of analytic literature into Russian. To this day, Woolf is happy if some obscure passage in Freud's writings becomes clear to him through new clinical findings and he can show that "Freud was right after all." Since he belonged to the first generation of analysts, Woolf did not undergo a personal analysis; however, he submits himself to daily self-analysis, from which he learns for his clinical work. Another even more important learning source for Woolf and the whole first generation of analysts was the regular publication of Freud's papers, each an eagerly awaited revelation. Woolf worked through Freud's writings so thoroughly that he knew them almost by heart. Even today, his knowledge of them is astonishing.

Having very early become a teacher and a fighting pioneer for the acknowledgment of psychoanalysis, Woolf exacts from his pupils clear and precise thinking. He is always at their disposal and gives generously of his knowledge and advice. He is a hard worker with an unfailing sense of duty and responsibility. His days and evenings are filled to the brim with analyses of patients and candidates, consultations, discussions, seminars, and supervision. In addition, he continues to write and is enthusiastic about new ideas and concepts that are striving for expression. Currently, he is responsible for the translation into Hebrew and the editing of Freud's nonclinical writings.

REFERENCES

Woolf, M. Beiträge zur infantilen Sexualität. *Zbl. Psychoanal. Psychother.*, 1912, 2, 6–17.

Woolf, M. Phantasie und Realität in der Psyche des Kindes. *Odessa* (Russian), 1926. (See also F. Lowtzky, *Imago*, 1927, 13, 129–130.)

Woolf, M. Phobie bei einem anderthalbjährigen Kinde. *Int. Z. Psychoanal.*, 1927, 13, 290–293. (See also *Int. J. Psycho-Anal.*, 1928, 9, 354–359.)

Woolf, M. Zur Psychologie der Kinderlaunen. *Imago*, 1929, 15, 263–282.

Woolf, M. Über einen interessanten oralen Symptomenkomplex und seine Beziehungen zur Sucht. *Int. Z. Psychoanal.*, 1932, 18, 281–302.

Woolf, M. Über den hysterischen Anfall. *Int. Z. Psychoanal.*, 1933, 19, 584–612.

Woolf, M. Phantasie und Wirklichkeit im Seelenleben des Kleinkindes. *Z. Psychoanal. Pädagog.*, 1934, 8, 306–318.

Woolf, M. Über einen Fall von männlicher Homosexualität. *Int. Z. Psychoanal.*, 1941, 26, 105–121.

Woolf, M. Prohibitions against the simultaneous consumption of milk and flesh in Orthodox Jewish law. *Int. J. Psycho-Anal.*, 1945, 26, 169–177.

Woolf, M. Fetishism and object choice in early childhood. *Psychoanal. Quart.*, 1946, 15, 450–471. (a)

Woolf, M. *Nefesh hayeled.* Israel: Sifriat Poalim, 1946. (b)

Woolf, M. The child's moral development. In K. R. Eissler (Ed.), *Searchlights on delinquency.* New York: International Universities Press, 1949. Pp. 263–272.

Woolf, M. The problem of neurotic manifestations in children of pre-Oedipal age. *Psychoanal. Stud. Child,* 1951, 6, 169–179.

Woolf, M. On castration anxiety. *Int. J. Psycho-Anal.*, 1955, 36, 95–104.

Woolf, M. Zur Psychologie des Selbstmordes. *Acta Psychother.*, 1958, 6, 317–326.

Abraham Arden Brill

1874–1948

FIRST AMERICAN TRANSLATOR OF FREUD

*

MAY E. ROMM

Brill was the American missionary and pioneer of psychoanalysis. He was the first psychoanalyst in the United States, and he was the first translator of Freud's writings—putting them at the disposal of the English-speaking public.

Abraham Arden Brill was born in Austria on October 12, 1874. He sailed alone to the United States at the age of fifteen. He was so naïve that during the trip he was defrauded of his meager funds. Thus, he arrived in the "land of golden opportunity" without a dollar in his pocket, knowing not a word of English, and without a friend to ease his poverty and loneliness. Somehow—in his native tongue and, doubtless, with gestures—he conveyed to the owner of a saloon his need for shelter and was given permission to sleep on the floor of the saloon in exchange for helping with some chores. Later on, as he learned the language, he taught English to foreigners for the munificent sum of twenty-five cents per lesson. He also taught mandolin.

Brill's situation improved when a physician befriended him, allowing him to sleep on the floor in his office. During this time, Brill taught billiards in pool parlors and frequently played chess, a game in which he excelled, for stakes. That he not only survived such inordinate vicissitudes but attained such heights in his professional, social, and personal life suggests that biology, as well as environmental factors, may play a role in man's development. Perhaps because he survived and triumphed over such a difficult background, Brill remained an optimist to his last breath. Although he frequently reminisced about his early days and hardships in this country, to my knowledge he never related the happenings of his childhood and adolescence to any of his friends.

It took Brill only three years in the United States to complete his elementary and high school education. From the time of his arrival until he acquired his medical degree from Columbia University College of Physicians and Surgeons in 1903, he worked at many jobs to support himself and pay for his tuition. There were painful times when lack of funds caused him to interrupt his studies. He would then work unceasingly, permitting himself only the bare necessities of life until he had saved enough money to resume them. Although understandably zealous to become a physician, Brill was even more determined to acquire an educational and cultural background before embarking on his professional career. Consequently, after graduating from New York City College in 1898, and before entering medical school, he obtained a scholarship from New York University and earned the Bachelor of Philosophy degree. Early in life, his father had inculcated in him the idea that he was destined to become a rabbi, a goal involving an inordinate amount of Talmudic study. By obtaining a good education and continually adding to his knowledge in a different, albeit related, field, Brill may have felt that he was in some measure carrying out his father's wishes.

After getting his medical degree, Brill spent four years working in Central Islip State Hospital, New York, with patients suffering from neurological and psychiatric disturbances. During this period, he carried on an extensive correspondence with Adolf Meyer, who influenced Brill to apply Meyerian therapeutic procedures with patients. The work was painstaking; an average case history covered twelve to sixteen pages—unusually long for state hospital records in those days. Not satisfied with the therapeutic results obtained with his psychiatric patients, Brill temporarily turned his attention to neurology. With his usual intense application, he rapidly learned enough to qualify as the hospital neuropathologist.

While learning neuropsychiatry, he read the psychiatric literature of Germany, Italy, and France. Not only did he master the languages, he translated a goodly number of foreign scientific papers into English. He was particularly interested in Kraepelin's studies and translated many of his works. Brill read everything available at that time on hysteria and other neuroses and concluded that the French offered him the best opportunities for further study. In 1907, he went to Paris, where he worked in the Hospice de Bicetre, under Pierre Marie. However, what was being taught there disappointed him, and, on the advice of Frederick Peterson, he went to Zurich to work in the Clinic of Psychiatry under the directorship of Eugen Bleuler.

Bleuler took notice of Brill and, when Karl Abraham resigned from the clinic to go into private practice, appointed Brill to fill the vacancy as third assistant. The technique there was based largely on Freud's psychoanalytic discoveries; the meaning and the dynamics of the patients' behavior and their verbal and nonverbal disclosures were utilized in the therapy. When Carl Jung, a senior staff member, analyzed one of Brill's dreams, Brill was greatly impressed. In addition to Bleuler and Jung, Brill became acquainted at the clinic with Karl Abraham, who was applying Freud's theories to the studies of psychosis.

In the process of gathering material and evaluating various techniques of psychotherapy, Brill was attracted by Forel's *hypnotismus*. He tried to apply hypnotism in cases of hysteria but soon gave this up. One particular experience, which Brill enjoyed recounting, may have influenced him in substituting other forms of psychotherapy for hypnotism: One of Brill's colleagues referred to him for hypnosis a male patient suffering from an involuntary spasmodic shriek—a cross between a hiccup and a shout—that occurred at frequent intervals. Brill attempted to hypnotize this patient, who resisted the command to fall asleep and continued to shake the office rafters with his strident noise. Since Brill had a tendency to lose his temper when thwarted, he turned to the patient and said, in a loud voice, "Shut up!" The man complied, and that was the end of the specific symptom. Brill then figured that, if he could produce a cure with a command instead of an hypnotic trance, hypnosis was not a very scientific method of psychotherapy.

Meeting Freud had the greatest impact on him. Brill was emphatic that his year in Switzerland was the turning point in his life—a spiritual rebirth. As he put it, the dynamic effect of the unconscious struck him like lightning. His admiration, veneration, and devotion to Freud engulfed every phase of his professional life, overflowing into his emotional life. At great financial sacrifice, he spent time in Vienna, where he and Freud would take long walks, discussing psychoanalysis, relating their dreams to each other, and analyzing them. This gave Brill the opportunity to grasp psychoanalysis at its original source. The correspondence between the two men continued until Freud's death. Brill often mentioned his great satisfaction in the thought that not only was he entrusted with the translation of Freud's works, but Freud had urged him to do so.

In 1908, Brill met Ernest Jones at Burghölzli, and together they attended the first International Psychoanalytical Congress in Salzburg. They traveled to Vienna and Budapest to visit Freud and S. Ferenczi. Both were dedicated to the task of spreading the knowledge of psychoanalysis—Brill in the United States, Jones in Canada.

Between 1908 and 1910, Brill was the only analyst in New York City—in fact, in the entire country. At that time, he had two pupils, James J. Putnam, a professor at Harvard University, and Smith Ely Jelliffe, who was credited by Freud and Brill with being the father of psychosomatic medicine. Jelliffe acknowledged that Brill made Freud and his writings vital and real to him.

On occasion, the quality of Brill's translations has been criticized. Although he was aware of criticism, with his usual intensity and discipline he continued his mission of offering Freud's work to the public in the English language. By 1924, he had translated ten of Freud's works and, in 1938, he published the *Basic Writings of Sigmund Freud*. Brill did not limit his translations to Freud's works; in 1909, he had translated Jung's *Psychology of Dementia Praecox*, and, in 1925, he edited the English edition of Bleuler's *Textbook of Psychiatry*.

In evaluating Freud's psychoanalytic concepts, Brill added a number of his own ideas, which he clarified through clinical examples from his practice. His empathic reaction to emotionally disturbed persons is clear in his statement that a disturbed sick individual is no more responsible for his symptoms—be they anxiety, perversions, or bizarre actions—than the victim of infantile paralysis is responsible for his malady. Although Brill occasionally contributed his own ideas and evaluations to the knowledge and teachings of Freud, on the major issues he agreed completely with the "master." He believed with Freud that, as a rule, the psychotic is unsuited for psychoanalytic treatment, because he cannot transfer sufficient libido to the analyst. Brill elaborated this view by saying that the psychotic is either too suspicious or too interested in his own inner world to pay any attention to the therapist. (This has since been proved erroneous; the psychotic is apt to develop an overly intense transference to the therapist.) Brill was also in full agreement with Freud's concept (also later disproved) that an individual who functions adequately sexually can under no condition develop a neurosis.

Brill was particularly interested in the dynamics of wit and humor. Slips of the tongue that expose the unconscious intrigued him. In relating them, he never spared himself if the slip concerned him. He enjoyed telling how a patient of his, whom he had charged an adequate fee, was once talking about a problem and, instead of saying, "It was a bitter pill to swallow," said, "It was a bitter bill to swallow." At the end of the therapeutic hour, Brill asked the patient whether his fee was a strain on him. The patient, amazed that Brill sensed the correct situation, admitted that he had difficulty in meeting the fee, which was promptly decreased. Brill evaluated wit as a conscious mechanism for the production of pleasure, labeling it "the highest development of civilized man." He felt that people like to tell jokes and to listen to them because in doing so, at least momentarily, they forget painful reality and obtain pleasure at the expense of either their own hardships or those of others.

According to Jones (1957, vol. 3, p. 38), Brill went through a painful emotional period in 1920, when he erroneously believed that Freud was displeased with him because of the unfavorable criticism his translations had received. When, through their correspondence, Freud became aware that Brill was crushed by the thought of his possible displeasure, he reassured Brill. It is interesting to note that, earlier, Jones had offered to help Brill improve his translations of Freud's works but had been rebuffed by Brill, whereupon Jones had commented to Freud that Brill's translations were inadequate. However, Freud had replied that he would rather have Brill as a good friend than as a good translator (Jones, 1955, vol. 2, p. 45). At no other time was Brill insecure in his relationship with Freud. He zealously continued to bring before the public the meaning of psychoanalysis, through lectures, debates, and teaching. He was a prolific writer, and his works are clear, concise, and illustrative.

Psychoanalysis: Its Theory and Application, which he wrote in 1912, was the first book on the subject of psychoanalysis in America. In 1921, he published *Fundamental Conceptions of Psycho-Analysis*, which was widely read by interested persons and served as a textbook for students. In 1944, he published *Freud's Contribution to Psychiatry*, which he presented in an interesting and original manner. This book included an account of Brill's own introduction to psychoanalysis. In 1946, he published a volume, *Lectures on Psychoanalytic Psychiatry*, which incorporated his own teaching experiences.

Among others, three of his manuscripts stand out as valuable scientific contributions. One is "Unconscious Insight: Some of Its Manifestations" (1929). There Brill designated neuroses and psychoses as fortresses erected to protect the patient from pain or displeasure. When an individual finds himself so blocked in his struggle with the outer world that he cannot function, an unconscious adjustment takes place that permits him to live with a minimum of effort. The price of the adjustment is illness. Brill considered a hypomanic or manic attack to be an unconscious reaction to a traumatic situation, disagreeing in this regard with Freud's explanation that a manic attack is "a typical psychic mechanism," and with Alexander's viewpoint that a manic attack is a form of bribe to the superego. Brill believed that the manic attack is an attempt to recapture the protective affect of the mother cathexis. According to Brill, the manic phase is a revolt of the ego that allows some tendencies of the id to come to the surface.

Brill had an intense interest in the dynamics of the functioning of schizophrenics; while working intensely with them, he came to the conclusion that their purposeless laughter is an active, unconscious defense mechanism. The schizophrenic fears and resists his feeling of helplessness and frustration and denies it to himself and to the world. His laughter is a cover-up for intense anger and deep sadness. As one of Brill's patients finally said, "When I wish to cry, I just laugh." In "Unconscious Insight: Some of Its Manifestations" (1929), Brill gives fascinating and clear clinical examples from his practice of the mechanisms of denial, projection, identification, and other methods used by the patient to avoid facing reality and to decrease inner pain.

In a paper written in 1932, "The Sense of Smell in the Neuroses and Psychoses," Brill contributed his knowledge of a subject about which very little had as yet been written. As a matter of fact, very little has since been added. He evaluated anthropologically the reaction to odors of human beings in the various cultures. He compared the olfactory sense of primitive people with children and adults in our civilization. Children are like the animals in making good use of their sense of smell. Usually they lose this sense to a great extent when they become adults; however, on occasion, an adult retains a hypersensitivity to odors. Brill quoted Bleuler, who claimed that smells are very rarely hallucinated. Brill agreed with Freud, who implied that, because of the connection between the sense of smell and the sexual instinct, the abandonment of pleasure in smell plays a part in the genesis of neurosis. Brill speculated that the sense of smell does not really atrophy but is repressed and functions on a nonconscious level. He suggested that the decrease of the sensitivity to smell may have started millions of years ago, when the human being assumed an erect posture and turned away from the earth.

In discussing the importance of perfumes in the lives of women, Brill mentioned the disagreeable origin of most perfumes, some of which come from undigested remnants of squids and octopuses found in whales and others from the sexual glands of the civet cat, musk ox, musk deer, and beaver. He referred to Havelock Ellis, who had pointed out that even perfumes made from flowers have a sexual origin, for flowers represent the mating period of plant life. Brill delighted in tracking down the origins of superstitions, and in this paper he stated his conviction that the ubiquitous superstitions about death following the advance of some specific bird or animal are based on the odor mortis that attracts them, implying, of course, that through their olfactory tracts these birds and animals sense the odor of deterioration in the individual shortly before he draws his last breath. Odors have always been used to please and appease the gods, as well as to drive away evil spirits. This is done through burnt offerings, which produce odors not relished by man. Brill concluded with his concept that the repression of pleasure in smell began at the dawn of civilization with the beginning of sex control and has continued ever since. With his usual candor and honesty, he admitted that he had once differed with Harry Stack Sullivan's belief that the prognosis of schizophrenics with olfactory hallucinations is invariably bad, but that, after further investigation, he had come to the conclusion that Sullivan was correct.

His interests within the psychiatric field included the study of the origin and meaning of superstition in relation to the functioning of individuals in our culture and among primitive peoples. He could hold an audience spell-bound when he discussed the effect of hexing on primitive people; he had collected a great deal of literature on deaths caused by this method.

In "The Concept of Psychic Suicide," Brill wrote that long before he received medical corroboration of "psychic suicide" in primitive people, he had become convinced that some of his own patients actually possessed the strange faculty of dying at will. Although psychic suicide is not as dramatic as hexing, once these patients give up the will to live, they silently and endopsychically proceed with the intensification of their conviction that they are dying, and become resigned to death.

Brill was fascinated by the fact that relatively intelligent and mature people take fortunetelling seriously and that others guide their lives by numerology, astrology, and like studies. He had a theory about fortunetelling: If a bright, intuitive person relates thirty to fifty statements in rapid succession to a total stranger, the "victim" invariably takes out the few ideas that apply to him, represses the others, and believes that he has received his money's worth in the evaluation of his qualities and in the hope offered him of an exciting future.

In "Reminiscences of Freud," Brill said that, although he was fully aware of Freud's advanced age and chronic illness of years' standing, he could not bring himself to accept the fact that death was imminent for his master. He related an incident from his early psychoanalytic career that demonstrates how completely Freud influenced him. He had complained to Freud that the burden of his work was heavy, expecting Freud to sympathize with him. Instead, Freud had looked at him and had said, "Well, you are young; you should not complain but act!" This was the last time Brill complained to anybody about the vicissitudes of his work. Perhaps more than anyone else Brill appreciated Freud's genius; nevertheless, he believed that, in the course of time, some of Freud's views would certainly be modified. Even so, he was convinced that the luster of the man and the glory of his great achievements would remain a permanent scientific milepost, whatever the future might bring.

Brill founded the New York Psychoanalytic Society in 1911 and was active in the formation of the American Psychoanalytic Association several months later. He was several times president of both organizations, and he attended practically all psychoanalytic meetings in New York and many in Europe. Brill never missed an opportunity to speak on psychoanalysis; always uppermost in his mind was his aim to educate the members of the medical profession in Freud's discoveries of the dynamics of emotional functioning, both in so-called healthy people and in persons suffering from emotional disturbances. He never weakened in his determination to win people over to Freud's concepts, especially in the field of sexuality.

I recall a meeting of the New York Society of Neurology and Psychiatry in the early thirties at which Brill referred to the importance of infantile sexuality in his paper. In discussing the paper, Bernard Sachs, at that time president of the Section on Neurology, said he could not accept Freud's ideas and concepts; poignantly Sachs declared he was under the impression, which he could not give up, that the penis was attached to the boy, whereas Freud and Brill were asking him to accept the concept that the boy was attached to the penis. There was a burst of applause—not because the audience agreed with Sachs, but because his graphic remark was so humorous. Brill applauded and laughed heartily. After the meeting, Brill had coffee with Sachs; probably his conversation included arguments to validate Freud's discoveries.

One of Brill's aims was to create academic recognition for psychoanalysis; he finally succeeded when he was appointed lecturer in psychoanalysis at Columbia University, in 1910. An appointment followed as clinical professor of psychiatry at New York University. In those days, most of the members of the faculty in psychiatry and neurology were opposed to many of Freud's concepts; they particularly resented the theory that sexuality plays an important role in human functioning. Brill never veered from his courageous determination to expound and teach what he believed so completely. He refused to modify his views to appease the powers-that-be in the academic echelon.

Brill never lost sight of the fact that he was essentially a physician; he took the Hippocratic oath literally and seriously. When asked about his specialty, he would reply that he was a psychiatrist who believed that psychoanalysis is a microscope for the study of the mind. He felt that, without the psychoanalytic contribution, psychiatry is descriptive and barren, offering the patient a haphazard and hopeless prognosis. He stressed his belief that only qualified medical people should be trained as psychoanalysts (1942). When questioned about the existing controversy among analysts, he would point out how difficult it is for an outsider to appreciate the patients, forbearance, and emotional self-denial that a psychoanalyst practices in his treatment of patients. He thought it small wonder that psychoanalysts, who, of necessity, pen up much tension during their dealings with patients, occasionally vent their aggression on their confreres. He would say, smilingly, that it is innocuous for psychoanalysts to call their colleagues crazy and gratuitously suggest that they need more personal psychoanalysis. With his usual wit, he would prognosticate that in due time every psychoanalyst would be a saint; until then, psychoanalysts will continue to be human.

In his introduction to *Basic Principles of Psychoanalysis*, Brill pointed out the broad aspects of his specialty—calling attention to the fact that not only does psychoanalysis deal with the exploration and treatment of emotionally disturbed human beings, but—through evaluation of the mysteries of dreams and the dynamics of wit, mythology, and fairy tales—it also throws much light on the history of civilization and on the development of philosophy and religion. Brill challenged the public to utilize the knowledge offered by Freud as a preventive measure against mental illness and as an addition to education in a number of fields.

Although dedicated to the pursuit of psychiatry and psychoanalysis in its manifold phases, Brill nevertheless managed to lead a rich personal and social life. In 1908, he married Rose K. Owen, also a psychiatrist, to whom he remained devoted until his last breath. Toward his two children, Gioia (named after Freud) and Edmund, he reacted with tender concern. He gloried in his grandchildren and frankly admitted that he adored them. On several occasions he told me with a twinkle in his eye that he did not follow the rules of the book in the handling of his grandchildren; he sheepishly admitted that he knew he was spoiling them, but that this was so much fun he could not resist it.

Brill was vitally interested in sports and took every opportunity to attend prize fights. Once, while he was describing with great gusto the particular round of a fight in which a skillful blow was inflicted by one of the contestants, I remarked that I found it difficult to understand how an intelligent and cultured person, particularly a psychoanalyst, could enjoy watching one human being inflict bodily injury—at times severe or even deadly—on another. I was unprepared for Brill's intense reaction: he informed me in no uncertain terms that, being a woman, I could not, or would not, understand how helpful prize fights are to an audience, allowing the observers to identify with the participants in the struggle for victory and thus releasing many ego-alien affects that otherwise might be used in a fashion detrimental to themselves or others. He practically told me that it is futile to attempt to explain to a woman the value to a male audience in watching a competitive sport. I could have given him a number of valid reasons for my viewpoint, but knowing from experience that Brill's anger and displeasure were short-lived, I let it pass. He was soon again his usual kind and warm self.

Although Brill did not revere the religion in which he found himself through an accident of fate, he never denied it. He knew Jewish history thoroughly, and at times talked with pride of Maimonides, Cordoza, and other great men of Jewish origin. He loved Jewish humor and Jewish food. Not infrequently, he would patronize Jewish restaurants on the East Side of New York and even would spend a few hours watching a Jewish play.

Brill had a large number of friends, who could always depend on his loyalty. He was an entertaining guest and an excellent host. The dinner parties he and his wife gave in their brownstone house were almost ritualistic: A very good dinner was served in the dining room downstairs. After dinner the men would remain seated around the table with their cigars and brandy; invariably the conversation was lively. Mrs. Brill and the other women would retire to an upstairs sitting room full of caged birds, where conversation took a less exciting form.

While a guest in my home, Brill once demonstrated facetiously how all-embracing psychiatry was for him; the conversation revolved about the personality make-up of the various persons present, most of whom were physicians, many psychiatrists. It became somewhat of a game for each person to identify the psychiatric group to which he himself belonged—whether schizoid, manic, or asthenic. Brill's turn came last. He thought for a while and then, in an emphatic tone, he announced that he belonged to the schizoid-manic group. This all-embracing trend was present in many phases of his life.

The statement that a busy man finds time to serve other people definitely applies to Brill. He was always ready and willing to see any person who wanted information about psychoanalysis, or any colleague who had problems or troubles. He freely offered help to one and all who reached out to him. He was particularly devoted to his students, and, even when he was past seventy years of age, he would return to his office Sunday evenings to interview students who applied for psychoanalytic training. Brill accomplished the foregoing despite the fact that he carried on an active practice, he taught consistently, and, in addition to writing several books, he produced well over 150 papers dealing with a wide variety of scientific problems. Most of his writings deal with psychiatry and psychoanalysis, but he also included amplified psychiatric topics and themes of general popular interest.

Brill's empathy toward human beings included his interest in the penal system. Somehow, he extracted time from his busy schedule to become a police surgeon. He gave lectures to the members of the Police

Department about the humane way of treating people who break the law. Brill stressed the relationship between psychopathology and criminal behavior, and he was instrumental in influencing the lawmakers to remove, insofar as possible, the stigma placed on homosexuals. Due to his efforts, homosexuals in the State of New York are no longer labeled criminals unless they seduce a minor or are guilty of sexual indecency in public.

Brill gave his wife a great deal of well-deserved credit for his success. She literally worshiped him and gave up the pursuit of her own medical career to devote all her time to her husband and her children. She approved of all his plans and at all times put his comfort and his preferences ahead of her own. Brill was fully aware of how fortunate he was in his choice of a mate.

Although Brill was definitely financially underprivileged until he was able to make his own living from the practice of psychiatry, at all times he was free with money and was flexible to a fault in what he charged for his time. In his opinion (which he voiced to me on several occasions), the emphasis placed by psychoanalysts on the patient's paying in person to the psychoanalyst as much as he can afford, and compulsively on time, reflects the subjective reaction of the psychoanalyst.

One of his therapeutic skills consisted in evaluating a patient *in toto*, taking into consideration his nonverbal as well as his verbal communication. I recall one hour of supervision with him, during which I mentioned that I was concerned about a woman patient I was treating, because she had several times threatened suicide. Brill asked me how the patient behaved when the therapeutic hour was concluded. I told him that, when she got up from the couch, invariably she powdered her nose and put on lipstick. His advice to me was, "Don't worry, she will not suicide." His prophecy was correct and, in time, she terminated her analysis successfully.

Brill's limitless energy was clearly demonstrated not only in his work but also in his favorite avocation. He made an intensive study of ornithology. Frequently he would get up at five o'clock in the morning and walk in Central Park, watching and evaluating the actions and habits of birds. His wife often joined him, and together they would spend hours getting first-hand information from what he called "his feathered friends." Brill's interest in music and literature gave him great pleasure. He frequently attended concerts. He read extensively, leaning toward writings on philosophy. He was greatly influenced by Spinoza, with whom he felt a spiritual kinship. Also, he had read widely in the Old Testament and the Talmud, from which he frequently quoted.

In 1933, Brill became the first chairman of the Department of Psychoanalysis within the American Psychiatric Association. Among the many honors conferred upon him, he was most pleased with the dedication of the Abraham A. Brill Library of the New York Psychoanalytic Institute, on December 16, 1947, at which time a bronze bust of Brill by the sculptor Olen Nemon was presented to him and placed in the library. Present at the ceremony were his wife, his children, and his grandchildren.

A few weeks before Brill died, representatives of a publishing house asked him to write his autobiography; however, he believed that this would be a complicated project, involving many prominent contemporary figures of the literary and artistic world as well as many of his colleagues. He feared it might assume the form of an exposé. On several occasions he confided to me that he literally had a "trunk full of letters" written to him by Freud. When I urged him to show or read some of them to me and perhaps publish them, he sadly refused; so many people were involved in the content of these letters, he felt it best they remain undisclosed.

In philosophizing about life and death, Brill stressed that, whereas it is most desirable to live adequately and courageously, this should not satisfy Homo sapiens. He pointed out that man must also meet death with fortitude and realistic acceptance, if his goal is self-esteem and the esteem of others. Many of his friends (myself included) noticed a definite change in him after Freud died. A good deal of his buoyancy, his enthusiasm, and his lust for life seemed to have evaporated. There was a sadness in him that he could not conceal. He told me that, when he was informed of Freud's death, some part of him also died. On the last few times that I saw him during my biannual attendance at psychoanalytic meetings, he repeatedly referred to his acceptance of the idea that life was running out for him. He died March 2, 1948, of a heart attack. His final illness lasted only several days, during which he expressed great concern for his family, his patients, and his students. He practiced what he preached. He lived fully and courageously, and he died without fear—giving of himself to the last minute of life.

REFERENCES

Brill, A. A. Unconscious insight; some of its manifestations. *Int. J. Psycho-Anal.*, 1929, 10, 145–161.

Brill, A. A. A psychoanalyst scans his past. *J. nerv. ment. Dis.*, 1942, 95, 537–549.

Jones, E. *Life and work of Sigmund Freud*. New York: Basic Books, 1953–1957. 3 vols.

Smith Ely Jelliffe

1866–1945

PSYCHOSOMATIC MEDICINE IN AMERICA

*

NOLAN D. C. LEWIS

Smith Ely Jelliffe, a pioneer in what is now termed psychosomatic medicine, was one of the most able and unique participants of his day in the disciplines of neurology and psychiatry. He was a man of wide and varied interests, of splendid mental endowments, of great vitality and persistent endeavor.

Jelliffe was born on October 27, 1866, in a brownstone house on West Thirty-eighth Street in New York City, and New York remained the center of his numerous activities for his entire life. He traced his ancestry to one "William," who came from Normandy, bringing a Joli or Jolif with him. In this line there was a certain priest and schoolmaster named Thomas Jolyffe, and so, down to Jelliffe's grandfather, a hatmaker in Danbury, Connecticut. His father, William, a teacher, was born in Darien, Connecticut. The elder Jelliffe became a principal in one of the public schools of Brooklyn.

After graduating from Brooklyn Polytechnic in 1886, Smith completed the medical degree at the College of Physicians and Surgeons, in New York. In 1894, he married Helena Dewey Lemming, whom he had known since childhood. They had three daughters and two sons. After her death, he married Bee Dobson.

Around 1896, Jelliffe's interests began to turn to psychology and clinical problems. He spent the summer of that year at the New York State Hospital at Binghamton, where he met William A. White, then a member of the staff. White was destined to exert a strong influence on Jelliffe's thinking and subsequent career. I once heard Jelliffe remark, "White and I have written and published so many things together that I am not at all certain when I quote from one of them whether to say 'White and Jelliffe,' or 'Jelliffe and White.' "

His first recorded publication, "List of Plants of Prospect Park" (1890) revealed his interest in botany. During the following fifteen years he published a total of eighty-two articles on various subjects: forty-eight of these—more than half—were in the field of descriptive botany or pharmacognosy of a variety of drugs of vegetable origin.

In 1899, Jelliffe wrote three books and twelve papers; he also became the associate editor of the *Journal of Nervous and Mental Disease*. His concentration of interest in this field probably should be dated from that period, for, in 1902, he became managing editor of the *Journal*, and, from 1900 to 1905, he wrote five books and twenty-seven papers covering a broad area of neurology and psychiatry.

At first, Jelliffe was not seriously impressed with psychoanalysis. In 1907, he attended the International Congress of Psychiatry and Neurology in Amsterdam, where he met C. G. Jung and listened to the actively open controversy between Jung, who at that time was a Freudian, and Hoche, who opposed him. Soon after this, Jelliffe became gradually more interested in psychoanalysis, but he was still in some doubt and not too enthusiastic, if one may judge from letters written to White from Austria, in March 1909.

By 1913, Jelliffe had become an active participant in the psychoanalytic movement. In this year, in the face of discouraging advice and many uncertainties, he and White launched the first psychoanalytic journal in English, *The Psychoanalytic Review*, which has been a potent force in spreading psychoanalytic information in America. Before the *Review* was created, Jelliffe, as editor of the *Journal of Nervous and Mental Disease*, was making some changes in the scope and contents of the *Journal*. He later wrote (1939):

> But all was not well with some of the older organic neurologists, especially as psychiatric material was given more and more notice, and more particularly since 1910, when psychoanalytic views, introduced from time to time, began to irk, even to irritate, the older solons of neurology and psychiatry. Some effort was made to mollify certain of the more outspoken op-

ponents to the Freudian conceptions. Thus I took out most of the psychoanalytic material and in 1913 with Dr. William A. White started our *Psychoanalytic Review*. But apparently this separate and independent venture only added insult to injury, and your very patient spokesman was actually threatened by the reigning patriarchs that "they would ruin the journal—withdraw their approval." They tried but were not successful, and it continued to grow.

Also in 1913, Jelliffe published a number of papers on psychoanalytic technique, on daydreams, and on transference. Between that time and 1937, his published contributions amount to 400 items. They cover a vast area of neurology, general psychiatry, psychoanalysis, and general literature, difficult to classify.

So far as I can determine, Jelliffe first personally met Freud in August 1921. Jelliffe wrote to White from Bad Gastein, Austria:

> He was very nice to me, and we spent the afternoon talking about everything. He was taller and larger than I had pictured him—heavier with a distinct stoop. The precise discussion of many points was not reached, but he had a fine stroke and cut into things very sharply and clearly. Bergson, he says, he does not understand. The indeterminism of pragmatism leaves him too uncertain, hence his Platonic-Kantian absolutism. As for Adler he has little use. Jung's recent material—particularly the prospective function of the dream—he called "trash," and he was content with the activities of his many pupils. He was very much interested in our organic work and told me of one of his pupils in Baden-Baden who was carrying on quite a similar type of analyses and with the same ideas we have been working on.

Jelliffe accepted everything that Freud said in general, but frequently he used these concepts in different, original settings. In the psychoanalytic movement in America, he not only contributed much general material of value, but he was a pioneer in the application of psychoanalytic knowledge and research in somatic diseases. Freud appreciated Jelliffe's work in this particular field, as well as in psychoanalysis in general. From time to time in the past, I have heard statements from psychoanalysts to the effect that "Jelliffe was not a Freudian analyst." Whatever Jelliffe's position may have been, the following previously unpublished letters selected from a rather large correspondence between them will show what Freud thought: Freud was not one to throw "bouquets" when he considered "clubs" were indicated.

A letter dated October 2, 1933, from Berggasse 19, reads:[1]

[1] Translated from the German.

DEAR DR. JELLIFFE:

What you sent me was indeed of the greatest interest to me. It is one more bit of that medicine of the future for which you are preparing the way.

The next issue of the *Internationale Zeitschrift* will contain an article by the German internist Weizsäcker—another contribution to what I believe you term Holism. I have learned to appreciate you, the multitude of your interests and the abundance of your knowledge, your freedom of thought, and your worth as one of the strongest supporters of analysis in America.

I am sorry to hear that you are troubled with an impairment of your hearing. Indeed, since my operation in 1923, I have only one ear at my disposal. The other still holds out; but to grow as old as I now have become makes things easy for the Death Instinct.

You will no longer expect of me numerous contributions to science, nor important ones, even if I should live a while longer. (My father and oldest brother died between the ages of 81 and 82.) However, I shall not cease to rejoice when other workers follow up the *Anregungen* which I have been able to give.

With many hearty greetings,
IHR FREUD

Freud wrote (in English) from London, on August 23, 1938:

DEAR DR. JELLIFFE:

Thank you so much for your kind words of sympathy. I am happy to be here after my experience in what is now Germany. Looking forward to the proofs you announce, I hope you are sure of all the assistance I can give you without influencing your judgment. I feel hurt by the behavior of American Analysts in the matter of Lay-Analysis. They, it seems, are not very fond of me. But this does not affect my relation to you, which is to remain undamaged.

Hoping you will be all right for a long time to come:

Yours sincerely,
FREUD

In October of 1938, Freud wrote, in English, from Maresfield Gardens, London:

DEAR DR. JELLIFFE:

Here I am at last settled in relative security, glad to have escaped the furor teutonicus, waiting for patients who so far have not arrived. I have overcome another of my habitual operations and am still fit to work.

Among the immigrants in New York there is one man, Dr. Jekels, not only a distinguished analyst but also a very good friend of mine. I would like to hear that you can do something to ease his situation by sending him patients, etc.

You promised to send me some proofs of an essay of yours in which I should be interested.

Yours with kind regards,
SIGM. FREUD

I find a final letter written in English in February, 1939 (the year of Freud's death), which reads:

DEAR DR. JELLIFFE:

Thanks for your highly interesting paper. No comments on my side forthcoming. I know you have been one of my sincerest and staunchest adherers through all these years. I now often laugh in remembrance of a bad reception I once gave you at Gastein because I had first seen you in company of Stekel.

A remark of yours saying that psychoanalysis has spread in U.S. more widely than deeply struck me as particularly true. I am by no means happy to see that analysis has become the handmaid of psychiatry in America and nothing else. I am reminded of the parallelism in the fate of our Vienna ladies, who by exile have been turned into housemaids serving in English households.

Yours with kindest regards,
SIGM. FREUD

It is well known that opponents of psychoanalysis were legion in the early days. Their arguments were usually demolished when they attacked Jelliffe's presentations in any meeting in which he discussed or read a paper. He could be very rough on opponents, as he always seemed to be well loaded with pertinent literature, of which he had a truly vast knowledge and memory; therefore he was more than a match for the average critic. As a journal editor, he had the advantage of having at hand a wide variety of American and foreign exchange journals, other scientific material, and books for review.

His list of personal publications from 1890 to 1902 includes sixty-seven works on clinical medicine and a variety of scientific subjects. With the passing years, he ventured ever deeper into the problems of psychosomatic relationships. As early as 1920 through 1922, he published papers on multiple sclerosis and psychoanalysis.

Among his early productions in psychosomatic medicine, one finds an article written with Elida Evans, "Psoriasis as an Hysterical Conversion" (1916); it is considered by some as the beginning of the trend. In successive years, there are "The Vegetative Nervous System and Dementia Praecox" (1917); again, with Elida Evans, "Psychotherapy and Tuberculosis" (1919); "Multiple Sclerosis, the Vegetative Nervous System and Psychoanalytic Research" (1920); "Psychopathology and Organic Disease" (1922); and "The Old Age Factor in Psychoanalytic Therapy" (1925). In 1926, Jelliffe published two outstanding articles: "Post-encephalitic Respiratory Disorders" and "Psychoanalyse and Organische Störung" (in *Internationale Zeitschrift für Psychoanalyse*, and, one year earlier, "Somatic Pathology and Psychopathology." This trend grew stronger, resulting in "The Mental Pictures in Schizophrenia and Epidemic Encephalitis" (1927). Shortly thereafter, he published "Oculogyric Crises as Compulsion Phenomena in Postencephalitis" (1929); and, ten years later, the book, *Sketches in Psychosomatic Medicine* (1939), containing a number of his former papers. From 1926 through 1932, no less than nine articles are listed on the psychopathological aspects of various postencephalitic syndromes alone.

As early as 1922, Jelliffe had begun to point out that medicine should take into account how forms of introversion, self-absorption, and rumination over one's own past initiate and maintain derangements in the deep layers of nervous activity within the physicochemical metabolic functions and organs of the body; how symbolic, in turn, these are of the very psychic factors that become the motivation of the physical phenomena; and how some organ or organs must bear the brunt of a continually precipitated conflict of unconscious origin. As A. A. Brill wrote (1947):

> Jelliffe is the father of psychosomatic medicine, and it is pleasing to know that Freud always gave him due credit for it. In those days it was a very dark realm for one to plunge into; but psychosomatic medicine, of which he was the American pioneer, was only a by-product of Jelliffe's striving to

establish a monism of body and mind. Endowed with a broad education, a searching mentality, a prodigious memory and a daring personality, Jelliffe had the proper equipment to venture into what he called *paleopsychology* (or paleology of the mind). He applied to the mind the methods naturalists such as Darwin and Haeckel did to the body. To be sure, a number of psychiatrists have sensed the influence of the psyche on the body and have . . . described it, but it remained for Jelliffe to demonstrate it by convincing case material.

However, Jelliffe was not at all satisfied with what he had learned concerning psychological determinants of somatic pathology and symptomatology. Although Jelliffe was an excellent neurologist, he felt that he suffered some handicap in not having a more intimate and detailed knowledge of general somatic pathology. I remember that, during one of our evenings together, he remarked, "Lewis, I feel that I could have made more headway with psychosomatic problems if I had had more basic training and experience in pathology." In 1923, he wrote, "An organ is a piece of structuralized experience and tissue memories": for him this became a sort of slogan to which he frequently referred throughout the subsequent years. In the field of psychosomatic medicine, he was frequently accused of presenting "only half of the truth"; however, it was likely to be the "half" that his critics had not previously recognized.

Jelliffe thoroughly enjoyed his fairly frequent *Wanderjahre* in Europe. During the 1908–1909 *Wanderjahre*, his letters and later conversations referred often to Theodor Ziehnen, Emil Kraepelin, Heinrich Oppenheimer, Paul Flechsig, Gabriel Anton, Hugo Liepmann, Paul Vogel, George Dreyfuss, Ludwig Merzbacher, Max Nonne, and Felix Lewandowsky.

During his 1921 trip to European centers, he wrote freely of his visits to, and his impressions of, the work and ideas of Robert Bing, Constantin von Monakoff, Eugen Bleuler, Carl Jung, Oskar Pfister, Ernst Strumpell, Hans Jacob, Giovanni Mingazzini, August Wimmer, Wilhelm Weygandt, Gottfried Foerster, Paul Schuster, Emil Kraepelin, August Kramer, Gustav Specht, Ernst Rüdin, Walther Spielmeyer, Karl Bonhoeffer, Hans Tandler, Hans Eppinger, Otto Pötzl, Sigmund Freud, Otto Rank, Wilhelm Stekel, Hans Silberer, Edward Hitschmann, Ernest Jones, and S. A. K. Wilson.

In Jelliffe's 1926 European period, he wrote much of Otto Marburg,

Julius Wagner von Jauregg, Joseph Gerstmann, and Paul Schilder. Concerning Jung he wrote:

> Jung is looking fine. He was very nice and cordial except when I read a part of my paper on Paleopsychology. He made quite a fuss about mixing physiology and psychology, mind and matter, body and mind, objective and subjective, and individual and environment. The things we have come to think of in terms of complements, he insists on regarding as separate—especially physiology and psychology, which he seems to think have nothing to do with each other. I really couldn't understand him on this score. The idea of the symbol as an energy container Jung accepts in principle but will not follow. As a consequence I think he is quite tired.

Nearly to the end of Jelliffe's life, he and Jung carried on an active correspondence—exchanging reprints and ideas, and discussing the various publications of others.

In attempting to evaluate and record the contributions of any individual to his professional field of activity, particular attention must be devoted to any influence he has had, or may have had, upon those whose lives or interests he has touched and stimulated, as a teacher, writer, or by personal service.

As editor, beginning in 1902 and throughout the rest of his life, he maintained the oldest journal of neuropsychiatry in this country, the *Journal of Nervous and Mental Disease*, a journal rather unique in that, along with articles from the most noted authors, it fosters the creative and expressive abilities of young, deserving workers whose offerings have been rejected by less sympathetic editors of professional journals. His co-editorship with W. A. White of the *Nervous and Mental Disease Monograph* Series, which was started in 1908, afforded him numerous contacts and an ever-widening scope of activity. By 1939, sixty-four of these monographs had been published, and a glance at a list of the famous contributors shows the sweep of interest. Among the early monographs, one finds Jung's *Psychology of Dementia Praecox*, Brill's translation of *Freud's Selected Papers*, Freud's *Three Essays on the Theory of Sexuality*, Sadger's *Sleep Walking and Moon Walking*, Maeder's *Wish Fulfillment and Symbolism in Fairy Tales*, Rank's *Myth of the Birth of the Hero*, Kraepelin's *General Paresis*, and André-Thomas' *Cerebellar Functions.*

Jelliffe made many acquaintances in foreign lands, not only by his frequent visits but also by a truly prodigious correspondence with scientific workers everywhere. During my own travels, when visiting professors in European universities, after the first words introducing me as an American, I was often greeted with the question, "How's Jelliffe?" The success of his editorial ventures was due, at least in part, to the fact that he knew personally and counted among his friends so many pioneers—the initiators and exponents of our present psychiatric and neurological theories and practices as they have developed in the active medical centers of the world, who were willing to co-operate with and contribute to his various projects.

Concerning his literary ability, had Jelliffe, with his many talents, chosen to devote himself exclusively to a literary career, he certainly would have attained fame as an essayist, a critic, or a novelist, and possibly as a dramatist. Jelliffe's historical and literary contributions can be roughly arranged in three groups or categories: (1) accounts of his journeys abroad—delightfully told and abounding in shrewdly recorded meetings with the leading psychiatrists and neurologists of his time, their laboratories and medical schools; (2) papers on purely historical research; and (3) his psychiatric interpretations of certain literary classics.

In the light of what I have already said regarding Jelliffe's activities, it should not be necessary to stress his love for books. He accumulated one of the largest private professional libraries in the country. Books overflowed his country place on Lake George, New York, as well as his town house in New York City. These books, about 12,000 of them, included treatises on general science, mathematics, botany, drama, art, and fiction, as well as volumes on neurology, psychiatry, and general medical subjects.

Jelliffe's early botanical studies gave him insight into the value of order, which he continued to express in his best-known contributions, and which is shown so clearly in his delineation of three levels of function, namely, the vegetative, the neuromuscular, and the symbolic. He called the nervous system the "master spirit in evolution." Adolf Meyer wrote of him (1939):

> Neurology to him spelled *action*, and what remained to too many an unknown and shunned world, he early saw as a *world of symbols* used for the plan and the direction of both action and vegetation.

He could not be limited to one aspect of the body or to any one concept of the mind, but was always reasonably open to new concepts.

However, he usually expressed himself in unmistakable positiveness.

It is conceded by all who knew him that Jelliffe was a rare individual, an example of a relative unpredictability in the midst of a steady output of literary activity. As his friend Foster Kennedy put it,

> His great attribute was zest. He had to drive right on, carried forward in time on the succeeding waves of every new idea—a powerful, vigorous, emotional man, with color that radiated every assembly in which he sat.

Jelliffe lived a full active social life, enjoyed good food and drink, and was such a witty conversationalist that, at various medical society dinners, I often noted considerable competition among his colleagues to obtain a seat at his table. He was handicapped by auricular fibrillation, which existed over an unusual number of years for such a condition, and in later years also by a slowly developing Paget's disease of the skull, which eventually took heavy toll on his hearing. In the last few years of his life, he suffered from a fluctuating impairment of memory and some confusion of thought, but despite these serious difficulties, on his "good days" he was an enjoyable companion to the end, which came at the age of seventy-eight.

His philosophy of life and living is contained in a statement in *Psychoanalysis and the Drama* (1922):

> There are two things which mark the complete success of man; his capacity for adapting himself to the demands of external life and that for living out satisfactorily his own inner self. In these is to be found the measure of health within himself individually and without himself, that is in his full moral relationship to Society . . . the function of life is to live more abundantly. Every agency created by life should be a servant to this end. Literature is not the least of such agencies, providing as it does interpretation of the hidden meanings of life and giving ever new groupings of the forces of life for the carrying out of the great function.

He lived for all that life was worth and enjoyed it thoroughly. Beyond any changes that may come from human endeavor and human institutions, the work and spirit of every great man live forever in the records of time.

REFERENCES

Brill, A. A. In memoriam: Smith Ely Jelliffe. *J. Nerv. ment. Dis.*, 1947, **106**, 221–227.

Jelliffe, S. E. The vegetative nervous system and dementia praecox. *New York Med. J.*, 1917, **105**, 968–975.

Jelliffe, S. E. Multiple sclerosis, the vegetative nervous system and psychoanalytic research. *Arch. Neurol. Psychiat.*, 1920, **4**, 593–603.

Jelliffe, S. E. Psychopathology and organic disease. *Arch. Neurol. Psychiat.*, 1922, **8**, 639–651.

Jelliffe, S. E. The old age factor in psychoanalytic therapy. *Med. J. Rec.*, 1925, **121**, 7–16.

Jelliffe, S. E. The mental pictures in schizophrenia and in epidemic encephalitis, etc.; a point of view. *Amer. J. Psychiat.*, 1927, **6**, 413–421.

Jelliffe, S. E. Oculogyric crises as compulsion phenomena in postencephalitis; their occurrence, phenomenology, and meaning. *J. Nerv. ment. Dis.*, 1929, **69**, 59–68, 165–173, 278–287, 415–420, 531–539, 660–679.

Jelliffe, S. E. Sketches in psychosomatic medicine. *Nervous and Mental Disease Monograph* Series. Washington & New York: Nervous and Mental Diseases Publishing Company, 1939. No. 69. (a)

Jelliffe, S. E. The editor himself and his adopted child. *J. Nerv. ment. Dis.*, 1939, **89**, 545–589. (b)

Jelliffe, S. E., & Louise Brink. *Psychoanalysis and the drama*. New York: Nervous & Mental Disease Publications, 1922.

Jelliffe, S. E., & Elida Evans. Psoriasis as an hysterical conversion symptom. *N.Y. med. J.*, 1916, **104**, 1077–1086.

Jelliffe, S. E., & Elida Evans. Psychotherapy and tuberculosis. *Amer. Rev. Tuberc.*, 1919, **3**, 417–428.

Meyer, A. Remarks. *J. Nerv. ment. Dis.*, 1939, **89**, 405–408.

Victor Tausk

1877–1919

THE INFLUENCING MACHINE

*

MARTIN GROTJAHN

AND

HANS A. ILLING

§ A Life in Search

Victor Tausk was born in Croatia—now a province of Yugoslavia, but at that time a part of the Austro-Hungarian empire. He studied law and was appointed judge in a small town in Bosnia. For unknown reasons, which Sigmund Freud later called a "very serious personal experience," he abandoned the practice of law and settled in Berlin as a reporter. From there, he moved to Vienna. Tausk took psychoanalysis so seriously that he changed professions for a third time and studied medicine. A year before the outbreak of World War I, he obtained a medical degree, in addition to the law degree he already held.

During World War I, Tausk became a high-ranking medical officer in the Imperial Austrian Army. On March 7, 1919, less than a year after the Armistice, he ended his career by suicide at the age of forty-two. Freud wrote to Lou Andreas-Salomé that poor Tausk, whom she had honored with her friendship, had ended his life. He had returned from war exhausted, worn out by its horrors. While trying to build up a new life under most unfavorable conditions in Vienna, he also had planned to include a new wife, whom he was to marry eight days later. In his farewell letters, written minutes before his suicide, he addressed his bride-to-be, his first wife, and Sigmund Freud. The notes are all tender and reaffirm his contact with reality. His decision to end his life, Tausk attributed to his "inadequacy and failure."

In his obituary, Freud described Tausk (whom he had once viewed with suspicion as "a wild man") as "intensely conscientious," and attributed to him a strong sense of observation, sure judgment, and special clarity of expression. In his letter to Lou Andreas-Salomé, who had been an intimate friend of Tausk, Freud made an attempt to understand the "problem of Tausk's personality." In answer to Freud, Lou Andreas-Salomé wrote (1958, p. 189):

> Poor Tausk. I was so fond of him. I thought I knew him well, and yet I never, never thought it would be suicide. . . . Had he chosen a weapon, then I could have imagined that his death was that of one who is simultaneously an aggressive and a passive person. For this was the *Tauskproblem,* its danger, which also was its stimulus; even in such a *strong* character, everything remains the impotence of a midget facing the inner giant of immoderation.

§ The Influencing Machine

It is rare in the history of psychoanalysis that a man secures his place in the annals of psychoanalytic research through the publication of a single major paper. Victor Tausk is perhaps the only analytic pioneer to have done so. The same year that saw Tausk's life end suddenly at the age of forty-two, 1919, also witnessed the publication of his famous paper, "On the Origin of the 'Influencing Machine' in Schizophrenia" (1933). Together with Freud's psychoanalysis of the Schreber Case of 1911 (1953, Vol. 17), this contribution opens the doors to the psychoanalytic study of psychosis. A third paper, on an equally high level, stands in close relationship to Tausk's; written at approximately the same time by Hanns Sachs, it is entitled, "The Delay of the Machine Age" (1933). Tausk's paper applies his general ideas that, in reality and illusion, machines are man's unconscious projection of his body image into the outer world.

When Robert Fliess chose Victor Tausk's work for inclusion in *The Psychoanalytic Reader,* his anthology of essential contributions to analysis, he said in introduction (1946, p. 53):

Yet the paper violates almost all pedestrian standards for publication. Much of the text is contained in footnotes, no section can be given an adequate heading; and the paper cannot be abstracted without being practically rewritten.

According to Tausk, the symbol of the machine represents the patient's genitals. In this way, the schizophrenic's hallucination is like the dream of the neurotic, for Freud had discovered that, as a rule, complicated machines appearing in dreams represent the patient's genitals. Tausk found that the machines stand in the service of masturbatory fantasies—partly serving wish-fulfillment, but mostly denying the wish and embellishing it with psychotic symptoms. The persecutory influencing machine is a representation of the patient's genitals projected onto the outer world. In machine dreams, the sleeper often awakens after having dreamed of manipulating parts of the machine. It is the frequent complaint of the schizophrenic that the apparatus causes erections and drainage of semen and weakens potency.

Frequently, the influencing machine makes the patient see pictures. Often the machine becomes a "cinematograph," although, unlike typical visual hallucinations, the pictures are not three-dimensional. The schizophrenic believes that, under the control of one or many persecutors, the machine may work in the transmission of thoughts or in the elimination of feelings. He believes that this machine may produce motor phenomena in the body, erections, or seminal emissions that weaken the patient and deprive him of his potency. This may be accomplished by suggestion, hypnosis, magnetism, or some type of ray; it creates the sensation of being influenced. The feelings cannot be described because they are strange to the patient himself; they are harmful and persecutory.

Tausk described schematically the different phenomena that are produced by the influencing machine but that may occur without it. These are: (1) sensations of inner change, both in psychic and physical functions within various parts of one's own body; (2) feelings of abnormal sensations; (3) feelings of awareness of an originator, who may not be the patient himself; (4) feelings accompanied by hallucinatory projection of the inner occurrence to the external world, without awareness of an originator; (5) feelings of inner change accompanied by awareness of an external originator, as a result of identification; (6) feelings accompanied by projection of the inner occurrence to the outer world, and belief in an originator produced by paranoid mechanism; and (7) feelings of change attributed to the workings of the influencing machine manipulated by enemies.

Tausk assumed three stages in the history of the development of the influencing machine: (1) the sense of internal alteration produced by the influx of libido into a given organ (hypochondria); (2) the feeling of estrangement produced by rejection whereby the pathologically altered organs and their functions are so-to-speak denied and eliminated as something alien to the wholly or partially sound organs and functions accepted by the ego; and (3) the sense of persecution (paranoia somatica) arising from projection of the pathological alteration onto the outer world, (a) by attribution of the alteration to a foreign hostile power, and (b) by the construction of the influencing machine as a summation of some or all of the psychologically altered organs projected outward.

Tausk concluded that the "evolution by distortion of the human apparatus into a machine is a projection that corresponds to the development of the pathological process which converts the ego into a diffuse sexual being or into a genital, a machine independent of the aims of the ego and subordinated to a foreign will. It is no longer subordinated to the will of the ego, but dominates it."

The few other earlier writings of Tausk deal with the problems of repression, ejaculatio praecox, libido tonus, delirium tremens, depersonalization, catatonia, ideas of persecution, and problems of melancholia.

§ The "Tausk Problem"

Tausk's best memorial is provided by his own writings about schizophrenia; they keep his memory alive, as does the sad and devoted obituary by Freud. One additional close friend, Lou Andreas-Salomé, has tried to deal with the "Tausk problem," as she called it: in her memoirs (Leavy, 1964), which demonstrate so well her gift for friendship and empathy with many of the great and famous men of the time, she devoted several chapters to Tausk, who was her teacher and friend. When she came to Vienna to "go to school with Freud," he recommended that she attend Tausk's lectures. In 1912, Tausk was probably the first analyst aside from Freud to combine the simultaneous teaching of psychiatry and psychoanalysis. On Wednesday evenings, both teacher and pupil attended the discussions on psychoanalysis at Freud's home.

On November 19, 1912, Lou Andreas-Salomé wrote concerning Tausk's lectures: "In fact one gets the impression not only of classical Freudian theory but also of an unusually loving and reverent approach to the essential discoveries of Freud . . ." (Leavy, 1964, p. 51). A further entry in her diary, dated November 27, 1912, reads: "It seems to me that in comparison with all the others, Tausk not only adheres completely to Freud's views, but he surpasses the rest. Perhaps this is bound to result in a direct, mutual conflict." "I think that Tausk is of all the most unconditionally devoted to Freud and at the same time the most prominently outstanding" (Leavy, 1964, p. 57).

It is only a short distance from an obscure Croatian village to the Vienna of pre-World War I times, but it is a long journey from "a serious personal experience" to the trust and friendship of two such personalities as Sigmund Freud and Lou Andreas-Salomé. Tausk responded to this friendship and trust with one great contribution to psychoanalysis. Then, like a marathon runner, he fell.

REFERENCES

Andreas-Salomé, Lou. *In der Schule bei Freud, Tagebuch eines Jahres 1912–1913.* Zurich: Max Neihans Verlag, 1958.

Fliess, R. *The psychoanalytic reader.* Vol. 1. New York: Int. Univer. Press, 1946.

Freud, S. The complete psychological works of. . . . London: Hogarth Press, 1953–. 24 vols.

Leavy, S. A. (Trans.) *The Freud Journal of Lou Andreas-Salomé.* New York: Basic Books, 1964.

Sachs, H. The delay of the machine age. Margaret J. Powers (Trans.) *Psychoanal. Quart.*, 1933, 2, 402–424.

Tausk, V. On the origin of the "influencing machine" in schizophrenia. *Psychoanal. Quart.*, 1933, 2, 519–556.

BIBLIOGRAPHY

Grinstein, A. *Index of psychoanalytic writings.* Vol. 4. New York: International Universities Press, 1958.

Jones, E. *The life and work of Sigmund Freud.* Vol. 2. *Years of Maturity.* New York: Basic Books, 1955.

Peters, H. F. *My sister, my spouse.* New York: W. W. Norton, 1963.

Victor Tausk, a review. *Int. Z. Psychoanal.*, 1919, 7, 225–227.

Sandor Rado

b. 1890

THE ADAPTATIONAL THEORY

*

FRANZ ALEXANDER

Sandor Rado belongs to the second generation of psychoanalytic pioneers; however, his scientific career deviates from the usual in this group. Rado began as a thorough student of Freud and became the most lucid interpreter of the master's teachings—an unparalleled teacher of psychoanalysis. For many years he was editor-in-chief of *Internationale Zeitschrift für Psychoanalyse;* nevertheless, he developed into a constructive critic of traditional concepts and treatment procedures.

Rado is one of the few "reformers" who have remained in the psychoanalytic fold and tried to advance psychoanalysis from within the fraternity. The crowning achievement of his scientific career was the formulation of "adaptational psychotherapy," which he considered a logical step in thought development. According to Rado, "adaptational technique is an attempt to restore the line of development initiated by Breuer's patient" (1956, p. 357). Some of his colleagues feel that Rado has introduced unnecessary neologisms for phenomena for which psychoanalysis had already created traditionally sanctioned terms, for example, "hedonic self-regulation" for "pleasure principle," "nonreporting desire" for "unconscious trends," "an obedient child" for "positive transference," and many similar semantic innovations. This is probably the main reason for Rado's controversial position in the psychoanalytic community. His classification of some fundamental concepts would have had a greater effect on many of his colleagues had he remained content with sharpening definitions and classifications of traditional terms and abstractions rather than renaming them.

Sandor Rado was born in Hungary, in 1890. He started to study law, and received a degree in political science in 1911. Four years later, he obtained a medical degree from the University of Budapest. Very early, he was attracted by psychoanalysis, which had received an early start in Budapest under Sándor Ferenczi's leadership. In 1913, Rado had already become the secretary of the Hungarian Psychoanalytic Society. He functioned in this capacity for ten years, until he left Hungary for Berlin in 1923. Rado served as secretary of the German Psychoanalytic Society for four years, from 1926 to 1930, and as secretary of the International Training Commission of the International Psychoanalytic Association, from 1927 to 1935. Rado was again and again elected as secretary of various psychoanalytic organizations. From the first, Rado demonstrated his unusual organizational talent and leadership qualities, persuasiveness in debate, determination, and that amount of stubbornness that leadership requires. Due perhaps to his training in law, he became a formidable debater—usually succeeding in rapidly ferreting out the weak spots in his opponent's argument. In polemics, he was terse, to the point, logical to the utmost, and often devastating. Although this did not contribute to universal popularity, even his enemies respected his brilliant cognitive abilities.

It is perhaps no overstatement that Rado was and is a lucid scholar and a concise writer in his chosen field. Among his collected papers, none is longer than twenty pages—unusual for a psychoanalyst. Discursiveness may usually be taken as an indication of an author's unsuccessful struggle for clarity.

The aggressive, uncompromising debater is only one facet of Rado's personality. Those near to him know him as a basically warm human being and a loyal friend. Perhaps Rado is known best by his patients; as a therapist he is anything but a passive onlooker at the gradual self-realization of the patient's unconscious; he is the active, determined ally of the patient, whom he tries to help with his penetrating mind and outstandingly practical judgment. In treatment, this brilliant theoretician becomes the energetic advocate of those who have entrusted themselves into his care.

Why did Rado, whose bent of mind should have driven him toward the natural sciences, become a medical psychologist? Most therapists who have chosen psychoanalysis as their vocation are primarily distinguished by their intuitive psychological propensity, and excel in empathy rather than in precise reasoning. Many of the finest representatives of our field are akin to poets and novelists, in both focus of interest and creative ability. The combination of intuitiveness and precise reasoning is indeed rare; because the majority of analysts are not primarily "thinkers" but "empathizers," this field is in dire need of men who combine both faculties.

Rado's own autobiographical account is most revealing. As a ten-year-old schoolboy, Rado began to wonder why various people act so differently under like circumstances. "Since nobody could explain it to me, I looked up in the Hungarian encyclopedia first the article on the mind, them the one on the brain, but could not understand either." The formulation of this question presaged the future scientific investigator: he keeps one variable constant (the situation) to establish the effect of the second variable (the human factor in the equation). But first of all he turns to the existing literature.

When he was nineteen years old, Rado discovered Freud's work from a pamphlet by Ferenczi. He was elated. Here was a study of motivation, and what a method! Rado decided to study medicine as the nearest road to the object of his curiosity, to become a physician specializing in psychoanalysis. This was a rare decision indeed to make at the beginning of the century. Most of us drifted gradually toward psychoanalysis, either from the humanities or, as this writer did, from brain research. Rado knew at once what *he* wanted.

Rado introduced himself to Ferenczi, who was delighted to meet a young man, not yet twenty, who was thoroughly conversant with Freud's writings. Among present candidates for training in psychoanalysis, not many have read even a few of Freud's works. Even after accomplishing their four to five years of training, many psychoanalysts do not know Freud's writings as well as Rado did *before* he started his psychoanalytic career. Ferenczi encouraged Rado's plan to study medicine with a view toward eventual practice of psychoanalysis.

The reader may interject: "Is this prestudy of Freud's works good? Perhaps it is because of this thorough indoctrination by Freud—through reading everything that Freud wrote—that it took Rado more than twenty years to become an independent thinker in this field. Because of his relative ignorance of the old contributions, the contemporary student may be freer and more likely to advance the field." The validity of this argument is dubious. Only by repeating past thought developments thoroughly, step by step, does one become fully aware of the inaccuracies of older concepts, and ready to make revisions in established views.

Ferenczi and Rado became close friends, and the young student helped Ferenczi organize the Hungarian Psychoanalytic Society. The Society was typical of the early informal organizations, which consisted of a group of friends seeking to learn from each other. At Ferenczi's suggestion, Rado journeyed to Vienna to attend one of Freud's weekly lectures at the Medical School of the University of Vienna; Freud's topic was the interpretation of dreams. He spoke for two hours without a note. In content, organization, and form, the lecture was fit to be printed without change. However, Freud made at least a dozen slips of the tongue during the lecture, and played almost incessantly with one of the rings he wore, turning it around and around on his finger. "Voilà!" Rado thought, "The knowledge of mental mechanisms does not protect the knower from being victimized by them." This observation "taught him a lesson for good."

In the Fall of 1918, a few weeks before the end of World War I, Freud came to Budapest to attend the International Psychoanalytic Congress. As secretary of the Hungarian Society, Rado served as Congress Secretary, a job that secured him some official contact with Freud. In addition, members of the Hungarian group had several informal meals with Freud, which provided ample opportunity for conversation and discussion. Rado began to know Freud, the human being.

In the Fall of 1922, Rado went to Berlin to be analyzed by Karl Abraham. He was immediately invited to join the faculty of the Berlin Psychoanalytic Institute and taught there from 1922 to 1931. He had an active role in devising the curriculum, which served for decades as a model for the rapidly multiplying institutes. In 1924 Freud appointed Rado managing editor of the *Internationale Zeitschrift für Psychoanalyse*, and three years later, managing editor of the *Imago* as well.

In the Fall of 1931, on the invitation of A. A. Brill, then president of the New York Psychoanalytic Society, Rado moved to New York, there to organize a Psychoanalytic Institute on the Berlin model.

Rado was appointed professor of psychiatry and head of the Psychoanalytic Institute of Columbia University, in 1944. This was the first psychoanalytic institute within a university. He met a great deal of resistance in this new venture; many of the psychoanalysts felt strongly that the teaching of psychoanalysis should remain under the control of the American Psychoanalytic Association, that universities were not yet ready to assimilate psychoanalysis. They feared compromise and dilution, a fear based on the early rejection of Freud by academic psychiatry in Vienna. Undisturbed by this opposition, Rado continued to organize an exceptionally good training program and a psychoanalytic society apart from the New York Society, in which he had once played a leading role. Rado remained within the fold, although his new institute's position remained tangential.

Once an active member of the central governing body of psychoanalysis, Rado now lived on the fringes of the organization. The quality and quantity of his scientific productivity during these years was in inverse proportion to his dwindling political and organizational influence in the American Psychoanalytic Association. Upon reaching the age limit for academic positions in 1957, Rado retired from his professorship, and soon organized a most progressive program in a new school of psychiatry, the New York School of Psychiatry, where he is continuing his intensive teaching activities.

As happens with all persons having truly creative minds, Rado's life focuses around his scientific activities. The development of his contributions must, therefore, serve as the center of his personality profile. In his collected papers, Rado divides his contributions into three phases: contributions to classical psychodynamics, quest for a basic conceptual system, and development of adaptational psychodynamics. His very first article, written in 1922, is a lucid epistemological discussion of the principle of causality, which Rado traced back to man's own internal perception of motivational sequences. This remarkably penetrating article is Rado's only philosophical writing, for, as he became more and more involved in psychoanalytic practices, he turned toward clinical observations.

Two early writings were on the problem of melancholia. The first, "An Anxious Mother," only six pages long, is one of the classical early writings in which Freud's new "ego-analysis" was applied to clinical observations. In the two articles, Rado added a second motivating force to the hitherto stressed self-punitive component in depressions: the appeal for love by display of suffering. "This disease," he wrote, "we can describe only as a great despairing cry for love." While these early articles are still couched in the abstract expressions of traditional instinct theory, we see the beginnings of Rado's search for understanding through psychological realities rather than abstractions.

The next subject Rado took up in this early phase of his development was the problem of drug addiction, a topic to which he later returned. His concept of "alimentary orgasm," which replaced genital supremacy in pharmacothymia, has been widely quoted. Writers on alcoholism have made extensive use of this concept.

Authors of various psychiatric and psychoanalytic papers have convincingly described a number of emotional inducements to drink, such as inferiority feelings resulting from excessive inhibitions and manifesting themselves in great shyness, pent-up and never expressed resentments, and inhibition of sexual cravings. Rado has perceptively characterized the gratification the alcoholic experiences from drinking as bliss derived from the re-establishment of the omnipotent feeling of the infant, as yet unhampered either by recognition of the hard facts of the external world, or by the self-critical faculties that—gradually, in the course of life—inexorably whittle down the illusion of infantile omnipotence. Rado first referred to this emotional state as "alimentary orgasm," later he called it "narcotic elation" or "narcotic superpleasure."

During the period between 1933 and 1945, Rado's work was characterized by its searching quality as he strove for the formulation of generally valid conceptual schemata. In such articles as "Fear of Castration in Women" and the "Concept of Bisexuality," he indulged in a great deal of speculation. However, in the latter article he devoted his critical talents to the discussion of such ill-defined concepts as "bisexuality." The idea of neurotic symptoms resulting from "emergency control" first appeared in this period; it has become the nucleus of his later adaptive psychodynamics. Neurosis is looked upon as a miscarried adaptational effort. It is noteworthy that in his article, "Training in Psychoanalysis," Rado (perhaps as a reaction to his own search for highly abstract formulations) took up the cudgels against "superlatively abstract general formulas," which, he warned, must be excluded from clinical discussions. He was placing more and more emphasis on observation, as opposed to theoretical, constructions. He warned us that "the student uses the patient to understand the theory and not the theory to understand the patient; and such a patient, too, will end by 'understanding' the theory but not himself" (1956, p. 127).

Rado's work culminates in his writings on "adaptational psychodynamics," which he conceives as a return to the original biological mechanistic approach from which, according to him, Freud gradually veered away in an "animistic" direction. In most respects, adaptational psychodynamics is a concise reformulation of what has come to be known as ego analysis. According to these theoretical developments, the ego's essential function consists in insuring that dynamic equilibrium we call the life process. Subjective needs are perceived by introspective awareness and acted upon by behavior suited to their gratification. This requires testing of reality, upon which the gratification of needs depends. The integrative act by which data of internal and external perceptions are brought into harmony, and then serve as the basis of adaptive behavior, is the function of the biological equipment called the mental apparatus. The nucleus of this objective process is what Freud has called the "reality principle." Although Rado's adaptational concepts are essentially identical with the basic tenets of psychoanalytic ego psychology, his formulations are concise and divested of the ballast of superfluous residues of earlier theoretical abstractions. Neurosis is considered as maladaptation achieved by emergency controls.

Rado's most important contribution, however, is not this theoretical framework, but his therapeutic conclusions and his critical evaluation of the standard psychoanalytic procedure. He maintains that the classical technique works on what he calls "the parentifying level of treatment." The patient continues practicing childlike emotional dependence (upon his therapist) throughout the treatment (1956, p. 261). Rado has questioned the value of so-called transference interpretations (1956, p. 261):

> In the transference procedure whenever the patient vents his rage on the physician, there follows a penetrating search for the infantile origins of his rage, resulting as a rule in the finding that he has again repeated his rage against his father. This procedure relieves neither the patient's true resentment of the physician nor his true resentment of his father; still less does it relieve the resentments of his current life situation, which are in no small measure responsible for his present suffering.

Rado criticizes the exclusive preoccupation of the therapist with the patient's past and the neglect of his present. In his own pungent words, "This fact is reflected in psychoanalytic literature, which refers neatly to the entirety of the patient's present life as his 'current conflict' " (1956, p. 261). He maintains that "the modifying power of the undoing of repressions is overrated" (1956, p. 261) in the classical technique. As some other psychoanalytic critics of the standard procedure (for example, T. French, F. Alexander) have done, Rado poses the cardinal question, a question frequently asked by the patients themselves: How does discovering the past origin of neurotic symptoms and behavior help one to lose his maladaptations? ". . . to recall the past is one thing; to learn from it and be able to act on the new knowledge, another" (1956, p. 262). Rado feels that these shortcomings of the classical technique can be overcome: "Psychoanalytic therapy surges with values and therapeutic resources; in its development, the classical technique is not the end but the beginning" (1956, p. 262). As a remedy he submits his "adaptational technique," which works no longer on the "parentifying" but on the "self-reliant" and the "aspiring level of treatment behavior." This approach emphasizes "welfare emotions (pleasurable desire, joy, love and pride)." It is a "re-educational process," as Freud had called it and, as Rado adds, is pre-eminently an "emotional re-education." With French, Rado believes that memories of failure can be neutralized by the recall of successful past performances; he calls this the "emotional redefinition of memories" that restores hope and lost self-confidence.

Rado's pre-eminently critical mind has succeeded in pointing out the weaker spots of the standard psychoanalytic procedure. The effective debater of his early years now emerges as a constructive critic of theories not fully thought through and of practices carried over from the past without re-examination. Here lies the merit of his adaptational theory, far more than in his detailed prescriptions for a modified procedure. True, the classical theory also holds that the final goal of psychoanalytic treatment is eventually to make the patient capable of dispensing with the therapist. The patient's inclination is to treat the latter as a parental figure. Also according to theory, this regressive repetition of the child–parent relationship is not the goal of treatment but a means of overcoming childhood's dependency needs. One cannot beat an enemy who is not present. The patient must relive his past maladjusted behavior patterns in order to correct them. The classical technique was originally devised for research and not for treatment. Freud felt that he had first to understand the nature of the disease he proposed to cure—that it was a fortunate coincidence that the aims of research and therapy coincide. Both patient and therapist must first understand the origins of the disturbance.

This apparent parallelism between aims of research and treatment has proved a grave overstatement. More and more it is becoming clear to many analysts that psychoanalytic treatment has bogged down in the first step: the understanding of the past, the origins of neurotic disturbances. Thus, psychoanalysis has not yet devised effective methods for modifying the maladaptive patterns that repeat themselves during the regressive manifestations of the treatment procedures. The clear recognition of this failure and its convincing demonstration constitute Rado's most important contribution. Other students of psychoanalysis are grappling with this same central issue.

Rado's groping efforts toward replacing neurotic maladaptation by actively helping readaptation are being paralleled by the work of others. The teachings of learning theory acquired in the last fifty years by experimental psychologists are available for application to that complex learning experience which is the essence of psychoanalytic treatment. At the height of his scientific evolution, Rado is engaged in the creative application of his great critical talents to a long overdue reexamination of the current practice of psychoanalysis.

REFERENCE

Rado, S. *Collected papers of* . . . . Vol. 1. *Psychoanalysis of behavior.* New York: Grune & Stratton, 1956.

Theodor Reik

b. 1888

MASOCHISM IN MODERN MAN

*

JOSEPH M. NATTERSON

§ Introduction

In 1948, Theodor Reik wrote, "Let me freely admit that in these thirty-five years of psychoanalytic practice, I have had this wish [to change professions] more than once. I have had moods in which being a psychoanalyst appeared to me less a profession than a calamity" (1948). This statement reflects Reik's remarkable candor and his dramatic style. He has never concealed his own associations or their unconscious meanings. Further, his remark tells us about his concept of psychoanalysis as an experience in which the analyst must respond deeply and honestly to the despair and joy of the patient. The analyst's pain causes him to wish to escape, but his moral courage enables him to persist in his profession.

Theodor Reik, now seventy-six years old and living in New York City, was born on May 12, 1888, in Vienna. He was the third of four children in the cultured, lower middle-class Jewish family of Max and Caroline Reik. His father was a civil servant. Reik's maternal grandfather became part of the crowded household when Reik was a boy. Reik attended the public schools of Vienna. His intellectual and aesthetic interests unfolded during adolescence, and he entered the University of Vienna at eighteen, shortly after the death of his father.

Reik's major subject at the university was psychology; his minor subjects were German and French literature. His interest in Freud was stimulated by a deprecating reference to Freud by Jodl; this led Reik to read Freud's *Interpretation of Dreams*. Reik's first book—published in 1910, when Reik was twenty-two years old—was a study of Beer-Hofmann; it included a reference to Freud.

Reik met Freud in 1910 and quickly became devoted to him. In 1912, Reik received his Ph.D. and, two years later, he became a member of the Vienna Psychoanalytic Society. He married his first wife, Ella, in 1914. She had been his childhood love. Their son Arthur was born in 1915.

From 1914 to 1915, Reik was in training analysis in Berlin with Karl Abraham. World War I interrupted Reik's professional life; from 1915 to 1918 he was an officer in the Austrian cavalry. During these years, he was in combat in Montenegro and Italy, was decorated for bravery, and emerged from the war a First Lieutenant. For the next ten years, until 1928, he lived and worked in Vienna, becoming Secretary of the Vienna Psychoanalytic Society after the resignation of Otto Rank. Reik then moved to Berlin, where he lived from 1928 until 1934. He taught in the Psychoanalytic Institute there and had a successful psychoanalytic practice. Thence, Reik moved to The Hague, where he continued his practice and teaching. During this period, his wife died, after a long illness. While in The Hague, Reik married his second wife, Marija. Their first daughter, Theodora, was born in The Hague in 1936. Two years later, still moving ahead of the Nazis, Reik emigrated to the United States. Marija was pregnant with their second daughter, Miriam, who was born after their arrival. Despite Reik's distinguished background, internal psychoanalytic politics prevented him from becoming a full member of the New York Psychoanalytic Society; but in the face of this and other adversities, he successfully re-established his private practice and continued his teaching and writing in psychoanalysis.

Theodor Reik has published a great many psychoanalytic books and articles. A complete listing and discussion of these would be impracticable here; nevertheless, trends and periods can be discerned in a brief review of them. His contributions to psychoanalysis are manifold and controversial. Some authorities doubtless hold that, while Reik is a fascinating person with great literary skill who has made impressive contributions, his contributions are, nevertheless, not in the main stream of psychoanalytic development and do not deserve primary and exhaustive attention. A detached and objective appraisal of Reik is necessary, but this is made difficult by Reik's consistent application in his writings of his conviction that, at this stage in psychoanalysis, systematization and precise formulation would be both premature and potentially stifling. The free-moving, anecdotal, and repetitive qualities of Reik's writings require creative reading.

Reik is probably best known, most widely respected, and least criticized among his fellow psychoanalysts for the theoretical contributions of his volume, *Masochism in Modern Man* (1949b).

Among professionals, Reik is equally well known, but much more often criticized, for his contributions in the area of psychoanalytic technique. The lay public probably knows Reik best for these. *Listening with the Third Ear* (1948), his most famous writing on technique, emphasizes the intensely intimate and intuitive nature of the psychoanalytic experience.

Reik's devotion to literature and music is evident throughout his published works. His earliest psychoanalytic efforts concerned the writers Beer-Hofmann, Flaubert, and Arthur Schnitzler. Other works, ranging from lengthy essays to brief, illustrative vignettes, treat a multitude of important creative artists, including Shakespeare, Goethe, Anatole France, Ferenc Molnar, and Gustav Mahler.

Theodor Reik's influence on the American lay public is immensely important. His presentation of psychoanalysis to the public has helped significantly to create in America the most favorable climate for psychoanalytic development in the world. His avoidance of technical language should not deceive the reader, however. He attempts to reach the periphery of the reader's consciousness and to promote creative analytic thought.

In his most recent tetralogy, dealing primarily with the Old Testament, he presents a psychoanalytically oriented exegesis, which he himself regards as the most important of all his contributions to psychoanalysis.

Reik might be termed an exemplar of the creative role of the European humanist in the first half of the twentieth century. His background in psychoanalysis, traditional psychology, philosophy, biographical history, religion, and belles-lettres has prepared him exceedingly well for this role.

§ Reik's Early Life

Theodor Reik grew from the vigorous, fermenting matrix that was late-nineteenth-century Vienna. According to Gustin's brief biography, he was an indifferent student as a youngster, with greater interest in athletics than in books, making no particular impression for intellectual or scholastic brilliance on his teachers, family, or peers.

The lusty, erotic, searching, anti-Semitic, and intensely political Vienna of Reik's youth seems reflected in all of his later works, which have any autobiographical qualities. The emotional experience of his childhood prepared him well for a later lifetime dedicated to psychology. Obviously, warmth, love, and basic acceptance characterized young Reik in his relationships with his family. However, in addition to love, there were multiple overlapping conflicts, which were apparently never resolved. First and foremost, on the basis of the frequency with which he mentioned it in his writings, was the conflict between Reik's father and his maternal grandfather. This was the conflict between the truth-seeking, tradition-rejecting father, who repudiated Jewish religious dogma, and the pious, orthodox, unquestioning grandfather. Later, Reik finally identified with his father and discarded religion, yet retained a deep and broad interest in the history and customs of the Jewish people.

Reik believes that masochism is an important requisite for the psychoanalyst, and identification with his loving but sad, long-suffering and hard-working mother may have been an important directing influence toward psychoanalysis. Another important trait of the psychoanalyst, according to Reik, is insatiable curiosity. In part, at least, he attributes the curiosity of the Jewish analyst to the necessary stimulation of this trait in a Jew living in a hostile climate. The anti-Semitism of the Viennese and their German cousins to the northwest has become legendary. The hatred that in its full flower eventually consumed the Jews of Central Europe had—in Reik's youth—a tonic effect on the Jewish men, stimulating their curiosity, wit, and creative ambition.

The other major area of childhood conflict was Reik's rivalry with his two older brothers. In later years, this manifested itself in similar neurotic attitudes toward Hanns Sachs and Otto Rank. In Vienna, Sachs, Rank, and Reik were very close; in Berlin they were known as the "psychoanalytic triad."

Despite difficulties presented by the university authorities, Reik was awarded the first Ph.D. ever given by the Department of Psychology of the University of Vienna for a thesis on a psychoanalytic subject. His paper dealt with Flaubert's "Temptation of St. Anthony."

§ The Young Psychoanalyst

Reik dates the beginning of his professional career in 1910, when he "first came to Freud." One year after this first meeting, Reik was awarded his Ph.D. Freud advised him to start psychoanalytic research and to relinquish the notion of becoming a psychoanalytic physician. Reik followed this advice. In 1911, he became a member of the Vienna Psychoanalytic Society. In this period, he wrote an article about Arthur Schnitzler, whom Freud regarded as a kind of "double."

Because Freud had by this time given up training analyses with local Viennese candidates, he sent Reik to Berlin for analysis with Karl Abraham during the year 1914-1915.

During that time Reik married Ella, his childhood sweetheart. She was half Jewish, with a pretentious and anti-Semitic father whom Reik hated and feared. For several years their relationship was painfully and sweetly covert. In this period Reik idealized Ella and noted the strong mother transference he brought to the relationship.

Because Reik had no money, Freud gave him 200 marks per month from 1913 to 1915, and Abraham charged no fee for the analysis. Freud knew Reik had much conflict over accepting this largesse. At one point there was a misunderstanding between Freud and Abraham as to which of them was supporting the young couple; in consequence, neither gave them any money. Reik starved himself and his bride to make ends meet, as Freud later learned with horror. In a touching letter to Reik in Berlin in 1914, he explained the confusion and promised to renew the "pension."

As early as 1913, Freud criticized Reik severely for being too biting and sarcastic with colleagues. Freud wrote him: "I know that you are again engaged in spoiling for yourself as many opportunities as possible. All this because of a few people you would like to kill. Too much repentance!"

Freud bluntly also told Reik he was dissipating his talents through his prolific writing habits, and on one occasion, using a urinary metaphor, asked Reik, "Why do you pee around so much? Just pee in one spot." This interpretation of urethral ambition was effective, for thereafter Reik stopped his literary promiscuity and concentrated on larger books and articles.

Although she dutifully copied all of Reik's manuscripts, Ella was uninterested in psychoanalysis. Reik was disappointed in her on this score, but in later years his resentment diminished. She adored Freud but felt defensive and competitive toward Frau Freud. In 1920, Ella developed subacute bacterial endocarditis. This illness and its chronic consequences had decisive and tragic effects on Reik's marriage. Ella Reik never regained her health. Guilt over his death wishes toward Ella and his extramarital activities made him consciously miserable, drove him to further labors, and symptoms of vertigo ultimately resulted in a resumption of personal analysis, this time, with Freud. The analysis, which occurred in the early 1930's, eased Reik's rage and his pained conscience.

The best known and lasting of Reik's works of the twenties and thirties concerned the application of psychoanalysis to religion and to problems of crime. These four papers are now available under the title, *Ritual* (1958). The first, "Couvade," was read at the Berlin Psychoanalytic Society in 1914 and published in *Imago* the same year. Reik explained couvade in its various forms as essentially a socially sanctioned way of identifying, first, with the laboring woman, and then with the newborn child. The pseudomaternal form helps control hostility to the woman in labor, as well as the sex drive of the man. The dietary form of couvade is regarded as a compromise between hostile and tender feelings toward the newborn child, as well as a way of expiating guilt for aggression. Emphasis is placed on the Oedipus complex and the father–son rivalry, with hostility to the child equaling hostility to the father. Freud had high praise for this paper.

In his second paper of this series, "Puberty Rites of Savages," for which Freud gave him the prize for the best work in applied psychoanalysis of that period, Reik proposed that circumcision and death rites reflect the widespread group resolution of conflict between sons and fathers, including aggression, guilt, and homosexuality. The important social problems of incest and parricide are dealt with through these puberty rites. The circumcision rites prevent incest, and the symbolic killing that is part of these rites prevents parricide. The resurrection of the symbolically killed son represents the tender and guilty undoing of the fathers' wishes to murder their own fathers.

The last two papers, "Kol Nidre" and "The Shofar," deal with the origins and significance of ancient phenomena in the Jewish religion and culture. Kol Nidre is a haunting and ancient Jewish song of obscure origin, and the Shofar is a primitive wind instrument, made of a ram's horn. Aside from psychoanalytic interpretation, Reik attempted to establish concrete historical facts about the times and places of origin of these phenomena, and these suggestions are credible, if not proved. Of more interest to the psychoanalyst, however, is Reik's ingenious, subtle working and reworking of the Oedipal theme in many variations as applied to these historical and religious phenomena.

In the mid-twenties, a series of papers on the problem of crime appeared, including "The Compulsion to Confess" (1959b) and "Freud's View on Capital Punishment." The subject is also developed in "The Unknown Murderer." These papers include many interesting clinical examples of case material and technical problems in psychoanalytic treatment, but the major concept is that unconscious guilt motivates both the crime itself and the criminal's need to be caught and punished.

Reik occupied a special position close to Freud, who remained his protector, patron, and advisor. This relationship was of transcendent importance for the young Reik. Probably his relations with the other psychoanalysts in Vienna were highly competitive and difficult, and although Reik's lack of a medical background put him at a disadvantage, his closeness to Freud tended to compensate for this difficulty.

Reik was a member of the group that met with Freud on Wednesday evenings. At one of these meetings, Freud said, "We do analysis for two reasons: to understand the unconscious and to make a living."

Reik regards himself as a "mediocre therapist" and has stated that he is like Freud in that he, too, lacks the *furor therapeuticus*. Early in Reik's career Freud asked him to provide German tutoring for a woman whom Freud was analyzing in the French language. This patient, a Russian, was the daughter of a famous painter. In her daily tutoring sessions with Reik, while Freud's patient would talk at length about her analysis, Reik listened with great interest. Freud was irritated by Reik's contribution to this patient's resistive behavior and ordered Reik to discontinue his interference, saying, "When I need the power of the river to drive mills, you build tributaries and take away my power."

Freud's capacities as a psychoanalytic consultant were evident when, for instance, Reik had difficulty in eliciting transference feelings from a female patient. Freud's advice was simple, "Make her jealous." So, on the next occasion, as this patient was leaving, Reik warmly greeted the next patient—also a woman—in the hearing of the problem patient. During the following session, the previously aloof patient became furious with Reik and freely expressed her anger, and the analysis proceeded more effectively.

Freud also contributed to the development of Reik's "surprise" technique. In dealing with a composer who molested little girls, Reik found himself completely baffled as to the significance of this acting-out symptom. Freud suggested, "He must have been seduced as a child." Confirmation by memories of seduction by governesses came as a "surprise" to Reik and to the patient. Reik also learned the technique of interrupting analysis for therapeutic purposes from Freud, who talked about "fractured analysis," in which interruptions necessitated by the patient's travels were discovered to have therapeutic value.

Freud was impressed by Reik's sense of humor. He responded with roars of laughter when Reik once called Paul Federn a "belligerent pacifist." The sharing of humor was reciprocated: at a meeting in which a methodologically elaborate paper with minimal substance was presented, Freud passed a brief note to Reik which read: "How would you like to be shown a menu, but served nothing to eat?"

Freud would not permit Reik to ignore or rationalize his sadomasochistic problem. For instance, in a letter to Reik in 1928, he wrote:

> . . . it grieves me much that you even need such therapy. Your hostility transgresses all justified measure, blasts the frontiers of what is permissible, spoils your presentation, and must sadden anyone who, as I, has the interest of a friend in you and highly appreciates your achievements. It cannot possibly go on like that.

§ Berlin and The Hague

Reik was successful in Berlin with his practice, a faculty appointment at the Berlin Institute, and his continued writing in psychoanalysis. He returned to Vienna frequently for consultations with Freud.

In 1928, Berlin was a most cosmopolitan city, prominent in science, dedicated to literature and the arts, beckoning to all members of the avant garde and apparently very attractive to Theodor Reik, who was incubating important innovations in psychoanalysis. At the same time, a cloud was forming over this remarkable city; at first casting a small shadow, it rapidly accumulated depth and darkness until, in 1933, the tornado of National Socialism destroyed the important new culture in Berlin, including the psychoanalytic movement.

As a Jew and a psychoanalyst, Reik was prudent enough for, in 1934, he moved with his family to The Hague in the Netherlands. A year earlier he had published "New Ways in Psychoanalytic Technique" (1933), in the *International Journal of Psychoanalysis*. This was the forerunner of his most controversial series of psychoanalytic publications, including *Surprise and the Psychoanalyst* (1935), and *Listening with the Third Ear* (1948). In "New Ways in Psychoanalytic Technique," Reik took direct but tactful issue with the psychoanalytic school of thought that emphasizes an orderly, methodical, surgical, approach to the unconscious.

Reik boldly asserted that psychoanalysis is not, and perhaps never will be, ready for such a systematic approach and that, in fact, such an approach can have the paradoxical effect of vitiating the psychoanalytic experience. He was aiming his guns mainly at Wilhelm Reich and Otto Fenichel, who achieved fame as systematizers of psychoanalytic knowledge. According to Reik, the essence of the psychoanalytic experience is that it is an unconscious duet between patient and analyst. The important insights arise from this unconscious interplay as surprises to both the analyst and patient, and reliance on consciously held theoretical assumptions by the analyst serve to interfere with, rather than implement, the arrival at the appropriate truths. Reik was aware of the consequences of the publication. He seems to have deliberately set himself up as a heretic and iconoclast because of his profound conviction of the correctness of his point of view and, perhaps also, for the sake of enraging his fellow medical practitioners.

In The Hague, he continued his hard work. Despite the difficulties of being a refugee and the increasing cardiac illness of his wife, Reik remained productive and worked hard on the most universally accepted of all his works, *Masochism in Modern Man* (1949b). Reik has said, "Suffering, consciously experienced and mastered, teaches us wisdom" (1933). According to Reik, the psychoanalyst searches for causes to relieve strong masochistic trends, hence it is appropriate that Reik's master work should be addressed to the problem of masochism. Freud died shortly before this book was completed; his death was especially disturbing to Reik because it repeated the frustration of his father's death prior to Reik's matriculation at the university. For the second time, Reik was thwarted in his wish and need for the unique filial enjoyment of the father's pride.

Masochism in Modern Man is a thick, idea-packed volume. Reik views the masochist as basically pleasure-seeking but, whereas the non-masochist seeks end-pleasure through a series of fore-pleasures, the masochist seeks end-pleasure through a series of fore-displeasures. The masochist wants orgasm, but the castration anxiety associated with this wish impels him into situations of torture in which he is suspended between increasing pain and sudden orgasm (suspense factor). Without fantasy, realistic pain is just as unpleasant for the masochist as for anyone else. The masochistic fantasies are mainly derived from sadistic fantasies of mastery; thus, masochism is a "secondary instinctual formation." Social masochism differs from the perversion in that it is neither associated with end-pleasure nor with any individual pain inflictor: the end-pleasure comes in paradise after death, and the world is the torturer. Social masochism is an important historical and sociological phenomenon. For example, the Christian martyrs were social masochists who sought "victory through defeat," and they exerted mighty influence on the course of human events. While the concept of primal masochism derived from the death instinct was not directly refuted by Reik, through selective inattention to this concept he has presented masochism as a reactive, or secondary, variation of the universal search for happiness.

It is amazing that this great work should have been completed and have made its first appearance when Reik's adult fortunes were at their lowest ebb. While in The Hague, Ella, ever more debilitated by her heart disease, took a lengthy trip to be with their son Arthur, who had married a Dutch girl and moved to Palestine. After this visit, she returned to her parents' home in Vienna, where she died within minutes after greeting them.

A grateful patient with access to confidential political information disclosed to Reik (at personal risk) that he should move from The Netherlands. This informant was an American, and his generosity and selflessness may have created in Reik excessively high expectations of his American welcome.

§ Reik's American Years

Reik expected to be received in America with the psychoanalytic equivalent of a brass band. He had an international reputation as a psychoanalytic practitioner, theorist, and teacher. He was Freud's protégé, and had had many years of close relationship with the founder of psychoanalysis. He neglected, however, to consider that he had already become a controversial figure among psychoanalysts and was not overly esteemed by those psychoanalysts who, opposed to lay analysis, wished for a firm reintegration of psychoanalysis into the medical fraternity. So, in 1938, his first year in America, his hopes were dashed. The New York Psychoanalytic Society refused to accept him as a full member; persons from whom he had expected much assistance refused to help him; and he had no money.

Reik has told me that beyond question he was paranoid in his response to the rejection by his psychoanalytic colleagues in America. The antagonism has abated, over the years, so that by now personal and some informal professional contacts with members of the New York Society have resumed.

If Reik's beginnings on this continent were inauspicious, subsequent developments have more than compensated for the early times. Reik has written and published a prodigious amount in the years since 1938. *Masochism in Modern Man* (1949b) appeared in English, shortly after Reik arrived in this country, but was actually the result of European labors. The greatest of his accomplishments in the United States is *Listening with the Third Ear* (1948). Among his other well-known books written and published in the United States are: *The Psychology of Sex Relations* (1961a), *The Search Within* (1956), *Fragment of a Great Confession* (1949a), *The Secret Self* (1953), *The Haunting Melody* (1960b), *Of Love and Lust* (1959a), and, subsequently, his Biblical tetralogy, *Mystery on the Mountain* (1958a), *Myth and Guilt* (1957), *The Creation of Woman* (1960a), and *The Temptation* (1961b). His latest book is *Jewish Wit* (1962).

In 1940, Reik's book, *From Thirty Years with Freud*, appeared in English. Intended as a personal tribute to Freud, it contains more on, and by, Reik than Freud. Reik here noted that, on each of Freud's birthdays, he had presented Freud with an anniversary essay concerning psychoanalysis. Since the essays are included, this book stands as a memorial to Freud. Reik's filial attitude toward Freud is conspicuous throughout the volume. He defers to Freud as the fair and powerful, although imperfect, originator and leader. Prominent are Reik's tender but ambivalent feelings toward his father and grandfather; this suggests some possible basis for the father transference to Freud, and also indicates possible reasons for Reik's intense preoccupation with Oedipal issues, including the negative Oedipus complex and his relative neglect of pre-Oedipal factors in psychoanalytic phenomena.

In 1945, Reik first published the *Psychology of Sex Relations* (1961a). This is the most iconoclastic of all Reik's works, wherein he has rejected the libido theory and, in the process, repudiated the classical psychoanalytic concepts of love, homosexuality, and the other perversions, as well as paranoid reactions. However, Reik has not contented himself in this book simply with negative statements, for he has offered a provocative theory of love. In essence, love is a late cultural accretion of mankind resulting from the complex interplay of sexual instincts and ego instincts (aggression and domination) in the setting of a cultural epoch that permits and necessitates the phenomenon of love.

Listening with the Third Ear (1948) extends the paper on technique published in 1933, and is regarded by many as Reik's finest work. This impassioned book sets forth Reik's concept of psychoanalysis as an exquisitely personal experience, in which the essential interaction goes on between the unconscious of the patient and that of the analyst. Understanding and insight come as a surprise to both patient and analyst, albeit usually first to the analyst. The setting aside of theoretical and technical theories and preconceptions is a *sine qua non* of successful psychoanalytic technique, and the nature of the psychoanalytic process defies systematization and codification.

Analysis cannot be viewed as a battle between analyst and patient in which logistics, terrain, and lines of defense are to be evaluated and manipulated, if the analyst is to triumph over the opposing patient. The key term in Reik's approach is "intuition," and he emphasizes the value of the analyst's free associations, his hunches, and surprise. The increased interest of analysts in the therapeutic importance of countertransference phenomena probably stems in part from Reik's contributions. His many years of devotion to the arts, particularly to literature and music, have undoubtedly been important in his preference for an "artistic" rather than "scientific" approach to psychoanalysis.

Masochism in Modern Man (1949b) and *Listening with the Third Ear*

(1948) are twin peaks of the Reik literary mountains. They firmly establish him as a master of psychoanalytic theory and technique.

Fragment of a Great Confession (1949a) draws many fascinating parallels between Goethe's love life and Reik's. Reik's candor in this book is truly remarkable and worthy of an analyst of his stature.

In the early 1950's, Reik continued with applied psychoanalysis, dealing with his beloved subjects of literature and music in two books, *The Secret Self* (1953) and *The Haunting Melody* (1960b). The former contains excellent examples of the unconscious creativity of the classic writers, especially Shakespeare and Goethe, in both of whom the timeless strivings and problems of mankind are unconsciously experienced and communicated in artistic form. This is especially impressive in Shakespeare, because his supreme mastery emerges, despite conscious attitudes that clearly partook of and deviated little from the stereotypes of his time. Shakespeare, Goethe, and Heine are all selectively treated in this volume, as though Reik were somewhat fearful of too global a treatment of these great men. However, Anatole France receives different treatment; Reik admires France greatly, but seems less intimidated. He suggests that France has an unconscious preoccupation with the primal scene, including the passive feminine attitude to the father, and he regards France's fascinating irony as indirectly related to this preoccupation. He implies that the employment by France of religious themes in an ironic and skeptical way reflects the author's Oedipal preoccupation and his attempt to cope with and resolve it. In addition in *The Secret Self*, the literary themes are mostly those of fathers and daughters. In this book, Reik refers often to his daughters Theodora and Miriam, but rarely to his wife or to his son Arthur.

The Search Within (1956) contains important biographical material from Reik's correspondence with Freud.

In the two decades from 1940 to 1960, Reik maintained an active career as a psychoanalytic practitioner and teacher. The increasing psychological sophistication of American intellectuals and Reik's increasing fame outside the organized psychoanalytic community have drawn many young, ambitious persons—particularly psychologists—to him for training, inspiration, and professional guidance. Many of his students have become well-known practitioners, teachers, and writers in this field.

In 1948, Reik, with a group of his American adherents, founded the National Psychological Association for Psychoanalysis. Owing to advancing age, Reik has in recent years withdrawn from active leadership of this training organization. However, he remains helpful and friendly to the group. In addition to these primary activities, he has lectured at many colleges and before other professional groups and has traveled extensively throughout America. He regards the American culture as woman-dominated. This seems to disturb him from a personal standpoint, since he is basically oriented to the masculine primacy of Continental culture. He sees the relations between men and women in America as more than an individual problem, inasmuch as they affect the social organization, the values, and the ultimate development of the American individual and society.

In 1961, Reik completed his Biblical tetralogy (1957, 1958a, 1960a, 1961b). He once told me that these are the most important contributions he has made—an opinion probably shared by only a few psychoanalysts and psychologists. The themes of these books include the revelations to Moses on Mount Sinai, the origins and result of the basic guilt of modern man, the legend of the creation of Eve, and the relationship between Abraham and Isaac. The purpose of these works seems to be the clarification of historical reality. Thus an effort is made to add to the body of historical knowledge, rather than to psychoanalytic theory, through the use of the historical past. In his introductory remarks to *The Temptation* (1961b), Reik has indicated that his advancing age is a significant element in his motivation for writing these books.

Reik did not pause for long after completing his tetralogy. Just one year later, his latest book, *Jewish Wit* (1962), was published. Reik has indicated to me that this will be his last. That remains to be seen.[1]

Jewish Wit is an excellent collection of Jewish jokes, through which Reik has attempted to understand the psychological significance of Jewish humor. He regards Freud and M. Grotjahn as important contributors to the unconscious psychology of Jewish humor. This humor consists of an "oscillation between masochistic self-humiliation and paranoid superiority feelings." According to Reik, "Jewish jokes started with heresies and allusions of timid aggression against the exaggerated demands made in the name of religion and will end with the abolishment of the illusion of religion." Thus, Jewish humor is an important part of the Jewish leadership in man's struggle for humanism and a rational morality.

[1] Since these lines were written, two books have appeared: *Voices from the Inaudible* (1964) and *Curiosities of the Self*, "Three Explanations" (1965).

Reik today lives on the west side of Manhattan in a deteriorating neighborhood. His apartment is on the top floor of an aging building, with a cramped, rickety elevator and dark, uncarpeted corridors. His quarters are simple, even austere. Reik's office-study is in his apartment. The view from his windows is of tenement walls and roofs, but much bright sunlight enters. His desk, couch, and chairs are ancient, sturdy, and utterly without style, as though their owner had no aesthetic pleasure in furnishings or felt that such sensual gratification would distract him from his primary task and interests.

Two walls are covered with photographic Freudiana. There are also portraits of Gustav Mahler, Arthur Schnitzler, Anatole France, Richard Beer-Hofmann, and Dostoevski, and a picture of Spinoza being stoned by the old Jews. A print of a mythical Oedipus, Nietzsche's death mask, and a cheap, miniature reproduction of Michelangelo's "Moses" are also visible.

Reik has grown a streaked, gray beard and bears a striking resemblance to a Jewish patriarch. In his long, beige smock, he gives the total effect of an aging but vigorous artist-scholar who lives and works in simple surroundings that complement his stimulating vigor and his lack of physical charm. He is lively, outgoing, cordial, and unassuming. Smugness and condescension are now gone, and Reik seems to be a wise and mellow old Jewish Talmudic scholar and gentleman.

In many ways, Reik is the epitome of the sensitive aesthete, the pleasure-loving, erotic, highly intellectual, secular Jewish scholar. These characteristics are to be treasured. They defy conformity and dehumanization and promise the confused and alienated cog in the machinery of our technological age some hope of pleasure, completeness, and understanding in the privacy of his own thoughts and through the sharing of the creative pleasures of great men of the arts. Thus, the little man with Reik's stone in his sling successfully holds the modern Goliath at bay, even if he does not defeat him. He avoids Philistinism and adds a drop to the great pool of human creativity.

REFERENCES

Reik, T. New ways in psychoanalytic technique. *Int. J. Psycho-Anal.*, 1933, **14**, 321–328.

Reik, T. *Surprise and the psychoanalyst.* London: G. Routledge & Sons, 1935.

Reik, T. *From thirty years with Freud.*

(R. Winston, Trans.) New York: Farrar, Rinehart, 1940.

Reik, T. *Listening with the third ear.* New York: Farrar, Straus, 1948.

Reik, T. *Fragment of a great confession.* New York: Farrar, Straus, 1949. (a)

Reik, T. *Masochism in modern man.* (M. H. Beigel, & G. M. Kurth, Trans.) New York: Farrar, Straus, 1949. (b) (See also New York: Grove Press, 1959.)

Reik, T. *The secret self.* New York: Farrar, Straus, 1953. (See also New York: Grove Press, 1960.)

Reik, T. *The search within.* New York: Farrar, Straus, 1956. (See also New York: Grove Press, 1958.)

Reik, T. *Myth and guilt.* New York: George Braziller, 1957.

Reik, T. *Mystery on the mountain.* New York: Harper Bros., 1958. (a)

Reik, T. *Ritual.* (Rev. ed.) New York: Int. Univ. Press, 1958. (b) (See also New York: Grove Press, 1962.)

Reik, T. *Of love and lust.* New York: Grove Press, 1959. (a)

Reik, T. *The compulsion to confess.* New York: Farrar, Straus & Cudahy, 1959. (b) (See also New York: Grove Press, 1961.)

Reik, T. *Creation of woman.* New York: George Braziller, 1960. (a)

Reik, T. *The haunting melody.* New York: Grove Press, 1960. (b)

Reik, T. *Sex in man and woman; its emotional variations.* New York: Noonday Press (Farrar, Straus & Cudahy), 1960. (c)

Reik, T. *The psychology of sex relations.* New York: Grove Press, 1961. (a)

Reik, T. *The temptation.* New York: George Braziller, 1961. (b)

Reik, T. *Jewish wit.* New York: Gamut Press, 1962.

Reik, T. *Voices from the inaudible.* New York: Farrar, Straus & Co., 1964.

Reik, T. *Curiosities of the self,* "Three explanations." New York: Farrar, Straus, 1965.

Ella Freeman Sharpe

1875–1947

THE SEARCH FOR EMPATHY

*

CHARLES WILLIAM WAHL

Ella Freeman Sharpe was born in the small market town of Haverhill, Suffolk, in the year 1875. The eldest of three daughters, she was closely attached to her father. One of her earliest recollections was sitting at his feet while he read the plays of Shakespeare to the family. She had about reached puberty when her father died. Feeling destined to fill his place, she took over the care of her mother and sisters, in whom she maintained an intense interest throughout her life, rather as an eldest son might have done. She developed, as had her father, an impassioned and almost encyclopedic knowledge and love of Shakespeare and of English literature, which lasted throughout her life and strongly directed its course.

After three years at Nottingham University, her ambition and intention was to pursue advanced study of English literature at Oxford. However, the necessity of supporting her family forced her to forego this opportunity. Instead, she taught English literature at a number of schools, finally becoming English mistress and co-head of the Huchnall Pupil Teachers' Center, where she taught with great success and dedication, from 1904 to 1917.

She was profoundly affected at this time by the dissolution of a long and close friendship and by the death of many of her former pupils on the battlefields of World War I. As a result, she suffered anxiety and depression. She went to the Medico-Psychological Clinic of Brunswick Square, where she was treated successfully by Jesse Murray and James Glover. As a consequence of this therapeutic help, she grasped the significance of Freud's work and became interested in psychoanalysis. In 1917, she gave up her teaching position and went to London to study psychoanalysis at the Clinic. Three years later, in 1920, she went to Berlin for analysis with Hanns Sachs; for several years, she continued her personal analysis with him during the summer holiday. She was elected to full membership in the British Psycho-Analytic Society in 1923.

Ella Sharpe quickly developed into an analyst of great capacity and depth, with an almost intuitive grasp of analytic material. To quote a fairly typical opinion voiced by one of her analysands:

> The most striking impression to me was Ella Sharpe's great sensitiveness to the nuances of verbal and nonverbal expression, and particularly to the implications hidden in the use of words and phrases which characterize most clichés. She had a great capacity for synthesis as well as analysis, and she could pick up and link together the material of the hour with a skill that always excited my admiration and envy. Not only would she remain alert and attentive to every detail of the material as it was being presented, but she was able to store, organize and convert it into something very meaningful by the end of the session.

Another said:

> I remember best the ease and persistence with which she was so unflaggingly attentive. She shared with you always her passion to understand.

A colleague who had known Miss Sharpe for many years supplied this vivid description:

> To think of "Brownie" Sharpe brings to my mind two contrasting pictures. One, of a rather slender, willowy woman, of uncertain age, with an eager, watchful, mobile face; shy, yet warm; gazing with sympathy and yet with a gentle and deprecatory curiosity at whomsoever came within her orbit. Twenty years later that willowy figure had given place to a stout, comfortable form that filled a capacious armchair, by the side of which stood a large ash tray filled with the stubs of the cigarettes she chain-smoked. Her face and lips had thickened a little, and her hair had almost fully greyed; but her eyes—deep, soft and brown—had an unaltered expression; they were still gentle, eager, primed with observant curiosity and understanding. She

was always a nervous woman with rather a marked hand tremor; she was frightened by noise (to her dying day, she could not bear to hear even a movie pistol shot), but as the years passed, bringing success in her chosen work, she acquired a placidity which, from an onlooker's point of view, was disturbed only when she launched forth in private on some of her favorite subjects—literature and art. Then she would almost stumble over herself in an eager expression of ideas. She lived for psychoanalysis, for art and for her patients. Her patients evoked in her understanding, compassion and a sublimated motherly interest that came to be regarded as her special characteristic. This sublimated maternity was also the keynote of her private life, for she collected her siblings around her and settled them in a house of their own, where on weekends she would dispense a warm hospitality and solicitude for her siblings and guests.

I don't know whether her life was ripened with romantic fulfillment, but certainly psychoanalysis was her longest and last love. She treated the hurt minds of those who came to her as if she were handling some fragile piece of pottery that she thought to restore.

Another colleague writes:

Her passion to understand was very evident in her attitude to Shakespeare, her interest in whom might be described as her main hobby. She shared this interest not only with her father but with her analyst, Hanns Sachs, and I doubt if she ever missed any stage production of Shakespeare that occurred during her life in London. She knew Shakespeare as a devoted priest knows the Bible.

As these accounts indicate, Ella Sharpe was first and foremost a clinician rather than a theoretician. She believed psychoanalysis to be a developing science. Discipleship was not one of her characteristics: thus, along with Marjorie Brierley and others, she was a member of the "middle group" of the British Psycho-Analytical Society.

Her scientific achievements embrace three main areas, all developed in concert with her early artistic and pedagogic interests. The first area is comprised of a series of papers on the psychoanalytic interpretations of art and the artist. These include: "Francis Thompson: A Psycho-Analytical Study," "The Impatience of Hamlet," "From *King Lear* to *The Tempest*," "Certain Aspects of Sublimation and Delusion," and "Similar and Divergent Unconscious Determinants Underlying the Sublimations of Pure Art and Pure Science." In the last-mentioned paper, she suggested that art is a sublimation rooted in primary identification with the parents; that this identification process is a magical incorporation of them, having its early unconscious conceptions in the child's cannibalistic wishes. As is true of all of her clinical papers, her work on sublimation is soundly based on actual clinical observation but also reflects her own life experiences with some accuracy.

Ella Sharpe was very interested in the differences between the creative artist and the neurotic. She concluded that the essential difference is not that the id wishes are less hostile or the superego less implacable in the artist; nor does the difference lie in an absence of magic or in less infantile omnipotence. She felt, rather, that in the artist—despite the pathologies he may have—there is a reality system of some kind in which the conflict is played out or annulled in connection with real people and real things. The eccentric differs from the neurotic in that his orbit is disciplined and regularized. Shakespeare, she believed, particularly epitomized this goal, for, even from the scanty facts of his biography, two facts are clear: first, that he had a rich, emotional life; and, second, that throughout his life he adhered to a stable purpose—to retrieve his father's lost property. Thus, Shakespeare's mind was free through empathy to invent his many beautifully delineated characters, while in life he played the role of Shakespeare rather than assuming the part of any creature of his fantasy. Here, it seemed to Sharpe, psychoanalysts can learn from the artist; for if the patient can externalize in his analysis the many roles the unconscious plays in fantasy, he can then build up an integrated ego in life.

The second area of productivity comprises a series of papers on the technique of psychoanalysis. These papers support the impression of her students that she was a brilliant and persuasive teacher. In her early years, she undertook more training analyses than any other analyst in England, and in these she persevered and continued to utilize the traditions and skills acquired during her former work as an educator. She had the reputation of being extremely practical, rather than theoretical. As one analysand has said:

> No student ever left her with a sharpened sense of inferiority or with that inner despair that so often affects the candidates when subject to the rigors of psychoanalytic training. Unlike many teachers of the subject, she could project herself into the minds of young and eager students and—knowing well their needs, doubts and requirements—leave them not only enriched, but unscathed.

Long before it was fashionable to speak of it, she was very much aware of the phenomenon of countertransference, and it was in the understanding of this aspect of psychoanalytic work that she made some of her finest contributions.

Her third and greatest contribution to psychoanalysis was in the area of dream analysis. In *Dream Analysis,* she first observed that the mechanisms of dream work and symbolization have their exact counterparts in poetic diction. Simile, metaphor, metonymy, synecdoche, onomatopoeia, euphemism, dramatization, and antithesis are processes clearly demonstrable in dreams as in poetry. Sharpe clearly implied that words and concepts originate not only from concrete percepts but, ultimately, from the fact of physical sensation. Although the words and concepts later acquire secondary and tertiary meanings, as far as the unconscious storehouse of the patient is concerned they do not lose the multiple and concretistic significances they possessed when first heard and used. The understanding of a word, therefore, consists in the sum of its present and past significations. Hence, the value of a dream lies not only in discovering the latent meaning by means of the manifest content: the language used in the narration of the dream and in giving the associations itself helps toward the elucidation, for though the disparate meanings of words are separate and discrete in the conscious mind, they are fused and stratified in the unconscious. An awareness of the exploitation in dreams of the concrete, idiomatic, and metaphorical uses of words and phrases is of enormous help in the technique of deep dream analysis.

Although they have yet to be exploited fully, these ideas constitute significant advances in the process of synthesis of our basic knowledge of primary-process thought. It is now clear that conceptualization—whether in dreams, in neurotic symptom formation, in psychotic delusion and hallucination, in the play and thinking of children, in mythopoesis, or in poetry—obeys the laws of primary-process logic. About each area of study has grown an isolated stalagmite of knowledge, but our science has still to produce a codification and fusion of these several areas into a set of general laws and processes. In *Dream Analysis,* Ella Sharpe has made a tentative and valuable beginning toward this goal. With Ernest Jones, she believed that symbolism must be freshly created out of individual material, and that when it occurs stereotypy springs from the fundamental and perennial interests of mankind. She felt deeply that man's artistic products—and particularly his language—provide the most significant clues to the broadest understanding of man.

Ella Sharpe was busy and active until the last weeks of her life. Before World War II, she had been warned that her high blood pressure was a danger and that she ought to take things easy, but she preferred to continue her work rather than take the rest that might have prolonged her life. Early in the Summer of 1947, she took a holiday in Aldeburgh. Coming back on the train from this last holiday, she was taken ill; she died in the hospital two weeks later. During the last months of her life, she had planned a book on the teaching of psychoanalysis and had completed the first chapter. It concludes with this description of what it means to be a psychoanalyst—a fitting description of Ella Sharpe's philosophy of life and her life's work.

> Leaving now the deep unconscious gratifications that our work can give, we must demand of ourselves that they be genuine sublimations. Apart from the obvious one of earning an income I will name a possible final one. Its roots are in the unconscious and they too are obvious. While our task lies primarily with the unconscious mind of the patient, yet personally I find the enrichment of one's ego through the experiences of other people not the least of my satisfactions. From the limited confines of an individual life, limited in time and space and environment, I experience a rich variety of living through my work. I contact all sorts and kinds of living, all imaginable circumstances, human tragedy and human comedy, humour and dourness, the pathos of the defeated, the incredible endurances and victories that some souls achieve over human fate. Perhaps for this I personally am most glad I made my choice of psycho-analysis, the rich variety of every type of human experience that has become part of me, that never would have been mine either to experience or to understand in a single mortal life, but for my work.

BIBLIOGRAPHY

Sharpe, Ella F. Vocation. In E. Jones (Ed.), *Social aspects of psychoanalysis*. London: Williams and Norgate, 1923.

Sharpe, Ella F. Francis Thompson: a psycho-analytic study. *Brit. J. Med. Psych.*, 1925, 5, 329–344.

Sharpe, Ella F. Contribution to "Symposium on child analysis." *Int. J. Psycho-Anal.*, 1927, 8, 380–384.

Sharpe, Ella F. The impatience of Hamlet. *Int. J. Psycho-Anal.*, 1929, 10, 270–279.

Sharpe, Ella F. Certain aspects of sublimation and delusion. *Int. J. Psycho-Anal.*, 1930, 11, 12–23.

Sharpe, Ella F. The technique of psychoanalysis. *Int. J. Psycho-Anal.*, 1930, 11, 251–277, 361–386.

Sharpe, Ella F. The technique of psychoanalysis. *Int. J. Psycho-Anal.*, 1931, **12**, 24–60.

Sharpe, Ella F. Similar and divergent unconscious determinants underlying the sublimations of pure art and pure science. *Int. J. Psycho-Anal.*, 1935, **16**, 186–202.

Sharpe, Ella F. *Dream analysis: a practical handbook for psychoanalysts.* London: Hogarth Press & Institute of Psycho-Analysis, 1937.

Sharpe, Ella F. Psychophysical problems revealed in language; an examination of metaphor. *Int. J. Psycho-Anal.*, 1940, **21**, 201–213.

Sharpe, Ella F. Cautionary tales. *Int. J. Psycho-Anal.*, 1943, **24**, 41–45.

Sharpe, Ella F. What the father means to a child. *New Era*, 1945, **26**, 7.

Sharpe, Ella F. From "King Lear" to "The Tempest." *Int. J. Psycho-Anal.*, 1946, **27**, 19–30.

Géza Róheim

1891–1953

PSYCHOANALYSIS AND ANTHROPOLOGY

*

WESTON LA BARRE

§ His Life

Géza Róheim was the only child of a prosperous bourgeois family in Budapest. His parents' home was known for its hospitality and fine foods, especially for the wines grown in the family vineyards; and Róheim retained throughout his life a robust enjoyment of food and drink. As a child, he was somewhat overprotected and overindulged, which may account for a certain imperiousness and categorical quality of his adult personality. He loved sports with a characteristic enthusiasm; he was a good oarsman and won prizes in fencing in Hungary, a country of fine swordsmen. But from early in life he was primarily a scholar, with a special interest in folk tales. René Spitz (1953) writes:

> I met him when he was five years old and I only a few years older. I remember him as a serious-eyed little boy, who was much less interested in the usual pursuits of his age than in exchanging books with me. To the last we both remembered that he introduced me to *Alice in Wonderland* and that I gave him his first book on folklore, *The Arabian Nights*. I like to think that the color and variety of the tales of Schehérazade kindled his interest in the various customs of the populations of the globe, in their usages, and in folklore, as did his grandfather's stories of the origin of man; that his

voyage to the far countries of the earth were inspired by the voyages of Sinbad the Sailor, many of whose itineraries he followed.

During Géza's early teens, his father opened an account for him in one of the oldest bookshops of Budapest, and an old assistant there fed his insatiable appetite for reading by directing his interest further toward the mythology, folklore, and ethnography of primitive peoples. While yet a high school student, he was invited to lecture to the Hungarian Ethnological Society; and before he was twenty he published his first paper, "Dragons and Dragon Killers," in the journal of the Society. He was already aware of psychoanalysis in 1911, and his paper is notable as the earliest use of psychoanalytic concepts by one who was later to become an anthropologist. There was then no chair of anthropology in Hungary, so young Róheim went to Leipzig and Berlin to study. But even there he had to take his Ph.D. examination by majoring in geography, with anthropology as a minor only. Some anthropologists trace their nonacceptance of him as a colleague to this flaw in professional training; and in the anthropological thinking of Britain and America, Róheim remained essentially an autodidact and even an amateur.

He was analyzed in 1915 and 1916 by Sándor Ferenczi, whose close friend he thereafter remained. On returning from Germany, Róheim joined the staff of the Ethnological Department of the Hungarian National Museum, but was forced to resign during the counter-revolution of 1919. In March 1918, Róheim was already a member of the Budapest Congress on Psychoanalysis; thenceforth, until the Paris Congress of 1938, he attended and presented a paper before nearly every congress, except for the years when he was away on ethnological field work. He was a voluble speaker and fluent in several languages: in one remembered feat, during the Innsbruck Congress, because of a shortage of papers in English and at the president's request, Róheim discarded his prepared German manuscript and gave his address in English, impromptu.

Meanwhile, his anthropological papers, notably "Das Selbst" and "Spiegelzauber," were attracting appreciative attention in psychoanalytic circles; and about this time, Róheim was also appointed professor of anthropology at the University of Budapest. In 1921, Freud awarded the prize for the best paper on applied psychoanalysis to Róheim's study, "Australian Totemism," the first such award having also gone to an anthropological study, Theodor Reik's "Puberty Rites of Savages." Building on the foundation laid by Karl Abraham, Riklin, and others for the psychoanalytic study of folklore, Róheim soon became recognized by both psychoanalysts and anthropologists as the foremost proponent of the combined disciplines. Róheim's scientific polemics were evoked primarily by the resistance of anthropologists to psychoanalysis, rather than by any question of his competence in psychoanalysis. Indeed, Róheim had analyses with both Ferenczi and Mrs. Vilma Kovács before going into the field; and, after returning, he continued his studies, was graduated as a therapeutic analyst, and eventually became a training analyst in the Budapest Institute of Psychoanalysis.

§ His Scientific Work

It is not as a psychoanalytic theorist or innovator that Róheim will be longest remembered, although—in common with most anthropologists —he came to reject the Atkinson-Darwin theory of the primal horde, which Freud had used in *Totem and Taboo*. Róheim's unique position, rather, is that he, first and foremost, introduced psychoanalysis into anthropological thinking, and for some decades bore the brunt of polemics and obloquy for his pains. It is as an anthropologist that Róheim must ultimately be judged and valued.

However, even at the time of his "Australian Totemism," Róheim's prodigious and encyclopedic knowledge of folklore was purely academic. He needed both the direct testing of psychoanalytic theory in the ethnographic field and the chance to collect empirical data, which the psychoanalytically unsophisticated observer neither sees nor records. To this end, Freud, Ferenczi, and Vilma Kovács organized a series of field trips for Róheim, all financed by the munificent generosity of Marie Bonaparte, Princess of Greece. From 1928 through 1931, Róheim pursued fieldwork in Somaliland (East Africa), Central Australia, and the Normanby Islands (Melanesia), and among the Yuma Indians of Arizona—a well assorted selection for anthropological sampling. These expeditions were the historic first ethnographic field trips ever undertaken by a psychoanalytically competent person with the explicit intent of studying the dreams and unconscious materials of primitive peoples.

Although the United States is perhaps the scene of the greatest intellectual success of psychoanalysis in a civilized country, Róheim was received most grudgingly in the U.S. by his fellow anthropologists. In part, this was because of the alien and inadequate nature of his anthropological training; in part, because he would not learn the methodological language of American anthropologists; and, finally, because of his intransigent and well-nigh Talmudic Freudianism, which made concessions to no man and no theory. On the other hand, few American anthropologists had made themselves competent to assess Freud's ideas, though—as had many laymen—many fancied themselves so. Franz Boas, the father of American anthropology, never came to serious intellectual grips with psychoanalysis, retaining what might best be described as a disciplined disapproval. Robert H. Lowie, an otherwise most judiciously minded scholar, suffered from angry misinformation concerning psychoanalysis, mostly revolving around the controversial person of Bronislaw Malinowski.[1] Alexander Goldenweiser used psychoanalytic concepts competently but was exiled for most of his professional life in a distant provincial university. Margaret Mead, whose scientific impetus owes much to psychoanalysis, defended Róheim and tried to interpret his ideas to colleagues for many years, until he broke with her over the study of modern cultures, notably the culture of Hungarians, whom he accused her of "treating like savages" with her method. Edward Sapir, the founder of culture-and-personality studies in America, was almost alone in his inclusion of Róheim's and other psychoanalytic books on his lists of required reading for graduate students in anthropology at Yale. Throughout his long professional career, A. L. Kroeber—at his death the universally acknowledged dean of American anthropologists—was thoroughly ambivalent to psychoanalytic theory in anthropology, although he himself practiced lay analysis for a time and wrote two remarkable reviews of *Totem and Taboo* (twenty years apart), which express both his early rejection and the ultimate grudging acceptance of Freud's ideas.

Even today, only Devereux and La Barre are outspoken proponents of psychoanalytic anthropology—though Wallace, Whiting, and others use analytic concepts—which both derive significantly from Róheim. Melville J. Herskovits (1934) expressed what can perhaps be considered a consensus among professional anthropologists in America:

[1] The details of this and other relevant scientific controversies (for example, A. L. Kroeber's positions on psychoanalysis) are contained in Weston La Barre's paper, "The Influence of Freud on Anthropology" (1958).

The method of the Freudians themselves has been one of clinical analysis, and when the psychoanalysts have stepped out of their clinics to apply their theories to society as a whole, and particularly to primitive man, their disregard of anthropologic methodology has carried its own conviction of insufficiency.

It was this stricture that, as polemicist, Róheim himself was never to overcome, and Herskovits considers that Róheim long prejudiced anthropologists against psychoanalysis as a working hypothesis. Nevertheless, in the same paper, Herskovits has ably and impeccably used the Freudian concepts of repression and compensation in a study of African materials—almost a pattern of the final capitulation of the more discerning anthropologists to these difficult and provocative, albeit, highly useful concepts.

Out of the great mass of his folkloristic papers of limited compass and perceptive *ad hoc* interpretations of individual myths, Róheim's major works emerge: *The Riddle of the Sphinx* and *The Origin and Function of Culture*. The first is the more characteristic of Róheim's prolix and sometimes undisciplined style; the second, in this writer's judgment, is one of the classic gems of both psychoanalytic and anthropological writing because of its (for Róheim unwonted) conciseness and clarity of style, recalling his own masters, Ferenczi and Abraham.

In an influential review of *The Riddle of the Sphinx*,[2] Margaret Mead (1935) has complained with some justice:

Dr. Róheim presents an argument bewildering in its tangle of unresolved complexities, elisions, and condensations. After a short introduction posing the problem of the origin of culture, he presents a long discussion of Australian aboriginal ceremonialism which is practically unintelligible in the terms in which he describes it here. If his previous publications on Australia have been read with great care, and if the reader possesses a good working knowledge of Freudian theory, and a detailed knowledge of Central Australian tribes drawn from other more formal sources, this section on Australia becomes relatively intelligible, and also very stimulating. In the present volume, however, it is interlarded with references to European folk-lore, on the basis of a frame of reference which is seldom more than implied.

[2] As Devereux wrote, "The problem was that Róheim took both anthropologic and psychoanalytic knowledge for granted and imagined that people could follow his big leaps easily, filling in the gaps for themselves," which few are competent to do.

It must be admitted, even by his warmest admirers, that the intense, insistent, and often inchoate cyclothymic style of Róheim was not usually a didactic success. But Mead (1935) has pointed her reviewer's rapier at the most vulnerable spot in Róheim's theoretical structure:

> . . . while Róheim reiterates that the [sociocultural] system is self-perpetuating, he suffers from the handicap which is apparent in so much work which stems from the life-history approach; he sees the plot of human life as beginning, in every sense, with the birth of a new generation, and in his final argument ignores the society into which the first group of children who suffer from this [cultural] trauma are born . . . His argument is not so much that ontogeny recapitulates phylogeny, as that the development of the human race and its cultural institutions can be derived from a study of the development of the character of a given human individual. He has left out of consideration the nature of society. . . . If one neglects to consider that societies are, after all, aggregations of individuals which have their own laws of integration, laws which may possibly be paralleled with the laws of integration of an organism, but which are not comparable to the laws which govern the psyche alone, the result is Róheim's theoretical statement.

In this book, Róheim was more clinically and psychoanalytically oriented than usual toward the ontogenetic origins of culture in the individual, and Mead has acknowledged the necessity of this view for our fuller understanding. But neither should the "phylogenetic" precipitates of other preceding individual lives, cumulatively and socially (viz. historical culture) be neglected. Mead's review goes on to say:

> It is necessary to recognize that because society is composed of individuals with a definite biological constitution, and because some social forms, especially the family, are so intimately linked with the biological nature of man that they are virtually inevitable, no explanation of the social order which does not take these factors into account is valid. But it is equally necessary to recognize that Society is composed of a *group* of individuals, and that the perpetuation of social forms follows different laws than those of individual consciousness, and social institutions subserve not only the survival of the individual but the survival of the group.

Róheim's *Riddle of the Sphinx* suffers, therefore, from its inadequate attention to the central subject of anthropology, the fact of *culture*, which, for all its cumulative ontogenetic origins, is, in one of its infinite historic varieties, *the* central environing influence on the life of the child in each society. The book therefore speaks more to the analyst than to the anthropologist.

Precisely because he has presented a theory of culture in his *Origin and Function of Culture*, Róheim is here the better anthropologist. Drawing on the findings of biology and physical anthropology (especially the concept of neoteny of the Dutch anatomist Bolk), Róheim propounded the stunningly provocative hypothesis that culture arises from man's neotenic retardation and biologically delayed maturity. In this incomplete form, Róheim's thesis is almost certainly inadequate, for much of secular and technological culture is surely object-oriented, "genital," and ecologically adaptive. Nevertheless, with respect to sacred culture, which is id- and superego-oriented, and refers rather more to individual-social conflicts than to physical reality, Róheim's thesis is brilliantly illuminating. Cultures are man's sets of defense-mechanisms; societies' systems vary even as individual personality-systems vary. Some defenses (that is, technology), we should say, are better—more adaptive—than others, for example, the institutionalized Oedipal fantasies of sacred culture. Róheim's anthropological theory of culture is profoundly psychoanalytic. In Spitz's words (1953), Róheim:

> . . . saw in culture a huge network of more or less successful attitudes to protect mankind against the danger of object loss, the colossal efforts made by a baby who is afraid of being left alone in the dark. This was the main stream of his entire work, as expressed in nearly two hundred papers and books.

And the work derives significantly from the man.[3]

§ The Man

Géza Róheim was a vehement and positive personality, insatiable of life. Many anecdotes are told of him—some of the best by Róheim himself. Toward the end of World War I, Róheim approached the di-

[3] Of Róheim's posthumous work, which is beginning to appear, *Magic and Schizophrenia* may prove of greatest value. Róheim believed that both individuals and societies pass through a stage of magical, symbolic thinking, a state of development that he relates to schizophrenia, to dreams, and to creativity. The cultural evolutionism of this argument is likely to be rejected by anthropologists, who are understandably wary of methodologically equating child, savage, and psychotic, however dynamically similar such processes in each may be. And, indeed, both anthropologists and analysts may come to agree that, as processes, these recur in all peoples and all times and are not confined to one putative stage of cultural evolutionary development.

rector of the Budapest Museum, saying that he was unhappy in his job and might have to leave unless granted two free hours a day for writing. The director replied, "We should be glad to grant you the time but, as you know, there is a shortage of paper"—an amused recognition by Róheim of his own prolixity.

Teased about being a huge eater, Róheim replied that his Uncle Ödön was so gluttonous an eater that, when the Róheim family invited guests, they made two equal portions, one for the guests, and one for Uncle Ödön; that on a boat trip from Germany to Denmark, Uncle Ödön settled down and ate throughout the entire trip. Róheim was proud of his uncle's feats of eating. Hungarian food was invariably served in Róheim's own home. He told one of his students that for at least the last forty years of his life, he had drunk no water, only wine.

He was physically fearless and even incautious. A passionate swimmer, he was once swimming in an estuary on Normanby island when a crocodile took his German shepherd dog from right beside him. Again, on Normanby, Róheim taught the village boys to play soccer, wrenching his knee in the process. He was incapacitated for a time and the old chief visited him, saying, "I did not tell you beforehand, but what do you expect when a grown man acts like an adolescent?" Róheim had several "affairs of honor," in one of which the tipsy offender later apologized, through seconds, in a written procès-verbal.

Róheim was violently against circumcision, on physiological grounds, and felt that in the United States the tendency is for all parents to castrate their children.

He was extremely hard on books, tearing them apart for use: sometimes very valuable works were damaged in this way, including Roscher's *Reallexikon*. Someone has said, with a touch of malice, that Róheim hated books that he himself had not written. When an anthropologist chided him for writing in a very undisciplined way, with illustrative examples not even in geographic or ethnic context, he acknowledged the justice of the criticism but said it was due to his day-long listening to patients' free associations. He wrote so voluminously that he himself was obliged to finance at least some of his publications. One friend, an analyst, said, "He was a genius, but also quite juvenile in many ways—though part of it was Hungarian national character, consciously and proudly cultivated: a deliberate Hungarian. I think he never ceased being homesick for Hungary."

Róheim infuriated American analysands by scrupulously observing

Hungarian holidays and often ignoring American ones; and, by testamentary wish, his coffin was covered with the Hungarian flag. Róheim was enraged when the Russians took possession of the "Holy Crown" of Hungary; it is said that, when he left Hungary, it was a toss-up whether he was in greater danger from the Communists or from the Fascists. The world-traveled ethnographer found it hard to leave his homeland, which he did most reluctantly at the insistence of his wife.

Róheim married Ilonka in 1918, and for more than thirty years she accompanied him everywhere. It was taken for granted that, in the field, Ilonka would take care of their material needs and also get data from native women and children. A friend wrote, "Their marriage was one of those which are inexplicable and incomprehensible to everyone except their most intimate friends. Géza and Ilonka quarrelled and disagreed all the time, but were inseparable." To a new acquaintance, a guest at their table, the casual savageness of their insults was disconcerting. And yet, close friends of Róheim are convinced that his death, which followed that of his wife by a few months, was due primarily to grief. Róheim successfully recovered from a masochistic operation—not very dangerous, perhaps even unnecessary—but he never recovered from Ilonka's death. His life ended essentially with hers.

A fellow-countryman writes of him:

> Géza was a spoilt and over-protected child, and in a way he remained such all his life. He had to be looked after by sympathetic people, and there were many, especially women, who were willing to do this. He responded with gratitude, sincere friendship, and often with more demands—as a child would do. His straightforwardness and sincerity were also that of a child; for diplomatic niceties and clever moves of power politics within the Society or Association, he had no understanding. If a dispute or a problem arose, one could be certain that Géza would take part in it with unbiased simplicity, insensitive to all the other implications—a really heartening experience. But, like every over-protected child, he was always insecure, always suspicious, always expecting some highly unscrupulous, uncalled-for attack, unconditionally devastating. Everyone who was not a proven friend was a potential, even an actual enemy—as is the case in primitive fairy tales.

Despite omnivorous reading in anthropology, Róheim was not equally interested or comprehensively informed in all areas, and he was often indifferent to intellectual or scientific problems that interested his colleagues. There is no doubt that he suffered from being an outsider in the U.S., but for this he himself was in part responsible: he lacked the techniques of being a sibling and knew only how to be a son, a rival, or a lover. His works reveal defects of structure and style; he wrote swiftly and intensely, relying on a remarkable memory, whereas a more careful scholar would have verified references meticulously.

But for all his defects of presentation, Géza Róheim was a fearless man, ready to incur criticism and even enmity in maintaining his position—for all that he was hungry for affection and professional approval, and sensitively vulnerable to abuse and lack of recognition. For decades he was the unique anthropologist who applied psychoanalysis to the understanding of human cultures—a true pioneer. He was not an important theorist in the development of psychoanalysis as such; perhaps he was not even a complete anthropologist. But he was a vital, warm, and lovable human being. And, as a theorist on the origin of culture, he was an authentic, although as yet largely unrecognized, genius.

REFERENCES

Balint, M. Obituary of Géza Róheim. *Int. J. Psychoanal.* 1954, 35, 434–436.

Herskovits, M. J. Freudian mechanisms in primitive Negro psychology. *Essays presented to C. G. Seligman.* London: Routledge, 1934.

La Barre, W. The influence of Freud on anthropology. *Amer. Imago,* 1958, 15, 275–327.

Mead, Margaret. Review of Géza Róheim's "The Riddle of the Sphinx." *Character and Personality,* 1935, 4, 85–90.

Spitz, R. Obituary of Géza Róheim. *Psychoanal. Quart.,* 1953, 22, 324–327.

The debt to the obituaries of Géza Róheim by René Spitz (1953) and Michael Balint (1954) is heavy, and gratefully acknowledged—W. L. B.

Helene Deutsch

b. 1884

THE MATURATION OF WOMAN

*

MARIE H. BRIEHL

Helene Deutsch is a pioneer in psychoanalysis in several senses.[1] She was among the first to explore the emotional life of woman and the first and only analyst to construct from her findings a comprehensive psychology of the life cycle of womanhood.

Of her works, Grinstein's *Index of Psychoanalytic Writings* lists forty-four items from 1919 to the present. Eight papers on female psychology, starting with "On the Psychoanalysis of the Female Sexual Functions" in 1925, culminated in 1945 in the two volumes *The Psychology of Women;* five complete case histories, originally presented in the Continuous Case Seminar in Vienna, were combined with additional material in the volume, *Psychoanalysis of the Neuroses;* numerous other papers range in theme from severe pathological states to universal affects and traits as seen in her own clinical material, in life, and in the intuitive presentations of great literature.

The story of Helene Deutsch's life is significant because of the startling unity of her youthful searchings with the completed research of her maturity. Born in 1884, in the small town of Przemyśl, Galicia, then an autonomous part of Poland under Austrian rule, she lived close to the Polish-Russian border at a time when it was seething with under-

[1] She was one of the first four women candidates in analysis with Freud.

ground traffic in revolutionary ideas. Przemyśl was a mélange of cultural contrasts, the isolation and orthodoxy of some Jews existing side by side with the sophistication of the Jewish "intelligentsia," which surpassed even the highest standards of Polish culture.

Her father, a scholar in international law, held, despite notorious Polish anti-Semitism, the important post of "Syndicus," juridical representative to the Federal Court in Vienna. At one time President of the Jewish Community, he considered himself a Pole and was held in high esteem by both Jews and Poles. From his broad cultural interests came her love of literature and learning, even in childhood. Her mother, proud, morbidly ambitious, and a social climber who attached the greatest importance for her daughters to status, reputation, and conformity, set a restricted conventional tone in the home. However, Helene's adolescent participation in smuggling books across the border opened for her a broad world of ideas.

For Helene and her generation, womanhood was epitomized in the figure of Vera Figner, Russian woman physician, revolutionary and martyr in the cause of freedom, and author of the widely read book *Night over Russia.* Woman's search for identity, for educational opportunity, and for social and political freedom was an integral part of the upheaval of those times. Helene's spiritual, literary, and cultural interests stemmed from all these influences, and it is against this background that her rejection of Victorian strictures and her pursuit of education can be understood.

Helene Deutsch was the youngest of four children. Her arrival, after an interval of eight years, was the expression of her parents' wish to have a second boy. At fourteen, she finished the prescribed schooling for girls at an excellent *Pensionat* and spent the next two years as a debutante under her mother's tutelage. Bored in the extreme, her sixteenth year marked a critical change; she joined those of her generation who were breaking from tradition. She found intellectual inspiration in a chance acquaintance with a young man her own age and, later, in a professor who encouraged her to study for the university matriculating examinations. Since no high schools were open to girls, the preparation involved secret study. Though she actually mastered the immense amount of material in two years, long interruptions extended the desperate struggle to six. Having passed some subjects brilliantly, she ran off to Vienna, only then informing her parents of her plans and threatening not to return unless they would, in a "written document," support her goal to take the university entrance examination. This won their reluctant assent and irregular financial support.

Now came the problem of choice of career. During those six years, Helene had earned some money by writing *feuilletons* and a regular newspaper column, but her journalistic ambitions had become somewhat obscured. Her second ambition, to become a lawyer, was closed to her as a woman. When later, as one of two suffragettes, she was instrumental in winning admission of women to the law school, it had become a matter of general principle rather than personal aim. The decision, in 1907, to enroll in the Medical School of Vienna University was thus a compromise among her many interests, the humanities and psychology, and her strong need for concrete activities. Even during her early studies she had felt that she would become a psychiatrist.

The first year of her university life was filled with deprivation, even hunger, because only after her first brilliant examination did infrequent support come from her parents. She married Dr. Felix Deutsch in 1912, during her last year at medical school. Later outstanding in internal medicine, he, too, eventually came to psychoanalysis, by way of his spontaneous awareness of the nonsomatic aspects of his patients' problems. Their son was born six years later during her most intensely productive scientific period.

After graduation in 1912, and a semester in pediatrics, she entered the Wagner-Jauregg Clinic of the University of Vienna Medical School for seven years of neurological and psychiatric training. During World War I, she became the first woman to receive an unofficial, unpaid assistantship from Wagner-Jauregg. Since almost all male psychiatrists were recruited for military service, she headed the civilian women's section of the Psychiatric Department at a time when the famous Otto Pötzl was in charge of the men's section. The experience was "wonderful because there was no one to train me, only the patients." Working indescribably hard, she had to add to her work with women the awful responsibilities for the mental illnesses of military men brought to the psychiatric hospital from the front or prison camps. In this function as "civilian war doctor," she was well paid for the first time in her career.

No member of her sex was allowed to serve as "clinical assistant," which she *de facto* was, but she never regretted having relinquished the ambition for an academic career in favor of analysis, on Freud's advice that "you cannot do both." In 1916, while studying with Emil Kraepelin in Munich, she had discovered Freud and *The Interpretation of*

Dreams. It opened a "new era" in her life; she read "all day and all night." Now that she could interpret the symbolic language of a schizophrenic patient, she became enthusiastic about psychoanalysis. Her reading and Freud's ex-official lectures for a small group so impressed her that her future was determined. She turned to Freud for analysis. To his question "What would you do if I sent you to someone else?" she promptly replied, "I would not go." The analysis with Freud lasted one year, from 1918 to 1919, and terminated because he needed the time to take the "Wolfman" back into treatment. Though he said, "You do not need any more; you are not neurotic," she felt frankly disappointed. In 1923, she went to Karl Abraham in Berlin for one further year. Her ideas for the later organization of the Vienna Institute emerged from this stay in Berlin.

During her year of analysis in 1918, she was admitted as a full member of the Vienna Psychoanalytic Society—the second woman member, following H. von Hug-Hellmuth—and started her first analytical cases, sent to her by Freud. There were no regular controls at that time, but during and after her analysis, Freud discussed with her the problems of her patients. His frequent remark, "You understand the patient better than I because you see him every day," indicated his confidence in her work.

Helene Deutsch speaks with frankness of her ensuing relationship with Freud. Her modesty and reserve kept her from taking greater advantage of the opportunities for more personal contact with her great teacher. Her membership for twenty years in the Vienna group "closest to Freud" enabled her to see the dynamics of the relationships between Freud and his pupils. In "Footnote to the History of the Psychoanalytic Movement," she explained sensitively: "He who attached himself to Freud at that time knew that he was going into exile, that he would have to renounce . . . the usual gratification of professional ambition. One might therefore expect these first pupils to have been revolutionists of the spirit . . . a select and courageous advance guard . . . an expectation . . . realized only in individual instances. . . . Many came out of an intuitive inner urge; others were impelled by their own neuroses, or were driven by contrariety or by an identification of their own lack of recognition with Freud's lot. . . . Each wished to be a favorite, and each demanded love and preference for having made the sacrifice of isolation." But Freud "loved those who were critical, who were independent, who were of interest for their brilliance, who were original. . . . Any impulse toward originality when it subserved other than *objective* purposes . . . made him impatient." Helene Deutsch's position among the second generation of the group around Freud for twenty years indicates not only her own "revolutionary" spirit and courage but her basic adherence to Freudian tenets.

Some of her publications were first discussed with Freud. During her analysis, Freud encouraged her to publish "The First Love Pangs of a Two-Year-Old Boy," a classical forerunner, in 1919, of studies in child observation.

The personal circumstances that brought about her decision, in 1933, to leave Vienna for America created some temporary distance between Freud and the Deutsches, because it seemed to imply disloyalty to the Institute in which she had become a leading figure and to Freud to whom she was deeply devoted. Events proved her decision timely; by 1938, the Hitler terror forced the Freuds, too, to leave Vienna. This foresight arose from her maternal desire to give her adolescent son the opportunity for life and education in a free country, as she had once sought it for herself when she left Poland. She had rejected a previous excellent opportunity in 1929. It so happened that during my supervisory hour with her she received the exciting long-distance telephone call in Vienna from Franz Alexander in Berlin, inviting her to the United States. Her refusal of the tempting offer, which Karen Horney then accepted, thus inadvertently contributed to a divergent trend in American psychoanalysis. Her eventual move extended to the United States her pioneering contributions and innovations in analytic training.

In 1924, enriched by the experience at the Berlin Institute, she had returned to Vienna to create a psychoanalytic institute along similar lines. With Freud's help, against the resistance of important members, the Vienna Psychoanalytic Institute was founded in 1925. She was elected Director and served in this position for ten years, until her departure for America. The Institute replaced and integrated the old "unincorporated teaching," transferring to its Educational Committee decisions about the nature and length of training heretofore left to private agreement between teacher and student. It worked closely with the Ambulatory Clinic, which she, together with Paul Federn and Edward Hitschmann, its first director, organized in 1922, and with the Child Guidance Center (created in 1924) attached to the clinic. The establishment of the Psychoanalytic Ambulatorium became possible only through the active collaboration of Felix Deutsch, who made available to it the facilities of the Clinic for Heart Diseases of which he was Director. At the Ninth International Psychoanalytic Congress in Bad Homburg in 1925, from which Freud was absent, Helene Deutsch represented the new Vienna Institute. At the tenth Congress, as a member of the newly founded International Training Commission, she, with S. Rado and H. Sachs, defined the basic training program for Institutes in which all national groups eventually concurred. She later played a leading and vitalizing part in the same transition in Boston, becoming a permanent member of its Institute in 1937.

The Vienna period of analytic growth was, in her words, "a glorious time." Freud was gradually restricting his activity to meetings at his home with a small, chosen group of members among whom she was included. The Society was enriched at that time by younger members, who were to continue their role as the avant-garde of analysis for years to come. Among her colleagues and students were Nunberg, the Bibrings, the Krises, the Waelders, the Hartmanns. Every Saturday they gathered at her house for dinner, and what was called a "game of poker" was in fact the most inspiring and productive exchange of ideas.

Helene Deutsch introduced the continuous case seminar, the now universally accepted clinical laboratory that psychoanalysis had previously lacked. It became a chief feature in the Vienna Institute's program. Her account of its origin gives an interesting sidelight on her dynamic qualities as teacher and organizer. Wilhelm Reich, brilliant and powerful, had aroused a prolonged controversy over his introduction of a "new technique which proved to be confusing to the students." Too many fruitless hours were spent fighting about "his" and "our" techniques. To resolve this, she suggested, "Let us have a seminar in which one person presents a case and shows how he works—and let Reich discuss it. I am not a candidate, but I will bring a case." The case she presented in weekly sessions of this original demonstration appeared later in her book, *Psychoanalysis of the Neuroses*, as the "Hysterical Fate Neurosis."

The continuous case seminar differed from present methods in that the teacher, instead of a candidate, demonstrated the case. It was attended by all candidates and some members. Ultimately it superseded the Berlin model of small groups of five or six in clinical supervision. I heard her report the lively psychological adventures of the patient with the hen-phobia, also included in the *Psychoanalysis of the Neuroses.*

She spoke from notes for the two hours without interruption. In this early clinical demonstration for the candidates, in order to protect the treatment process as well as the clarity of the presentation, there were no interruptions for discussion. Her reporting style revealed how the genesis of the patient's problems was tied up with his life story and, in a rare manner, coordinated the clinical process with analytic theory.

Helene Deutsch entered on the analytic scene in the United States well in advance of other notable Europeans. Her first visit in May 1930, as a guest lecturer for the International Congress of Psychic Hygiene, and the visits of Dr. Felix in 1931 and 1934, prepared them to accept the invitation to move to Boston in 1935, still unaware that their sojourn in America would be permanent.

From the beginning, she found the work in this country "exciting and productive," parallel to the early Viennese activities. Her collaboration at the Boston Psychoanalytic Institute was welcomed, and her affiliations with hospitals brought her back to the work she had loved but which had been impossible in Vienna. In recent years, she has gradually retired from teaching. Never has she really adjusted to the "big machinery" of the American Psychoanalytic Association; she has accepted only with resignation the "grandiose" development of analysis in this country. "I believe it is deeply historically determined," she says, "but I still carry in my mind the tradition of this Viennese epoch of which I was a part." American psychoanalysis has recognized her epochal contributions with the Menninger Award of 1962.

At this point, we may pause to limn those intangible qualities of personality that pervade Helene Deutsch's work. Watching her lecture, report a case in seminar, or listen in supervision, as I did, one was always aware of an exquisitely keen mind, empathically dedicated to her subject and intuitively responsive to the dynamic import of the patient's material, both in its individual human drama and its objective psychological significance. My memory retains the physical image of Helene Deutsch thirty-five years ago. Her personal beauty—the classic structure of her features, the robust color of her skin, her penetrating blue eyes softened by the halo of brown hair, and the tall, rounded figure clad in attractive and fashionable silks—bespoke a graciousness that did not conceal the strength of character within. In the Slavic rhythm of her speech, her face was dramatically mobile and animated; at rest, it revealed kindliness and feminine softness.

Recently I saw her, at seventy-eight years of age, standing in the leafy sunshine of her white-frame cottage doorway in Cambridge, Massachusetts, a thinner figure, straight, tall, and plainly dressed, one which, except for its emanation of innate elegance, could be mistaken for that of a typical New England woman. In this her third home, the cultural influences of her European background, her Polish youth, and her productive Viennese middle life, are reflected. The warm brown living room with a few pictures and wood sculptures leads to the consulting room, where the desk and a cheerful wall of books are the predominant features, while the low analytic couch covered in dark velvet inconspicuously rests against the entering wall. Entrance and exit to this room are through the garden, apart from the house, and do not conflict with a similar separate arrangement for Dr. Felix[2] in the opposite wing of the house. A serene old-world quality fills the house and the small, glass-enclosed patio extending into the garden, where after several hours of concentrated talk in her office, we enjoyed tea.

In the relaxed atmosphere of this setting, I could not help but remember my first visit to her Vienna office in the crowded and busy Wollzeilgasse, up some narrow flights of stairs into a bare, square waiting room with hardwood benches lining the wooden walls. Access to Helene's consultation room was through a very long, enclosed narrow corridor. In this large darkened room, the couch was also inconspicuous against a dark wall. I sat before a window facing a desk chaotic with books and papers. I felt she could barely take time for the hour; yet, in that time, I had her full attention for my material, which she interrupted only for sparse, perceptive comments interspersed with nods of approval. If not everyone had the same response to her supervisions, it was because her piercing mind, in its own special intuitive and keenly critical way, could also be intolerant of minds that worked differently. But one always felt that added to her scientific gift was the warm human touch so essential to a whole understanding of the person and problem.

The *Psychoanalysis of the Neuroses*, published in 1930, for the first time supplied in its eleven lectures a clinical text for analysts and students, adding new explorations and additional corroboration of what was already known and accepted. The essential features of the transference neuroses—hysteria, phobia, compulsion neurosis—are described; and a narcissistic neurosis, melancholic depression, is added for compar-

[2] The sad news of the death of Dr. Felix Deutsch on January 2, 1964, arrived during the writing of this paper.

ison. Differences and similarities in the genesis and structure of each type are pointed up, in respect to the libidinal phase of regression or fixation and its depth, the fate of the object relationship, the tension and conflict between the superego and the ego regarding the claims of the instinctual sexual and aggressive drives, and the extent of the process of instinct defusion and decomposition in releasing destructive tendencies.

Raising the question under what circumstances latent neuroses become mobilized, Deutsch starts with the "actual" neurosis, describing and defining it in terms of the internal and external problems that the ego fails to solve. She demonstrates also the technical ways by which the actual neurosis in each type is traced back and connected with the infantile neurosis.

The fate neurosis is a "model" for the dynamics of anxiety hysteria, involving fixation of object choice at the infantile genital level. Conversion hysteria, in contrast, demonstrates assimilation of infantile disharmonies into the ego through secondary gains of physical suffering used to discharge guilt, to relieve anxiety, and to leave the ego freer to adapt to changed external circumstances. The nucleus of infantile anxiety states is the masturbation conflict. Insightful formulations condense the dynamic connections, for example, "the night cry of the child is a call for help from the father against the dangers of masturbation." The decreasing frequency of certain hysterical symptomatology is attributed to wider involvement in such interests as telepathy and spiritualism in which a symbiosis between libidinal and destructive impulses is effected in a socially acceptable form.

"On Pathological Lying," published in 1922, discusses *pseudologia fantastica* as resembling hysteria in that it is the distorted reappearance of a repressed real experience. "Occult Happenings during Analysis," which was published in 1926, explains "telepathic" experiences between analyst and patient on the basis of unconscious affective communication between them in the transference.

The structure of phobia and phobic states is set forth in a case of cat-phobia and another of hen-phobia; obsessional neurosis is represented by a severe case of stuporous immobility. Finally, a case of melancholia illustrates the most deeply regressive pathology. Deutsch shows in detail how the agoraphobe converts his companion into a "protected protector" whom he protects against his own rage, thus diminishing his death anxiety. To the dynamics of the obsessional neurosis are added newer formulations regarding aggression in the superego and its unrelenting severity against the ego, neatly described in her phrase "aggression against aggression." In tracing melancholia to its deepest regressive phase, the cannibalistic incorporation and identification mechanisms, she demonstrates clinically the transitions between the other forms of neurosis by which the patient had, at various critical periods, attempted to inhibit or resolve the destructive impulses, and compares the neurotic accomplishment of each type in the mechanisms used.

In each case described, the anatomy of the pathology is always cloaked with the flesh and blood of the affects.

Within the main stream of Helene Deutsch's publications on female psychology and the neuroses, two main areas can be discerned: the problem of affects in neuroses and normal character, and the dynamics producing defense mechanisms in normal and pathological states.

"The Psychology of Mistrust," published in 1921, which she considers her best work, is the model for her investigation of universal affects and their disturbances. The quality of mistrust originates in the ambivalent inner conflict over childhood disappointments projected onto external objects. In isolating its dynamics, Deutsch became by many years a forerunner of the more recent child-directed research on this problem (Spitz, Erikson) in the development of early object relations.

"Contentment, Happiness and Ecstasy," written in 1927, explores positive feelings that are ordinarily beyond the analyst's observation. The normal mode of resolution of tension states within the ego, which leads to a feeling of happiness, is attained through a process of ego-boundary expansion involving object cathexis and sublimation. Its transient character is a manifestation of the continuous struggle for mastery over the ambivalent forces, and of the fact that satisfaction is followed by new strivings.

"Absence of Grief" was published in 1937. It adds to Freud's work on mourning the idea that permanent suppression may mean the death of the entire emotional life and lead to "unmotivated" depressions.

The "as if" personality described in the well known 1934 paper, "Some Forms of Emotional Disturbance and Their Relation to Schizophrenia," is a study of the deficiency in the affective life of an apparently normal personality who gives a good semblance of adaptation to reality, yet is actually devoid of genuine emotion. The 1937 paper, "Folie à Deux," is based on clinical observations published as early as 1918 in the Wiener *Klinische Wochenschrift*. In the induction of another person into the delusions of the primarily diseased person, the common delusion attempts to rescue the lost object through identification with it or its delusional system. The universal implications of this process are evident in the state of being in love, as well as in mass psychological phenomena in social and political movements, where world approval or disapproval is the only criterion of the value of the idea as heroic or mad. One surmises that this is a reference to the mass psychosis of Hitlerism, with the effects of which the author and her colleagues had had bitter personal experience.

As is evident, ego-psychological problems are dealt with in the scope of other investigations. As early as 1925, "A Contribution to the Psychology of Sport" sets forth the mechanism of projection as an ego defense, to explain the transformation and sublimation of castration and death anxiety into ego-syntonic aggressive activities that re-establish the reality relationship between the ego and the outside world. And the 1933 paper, "The Psychology of the Manic-Depressive States" (still untranslated from the German),[3] discusses, for the first time in analytical literature, the defense of denial.

Many other papers have to do with ego dynamics. The 1930 paper, "On the Genesis of Fantasies of Descent," attributes the universal fantasy of belonging to other parents than one's own to a split between the image of the overevaluated pre-Oedipal parent and the correction of it after the building of the superego. Deutsch's psychoanalysis of Don Quixote, "Don Quixote and Quixotism" (1937), published in 1934, explains the character on the basis of such a split in the ego of man. Such a person is the child-idealist who demands that the real world adjust to his ego ideal. Sancho Panza, his dissociated counterpart, is necessary to him as the tender but ridiculed parent who serves as a bridge to reality. The two antitheses constitute a unity in man. In the deprecatory caricaturing elements of glorified castrated son and devaluated Philistine father, the reader's pleasure is served by providing a bit of ego mastery of his own infantile past.

"The Impostor," delivered as the 1955 A. A. Brill Memorial Lecture, presents a brilliant analysis of the development of the "nonego ego" of the psychopath. To eliminate friction between his exaggerated ego ideal and his own inferior guilt-laden ego, he assumes the role of one

[3] A new edition of *Psychoanalysis of the Neuroses*, to be published by Hogarth Press, includes this paper in English translation, along with additional clinical publications after 1937.

who fulfills his "magnificent" ideal and behaves as if it coincided with his own by trying to force the world to accept these pretensions. Illustrating her thesis with Thomas Mann's character, Felix Krull, Deutsch marvels "how the genius of a writer is able to grasp intuitively the insights we arrive at so laboriously through clinical empiricism." Her own insights reveal her kinship with this intuition of literature.

Extending chronologically from the beginning of her psychoanalysis with Freud to the present day, Helene Deutsch's work is climaxed by the two volumes, *The Psychology of Women*, which alone would assure her a unique place in psychoanalytic history. Zilboorg aptly said that this work belongs to the continuity of psychoanalytic history that goes on quietly under all the disagreement and controversies. Published in 1944 and 1945, it is the first and only integrated, chronological, and comprehensive study in depth of the psychological development of woman, and it remains the classic work on the subject. In addition to the contents of her papers of the two preceding decades, it includes further empirical material from the Boston period of her supervisory social case work, as well as data from creative literature. It constitutes the major contribution to one of the few areas of psychoanalysis that Freud had left "admittedly incomplete and fragmentary."

Early in his career, Freud had said the enigma of woman could be fully understood neither by men, nor yet by women, who "are the riddle themselves." "If you want to know more about femininity," he had concluded, "you must interrogate your own experience, or turn to the poets, or else wait until science can give you more profound and more coherent information." To this subject, Helene Deutsch came as a woman, with the clinical acumen of the scientist and the feeling of a poet. In eight papers on female psychology, she followed collaboratively in the direction pointed by Freud, adding, on the basis of her clinical findings, her own theoretical enlargements. Her first contributions, "The Psychology of Women in Relation to the Functions of Reproduction" of 1924, and "On the Psychoanalysis of the Female Sexual Functions" of 1925, were followed by "The Significance of Masochism in the Mental Life of Women," in 1930, and "On Female Homosexuality," in 1932. These coincide in time with Freud's first and final papers on the same subject—1925 and 1931. Freud gave full credit to the women, chiefly Deutsch and Jeanne Lampl de Groot, for having broken new ground and added new insights. Because of their advantage over men in being suitable mother substitutes in the transference situation, he had come to feel that "they were able to perceive the facts more easily and clearly" than men, particularly in respect to the earliest, strong and elusive mother attachment. As Fliess picturesquely put it, Freud had, Pygmalion-like, "caused the female hewn by the chisel of his own research to come alive and respond with discoveries of her own."

The sum of Deutsch's insights about the feminine core of woman's ego, the manner of its genetic formation, development, and manifestation in the feminine functions, in the ramifications of woman's personality, character, and behavior, and in neuroses, has clarified though by no means simplified the "riddle," and it belies Deutsch's own statement that Freud had "left nothing to discover."

The "facts" studied in these papers supplemented Freud's and Abraham's basic theses and underscored the significance of feminine masochism in the functions of reproduction, in frigidity, in female homosexuality, in femininity, in the relationship between motherhood and sexuality, and in other problems of normal and neurotic development.

The *Psychology of Women* examines the total life cycle of woman, from the time before "the female child becomes a woman" through the climacterium. The central phenomenon of motherhood is shown to conceal a complex world within itself: "physiologic processes, the operation of biologic laws of heredity and adjustment, rational and seemingly absurd processes, historical and individual psychic elements," within a setting of sociocultural influences. This complex of factors reveals the deeply-rooted universal human dynamic components in female development that are basically accountable for her normal character and personality, as well as for her neurotic disturbances and deviations.

In "The Significance of Masochism in the Mental Life of Woman," she had established, in 1929, the concept that the genesis of "femininity" lies in the essential passive-masochistic disposition of woman, which is the elemental force in her mental life and ties her instinctual functions closely to her anatomical destiny in the function of reproduction. Because of the lengthy and circuitous regressive route by which a masochistic conversion of the girl's constant struggles with her never wholly-effaced bisexuality is brought about, it had been easier to recognize the masculine pathological element in woman than to see the specifically feminine nucleus of her disposition and its development.

The original phase of passive attachment of the infant to mother plays the fundamental role in the girl's feminine development, not alone in the primary oral phase but—differentially from the boy's—also in the later regressive movement away from the active phallic phase. It is the startling perception that the clitoris is not an adequate phallus like the boy's that begins the regressive movement to the earlier passive positions in which the girl received mother's active love and care on the oral and anal levels. "The thrust to passivity" with the wish for an anal child from mother, replacing the wish for a penis, is central to the evolution of femininity. The girl's ambivalence to mother motivates the transition to father as object; however, identification with her in her masochistic genital relationship with father is the basis for the hope of attaining the missing penis-child from him, through the third receptive organ, the vagina. The dynamics of the girl, thus involving a change of zone, of aim, and of object, develops, from a fundamental dispositional factor, the essential masochism based in her anatomical and biological structure.

The difficulties attending the feminine position center around these changes: the abandonment of the clitoris before a cathexis of the vagina is possible; the regressive deflection in aim of the active-sadistic tendencies to the masochistic wish to be castrated, which constitutes the first libidinal relationship to the father; and the maintenance of the passive position, despite the reality of the father's inhibiting influence. When this essential libidinal masochism cathects the new object of father, the girl is on her way to femininity. All the processes in the ego and the instincts, the constitutional, the anatomical, and the environmental factors work together to produce it. Nevertheless, the masculine bisexual element flares up and must be repeatedly subdued in every phase of later feminine manifestations. The processes of menstruation, pregnancy, and parturition, involving powerful upheavals in the libidinal economy, may assume traumatic proportions as a result of the conflicts between the ego and the reproductive tendencies.

In puberty the "wave of activity" must again be deflected into a secondary reinforcement of the primary erotogenic masochism. The fact of menstruation settles for good the phallic, organic deficiency, and the resulting masochistic fantasies prepare the way for defloration and ultimate vaginal cathexis. For the woman to succeed in exchanging the penis wish for a real and valuable vagina, the hostile impulses aroused by the narcissistic injury must be overcome by feelings of love. The vagina then becomes, in miniature, the ego of the woman.

Coitus represents the mastery of both the weaning trauma and the castration trauma. In this act, the woman restores the first unity experienced through the displacement of oral libido to the vagina and is enabled, by an "identification series" with her mother, to surrender the clitoral attachment to the vagina and to identify with the incorporated penis of the partner. The latter is symbolically retained during pregnancy, released in the process of parturition, and restored again in the libidinal relationship to the child.

In Helene Deutsch's formulations, the female sexual act is performed in two parts. To the vaginal orgasm of coitus is added the final "orgy of masochistic pleasure" in delivery, which contains the acme of pleasure and relief analogous to male ejaculation. The interval in time between the two acts is filled with complicated processes in the economy of the libido and the ego. Ambivalent tendencies, containing deposits from all earlier phases—oral, anal and phallic—become manifest during pregnancy, disturbing the original regressive unity. In this process, the libidinal relationship to the child is formed, which must be worked out within the ego, in an interaction of its parts. The child *in utero,* at first part of the ego and increasing its narcissism, becomes in later phases also an outside object around whom the old ambivalent conflicts are repeated.

According to their reaction to pregnancy, women show favorable or unfavorable changes, blooming through a heightening of secondary narcissism when libido is directed toward the child as part of her ego, or shrinking and depressed when her narcissism is sacrificed to the child and the superego has impoverished her ego. The ambivalence toward the child *in utero* is manifested in the final struggle of delivery, in which the hostile impulses are mobilized for the expulsion of the incorporated object. The deepest and final regression is thus the trauma of giving birth, in which the repetition of anxiety attached to birth is discharged by actual reproduction.

This discharge, which men can attain only in intercourse and which therefore impels them to sublimation, women can attain in reproduction. Normally, as men derive forces for sublimation from the sadistic tendencies, women draw on the masochistic ones for maternity. In the mental economy of woman, employment of the masochistic instinctual forces for purposes of race preservation is an act of sublimation. The child inaugurates the work of sublimation, even before he becomes a reality in the outside world, as the incarnation of the ego ideal modeled after father. After delivery, the feeling of emptiness is filled with the beginning of the new relationship to the newborn child. The physiological and psychological factors in lactation complete the circle begun by coitus, reproducing physiologically and psychologically the same situation at the end as at the beginning, and the girl child has now become the mother in reality. This is the normal course of feminine psychological adaptation.

A wide range of outcomes is possible, in the fate of the earliest feminine masochistic identification and its conflict with the active-phallic drive, in disturbing this psychological adaptation. The dangers of neurosis arising in the development of the primary feminine libidinal masochism, as in exacerbation of masculinity, come from intense penis envy and excessively vigorous, active phallic tendencies, which can result from flight from the incest wish and the masochistic dangers threatening the ego in identifying with mother.

Maternal and sexual capacity do not always develop together. They may be incompatible where the ego is torn between the rival urges to be motherly and to be erotic. Various grades of detachment of these two tendencies show that there is a connection between repudiation of the erotic impulse and the impaired capacity for maternity. In the normal, passive identification with mother, repudiation of the maternal role may result from excessive Oedipal guilt for rivalry with her. Strong pre-Oedipal fixation may give the libido a homosexual position. Father as a sexual object may be renounced, sexuality degraded and denied, and the maternal role overestimated or regarded as parthenogenic, as in the fantasy of immaculate conception; or the masochistic tendencies can be so fully satisfied by maternity, as in the *mater dolorosa* attitude, that sexuality becomes insignificant. In the symptom of frigidity, the libido never attains a central vaginal organization. Both sexual and maternal capacities may be impaired because the ego, feeling the danger from masochistic gratifications in both capacities, protests against the passive feminine role by escaping from an identification with mother into an identification with father, thus also shunning the danger from the incest wish. The problem in neurotic diseases is that the primary-libidinal feminine masochism is interwoven with moral masochism because of excessive guilt reactions.

The association between pleasure and pain in woman derives directly from the reproductive function. Masochism plays a dual role in feminine sexual and reproductive functions, on the one hand helping in the adjustment to reality through the necessary consent to pain, and on the other provoking, through excess, the danger of distortions and defenses that can only result in disturbance. The destiny of woman's femininity depends on the harmonious co-operation of masochism and narcissism.

One must look behind the castration anxiety to find the masochistic wish characteristic of the infantile phase of the normal feminine libido. In woman's life in the relationship of mother to the child, the libidinal forces that come into play are closely allied to the masochism that finds its greatest gratification in the relationship between man and woman.

While the basis of these summarized constructions are to be found in the analytic source material of Deutsch's cases, the conviction of their perceptiveness also comes to the reader affectively, from her numerous illustrative studies of female characters in world literature, whose gifted authors (Balzac, Tolstoy, Ibsen, Gorky, Colette, and others) intuitively understood and described these same aspects of female character and conflict. And in the scientific search for the individual ontogenetic factors in the psychological gamut of variation from normality to pathology, Deutsch does not overlook the possible connections of the various manifestations with the phylogenetic history of the race, as well as anthropological, social, cultural, and environmental effects of the historical processes and attitudes toward women.

Helene Deutsch is essentially a clinician, in the words of Ernst Kris, "a great clinician—not only one who deals with nosology, with groups of afflictions—but in a wider sense, germane to psychoanalysis, a clinician of psychological understanding."

If the modern reader of psychoanalysis finds himself familiar with the main line of structural and dynamic formulations, it is because Deutsch has set the classical mode for the clinical presentation. He will be impressed by her clinical acumen, the incisive brilliance of her mind, and refreshed by the scope and richness of her familiarity with literature as well as life.

Felix Deutsch

1884–1964

PSYCHOANALYSIS AND INTERNAL MEDICINE

*

GLENN W. FLAGG

Felix Deutsch was born on August 9, 1884, in Vienna, Austria. His parents were well-to-do—his father a bank official, and his mother from a business family in Vienna. When he was five years of age, his father died, leaving his mother, an older brother, Felix, and a younger sister.

In his youth, Deutsch was an accomplished pianist, and for a time he was undecided whether to pursue a musical career or to study medicine. During his student days, he was very active in athletics at the university, where he was known for his principles and his allegiance to friends.

Although he grew up without any formal religious background, when Deutsch encountered the very anti-Semitic environment of the university he became a leader in a Zionist student organization; in this capacity he not only spoke for the group but often served as front fighter for the organization. While functioning as a defender of the student minority group, he suffered two life-long injuries and achieved the reputation of being on the side of the weak. It was during this period of his life that Deutsch met Freud's son Martin, who belonged to the same student group. Deutsch became Martin's tutor and through him met Freud and the other members of the family. Although Deutsch and Freud belonged to the same intellectual Jewish social organization, Deutsch felt that this relationship played little part in his scientific endeavors relative to analysis; it was almost never mentioned. His experiences as a champion in student organizations, however, developed Deutsch's fighting spirit for psychoanalysis, which was then in need of defense at the university. He decided at that time "never to make any compromise when the matter of truth was in question."

As of January 1, 1963, Deutsch's bibliography exceeded 140 items; their titles reveal the depth and breadth of his knowledge. As a researcher in psychosomatic problems, I have been impressed by the fact that a well-trained internist such as he is, respected by his medical colleagues, was willing, despite the hostile environment, to lend his prestige to the struggling science of psychoanalysis. To a certain extent, this was a consciously planned program. Upon delivering his first open lectures before the Society of Internal Medicine, "Mind and Body," studied from the psychoanalytic vantage point, Deutsch met with great hostility. He recalled that former friends avoided him: he was warned that he was digging his scientific grave and some labeled him a socialist. The Neurologic Society, to which he belonged, challenged him to make his position clear: Was he an internist, or an analyst?

Deutsch states that he was advised to "go underground" for awhile. As a result, he made an almost 180 degree turn scientifically and began a program of extensive research on the heart in athletics, and on the influence of sports on bodily processes. While conducting physiological research, Deutsch founded the publication known as *Sports Medicine* and wrote a standard textbook on the subject. Also, he wrote a book on insurance medicine, in which he deals with the longevity of neuroses. He was already analyzing psychosomatic patients at the hospital without charge and, on the advice of Freud, went into analysis with Siegfried Bernfeld.

In 1919, while on the faculty of the Internal Medicine Section of the Weidener Krankenhaus, he established the first clinic on "organ neurosis" and each year gave an official course for students on organic neurosis, psychoanalysis, and internal medicine. He presented the first seminar on organ neurosis at the Psychoanalytic Institute. Papers on this subject that he delivered before the Society were discussed at the meetings by Freud. At these meetings, Deutsch also presented the first analytically treated cases of angina pectoris, asthma, colitis, Buerger's disease, and blepharospasm.

At the International Psychoanalytic Meeting in Berlin in 1921, he suggested a broader application of the term "conversion symptom." Subsequent seminars on hypnosis and psychoanalysis, which he gave on request, were attended by Anna Freud, Hug-Hellmuth, Edward Hitschmann, and other leading analysts. Freud himself went with Deutsch to a demonstration, at the Heart Station, of hypnosis in a patient with Raynaud's disease. Freud was greatly interested in the demonstration because it reminded him of his days with Charcot and Forel. (Deutsch's personal account of his relationship with Freud has been deposited in the Library of Congress, to be published after his death.)

It was through the influence of Deutsch that the first permanent home of the Psychoanalytic Institute was established, in 1922, at the Heart Station. One of his papers in the psychosomatic field, published in that same year, is titled "The Meaning of Psychoanalytic Knowledge for Internal Medicine." In this paper, designed for practicing physicians, one can already see a major interest that has continued to this day. As M. Ralph Kaufman demonstrated in a paper read at the Boston Psychoanalytic Institute on May 21, 1955, in honor of the seventieth birthdays of Helene and Felix Deutsch, the first ten papers of Felix Deutsch contain the kernel of his later contributions.

"The Value of Psychoanalytic Knowledge in the Practice of Internal Medicine" (1922) emphasizes that constitutional factors alone do not clarify the total clinical picture, and that the course of a clinical illness can be understood only in terms of the individual reaction pattern of the patient. Deutsch also outlined there the role of instinct and instinctual repression in organic illness. In this very early paper Deutsch pointed out that the course of an illness may be influenced by emotional situations entirely independent of constitutional factors; he was already foreshadowing that aspect of his work which led to the technique of "associative anamnesis," believed by many to be his most important contribution to clinical psychiatry. In addition to the information obtained in a conventional medical history, this method elicits data on the patient's emotional development and thus enriches the understanding and treatment of the patient.

Deutsch continually exhibited his orientation to clinical medicine by referring to specific cases in many of his papers. Like Franz Alexander, he was early to recognize that continued stimulation of the sympathetic and parasympathetic nervous systems from emotional causes can result in organic disease. However, like Georg Groddeck (but unlike Alexander, Roy R. Grinker, and so on), Deutsch felt that activation of the autonomic nervous system tends to release emotional conflict, and that, as a result, autonomic symptoms express repressed symbolic content rather than being purely physiological concomitants or adaptive preparatory states, which remain prolonged and unreleased because of repressive forces. According to Deutsch, the neurotic symptom complex must be understood before we can know the language of the illness and what the patient is trying to communicate through his particular symptoms.

Deutsch has always maintained an organismic point of view that has been especially important in psychosomatic medicine, inasmuch as it maintains that the homeostatic balance within the organism between organic functions and psychic processes makes it possible for each to influence the other. Some have said that his emphasis on this interrelationship of all psychobiological reactions was already a formulation of the unitary field hypothesis.

In "Psychoanalysis and Internal Medicine," published in 1927, Deutsch not only used the term "psychosomatic" but formulated some of the basic concepts recognized today. He and Emil Kauf conducted basic psychosomatic research, demonstrating the influence of psychic and physical factors on heart functions and on the circulatory tonus, pulse, and blood pressure changes in hypnotized subjects. Also included were studies of the effect of psychic experiences on metabolism.

Other papers by Deutsch include: "Capillary Studies on Raynaud's Disease," "Autonomic Skin Test with Electrophoresis," "The Production of Somatic Disease by Emotional Disturbance," "The Choice of Organ in Organ Neurosis," "Psychophysical Reactions of the Vascular System to Influence of Light and to Impressions Gained through Light," "Psychological Methods of Obtaining Medical Information," "Psychosomatic Aspects of Dermatology, with Special Consideration of Allergic Phenomena," "Prophylactic Aspects of Malnutritional Problems," and "Instinctual Drives in Intersensory Perceptions During the Analytic Procedure."

In a paper presented in 1953, "Basic Psychoanalytic Principles in Psychosomatic Disorders," Deutsch summarized the then current evaluations of his point of view. He objected to the labeling of certain reactions as psychogenically conditioned, suggesting that the term be abandoned because:

> . . . by implication it denies the innate permanent psychic elements as always present in all homeostatic physiological functions since this term al-

ways refers to pathologic occurrences. From the dynamic analytic point of view all biologic functions are continually governed by emotional needs apart from the neuro-chemo-humoral regulatory mechanisms. Only if these psychophysiological mechanisms are tuned up to each other, a homeostasis is guaranteed—a condition called health (p. 103).

In "The Healthy and Sick Body under Psychoanalytic Consideration," published in 1926, he had already stated:

Health and sickness are biologically not essentially different. Health is the basis of illness, and in sickness one may recognize the elements of health. Even psychoanalysis discovered the normal primarily by way of the morbid. Psychoanalysis is an empirical science, devoted—as the very name indicates—to the investigation of psychic processes. The body—or better—the physical world, aroused its interest only insofar as it always contains psychic elements, or insofar as manifest organic symptom formations become conscious, replacing the repressed unconscious ones. Thus, the interest once aroused became greatly intensified when it appeared how far the psychic could be pursued into the realm of the organic.

This statement contains the essential elements of Deutsch's psychosomatic point of view and has served as a guidepost to many other investigators. His emphasis on the fused relationship of all psychobiological phenomena from earliest infancy is based on the fact that, at an early level of development, all sensory perceptions "have no other objectifications than those related to one's own body, [therefore] purely organic disturbances, i.e. diseases . . . will be of great importance for an unharmonious, uneven psychosomatic development."

Thus, the feeling stimulus becomes the most important factor in the foundation of the ego structure, "because it leads to acquisition of an extraneous reality which can be reached, accepted, rejected, unified with or separated from the body reality. . . . This psychosomatic process begins on a primary narcissistic level, passes through the oral and anal up to the genital stage, forever retaining elements of each level throughout life. This structural organization of the body ego may be disarranged at any level of development. It can be transitorily distorted, interrupted, arrested or fixed." In one aspect of this paper Deutsch pointed to the necessity for considering prenatal factors to understand certain regressive modes of behavior, and he postulated that a regressive pattern of behavior is laid down before birth. In this paper he formulated fourteen factors that enter into a psychosomatic disorder:

1. The occurrence of an organic dysfunction (hyper or hypo) in the neonatal or early infancy period.
2. The coincidence of this dysfunction with instinctual conflicts on a specific level of psychic development.
3. The frequency of the simultaneous repetition of this dysfunction and of the specific conflict.
4. The extent and number of sense perceptions involved in the psychosomatic process.
5. The fusion of these two processes.
6. The repression of the original experience which provoked the conflict.
7. The consistency of using the organic dysfunction as the preverbal expression of the repressed conflicts and their related memories.
8. The factors and figures in the past environment which stimulated the specific conflict.
9. The early symbolization and personification of these figures in parts of the body involved.
10. The degree of the ego weakness and its inability of solving the conflicts otherwise.
11. The degree of the resulting ego defect and organic defect.
12. The type of behavior disorder or neurosis which has finally developed.
13. The type of neurosis of the parental and family figures.
14. Other incidental and accidental life experiences.

To investigate the meaning, the purpose, the tenacity, the choice, and the development of symptoms, Deutsch stated that one needs

> a vertical cross-section through the historical layers of the personality. The theoretical concept is that of determinism, causality, regression and repetition compulsion, which elucidate the development of the symptoms by a consideration of the sense perceptions involved in the symptom complex. Their efficacy as conditioning factors lies in a dispositional fusion and interaction of psychic and somatic phenomena which persist during the entire life.

To obtain data for understanding his patients, Deutsch developed the method of associative anamnesis, which he later expanded to include sector psychotherapy. His refinement of the technique of the associative anamnesis has led to a number of major contributions. One of these is the book *Applied Psychoanalysis* (1949), which presents the new technique of sector psychotherapy. He stated there that "the technic of the 'associative anamnesis,' as therapy, aims to avoid the spreading of the field of therapeutic approach too far and to keep the material centered around certain symptoms or certain conscious and unconscious conflicts" (p. 23). His concept of goal-limited adjustment grew out of the utilization of this technique. It should be noted in passing that Franz Alexander and the Chicago School gave him credit for the technique of the associative anamnesis, which they found to be the best procedure for research purposes, in their work on the problem of specificity. Another major contribution that has grown out of this is the excellent work, *The Clinical Interview,* published together with Murphy.

Another major area of Deutsch's interest has been the investigation of sources of, and motivations for, the correlations and interrelations of emotional and bodily behavior. This work has been outlined by a series of papers titled, "Thus Speaks the Body" (1949). They outline the study of unconscious motivations of postural behavior.

Every individual has a basic posture. Every posture is meaningful and consists of a combination of different, well-determined postures of single parts. All postures of the different parts of the body are attuned to each other, and the change of one partial posture leads to a re-arrangement of the total configuration. The movement from one posture to another and the following position of the different limbs to each other is preconditioned by the representation of these parts in the unconscious. The configurations of the posture are bound to be characteristic for the person in question and depend on the firmness of the synthesization of the postural pattern within the personality. Drives and defenses once entrenched firmly in the basic posture lead to a postural defense line, which can be pierced only to a certain degree.

The repetition compulsion is an essential factor in the establishment of the basic posture. During the free associative procedure, unconsciously determined involuntary movements break through. This break-through depends on the degree of regression at a certain moment and on the kind of symbolization of the part of the body in question, or on the sort of inhibitory and defensive factors involved.

The posture changes whenever a shift in the psychodynamic situation takes place for which another postural expression is needed. The postural behavior substitutes and may precede the verbalization of the unconscious material. Emerging postures seem to be the product of a long developmental process and have their roots in the earliest childhood. Some betray their early origin by their similarity with infantile postures.

The change of posture seems to aim at the relief of tension. If the psychologic stimulus is insufficiently discharged, the postural configuration will continue or will be repeated. Observations of hand and finger postures how

how minutely the postural pattern is laid down. The tenacity of basic posture is clearly proven by their repetition even after a long interruption of analysis (1949, p. 62).

Deutsch extended his earlier interest in sensory perception, and he reiterated the need for the patient to include in analysis not only verbalizations but also body sensations, feelings, and affects. He presented his views in the paper "Analytic Synesthesiology" (1954). In brief, what has been reported here constitutes a recommendation for analytic research into preverbal expressions of the unconscious or preconscious during the analytic procedure. The appearance of certain intersensory forms of behavior is a precursory expression of the conflictive relationship to certain objects of the past. These preverbal sensory expressions disappear when the corresponding instinctual conflicts are settled.

Dissolution of the patterned sensory complex is an essential purpose of psychoanalytic therapy. Therefore, the scrutiny of the changes in sensory behavior can be used for the evaluation of the therapeutic process, of its result and—when we are engaged in therapy—as an adjuvant to know why we do what we are doing (1954, p. 300).

The last refinement to the method of interviewing by associative anamnesis is that the anamnesis is initiated by a sensory stimulus. Here an external sensory stimulus is an initial key signal for further associations. Thus, when a patient is interviewed while he is exposed to an external stimulus, his ego will react as if it were a stimulus from within, and he will produce verbal associations to it which reveal his defenses.

Last, but by no means least, since coming to the United States in 1935, Deutsch was an active teacher and educator, as a research fellow in psychiatry at Harvard University. Besides his teaching of physicians, he was influential in the training of social workers at the Simmons and Smith College schools of social work. He served as a consultant at many hospitals and clinics, was a member of numerous professional and honorary societies, and was Senior Lecturer and Training Analyst with the Boston Psychoanalytic Institute, from 1936 until his recent death, as well as Honorary Professor of Psychiatry at the Boston University Medical School from 1959.

REFERENCES

Deutsch, F. Die Bedeutung Psychoanalytischer Kenntnisse für die innere Medizin (The value of psychoanalytic knowledge in the practice of internal medicine). *Mitteilungen der Gesellschaft für inn Med. und Kinderheilkunde* (Vienna), 1922, **21** (1).

Deutsch, F. Psychoanalyse un innere Medizin (Psychoanalysis and internal medicine). *Berl Allg ärtzl Kong Psychother.*, 1927, **2**, 53–59.

Deutsch, F. Basic psychoanalytic principles in psychosomatic disorders. *Acta Psychother. Psychosom. Orthopaedagog.* (Basel), 1953, **1**, 102–111.

Deutsch, F. *Applied psychoanalysis. Selected objectives of psychotherapy.* New York: Grune & Stratton, 1949.

Deutsch, F. Thus speaks the body. I. An analysis of postural behavior. *Trans. N.Y. Acad. Sci.*, 1949, series 2, **19** (2).

Deutsch, F. Der gesunde und der kranke Körper in psychoanalytischer Betrachtung (The healthy and sick body under psychoanalytic consideration). Z., 1926, **12**, 493–503.

Deutsch, F. Analytic synesthesiology. *Int. J.*, 1954, **35**, 293–301.

While writing this brief chapter in the summer of 1962, I enjoyed an exchange of letters with Dr. Deutsch. It was with great regret that I learned of the death of Felix Deutsch on January 2, 1964—G. W. F.

A brief but very promising career ended April 1, 1965, when Dr. Glenn W. Flagg died in a plane accident. Dr. Flagg was the author of several papers on psychosomatic medicine and at the time of his death was the director for research for the Franz Alexander Psychosomatic Research Foundation.

Georg Groddeck

1866–1934

THE UNTAMED ANALYST

*

MARTIN GROTJAHN

Georg Groddeck was born in Baden-Baden, South Germany, in 1866. The son of Karl Groddeck, a physician he revered as wise and profound, Groddeck came to be known as the "father of psychosomatic medicine," a term he despised as shallow and misleading.

Georg remembered his mother as beautiful but aloof. He was the fifth and last child. There were three older brothers; Lina, the fourth child and only girl, was the mother's favorite and Georg's playmate. For a time he attended a girls' school with Lina. Georg assumed that his life-long close relationship with Lina helped him to understand man's bisexual nature, pregnancy envy in men, creativity, and how to be a good healer—a "mother-father."

After Karl Groddeck was ruined financially, the family moved to Berlin, where Karl became a physician to the poor. Georg was encouraged to study medicine; while arranging for medical training, he was required to sign up for eight years of Army service.

Georg's favorite teacher was Ernst Schweninger, whom he considered the greatest living physician. Schweninger was tyrannical, brutal, and bizarre; he antagonized everyone. Through the influence of a grateful patient, Otto von Bismarck, Schweninger was permitted to teach his eccentric physiotherapeutic ideas at one of the university hospitals.

Between 1889 and 1897, Groddeck endured Army service. During this unhappy time, his mother died; he turned to Else, a married woman with two small children, whom he married after her divorce and his army discharge. Georg moved his family to Baden-Baden, where he became Medical Director, and eventually the owner, of a small sanitarium originally founded by Schweninger. His sister Lina was Georg's devoted helper.

Groddeck spent the rest of his life here, developing around his stern-faced but curtly polite person an aura and sanitarium regime that eventually brought patients, including other psychoanalytic pioneers, from all over Europe. He dominated the daily routine of his patients, prescribing diets and massages—often administering the massages himself.

Groddeck believed that no one should be allowed to die alone, as had both of his parents. Although seeming almost brutal at times, he gently tended his sister Lina on her deathbed. Soon thereafter, the deaths of his three brothers, one by one, led Groddeck to the dark feeling that he was the sole survivor of a family marked for early death.

His publications began at about this time—1903—and covered a wide range: Schweninger's methods, novels, essays, and literary criticism—Ibsen's plays (Grinstein, 1957, pp. 790–792). He organized two clubs, one devoted to the education of the working man, the second designed to advance his father's ideas concerning the building of inexpensive homes for working people.

Despite his busy medical and literary life, Groddeck found himself becoming bored, dissatisfied, and unable to understand his patients; but when he became aware of the ubiquitous symbolism of his patients' communications, his boredom disappeared. He then saw illness as a physical reaction of the body to trauma and also as a symbolic creation, expressing the inner needs of unknown forces of the "It" by which we are ruled. His term was later adopted by Freud, whose translators preferred "id" as a less mystical rendering of *Das Es*. At first, Groddeck did not see that his opinions were related to psychoanalysis. In 1912, he published a novel, which became quite popular for a remarkable and unfortunate reason: it attacked psychoanalysis and deplored its Freudian emphasis on sexuality. Later, Groddeck freely admitted that he had attacked psychoanalysis before he had studied it.

In 1914, he separated from his first wife, who had gradually drifted into melancholic isolation. He began to live with Emmy, a young woman who had taken Lina's place at the sanitarium and whom he eventually married. During World War I, he was recalled to duty as an Army surgeon. In trying to run his Army hospital as he had what he often called his "Satan-Arium," he antagonized everyone and was soon dismissed, despite the intervention of his grateful patients, who included the Kaiser's sister and her husband.

In May 1917, Groddeck wrote his first long letter to Freud. He began by thanking Freud and recognizing him, especially for the concepts of transference and resistance. He apologized for having written unfavorably about psychoanalysis, admitting that his attack had been rooted in envy. He was still unable to finish reading *The Psychopathology of Everyday Life* and *The Interpretation of Dreams*. The difference between Freud's scientific clarifications and his own intuitive knowledge of the It was more than he could reconcile. Groddeck included pages of clinical material in his letter and shyly asked whether he would have the right to call himself an analyst and whether he would be acceptable to the Berlin Psychoanalytic Society. Freud replied that although Groddeck wanted to be treated as incorrigible and rejected, he regretted that he couldn't oblige: "I must lay claim to you and must state that you are an analyst of the first order." Their mutual respect and affection survived the many storms that could have been anticipated in the relationship between a devotee of "It mysticism," as Freud later called it, and his more controlled scientific colleague.

Groddeck transferred to Freud all the images lost by death in his past—father, mother, sister, brothers, and Schweninger—and loved Freud with guilty, melancholic, masochistic devotion. Freud's friendly warning about "It mysticism" wounded Groddeck deeply. Freud saw in him a gifted, intuitive, demonic innovator: perhaps Freud recognized in Groddeck his own inner demon, his own unconscious. He tried to tame, train, and love Groddeck as one would a favorite stepchild. Freud greatly respected a revolutionary flame and did not want to see it extinguished in any man or movement.

Groddeck's symbolic and definitely unscientific novel, *Der Seelensucher* ("The Soul Seeker"), was rejected by many publishers but delighted Freud, who, in 1919, offered to issue it through the Psychoanalytic Publishing House. "We will ask you to allow us this heretic work for publication because I myself am a heretic who has not yet turned into a fanatic," he wrote, ending with a great and sincere compliment, "I do not think I could easily get along without you." Freud showed undisguised amusement at the horror of some of his colleagues when the novel appeared.

§ Der Seelensucher

Der Seelensucher, which was published in 1921 but has never been translated into English, concerns a retired bachelor who gives up a hopeless battle against bedbugs and, as a result, leaves his home to become a wanderer. He assumes a new name, Thomas Weltlein (Thomas Littleworld), and wanders throughout the land seeking the meaning of life. He slips into a joyous madness in which he makes uninhibited depth interpretations—utilizing philology, mythology, and literature—in all manner of unexpected situations. He lectures at a ladies' luncheon, asking them to educate their daughters for the great joy they have to give to men. At his place on the speaker's platform, he plays upon everyone's interest in railroads by imitating locomotives having intercourse. His disgusting noises and obscene movements interpret, convince, and infuriate. Never has a more hilarious interpretation been given. The presiding officer, frantically swinging her bell, throws Thomas Weltlein out, while he excitedly continues to interpret the meaning and function of the ringing bell.

Weltlein is a fool and a madman. At a labor union meeting, he surprises everyone by speaking reasonably but with passion as he joins the men in their fight for freedom and equality. He is all in favor of creeping socialism.

At the book's close, he is killed in a train wreck. His stuffy sister identifies him by his gold pencil and a scar high up—very high up—on his left thigh.

§ The Book of the It

Groddeck's writings fitted well into the thoughts of Freud, who, in 1922, was working on *The Ego and the Id.* In that book, Freud acknowledged his indebtedness to Groddeck. Around the same time, in 1920 at the International Conference at The Hague, many analysts were shocked by Groddeck's describing himself as a "wild analyst" and by his associating freely, instead of reading his prepared paper. Only a few—among them, O. Rank, S. Ferenczi, K. Horney, Frieda Fromm-Reichmann, and E. Simmel—shared Freud's interest and affection. Groddeck was accompanied to the Conference by Emmy, who had not yet become his wife. It was not until the Groddecks had been properly married that Freud admitted that, being somewhat of a Victorian himself, he had been displeased when Groddeck had brought his mistress to their first meeting.

Groddeck feared that the word might kill the thought. He did not want to become a scientist, but to write and live in a freely associative manner. In his disappointment about his reception at the Congress, he tried to stay away from all analysts but Freud, who admonished him against erecting such a wall.

Ernst Simmel became his friend and a visitor in Baden-Baden. Simmel quoted Groddeck, who was fluent in English, as saying: "The Eye is I, and anyone who is short-sighted does not want to see far ahead. . . ." Under Groddeck's personal influence, Simmel could read a clock several miles away and conduct a Psychotherapeutic Congress in Baden-Baden without glasses, although in Berlin he was again badly in need of them.

In 1921, Groddeck began *The Book of the It,* a series of letters presumably written to an intelligent young woman interested in his analytic ideas. It was published in 1923. Freud found the work charming and irresistible. Even skeptical Anna Freud was interested. Ernest Jones found it amusing and "racy." Oskar Pfister, analyst and clergyman in Switzerland, was shocked and complained to Freud, who answered: "I am defending Groddeck energetically against your respectability. What would you have said had you been a contemporary of Rabelais?"

Groddeck wrote with frankness, honesty, and dignity. For the most part he avoided being exhibitionistic or masochistic. He insisted on calling his method "wild" and artistic; he could not have cared less about scientific proof. His central theme was: Man is lived by his It. He is born with this knowledge, but later loses it.

Groddeck wrote freely about his and every man's envy of mothers: His big belly expresses his wish for a child; or man wants a brain-child like Pallas Athene, who was born from the head of her father, Zeus. Writing a book brings him the worries and tortures of delivery. His goiter of many years disappeared only after he had learned about his unconscious pregnancy fantasies, which he believes caused the goiter.

Whether his interpretations are right or wrong, he does not know. He knows that talking and explaining the It helps patients. The It does not study medicine and can use any organ of the body as a symbol.

Groddeck credits Freud with anything that makes sense; anything that sounds silly and fantastic is his own—a most ambivalent compliment.

The It is the wish to become sick and the wish to become well. To be helped, patients must again become children, to whom God will give insight while they sleep. They should trust their mother-doctor with innocence and in love and read this book the way children read fairy tales.

It is silly for any woman to miss the highest pleasure in life: the pain and lust of delivery. Natural childbirth is the way a natural woman wants to have her baby. The arrogant, conceited doctor should not interfere.

A mother may fear that her child is an avenger for her sin of masturbation or incest. No one is so holy as to be able always to love an avenger.

Man can never cease longing to return to the womb of his mother.

A good woman does not feel castrated and does not suffer menstrual cramps. She knows well that blood and pain do not stand in the way of lust, but she may feel tempted to test a man's strength and knowledge by putting the menstrual taboo between his and her desires.

Our unconscious expresses itself in symbols: in love for God, crime and heroism, good deeds and evil ones, religion and blasphemy; in staining the tablecloth and breaking glass; in the invention of tools and machines; in art, sickness, and death—in every aspect of our lives.

Accidents may be understood as dreams and symbols. Whoever breaks an arm has either sinned or wished to commit a sin with that arm—murder, incest, or masturbation. Whoever goes blind desires to see no more, has sinned with his eyes, or wishes to see what he dares not see. Whoever gets hoarse has a secret he dares not tell.

The language of the unconscious is hard to decipher. The child in us will understand the language of the unconscious in sleep, or not at all. Some may consider this madness, but they should respect this madness since it has method.

Insight into the importance of mother transference illuminates all Groddeck's case histories. Every sick man is a child. Everyone who cares for a sick child becomes a mother. We owe our lives to the mother—and our deaths, too. All die on the Cross, the *os sacrum,* which is the mother. Love for mother is expressed in the Cross of Christianity, in Michelangelo's "Pièta," in the writings of Shakespeare and Sophocles. All are interpreted by Groddeck with great poetry, intensity, and a phenomenal literary knowledge. He seduces his readers into exposing themselves to the curative and maturing experience of art. He shows how to endure creative anxiety.

The reader is encouraged by Groddeck to acquire a new, perhaps mad (or maddening) way of looking at life. The mouse reminds Groddeck of a woman's penis, cut off and left alive. The horror we feel about a wounded bird also reminds him of castration anxiety.

For the It, love and death are alike, since in the sex act love dies.

Mother took care of us, made us feel our bodies, seduced us, taught us to masturbate and then punished us for it, because this is a mother's destiny. We all commit the original sin against mother. In our guilt, our It invents cancer and consumption; it does so in the same way it grows eyes, hair, nails, teeth. A fantastic explanation is better than none.

The doctor has two questions to decide: By what means is the It contriving to remain sick, and by what means can it again be induced to want to be healthy? The It must be helped by analysis, by hot baths, by massages, by masterful commands, and by that kind of love which a sick child expects from its mother.

In 1920, Groddeck became a member of the Berlin Psychoanalytic Society. In one of his communications to the Society, he suggested, "Put off action as long as you can, and watch for signs of the patient's It. Sooner or later, it will probably whisper to you advice you can pass on to the patient." He cautiously tried to explain his opinions about the psychogenic factors in disease, agreeing with his Berlin colleagues on one point: All medical treatment succeeds or fails with the transference.

One of his patients, a woman, suffered from severe, generalized edema, despite treatment for her heart condition with medication and with the special massage Groddeck had learned from Schweniger. The patient then confessed her "sin"—that she had vowed to remain a virgin and to become a nun, but she had since married and was no longer a virgin. After her "confession," she passed enormous quantities of urine; a veritable sin-flood was released. Within twenty-four hours, she had lost fifteen pounds.

Another patient, a shepherd, had developed retinal hemorrhages, which threatened him with blindness. Against great resistance, he told Groddeck that he had once stoned a crucifix, knocking the figure of Christ to the ground. His It had punished him severely. The effect of this short and deeply penetrating interview was that no hemorrhages occurred thereafter; and, thirteen years later, the patient worked as an accountant, which calls for constant use of the eyes.

In his own way, Georg Groddeck was a profoundly religious man. "The It and the Gospels," published in 1926, is one of his most original and profound writings.

"Coughs and Colds," which appeared in 1928, is a truly revealing self-analysis, relating his own heavy cough to the famous Groddeck family cough, which all the members of his family had developed during their lifetimes.

Having seen his entire family die—father, mother, three brothers, and his only sister—Groddeck felt near to death, and he believed that death meant nearness to the unconscious. Facing death calls for courage to face the It. Groddeck's wild and often desperate courage and temper was respected by Freud, who also lived close to death.

Ferenczi never tired of singing Groddeck's praises and telling others of the benefit he derived from his regular, annual "analytic holiday" in Groddeck's sanitarium, to which Ferenczi brought his analytic patients. Another guest was Karen Horney, who retreated to the sanitarium in deep grief after the sudden death of her beloved brother.

When Groddeck toyed with opening a special ward for maternity cases, he consulted Frieda Fromm-Reichmann, who became his good friend. Later, she often gave Groddeck credit for her method of treating hospitalized schizophrenics.

In 1926, Groddeck fought the taboo against applying psychoanalysis in the field of medicine—the taboo against relating dream work to psychic or organic symptoms. As he pointed out, both show the same relationship between the manifest form and the latent unconscious conflicts.

Groddeck had proudly and challengingly called himself a "wild analyst." At Groddeck's sixtieth birthday celebration, Ernst Simmel added:

> Groddeck may be permitted to style himself "wild"—in relation to the movement of which he is a supporter—in the sense that he owes his training to no one but himself. He may also be termed "wild" by virtue of his passionate temperament, which impels him to action where others throw up a case as hopeless or disguise their real helplessness under the cover of "accurate diagnosis."

§ The Unknown Self

In this collection of articles published between 1925 and 1929, Groddeck gave his imagination free rein. He wrote frankly about himself—more so than any analyst, with the possible exception of Sigmund Freud. Groddeck expressed himself joyously, loudly, innocently—perhaps with masochistic honesty. By offering himself as if constantly in analysis, he invited his patients to follow his example.

Groddeck's recollections go back to his school years and a few teachers he loved. The end of boyhood came to him when his father died. Before then, Groddeck had believed in his own special power to help and heal. After his father's death, he gained insight into his megalomania, which he recognized as a triumphant introjection of his parents into his unconscious.

The last part of *The Unknown Self* contains Groddeck's interpretations of German mythology (*The Ring of the Nibelungen*), *Peer Gynt*, and Goethe's *Faust*. The symbolic meaning of the Siegfried-Brünhilde relationship is a warning that mother and son will love each other but shall destroy each other. Siegfried recognizes his mother in Brünhilde. From all her teachings, he learned little; he remains a boy and a fool. He knows that, in front of her, he is not a hero and that he succumbs to her. The man dies in her arms and becomes a child again. The figure of the dwarf symbolizes another aspect of male sexuality: He is small, old and ugly, but has great hidden strength and will finally triumph over the enormous giant.

Sigmund and Siglinde are twin brother and sister, symbolizing the Janus face of every man, since man is bisexual.

Groddeck's interpretation of Peer Gynt follows similar lines. To his mother, Aase, Peer was always a little boy, while she remained a never-aging mother. The women in Peer's life are different incarnations of the eternally desired and dreaded mother.

For Groddeck, Goethe's Faust represents Every Man. Goethe wanted us to understand Faust as a man who finally recognized his unconscious ("Der dunkle Drang," the dark impulses of man) as his most human part. Faust wanted to live in harmony with his It, not in combat and in surrender. Groddeck found the final confirmation of his opinion in Goethe's definition of symbolic reality: "Alles Vergaengliche ist nur ein Gleichnis" (All that is mortal is but an image).

Late in 1930, Freud received the Goethe Prize. Although desperately ill, Groddeck wrote to "my most honored teacher and my most dearly beloved man" about his life-long passion for Goethe. His letter shows deep insight into Goethe's writings. Groddeck concluded by asking whether Freud agreed with Groddeck's interpretation of Goethe's Faust. Freud replied briefly, kindly, and with benevolent skepticism that he could not settle the controversy about Goethe, since "I do not understand Goethe in that any better than I understand Groddeck."

§ The World of Man

In Groddeck's last book, *Der Mensch als Symbol* ("Man as Symbol"), which appeared in 1933, Groddeck took up problems of art and language, of sickness, and of man's relation to the symbol. In many places he combined his intuition for language with the knowledge of the philologist. For Groddeck, the true artist is neither a spectator nor a master: he is an interpreter of the unconscious. Long before the brain came into existence, the It was already active.

Man is forever striving toward what he was and had in infancy. His choice lies between becoming either childlike or childish. A child fears no king, and even the majesty of death does not awe him. As Groddeck put it: "In this respect I have remained a child; death says nothing to me."

The best written and probably most personal chapters of *Der Mensch als Symbol* are the last two, "Love and Death" and "Death and Transfiguration." Love and death are closely connected because the man dies in the woman while having intercourse. Eros and death are similar since life begins with death, finds its fulfillment in sexual union, and ends in death. Dying is a pleasant experience, like falling asleep. Like dreaming, talking, loving, painting, or becoming ill, dying, too, is an expression of the It. Groddeck was convinced that every man's death is the fulfillment of a last wish.

Groddeck hesitated to trouble Freud with the manuscript for, by then, the German world was too sad in reality to allow escape into literature. However, he finally did send it to him, together with a letter that closed with the words, "Your unfortunately somewhat senile and feeble, but still grateful student." Freud did not personally acknowledge the receipt of the manuscript, but his daughter Anna wrote to

Groddeck that Freud had read it from beginning to end with great interest and did not believe "in your mental infirmities or senility."

Ferenczi wrote from his sickbed in Capri that he loved the new book, *Der Mensch als Symbol.* At the time, he was in the final stages of pernicious anemia, traveling was difficult, and he could not go to see his friend Groddeck. Ferenczi called himself "an atomizer of the soul"; Groddeck had tried to save his friend from this danger. After Ferenczi's death in May of 1933, his wife wrote that Lou Andreas-Salomé, a close friend of Freud, Groddeck, and many great men, had said: "Groddeck would have saved him." Troubled greatly that he might have neglected Ferenczi, in a long letter to Ferenczi's widow, Groddeck tried to show that probably he could not have helped:

> Just as one cannot stop the raging storm with the bare hand, so I could not have helped Sándor. As close as we were, he was already far removed from me in a flight to the stars in which I could not and would not join.

Once again Groddeck was alone. Turning to the world around him, he refused to recognize its reality. He refused to believe that Hitler was anti-Semitic. He firmly believed that if only he could have had one interview with Hitler, he could have corrected Hitler's mistaken thinking.

A year after Ferenczi's death, Groddeck suffered a severe heart attack. At the time, the authorities were on the way to arrest this strange doctor who wrote mad letters to the Leader. Frieda Fromm-Reichmann arranged an invitation for Groddeck to lecture before the Swiss Psychoanalytic Society, and he reluctantly agreed to go. In Zurich, he talked once more about the eyes, vision, and vision without eyes. He collapsed and was taken to the sanitarium run by M. Boss, a noted psychoanalyst.

In his last days, Groddeck was preoccupied with the cure for cancer and with the fight against death in his patients and in the German people. He believed that he could rid the world of all evil. One of his last visitors was Frieda Fromm-Reichmann, who was on her way to America. He got out of bed and, without any sign of sickness, walked her to the station. Shortly afterward he became decompensated and showed signs of agitation and delirium; then came the peaceful end.

§ Summing Up: Man's Innate Need to Symbolize

Georg Groddeck believed in man's innate urge to symbolize. As a physician and a linguist, he disliked artificial terms and preferred the talk of children and artists: they do not have the kind of defenses that interfere with the free creation of the It. But it would be wrong to call Groddeck an artist (which he was) as opposed to a clinical observer (which he also was).

Freud was always careful and cautious but not defensive toward Groddeck's approach, for Freud also recognized an indebtedness to art and literature. Although skeptical of Groddeck's "It mysticism," Freud saw considerable merit in Groddeck's poetic and original ways of dealing with the sick and their illness.

Georg Groddeck had pride in the correctness of his intuition. His insight and conjectures were confirmed by Freud's work. Whereas Freud had always claimed to be a scientist, Groddeck made no such claim. For him, life was divine.

Many men have continued Groddeck's work: Grantly Dick Read's theory and technique of *natural childbirth* are the final confirmation of some of Groddeck's early ideas. John Rosen has applied Groddeck's approach in the "direct analysis" of schizophrenic patients. In Switzerland, Madame Sechehaye has followed Groddeck's ways of thinking and acting in her method of *symbolic realization.* Many of Groddeck's thoughts have found their expression in the system developed by Melanie Klein. Still another application of Groddeck's technique led to Jacob Moreno's Psychodrama. The work of René Spitz with anaclitic depression confirms Groddeck's intuition and continues where he left off. The influence of Groddeck's ideas can be seen in Géza Róheim's work. Psychoanalysis has always postulated the pleasure principle as restricted by the reality principle. Recently, a third principle has been formulated, which might be called the principle of magic-mystic, or symbolic, thinking. All human mental activity starts this way, and Groddeck expressed it and applied it consistently in his praxis of healing.

Georg Groddeck loved the symbol and understood it. He lived by it and he worked with it. As an analyst and friend of Freud, he remained untamed and much loved.

BIBLIOGRAPHY

Freud, E. L. (Ed.) *The selected letters of Sigmund Freud.* Nos. 176, 188, 201, 212. New York: Basic Books, 1960.

Freud, E. L. (Ed.) Sigmund Freud-Oskar Pfister Briefe. 1909–1939. Frankfurt am Main: S. Fischer Verlag, 1963.

Grinstein, A. Index of psychoanalytic writings. Vol. 2, Nos. 12701–12726, 22308, 30944. New York: Int. Univer. Press, 1953.

Groddeck, G. *The book of the It.* (Vintage Books—V 195; Introduction by L. Durrell) New York: Random House, 1961. (See also Groddeck, G. *The book of the It.* [Mentor—MT 352; Introduction by A. Montagu] New York: New Amer. Library, 1961.)

Grossman, C. M., & Sylvia Grossman. *The wild Analyst: the life and work of Georg Groddeck.* New York: George Braziller, 1965.

Grotjahn, M. The importance and meaning of Ferdinand the Bull and Mickey Mouse. In *Beyond laughter.* New York: McGraw-Hill, 1957.

Grotjahn, M. Georg Groddeck and his teachings about man's innate need for symbolization. *Psychoanal. Rev.*, 1945, 32, 9–24.

Jones, E. *The life and work of Sigmund Freud.* Vols. 2, 3. New York: Basic Books, 1953–1957.

My thanks are due to Roderick Gorney, M.D., of the University of California, for his help in writing this essay. I also wish to thank Carl and Sylvia Grossman for making available to me their material on Groddeck. I especially appreciate having been able to compare their selection of Groddeck's letters to Freud with autobiographical notes in Groddeck's published work. (See the Bibliography.) —M.G.

August Stärcke

1880–1954

THE SOURCES OF CASTRATION ANXIETY

*

JACOB SPANJAARD

Only a few of Holland's contemporary analysts knew Stärcke. It is more than twenty-five years since he ceased attending the meetings of the Dutch Psychoanalytic Society; but, for ten years previous to that time, he had occupied himself mainly with his entomological work. However, his analytic interest had remained keen and productive.

Stärcke himself was never analyzed, nor was he a practicing analyst. He worked for almost his entire life as a resident physician in a single institution, treating an occasional patient suffering from a neurosis.

Stärcke was deeply interested in biology and had an extensive knowledge in this field. Living in bucolic surroundings and experimenting with plants and ants were of paramount importance to him. His garden was sacred ground, his greatest dread being that a reckless visitor would start picking flowers! To those who knew him in his own domain—the patch of unspoiled nature he had recreated, wherein he strolled wrapped up in all he observed—his image remains unforgettable. His artistic head, with a *fin-de-siècle* beard, topped a tall, stooped figure, invariably attired in a black suit. He would talk about his observations and discoveries by the hour, always mildly shocking listeners by his paradoxes, his bizarre comparisons, or his revolutionary speculations.

His scientific bent stemmed from his father, who must likewise have been an exceptionally intelligent man. Stärcke's father was the son of an old-fashioned German artisan, a joiner, who had fled industrialization and had settled in Amsterdam. Having grown up under very difficult circumstances, the elder Stärcke had nevertheless managed to make himself into one of the foremost accountants in the Netherlands, earning his living by keeping books for various firms and by teaching, although he never attained prosperity. One facet of his life was a keen interest in biology.

August was his oldest son. From childhood on, August was reticent and poetical, whereas Johan, his younger brother, who was his mother's favorite, was more sociable and had more friends. Being precocious, August was able to read and write before he entered elementary school; he skipped the first grade and had already completed his medical studies at twenty-one. He specialized in psychiatry and neurology with Johannes Wertheim-Salomonson and Cornelis Winkler, in Amsterdam, and subsequently pursued his studies for a few years in an asylum at Zutphen in eastern Holland. He next spent one year as private physician to a very wealthy lady whose psychotic son lived with her on her country estate. As "court physician" he was provided with his own well-equipped laboratory and had sufficient time to continue his studies of histology and microscopic techniques. It was during this amazing interval that he met his future wife, the daughter of a country doctor, who proved an ideal helpmate. Stärcke was then twenty-eight years old, a romantic, courteous, and extremely pleasant person, who, in his severe black suit and scarlet waistcoat, looked every inch the poet.

After 1910, he became resident physician at the Willem Arntz Foundation and remained there for the rest of his life.

Even before World War II, August's health had begun to fail. As a consequence, his faculties dimmed at such a rapid rate that from then on he achieved less and less, and his life became a gloomy and long-drawn-out ordeal. A few years before his death, the Dutch Society of Psychoanalysis made him an honorary member.

Stärcke's scientific achievements can be summarized under a few distinct headings; one comprises his more than 100 entomological publications. Another comprises his writings on psychoanalysis. I am happy that at last I have the opportunity of complying with Stärcke's request some years before his death, when he begged me to take down a few pronouncements of his that he considered noteworthy and to make them known at some future time.

In 1952, he codified a few sociological laws, which he requested me to emphasize, should the occasion present itself. A few are highly specialized in the field of entomology. Two, however, that are relevant to the analyst are striking examples of Stärcke's peculiar, original, and revolutionary way of thinking:

1. *The Law of Retrogenesis:* Development is not a product of evolution but of revolution. It does not build onto the highest point reached but harks back to a former and more primitive stage of development.

2. *The Law of Development Brought About by Need and Anguish:* Individual development that has already been established may be obliterated by general social development. When this happens, co-ordinated defense by society supersedes defense dependent on the individual intellect. Stärcke found cases in point among the ants; in his opinion, this law explains why Homo recens, with his cranial volume of 1400 to 1500 cc., fell behind Cro-Magnon man and the Chancelade prehistoric Eskimo, with their cranial volume of 1600 to 1700 cc. The latter two are responsible for the important inventions of their day.

August Stärcke's first acquaintance with psychoanalysis dates from 1905, when he happened on a copy of Freud's "On Dreams," which fascinated him. Even before this he had started out on a new tangent as a result of reading Otto Weininger's curious *Geschlecht und Charakter,* which apparently predisposed him to psychoanalysis. His brother Johan also became involved in August's new interest. Johan Stärcke came into contact with Freud later and is also mentioned in Freud's *The Interpretation of Dreams.* Johan translated "On Dreams" into Dutch in 1913; his promising career was cut short by his untimely death in 1917.

The first of August Stärcke's psychoanalytic articles, which discussed the dream, was published in 1911 by the *Zentralblatt für Psychoanalyse.* Subsequently, nineteen articles appeared in analytic periodicals, and numerous treatises on the same and related subjects were printed in other scientific journals. Some of his more general papers in Dutch and German publications deserve specific mention. His important lecture before the Dutch Society of Psychiatry and Neurology in 1912 introduced psychoanalysis to the official psychiatric world of the Netherlands; and, in 1914, he translated Freud's "Civilized Sexual Morality and Modern Nervousness" into Dutch.

Some articles on psychoanalysis that appeared after 1918 have become classics in their field showing Stärcke's preponderant experience with psychotics. The earliest of these is "The Reversal of the Libido-Sign in Delusions of Persecution" (1919; 1920), in which we find an elaboration of the psychoanalytic explanation of the delusions of persecution. The contents of these delusions must frequently be an anal persecution. Patients often reveal as an important secret their feeling that the essence of the matter consists of an inconceivable piece of villainy. The loved object, well known as the kernel of the persecuting agent, must be unconsciously identified with the scybalum. The scybalum is the primary persecutor. With pain and pleasure in rapid succession, it commits anal acts of violence, leading to one of the most primitive attitudes of ambivalence, which is subsequently strengthened by the punishing authorities in toilet training.

In "The Castration Complex" (1921a; 1921b), Stärcke extended the meaning of castration to the withdrawal of the mother's nipple from the infant who is not fully satisfied. The mother's nipple is certainly a part of the infant's body; and Stärcke was convinced that the premature withdrawal of the mother's nipple is a constant and universal fact in each nursing. He added some hypotheses (calling for further empirical confirmation) concerning the relation of sucking experiences with the development of the mind, cracked nipples with sadism, and the use of the little hand of the infant during suckling with pleasure in striking buttocks. The removal of the nipple makes it possible for feces, urine, and, perhaps, clothing to become "bridges from the ego to the comprehension of the external world." Happiness is bound up with the undoing of the separation between ego and the external world; sucking is its most primitive nucleus.

"Psychoanalysis and Psychiatry" (1921c; 1921d), which may be considered Stärcke's main psychoanalytic work, won for him the Freud award. He treasured the memory doubly because Lou Andreas-Salomé was his table partner at the banquet at which the presentation was made. "Psychoanalysis and Psychiatry" is a very stimulating paper of great vision, albeit speculative and perhaps marred by "lapidary" theses. Although Stärcke's experience had been primarily with psychoses, this work clearly demonstrates a broad biological and clinical approach, as well as a pioneer position in ego psychology. No signs of the "structural hypothesis" can be detected here, although this was to be developed only two years later. Stärcke's conception of the ego remains isolated, and his treatment lacks the kind of "empathic" material that the analysis of neuroses may provide. He did not recognize conscious meanings or empathy as conclusive psychological evidence; throughout his life he remained a psychoanalyst belonging to the first years of our science —a fervent adherent of "ego instincts" in accord with his biological approach.

On the first page of "Psychoanalysis and Psychiatry" we find his adage: The analyst is not hampered by scotomata as the psychiatrist is. According to Stärcke, the analyst works with the unconscious, the libido, and ego impulses as hypothetical correlates. Although psychoanalysis could not become a therapy of psychoses, there are many points in which psychoanalysis has great advantages over clinical psychiatry, for example, as a method of investigation, and in the comprehension of symptoms.

From Stärcke's viewpoint, psychosis is an illness existing only in relation to a society regarded as normal; the nature of this relationship alone determines the differences among criminals, heroes, and psychotics. Diagnosis depends on unconscious criteria on the part of the observer, consisting of an inability to influence and cure the patient, along with a strong narcissistic frustration in contact and exchange with him: "Society considers him mad who threatens to reveal to Man his unconscious, and knows no other means of defense against such revelation than to isolate the madman." By providing criteria in terms of instinctual forces and their quantities, psychoanalysis allows us an understanding of the differences among normal persons, neurotics, and psychotics. The idea of a "normal" society, indispensable to his concept of psychosis, leads to profound and speculative considerations about modern civilisation. The result is rather gloomy. Stärcke coined the term "metaphrenia" for the kind of obsessional neurosis belonging to a society of individuals "dominated by time and money compulsion." (In accord with the course of the manic psychoses, repressed material periodically breaks through in wars and revolutions.) The preceding stage he called "orthophrenia," a normal and primitive form of society with a less anal and more genital production compulsion, directed at reproduction.

The psychotic person refuses the ethical repression of impulses, whereas the normal one submits to it. The neurotic has an in-between position, displaying a tendency to compromise. Psychoses are characterized by a high degree of fixation, a greater number of primitive fixations, and consequently a preponderance of narcissism. But there is no increase in the actual quantity of narcissism.

Stärcke quoted Freud as showing the indefiniteness of the conventional nosological concepts and the mixed character of all neuroses and psychoses. There is a correspondence of contents in neuroses and psychoses, but Stärcke leaves open to discussion a possible difference in the part played by the Oedipus complex and the castration complex. He undertakes to delineate a separate development of both complexes, in the course of which the latter may become the weightier factor in the mental make-up of, for example, most institutional patients. In psychosis, conflicts—ubiquitously present in psychic processes—reassume the form they have in the small child.

After this train of thought, which is not explicitly brought to a conclusion, come the most important formulations of this paper—those concerning ego impulses and their regression. In general, the degree of regression or development of the ego impulses keeps pace with those of the libido. Stärcke then considers the consecutive stages of the ego impulses, and, starting from Freud's remark on repetition developing into memory, he relates this development to the motor inhibition of the libido. So long as there is a direct overflow of energy into motility, a euphoria occurs together with the discharge, in accordance with the well known "feeling of omnipotence." When the libido is dammed up, anxiety results, and the transition from anxiety to euphoria is experienced as pleasure. The ego impulses are thus classified as damming up, and the libido as a pleasure impulse. Further development must now be seen as a repetition of these processes in successive stages, wherein the ego impulses raise the threshold of discharge.

Stärcke has enumerated these stages as follows:

1. *The tonic stages.* At first, discharges are tonic; genital forepleasure at this stage remains correlated with the sympathetic nervous system. With the development of the axial nervous system, tonus with interruption appears. These tonic stages are recognizable in the two kinds of muscle innervation.

2. *The epileptic stage.* Examples are the reactions of flight and defense of lower animals in a state of violent terror, and the genital motility of the end pleasure in men. Laughing, sneezing, and yawning are likewise expressions of this stage, and the deep feeling of satisfaction that accompanies these discharges is striking.

3. *Stage of rhythmical repetition.* Instances of this are breathing, sucking, coitus, dancing, and many psychotic phenomena, for example,

stereotyped movements. In consciousness this stage corresponds to the feeling of desire.

4. *Stage of reactive repetition.* The motility consists of automatic and stereotyped mechanisms of attack, defense, and flight that result from stimuli (for example, the flight of butterflies). In human pathology we might mention the fugues of epileptic and other psychoses. A transition to the fifth stage occurs.

5. *Stage of postponed repetition* (stage of transference). Reality testing and the dissociation of the preconscious come to the fore. Although the motility in the genital branches remains on a low developmental level, in other spheres, such as the nutritive one, the libido becomes subjected to the ego impulses, along with a further extension of gratification. As soon as desiring is perceived too strongly and anxiety arises, censorship is initiated—originally subordinated to narcissistic purposes and, later, to reality testing. In this function of censorship, under pathological conditions, regression may occur. However, regression also occurs in science and religion. In science, one has the purpose of obtaining secondary gain, and again submits the thoughts gained along magic paths to the test of reality. Stärcke deals with censorship as a form of inhibition of movement (called "repression" in contradistinction to "suppression") and with conscience as a parallel to the test of reality but directed at examining the ego, that is, correcting it from the point of view of the ideal. On the highest stage of development, thinking as an experimental action is inhibited by repression. The imago, robbed of its lower tendencies, remains conscious as a memory. Memory thus originates through the repression of something else. This substitute memory may be a "feeling." Part of the ideas are always withdrawn into the unconscious.

The stages of postponed repetition comprise by far the greater part of life after the period of sucking, although in adults many actions remain fixated at lower stages.

In the end one can distinguish the *stage of lies and dissimulation* and the *idealistic stage*, both belonging to social maturity. As observation shows, fantasy is cathected when motor discharge is inhibited. Between fantasy and action there are several transitions, such as gestures, of which language is the latest offshoot.

In a long paper on psychoanalysis and aesthetics (1922), classical drama is said to be conceivable materially as representing conflicts of a primitive erotic kind, formally as a still more primitive rhythmic kind of utterance. Condensation and omission (ellipsis) ultimately result in a product acceptable to us as civilized people. Like the dream, the work of art has a significant discharging function and is of social benefit as well. Although analogous to religion, it is less rigid in form, continually creating new symbols. In a different respect there is a parallel with play. Aesthetics are widening the scope of the ego, albeit on a magic level, in contrast to logic.

In "Conscience and Repetition" (1929a), Stärcke begins with the psychoses in which we find hallucinations conveying a command—hallucinations that have inescapable force. These must be related to conscience. He then works out the conception of a stratified superego having conflicting layers that represent the different sequences of social organization, beginning with the mother–child relationship. This stratification develops by means of successive revolutions according to the "law of retrogenesis." Recent structures of the conscience originate not from the upper strata of the system but from those covered long ago. As an example, Stärcke adduces crimes committed in the name of the state. The superego is comparable to the stimuli in Pavlovian conditioned reflexes, stressing the driving force and resistance to reality, which were conditioned by an intensive and regular rewarding of the id impulses during a receptive period. In this way our imperative instincts develop into the categorical imperative of conscience: "Conscience is the power which shifts the repetition of action to self-punishment and repentance."

In 1933, Stärcke introduced the term "paradosis" to designate the passing on of character traits, psychosis, and the like to the next generation along other than hereditary paths (Stärcke, 1933).

His last original paper on psychoanalysis is "The Role of Anal and Oral Quantities in Persecutory Delusions and Analogous Thought Systems" (1935). Here he has emphasized again that every libidinal fixation is liable to social adjustment, and that the psychotic is incapable of making this adjustment. The drives are the same in psychotics, criminals, and normal individuals; what makes the difference is the possibility of delaying the impulses in order to achieve a secondary gain. Narcissism is pathological only when, if necessary, it cannot be moved temporarily to other positions.

One may consider religion a delusion, but this means that one overlooks its social aspect: the forming of groups, as opposed to the psychotic solitude. In the psychology of religion one must keep two things apart: a universal inclination to compose systems of thought inaccessible to logic, and a tendency in paranoiacs to keep these systems in isolation. The question then becomes: What determines the truth of a thought? "A thought is 'true' for us if it is repeated often enough but not rejected often enough." As examples of this, Stärcke has advanced some common methods of advertising. What is decisive is whether the drive—"objectivated" in thought or perception (hallucination)—is accepted by the superego or the ego, respectively. Social consent is therefore of great importance; it arises through frequent repetition on a small scale.

Delusion is related to normal thinking as stereotyped movements are related to normal action; it remains on the level of rhythmic or reactive repetition. The high frequency of repetition in unmodified form gives a truth value to delusion. Even as doubt is characteristic of adult thinking, delusion must be infantile in form and content. Here again Stärcke has emphasized that the determining factor in psychosis is not the depth of regression but, rather, the quantitative relation between available libido positions, that is, socialized versus other regressions.

In his lecture, "Parapraxes" (1937), given in honor of Freud's eightieth birthday in 1936, there are several interesting remarks.

In relating forgetting to infantile amnesia, Stärcke wrote:

> In the period of life in which the forgotten events happened, the things and persons involved meant subjectively so infinitely more to us than now, they cannot be expressed in our crumbled adult representations. The objective situations are not really being remembered, but made plausible with an accompanying feeling of certainty.

In so-called normal persons, the forbidden inclination finds an outlet that is socially acceptable. Because the notion of its origin is entirely lost, there is a need to look into the future for a good motive for the action: "Causal thinking is being replaced by final thinking, pessimism by optimism." But in considering what is more beneficial for life, one may often wonder whether the parapraxis or the "right" action is the real failure. Parapraxis may be thus labeled in the light of conscious intention. Since the mistake is often prompted by social interaction, it may be analyzed as a meaningful social ("Metaphrenic") symptom, especially when accidents are concerned. Parapraxes belong to the language of gestures and are useful social signals.

As has already been stated, the correspondence between Stärcke and Freud between 1912 and 1922 has been preserved. The letters indicate some disagreement, especially concerning the theories of *Beyond the Pleasure Principle*. Stärcke's criticisms[1] may be summarized as follows: by positing the libido as a force that preserves living matter and builds it up into ever larger entities, one does away with the autoerotic aspect of sexuality and again founds the theory on procreation. Freud's original libido is itself the death instinct. If we want to conceive of instinctual life as consisting of two components, every manifestation of life must contain both components. There is a close connection between procreation and destructive force. The act of fecundation is essentially an injury. The fundamental difference between an instinct of self-preservation and an instinct toward preservation of the species, resulting in an Eros composed of contradicting forces, is being glossed over. The hate–love dichotomy, one of the pillars of Freud's explanation, is incorrect. Hate means the approaching of an object with the intention to destroy it, whereas aversion is the term for removing oneself from an object. Consequently, the opposition of a destructive instinct and Eros seems incorrect.

Stärcke's idea of a destructive libido component, which is quoted by Freud in *Beyond the Pleasure Principle*, dates as far back as 1914, and may be found in the preface to Stärcke's Dutch translation of *Civilized Sexual Morality and Modern Nervousness*. It was Stärcke's belief that the ego instincts are centripetal and tend toward the enlargement and prolongation of life; in contrast, the libido is centrifugal and tends to give up and renounce life, ending in death. Copulation is connected with regression; the deeper the regression, the more the act resembles dying. In his letters to Freud, Stärcke dwelt extensively on his idea of the ego impulses. He pointed to the regression that the forms of motility show during agony, deriving from this the identity of the "instinct of life" with the ego impulses. Freud politely disagreed, after which Stärcke continued to protest, making use of a peculiar argument: "My objection stems from an inner observation: loving means wanting to die." Freud read "living," instead of "loving," and wrote very kindly: ". . . the comparison living = wishing to die is perhaps an expression of a subjective orientation toward life, for which I feel very sorry for you." Later on Freud apologized for his parapraxis, writing that the

[1] From the letters and from a discussion report of 1934.

antinomy of Eros and the death instinct was urging itself upon him with ever increasing force.

This is the last letter of the correspondence, in which additional "errors" and Freud's suggestion that they suspend the exchange of letters for six months may be the signs of a breach that was becoming insurmountable.

Perhaps these abstracts from his psychoanalytic work have conveyed some idea of Stärcke's genius. Apart from his originality, his erudition, and his broad grip on psychological and biological phenomena, one is struck by his tendency to unmask and contradict conventional opinions; this undoubtedly was one of the most important grounds for his fascination with psychoanalysis. As a further illustration, there are two ideas that, toward the end of his life, he wanted preserved. The first is that the idea of "personality" is a fiction. What we call personality can only be compared to the entirely fortuitous intersection of numerous and ever-varying lines, in which no unity is to be found. It is analogous to a swarm.

The second statement, a witty play on words, is: "Repentance is repining the lost crime."

Stärcke was a brilliant speaker, pugnacious, and witty. He entered readily into argument and took delight in staggering people with paradoxes and apodictical pronouncements. With his ready wit, he immediately captivated his audience on his first appearance at the Congress in The Hague in 1920. An account of this appears in a letter he wrote to his father-in-law. At the very moment he was to start his lecture on the castration complex (1921a; 1921b), the president begged him to shorten his meticulously timed paper by ten minutes—not to read it, but to speak extemporaneously. He became very agitated, for Freud was present. Almost immediately he hit upon a beautiful introduction, saying among other things:

> Fortunately I just remember that the American poet Edgar Allan Poe fixed the maximum duration of a speech as five minutes, as nobody is able to remain attentive for a longer period. I am forced to resort to a compromise which, in keeping with a fact from cultural history, will have the purpose of preserving the essential and removing the irrelevant—i.e., to a kind of circumcision—in the hope that the God—Father—President will be satisfied!

Stärcke's most essential contributions to psychoanalysis may be summarized in this manner: He saw the scybalum as the primary persecutor in the delusion of persecution, and he criticized the classical nosological system. He believed that the castration complex has its forerunners in oral deprivation. Consequently he became involved in the developmental stages of the ego apparent in all living individuals and ending in social adjustment; he qualified this social adjustment in a very striking manner.

In spite of the speculative and sometimes obscure character of Stärcke's treatises, a great many of his remarks show deep insight into, and understanding of, psychology. Next to Freud, Ferenczi had considerable influence on him. Stärcke often mentioned Ferenczi's "Stages in the Development of the Sense of Reality," which preceded his own conception of the development of ego impulses. But Stärcke was the first to speak of developmental stages of the ego impulses, thus providing a classification of primary ego functions.

Stärcke remained convinced, however, of the inevitability of the concept of ego instincts, and only partially accepted more recent developments of the theory of the structural hypothesis.

REFERENCES

Stärcke, A. Die Umkehrung des Libidovorzeichens beim Verfolgungswahn. *Int. Z. ärztl. Psychoanal.*, 1919, **5**, 285–287.

Stärcke, A. The reversal of the libido-sign in delusions of persecution. *Int. J. Psycho-Anal.*, 1920, **1**, 231–234.

Stärcke, A. The castration complex. *Int. J. Psycho-Anal.*, 1921, **2**, 179–201. (a)

Stärcke, A. Der Kastrationskomplex. *Int. Z. ärztl. Psychoanal.*, 1921, **7**, 9–32. (b)

Stärcke, A. Psychoanalyse und Psychiatrie. *Beiheft Int. Z. Psychoanal.*, 1921, No. 4. (c)

Stärcke, A. Psychoanalysis and psychiatry. *Int. J. Psycho-Anal.*, 1921, **2**, 361–415. (d)

Stärcke, A. De weg terug; Psychoanalyse en Aesthetiek. *Uit Zenuw- en Zieleleven.* Serie VII. Baarn: Hollandia-Drukkerij, 1922.

Stärcke, A. Das Gewissen und die Wiederholung. *Int. Z. Psychoanal.*, 1929, **15**, 222–230. (a)

Stärcke, A. Het geweten. *Psych. en. Neurol. Bl.*, 1929, **32**, 219–220. (b)

Stärcke, A. Paradosis. *Psych. Neurol. Bl.*, 1933, **36**. (a)

Stärcke, A. Die Rolle der analen und oralen Quantitäten im Verfolgungswahn und analogen Systemgedanken. *Int. Z. Psychoanal.*, 1935, **21**, 5–22.

Heinrich Meng

b. 1887

PSYCHOANALYSIS AND MENTAL HYGIENE

*

ADOLF FRIEDEMANN

Vividly before my eyes stands a man whom I was fortunate to encounter some thirty years ago, at a time when he was in his best form. He was tall, carried himself with dignity, and had a face that revealed the work and suffering he had experienced and seen. This was a man who knew what to say and what had to be said, and also knew when to remain silent. This attitude was emphasized by a slight turn of the head, as if always ready to listen.

Our encounter took place at a meeting of the Psychiatric Congress in Zurich, and at the end of our conversation I learned that this was a man I had heard and read about for many years. By that evening, I had found a new friend, Heinrich Meng, who was called one of the great hopes of psychoanalysis by Sigmund Freud. He is a pioneer of psychoanalysis in the truest sense: a pathfinder in mental hygiene, or, as he calls it, "psycho-hygiene." He is one of the great men who tore down the walls erected by the hate and anxiety of human misunderstanding. From early childhood, Meng knew what it meant to live in serious danger. He experienced the way in which the power of knowledge and insight and love can free men from stupefying anxiety; he knew how much humble acceptance of being human can prepare the way to change misery into energy, which might then help men to rise above their weakness. This is the fight that personifies the life and work of Heinrich Meng.

During the first three years after his birth on July 9, 1887, Heinrich Meng lived in Hohnhurst, a small village near Strasbourg. He vaguely remembers the Sundays, an old woman, her chickens and ducks. He grew up in a peasant's home. In 1889, a severe epidemic of polioencephalitis erupted in his idyllic village, whose population of about 100 people included seven children. Five of the children died within a very short time. Little Heinrich had been given up as hopeless and was in danger for four and a half months. A loving grandmother, a devoted country family physician, and a self-sacrificing mother fought for the life of the dying child. Heinrich remembers to this day how for weeks his mother gave the strength and warmth of her own life to restore him to health: "It seems to me this experience determined the choice of a medical profession. Here all help and all deeds are aimed to help the patient. What I had experienced passively as a child later gave impetus to do the same actively."

Little Heinrich attended the village school of Rüppurr, where his father was the Principal, near Karlsruhe, the capital of Baden. Baden enjoyed a privileged position within the German empire. In contrast to the rigid, supposedly God-given authority of the emperor, Baden was dominated by a democratic spirit.

Until Heinrich was eight years of age, he was the youngest of three children. Then another brother was born, and shortly thereafter, at the age of nine, Heinrich went to the *Gymnasium*. Little is known about the inner conflict of young Heinrich with his newly born brother. It is certain, however, that he managed it well.

Heinrich did not become a model student, as his older brother had been, but remained well within the middle of the class, although he was the youngest. He was well accepted by his classmates and was called upon to settle their disagreements and fights, receiving the honorable title of "Father."

Without being fully aware of it, Heinrich Meng experienced the effects of transference toward his teachers. From the beginning, athletics were his favorite hours; later he became attracted to history, natural science, and mathematics. This usually depended on how much he liked or disliked his teacher. The physical appearance of a teacher's strong and handsome looks played a part, in addition to the psychological rapport. The soccer game was more liked than school lessons, to the sadness of most teachers. Any failure in school was always principally related to playing soccer.

When Heinrich was fifteen years old, he grew tired of school but successfully passed the *Gymnasium* examinations that entitled him to a reduction of his term of military duty from three years to only one year.

Heinrich Meng won a victory against the wishes of his parents and became an apprentice violin-maker. The house he went to was frequented by artists and buyers of musical instruments and was also a place where every suffering creature was lovingly nursed—exactly as Heinrich had experienced during his illness at three. In addition to the six people who lived in this ten-room house, there were sick and wounded animals that had been brought there to be taken care of. There were dogs, parrots, pigeons, and a deer. The basement was populated by cats. They were cared for and frequently spoiled. Usually there were some animals in Heinrich's bed. He remembers well the continental porcupine with his peculiar habits.

At that time work stretched from seven in the morning until seven in the evening, with perhaps an hour's interruption at lunch. For two years the apprentice listened to the foreman and his men talking as he had never heard people talk in his father's home or in the *Gymnasium.* What he heard surprised and often horrified him. Young Heinrich often had to take instruments back and forth to the court theater, where the rehearsals opened his eyes and ears and filled him with enthusiasm. The violinist particularly appealed to him: "I admired him as if he were a half-god." Although he then began to practice the violin, Heinrich found the lessons joyless.

At seventeen, Heinrich went through a maturational crisis. The peculiar atmosphere of the workshop worried the sensitive young man. Working with wood did not seem right to him so he turned to the creatures, to the animals, and finally to his friends; homesickness did the rest. He returned to school and easily made up for the lost years. He was interested in physiology, religion, philosophy, and, particularly, in nutrition and diet. With a friend, he studied theosophy, Christianity, and Buddhism. He also became acquainted with the physician, Dr. Bircher-Benner, the famous nutrition expert and vegetarian. Heinrich offered himself for experimentation and participated in sport competitions so he could study the relationships of training, efficiency, and diet. Despite the time spent in violin-making, in two years he prepared for the college entrance examination and succeeded.

He went to the University of Freiburg, in Breisgau, to study medicine. The sensitive young student, so receptive to beauty, was deeply impressed by the magnificent surroundings. The beauty of this city near the Black Forest, so peaceful at that time, only a three- or four-hour walk from the Rhine and not much farther from the Feldberg, had a special fascination for him.

He was greatly impressed when he visited a centuries-old Trappist monastery in Alsace, where the monks enjoyed especially good health without eating meat. Meng participated in dietary experimentation, especially with the problem of protein and its minimum requirements. Even then he concluded: "Not only nutrition, but mental attitude is important for efficiency." Clinical studies brought Meng to Leipzig, Würzburg, and Heidelberg. He also became involved in the social problems he witnessed on his visits to the poor. He tried to deal with the problems of unmarried mothers and their children, unable to understand why a child was degraded because of its parents.

Meng was alarmed when the famous brain anatomist, Nissl, said: "You have probably heard that there exists something called 'psychoanalysis.' It is enough to call this pornography, and we will now proceed to the discussion of general paralysis." A year later, at twenty-four, Meng completed his medical studies and wrote his doctoral thesis in orthopedics. He did not specialize prematurely, later saying that to become a good physician it was important for him to keep his interest broad; he took postgraduate training in psychiatry, internal medicine, and pediatric surgery. In 1913, he published an important paper on the treatment of alcoholism, encouraged by the great August Forel. It was Meng's intention to settle down as a general practitioner, but World War I interrupted these plans. For four years Meng served at the front, in hospitals and in prison camps. He has spoken little about his war experience. From childhood, he felt a deep empathy with all suffering by all creatures and had become a physician in order to help. He had deep respect for human beings and the divine in everyone, even if deeply hidden under human miseries.

World order broke down from 1914 through 1918; only after a bloody revolution did a great part of the population become aware of the breakdown. Meng had seen the signs even when German generals talked about great victories.

Meng fought great inner turmoil during the war years. Fortunately, fate brought him in contact with an extraordinarily sensitive man, a psychoanalytically trained psychiatrist who worked quietly and exercised great influence on everyone who knew him. This man fascinated people who met him; he had the power to live according to his inner convictions. This true hero whose praise has not yet been sung was Karl Landauer. During those years of war and misery these two great men met.

The talks with Landauer about psychoanalysis were a turning point in Meng's life; Landauer advised Meng to study psychoanalysis and to go to Vienna.

In 1918, the war over, Meng went to Vienna. The first encounter with Sigmund Freud confirmed the expectations of the thirty-three-year-old physician. He was impressed by the personality of the Viennese scientist, whose behavior during the meeting was charming, comforting, yet skeptical and reserved.

Freud had the reputation of having created something new in medicine; here was the man of the dream interpretations, and, most fascinating, a man who lived tête à tête with the irrational, that region which had impressed the young man who had always been an admirer of Hoelderlin and Novalis. Meng had come to Vienna in order to study psychoanalysis, and Freud—after the interview of less than an hour—gave him the names of three analysts in Vienna whom he recommended for the analysis: two lay analysts, Reik and Rank, and the physician, Federn. He left the decision to Meng after he had briefly characterized these three men to the newcomer. It was stipulated that the analysand had the permission to consult Freud once in a while after the analysis had started. Freud himself began his three months' vacation the following day.

Heinrich Meng had come to Vienna to look for the "homines sapientes" and found a true Homo sapiens in the person of fifty-year-old Paul Federn. Of him Meng said that the first interviews with him were conducted in the spirit of confidence by an apprentice to his master. Federn, a man with the head of an Old Testament Prophet, seemed to Meng to be intelligent, vital, empathic, and open to the world of his partner in the situation. It is difficult to say how this quickly growing basis of trust and confidence was established.

Today Meng sees the bonds that were then formed as mainly his readiness to experience a genuine encounter with another person. Simultaneously, Meng was suffering from severe wounds received during the war, and Paul Federn was suffering from the death of his father. There was increased readiness on Federn's part to play the role of the father who adopts and brings up a son. Their age difference, accentuated by their differences in background, character, and faith, favored this transference-countertransference milieu. The contrasts deepened the analytic work, since both partners were moving toward the same goal. One statement of Federn, "The analyst experiences a never-ending learning and maturing process because of his unities of giving and taking," so impressed Meng that he remembered it twenty-five years later. Without this quality Federn could not have formulated his ego analysis, and Meng could not have shown the fateful connection between psychoanalysis and human development, the working through of aggressiveness and the anxiety connected with it.

Meng kept his unique position as student-teacher, just as Federn kept his special position of independence from Freud. In this way it was possible for Freud, Federn, and Meng not to subscribe to any orthodox dogma. All three, Freud especially, demanded exact self-knowledge of the analyst and knowledge of psychoanalysis as a science, as well as the mastery of psychoanalytic technique as a tool of therapy. Meng said that to be a student and co-worker means to work through and to independently re-experience the scientific insights of Freud and to apply them therapeutically on the basis of one's own empirical experience. Freud's theories are an important stimulus for thought and categorization of observation. Compared with the impact of experience, theories are of secondary importance. The student must not become a slave to his master; he should not be a castrated servant, but a fellow citizen in the world of science. Meng felt that the analyst must remain independent in personality, character, thought, and critique and as a clinical observer. He is not allowed to relinquish his own individuality in identification with Freud. In his years of learning and teaching, a beginner will assume that the discoverer of psychoanalysis has more experience and intuition.

Freud had told Meng that it takes time to know whether one is suited to become an analyst. He added that when you have experienced in Vienna what analysis is and what analysis demands from you is the time to work with it in your practice for the next five years. Then one should then return to Vienna or go to Berlin where one will find Hanns Sachs and the Out-Patient Clinic. Freud further advised Meng to undergo a second analysis with another analyst. He stated that Vienna was always open to him—if that was what he wanted.

Meng used the considerable freedom that was then granted to students in analytic training for discussions with Alfred Adler and Wilhelm Stekel. He also used his time in Vienna to continue his psychiatric training. He visited with Wagner-Jauregg, Pötzl, and Paul Schilder.

Heinrich Meng was fond of quoting Freud's remark in 1926 that psychoanalysis is not a systematized philosophy. Psychoanalysis does not tend to include the world as a whole without providing space for new findings and better insight. Psychoanalysis clings to facts of everyday experience. Psychoanalysis is always unfinished. The foundations of psychoanalytic theory remain (as Freud had formulated them in 1926): recognition of the unconscious, of resistance, of repression, of infantile sexuality, and of the Oedipus complex—these are the main points of psychoanalysis and the foundation of analytic theories.

After completing his analytic work in Vienna, Meng went to Berlin. In the Out-Patient Clinic of the Psychoanalytic Institute, he met Max Eitingon, who also belonged to the intimate circle of friends around Sigmund Freud. Meng also worked in other fields in Berlin. He had worked in Vienna with Steinach on sexual hormones, and he used the opportunity in Berlin to meet the sexologist, Magnus Hirschfeld. He also worked with the famous neurologist, Paul Schuster. Meng had by then gained such a reputation as to be called upon for consultations with the neurologist, Gottfried Forster, and, in Moscow, with the brain specialist, Oskar Vogt. There Meng studied Pavlov's theories and experiments. In Berlin, Meng had contact with August Bier, then one of Germany's leading surgeons, one of the first to introduce the climatic therapy of tuberculosis, and a firm believer in homeopathic medicine.

In 1925, Meng was appointed Chief Physician for Internal Medicine at the Robert-Bosch Hospital in Stuttgart. The founder of this hospital was a homeopathic physician to whom Meng posed the question of how to popularize mental and physical hygiene. Together they founded a publishing house that reflected many of Meng's traits: economic gain was not important but the enterprise should be self-supporting, and it must serve the common good; profits were to be given to charity. This publishing house made possible *The Popular Book on Psychoanalysis*, with Paul Federn as co-editor, in 1924. In 1928, the journal, *Hippokrates*, was founded to advance a united concept of medicine.

The insight of psychoanalysis had outgrown the limits of psychotherapy. Psychoanalysis had started to influence psychology and education. Together with Meng, Ernst Schneider, originally director of the Seminary in Bern, Hans Zulliger's teacher, and later professor of education at the University of Riga, founded *The Journal for Psychoanalytic Education.* This was one of the few German analytic publications that continued publishing until 1938, in spite of the National Socialist Regime.

Meng's medical successes and scientific reputation made it possible to introduce psychoanalysis into the University of Frankfurt. Meng and Karl Landauer were assigned to the directorship of the newly founded Institute for Psychoanalysis, which had the privileges of a "Guest Institute" at the University of Frankfurt.

Ever since his days in Vienna, Meng had become more and more convinced of the possibility that the knowledge of the unconscious, coupled with the science of psychiatry, could lead to a well-rounded mental hygiene movement. Meng, with the co-operation of the Institute for Social Research under Horkheimer, organized seminars for the psychological and sociological fields. With specialists from all fields, particularly those in internal medicine, psychoanalytic courses were organized and a consultation service established.

In treating girls with anorexia nervosa, Meng introduced the concept of "organ-psychosis." This term seemed to him to be a happier choice than the later term "psychosomatic medicine." Organ-psychosis, like the psychosis of the insane, is a disintegration process that interferes with normal function. Meng became a specialist in the psychology of organic sickness, especially with patients suffering from gastrointestinal diseases, and of vascular and metabolic disturbances.

The Frankfurt Institute developed a unique and outstanding faculty: Meng, Karl Landauer, Erich Fromm, Frieda Fromm-Reichmann, and Foulkes, who became one of the leaders of group psychotherapy in England. The great and unforgettable Karl Landauer was later destroyed by the horror of the Nazi concentration camp.

The Institute vanished after 1933 when hate and blindness prevailed, but its spirit could not be killed. The teachers of the Frankfurt Institute carried their thoughts to the world. Meng went to Basel, where he lectured on preventive mental hygiene, education, and psychoanalysis. Four years later, the University in Basel appointed Meng to the medical faculty. For twenty years Meng continued to develop his school at

Basel, which aimed to teach preventive mental hygiene and spread mental health beyond all national boundaries.

At a time when the spirit of progress was silenced and only words of hatred were heard in Germany, Heinrich Meng succeeded in interesting Hans Huber in Berne and Benno Schwabe in Basel in his ideas, and they agreed to publish the *Bücher des Werdenden* and continue to publish a standard library devoted to the science and practice of preventive mental hygiene and social psychiatry on a psychoanalytic basis.

Meng went through the school of hard knocks. He received much love, but he also suffered much grief and bitterness. The hate and deprivation of World War I had threatened him seriously. Meng withstood these dangers bravely and worked them through, with great personal courage. He damned the flood of hatred with human understanding. When the Hitler sickness spread to the Western World, Heinrich Meng was protected against the psychosis of hatred by his maturity and integrity. Even the catastrophe of World War II did not cloud his view of the essential and the important. He calmly and consistently continued his work.

I lived with Heinrich Meng during the challenging years of World War II and observed how he reacted with self-discipline, courage, and readiness to help. Meng's integrity and strength of character served him well and was proof for the ethical basis of psychoanalysis. The ethos of psychoanalysis was for Sigmund Freud a matter of course, so he had little need to discuss it. Meng found himself in deep opposition to the Nazi spirit of that time. For him the Germans were a people of thinkers and poets, best expressed in the genius of Goethe. Meng's wife has equal inner strength; calm, sensitive, and thoughtful, she has shielded her husband against the smallness of everyday life. She has made it possible for him to live entirely for his work and yet she has been able to develop her own independent ways, making their's a model example of a good marriage, both enriching each other's lives without pressuring each other to do anything not genuine to each. This maturity was imbedded in the Meng household.

In 1957, at the age of seventy, Heinrich Meng resigned as a teacher at the university but has gone on working as physician, healer, and consultant to numerous physicians. He continues to harvest the results of his extraordinary experiences, and we can expect many more worthwhile works from him.

Translated and adapted from the German by Martin Grotjahn.

Hans Zulliger

b. 1893

PSYCHOANALYSIS AND EDUCATION

*

ADOLF FRIEDEMANN

Hans Zulliger was born in Switzerland on February 21, 1893. He remembers his father as a modest and kindly man who originally worked for meager wages in a watch factory, but whose ability to manage his wages freed Hans's mother from working as a diamond cutter to devote her time to Hans and his three younger brothers. Hans Zulliger describes his mother as a "petite, gay woman, who frequently sang, taught me many nursery rhymes, and had a natural gift of saying the right thing at the right moment, reassuring me in my childhood miseries."

During a period when both parents had to work, little Hans was placed with friends who lived in another village. Hans was happy with this situation, and Frau Kuhn became "a second mother." Hans built a "little house" at the edge of the nearby forest, where he was allowed to play as much as he wished and where Father Kuhn taught him to fish in the brook that ran through the forest. Hans soon became skilled enough at fishing to earn money by selling his catch to the "Sunday fishermen." All of this stimulated the fantasy and imagination of the boy, and a longing for the Swiss lake country always remained with him. He also visited his uncle, Hans Zulliger, a baker for whom he often delivered bread.

By carefully saving their money, Hans's parents eventually succeeded in buying a piece of land where they built their own small home. Later they were able to afford a few domestic animals and their own vegetable and flower gardens. Hans, however, remained loyal to his fishing, and when he went out he never forgot to visit his old friends, the Kuhns, with whom he had a second home. It was in this setting and with these fine people that Hans Zulliger was formed and developed.

Learning was easy for him, and he was accepted in the *Gymnasium*, where tough discipline was applied and incarceration and restriction often used. A fellow student of Hans once cautiously said, "Perhaps there were some good psychologists among the teachers. We certainly were not aware of that."

After completing the *Gymnasium*, Hans had to choose between becoming a teacher or a forester. Requirements for acceptance as a teacher were very difficult, but he became one of those pupils to whom later generations referred with pride. He had also gained a reputation as a cornet player and had started to practice the violin. He would have liked to become a musician or a painter, but as the son of hard-working parents and the oldest of four brothers—all waiting to go to school—this was a "breadless art" that he could not afford.

At about that time, Hans first met up with psychoanalysis. Sigmund Freud, Eugene Bleuler and C. G. Jung had found their way into Swiss literature. The pastor, Oskar Pfister, had already introduced psychoanalysis into theology. Hans had the good fortune to meet Ernst Schneider, Professor of Psychology at Dorpat, who was perhaps the first to attempt to apply psychoanalysis to education, a dangerous idea at that time. Freud had disturbed the sleep of the world, and the sleeper felt brusquely awakened, reacting with displeasure, disgust, and hatred. The attitude of Ernst Schneider irritated the people in the Canton of Berne so violently that he had to abandon his position—to the sorrow of his students.

Finishing his studies in the spring of 1912, Hans took a job as a teacher of sixty-three pupils in Ittigen, a little village near Berne. In his class were children of different social levels who would be spending four to five years together. Hans Zulliger rooted himself deeply in this environment for forty-seven years. Here he built his home and here he lives to this day. Here he became the man who made the name of Ittigen famous the world over as the birthplace of "paedoanalysis."

It also became known as the home of the man who introduced child analysis into education as a special field of mental hygiene. Hans Zulliger is the only analyst who has the rare delight of knowing the children and grandchildren of his first pupils.

Hans Zulliger tells a story about the beginning of his work as a teacher that characterizes his spirit of adventure, generosity, and carefreeness. Teachers at that time were paid very little, but Zulliger had been brought up to save money; he felt rich with his first savings and had an urge to visit abroad. Because he wanted to share this enjoyment, he invited his father to accompany him to Genoa. "With a kind smile, he accepted. He found it even more amusing that I had to ask him for a loan within three days in the strange city. I no longer thought of myself as a rich man." In spite of his small salary, Hans Zulliger was able to visit Austria, Hungary, Italy, Spain, France, Holland, Denmark, and Germany. "Travel, I found out, is the best way to keep from becoming bitter and settling down as a teacher who does not know the world."

As a young teacher, Zulliger had met Fräulein Martha Urfer while she was looking for Christmas poems. She and Hans could not accept the sentimental trash fashionable at that time: "I found in such poems only artificial and infantile language. Suddenly I was inspired to write poems—perhaps half a dozen. I sent them to the teacher, and later my superintendent found the copies on my desk. He considered them ready to be published, and that was the beginning of my literary career. The Christmas poems multiplied after I had married Fräulein Martha in 1915, and after we had our own child." Poems, ballads, stories, and plays appeared partly in the local Swiss dialect, but other stories, fairy tales, and novels written in high German made the name Hans Zulliger famous the world over. Hans Zulliger is living proof that psychoanalysis does not destroy poetic creativity.

Upon hearing that Pastor Oskar could help his community by applying psychoanalysis to education, Zulliger began to ask himself whether he could help his own students, who were much younger than those with whom Pfister worked. His assignment was to adapt psychoanalysis to the needs of the school. "As soon as I had prepared myself properly," he has said, "I started my first attempts at analyzing, before the onset of World War I, and was favored by beginner's luck."

In 1921, Zulliger published "The Psychoanalytic Observations from Public Schools," and, two years later, a short book, *From the Unconscious Life of Our School Youth.* Both came into my hands when I was dealing with the challenge of psychoanalysis. Through Zulliger, I was introduced to psychoanalysis and a new world was opened to me.

His first publication marked a milestone in Zulliger's development. It put him in touch—initially by letter and later by personal acquaintance—with Sigmund Freud. Zulliger was soon invited to join the Swiss Society for Psychoanalysis, which had been founded two years previously. Among the officers of the Society was Herman Rorschach, who, shortly before his tragic death, introduced Zulliger to his tests. Since then, the name of Hans Zulliger has been intimately connected with that of Rorschach. Through Zulliger's work, the Behn-Rorschach Test was developed, and finally Zulliger evolved his own Zulliger Test.

Zulliger proved himself a sensitive thinker and interpreter and teacher of psychodiagnostic tests. His books on testing are the best introduction into experimental psychodiagnostics. These works show the special features of Zulliger's approach to child analysis: the loving, understanding, developmental approach to the human peculiarity of the individual child who is on the way to maturity.

Although Zulliger had gained some recognition as a child analyst before he was thirty years old, it was a long time before he received wider recognition. More privileged than Rorschach, it was his destiny finally to experience full recognition of his work by the world at large.

When the Society for Mental Hygiene opened the Institute for Mental Hygiene in 1949, in Biel, Hans Zulliger was elected first honorary member.

During World War II, Zulliger served in the Swiss Organization of Psychological Warfare. His experience with the Rorschach methods and his psychoanalytic background led him to develop a method for group testing. At the age of fifty, he could look back with pride at his life's work.

Local authorities gave him no opportunity to collect the results of his work in peace; he was forced to continue the everyday duties of schoolteaching until the Foundation of the Biel Institute for Mental Hygiene enabled Zulliger, in 1950, to devote himself to research. Although he had to return to teaching, he found it possible to lecture extensively, combining his natural gift for teaching with his scientific knowledge.

In 1952, the philosophy faculty of the University of Berne presented Zulliger with the title of Honorary Doctor, at which time the author of this essay summarized his work as follows: For over thirty years, Hans

Zulliger has been one of the ambassadors of Swiss culture. Zulliger began as a teacher who soon proved himself to the scientific world as an especially gifted psychotherapist. A small work of his, *Psychoanalytic Observations from Public Schools,* received attention in 1921, at a time when Sigmund Freud's psychoanalysis was a controversial subject—taboo at most universities—but had found a home in Switzerland through Eugen Bleuler and Pastor Oskar Pfister in Zurich, who was probably the first to attempt to introduce psychoanalysis into the service of pastoral care and education.

Hans Zulliger remained loyal to his profession as a teacher and to his vocation as a therapist. He taught in the same village for more than forty years and is probably the only psychotherapist in the entire world who has had the opportunity to watch so many children from an average population, follow their development, lead them through their difficulties, and to then see the success of his educational and therapeutic efforts through three generations.

Careful of every detail, he developed an impressive scientific work that has taken its place in psychology and mental hygiene. Without trying to be complete, the following books by Hans Zulliger should be mentioned: *From the Unsconscious Life of Our School Youth, Loosened Chains, Problem School Children,* and *Therapeutic Values in Play Activities.*

Zulliger's scientific methods were shown in his works on the Behn-Rorschach Test and on young thieves and their Rorschach Test responses. He developed his Z-Test, which is applicable not only in group situations but also for individuals.

To describe all of Zulliger's works would fill an entire monograph. His more than 100 articles and books were translated into many languages. He must be described as scientist, educator, and therapist. More could be said about him as a poet, about his humor, his artistic skill, and his being a good man. More should be said about his untiring readiness to help and about his work as Secretary for the Swiss Society for Psychoanalysis. Zulliger's work can be summarized as follows: All neuroses are caused by repression, as described by Sigmund Freud. The child's play is an expression of the child's unconscious. It is possible to interpret the play analytically, so it is possible to use play for treatment. Therapy proceeds without interpretation of the unconscious, which means the child is not given interpretations. A cure will take place only when ethical behavior becomes a matter of course to the child. Therefore, Zulliger rejects punishment as a means of education. He applies it only where there is confidence between child and educator. The basis for successful treatment is the exact knowledge of the work of Sigmund Freud, the knowledge of the child's magic-mystic thinking and its relationship to the development of conscience. The entire treatment stands and falls with the therapist. Fröbel's statement, "Education is example and love and nothing else!" could be called the theme of Zulliger's work, helping and healing.

Zulliger's deep religiosity is free from dogma and is an expression of an honest search for truth. Every insight is recognized with gratitude and what cannot be researched is faced with devotion and respect.

This attitude leads to a firm trust in the natural order of things, in a natural acceptance of such order, and in curative forces that become clear to the man who knows how to activate them. This explains why Hans Zulliger developed a special technique that allows him to transform parents into helpers in child psychotherapy. He knows how to interpret their behavior, but more, he heeds his insight for himself and does not give interpretation. He lets interpretation become effective without formulating it.

Quoting from a popular poem, Hans Zulliger once said, "What matters is the work; the creator is not important." This characterizes Hans Zulliger the scientist. He humbly lets his work speak for itself.

Translated and adapted from the German by Martin Grotjahn.

August Aichhorn

1878–1949

FRIEND OF THE WAYWARD YOUTH

*

GEORGE J. MOHR

From a quiet start as a schoolmaster in Vienna at the close of the nineteenth century, August Aichhorn advanced to a career that was to bring him recognition as a pioneer in the application of psychoanalysis to the field of juvenile delinquency.

In the classroom and later at the reformatory schools at Ober-Hollabrunn and St. Andrä, Aichhorn was guided by an intuitive understanding of dissocial behavior, based on an extraordinary capacity for empathy and identification with the delinquent. As he himself said, "Without really knowing what we were doing, we worked out what might be called a practical psychology of reconciliation" (1935, p. 150).

Aichhorn sought a language of expression that could explain the dynamic aspects of antisocial behavior and facilitate insight into the interplay of psychic forces operating in the development of delinquency. He could not accept the then current research into criminology and delinquency, which stressed as causal factors either heredity and constitutionally determined elements or environmental factors. Psychoanalysis gave Aichhorn the key to his enquiries; his practical therapeutic work enriched and broadened the application of psychoanalysis in the field of juvenile delinquency.

Aichhorn recognized that some states of delinquency include an admixture of neurotic and delinquent elements. In his own words, "When the neurotic factors predominate, the usual educational methods are therapeutically inadequate. In such cases psychoanalytic understanding of neurosis offers the most effective contribution to our work. When symptoms of delinquency are not predominantly neurotically determined, pedagogical skill is important because of the necessity to regulate the child's environment" (1935, p. 9). Some cases require a combination of both approaches. As the offender's irresponsibility, lack of motivation, and conscious acceptance of his delinquent impulses preclude the initial use of psychoanalytic treatment, changes—that include strengthening of the superego—must first be effected through educational procedures. Then, when the delinquent begins to suffer from his symptoms, the therapist can proceed with psychoanalytic treatment.

Aichhorn's concept of "latent delinquency," as distinguished from manifest delinquency, was of decisive importance in that it redirected inquiry into the causes and treatment of delinquency. Aichhorn believed that an arrest in personality development predisposes to antisocial behavior. The arrest arises from a disturbance in early child–parent relationships, for example, lack of parental acceptance or death of the parents. In the absence of appropriate object relationships that serve the child's needs for identification, the weak ego—lacking the capacity for sublimation and such defenses as reaction formation—cannot exercise choice for action in keeping with realistic requirements. It is primarily because of inadequate superego functioning that the child is unable to postpone gratification and the urge to satisfy drives at once prevails. People in the environment are important to the degree that they can gratify wishes; they are hated as disappointing adults if they prevent the securing of satisfactions. Inadequate character structure, which Aichhorn termed "latent delinquency," can be triggered into manifest delinquency by unfavorable influences during the latency period and adolescence.

In keeping with his view of the pathogenesis of delinquency, Aichhorn emphasized the necessity for dealing with the underlying determinants of latent delinquency rather than with the symptoms seen in manifest delinquency. He recognized that, in treatment, it is important to provide an experience in relationships that will undo the effects of the deficient or inadequate relationships of the past. This demands of the therapist a subtle exploitation of the transference situation, so that the patient—drawn to the therapist as the more suitable parental representative—can then experience needed gratifications hitherto denied him, establish healthier identifications, and, in the strengthening of his ego, make further advances in his personality development. In modern terminology, this use of transference provides a "corrective emotional experience." Aichhorn's formulations have remained essentially unchallenged and have provided the basis for extensive studies by many later experts.

While still a schoolteacher, Aichhorn attracted the attention of the authorities through his success in dealing with incorrigible youths; in 1918, he was commissioned to establish and direct a reformatory school at Ober-Hollabrunn and another two years later at St. Andrä. Anna Freud was so impressed with Aichhorn's work and with the degree to which Aichhorn's observations conformed with psychoanalytic views that she encouraged him to get in touch with the Vienna Psychoanalytical Society. Accordingly, in 1922 when he was forty-four, Aichhorn entered the Society to begin his training with Paul Federn. There, as Anna Freud wrote, he "took his place . . . at the bottom of the table" (1951). At ease and superbly self-confident in his own work, Aichhorn was uncomfortable and out of place in the atmosphere of the Society. He was not accustomed to the quick exchanges of the brilliant young theoreticians and stayed outside their discussions. Fortunately, through the help and understanding of Federn and his colleagues, Aichhorn gradually found a place in the group. He continued his work in the child guidance centers of Vienna and trained social workers and child guidance personnel as before; once his training was completed he began practical work in the analytic field, treating neurotic patients as well as delinquents. He published his first book, *Verwahrloste Jugend* (*Wayward Youth*), in 1925, as a basic guide to the principles of psychoanalysis for workers in delinquency, summarizing for psychoanalysts the guiding principles for work with delinquents. In 1935, a group of Americans working in psychoanalysis in Vienna, who recognized this book's importance, translated it into English, and it quickly attracted wide attention. It has become a basic textbook in child guidance and juvenile delinquency.

In *Wayward Youth*, which is written informally and in the first person, Aichhorn's exchanges with patients and their parents reveal not only the problems of the youth, but also the distinctive flavor of Aichhorn's own personality as therapist. Here is an account of his effort to bring together a father and son:

> I started the conversation then left them alone. . . . After about twenty minutes, I came back to find them both red-eyed and silent. The father said in answer to my look of astonishment, "It's no use; he won't talk." . . . I was angry and disappointed in him. I had worked with him for over two hours to show him how the situation had arisen and had tried to show him what he must do to bring the poor boy back into a sympathetic relation to him, and now he was behaving like this! Without looking at the father, I went over to the boy, put my hand on his head, and said, "Never mind, one doesn't always have to talk. Two people can understand one another without saying a word." At that, the boy began to cry violently. I do not know just how it came about—but the next minute they were in each other's arms. I must admit I was not untouched by the scene (1935, p. 101).

What was the quality that brought such impressive success in the treatment of delinquency to this man when others so frequently failed? Patients, friends, colleagues, and students attest to the extraordinary personality that so quickly could find a rapprochement with the transgressor, soften his bitterness and hate, and lead him to the acceptance of a healthier way of life. A favorite photograph of Aichhorn reveals a smiling *bon vivant* with a cavalier beard and hat tilted at a rakish angle. This was no thin-lipped pedagogue but a lover of life, and indeed this was Aichhorn—whether playing with his favorite little granddaughter Christine, teaching himself English, or explaining his roulette system to friends. Of Aichhorn the healer, Freud observed in the preface of *Wayward Youth*, "His treatment of his charges had its source in a warm sympathy for the fate of these unfortunates and was rightly guided by his intuitive understanding of their psychic needs."

Aichhorn's interest in delinquency can be traced to elements in his own background. He came of an old Catholic family and was proud of his tie to the soil through peasant forebears who had lived on the land for some centuries. In the move to the city the family turned to trades and crafts. Aichhornstrasse, in a district in Vienna where Aichhorn lived for many years, honors a bygone *Stadtvater* (city father).

Aichhorn grew up in extremely modest circumstances. After financial ruin in the crisis of 1873, Aichhorn's father, formerly director of a bank in Vienna, had taken over his mother-in-law's family bakery. Aichhorn and his twin brother were born in 1878, during lean days for the family. Throughout Aichhorn's life he was sensitive because his parents had been unable to provide the academic training he had longed for. Aichhorn unwittingly garnered a firsthand understanding of delinquency through his daily contact with the young fellows who worked in his father's bakery. They taught him to play cards, frequently relieving him of all his pocket money. Even their slang and patois became a valuable asset in helping him "speak the same language" as his charges later in his career.

In his own analysis Aichhorn realized that a slight tilting of circumstances had saved him from becoming delinquent himself. This personal understanding deepened his capacity for empathy with the delinquent and gave him a particular adroitness in establishing and using the transference relationship. He understood that in order to protect himself from the inimical world—including the therapist—the lad who was brought to him under legal duress or parental pressure would plot, lie, and otherwise try to wriggle out of the situation in which he found himself. Matching wits from the first moment of their meeting, a time of prime importance in establishing the foundation for their relationship, Aichhorn was on the alert for cues—a defiant shrug, an appraising glance—knowing that he must avoid the extremes of severity and leniency. Undue severity would invite rejection from the rebellious or intractable, sulkiness from the timid, whereas excessive leniency would be mistaken for weakness. With infinite balance and delicacy, Aichhorn managed to create the impression that he was an ally, albeit with a faint adumbration of power. He avoided all reference to the dissocial behavior; fully alert to the critical issue of the child's immediate emotional state, he concentrated on topics dear to the hearts of boys and girls, a favorite football player, a movie star, fairy tales, or tales of adventure. His sincerity flowed from a natural zest for these pleasures. I remember how Aichhorn's consulting room in Vienna reflected the boy in the man. His simple bookshelves, the pride of his own carpentering, were crammed with the works of James Fenimore Cooper and Karl May, the "German Zane Grey," whom he adored.

Aichhorn was adept at introducing his students to the patient–therapist setting. For example, I remember how he introduced me to his first patient. After presenting the youth's name, Aichhorn exclaimed, "Ist er ein Gauner!" (Is this one a scamp!). "If he keeps it up he's going to be a pimp on the Kaerntnerstrasse." To which the young man, in a comfortable comradeship with Aichhorn, replied, "But I *am* a pimp on the Kaerntnerstrasse."

Aichhorn gained further insight into the dynamics of delinquency and the requisite techniques for dealing with it in his encounter with two especially intractable types of delinquent, the aggressive youngster (1935) and the adolescent impostor.

At Ober-Hollabrunn, he was confronted with the problem of handling twelve particularly aggressive boys between the ages of fifteen and twenty, whose insufferable behavior could not be tolerated in any group. All were products of a violent past. Beaten and brutalized by parents who were constantly at loggerheads with each other, as well as with their children, these boys were starved for friendliness and tenderness and expressed their hatred in open violence and mistreatment of others, particularly those weaker than themselves. They would start a fight in a flash, sending table silver and dishes flying. In the dissension among the staff as to the best method of handling this problem, the situation deteriorated. The majority of the workers felt that these incorrigibles could be brought to heel only by the strictest discipline and the hardest physical labor.

But this ran counter to Aichhorn's principles in the treatment of delinquency, principles based on the recognition that delinquents are human beings who have found life too hard and are justified in their antagonism to society. He felt that the official attitudes of stern moralism and strict discipline prevailing in the older institutions merely reintroduce the child to his original conflict. Therefore, if the educator was to make any progress in the treatment, Aichhorn thought it necessary to create an environment for these children in which they could feel comfortable. As he later said, "I have never felt the need of changing my attitude in this respect but have continued to find it justified" (1935, p. 150).

In this new situation of the aggressive group, Aichhorn's intuition forced him to challenge the majority opinion. With characteristic daring, he announced that with the help of two women workers he himself would take charge of the boys. He then proceeded to allow their aggression full rein, short of mayhem or murder. Writing of this decision later, he said, "Aggression can rise only to a certain pitch. . . . Since we did not oppose the destructive behavior of the group, their aggression was bound to reach a climax" (1935, p. 175). As a first consequence, this attitude invited even more acts of aggression—increasing in intensity. When they did not get corporeal punishment for their provocations, these boys, conditioned by their pasts, interpreted it as weakness in the workers; they became even more aggressive, deriving revenge for their own deprivations by inflicting pain on others. When Aichhorn and his workers met this behavior passively, an unconscious wish for severity (which could justify hatred for the workers) drove the boys to still further hostility and aggression. They practically demolished the premises. They abandoned the dining table to devour their food in corners and created such bedlam that an aroused community repeatedly sent for the police and demanded action. Aichhorn unwaveringly kept to his course although his confidence was sometimes tested, for as he said, "We had set ourselves against majority opinion and were forced to carry on or admit defeat" (1935, p. 179).

The first change in the boys was observed when a "performance" of rage took the place of genuine rage. Aichhorn recalls such an incident when one of the boys assailed another with a knife, threatening to slit his throat. Recognizing this as an "act," Aichhorn quietly stood by as if nothing was unusual in such behavior. The boy threw the knife on the ground and, howling and weeping with frustration, finally fell into an exhausted sleep. Similar scenes occurred with each of the twelve boys. A period of instability followed, during which they sometimes behaved so well together it was thought they were cured. Then, without warning, as if they were magma thrown up from a volcano, the outbreaks began again. This continued for about three months, during which time the outbursts became less frequent and an emotional bond began to develop between the boys and the workers.

Aichhorn continued his friendly approach, having frequent talks with the delinquents and siphoning off their aggression by offering them suitable occupation and play. In this labile period, he was able to heighten some strong pleasurable emotions. At Christmas, for instance, he gave the boys a tree of their own and special presents, such as other children had. "It was a joy," he wrote, "to observe what these children experienced on that occasion." These aggressive boys finally developed into an integrated group, presenting no more problems than other groups. Aichhorn noted with interest that, when the aggressive behavior ceased, many of the boys who had formerly been backward in their studies showed superior mental performance in making up their school work. At this point, Aichhorn relinquished the leadership to a psychologist who had the task of training the boys to meet the demands of life outside the institution. Because of the identification of each boy with the all-loving leader and the emotional bonds between members of the group as a result of their common attachment to the leader, the groundwork had been laid for a positive response to the attitudes and expectations of the therapist.

Unlike the aggressive group, which expresses itself in open violence, the "adolescent impostor" is the smooth "con" man or, in psychiatric classification, the psychopathic liar and swindler. Seemingly he is incapable of forming a therapeutically useful transference relationship and is more likely to add the therapist to his list of victims than to respond to the therapist in the service of further development. Nevertheless, in spite of a boy's inability to establish object relationships, Aichhorn observed that the impostor can become attached to the therapist "through an overflow of narcissistic libido" (1951, p. 55), it is possible to evoke emotional responses useful in treatment. In the therapeutic relationship the adolescent impostor can love the therapist as if the therapist were a part of himself and not an object in the outer world which he can victimize.

According to Aichhorn, the ego ideal of the impostor is modeled on a father who has never become depreciated, even though the boy has suffered through his deceit and lies. "Father did this and so it's all right for me," is his philosophy. Aware both of his mounting power in the transference relationship and the child's libidinal ties to the objects of his earliest environment, Aichhorn set out to "unmask" this ego ideal by making himself superior to it. In the establishment of this narcissistic transference relationship, his main device was to arouse surprise without evoking fear, to show strength without using threats, and to dangle promises without making commitments. The patient then came to feel that Aichhorn had assumed the role that he himself had toward his victims, and thus seeing Aichhorn as an extension of his own ego or ego ideal, he stood in awe of the therapist. Less secure in his identification with the hitherto dependable ego ideal and less sure of himself, the patient would come to depend more and more upon the therapist, so that in the transference everything that had seemed powerful and potent in childhood was now embodied in the person of the therapist. At this stage, the affects usually manifest in the infantile neurosis come to the fore, opening the way to further treatment more in keeping with that of the neurotic patient.

Concurrent with his use of the transference relationship in the treatment of delinquents, Aichhorn sought to establish a similar relationship with each family member, thus providing in the kindly father figure a link between the hostile factions.

Aichhorn set forth his approach to the treatment of parents of emotionally disturbed children in a comprehensive paper, "On the Technique of Educational Guidance," which he wrote in 1936 to honor Freud's eightieth birthday. This was intended as a textbook of Aichhorn's treatment methods, and though its circulation was limited in the absence of an English translation, much of the material has found its way into the current casework and counseling approach. Such modern students of delinquency as Szurek and Johnson (1948) have further elaborated on the therapeutic implications in Aichhorn's emphasis on the need to understand the operation of the parental superego, its relationship to the superego structure of the delinquent, and the importance of parental superego potential for empathy with the therapist. In this work, Aichhorn also discusses the establishment by the therapist of a libidinal relationship with the parents, to influence various types of parents in given ways for therapeutic ends. He points out the importance of the establishment, maintenance, and resolution of strong transference attitudes of the parent toward the therapist as a means of bringing about modification of disturbances in the relations to the parents. And he indicates how in other areas—under the pressure of transference reactions—the behavior or action of parents can be influenced in a given direction and utilized advantageously.

Knowing from experience the fundamental importance of the correct use of transference in retraining the delinquent and the special qualifications this demands of the workers, Aichhorn chose his counselors and co-workers with scrupulous care. At Ober-Hollabrunn and St. Andrä, they were chosen according to age, sex, and qualifications of character best suited to the special requirements of each group.

In essence, the treatment of delinquency requires of the worker a capacity for empathy with the delinquent that can lead to a successful use of the transference. Correct use of transference encourages essential ego strengthening, with advance toward an increasingly independent ability to learn and to develop more mature relationships. Unskillful handling increases the risk of regressive augmentation of infantile libidinal attachments and impedes normal development toward a mature character structure.

As Anna Freud has said, the worker in delinquency must have "the capacity for double allegiance and identification with society on the one hand and the world of the delinquent on the other" (1951, p. 55). His personality must be sufficiently flexible to permit him to accept the delinquent despite his dissocial behavior and perhaps even temporarily to step outside his own identification with society and enter into a conspiracy of comradeship with the youth in his delinquent schemes. Aichhorn set the pattern of performance by his own genius for "topping" these adventurous plans. Ostensibly he would "go along" with the delinquent, weighing and considering the gratifications and dangers of the proposal, while at the same time subtly influencing him to accept the socially acceptable plan as the "better" one.

Aichhorn retired from public service in 1932 and entered private practice. He then organized a Child Guidance Service for the Vienna Psychoanalytical Society and conducted a seminar for problems of child guidance under the auspices of the Vienna Institute.

With the Anschluss of 1938 and the entry of the Nazis into Austria, the Society was dissolved; in the emigration of its members, Aichhorn lost his friends, pupils, and colleagues. As a non-Jew he faced a difficult choice. Although his decision to remain in Vienna was influenced by his son's internment at Dachau, it also probably met Aichhorn's deepest longing to remain on the family soil that had nourished his vitality and genius.

In his new isolation from his past, Aichhorn showed his own special brand of courage. He was an old hand at dealing with gangsters and was on familiar ground with the Nazis. Under cover of their new designation of "therapeutic education," he quietly proceeded to analyze a number of young psychiatrists in optimistic readiness for the future. Even during the Nazi occupation of Vienna, his contacts with leading personalities in the juvenile court and the Red Cross won for him invitations to lecture before the Hungarian Psychoanalytical Society.

At the war's end in 1946, Aichhorn immediately took the legal steps necessary to reopen the Vienna Psychoanalytical Society and Institute. Through the generosity of anonymous sources in America, the Society —renamed the "August Aichhorn Gesellschaft"—was re-established in elegant premises at I. Rathausstrasse 20, with Aichhorn's rooms adjoining. Aichhorn resumed his private practice and became chairman of the newly established Society, as well as training analyst, supervising analyst, and lecturer.

On Aichhorn's seventieth birthday in 1948, the president of the Austrian Republic honored Aichhorn's services by conferring on him the title of professor. And to mark the occasion, his friends in the International Psychoanalytic Association collaborated on a commemorative volume of essays under the title *Searchlights on Delinquency*, edited by K. R. Eissler (1949). With characteristic graciousness, Aichhorn honored his colleagues and friends with a handsomely inscribed bronze medal bearing his profile. This memento of himself in enduring bronze must also have pleased Aichhorn, who always enjoyed having his picture taken.

Aichhorn wrote relatively little during his lifetime, but his published works have had an enormous impact on later research and clinical practice in the field of juvenile delinquency.

During a discussion at a children's home in Budapest in 1948, Aichhorn was overcome by a sudden fainting spell: this was the onset of the illness that ended in his death from a cerebral hemorrhage the following year. Perhaps a sense of urgency drove him to start plans in 1949 for a publication that would co-ordinate the findings of his later days concerning delinquency; this was destined not to be completed. As a supplement to *Verwahrloste Jugend*, a collection of some of his writings originally delivered as lectures was published posthumously in Berne, under the title *Erziehungsberatung und Erziehungshilfe* ("Educational Counseling and Remedial Education") (1959). This volume contains Aichhorn's basic viewpoints and analyses of illustrative cases from his practice, together with a classification of categories of delinquency.

Through his unique gift for understanding the child in conflict with the world about him, Aichhorn stands as a pioneer who has advanced the application of psychoanalysis to the field of juvenile delinquency.

REFERENCES

Aichhorn, A. *Wayward youth*. New York: Viking Press, 1935.

Eissler, K. R. (Ed.) *Searchlights on delinquency*. New York: International Universities Press, 1949.

Freud, Anna. Obituary of August Aichhorn. *Int. J. Psycho-Anal.*, 1951, 32, 51–56.

Johnson, A. M. Sanctions for super-ego lacunae of adolescents. In K. R. Eissler (Ed.), *Searchlights on delinquency*. New York: International Universities Press, 1948.

Meng, H. (Ed.) *Erziehungsberatung und Erziehungshilfe*. Bern & Stuttgart: Verlag Hans Huber, 1959.

The author is indebted to Dr. Howard Hansen for valuable aid.

Dr. George Mohr died suddenly March 6, 1965, at the age of sixty-nine. He was a most admired and beloved teacher and colleague and his early work with children and his numerous publications in the field of psychiatry and psychosomatic medicine and psychoanalysis make him a pioneer on his own merit.

Melanie Klein

1882–1960

HER VIEW OF THE UNCONSCIOUS

*

JOHN ARNOLD LINDON

§ The Person

Melanie Reizes Klein was born in Vienna on March 30, 1882. She was the youngest of four children. Her father was a Doctor of Medicine. Melanie had great admiration for the independent spirit and scientific attitude of her father, but their relationship was never close—perhaps because of the age difference of more than half a century. She felt closer to her beautiful and intellectual mother, Libussa, of whom she was deeply fond.

Melanie was only fourteen when she decided to study medicine. Coached by her brother, she passed the entrance examination to the Vienna *Gymnasium*, the only school preparing girls for the university at that time. Soon after her matriculation, at the age of seventeen, she became engaged to Arthur Klein, an industrial chemist. Because of her early engagement and her marriage at twenty-one, her plans were changed. She studied art and history at the University of Vienna, but never received a degree.

Arthur and Melanie Klein had three children, Melitta, Hans, and Eric. The family settled in Budapest, where Melanie happened upon a book by Sigmund Freud. Her interest in the new science of psychoanalysis was immediate. She sought analysis with Sándor Ferenczi and continued with him for several years.

She read her first paper on child development before the Budapest Psychoanalytic Society on July 19, 1919. The paper was later expanded and appeared as her first published work, "The Development of a Child." In late 1919, she was elected a member of the Budapest Society. At the Psychoanalytic Congress in the Hague in 1920, she met Freud and Abraham. Karl Abraham was impressed with her and invited her to practice in Berlin.

In January 1921, Arthur Klein went to Sweden, and Melanie moved with her children to Berlin. This separation was the first step toward their divorce, in 1923. Her first patient, a five-year-old boy, was treated in his own home. From the start, she recognized that this child expressed his fantasies and anxieties mainly in play with his toys. She tried interpreting what he dramatized in a manner similar to Freud's interpretation of dreams. Thus began the development of her psychoanalytic play technique.

For the next five years, Melanie Klein worked in Berlin. Her findings about the horrifying and unrealistic nature of her young patients' fantasies gave rise to dissension among many of her colleagues, especially those who worked only with adults. Her insistance on the feasibility of child analysis without any educative or reassuring concomitants was rarely accepted.

At the invitation of Ernest Jones, Klein presented a course of lectures in London during the summer of 1925, and, when in 1926 he asked her to move to England and work in the British Psychoanalytic Society, she accepted and moved to London. It was a decision she never regretted. Ernest Jones was the third great analyst to recognize and sponsor Melanie Klein. With his support, she continued her work with children. Many British analysts were eager to learn child analysis from her, and she undertook the supervision of their cases involving children. By the early 1930s she had begun to analyze adults, as well as children and to develop her technique of adult analysis.

Although her analytic work flourished, tragedy entered her private life in the spring of 1934, when her twenty-seven-year-old elder son, Hans, was killed in a mountaineering accident. Her daughter, Melitta Schmideberg, had studied medicine and had become an analyst. Melitta Schmideberg became an outstanding therapist and analytic research worker in New York; she has recently returned to London.

Controversy concerning Klein's work grew. The technique to which she was led by her findings about mood fluctuations caused by immediate introjection and projection processes involved early and frequent interpretations and was out of line with the views of other analysts. The ensuing decade of controversy cost Klein the full support of many British analysts who had formerly welcomed her. She drew around her a group of pupils who later became known in the British Society as "the Kleinians." Although the Society-Institute avoided formal division, the schism was deep and persistent. Within the Institute, there exists a large Kleinian school, which has trained many analysts who practice in England, South America, and on the Continent. As a supervising analyst in the London Institute, Klein was considered a perceptive, illuminating teacher.

Klein treated her last child patient in the late 1940's, but until her death in 1960 she retained links with child analysis by supervising many students who used her technique and conceptual systems. Her main work was to teach and analyze psychoanalytic students, to treat adult patients, and to write. That her creativity remained to the end is apparent from her study of schizoid mechanisms, her formulation of the paranoid-schizoid position, her study of the psychoses, and her work in infantile and oral envy. *Envy and Gratitude* was written four years before her death. During the succeeding two years she completed one of her most ambitious works, *Narrative of a Child Analysis*. More than seventy-eight years old at her death, she was still engaged in creative work, writing "The Psychoanalytic Study of Oresteia of Aeschylus," which she was preparing for the Edinburgh International Psychoanalytic Congress.

In 1960, a slowly growing malignancy was discovered and successfully removed by surgery. Her postoperative course seemed satisfactory, and she enjoyed a visit with her son Eric on September 22. Two hours afterward she died, suddenly and quietly, of a pulmonary embolus.

§ Her Work

Melanie Klein considered herself to be a faithful adherent of Sigmund Freud. At no time did she regard her work as an independent set of theories of mental function, complete in itself to replace Freudian theory. Rather, she considered her work as contributing to psychoanalysis—as extending psychoanalytic understanding into the very early stages of infancy and the deeper layers of the unconscious.

§ Her Work with Children

In 1919, with Ferenczi's encouragement, Mrs. Klein began to work with children. She treated her first child analytic patient, five-year-old Fritz, in his own home. She soon recognized that in play the child was using his toys mainly to express symbolically his experiences, fantasies, and anxieties. Klein recognized that this mode of expression was also the language of dreams and, using Freud's method of dream interpretation as her guide, she interpreted these meanings to Fritz. The result was that additional material came into his play and verbalization. By interpreting both the child's verbalizations and his play, Klein applied the basic principle of free association.

A definite step in the development of play technique occurred in 1923 when she analyzed Rita, her youngest patient, who was two years and nine months old. Klein decided that treatment should not take place in the child's home because she believed the transference situation could only be established and maintained if the patient were able to feel that the consulting room or playroom—indeed the whole analysis—was something separate from her home life. Only under such conditions can the patient overcome resistances against experiencing and expressing thoughts, feelings, and desires incompatible with convention and which, for children, are apparently in contrast to much that they have been taught.

Klein was convinced that with the child one can achieve an analytic relationship free from educational, moral, or reassuring interferences, in which a proper analysis can be carried out. She noted that every therapist who begins to work with children finds, to his surprise, that even in very young children the capacity for insight is often far greater than in adults. She believed that, to some extent, the explanation is that the connections between the conscious and the unconscious are closer in young children than in adults, that infantile repressions are less powerful, and that the infant's intellectual capacities are often underrated.

Her concern with the necessity for reaching the level at which the unconscious anxiety was active led her deeper and deeper into the mind of the child.

From her work with children, Klein became convinced that the superego, as conceived by Freud, is the product of a development that begins in early infancy. She observed that the superego is experienced as a variety of figures that the child unconsciously feels actually exist within him and actually function within his body. These internal figures or objects were once external objects that were later introjected. Klein discovered the vital part that reparation plays in mental life and believed that reparation includes the variety of processes by which the ego undoes harm done in fantasy and restores, preserves, and revives objects. The importance of reparation, bound up as it is with feelings of guilt, lies also in the major contribution it makes to all sublimations and thus to mental health.

From 1924 to 1926, her analysis of a paranoid girl, Erna, helped prepare the ground for a number of conclusions, in particular the view that the early superego, built up when oral sadistic impulses and fantasies are at their height, underlies psychoses. By 1930, Klein had begun working with adult neurotics. From clinical and theoretical points of view she found it of great value to analyze adults and children simultaneously. Her work with neurotic adults and neurotic and psychotic children resulted in her hypothesis that anxiety of a psychotic nature is, in some measure, part of normal infantile development and is expressed and worked through in the course of infantile neuroses. These psychoticlike paranoid and depressive anxieties are transient. Klein emphasized that she did not suggest that children go through an infantile psychosis, but rather that they suffer transient periods with psychoticlike anxieties.

The importance Klein attributed to symbolism led her to theoretical conclusions about the processes of symbol formation. Play analysis had shown that symbolism had enabled the child to transfer not only objects but also fantasies, anxieties, and guilt to objects other than people. Klein believed that in children a severe inhibition of the capacity to form and use symbols, and so to develop fantasy life, is a sign of serious disturbance. Such inhibitions and the resulting disturbance in relation to the external world and to reality are characteristic of schizophrenia.

It was at this time, in 1932, that Klein published *The Psychoanalysis of Children.* Although some of her major ideas appear in this book, her views were modified considerably with later analytic experience; for example, only very late did she realize the fundamental importance of envy and its essentially aggressive nature. The major steps in the development of her ideas are: (1) discovery of the early forms of the ego, projective and introjective mechanisms for building up the child's internal world, and the early forms of the Oedipus complex; (2) discovery of the crucial place in development of the depressive position, linked with the infant's awareness of his mother as a whole and separate person; (3) discovery of the anxieties and the mechanisms that she termed the "paranoid-schizoid position," a point of fixation in psychotic illness; and (4) discovery of early oral envy and its influence on the early stages of development.

Of particular importance is her study of the changes in ego structure and the types of anxiety in object relationships that occur between the paranoid-schizoid and the depressive positions. To persons who follow her teachings, these discoveries are fundamental milestones in the understanding of early development.

§ The Early Stages of Infancy and the Unconscious

In describing her theories to her critics, Klein has pointed out, "Allowance must be made for the great difficulty of expressing a young child's feelings and phantasies in adult language. All descriptions of early unconscious phantasies—and, for that matter, of unconscious phantasies in general—can therefore only be considered as pointers to the contents rather than to the form of such phantasies" (1932).

In the earliest stages, love and understanding (and hate) are expressed through the mother's handling of her baby and lead to a kind of oneness that is based on the unconscious of the mother and of the child, being in close relation to each other. The infant's feeling of being understood underlies the first and fundamental relationship in his life, the relation to his mother.

At the same time as he experiences love, he also experiences discomfort, pain, and frustration. Frustration, to some extent unavoidable, strengthens hate and aggressiveness. Frustration does not only mean that the infant is not fed when he wants to be. There are unconscious desires, not always perceptible in the infant's behavior, that demand the continuous presence of the mother and her exclusive love. That he is greedy and wants more than even the best external situation can fulfill is part of the emotional life of the infant. These painful emotions are experienced as persecution and enter into the infant's feelings about his mother, who, in his first few months, represents his whole external world; to his mind, both good and bad come from her, and this leads to a two-fold attitude toward the mother, even under the best possible conditions.

Innate aggressiveness is bound to be activated by unfavorable external circumstances and, conversely, is mitigated by the love and understanding the young child receives. Although the importance of external circumstances is recognized increasingly today, the importance of internal factors is still underrated. Destructive impulses, varying from individual to individual, are an integral part of mental life, even in favorable circumstances. Development of the child and attitudes of the adult must be considered as resulting from the interaction between internal and external influences. The struggle between love and hate can be recognized to some extent through careful observation of babies. Some babies experience strong resentment about any frustration and show this by being unable to accept gratification when it follows a deprivation; such children have a stronger innate aggressiveness and greed than do infants whose occasional outbursts of rage are soon over. In the latter group, when gratification is again provided, the feeling of love is regained.

In her analyses of children, Klein saw the strength and speed of introjection and projection and the importance of their constant fluctuations in the minds of her little patients. Introjection and projection function from the beginning of postnatal life as some of the earliest activities of the ego. Introjection implies that the outer world—with the situations the infant lives through and the objects he encounters—is experienced as taken into the self and thus becomes part of the infant's inner life.

As Klein discovered, introjected external objects are experienced as being concretely present within the body. Klein has always stated clearly that she is in agreement with Abraham's theory that only "part objects" can be introjected by the infant, until he is of an age to realize the mother as a whole and separate person. In the child's perception, mother's breast, face, hands, and so on first come together as parts of a whole person in the latter half of the first year of life. The internalized breast, face, and hands are the precursors of the internalized mother herself. The core of the ego structure is the internalized breast. Klein's theory regarding "internal objects" was a milestone in her work.

Even in adults, mental life cannot be evaluated without considering additions to the personality that come from continuous introjection. Projection, which goes on simultaneously, refers to a process whereby the infant attributes to other people around him feelings that operate within him. Love and hate toward the mother are bound up with the infant's capacity to project all his emotions onto her, thereby making her a good, as well as a bad, object.

Projection alters the infant's impression of his environment, and by introjection this changed picture of his environment influences what goes on in his mind. Thus an inner world is built up that is partly a reflection of the external one. In the same way, introjection and projection go on throughout life; although modified in the course of maturation, they never lose their importance to the individual's relationship with the world about him. Therefore, even in the "normal" adult, the judgment of reality is never free from the influence of his internal world.

The processes of projection and introjection must be considered as unconscious fantasy products. "Phantasy is in the first instance the mental corollary, the psychic representative of instinct. There is no impulse, no instinctual urge or response which is not experienced as unconscious phantasy. . . . A phantasy represents the particular content of the urges or feelings dominating the mind at the moment" (1937).

"Unconscious fantasies" are mental activities that accompany every impulse experienced by the infant. For example, a hungry baby can deal with his hunger temporarily by hallucinating the satisfaction of being given the breast, with all the pleasures he normally derives—the taste of milk, the warm feeling of the breast, and being held and loved by the mother. But, in the same way, unconscious fantasy also takes the opposite form—of feeling deprived and persecuted by the breast that refuses to give satisfaction. The continuing interplay between introjection and projection, if not excessive and if not dominated by hostility, leads to enrichment of the inner world and improvement of relations with the external world.

Another of the primal activities of the infantile mind is "splitting," which is the tendency to separate impulses and objects into various aspects, good, bad, undamaged, damaged, and the like. This occurs in part because the early ego lacks coherence and because persecutive anxiety reinforces the need to keep the loved object separate from the dangerous one, thereby leading to a splitting of love from hate. The young infant's self-preservation depends on his trust in a good mother. By splitting good from bad aspects and clinging to the good, he preserves his belief in a good object and in his capacity to love it; this is an essential condition for keeping alive. Without at least some of this feeling, he would feel exposed to an entirely hostile world, which he fears might destroy him; this hostile world would also be built up within him by introjection.

Splitting processes diminish with growing integration of the ego during normal development. The infant's increasing capacity to understand external reality and to some extent bring together his contradictory impulses also lead to a greater synthesis of the good and bad aspects of the object. People can be loved in spite of their faults; the world is no longer seen only in terms of black and white.

Splitting processes change in form and content as development progresses, but are never entirely eliminated. Omnipotent destructive impulses, persecutory anxiety, and splitting are predominant in the first three to four months of life. Introjection during this period has been of "part objects." Melanie Klein described this combination of mechanisms and anxieties as "the paranoid-schizoid position," which, in extreme cases, becomes the basis for later paranoia and schizophrenia when excessive. Persecutory anxiety interferes with the gradual integration of the ego.

Allied with splitting is "projective identification," another of the primal activities of the infantile mind that Klein has described. Projective identification involves the splitting off of those qualities of one's own mind that are experienced as dangerous by the weak, infantile mind, projecting them onto some other person, and then identifying with that person. This defense is employed before the ego is strong enough to use repression. Projective identification has many repercussions: the ego feels depleted; there is the wish to, and the fear of, regaining this split-off fragment; there is the need to control omnipotently the person who has the projected part, lest the dangerous impulse be acted out or that portion of one's mind be lost forever.

Klein and her co-workers made considerable clinical contributions to the understanding of schizophrenia, paranoia, and manic-depressive psychoses. Projective indentification, splitting, introjection, and projection have been shown to be major defenses employed along with others in these psychoses because excessive persecutory anxiety has interfered with the gradual integration of the ego, leaving it fixated at the paranoid-schizoid position.

Klein accepted Freud's hypothesis of a death instinct that must be deflected from the self and is converted into aggressiveness toward outer objects. She believed that anxiety does not spring from the libidinal component of the fused Eros-Thanatos drives, but from the child's fear of his own aggression, which he can only partially control to his own satisfaction. The child is anxious about the damage he may have done to himself by uncontrolled aggression, for example, in screaming fits, and also is anxious about the harm that his aggression may have caused others. Even the adolescent does not feel anxious about his increasing libidinal drives as such, but always about the sadistic component of these drives.

Concomitants of destructive feelings are of great importance; greed and envy are particularly disturbing factors—first in relation to the mother, then throughout life. Because of constitutional factors, greed varies considerably from one infant to another. At one extreme, are babies who never can be satisfied. With greed goes the urge to empty mother's breast and to exploit all sources of satisfaction without consideration for anyone else. A very greedy infant may for the time being enjoy whatever he receives, but as soon as the gratification is gone, he becomes dissatisfied and is driven to exploit first the mother and soon everybody in the family who can give him attention, food, or any other gratification—initially in fantasy, later in reality as well as in fantasy. Greed is increased by anxiety, the anxiety of being deprived, being robbed, and of not being good enough to be loved. The infant so greedy for love and attention is also uncertain about his own capacity to love, because so much hate is stirred by the frustration he experiences. These dynamics, fundamentally unchanged, are seen in the greed of the older child and the adult.

Whenever the infant is hungry or feels neglected, his frustration leads to the fantasy that the milk and love are being deliberately withheld from him or are kept by the mother for her own benefit. Such suspicions are the basis of envy. Inherent in the feeling of envy is the urge to possess the object and also a strong urge to spoil the object. If envy is strong, its spoiling quality results in a disturbed relation to the mother and, later on, to other people; it means also that nothing can be enjoyed fully because the desired thing has already been spoiled by envy. Furthermore, if envy is strong, goodness cannot be assimilated and become part of one's inner life, giving rise to gratitude.

By contrast, the capacity to enjoy fully what has been received and to experience gratitude toward the person who gives it influences strongly both the child's character and his relations with other people.

Gratitude, a component of love, mitigates the hateful feelings; therefore, through the continuing projection and introjection, the child experiences both the real external world and his psychic inner world as friendlier environments.

The superego begins to operate, in Klein's opinion, much earlier than it does according to Freud's views. From babyhood on, the perceived parts of the mother—and soon the perceived parts of other people in the child's surroundings—are taken into the self as part objects, forming the basis for a variety of identifications, favorable and unfavorable. In the fifth or sixth month of life, with the increasing integration of the ego, the infant begins to realize, at first only intermittently, that the gratifying objects he needs and loves are aspects of the frustrating ones he hates and, in fantasy, destroys. He has matured to the point of perceiving whole objects.

With this discovery, he begins to feel concern about these loved objects, for he cannot yet distinguish between his fantasies and their lack of actual effects. He experiences feelings of guilt and the urge to preserve these objects and to make reparation to them for harm done. The anxiety now experienced is of a predominantly depressive nature; the emotions accompanying it, as well as the defenses involved against them, are part of normal development and are termed "the depressive position." Feelings of guilt, such as occasionally arise in everyone, have very deep roots in infancy, and the tendency to make reparations plays an important role in one's sublimations and object relations. This leads to a completely new approach to the understanding of Adam and Eve's original sin and guilt.

A working-through process occurs in all normal individual development. Adaptation to external reality increases, and with it the infant achieves a less fantastic picture of the world around him; for example, mother's coming back to him makes her absence less frightening, and therefore his suspicion of her diminishes. In this way, the infant gradually works through his early fears and comes to terms with his conflicting impulses and emotions. Depressive anxiety predominates at this stage, and persecutory anxiety lessens. Many apparently odd manifestations, such as inexplicable phobias of infancy, are indications of working through the depressive position. If guilt is not excessive, the urge to make reparation brings relief, along with other processes that are part of mental growth. Depressive and persecutory anxieties are never entirely overcome; they may recur temporarily under pressure, but a relatively normal person can cope with this recurrence and regain his balance.

In talking of the paranoid-schizoid position and the depressive position, Klein uses the terms "positions" rather than "stages of development" to emphasize the coexistance of earlier stages with later ones, owing to fixation and regression.

The early wish to make reparation adds to the innate capacity for love. In the sublimations that grow out of the earliest interests of the child, constructive activities gain impetus because the child unconsciously feels that in this way he is restoring loved people whom he has damaged in his inner world. The irrevocable fact that no one is entirely free from guilt has very valuable aspects, because it implies the never fully exhausted wish to make reparation and to create, in whatever way one can. Melanie Klein's views could lead to completely new insights into the dynamics of all creativity as variations of reparation.

Even if development is satisfactory and leads to enjoyment from various sources, the deeper layers of the mind hold some feeling of mourning for irretrievably lost pleasures of infancy and for unfulfilled possibilities. Emotional maturity means that, up to a point, these feelings of loss can be counteracted by the ability to accept substitutes and that infantile fantasies do not disturb adult emotional life. At any age, the ability to enjoy available pleasures presupposes a relative freedom from envy and grievances. Therefore, one way in which contentment can be found at a later stage in life is to enjoy vicariously the pleasures of young people, particularly the pleasures of one's children and grandchildren. Another source of gratification, even before old age, is the richness of memories that keep the past alive.

Klein believes that the infant's fear of loss of the loved object as a consequence of his hatred and aggression enters into his object relations and Oedipus complex from the beginning and influences his passage through subsequent conflict-filled anal, phallic, and Oedipal stages of development. She states that "the infant's emotional life, the early defenses built up under the stress of the conflict between love, hatred, and guilt, and the vicissitudes of the child's identification's—all these are topics which may well occupy analytic research for a long time to come . . . and lead us to a fuller understanding of the personality which implies a fuller understanding of the Oedipus complex and of sexual development" (1932).

REFERENCES

Klein, Melanie. Love, guilt, and reparation. In Melanie Klein & Joan Riviere (Eds.), *Love, hate and reparation.* London: Woolf & Hogarth Press, 1937.

Klein, Melanie. *The psycho-analysis of children.* London: Hogarth Press, 1932.

Segal, Hanna. *Introduction to the Work of Melanie Klein.* New York: Basic Books, 1964.

I am particularly indebted to Dr. Martin Grotjahn for his invaluable suggestions. Also of great help were my personal communications with Melanie Klein, her daughter Melitta Schmideberg, her son Eric Clyne, Eliot Jacques, and Dr. Sigmund Gabe. Especially helpful was Margaret Evans, training analyst of the Melanie Klein group of the London Institute—J. A. L.

Ernst Simmel

1882–1947

PSYCHOANALYTIC PIONEERING IN CALIFORNIA

*

JOHN S. PECK

Simmel was born in Breslau, Germany, in 1882. Little is known of his father, but Ernst was the youngest of nine children, presumably from more than one marriage. Most of Ernst's childhood was spent in Berlin, where his mother maintained an employment agency for domestic servants.

One of Simmel's original goals was to become an actor, but his less than average height—he was five feet six inches tall—was against this. He came into medicine by way of the study of pharmacy, obtaining his medical degree in 1908. He wrote a dissertation on the psychogenetic theory of the origin of dementia praecox.

Simmel began the practice of general medicine in a very poor section of Berlin, where he worked until the war began in 1914. His first war service was with combat troops. He was later put in charge of a hospital for psychiatric battle casualties; he obtained considerable success in treating these conditions by hypnosis and psychoanalytic techniques. In his treatment, he used a dummy on which the patient could discharge his repressed aggressions.

After the war, Simmel was instrumental in the founding of the Berlin Institute. With the aid of Max Eitingon, he established a psychoanalytic clinic and, with great enthusiasm, pushed for its expansion. Spurred by

Simmel's organizing and recruiting talents, the Berlin Institute and Clinic became a center for psychoanalytic training for physicians and members of such ancillary disciplines as marriage counseling and court work.

A paper in 1930, commemorating ten years of the Berlin Institute, gives evidence of Simmel's feelings and enthusiasm. He pointed out that society's debt to the neurotic remains unpaid; the state should provide treatment centers, but the Berlin Clinic was possible only through private financial arrangements. Supervised analyses and clinical case seminars were developed at the Berlin Institute and Clinic under Simmel's direction.

Upon the death of Karl Abraham in 1925, Simmel became president of the Berlin Psychoanalytic Society. In 1926, he established his psychoanalytic sanitarium, on the grounds of a large and beautiful castle on the outskirts of Berlin. Simmel pioneered in the development of the hospital care of patients using psychoanalytic principles. His papers on this subject are some of his most important contributions to psychoanalytic literature. Simmel's sanitarium was beset with financial troubles, in part a result of some impractical aspects of its construction and in part of Simmel's poor judgment in money matters, one of his lifelong characteristics.

The sanitarium was used as a resting place by Sigmund Freud during three visits to Berlin for treatment of his carcinoma. Freud was able to enjoy the beautiful surroundings and felt that his privacy was respected by the patients. Freud took an interest in attempting to continue Simmel's sanitarium in spite of its financial difficulties and lent his name to efforts to obtain additional financing.

Simmel's providing Freud with a refuge during his visits to Berlin was part of the friendly relationship between the two men that continued over many years. When Simmel was full of plans for establishing a psychoanalytic sanitarium and clinic in California, he intended to name it after Freud. Characteristically, in 1939 Freud suggested that Simmel wait and see if Freud lived. In token of their relationship, Freud gave Simmel one of the rings that had been worn by members of the original "inner circle."

With the rise of the Nazis in Germany, Simmel suffered the difficulties experienced by many analysts. A Jew of very liberal political beliefs, he was president of the Society for Socialist Physicians. There were several narrow escapes, and at least one period in jail before Simmel was able to leave the country. He fled by way of Zurich.

David Brunswick met Simmel in Europe in the 1930s. Largely through his invitation and the recommendation of Franz Alexander and Hanns Sachs, Simmel was invited to come to Los Angeles and to join a group of therapists who were interested in the study of psychoanalysis. With their financial and legal assistance, Simmel arrived in Los Angeles in 1934 with his second wife and small son. Simmel also had a son by his first wife; both she and the boy subsequently came to Los Angeles with Simmel's assistance.

On arriving in Los Angeles, Simmel helped organize a formal psychoanalytic study group. He took the lead in spreading psychoanalytic understanding into such areas as education, criminology, and social work. The Los Angeles group remained under the auspices of the Chicago and Topeka psychoanalytic institutes until 1942, when it became affiliated with the newly formed San Francisco Psychoanalytic Society, with Simmel as its first president. By 1946, after the arrival of Mrs. Frances Deri, Otto Fenichel, May Romm, Charles Tidd, and others, the Los Angeles Institute was formed.

Simmel wrote papers on purely theoretical topics, brief clinical notes, and the application of psychoanalysis to war neuroses, sanitarium treatment, organic illnesses, and broad social phenomena. He did not publish all he wanted to publish, and many of his contributions to psychoanalysis were communicated verbally to his colleagues.

At the time of his death, Simmel was accumulating material for a book that was to be entitled *Regression, Repression, and Organic Disease.* He also was engaged in research on relationships between psychoanalysis and epilepsy. One incomplete paper on alcoholism and addictions was published after his death.

Simmel's earliest significant contributions to psychoanalytic literature developed out of his war experiences. His book on war neuroses, *Zur Psychoanalyse der Kriegsneurosen*, was the first psychoanalytic book published after World War I with international co-operation. It includes chapters by Ernest Jones, Karl Abraham, and Sándor Ferenczi; Freud wrote the introduction. This book remained the only psychodynamic work available on war neuroses until new studies were begun during World War II, more than twenty years later. With his formulations, Simmel (first in 1918 and again in 1944) gave a workable hypothesis for the study of the psychoneurotic military casualties that occurred in such large numbers during both world wars.

Simmel told how he first attempted to remove the symptoms of war neuroses through hypnotic suggestion but found that this usually led to an increase in other symptoms. He developed a combination of cathartic abreactions under the influence of hypnosis, with analytic conversations and dream interpretations carried out during waking interviews, as well as in deep hypnosis. Simmel was able to confirm the symbolic importance of the symptom and that the body is used as the instrument to express the unconscious.

Although sexuality in the usual sense appears not to be involved in the development of war neuroses, Simmel recognized that the psychosexual make-up of the soldier contributes to his relative susceptibility to the strain of war service. In the soldiers' dreams elements can be seen that lead to deeper levels in infantile sexuality. Simmel recognized not only that the war neuroses symbolically preserve the physical existence of the soldier but also that, in a psychic sense, they may protect him against the development of a psychosis. He felt that the patient's dreams are an attempt at self-cure.

Simmel felt that abreaction in the form of words is not enough. He developed the use of a dummy; with the patient under hypnosis, this was used to represent the enemy and the bad father objects. The neurotic soldier was encouraged to act out his aggression toward this dummy. In many cases the discharge of the aggression was the beginning of the cure.

Twenty-five years later, Simmel again described his treatment and showed how, during World War I, he had developed a treatment that could be shown to fit well into more sophisticated psychoanalytic theory. In this later paper, Simmel emphasized the changes in the internal psychic structure that occur within the ego and the superego of the soldier. He develops what Simmel called "the military ego," in which the internalized parental superego is replaced by the military unit, so that the group leader comes to represent the externalized superego. Thus the soldier (and Simmel pointed out the use of the word "infantry") finds himself in the emotional position of a child before it has developed a superego.

The soldier's shattered ego is supported by the group identity, the wearing of the uniform, and the like. An important element in the predisposition to the development of war neuroses is the occurrence of personal disappointments and narcissistic blows, interfering with the soldier's sense of group identity and leading to a sense of isolation. Narcissistic wounds at the hands of superior officers are particularly likely to predispose soldiers to the development of war neuroses. In this situation, the superior officer may lose his role as a good father and become a hated father whom the soldier is tempted to kill. With the weakened superego characteristic of the military personality, the soldier may then become paralyzed with anxiety and guilt about his hostile impulses, which are now directed toward his superior officer, as well as toward the enemy of the country—both representing the father. Some soldiers react to this complex by becoming overly aggressive.

Simmel felt strongly that psychoanalysis has an important contribution to make in the treatment of organic disease, even if the disease is not, strictly speaking, psychogenic. Thus, in a 1922 paper entitled, "Psychoanalytic Considerations Concerning the Origin and Progress of Disease," he expressed the feeling that there is an identity between physiopathological and psychopathological processes. Every disease, physical as well as neurotic, is a social disturbance, and there is a direct continuum from the individual cell within the community of cells that make up the human being to the human being as an individual within the organism of human society.

In another paper, "The Psychogenesis of Organic Disturbances and Their Psychoanalytic Treatment" which appeared in 1931, Simmel presented the case report of a man dying of cardiac failure. Simmel felt that during psychoanalytic therapy the patient's fluid retention had been disclosed to be a derivative of the patient's death wish, the unconscious attempt of the patient to drown himself in compensation for his guilt feelings concerning the death of his first wife, who had committed suicide by drowning. In a 1945 paper presented as part of a symposium on psychogenic factors in obstetrics and gynecology, Simmel emphasized the importance of the death instinct and its potential as a source of interference in the normal physiological functioning of the organs.

In the short 1925 paper, "A Screen Memory in Statu Nascendi," Simmel based a clinical note on an observation of his own son, who developed a screen memory following an episode in which a surgeon jestingly threatened to cut off the little boy's penis. Simmel showed how, one year after the incident, the child remembered it as the surgeon having threatened to cut off his hair.

In 1926, Simmel published "The Doctor Game, Illness, and the Profession of Medicine." Here he formulated psychodynamic insights gained from an examination of the common game in which children play at being a doctor. Children act out many of their sadomasochistic concepts of sexual intercourse in this game; depending on his orientation, the child chooses to identify with either the doctor or the patient. The doctor game permits children to indulge in many pregenital and sexual activities, such as investigating the bodies of others, working with urine and feces, and exploring the mysteries of the differences between the sexes.

The doctor game is then connected with the transference "game," as seen in the analytic relationship. Here, again, there is a polarity between passive submission and active aggression. Many patients react to this situation by attempting to analyze the doctor, as a defense against submitting to their own analysis. Simmel pointed out that the choice of profession sometimes seems influenced by unconscious submissive tendencies, and he correlated this with an observation that many doctors become ill with the very illnesses in which they have been specialists.

This paper ends with a discussion of the role of the physician in the service of the pleasure principle as the guardian of life, helping patients in their struggles against the death instinct. Simmel emphasized the physician's duty to consider the patient's libidinal constitution and its role in organic illnesses.

Simmel's pioneering establishment of a psychoanalytic sanitarium in Berlin, at Schloss-Tegel, from 1927 to 1931, was the basis for another group of important contributions to the literature. It is striking that, in 1927, Simmel described principles that are even yet used in far too few institutions for the inpatient care of neurotic and psychotic patients. The neurotic may live in an environment in which he is surrounded by individuals who are part of a collective neurosis and whose complementary neuroses may cause them to gratify and infantilize the neurotic patient. One important gain from hospitalizing a neurotic patient is often his removal from this neurotic constellation. He is placed in surroundings in which the individuals around him react not with infantilizing gratifications but with a neutral feeling. This forces the patient to turn increasingly to the analyst to obtain infantile gratifications, thus tending to intensify the transference. The sanitarium milieu acts against the primary and secondary gains of the patient's neurosis. Simmel was aware that, to the patient, the sanitarium comes to represent an extension of the analyst and that different aspects of the sanitarium may be identified with mother, father, and siblings.

Simmel used sanitarium treatment particularly in cases of addiction, for he felt it was less difficult to counteract the addicts' self-destructive tendencies under these conditions than when treating them as outpatients. In addition, he realized that the sanitarium environment might itself provide sufficient gratification to enable the addict to give up his addiction. Simmel also recognized the importance to the addict of having the analyst continuously on call during the withdrawal period. Nonetheless, he was aware that some patients use the sanitarium as a refuge and a kind of intra-uterine existence, a situation that usually disappears spontaneously under analysis but on some occasions may become a source of resistance.

As a part of a Freud birthday number of the *Bulletin of the Menninger Clinic* in 1937, Simmel published an article on sanitarium treatment. In this paper, he has pointed out that the work initiated by him in his short-lived clinic is being continued at the Menninger Foundation. In this late paper, Simmel emphasized the importance of the terrible, destructive tendencies within human beings that he had first noted during World War I. He suggested that the main problem of psychoanalytic mental hygiene is the treatment of the death instinct.

According to Simmel, Freud was much impressed by the use of sanitariums in psychoanalytic treatment and had once stated that every psychoanalytic candidate should spend some time in a sanitarium—not only as a therapist but as an attendant. Simmel has reported that Freud also shared his interest in the connections between psychic and somatic approaches to illness, quoting Freud as having predicted that, as our knowledge of hormones increases, the endocrinologist may some day succeed in using hormones to produce psychic changes.

As a corollary to his work with sanitarium patients, Simmel was keenly interested in the problems of addiction; at various periods in his life he wrote several papers dealing with this topic. Generally, Simmel emphasized the addict's orality, in which object relationships are replaced by hate—expressed in terms of devouring and destroying the object. He described all addiction as protection against the depression that results from the introjection of a disappointing love object. The addict has only pseudolibidinous object relationships, and his only real external object becomes the drug or alcohol. The addiction of the alcoholic is chronic murder and chronic suicide.

His longest paper on this topic, "Alcoholism and Addiction," was incomplete at Simmel's death but was nevertheless published posthumously in 1948. It includes the recommendation that the addict usually needs hospital care during his analytic treatment and that occupational therapy must be used to help discharge aggressive and destructive tendencies. He recommended the formation in cities of small hospital units where alcoholics could be placed temporarily, with adequate care and supervision. The end of the paper is a discussion of Alcoholics Anonymous and how some of its principles correspond to psychoanalytic findings.

In 1946, following a symposium on anti-Semitism held by the San Francisco Psychoanalytic Society, Simmel edited a collection of the papers under the title, *Anti-Semitism, a Social Disease*. In his introduction, Simmel described the centuries-long history of anti-Semitism, warning that it is not limited to Germany, that it could develop to a similar degree in other countries. In addition to the introduction, Simmel has contributed a long article to the book, *Anti-Semitism and Mass Psychopathology*. Simmel expressed the belief that, in individual anti-Semites, the prejudice is often a defense against latent homosexuality. As a mass phenomena, however, Simmel felt that anti-Semitism is a mass psychosis developing by a gradual transformation from an illusion into a delusion and, finally, the discharge of unrestricted destructive instincts. He felt it could develop during group formation under pathological conditions that may disintegrate the ego system of the individual members of the group. Simmel emphasized the superego as the source of maturity and strength and that the psychotic ego regresses to an infantile stage in which there is neither superego nor internalized parent. The man in the crowd may thus submerge his ego and regress to a state of unrestricted acting out of primary process destructiveness. The group formation is called pathological when it arises out of a need to endow the powerless individual with the capacity for discharging unrestricted destructive instinct energies.

Simmel felt that Jews are particularly vulnerable to becoming the objects for projection and paranoid feelings that arise out of unresolved ambivalent and hostile parental relationships. This he analyzes in terms of specific accusations against the Jews—such as their killing of Christ and their stealing of Christian children to slaughter them and use their blood in Jewish ceremonies. As Freud pointed out, by giving up animal sacrifices and making God invisible, the Jews transformed him from a material parental image to a spiritual collective superego that, according to Simmel, demanded greater mental sacrifice from the human race than it was ready for. Christianity, by reintroducing the primeval totem feast in the form of Holy Communion, again allowed some gratification of the devouring instincts.

Again and again throughout this article on anti-Semitism, Simmel refers to the importance of superego development as a source of mental health. He also comments on developments in modern society that he deplores, such as the loss of any sense of satisfaction at the completion of the workers' tasks and the decline in entertainment from what people *should* see to what they *want* to see; he calls for governmental prohibition of any anti-minority activities.

A central theme runs through Simmel's work. It is his emphasis on the death instinct and the presence of strong destructive and self-destructive drives within the human personality. The death instinct may make internal bodily organs its targets for destruction and result in disease. The chief task of psychoanalytic treatment is to combat the death instinct.

One of Simmel's most important theoretical papers, "Self-Preservation and the Death Instinct," was read before the San Francisco Psychoanalytic Society in April, 1943, and published in the *Psychoanalytic Quarterly* in 1944. According to Simmel, it represents a modification of Freud's dualistic theory of the life and death instincts and arose out of twenty years of psychoanalytic practice. Man's destructive energies, he wrote, are not manifestations of the death instinct but, rather, manifestations of "an instinct of self-preservation." This instinct of self-preservation is connected with oral cannibalistic instincts, under the heading of a gastrointestinal instinct. Gratification of this instinct results in the destruction of the object by incorporation, but in the service of self-preservation. Simmel felt that, in referring to hunger and love as the two principal forces in the world, Freud had anticipated this theoretical modification.

Simmel applied this formulation to the understanding of the genesis of both psychoneuroses and psychoses. The ultimate self-destruction of death, and its resulting peace, is not simply a manifestation of a death instinct but, rather, that of the instinct of self-preservation, the destructive energy of which has been turned upon itself. Thus the destructive energy of this instinct of self-preservation belongs in the category of libidinal energies, since it aims at the synthesis of living substances. The instinct of self-preservation has an internal goal, whereas the sex instinct extends beyond the borderline of the individual.

This self-preservative instinct develops from the very beginning of life, when the preservation of self is associated with the tendency to preserve or regain complete instinct repose—as the infant, his hunger satisfied, returns to a state of unconsciousness. It is through incorporation and identification in the solution of the Oedipus complex, which is really part of this gastrointestinal self-preservative instinct, that the individual attains his final identity. This self-preservative instinct also acts as a solution for the rage toward the frustrating object, since incorporation of the object destroys it but also helps achieve a self-preserving identity.

In this paper, Simmel seems to be saying that all destruction takes the form of incorporation. In saying this, he seems to imply that rage results in incorporation of the object and is really self-preservative. Simmel ends the paper by saying that he considers this contribution an extension of Freud's theories and feels that Freud would have reached the same conclusion, had he continued his researches rather than turning more toward the psychoanalytic study of culture toward the end of his life.

Ernst Simmel died in Los Angeles from coronary heart disease, on November 27, 1947. He had suffered his first coronary thrombosis in 1944, the same year in which his paper on self-preservation and the death instinct was published. Simmel's last years were marked by difficulties developing in the rapidly expanding psychoanalytic community in Los Angeles. To the end of his life he remained active, showed no fear of the approaching end, and, three days before his death, expressed regret at the amount of his unfinished work. He was annoyed, frustrated, and bitterly rebellious against the necessary limitation of his activities.

Simmel was a pioneer in the application of psychoanalytic principles to the study of war neuroses and the hospitalization of patients, and he established the first psychoanalytic sanitarium. He introduced many of the concepts and techniques of training accepted in all analytic institutes today, and he contributed to the literature important theoretical papers, one of which offered a possible fundamental modification of

Freud's original theories. As one of the European analysts who immigrated to the United States, Simmel was instrumental in organizing the psychoanalytic movement in Southern California. Simmel lived his life through and with psychoanalysis. He felt that its discoveries offered a route toward a better way of life for mankind.

BIBLIOGRAPHY

Simmel, E. *Kriegsneurosen und psychische Trauma:* Ihre gegenseitigen Beziehungen, dargestellt auf Grund psychoanalytischer, hypnotischer Studien. Munich & Leipzig: O. Nemnich, 1918.

Simmel, E. *Psychoanalysis and the war neuroses*. London: Int. Psycho-Anal. Press, 1921.

Simmel, E. A screen memory in *statu nascendi. Int. J. Psycho-Anal.*, 1925, 6, 454–457.

Simmel, E. The "doctor-game," illness and the profession of medicine. *Int. J. Psycho-Anal.*, 1926, 7, 470–483.

Simmel, E. Georg Groddeck zum sechzigsten Geburtstag. *Int. Z. Psychoanal.*, 1926, **12**, 591–595.

Simmel, E. Psychoanalytic treatment in a sanitarium. *Int. J. Psycho-Anal.*, 1929, 10, 70–89.

Simmel, E. The psychoanalytic sanitarium and the psychoanalytic movement. *Bull. Menninger Clinic,* 1937, 1, 133–143.

Simmel, E. Self-preservation and the death instinct. *Psychoanal. Quart.*, 1944, 13, 160–185. (Also in *Yearbook of Psychoanalysis,* 1944, 1, 143–162.)

The author is indebted to the following people, who helped immeasurably with their personal reminiscences about Simmel: Dr. David Brunswick, Mrs. Frances Deri, Dr. Martin Grotjahn, Dr. Joachim Haenel, Miss Diana Howard, and Dr. George Frumkes.

Franz Alexander

1891–1964

THE WESTERN MIND IN TRANSITION

*

MARTIN GROTJAHN

The life of Franz Alexander illustrates well the complexity of growth and maturation of a scientist in our time, a time of transition and change. During these seventy-three years, more important changes have taken place than in the previous 500 years of human history. Franz Alexander has observed the evolution in Western culture as a psychoanalyst. He has studied this culture and his own role as participant-observer. His development throughout his lifetime exemplifies the fate of an individual in our time. To write a profile of Franz Alexander is to present a panoramic view of psychoanalytic development in Europe and in the United States of America.

Franz Alexander was born in Budapest in 1891. His childhood was dominated by humanistic tradition and by a father who was a professor at the university. Knowledge for its own sake was a guiding principle, and search for absolute truth and for absolute beauty was still believed possible. Franz Alexander had to proceed from a world of absolute values to a world of relativity. We must adjust to a free-floating, relative reality—and this is not easy.

§ The European Period

In many carefully censored analytic-autobiographical notes, for example, in "The Natural History of an Inner-Directed Person," Franz Alexander mentions his father, Bernard Alexander. The son is neither apologetic nor defensive about his devotion to his father, who was to him teacher, friend, and mentor. Bernard, a professor of philosophy at the University of Budapest, was well known for teaching in philosophy and his knowledge of Shakespeare. He gave his son Freud's book on dream interpretation to read and review. Later, the son showed the father that an understanding of the unconscious could provide a new approach to understanding Shakespeare.

After an abortive attempt to study archaeology, as his father had urged, Franz Alexander moved from Budapest to Göttingen or, one might say, to the Café National in that city. Soon he decided to study medicine.

Freud's demonstration of irrational trends in man challenged Bernard Alexander's belief in the power of reason; the father's basically Apollonian world was shaken by the discovery of the Dionysian underground. At first, the son turned with righteous indignation from confusing psychology to orderly neurophysiology. Only after World War I, when trying to deal with patients, did he begin to appreciate the psychology of the unconscious.

The lesson of World War I was difficult to accept for a man brought up in the philosophy of democratic individualism; suddenly, decisions of the state, the army, and the country were all important, and the individual had become less so. The nation as an autonomous political unit replaced the separate, self-determining being. The war was a severe threat to the development of an ego identity, and the outer-directed person emerged, opposing the inner-directed person.

In 1914, Alexander was caught up in this catastrophic change with overwhelming suddenness. Although already aware that war was an anachronism, he had to join the army. His enthusiasm for the nation tried to save the illusion but did not carry him through the entire war. When the war was over and Hungary defeated, Alexander moved from Budapest to Berlin.

He became the first student of the Berlin Institute for Psychoanalysis, thereby abandoning hopes for an academic psychiatric career in

Germany. Many years later, in "A Jury Trial of Psychoanalysis," Alexander described the conflict he had felt about his decision to study psychoanalysis, which was regarded by all academic thinkers as an unscientific horror.

Moving to Berlin, Alexander observed the Teutonic heritage expressed in the antirational German romanticism of that time; it contrasts with the German emphasis on organization, which simultaneously combines a pro-individualistic with an anti-individualistic attitude.

In "Recollections of Bergasse 19," Alexander has described his psychoanalytic training and his visits with Sigmund Freud. Alexander was deeply impressed by the personality of Freud, his devotion to one great cause, and his ability to function simultaneously as the great revolutionary scientist, the well-settled, cultured, conservative physician, and the home-loving husband and father. During one visit, Freud and Alexander discussed the life of the termites. Freud hoped that man would not imitate the example of the termites and asked, "Who is man's enemy against whom he must organize himself in such a rigid fashion?" Freud was sensitive to Oedipal tendencies in his student-sons. Alexander also observed how carefully Freud defended himself against outside influence in order to devote himself to the task he had set himself.

In 1921, after his analysis with Hanns Sachs, Alexander became an assistant at the Psychoanalytic Institute in Berlin. Earlier in the year, Freud had awarded Alexander a prize for the best clinical essay of the year. The essay, "Castration-Complex and Character," is incorporated as a chapter in Alexander's early work of this Berlin period, *Analysis of the Total Personality*. Bertram Lewin, the translator, has called *Analysis of the Total Personality* the first comprehensive exposition of analytic ego psychology, well describing the ego's dominance over the instincts. Perhaps this book, which combines analytic ego psychology with clinical psychiatry, already shows Alexander's special fitness for the American scene.

While in Berlin, Alexander developed an interest in the analytic study of the criminal. Together with his former student and friend, Hugo Staub, he published in 1929 the first comprehensive psychoanalytic study on criminology, *The Criminal, the Judge, and the Public;* it was republished in 1957.

Around 1930, Berlin became the center of analytic progress. By then Alexander had analyzed and trained many physicians, among them many visiting Americans who acquainted him with American thinking, which was directed toward treatment. In contrast, European psychoanalysts followed Freud's example and were primarily interested in understanding the structure and functions of personality. Continental analysts believed that analytic knowledge was not far enough advanced to provide effective treatment. Psychoanalysis was accepted more as a source of knowledge, which at some future time might serve as the basis for improved treatment technique. A skeptical but treatment-directed attitude has guided Franz Alexander throughout his life and is visible in his latest attempts to crystallize the essentials of the therapeutic process.

§ Twenty-five Years in Chicago

In 1930, Alexander visited America and started to work in Chicago, where he occupied the first University Chair for Psychoanalysis. Sigmund Freud was skeptical about the future in America; his parting statement was, "I hope America will leave something intact of the real Alexander."

After some experimentation in Chicago and an interlude in Boston, Alexander realized that at that time universities were unwilling to accept psychoanalysis. Freud had set up a separate psychoanalytic institute in Vienna, which he regarded as permanently independent. Alexander believed that a separate psychoanalytic institute is necessary only until such time as universities will accept psychoanalysis.

The Chicago Institute for Psychoanalysis was modeled after the Berlin Institute, and for twenty-five years Alexander remained its director. His analytic research and teamwork became a historical event and model in American psychiatry. In addition to his personal pioneering research, out of which a new chapter of American psychoanalytic psychiatry has developed, Alexander must also be recognized for his gift in organizing an analytic team. During the Chicago years, he trained people, welding them into the first analytic community. Only persons who have lived in this kind of psychoanalytic family know the intrinsic difficulties and special aspects of getting individualists, such as analysts must be, together in a group—keeping them together and making them work.

After an initial enthusiasm in psychoanalytic research, Alexander noticed the inescapable trend toward organization and uniformity that endangers all institutions, analytic ones included. Work at the Institute led him to the investigation of the essentials of the therapeutic analytic process and its relationship to training. His ideas are recorded in several books on therapeutic technique. In 1938 he became Professor of Psychiatry at the University of Illinois, and later organized the Associated Psychiatric Faculties of Chicago.

Alexander felt the need for progress in psychoanalytic therapy and training. Many of the teachings of psychoanalysis had become a codification of errors, which split psychoanalytic organizations into warring factions. Not differences in principle but varying degrees of dissatisfaction with the status quo have led to what Alexander has described as "analytic in-fighting." Some analysts have been inclined to overcome their doubts and dissatisfactions by appealing to administrative conservatism, whereas other more progressive and less dogmatic groups have aimed more at therapy than at theory.

Alexander has examined the therapeutic field in the light of three questions: (1) what are the advantages of rigid standards; (2) how can psychoanalysts learn from outside experience; (3) how can we test our methods clinically?

Alexander has worried about the decreasing autonomy of institutes and places of teaching and learning analysis. He sees threats to individual creativity in increasing administration, rigidity, conformity, and excessive rules and regulations that endanger the sense of responsibility in the teacher or therapist. Despite the change and rapid growth of analytic knowledge and clinical experience during the last fifty years, almost no change in technique has occurred since 1913–15, when Freud described his approach to psychoanalytic technique. We assume that our analytic technique must be conserved. Changes in analytic technique should be studied, not refused for dogmatic reasons.

Psychoanalytic therapy started with catharsis and shifted to insight. The importance of transference was recognized later, and Alexander directed his attention to the study of the emotional experience in the therapeutic situation: He studied the roles of countertransference, of management, and of manipulations such as flexibility in the number of interviews and fragmentation of treatment; he investigated the processes of learning, growth, and maturation, within and without the therapeutic situation.

The knowledge of countertransference has become of decisive importance. The therapist's countertransference is not an impurity but a necessary tool for empathy, for understanding and handling the therapeutic situation. There are many ways of communication besides verbal interpretation; we have learned much recently about nonverbal and multilevel communications and subliminal cues.

Alexander always suspected that a very long analysis is not, as a rule, a successful one. This has led to planned interruptions of treatment, designed to stimulate progress. Patients do not mature on the couch but after they have left the analyst. Alexander has also questioned the analytic slogan, "Transference cures cannot last"; he suggests that such cases should be investigated for long-lasting results.

In his papers about two kinds of regression, Alexander set forth his main objections against a rigid, standardized, formal approach to analytic treatment. One kind of regression is a retreat to the time before the patient failed and developed his neurosis. The second is a therapeutic one that leads to the unsolved conflict and to a traumatic situation, wherein the patient returns to the scene of failure in a search for mastery. This is where the analyst can be of most help: through his interpretation he can offer aid to the integrative powers of the ego.

Little is wrong with psychoanalysis, but much is wrong with the narrow-minded spirit of dogmatism. The skillful therapist must employ a flexible analytic technique leading to a "corrective emotional experience." Alexander's main thesis is that neurotic patterns that originate in early emotional experiences can be corrected by the new emotional experiences of the therapeutic situation. Cognitive insight into early experiences is not equivalent to alterations in these ingrained patterns of feeling and behavior. A person may recognize his repressed resentment against another person; he may even recognize its motivational background, yet be unable to change. In psychoanalysis, the principal therapeutic agent is the repeated experiencing of the difference between the present and the past interpersonal setting—the repeated experience that fixed emotional responses, developed in the past toward members of the family, are inadequate when directed toward the therapist.

The patient unconsciously attempts to manipulate the therapeutic situation in the way in which he has experienced his infantile neurosis. For instance, the patient may try to maneuver his analyst into the position, attitude, and reaction of the tyrannical father of his youth, to whom the patient had adjusted in a neurotic way. It is the task of the therapist to understand the dynamics of the patient's fixed reactions and to help the patient to understand and to experience the inadequacy of these old reactions, which are inappropriate to the therapist's behavior and personality. Through interpretation, appropriate response, and perhaps restrained action, the analytic therapist will help the patient to gain insight. He may also stimulate the relearning process by working through the situation in an atmosphere that is different emotionally from the traumatic situation of the patient's infantile past. This vivid and repeated re-experiencing of past reactions in the new and different setting of the actual patient-physician relationship, which the old reaction patterns do not fit, is what Alexander has called the "corrective emotional experiences." It adds to analytic insight an important factor closely related to the process of all learning necessary for the kind of emotional maturation needed to make analysis effective.

Franz Alexander's opinions have become controversial, symbolizing for some progress and for others analytic impurity. It might be said that Sigmund Freud disturbed the sleep of the world and that Franz Alexander disturbed the sleep of the psychiatrists and psychoanalysts. This is not easily forgiven.

Alexander's therapeutic opinions led to a new version of analytic training. To his way of thinking, students of our big psychoanalytic institutes are not encouraged to learn from their own experiences but are taught to follow standard procedures. It is an illusion to think that an analyst can continue without influence on his patients. Freud separated from Breuer because Breuer was horrified by the transference, whereas Freud used transference as a theraputic tool. I understand Alexander to mean that today the modern psychotherapist uses countertransference to react with spontaneity to the needs of the patient, especially to the unconscious needs. This is quite different, as I see it, from Ferenczi's suggestion to react and to fulfill partly the wishes and desires of his patients.

Alexander emphasizes that the complex emotional transactions between patient and therapist cannot be exhaustively described by the concepts of transference and countertransference. This interaction includes an interplay between two distinct personalities, who interact as two human beings within the reality of the transference situation.

The therapeutic needs are expressed in the patient's behavior and production, and they must be perceived by the analyst. The responses of the analyst to the needs of his patient are determined in part by his countertransference, in part by his and the patient's specific personality features, and in final measure by the therapist's consciously controlled reaction. The resulting therapeutic communication goes beyond verbalization and insight. Expressed in many cues and simultaneously on many levels of interaction, it reaches great emotional impact and aids therapeutic efficiency.

Analysts are better therapists than teachers. As teachers, we are directed toward the past, whereas we should be looking into the future. We should teach psychodynamic reasoning, which is more important than procedure. Alexander always tried to live up to this maxim.

Therapy becomes analytic not by avoiding manipulation—and to lie on the couch is a form of manipulation—but through the understanding of unconscious communication and interaction. Planned manipulation and role-playing are terms and concepts *not* originated by Franz Alexander, who never suggested active role-playing (if I understand him correctly). He realized that during the therapeutic situation the analyst becomes aware of conscious and unconscious wishes and needs of the patient. The analyst does not allow his patient to manipulate him into satisfying the patient's neurotic, infantile, regressive wishes. However, the analyst may respond to the conscious or unconscious processes of the patient, partially intuitively and partially by plan, in such a way as to help the patient's struggle for maturation and greater integration. In Alexander's opinion, all this asks not for new methods but for consistent application of Freud's principles.

Franz Alexander had many aspects to his personality. His friends recognized him at his best when he spoke as the courageous, original healer, unafraid of his patients and unafraid of his colleagues. In this aspect he approached most nearly the ideal of the truly free man. In therapy and teaching, he occasionally called himself a "conservative anarchist."

For twenty-five years, Alexander trained and directed his research team in Chicago. He and his staff devoted much time to research in psychosomatic medicine. In 1939 he founded, together with Flanders Dunbar, Stanley Cobb, Carl Binger, and others, the journal, *Psychosomatic Medicine*, for which he wrote the opening article and in which he published most of his reports on psychoanalytic medicine.

In this research, he has always advocated the necessity of a multidisciplinary approach, which is almost self-evident for a man with his background in scientific methodology. However, to start his pioneering work, he was obliged to concentrate his investigations on the psychological aspects of psychosomatic disease.

At first, Alexander had to define the concept of truly psychosomatic illness and differentiate it from hysterical symptoms and other conversions. The hysterical symptom was seen as a symbolic expression of a conflict with the help of the body; psychosomatic sickness is not a symbolization but a result of the "logic of emotions," which is expressed in tension and in this way causes dysfunction.

Alexander introduced the concept of "vector analysis." Almost all organs of the body can be disturbed by different emotions, heading in different dynamic directions: the wish to receive, to retain, and to eliminate. All vectors have loving as well as aggressive, hateful connotations. Receiving can turn to hostile taking; elimination can be generous giving or hostile-aggressive. The three vector qualities of incorporation, retention, and elimination are actually the dynamics of the life process.

A vegetative neurosis, for example, emotional hypertension, is not an attempt to express an emotional conflict as is conversion hysteria. It is the physiological concomitant of constant or periodically recurring emotional states. The hypertensive patient is under a constant but unexpressed emotional tension that is not drained by neurotic symptoms.

Chronic, inhibited rage may lead to a chronic elevation of the blood pressure. Analysis may help solve the conflict between passive-dependent, feminine, receptive wishes and overcompensatory, competitive, aggressive-hostile impulses.

In 1934, he pointed out that with the help of vector analysis, many gastrointestinal syndromes can be understood. The most outstanding feature in the psychoanalysis of the gastric cases is intense receptive wishes that conflict with the patient's fight for his independence. Alexander developed a sloganlike working hypothesis summarizing the ulcer personality, "I do not want to take or to receive; I am active, competitive and efficient and have no wishes for passivity and dependency."

The typical situation in which a man may develop an ulcer is the Tantalus situation. It is the always-hungry man who does not allow himself to accept. He is like Pavlov's dog, who was fed but could not retain his food and so developed ulcers.

The psychoanalytic formula for five patients undergoing analysis because of ulcerative colitis was different: "I have the right to take and demand, for I always give sufficiently. I need not feel inferior or guilty for my desires to take, because I am giving the best I have in exchange for what I take." As Freud, Abraham, and Jones established early in their studies, the eliminative function psychologically becomes the equivalent for giving and also for accomplishment. The most common onset situation, particularly in colitis cases, is one in which the patient has lost hope and is convinced that he cannot accomplish the task at hand. He then regresses to an infantile form of accomplishment, which is gastrointestinal elimination. Dynamic formulation of the conflict in patients with constipation seems to be: "I do not take or receive, and therefore I do not need to give anything."

The Chicago group also studied the psychodynamics of asthma, their research following suggestions given by Sigmund Freud and continued by Edoardo Weiss. The analysis of the asthma cases revealed a conflict between aggressive-masculine and passive-feminine tendencies. The patient in his asthma cries out for help from his mother and is afraid of separation from her. The prototype of the asthma attack is the cry of the newborn baby for his mother with his first drawn breath. In analysis, the asthma attack can be replaced by confession of crime or guilt. A crying spell or a confession may relieve the asthma and may restore good relationship with the mother (or her image). It is as if the asthma patient were acting according to the slogan, "I cannot love because this would imply the loss of my mother's love."

In later years, the Chicago research team turned their attention to the analysis of thirty-three cases of rheumatoid arthritis. The typical unconscious conflict of the arthritic patients, the majority of whom are women, is what is commonly called "masculine protest." The early history reveals dominating parents, mostly mothers, against whom the arthritic patients rebel and then submit. This produces a kind of emotional strait-jacket situation. Arthritic patients are frequently masochistic, self-sacrificing types.

There is much work of the Chicago Institute for Psychoanalysis that has not yet been reported or has been reported only in preliminary fashion, for example, study of fatigue due to hyperinsulinism (or hypoglycemia), found in situations of vegetative retreat. Initial research in diabetes mellitus, accident proneness, longevity, and tuberculosis has yielded preliminary hypotheses. A wealth of analytic observations has been collected about the personality of patients with cancer.

Profound changes in psychosomatic medicine are taking place, and the future may show that all its pioneers have made unavoidable mistakes in their conceptional thinking, in their clinical observations, or in their interpretations. Mistakes have also been made in multidisciplinary co-operation. As a consequence, Alexander turned with increased interest to the problem of specificity. It is this multidisciplinary approach that points to the future.

During his twenty-five years as Director of the Chicago Institute for Psychoanalysis and as the head of a research team, Franz Alexander never lost sight of the general cultural situation. He recognized the "advent of the statistical man" and described the correlation between scientific advancement and social change that has become apparent in the last 150 years. The scientist became a public figure and the government discovered his importance. No longer an elegant pastime, basic research has become a realistic necessity. To impose organization upon research is futile and retarding. True creativity stems from the unconscious, and systematic teamwork can help only after the individual has communicated his discovery. The more we learn about the person of Sigmund Freud and his way of living and working, the more we see the "empire-builder," who spent an unbelievable amount of time and effort in organizing "mein Reich," as he called it. A man with the great and symbolic name of Alexander had to follow his destiny, continuing Freud's empire-building in the setting of Chicago in the mid-century.

By 1955, Alexander had spent a year's leave from Chicago at the Center for Advanced Study in Behavioral Science (Ford Foundation, Palo Alto). In this creative retreat he returned to his favorite philosophers and mathematicians and studied once more the relativity theory of Einstein, the quantum theory of Max Planck, and the indeterminancy principle of Werner Heisenberg. Following Heisenberg's uncertainty principle, Alexander modified his concept of the determination of natural events, and adopted the concept of potentiality and probability. Modern science increases distance between man and nature. The other branches of science must follow, and psychoanalysis is beginning to do so. This development deepens man's estrangement from nature. Man is already threatened by technological applications of science. These are the two trends leading to the feeling of alienation in modern man, which find expression in man's feeling of loneliness, in his existential despair, in his lack of identity and of direction. It is his task now to adjust to a new world, a world of free-floating, relative reality.

The revolution in science has been followed by a revolution in modern art. Alexander has questioned, "In what way does contemporary art express the spirit of our era, as Byzantine art expressed the mentality of the Middle Ages, or as Impressionism did the outlook of the second half of the nineteenth century?" Modern art does not represent the world we live in, but transforms this world according to a consistent formula of its own. The nihilistic rejection of everything that even reminds one of the real world initiated the revolution in art. However, rejection and rebellion against reality do not constitute a static mental condition; they represent no final solution. Alexander concludes that modern art in its present form may not be the final answer. After the scientific mastery of the unconscious, artistic mastery will follow.

The revolution in science and art is related to the birth of existential philosophy. In the fervor of the extroverted mastery of the world around him, man has partly lost self-mastery. He has conquered the world but has had to neglect his own self. Heidegger's philosophy offers no operational clues to which profound insights can be applied; Freud's method puts his philosophical postulates to work. As a philosopher's son, Alexander gave respectful attention to the study of existential philosophy, but his opposition is clear. His philosophy was first brought out in "Our Age of Unreason" in 1942 and restated with increased breadth and depth in *The Western Mind in Transition*, published in 1960, which had its roots in the Chicago experience but was actually written in Los Angeles.

§ Harvest Years in Los Angeles

In 1956, Alexander accepted an invitation to become the Director of a new Psychiatric Research Department at the Mount Sinai Hospital in Los Angeles. Here he started organization and work on a new research project, supported by the Ford Foundation. It was his aim to study the psychotherapeutic process by direct observation of patients and therapists in action.

The investigation lasted several years. The results are in the process of being described, discussed, co-ordinated, evaluated, interpreted, and summarized. This unique (and perhaps unmanageable) accumulation of detailed clinical observations and recordings may exert great influence on psychotherapeutic research and technique in American psychiatry for many years to come.

Once more Franz Alexander organized a research team, put it to work, held it together, supervised efforts and organized reports to the scientific world. The fact of this objective investigation of the therapeutic process has already had an impact on workers in the field: the veil of intimacy and mysticism overhanging the unique one-to-one relationship between patient and therapist has been lifted. Perhaps it is not yet possible to describe the essentials of the psychotherapeutic process, but at least Franz Alexander and his research team suspended speculation and invited witnesses to join the therapist, who thus far had filled the difficult dual role of participant-observer. Therapeutic communication has been subjected to the scrutiny of schooled observers, whose trained eyes and ears have been supplemented by electronic eyes, ears, and memory.

The report based on this research promises to deepen our knowledge about the central position of the therapist, the importance of the therapeutic atmosphere, the essential role in interpretation of nonverbal communication, the nature of multileveled communication, and the proper use of overcommunication at the beginning of any encounter. We may gain information about possible incorrectness and distortion of impressionistic anecdotal case reporting, about the relationship between countertransference and behavioral action, and about the meaning of interacting, role-playing, and innumerable technical and theoretical problems that plague the intuitive therapist.

As during most of his lifetime, Franz Alexander will again be in the limelight, standing, as it were, in the eye of a controversial hurricane. Some will see him as the hero of progress, others, as the executioner of psychoanalysis. True to his character, Alexander was hardly aware of the personal and emotional undercurrents of such controversy. No one knows whether this attitude of denial was real and genuine or defensive and purposeful. Franz Alexander learned to adjust his personality to work efficiently in the realm of science, without undue reactions to personal issues.

There are two trends that Franz Alexander liked to watch from his observation post in Los Angeles: First, he wanted to see the slow and safe integration of psychoanalysis into academic psychiatry. So far as Alexander was concerned, psychoanalysis is one of the basic sciences of psychiatry. A logical consequence of this development would be the integration of psychoanalytic institutes into departments of psychiatry in American universities. As a prophet, Alexander was careful and cautious, and he did not predict how many years such integration would take. Although the trend was clear to him, he realized that neither all the universities nor all of organized psychoanalysis is ready for such integration.

Second, Alexander wanted to delve further into the future of psychoanalysis as a science; he wanted to describe, clearly and definitely, the difference between psychoanalysis as a science and as an instrument of treatment. This difference, noted by Sigmund Freud in his later years, will become even more obvious after completion of the research into the essentials of the psychotherapeutic process begun by Alexander.

During his years in Los Angeles, Franz Alexander prepared several books, most of which deal with problems of history. In 1960, he published *The Western Mind in Transition,* in which he quoted his father, Bernard Alexander, as saying, "Only one who can escape into the desert, or who can create a desert around himself, can save his art in our days." Symbolically and realistically, the son heard his father and took his advice to heart.

The Western Mind in Transition is a frankly autobiographical book, reflecting Europe at the turn of the century, recalling the author's family and background, tracing his early intellectual development. In the second part, Alexander describes the origins and the growth of the psychoanalytic movement as he saw it from the early days. He gives his opinions on modern science and technology, on art and existentialism, on problems of ego identity and on modern life.

Alexander does not relate modern man's unstable ego identity and his sense of futility solely to early, infantile events. The sense of ego identity in previous generations probably was related to the identification with the "strong" father. It probably was also genetically connected with the closer relationship to the old-fashioned mother, longer and less scheduled breast feeding, and the unquestioned assumption by mother and nurses that the care of babies is a full-time, engrossing and fulfilling occupation, not a sacrifice. Modern man's insecurity may be rooted in his early infantile care and neglect. The later strengthening of ego identity through ideology and through religion and a firm set of values is more important in Alexander's present focus of interest than the genesis in early infancy.

Alexander postulates that surplus energy is a source of creativity. Man's creativity is most productive when he is relieved of the immediate pressures of his survival needs. The affinity between play and creativity was long recognized by Alexander, whose own way of life was always a peculiar combination of play and hard work.

At a point in history when technology offers more time for play and luxury than ever before, man looks longingly at the creative centuries of the past, during which man took time for play and creativity without feeling guilty. The obsessive need for production for its own sake, rather than as a means of creativity, leads to the secret of the crisis of Western civilization.

The solution will come not from psychiatry but from new educational principles that should change the ethos of our "overadjusted" society. The hope lies not with the maladjusted but with the "unadjusted" person, in the sense of nonconformist, not overadjusted, man. In all his life and in all his work, Franz Alexander was an example of this.

There was a time—only fifty years ago—when man could answer the question, "What is the purpose and the sense of existence?" with a vital and concrete answer, "To build a technically efficient world, with a steadily rising material standard of living for everyone."

Full life means self-realization, not merely filling a social role; maturation and integration must also take place on symbolic and cultural levels. The security-seeking, conforming mass-man, bound to his machine, is not here to stay forever—if Alexander can help it.

§ Postscript

In the second week of March, 1964, Franz Alexander died. To the end he continued to work with his doctors in training analysis. His desk was piled high with manuscripts, galley proofs, and the many letters Freud had written him, from which he was planning to quote during forthcoming lectures.

There was also the entire correspondence between Sigmund Freud and Eugen Bleuler, which he was preparing for publication. On Sunday morning, March 8, 1964, shortly after having returned to his home in Palm Springs, he died.

He believed himself to have been his mother's favorite; certainly he was beloved and needed by all who knew him and learned from him.

Marie Bonaparte

1882–1962

THE PROBLEM OF FEMALE SEXUALITY

*

CLAUDE STEIN-MONOD

§ Her Forgotten Childhood and Analysis with Freud

Princess Marie Bonaparte writing at the time of Freud's death, said:

> A descendant myself of a line that gave to the world one of its greatest conquerors, yet the daughter of one of the Emperor's great-nephews, who devoted himself to labors of thought, I learned from my childhood to put spiritual triumphs above feats of strength and power; it is no doubt this that turned me in my declining years toward Freud, whose disciple I am proud to be (1939).

On August 13, 1937, Freud had written to her:

> MEINE LIEBE MARIE,
>
> . . . To the writer, immortality means being loved by any number of anonymous people. Well, I know I won't mourn your death, for you will survive me by years, and over mine I hope you will quickly console yourself and let me live in your friendly memory—the only form of limited immortality I recognize (E. Freud, 1960, p. 436).

Marie Bonaparte centered her entire work on psychoanalysis, the greatest experience of her life. She made use of all the material Freud had brought her, remembered his conversations and remarks. Furthermore, from 1926 onward, she kept up a correspondence with her master. Thanks to her systematic mind and to the respect and admiration that prompted her to remember the words of the man whose disciple and friend she was, she presents us with an actual, living Freud (1939).

Psychoanalysis came to France rather late. In the company in which she moved, Princess Marie Bonaparte had the opportunity to talk of psychoanalysis with Madame Sokolnicka, a pupil of Freud and Ferenczi. At her father's deathbed in 1924, she read *Introduction to Psychoanalysis*. Upon this loss of her father, to whom she had been so deeply attached, she felt the desire to find a second "father." There was another reason, apart from her personal problems, that led her to ask Freud for an analysis: the discovery, among her father's papers, of five little black notebooks she had written between seven and a half and ten years of age. She had no recollection of them, and, even after studying their contents, she could never remember writing them. The enigma of these copybooks with their fantasies troubled her. She had to find out their meaning. Fearing the caprice of a lady of fashion, Freud at first refused to take her in analysis; but he finally accepted her, and from 1925 she went to Vienna for several months each year for several years.

In spite of her strong wish to do so, Marie Bonaparte was not able to study medicine. Her father objected, fearing that the profession might prove an obstacle to the brilliant marriage he desired for her. Marie complied, but avidly studied everything connected with the field in which she was so interested and acquired a solid knowledge of it. She assiduously attended consultations at Sainte-Anne Hospital in Paris to learn psychiatry and make contact with mental patients. Surgery, as well, seems to have had a certain attraction for her. It is interesting that in 1924, before her analysis, she published an article under the pseudonym of "Narjani," called "Considérations sur les Causes Anatomiques de la Frigidité chez la Femme" ("Notes on the Anatomical Causes of Frigidity in Women"). She was always interested in the problems of female sexuality and frigidity. She tells us that she always had attracted confidences from women and that she had been struck by the number of women who were clitoridal.

Freud had once told her he thought that, in removing the clitoris, certain primitive tribes tried to feminize woman and desired to complete her biological castration. But Marie Bonaparte wondered if there were not another reason: the Oedipal jealousy of the old women who generally performed the task.

This conclusion recalls one of the principal themes of the five copybooks where, in story form, the theme of phallic castration and hole anxiety frequently occurs. For Mimi (her childhood nickname), the hole was the symbol of womanhood.

The commentaries on the copybooks were not written immediately after Marie Bonaparte's analysis. She often discussed with Freud the possible interest of this denouement. He dissuaded her from writing it too soon, since he thought the latent contents, underlying the manifest contents, should be made clear.

Marie Bonaparte's childhood was sad and lonely. In 1880, her mother, Marie-Félix, daughter of François Blane (the originator of the Casino at Monte Carlo) and heiress to a vast fortune, married Prince Roland Bonaparte, the son of Pierre Bonaparte and grandson of Lucien Bonaparte, the brother of Napoleon I. Marie Bonaparte was born on July 2, 1882, at Saint-Cloud, near Paris. A month later her mother died of an embolism.

The atmosphere in the house was gloomy; Marie was allowed very few friends other than her cousins, the children of her father's sister. Furthermore, her grandmother forced a hateful regimen on her for fear she should fall ill. This family atmosphere is described here briefly, for it was largely to escape from its sadness that Marie wrote the copybooks. She did not like her grandmother. The latter appeared to her (as she said later in analysis) like a "veritable Jocasta." Similarly, her father appeared like a "real Oedipus": it was as though he were remarried—to her. She wrote short stories, finding an escape from her melancholia in words. As soon as she knew how to write, she noted down her dreams on slips of paper. To her, they were the supreme enigma of the life of the mind; they interested her intellectually, and as an artist she delighted in them.

Her vocation for literature showed itself very early. At seven, she already wanted to write "something lasting." She attached great importance to her writings, reading and rereading them, correcting them, and carefully drawing up a table of contents. She had a feeling for words and writing was a real pleasure. She expressed herself in a language of images and symbols: it was also a secret language, since she wrote in English, which she knew well. (Her father had made her learn English and German from the age of four.)

The striking thing about Marie Bonaparte's life and work is this path from which she never seemed to swerve. "All my life I was to care about the opinions, approval and love of only a few 'fathers,' selected ever higher and of whom the last was to be my grand master Freud." From her infancy she needed to find a "father" of this kind; at the age of forty she was still looking.

All her life Marie strove to escape from the anxiety of transientness and death. Very early—from the age of four, she says—she had "a poignant feeling of the passage of time." When Freud remarked, "Why should anything that comes out of man last if the whole universe is perishing?" she replied, "What you say is fine—but how sad!"

In her autobiography Marie stresses the fact that she had no religious education other than the prayers which her maid, Mimau, secretly made her say. She had read the Bible, but the God of Abraham appeared to her as cruel and unjust, and she preferred the gods of Olympus.

After a few weeks of analysis, Freud discovered, after hearing the account of one of her dreams, that as a baby she had been present at scenes of coitus. Marie Bonaparte at first strongly resisted and rejected this reconstruction. But when all her unconscious memories pointed in the same direction, she finally yielded in face of the evidence. Furthermore, she chanced to meet again one of her father's grooms (a bastard son of her grandfather), who after considerable questioning, confirmed what Freud had guessed: that he had had sexual relations with the wet nurse in the presence of Marie who at that time was less than a year old. She wrote to Freud of the result of this meeting. Delighted at the confirmation, Freud replied, "Now you understand how contradiction and recognition can be completely indifferent when one knows oneself to possess a real certainty. That was my case, and it was why I have held out against scorn and disbelief without even getting bitter" (Jones, Vol. 3, p. 122).

This precocious sight, which she interpreted as sadistic, as all children who witness sexual relations do, explains many of the purple passages in the copybooks. It explains the terror of the little girl, who tries to get away from male agression and regards the "hole," the very condition of woman, as fearful punishment.

Inseparable from hole anxiety is castration anxiety. The masculine grandmother, whom Marie admires but does not like, a woman in public life, appears as a phallic woman. The fear of feminine sexuality appears in all the stories she wrote as a child. The very fact of her mother's death gave her the unconscious conviction that all women are doomed to death. As for man, he outlives his sexuality, which is why she wants to be a man. Motherhood is dangerous and being a woman implies "intellectual shame."

§ The Bisexual Constitution of Woman

Thus Marie Bonaparte seemed destined to deal with female sexuality. In 1935, Freud drew her attention to the many psychoanalytic works dealing with this matter and to their tendency to deny the fundamental primitive "phallicity" of woman. Freud reckoned that his disciple had come so close to his own views on the subject that he advised her to write something on it. He shared Marie Bonaparte's main view, namely, that frigidity in woman is provoked by her vital fear of penetration inside her body. This theory appeared in "Passivity, Masochism and Femininity," published in 1935. This anxiety is related to bisexuality, for the young girl recoils before the sexual aggression of man in proportion to the bisexuality in her make-up.

At the end of the nineteenth century, Fliess introduced the question of bisexuality. Freud took this up in 1905, stating that neither pure masculinity nor pure femininity is ever seen.

In *Female Sexuality* (1953), Marie Bonaparte sketched a biological theory of bisexuality, which is necessary to explain why a masculinity complex in women is more common than a femininity complex in men. She criticizes Karen Horney, Melanie Klein, and Ernest Jones for not taking account of this fact and for putting forward the primary nature of femininity.

Whereas Abraham thought that the early phallic stage of genital organization corresponded to an object-love stage, with exclusion of the genitals, Marie Bonaparte considers that exclusion of the phallus happens in the late phallic stage and results from rejection of the early phallic stage. It is the castration complex that brings the late anal-sadistic stage to an end; Marie Bonaparte considers that what Abraham calls the phallic stage with exclusion of the genitals is the phallic stage after the castration.

To become truly a woman, the girl must grieve for and accept the loss of her penis. If she does not, but aspires to take it from the male, she runs the risk of not accepting the penis lovingly.

Marie Bonaparte points out that for the boy the castration complex is cultural, whereas for the girl it is biological. The girl must pass from penis envy to envy of the cloacal child.

She criticizes Karen Horney's theory that the young girl's vagina is awakened very early and that she later develops male clitoral sensitivity as a defense. Also, she opposes Melanie Klein's idea that one cause of frigidity is a concave cloacal castration complex in the young girl. Both of these theories go against the primary nature of masculinity, that is, of bisexuality.

As Freud established no prehistory of the vagina, Marie Bonaparte says he could be criticized for not stressing the primary nature of femininity. But she finds that one does not necessarily exclude the other and is convinced that there is a vaginal prehistory in the young girl. Marie Bonaparte is the first to observe an active phallic stage in the young girl, in which the clitoris corresponds to the phallus. The passive prehistory of the phallus is more important to the girl than to the boy. This passive stage is succeeded by an active stage, in which the young girl, lacking the penetrating organ, envies the mother. This active phallic stage is sandwiched between the two passive phallic stages.

Too strong a clitoral fixation on the mother may do more to thwart the erotic function than too strong a fixation on the father. A condition of vaginalization is the transfer of envy from the penis to the child, that is, the acceptance of motherhood. Fear of motherhood may often spring from fear of pain, danger, or death, wherein the large penis appears to the young girl as threatening or perforating. Also, the young girl who wants to usurp her mother's place fears the mother's vengeance. Melanie Klein thought it was fear of the mother's vengeance that made the young girl abandon her cloacal envy for that of the phallus; a marked sadism would predispose her in this direction. But Marie Bonaparte holds that Melanie Klein does not give enough consideration to the bisexual components, for sadism is a male attribute. The extremely important conclusion is that sadism and aggression favor masculinity and the male function, whereas in the same proportion they disfavor femininity and the female function.

The role of the female is to wait. Girls who do not want to wait have a strongly bisexual constitution. It would be interesting to know how much of this springs from wanting to be masculine and how much from actually being masculine.

More than once Marie Bonaparte has warned parents and pedagogues against too severely repressing masturbation, which is essential to the libidinal development of every human being.

The conclusion of the first part of *Female Sexuality* is that there are three obstacles to the full erotic function of woman: her femininity (she has less libidinal energy than man and fewer chances to sublimate it), her masculinity, and her morality.

A long chapter is devoted to essential feminine masochism. Marie Bonaparte disagrees with Helene Deutsch, who saw it as a primordial condition for establishing the erotic function in woman.

Masochism is biologically intrinsic to the female, for the female germinal cell is essentially an object that is broken into. Similarly, during her libidinal development the young girl is faced with masochistic relationships of different kinds: in the oral stage, to be eaten by the father; in the anal stage, to be beaten by him; in the phallic stage, to be castrated; in the adult feminine stage, to be penetrated or fertilized by the man, who is the substitute father. For the author, vaginal coitus is stamped with a "masochistic passive positive Oedipus toward the father, whom she never completely abandons . . . since woman, more than man, remains subject to the libidinal impulses of her childhood." Woman is, therefore, destined to accept the masochism that "man should refuse." This is even more inevitable because libidinal and aggressive impulses remain closely linked in woman. Hence the increased erotization of the masochistic relationship; this relationship is seen as an attack by the large paternal penis on the small clitoral penis, which was originally the erotogenic basis of active erotic impulses. Refusal to submit to vaginal coitus can lead, first, to an attitude of "masculine protest," second, to refusal of the "sexual mission," and third, to total frigidity connected to a greater or lesser extent with moral masochism.

These considerations lead to the description of three types of women: (1) feminine, vaginal, corresponding to a cloacal libido position; (2) bisexual, where the libido is centered, as in men, on the little phallus, the clitoris; and (3) clitoral-vaginal, possessing two erotogenic zones. These are the most favored.

§ Marie Bonaparte and Edgar Allan Poe

"The Identification of a Daughter with her Dead Mother," which appeared in 1928, two years after Marie Bonaparte's analysis had begun, is one of her most important works. Because of the honesty and frankness with which the author has set out, in a few pages, the course of her own analysis, it constitutes a lesson in psychoanalysis and an exceptional document.

At the age of four, Marie Bonaparte had a violent attack of hemoptysis, and it was thought she would die. Her memory of the incident did not include the spitting of blood, but she remembered a wonderful hallucination in which a large rainbow-colored bird with a long beak stood on one leg on the lower part of her stomach and looked at her with one eye. In the course of her analysis forty years later, she managed to solve the enigma of this mysterious bird.

This short work is of literary as well as scientific value. In a few sentences, the author conveys the oppressive atmosphere of her childhood. She even sketches the main events of her life, which she later developed in her autobiography, *A la Mémoire des Disparus* (in Memory of the Departed). The mysterious bird recalls the marabous and flamingos that had intrigued her in the zoological gardens. It is also reminiscent of a stork from her picturebook, a stork that delivers babies. As for the rainbow-colored feathers, she remembered hearing about a large and beautiful opal that had belonged to her mother. The opal had a magic halo and was said to bring bad luck. And, indeed, her mother died at twenty-two. This bird, then, is the bearer of both babies and bad luck, since its plumage recalls the rainbow-colored opal. The child retained a feeling of aesthetic delight from this hallucination, but also a certain dread, a deep feeling of guilt, of having killed her mother.

From her childhood she had been fascinated by the attractive but hostile sea, which was the more hostile for the fact that she was not allowed to bathe in it. She sometimes wrote of this great mother symbol, and one of her literary compositions is a poetic story about the legend of Flyda of the Seas. The same theme frequently recurs in Edgar Allan Poe's works.

At seventeen, after a period of revolt during which her relationship with her father and grandmother had been very difficult, she imagined she had tuberculosis, as her mother had. She was convinced the doctors were concealing her true state from her and that she would shortly die. Her reaction—uncommon, but true to character—was to begin to work like mad. She was proud to be able to talk with her father of her scientific studies.

When she was nineteen, her father, who did not worry much about her literary education, gave her Edgar Allan Poe's stories to read. She could not bear to read "Ligeia," the story of a vengeful woman who returned to life in Rowena's body. At the time, she did not understand this fear. As is seen from the five copybooks, dead women were more terrifying to her than dead men. She did not really believe that men die. Marie Bonaparte's identification with Poe rests on their both having been haunted by representations of a vengeful mother.

For her, being ill was both a protection against marriage and murderous pregnancy, and faithfulness to her father; yet on her twenty-second birthday her father had said to her, "It's high time you took yourself in hand and got over your absurd ideas." High time, therefore, to abandon identification with her dead mother. She resented this advice as if it were a rejection of love. But she felt that she had overcome the identification with her mother and was free to marry. At twenty-five, she became engaged to Prince George of Greece, whose age (thirteen years older than she) and position enabled her to transfer to him her love for her father. She hesitated long before letting the Prince have her hand, for she was terrified of exile. But she was in love and the wedding was fixed for December 12, 1907. When leaving Paris, however, she said it would take a lot of happiness to make up for the loss of intellectual life that her new life would entail. But she overcame this obstacle; she managed to reconcile the life of the intellectual with that of the princess and sacrificed nothing of either.

In "The Identification of a Daughter with her Dead Mother," she tells us that Prince Roland gave her Poe's stories to read. She had to abandon them. Every evening, Ligeia's corpse came near her. In spite of her father's care to rid her of all superstition, she—who feared neither robber nor murderer—was frightened of ghosts. She tried to read another story, "The Masque of the Red Death," but, again, the temptation to identify herself was too strong; she came back to the book only when "healed by the Master of Vienna of my fear of ghosts; and to get my own back for the terrors of my youth, I was, in my turn, to analyze, to dissect, the sadist, the necrophile, Edgar Allan Poe." What had made her close the book was fear lest her dead mother, whom she had killed in being born, should return—an Oedipus ogress—in vengeance.

In her analysis of the life and works of Edgar Allan Poe, Marie Bonaparte made her most important contribution, both from a literary and from a psychoanalytic point of view. She based her work on Freud's theory that "the same mechanisms which, in dreams or nightmares, govern the manner in which our strongest, though most carefully concealed desires are elaborated—desires which often are the most repugnant to consciousness—also govern the elaboration of the work of art" (S. Freud, 1908). Using the laws Freud laid down in *The Interpretation of Dreams*, she interprets the symbolism of Poe's works. She sets about analyzing a story in the same way as she would analyze a dream.

Marie Bonaparte anticipates the possible objection that literary creation is fundamentally different from the dream, because literary creation is subject to logic, whereas the dream is not. But in the work of art, beneath the manifest story, another story is being told. Poe's work resembles a dream or a nightmare in that, in both, an image sinks into the unconscious to re-emerge in another, unrecognizable form.

Marie Bonaparte arranged the tales she thought most characteristic in two large groups: tales of the father and tales of the mother. This division brings home Poe's ambivalence; throughout his life, he oscillated between the mother, loved and hated, and the father-castrator, to whom he passively submitted. This was to be the subject of one of the most meaningful and significant of all the stories, "The Pit and the Pendulum."

In this tale, two great latent themes are broached: return into the body of the mother and masochistic, homosexual passivity in the son, accompanied with anxiety.

The fantasy of return to the mother's womb is common to all mankind. Marie Bonaparte, relying on an example drawn from her own life, thinks this fantasy is not necessarily one of anxiety but could sometimes be a pleasure dream. She remembers that as a little girl she used to build houses by stretching shawls over two chairs. She would spend hours there, feeling protected and warm, drawn in upon herself. For Poe the same fantasy, accompanied with anxiety, results in a fear of being buried alive. Like Freud, Marie Bonaparte rejects Rank's theory that the anxiety of birth represents a psychological memory, that is of greater importance than castration anxiety. The example of Poe confirms her point of view. Here death takes the form of return to the womb, of return to the primitive fetal state, which is already marked with the state of after-death.

The hideous figures seen by the prisoner on the walls of his cell represent totemic animals; in several stories the totemic animal represents the mother, for instance the horse in "Metzengerstein" or the cat in "The Black Cat." In other stories, the figures represent the father. Time with his scythe is the father-castrator and, in the torture of the pendulum, the son, bound, is masochistically delivered into the hands of the father. The fantasy of the bound prisoner as he watches the slow movements of the pendulum recalls fantasies of some subjects who reproduce in analysis the observation of intrauterine coitus. The unconscious desire that creates such a fantasy is sexual. The child present at a scene of coitus identifies himself, according to his nature, with one parent or the other. Marie Bonaparte here recalls the importance of bisexuality. The victim's fantasy under the pendulum again proves how defenseless Poe's masculinity was.

This tale is particularly filled with anxiety, for the victim is held in two anxieties, that of the pit and that of the pendulum. The first represents the mother with her cloacal hole, the second the phallus-castrator. In reality, therefore, the fictional tale of "The Pit and the Pendulum" is a faithful biographical account of the oscillations in Poe's bisexuality between the male and female attitudes, oscillations that in both directions ran up against the threat of castration.

Throughout his life, Poe was "excluded from woman's ecstatic attraction toward libidinal subjection to man." In spite of the threatening presence of the father, it is the presence of the mother that dominates Poe's works. He was always dependent on women—especially on Maria Clemm, who gave him a home. For him, woman is mother, and he displaces the affects originally proper to mother to imaginary women.

Poe's sexual impotence was linked with his fixation on his dying mother, for his sexuality could be only sadonecrophilic, and against this his morality revolted. He was subject to both a passionate attraction and a horrified revulsion. In going from one woman to another, he was seeking as much to escape from as to return to his fixation on his mother.

In 1930, Marie Bonaparte wrote an article "Deuil, Necrophilie et Sadisme" ("Grief, Necrophilia and Sadism"), in which she compared Poe's necrophilia and Baudelaire's sadism. The necrophile is a sadist who, intimidated by fear of the father, dares not identify himself entirely with the murderous father and contents himself with the father's remains. Because of the murderous father, Poe was left only the pleasure of the already dead mother. "Baudelaire must prepare the banquet himself, while Poe has only to start eating." Because of his fixation on his mother, Poe could never be initiated in sexuality by any other woman.

§ Other Works

For a long time, the Hungarian ethnologist, Géza Róheim, who had been analyzed, was the only ethnologist who advocated working together with psychoanalysts. He endeavored to show that analytic investigation could widen the understanding of the primitive mind.

In 1921, Róheim was awarded the Freud Prize for work on "Australian Totemism" and "The Self." Róheim had long wanted to make an expedition to Australia "to analyze his primitive natives." With Marie Bonaparte's financial support, he was able to carry out this plan and make field studies of the natives of Somaliland, Central Australia, and Normanby Island, and of the Yuma Indians in Arizona. His findings were of great value to psychoanalysis, inasmuch as he invalidated Malinowski's point of view and confirmed the universality of the Oedipus complex—even in tribes that deny real paternity by attributing pregnancy to magic influences activated by the phallic symbol of their ancestors.

In 1927, Marie Bonaparte wrote an article, "Du Symbolisme des Trophées de Têtes" ("The Symbolism of Head Trophies"), in which she treats of how horns—symbols of strength, of virility and, in many religions, of the most powerful gods—had become symbolic of the ridiculous figure of the wronged husband. This is a problem that goes back to ancient times, for the metaphor already existed in ancient Greece.

§ Marie Bonaparte and the Psychoanalytic Movement

Marie Bonaparte filled an eminent role in the history of the French psychoanalytic movement, not only because of her considerable writings, but also because of her activity, her closeness to Freud, and the position she held in the different international organizations. She was a member for many years, and then vice-president, of the Council of the International Psychoanalytical Association.

In 1926, she was a Founder-Member of the "Société Psychanalytique de Paris," of which she was made an honorary president shortly before her death in 1962. In 1927, the *Revue Française de Psychanalyse* was founded with her financial support, and she edited the nonmedical section. In 1934, she devoted herself to the foundation of the Institut de Psychanalyse in the Boulevard St. Germain in Paris, to propagate the theory of psychoanalysis and training practitioners. It was there that she gave her first lecture on the theory of instincts. Her role has been a varied one, organizer, teacher, and translator of a number of Freud's works. She enjoyed unchallenged authority among her colleagues, partly because of her personality but also because she was the only person to have spent many years in analysis with Freud, and she was afterward his disciple and friend.

Although they may have handicapped Marie's career, her titles of Princess Marie Bonaparte and Princess of Greece and Denmark enabled her to help Freud in many ways. She lent her name and fortune to the service of his cause.

Freud had had endless difficulties with the publication of books and periodicals. During the winter of 1929, when the publishing house Verlag was going through a financial crisis, Marie Bonaparte saved it from bankruptcy. Freud was extremely grateful.

One of the Princess' most glorious deeds was to save Freud's letters to Fliess from destruction. She had bought the letters from the Berlin bookshop to which Frau Fliess had sold them and had brought them to France. When Freud heard that these papers were in Marie's possession, he wanted to buy them back, for he did not want them published. Fearing he might destroy them, she was bold enough to refuse; she put them in safe keeping, and after many incidents they were removed to London. A dozen or so years after Freud's death, Marie published some important extracts from the letters, in collaboration with Anna Freud and Ernst Kris.

All those who ever met Marie Bonaparte agree that one of her outstanding qualities was frankness. She believed her character was deeply influenced by studying the fables of La Fontaine as a child. "The Miller, His Son and the Donkey" showed her the way to independence of thought and an attitude of mind that enabled her to disregard common opinion when she believed she was right.

Marie always espoused causes she thought just. As an adolescent, she was passionately interested in the Dreyfus case. She, who was to uphold the cause of the Jews all her life, was unable to contain her indignation. In 1933, Freud wrote to her, "I am glad and it makes me proud to hear how much sympathy you are showing the victims of the persecution in Germany. . . ." She saved 200 Jews from the Nazi persecution.

In the same spirit, she acted as hostess in France to refugee psychoanalysts from Central Europe and Germany, before their departure for the United States, and lent them her support. Among these was R. M. Loewenstein, who, before his departure, actively contributed to the French psychoanalytic movement by training many analysts.

The death penalty was repugnant to her. When she heard that Caryl Chessman was to be executed, without hesitation she flew to San Francisco. She saw the condemned man, talked at length with him, and interceded for him with the governor.

She always remained a fervent disciple and admirer of Freud, to whom she often referred as "the Master of Vienna," but she also became his devoted friend and, to some extent, protector. As Ernest Jones has pointed out, Freud liked being surrounded by women who were a bit masculine, such as Minna Bernays, Emma Eckstein, Lee Kahn, Lou Andreas-Salomé, and Joan Riviere.

The tone of their correspondence shows that already in 1926 their relationship was one of confidence and friendship. They broached every topic: psychoanalysis (some of Freud's letters are veritable lessons), politics, art, literature, and books. Although he barely liked it, Freud finished reading Céline's "*Voyage au Bout de la Nuit;* . . . I am reading it because you wished me to," he wrote in March, 1933.

It is clear from many of these letters that Freud had a great respect for the Princess's judgment; as he wrote in April, 1926, "I have once more admired your judgment (about the trauma of weaning)."

In 1929, Marie Bonaparte adopted her protective attitude toward Freud. She advised him to put himself under regular medical care and recommended Max Schur, an excellent internist who also was analytically trained. The choice turned out very well, and Freud was delighted.

When the political situation deteriorated in 1933 and the persecution of the Jews in Austria worsened, Freud grew worried about the future of psychoanalysis. He wrote a very moving letter to Marie Bonaparte, who invited him to come and stay in the house where she was born, in

Saint-Cloud. Freud turned down the invitation because he thought the persecutions were becoming less active. During these anxious times, he still wrote to her, "There are times when one is not inclined to write, but I should not like not to be in contact with you."

During the last years of Freud's life, Marie Bonaparte became more useful to him than ever. In 1938, Austria was invaded by the Nazis. Freud had to leave Vienna, and England was ready to receive him. But Ernest Jones had the greatest difficulty in persuading the master that it was necessary to leave; Marie Bonaparte also tried. She arrived in Vienna in March and, with Anna Freud, read Freud's notes and correspondence. They burnt everything they considered of secondary importance. The Nazis claimed a large sum of money from Freud, which he did not have. Marie Bonaparte lent the money to him, and he repaid it to her in England the following summer. She then used this sum to reprint Freud's *Gesammelte Werke* ("Collected Works") in London, to take the place of the edition that had been burnt by the Germans.

From early in 1938 until their departure for England, a period of anxious waiting, Freud found some distraction in translating, with his daughter, a little book of Marie Bonaparte's that he had much appreciated, "Topsy, the Story of a Golden-Haired Chow." The master and the disciple shared a common passion for chows. Freud had owned one, which had died a short while before, leaving a grieving master. Again Freud expressed his admiration for the delicacy with which the writer had analyzed her feelings for the animal and had described the beauty of an existence that was complete in itself.

When Freud finally left for London, he was infinitely touched by the welcome he received from the Princess on his way through Paris. The hours he passed with her furnished him with a memory from which he derived strength and peace.

During the last year of Freud's life, Marie Bonaparte went to London several times. Freud regretted that because of ill health he had been unable to receive her as he would have liked or to devote much time to her. In a depressed letter, he told her how ill he felt and asked her to come and see him in London. She went there for his eighty-third birthday, following which Freud wrote, telling her how much pleasure her visit had given him.

In June, 1939, Marie Bonaparte went to London and saw Freud for the last time. On June 16, she received his last letter, telling her how much he was looking forward to her next visit, when they would again be able to discuss their work. In September of the same year, she again returned to England, to attend Freud's funeral.

Marie Bonaparte spent the war years successively in France, in Greece, and at the Cape. On returning to France in 1945, after the war, she again took up her activities as writer, psychoanalyst, and teacher at the Institute in the rue Saint-Jacques (which had replaced the first Institute after the war and had become an important and representative center of French psychoanalysis).

On the occasion of her seventieth birthday in 1952, Rudolph Loewenstein edited *Essays in Honor of Marie Bonaparte*, under the title *Drives, Affects and Behaviour*. This work, the result of the collaboration of twenty-four authors and with a highly scientific approach, is an appreciation of the Princess's work and personality. It also bears witness to the affection in which she was held and to the gratitude felt for her ceaseless activities in all branches of psychoanalysis.

Nothing could show the role she has filled in the psychoanalytic movement better than Freud's letter to her dated November 12, 1938:

MEINE LIEBE MARIE,

I am always prepared to acknowledge, in addition to your indefatigable diligence, the self-effacement with which you give your energy to the introductions and popular expositions of psychoanalysis.

And yet you claim to be so very ambitious and to long for immortality at any price! Well, your actions testify to a nobler character (E. Freud, pp. 454–455).

REFERENCES

Bonaparte, Marie. Du symbolisme des trophées de tête. *Rev. Francaise Psychanal.*, 1927, 1, 637–732.

Bonaparte, Marie. *Female sexuality*. New York: Int. Univer. Press, 1953.

Freud, E. L. (Ed.) *The selected letters of Sigmund Freud*. New York: Basic Books, 1960.

Freud. S. Der dichter und das phantasieren. *Neue Rev.*, 1908, I.

Jones, E. *The life and work of Sigmund Freud*. New York: Basic Books, 1953–1957. 3 vols.

This chapter was written before the death of Marie Bonaparte in 1962 and has been abridged by the editors.

Siegfried Bernfeld

1892–1953

SISYPHUS OR THE BOUNDARIES OF EDUCATION

*

RUDOLF EKSTEIN

Because the life and work of Bernfeld and the times and places in which he lived are so interwoven, it seems to me best to discuss them simultaneously.

He was born on May 7, 1892, in Lemberg, part of the Austro-Hungarian Empire at that time. His parents were settled in Vienna, the Empire's capital, but his young mother, only nineteen then, returned to her parents in Lemberg, in order to be with her mother when she gave birth to her first child. His father, much older than his mother, was a Hungarian Jew, a self-made man who, although he came from a poor background, was quite well educated and well read. His mother, who had more formal education, was also widely read. A maternal uncle who was a psychiatrist, may have stimulated the boy's interests. The father was in the clothing business, and the family had advanced so far on the economic ladder that they owned a house in Hietzing, one of the Viennese suburbs.

Siegfried Bernfeld had a younger brother and a sister. The sister is now living in the United States; the brother was killed during Hitler's invasion of Czechoslovakia.

Young Siegfried was considered very "special" by his mother; his brother and sister, who identified with the parental view, also looked up to him with great respect. Most of his schooling took place in Vienna, where he finished the *Humanistisches Gymnasium* in 1910. He is said to have had a great deal of interest in plant physiology, having been inspired by a much admired high school professor, who interested him in botany and zoology. He actually registered at the University of Vienna to study that subject, then his major interest. I possess an editorial written by the twenty-year-old Bernfeld and published in 1913 in the *Neues Wiener Tagblatt,* in which he identifies himself with a concept of academic life that requires that one work and study intensively and warns against those who may whisper to the young high school graduate, "During the first years enjoy *Akademische Freiheit!*"

In 1964 one of his daughters quoted an anecdote Bernfeld used to tell on himself. He felt he was unable, because of lack of manual dexterity, to satisfy the demands of the botany professor, who required that the students prepare microscopic sections of leaves by hand. Because of that, he said, he switched to pedagogy and psychology. A journalist formerly from Vienna recalls Bernfeld, who was his tutor at that time. He remembers walking down the street with Bernfeld, who was holding a stopwatch in his hand and giving the boy free association tests, obviously in connection with Bernfeld's studies at the University. That was about 1912, when Bernfeld was only twenty years old.

Very early Bernfeld joined youth movements and was deeply identified with socialist and Zionist causes; much of his early writing for high school organizations and socialist and Jewish youth movement organs was an attempt to translate psychological insights into educational and political propositions.

Family lore has it that he founded a *Schimpfverein* when very young. The members of this high school club met together to complain about, and undermine, their elders. The task was to attack parental authority, to *schimpfen.*

The first phase of his adult life found him, then, with children and adolescents, with political and social reform, with educational tasks, and with the use of psychological and psychoanalytic insights for a new kind of education that was to make the world a better place to live in. Although he first chose plant physiology as his major study, he had psychological interests even during high school days; he described to his family how he had attempted to hypnotize his younger brother and how terribly frightened he was when he succeeded but at first could not remember how to reverse the process.

Before he became actively interested in psychoanalysis, he was associated with socialist and Zionist leaders. One of his early associations was with Martin Buber, and his contributions to Zionist and socialist papers began to appear at the end of World War I. In these writings he identified himself with active Zionism, discussing the peace treaties and the goal of Palestine as a Jewish home; he believed that youth should not wait passively for an ideal future but should work in the present. Very early he gave both the socialist and the Zionist movements insights from modern pedagogy, from psychology, and from psychoanalysis.

In 1922, he wrote about secret languages and secret writings of children and adolescents, as well as the language development of Yiddish children. He discussed age limits for the capacity of education in severe behavior problems, and he constantly tried to influence the educational policy of socialist groups. He also discussed such issues as punishment and institutional education. He took issue, as late as 1930, with those who did not want to include psychotherapy as a part of health insurance. After that time, his contributions were published in professional and scientific journals only.

Although he had spent part of his student years at a number of other universities in Germany, he received his Ph.D. from the University of Vienna. He married his first wife, Anne Salomon, in Freiburg in Breisgau in 1914 at the outbreak of the war. She, a medical student, then continued her studies in Vienna. He saw service during the war, but, as one can see from his writings, he had no conviction about the purpose of that war.

Despite his burning and passionate political and social commitments, he was a thorough research worker, as can be demonstrated from his first publications in scientific journals, which go back as far as 1914. It must also be stated that his prepolitical commitments never touched his scientific integrity. He was extremely tolerant toward the scientific views of other people, and endlessly curious. In the articles of that period he discussed the methods to be used to study scientifically the documents of youth, such as their diaries, their poetry and novels, and their reading matter.

Bernfeld's first book of psychoanalytic significance contains a report on *Kinderheim Baumgarten* and a discussion of serious experiments with new education. This book describes the experiences in a children's home for Polish Jewish refugee children, most of them war orphans.

This home, founded in 1919, hardly survived its first year. Bernfeld was at that time identified with Zionist education, and both he and his friend and co-worker Willi Hoffer enthusiastically gave their time to these orphans. This failed, as did similar experiments of others, because the experiment was not supported administratively and because it had insufficient trained personnel. Bernfeld wrote angrily about the autocratic powers that he considered to be in the way of his pedagogical activity. He described how difficult it was to detach himself from the children. He viewed himself, the staff, and the children as "victims" of a battle for a great idea, new Zionist education.

Many of the educational principles described, then part of the first experimental applications of psychoanalytic principles to education, are now well known in progressive education.

At the time of *Kinderheim Baumgarten,* Bernfeld was already deeply immersed in psychoanalysis. He had taken many of the available lecture courses, had known Freud, and he reported:

> In 1922 I discussed with Freud my intention of establishing myself in Vienna as a practicing analyst. I had been told that our Berlin group encouraged psychoanalysts, especially beginners, to have a didactic analysis before starting their practice, and I asked Freud whether he thought this preparation desirable for me. His answer was, "Nonsense. Go right ahead. You certainly will have difficulties. When you get into trouble we will see what we can do about it." Only a week later he sent me my first didactic case, an English professor who wished to study psychoanalysis and planned to stay in Vienna about one month. Alarmed by the task and the conditions, I went back to Freud, who only said, "You know more than he does. Show him as much as you can."

It was only later that he completed his formal training analysis in Germany with Hanns Sachs. He was one of the most brilliant contributors at that time. When he published *Kinderheim Baumgarten* he was about twenty-eight years old. Long before that, in 1914, he had published *The New Youth and the Women* and *The Jewish People and Its Youth.* In 1922, he edited a volume concerning the community life of youth, which contributed to research on youth. G. Fuchs, Hoffer, and Erwin Kohn were co-contributors. Hoffer was also a contributor to Bernfeld's volume, *Concerning the Poetic Creativeness of Youth,* published in 1924.

One year later, Bernfeld published two more volumes. The first, an innovation and a classic, concerns *The Psychology of the Infant,* unfortunately the only one of these books translated into English—by Rosetta Hurwitz in 1929. This volume is an extraordinary compendium in which he expressed himself in favor of the idea that instinctual life should be the foundation of a theoretical synthesis; thus Freudian psychology would become the basis for the new psychology, since there was no other instinct theory in psychology at that time. He hoped that this book would advance child psychology through the findings of analysis and the theories of Freud, and that their contribution to the understanding of facts found elsewhere and the enlargement of fundamental theories of other schools would be proved. He defined infancy as the period between the trauma of birth and the trauma of weaning. This definition indicates the limitations of the work. Published in 1925, it contained no psychological considerations of the ego, although a publication of three years earlier concerning sublimation indicates that he was occupied even then with notions of adaptation and an understanding of play; he discussed play not only as instinctual expression but also as an activity in which early repetition of unconscious conflict is combined with "an old theory of play," that of mastery. That text is a monumental work, but it led to a dead end, since it did not attempt to go beyond current theory.

The other book, the title of which I have chosen to characterize the life work of Bernfeld, is *Sisyphus or the Boundaries of Education.* In this book, published in 1925 and written in a powerful style as persuasive as was his political oratory and his skill as an eloquent teacher, he attacks idealistic notions of education that view the educator as one who molds the child's character, as a sculptor turns the marble block into a piece of perfection. He speaks of the sociological and the psychological boundaries of education. He uses insights from economics and sociology and from Marxist philosophy, to show the social boundaries of education, and he uses the theory of the unconscious to demonstrate inner boundaries. These boundaries turn the teacher into a Sisyphus, who sees them as limits, as chains that tie him down and force upon him impossible tasks. But if these boundaries are regarded as lawful, they can lead to insights that permit the creation of educational theory, based not on narcissistic idealism but on science. It was the latter view that Bernfeld was identified with, although there remained in him something of the idealistic teacher who from time to time overidentified with his task and became a passionate, suffering, and ever-trying Sisyphus, rather than a mere scientific technician.

His last paper, "Psychoanalytic Education," published ten years after his death, conveys much of that Sisyphean quality. How much this reminds one of Hannibal *ante portas*, the hero of Freud's adolescent years.

Of course, Bernfeld had not only psychological but also deep political awareness. It is pathetic that, as early as 1925, men like himself understood the problems of Central Europe well but were not strong enough to stem the tide of totalitarianism that led to World War II.

In this book he creates a fantasy, the precursor of Orwell's *1984*, in which Citizen Machiavell, a reactionary who seems to know both Marxism and psychoanalysis, is appointed Minister of Education. Machiavell addresses the Council and the experts of his Ministry to acquaint them with the new task. A few excerpts from that speech, even though in an imperfect translation, will convey much of the Bernfeld of that period, identified with children and with youth, dedicated to a new education, and utilizing the new science of psychoanalysis, which at that time was still considered a movement, *die Psychoanalytische Bewegung*. These are the words Bernfeld has Citizen Machiavell speak —a fantasy forerunner of Goebbels:

> . . . in order to achieve our aim I propose to you the following administrative measures. For you must understand that the organization of the educational system is the decisive problem that consequently must be kept, completely and relentlessly, within our own sphere of influence, while we may leave the curriculum, the didactic questions, and even educational questions safely to the pedagogues, the ideologists, and, yes, even to the Social Democrats. Yet even this concession I shall turn into a question of tactics. It must be demanded of us; we will make them fight a long time for it and grant it as a concession, always at that time when we feel the need for diverting the attention of the public.
>
> . . . As for the rest, youth must be educated toward a feeling of self-consciousness. It must feel convinced of its nobility, its beauty, and its cultural mission. . . . We will speak naturally about the German "Folk," and not about bourgeoisie. Certainly, the German nation is very much inclined not to accept this concept of Folk. This is an enormously dangerous fact. This fact can be offset, however, by means of a relatively simple reform. It only necessitates the courage to maintain complete stupidity. One just has to turn the unconscious anxiety of the German people, arising from deep inferiority feelings, into aggression. One would need to lead the Germans to believe that they have an enormously powerful, common enemy who endangers those parts of our, I mean, the people's holiest cultural values and

who would have to be annihilated through a stupendous, common deed. It must not be a realistically dangerous enemy, naturally, such as the French, since this would produce realistic fear. And if, then, we beat that real enemy, we would be in the same position as before. Such an enemy would need to be a fly, a nothing. It would also have the advantage that we could make use of the romantic element inherent in the minds of the Germans and their youth.

What do you think of a secret society of foreigners persecuting Germans? Large masses of people can be brought into deep identification with one another or any given person if they share a common sinister danger and if someone steps forward and saves them. Do you begin to understand what I have in mind? We will put youth . . . and with it the whole nation . . . and first of all the quasi-bourgeois youth, into a state of panicky fear of a sinister power that threatens them, and then we shall step forward as their saviors and leaders. Read Professor Freud on mass psychology . . . a very useful author, I assure you, if only the socialists do not begin to be aware of this too, but luckily they seem to consider him a bourgeois. . . . Well, from Freud you can obtain the conviction that my proposal must work. The bourgeois type, the most bourgeois individuals would become the ideals of youth, and it would form through this ideal a self-confident, proud, exclusive community that simultaneously could be easily led. If only we had the enemy at hand. It is a difficult task to find such an enemy, since he must be not present and yet credible. I recommend that we nominate the Jews to be this enemy. They actually are not at all dangerous. In Germany there exist 600,000 of them against 60,000,000. That is a good ratio. And they really are in every respect a utilizable people; they themselves will help us in one way or another. If they should, however, be beaten up or murdered, then there are enough of them in other cities and countries to maintain the fright they cause permanently before our eyes. With the help of such carefully nursed and applied anti-Semitism we shall maintain that proud, self-confident bourgeois youth, that youth, namely, which is permeated with the feeling of its own value and a belief in the nobility of its Folk and racial superiority, which will arouse identifying aspirations down to the deepest layers of the working classes. And it is this attitude of the proletariat that is important to us. . . . I have found that the year most suitable for our ends for starting school is the sixth year. The child has just got over or is still in the midst of an exceedingly important catastrophe, viewed psychologically, yes, psychoanalytically. The little boy has capitulated in the face of father's property rights with the development of strong anxiety, and he has renounced possession of his beloved mother. He now seeks new objects for his uninvested love. They shall come forward in the person of his teachers. It would be preferable if we had only unmarried women teachers as our agents. At the same time, he has gained a deep insight into his own insufficiency and with it the readiness to submit to authority, which is also supported by the resulting formations during these early infantile struggles and detachments of an agency in the ego, the guilt feeling, the readiness for punishment. If any impulse of defiance awakens, it will instantly suffer lasting defeat through the authority of the school.

. . . as there is no room in this tight circle of factory and family for any higher forms of sublimations, puberty, a period of intense sexual upheavals, will drive youth to sexualize their economic activities. The economic field will be merged in the unconscious thinking with the sexual. The excluding owner, the entrepreneur, or even his director or foreman will represent the father to youth. Thus the overwhelming majority of them will be broken of their inner aggression and revolt, however noisily it might make its appearance, because youth will be paralyzed by the memory of the infantile catastrophe that arose from the same basic situation and that will be bound by the same unconscious love and identifying tendencies with the father-entrepreneur. Economic independence of youth will strengthen these identifications. And, should some, in spite of this search for a way out of their situation, recognize what is keeping them in economic bondage, they will probably strive toward the life of that bourgeois youth that is separated from them, and they will seek that education which they think represents the value and the power of the bourgeois youth and society, influenced as they are by the school and by public opinion, by the cleverly prepared confusion of the concepts of culture and education, which even the workers' parties will only be able to see through with difficulty. They will not find it. . . .

He ends his volume with the comment that there "is no way out from ambivalences and doubts. The scientist is not ashamed of them; he exaggerates them, in order, as he hopes, to overcome them in the future."

Two daughters were born to Bernfeld and his wife, one during World War I and the other shortly after the War. When he and his wife separated in 1926, she left Central Europe to move East and Bernfeld in a few years moved West. The first period of *Sturm und Drang* perhaps ended then.

Bernfeld's life then entered a new phase. Of course, he had not given up his interest in adolescence and childhood. Many important contributions were published, such as his summary on the psychology of puberty in 1927, the papers on Pestalozzi and the "Diaries of Youth," the beautiful study, "Fascination," the contribution to the suicide issue of the *Zeitschrift für Psychoanalytische Pädagogik* in 1929, the 1935 paper, "Simple Male Puberty," and one in 1938, "Types of Adolescents," also published in English. But a new interest was slowly ascending, introducing the second period of Bernfeld's scientific life.

In 1926, he settled in Berlin and remained there until 1932. During that time, he taught and worked as an analyst in association with the first psychoanalytic institute, the Berlin Institute for Psychoanalysis. His experiences as a teacher and his reactions are described in his last posthumous paper, published in 1962. He was a brilliant and dedicated teacher. A part of his creativity was fed by the feeling that he was "never closely identified" with any of the teaching organizations, whether in Vienna, Berlin, or San Francisco. He was skeptical about training systems, the institutional setting, and its requirements; nevertheless, he was one of the great teachers of psychoanalysis and was deeply admired by his students. During the days in Berlin, he was still actively occupied with political issues. He lectured to workers' groups and continued to participate in social and political life, as one can see from his nonscientific publications during the early years of this second phase of his life.

After Hitler's enormous election victory in 1932, Bernfeld saw the handwriting on the wall and left Germany. He went to Vienna but remained there for only a short time.

The actress Liesl Neumann, an old friend from Vienna, became his second wife during the Berlin years, from 1926 to 1932.

Bernfeld's interests moved to issues of theory, to a critical analysis of the scientific basis of our science, the result of which is reflected in a number of important and lasting contributions. Some of these were an attempt to free psychoanalysis from ideological components; among these was the rather critical paper on Wilhelm Reich, who asserted in 1932 that there was no such thing as a biological striving for unpleasure, no death instinct, and reasoned that the problem of masochism remained the exclusive achievement of sex economy. Bernfeld held, in his "The Communistic Discussion Concerning Psychoanalysis" and Reich's *Denial of the Death Instinct Hypothesis* of 1932, that Reich was guided primarily by political and emotional motives. This discussion hid a powerful struggle, which ended with Reich's separation from organized psychoanalysis and later from psychoanalysis altogether. Many of these papers, such as that of 1935 on "The Classification of the Instincts," dealt with issues of instinct theory and the biological basis of analysis.

Bernfeld analyzed the concept of sublimation and agreed with Richard Sterba on stages of sublimation, a concept reminiscent of today's concept of a hierarchy of ego organization. He returned to some of his earlier interests in biology, contributing a number of papers and monographs with his friend Sergei Feitelberg. The best-known and most discussed of these is his attempt to introduce quantification into psychoanalytic instinct theory. I refer to his paper "Concerning Psychic Energy, Libido and Their Measurement," published in 1930. These attempts to measure pleasure and libido are beyond the scope of this paper; however, I recall vividly one of the seminars with Moritz Schlick, the leader of the *Wiener Kreis*, identified with the philosophy of science. It became clear in the discussion with Bernfeld that, as much as the idea of quantification must be a goal of scientific development, the attempt by Feitelberg and Bernfeld had not yet succeeded and was at best a beginning. In spite of the untenable position Bernfeld took, I recall his persuasive intellectual power, the burning eyes set deeply in the face of the gaunt, tall man. These studies raised questions that have again today become a vital part of psychoanalytic discussions on methodology. Bernfeld was aware of modern philosophical discussions, and his unpublished manuscripts show that he discussed with the philosopher Hans Reichenbach the use of scientific self-observation and attempted to clarify philosophically and methodologically the validity of propositions that are to be considered as statements of self-observation. One of his most beautiful papers, "The Facts of Observation in Psychoanalysis," published in 1941, has been translated into English. In it he defined the observational facts of psychoanalysis according to "the specific techniques by which they are procured":

> Some of these techniques will belong to the well-known and well-reputed methods of observation. Some of them are new: commonplace ways of knowing and handling men and their affairs used in psychoanalysis as means of research. These techniques, as far as they are equivalent to new observation instruments, will be physically isolated from psychoanalysis and subjected to specific, appropriate study of their structure and function, in general, by experimental psychology. Thus hallmarked and improved they can be freely used by psychology and psychoanalysis and will yield various applications to theory and practice.

In this paper he discussed methods of observation, which include those necessary to remove obstacles of observation, and he described and improved the instrument of the psychoanalytic interview. He is in favor of the use of the basic methods of psychoanalysis in the laboratory of experimental psychology. He suggests that "similarly, our pattern—secret, interpretation, confession—must become the object of research that is not interested in the confessions as observed facts but in the *procedure* itself as a means of producing facts."

He believes, then, as he did throughout his career, that psychoanalysis should not remain isolated but should build bridges to the other behavioral sciences.

One of the papers of that period, published in 1932, concerns "The Concept of 'Interpretation' in Psychoanalysis." Bernfeld discusses the psychoanalytic interpretation of neurotic symptoms, daydreams, parapraxis, or works of art as nothing but the attempt to order these facts into the total personality. He speaks of interpretation as the search for the total *Gestalt*, and he discusses the operations of interpretation, their methodology, as well as the technical act of interpretation, the inner experience connected with it. He suggests that as yet psychoanalysis has had no procedure for interpretation. He suggests that the interpretive method itself is but a method to procure material, but that we do not yet have experimental conditions for verification.

While he lived in Berlin, attempts were made to procure for him a professorship in Braunschweig. The hope was expressed in a report by the representatives of organizations of teachers that he would be appointed a professor of education and psychology. He was to bring his insights and his background to the education of teachers. Rudolf Olden asked Freud whether he would make a statement. Freud's statement reads as follows:

January 22, 1931

Prof. Dr. Freud *Wien IX Berggasse 19*

DEAR SIR:

You want my judgment about Dr. Siegfried Bernfeld? This is easy to render, since he is an unambiguous personality. He is an outstanding expert of psychoanalysis. I consider him perhaps the strongest head among my students and followers. In addition he is of superior knowledge, an overwhelming speaker and an extremely powerful teacher. Thus I can say all in all only the very best about him and we deeply regretted it when he left for Berlin.

Sincerely yours,

FREUD

Of course, one should not expect that in 1931 the author of Sisyphus would be appointed a professor of education.

He remained in Vienna only a short time and left when the Republic gave way to an Austrian dictatorship. He left for Southern France, where he married his third wife, Suzanne Cassirer Paret, who had studied philosophy and had also been analyzed by Sachs and later by Freud. She became his co-worker in the third phase of his life.

In France he saw comparatively few patients and spent most of his time on studies concerning the relationship between biology and analysis, thus taking up once more an early interest, but in a different way. Some of his work has been communicated in papers presented before the biological society in London. There are unfinished manuscripts of that time, including numerous correspondence with biologists and with his old co-worker Feitelberg. One publication from 1937 concerns "The Revision of Bioanalysis," in which he raises the question of what one could do with many of the analogies between the person and his body organs, which Ferenczi discusses, to put them into a form that offers concise psychological propositions by which the implied assertions can be examined and verified. He suggests that the instrument for such examination is available in the mathematical discipline of topology. An unpublished manuscript, "The Geometry of Organisms," which is dated 1940, deals with some of these issues.

Whereas the first phase of Bernfeld's work expressed the early enthusiasm, the political optimism, and the hope for a new world order, we find that in the second phase he limited himself more and more to issues of theory, scientific methodology, and critical review of the questions that psychoanalysis has raised.

He never quite felt like a settled person. Even though he came from a stable home, he was restless and was not identified with the kind of family tradition that he had found in his own childhood home, even though he was accepted and admired. He rebelled against the social order, and, as the values of the generation before World War I were shattered, he discovered that the safety of the home was an illusion. He hoped that the new education would create a new world, an illusion that he shared with many in the aftermath of the Great War.

Psychoanalysis as a science and as a movement gave him a new home in which creativity and early rebellion were now disciplined. He became more and more the scientist, the ever-questioning scientist. But the social unrest never allowed him to settle. The professorship failed, and he left one country after another, always a jump ahead of the anticipated disorder. Thus he was never technically a refugee. As much as he loved France, it did not offer a settled home, and "Brassi" (Bernfeld's nickname) had to move on. Family lore has it that the name Brassi comes from Brassbulla, the legendary ruler of a mythical domain he invented in his childhood. Brassi was still seeking that mythical domain.

In 1936, Bernfeld and his wife wrote off Europe as a place for creative work and decided to try anew. Often after 1918 he had tried unsuccessfully to go to Palestine; now he succeeded in getting visas, first for England and then, in August, 1937, for the United States. His old friends F. Deri, Fenichel, and Simmel prevailed upon him to move to San Francisco, where he was needed, and 1937 saw the beginning of his and his wife's work there.

If we look at his scientific contributions during that period, we see a third phase emerging. Obviously something had happened to that early *Schimpfverein.* His critical and productive examination of psychoanalytic concepts and theories slowly turned into a creative study of the work of the originator of psychoanalysis. He turned to Freud, tracing the development of the man and his work. I remember that in a personal conversation he once spoke to me of Freud's work as finished. He looked at it as supreme and complete. At the same time, he seemed overcome by pessimism—as if he himself had nothing new to contribute. I suggest, though, that he had never given up the hope that research in biology and topology might reveal new avenues that would give psychoanalysis new impetus. Also, he contributed then, in part with Suzanne Bernfeld, a number of magnificent papers on Freud that play an outstanding part in Jones's monumental biography of Freud. In 1944, he traced the connection of Freud's early theories with the school of Helmholtz and described Freud's early childhood; analyzed an unknown autobiographical fragment by Freud, in 1946; and studied Freud's scientific beginnings in 1949, his medical studies in 1951, his first year in medical practice in 1952, and his studies on cocaine in 1953. He had other manuscripts in preparation, such as one on hypnosis. His wife contributed one on Freud's use of archaeology, in 1951, comparing it with psychoanalysis, and exploring the use of archaeological metaphors.

I saw their rich archives and watched some of the painstaking search for material that would yield insight into the early creative years of Freud. Each paper, a true masterpiece, was carefully documented.

As pessimistic as he was in some private conversations, he remained an inspiring teacher and a great contributor to the work of the institute in his community. He felt identified with his new country. Robert Waelder once jokingly wondered whether America had made a bourgeois out of Bernfeld. Bernfeld was said to have remarked that, if Waelder meant that he was fairly content with the present government of his country, he was absolutely right. Bernfeld, the wanderer, had found a home, but he remained a restless and searching man. All his friends loved and admired him, although he was not an institution man. His last paper, given a few months before his death, the last paper before the San Francisco Society, which was presented in 1952 and published in 1962, testifies to that. He had given up his status as training analyst, as a protest, and against the wish of his collaborators. He was always a dedicated, serious, and well-disciplined scientist, as well as teacher, but he was not a disciplined institution man. Can one be a dedicated scientist, a searcher for the new, a teacher who makes students think, and still completely satisfy institutional requirements? He was deeply dedicated to education, to children and adolescents, and to young analysts. They were the recipients of his skill, his love, his warmth, and his critical endeavor to advance the cause of psychological truth. But although he had deep insight into the boundaries of human institutions and the human mind, he remained a Sisyphus all his life. He died in 1953, after a prolonged illness. He carried on his work to the last. He never withdrew to an analytic ivory tower. Psychoanalysis for him was interwoven with social responsibility.

One cannot attempt a biographical statement without discovering that one has also been tempted to be autobiographical. But the trouble with autobiography—following Bernfeld's *bon mot* concerning the difficulty of self-analysis—is the countertransference. Both transference and countertransference guide and limit the biographical task. One cannot help but see the traces of identification in it. As one follows the three phases in Bernfeld's life, one rediscovers also three phases in the development of psychoanalysis itself. Once more ontogeny reflects phylogeny. Early psychoanalytic science was at first a psychoanalytic movement. As it became critical and examined its theories, its concepts, its methodology, its therapeutic results, and began building bridges to the other behavioral sciences, it achieved a new stage of maturity. The upheaval of Europe brought it to America, where it found a new and settled home. But settling means institutionalization. Institutionalization has new dangers that can only be overcome if there are enough people like Bernfeld within the institutional setting to help maintain the spirit of objective inquiry, the spirit of scientific curiosity, the passionate, social spirit of the early psychoanalytic movement—people who may become like Bernfeld, in Schafer's phrase, "the loving and beloved superego of classical psychoanalysis."

BIBLIOGRAPHY

Bernfeld, S. *Kinderheim Baumgarten. Bericht über einen ernsthaften Versuch mit neuer Erziehung.* Berlin: Judischer Verlag, 1921.

Bernfeld, S. *Sisyphos oder die Grenzen der Erziehung.* Leipzig & Vienna: Internationaler Psychoanalytischer Verlag, 1928.

Bernfeld, S. Über Faszination. *Imago,* 1928, **14,** 76–87.

Bernfeld, S. *Psychologie des Säuglings.* Vienna: Springer, 1925. (English edition: *The psychology of the infant.* [Rosetta Hurwitz, Trans.] New York: Brentano, 1929.)

Bernfeld, S. Der Begriff der Deutung in der Psychoanalyse. *Z. agnew. Psychol.,* 1932, **42,** 448–497.

Bernfeld, S. Zur Revision der Bioanalyse. *Imago,* 1937, **23,** 197–236.

Bernfeld, S. Types of adolescence. *Psychoanal. Quart.,* 1938, **7,** 243–253.

Bernfeld, S. The facts of observation in psychoanalysis. *J. Psychol.,* 1941, **12,** 289–305.

Bernfeld, S. Freud's earliest theories and the school of Helmholtz. *Psychoanal. Quart.,* 1944, **13,** 341–362.

Bernfeld, S. An unknown autobiographical fragment by Freud. *Amer. Imago,* 1946, **4,** 3–19.

Bernfeld, S. Freud's scientific beginnings. *Amer. Imago,* 1949, **6,** 163–196.

Bernfeld, S. Sigmund Freud—1882–1885. *Int. J. Psycho-Anal.,* 1951, **32,** 1–14.

Bernfeld, S. Freud's studies on cocaine: 1884–1887. *J. Amer. Psychoanal. Ass.,* 1953, **1** (4), 581–613.

Bernfeld, S. On psychoanalytic training (1952). *Psychoanal. Quart.,* 1962, **31,** 453–482.

Bernfeld, S., & Suzanne Cassirer Bernfeld. Freud's early childhood. *Bull. Menninger Clinic,* 1944, **8,** 105–115.

Bernfeld, S., & Suzanne Cassirer Bernfeld. Freud's first year in practice: 1886–1887. *Bull. Menninger Clinic,* 1952, **16,** 37–49.

Bernfeld, S., & S. Feitelberg. Über psychische Energie, Libido und deren Messbarkeit. *Imago,* 1939, **16,** 66–118.

Bernfeld, Suzanne Cassirer. Freud and archeology. *Amer. Imago,* 1951, **8,** 107–128.

Wilhelm Reich

1897–1957

CHARACTER ANALYSIS

*

WALTER BRIEHL

Of the many psychoanalysts who have contributed to the theoretical and technical aspects of the science, Wilhelm Reich stands out because of his overwhelming preoccupation with the problems of technique.

Reich was born in 1897 in Austria, where his father was a farmer. He became interested in biology early in life and, prior to his military service during World War I, maintained plant and insect collections and his own breeding laboratory. In 1918, at the age of twenty-one, he matriculated at the University of Vienna School of Medicine where he was awarded the Doctor of Medicine degree "with distinction." His postgraduate work was carried on at the Vienna Neuropsychiatric Institute under Julius von Wagner-Jauregg and Paul Schilder. At the age of twenty-three, while still a medical student, he attained membership in the Vienna Psychoanalytic Society, a recognition that could only be bestowed on one who showed promise in this field. The position of older members in the society—Federn, Hitschmann, Nunberg, and others—had already been firmly established by virtue of maturity and talent. Nevertheless, Reich's driving energy (expended in analysis, teaching, lecturing, writing, and administration) advanced his prestige rapidly. Temperamental clashes between Reich and other members of the group and differences of opinion concerning some of his ideas and technical procedures at times required the dispassionate intercession of Dr. Federn for the re-establishment of objectivity and soberness.

A basis for Reich's work seems to have been laid by Ferenczi of

Budapest. Having been Freud's closest friend, Ferenczi was highly regarded in Vienna, even though his technique varied so sharply later in life from even the bold therapeutic innovations embodied in his "active therapy" that he and Freud parted psychoanalytic company. As Ferenczi had developed his active therapeutic procedures for use when and where a long trial of classical analysis is unable to penetrate ego structures, so Reich developed his theory and practice of character analysis after he discovered that all too frequently the therapeutic efforts of analysts had been thwarted, but because of countertransference this outcome had ended in a blind alley (*Sackgasse*) rationalized as the patient's resistance against getting well.

Reich was director of the Seminar for Psychoanalytic Therapy in Vienna from 1924 to 1930. This seminar was designed to work exclusively with case histories of stalemates and analytic failures; by its nature it proved a most stimulating and provocative undertaking. Contributions from this seminar and from his analyses furnished the material for his most important paper, "Über Charakteranalyse," 1928b, although before this publication numerous forerunners had appeared that had already created American interest in Reich as the representative of a more active psychoanalytic therapy in Vienna. Because of the inaccessibilityof Freud (whose time and energy were reserved for such older and established colleagues as Clarence Oberndorf, Abram Kardiner, George Amsden, Smiley Blanton, Monroe Meyer, and Ruth Mack Brunswick), analysands who wished to go abroad to the psychoanalytic mecca, Vienna, were advised by training analysts in New York and by Ferenczi (who was lecturing in New York during 1926–1927) to go to Reich for their personal analyses. Accordingly, a number of persons who became prominent were brought into close contact with the personality and theories of Reich.

One of Reich's early papers lays down several rather categorical standards for successful or unsuccessful treatment. One, perhaps of greatest validity at that time, is this: "If the genital period is not reached either by genital masturbation, or genital exhibitionism or genital incestuous wishes, such cases have a bad prognosis" (1924). Reich supplemented some of the hypotheses of this paper with some technical principles in a report given before the Eighth International Association Congress in Salzburg in 1924:

As a criterion of the genital or pregenital organization of adult patients, it is advisable to observe the specific form which onanism may assume in them. Here one must not hesitate to forbid absolutely every extra-genital form of onanism, but to encourage the genital form. And an analysis cannot be accounted complete until the patient has freed his genitality from the sense of guilt and withdrawn it from the incestuous object and also has finally risen above his prepregenital level of organization. The criteria of this change are to be found in the phantasies and dreams of the transference (1924, Vol. 5, pp. 398–399).

In 1926 Reich delivered a paper before the Vienna Seminar for Psychoanalytic Therapy that was the forerunner of his most distinguished work, *Character Analysis* (1945). This earlier presentation, which also appeared in the *Zeitschrift* (1927a), was titled "The Technique of Interpretation and of Resistance Analysis." It is strange that this excellent paper never has been translated into English, dealing as it does with one of the most significant aspects of analytic therapy, the transference neurosis in its repressed and disguised manifestations—particularly in its negative aspects. In this paper, Reich laid special emphasis on, in essence, "no interpretation of content without first interpreting the resistance to the process of free association." (During this period of psychoanalysis the term "resistance" was used, later giving way to the broader term, "defense.")

Many of the ideas of technique that Reich was formulating in the later twenties accrued not only from his own experience but from the suggestions of members of the therapy seminar. He may not have been the originator of such ideas, but it must be said that in Vienna he was the dynamic power behind their organization. Freud often expressed regret that the teaching of psychoanalysis precludes the presence of an observer, as is possible in hospital bedside teaching. To reduce this inadequacy to a minimum, Reich conducted his seminar with informality and spontaneity. He placed emphasis on two main themes: the study of individualized resistance problems and the study of the reasons for analytic failures, which up to this time had been considered due to individual inexperience or errors, rather than to limitations of technique.

From these studies Reich published several books: *Der Triebhafte Charakter*, in 1925, *Die Funktion des Orgasmus*, in 1927, and in 1933 his most important work, *Charakteranalyse*, which appeared in an English edition (1945). In later editions, so much material of a nonpsychoanalytic nature is interspersed and admixed that one reviewer has stated: "It is not the translation of the German book which Reich published in 1928 and which became a marking stone in psychoanalysis as a scientific technique, deeply influencing almost the entire generations of English psychoanalysts." An abstract or reading would only detract from the prestige that was Reich's during the period of his psychoanalytic accreditation, a prestige well-earned by his work.

Although Karl Abraham's *Psycho-Analytic Studies on Character Development* preceded Reich's papers on character analysis, Abraham's studies are primarily restricted to what might be called the phenomenological aspects of character formation, that is, character formation as an outgrowth and development of oral, anal, and genital ego types. Nevertheless, one of Abraham's papers deserves mention at this point. Here Abraham writes of encountering marked narcissistic resistance in some patients and not being able to proceed analytically until he had made known to them the nature of such narcissistic resistance at the very beginning of treatment (1919). In brief, Abraham's approach regards the character of narcissistic resistance as a transient one, whereas in Reich's approach such resistance is considered as a more or less chronic, structured ego function, the dissolution of which becomes the focal point of therapy.

Freud, as is known, modified his technique from that of direct interpretation of symptoms to that of analyzing and overcoming resistances and defenses. Reich would not have changed the term "resistance analysis" to that of "character analysis" had not particular circumstances made the latter term preferable to him. Of the various types of resistance encountered in practice, Reich noted a particular group to which he gave the name "character resistance." To quote:

> These acquire their specific imprint, not from their content, but from the patient's individual mode of behavior. . . . The form taken by the reactions of the ego—a form which in the face of similarity of experiential content differs according to the character—is just as much determined by infantile experiences as is the content of the symptoms and phantasies (1948, p. 131).

Although other psychoanalysts, Edward Glover and Franz Alexander foremost among them, have differentiated character and symptom neurosis as nosological entities, Reich was of the opinion that a neurotic character is invariably the underlying basis of a symptom neurosis, that is, that, rather than being separate and somewhat unrelated entities, they have a direct, causal relationship.

> The difference between character neuroses and symptom neuroses is simply that in the latter the neurotic character has produced symptoms as well—

that the neurotic symptoms are, so to speak, a concentrate of the neurotic character . . . the more deeply we penetrate into its [the symptom's] determinants, the further we get from the field of symptomatology proper and the more does the characterological substratum come to the fore (1948, p. 131).

Coming to the fore, this characterological substratum serves as a compact defense mechanism against therapeutic efforts, a phenomenon to which Reich gave the name "character armor."

How did Reich put his theories of character analysis into a system of technique? This problem involves the therapeutic viewpoint, that is, does the therapist interpret the id striving, or, without touching upon the id striving, does he preferably approach the aspect of resistance, which is more closely related to the conscious ego, the ego defense, the rejection? From the latter aspect of therapy, Reich postulated that every defense ultimately must end in a negative transference and the character, the armor of the ego likewise, revealed and uncovered.

The turning point necessary for a successful analysis is the emotional outburst or activated aggressiveness in the sense of a negative transference. Observing in a patient a major "character armor" trait, for example, affectlessness and indifference, Reich would continually belabor him with it—practically to the exclusion of all other interpretations. The patient would then have the choice of either discontinuing therapy or of mobilizing a reaction—aggression or hostility—against the repetitive therapeutic provocation aimed at his characterological armor. When such a situation has been brought about, the blocking of affect has been broken down, and the patient becomes analyzable. Whether the armor be of the nature of affectlessness or some mannerism of speech or motility, the technique remains the same.

Reich followed the publication of his work *Über Characteranalyse* in 1928 with another significant contribution, "The Genital and the Neurotic Character" (1929), devoted mainly to the psychoanalytic theory of character. This he defined as the typical mode of reaction of the ego toward the id and the outer world. "Character resistance" is not to be confused with Freud's "ego resistance," which is resistance with a specific content offered by the ego. Character resistance refers to the typical form of resistance adopted in defense and remains the same whether of id or superego origin. Thus there is a close relationship between repression of instinctual demands and character that, once formed, makes a great deal of repression needless, since the instinctual energies that float freely in ordinary repression are consumed by the character formation in rigid ego-syntonic reactions and behavior. Repressions that have resulted in well-established character traits are more difficult to eliminate than those at the basis of a symptom.

In this paper, Reich places much emphasis on sublimation and reaction formation. Reaction formation and reactive achievement are largely responsible for increased damming up of the libido.

Reich's third important contribution, *Character Formation and the Phobias of Childhood* (1930), is an attempt to develop further the theoretical aspects of the two above-mentioned papers. Reich's acceptable contributions to psychoanalytic literature came to an end shortly thereafter. In 1934, he officially resigned from membership in the psychoanalytic movement, and from that time on he became further and further removed from analytic associations.

What relationship and attitudes might have existed between Freud and Reich? What previous set of circumstances might have effected such a resignation? What was the dramatic last link in the association? In his biography of Freud, Jones wrote that Freud thought highly of Reich in early days, but, "Reich's political fanaticism has led to both personal and scientific estrangement" (1953–1957, Vol. 3, p. 191). Although Reich was considered an alarmist and a political fanatic, the fact remains that his conjecture on the course of events and the dangers of the Nazi regime, as elucidated in his book on Fascism, were realistic and correct—though too premature for current acceptance. However, when he blended his political ideology and psychoanalytic theory, he raised a storm of conflict. A paper in this vein was published in the *Zeitschrift* and, according to Freud, "culminated in the nonsensical statement that what we have called the death instinct is a product of the capitalistic system."

But perhaps other and subtle factors of a personal nature were operative. Reich was still esteemed for his work in the late twenties and early thirties, yet there was an aura of misgiving about his future. Perhaps Freud sensed the presence of an intrapsychic conflict, and, as a result, Reich's resignation met with no great opposition. Alienated from psychoanalysis, Reich also fell into disfavor with Marxist groups as he sought to introduce ideas of sexual reform and enlightenment to them.

Reich left Vienna in 1930 and worked in Berlin, Copenhagen, and, finally, Oslo, from whence he had to flee following the threat of the Nazi occupation of Norway. At these places, he won adherents who shared his thinking and activity and who, under the name *Sexpol,* issued a *Journal of Political Psychology and Sexual Economy*, as well as pamphlets on related themes. He also practiced a form of psychotherapy to which he gave the name "vegetotherapy," which he considered an extension of character analysis to its deepest repository of resistance, the autonomic system. Here, he believed, dammed-up libido and orgastic impotence cause the tensions and malfunctioning of psyche and soma alike. Related to this and with the aid of a well-equipped laboratory in Oslo, he carried on extensive experimentation that I shall not discuss in detail, but which can be pinpointed from a pamphlet title, *Electric Function of Sexuality and Anxiety* (1937). It is worthy of mention that, according to Reich's own judgment, he had never repudiated basic psychoanalytic principles. Rather, he believed that all he had accomplished—however unacceptable to analysts—was but of the nature of profoundest penetration into hitherto unknown areas.

In 1939, during the years of the Hitler nightmare in Europe, Reich came to the United States through the efforts of American colleagues who, with funds and affidavits, brought as many European analysts as possible to our shores, to spare them the concentration camp or to save their lives.

Shortly after his arrival here, friendly overtures were made to Reich, but he avoided them. He established himself on Long Island with the extensive laboratory equipment he had brought from Oslo and attracted about himself a group of friends and interested persons. At the first, I was a member of this group, but it was obvious that personality changes had occurred and that he was not the Reich of old, of the psychoanalytic therapy seminars in Vienna. Finally, he began to react with increasing irritability and projected hostility to helpful advice offered in various categories (for example, whether to avoid conflict, how to effect adjustment, or suggestions pertaining to medical licensure); with this state of affairs—offering no basis for personal or professional understanding—further association became impossible and our relationship was terminated.

Reich finally settled in Maine, where he obtained a large estate to carry on the experimentation on "biones" that he had begun in Oslo. He claimed that his discovery of biones had fundamentally advanced a theory concerning the origin of life, and that it was also related to the cancer problem. Going beyond his theory of biones, Reich claimed that he had discovered a method for gathering cosmic radiation that, with a device he used on patients, had therapeutic value. But these claims brought him into legal difficulty with the U.S. Food and Drug Administration. When Reich took the position that the Court had no jurisdiction to render opinions or judgment on truth and error in matters of natural science, he was held guilty of contempt of court. Subsequently, he was fined and given a two-year sentence, and by court order his devices and the printed matter pertaining thereto were destroyed. He had served several months of this sentence when, in 1957, death intervened. Reich left behind a sealed legacy to be opened fifty years after his death. Does this legacy contain the answer to the question: What ego identity did he seek that motivated him to change from one object relationship to another, to establish through his scientific experimentation a world of his own, only to destroy himself in the process?

Notwithstanding the opinion of practically all of Reich's colleagues that he had disassociated himself from acceptable psychoanalytic theory and practice, there is unanimity of opinion that his thinking and earlier works have earned a permanent place in the archives of psychoanalytic literature.

REFERENCES

Abraham, K. *Psychoanalytische Studien zür Charakterbildung.* Leipzig, Vienna, Zurich: International Psychiatric Verlag, 1925.

Abraham, K. *Selected papers on psychoanalysis.* A particular form of neurotic resistance against the psycho-analytic method (1919). In Ernest Jones (Ed.) (5th ed.) New York: Basic Books, 1960. Pp. 303–311.

Jones, E. *The life and work of Sigmund Freud.* Vol. 3. New York: Basic Books, 1953–57. P. 191.

Reich, W. Concerning genitality from the standpoint of psychoanalytic prognosis and therapy. *Int. Z. Psychoanal.,* 1924, 10, 164–179.

Reich, W. The technique of interpretation and of resistance analysis. *Int. Z. Psychoanal.,* 1927, 13, 142–159. (a)

Reich, W. Über Characteranalyse. *Int. Z. Psychoanal.,* 1928, 14, 180–196. (b) (English trans. On character analysis. In R. Fliess (Ed.), *Psychoanalytic Reader.* Vol. 1. New York: International Universities Press, 1948. P. 129.

Reich, W. Electric function of sexuality and anxiety. In *Experimentelle Ergenbisse über die elektrische Funktion von Sexualität und Angst.* (Results on the Electric Function of Sexuality and Anxiety.) Copenhagen: Sexpol-Verlag, 1937.

Reich, W. Character formation and the phobias of childhood. In R. Fliess (Ed.), *Psychoanalytic reader.* Vol. 1.

New York: International Universities Press, 1948. Pp. 170–182.

Reich, W. *Character analysis.* (Trans. Theodore P. Wolfe) (2nd ed.) New York: Orgone Institute Press, 1945.

Reich, W. The genital and the neurotic character. In R. Fliess (Ed.), *Psychoanalytic Reader*. Vol. 1. New York: International Universities Press, 1948. Pp. 148–169.

Otto Fenichel

1898–1946

THE ENCYCLOPEDIA OF PSYCHOANALYSIS

*

RALPH R. GREENSON

I met Otto Fenichel early in 1938, shortly after he had settled in Los Angeles, and I knew him until his untimely death in January of 1946. In that short span of less than eight years, I had the opportunity of knowing him as therapist, teacher, supervisor, and, for a brief period, as friend. He was by far the most important influence in my psychoanalytic life, and I consider myself most fortunate to have had so extraordinary an opportunity. It is true that my many-sided emotional involvement with him has limited my objectivity, but it has also afforded me many firsthand insights into the man and his work. Furthermore, the twenty-six years that have passed since we met have been for me twenty-six years of continuous work in psychoanalysis, so that I, who met him as a beginner in the field, now write from the vantage point of an old-timer, albeit a young old-timer. In any case, I hope that whatever my portrait of Otto Fenichel may lack in objectivity will be compensated for by the intimacy of my observations.

When I went to meet the renowned Otto Fenichel in 1938, I was prepared to meet the man who had accomplished that awesome feat of producing the first textbook of psychoanalysis written for psychoanalysts. The book, *The Outline of Clinical Psychoanalysis* (1934), was far beyond my modest understanding, but I was impressed by its vast scope, the close-knit, detailed reasoning, and the systematic clarity. Above all, I was struck by the high respect with which this book was held by all the analysts, the candidates, and even the antianalytic psychiatrists. I had expected that a man who could write such an erudite and disciplined work would be a remote and austere academician. To my surprise and delight, I found him disarmingly warm, attentive, and straightforward. I had come to discuss with him the possibility of becoming his patient (today it is fashionable to say "analysand for didactic analysis"), and he behaved as a therapist who was interested in me as a person, concerned with my problems, honest in his appraisal—all this without a single technical term and with no hint of that aloof air of superiority so often found in experts.

After a few sessions he openly pointed out to me where he had some misgivings and also where he saw some positive factors. He said simply that we might try to work together for a period of time and then we would have a better idea of the prospects. I must confess that I was disappointed. I had hoped that what I considered my flair for quick personal contact would have overridden his doubts, but I learned then of a basic Fenichel trait. He noticed the so-called "charm," he mentioned it, he even seemed to enjoy it; but it in no way obscured his judgment. He was incorruptible; what he enjoyed he also noted; therefore it never seduced his reason.

This was equally true when I was in the throes of hostile transference feelings. He would listen carefully and patiently to my outbursts and would usually encourage me to go on describing what I hated about him. He never seemed to be defensive or retaliative or anxious; he went on analyzing just as he would any other kind of material. I do not mean to give the impression that he was bland or wooden in his responses. There were marked changes in his emotional tone, but they were within the limits of his therapeutic working relationship to me. For example, I could hear his pleasure when we succeeded in unraveling something particularly obscure, or his tone of disappointment when he would say sadly at the end of an hour that he didn't understand what was going on.

Fenichel was certainly considered the epitome of a classical analyst, yet I remember a few occasions when he would laugh heartily at something funny and even tell a joke himself. I recall an hour in which I was in agony from a terrible sunburn and he interrupted the hour to get me some sunburn lotion from his bathroom. As one can imagine, this action of his stirred up many feelings and fantasies in me. At the end of the hour, after he interpreted what was interpretable, he said he felt he had made an error in getting the lotion from the bathroom and encouraged me to pursue this theme in the next session.

The first seminar of Fenichel's I attended was in 1939, a Freud's Literature Seminar, and the first paper was to be the famous "Three Essays on Sexuality." There were three candidates in training at that time, and we all read the entire work carefully, prepared for all eventualities, or so we thought. The session began at 8 P.M.; by 11 P.M., when we had to stop, we had not got beyond the second sentence of the first essay. The term "libido" occurs there, and we spent two and one-half hours amplifying our notions on what we thought the term meant, what it should have meant, what was wrong with it, right with it, and so on. Fenichel encouraged us all to express our views fully, trying to follow our reasoning and helping us to be clear and comprehensible. Eventually he would express his opinion about the different points of view we had expounded. He was quite outspoken about whether he thought an individual's ideas were right or wrong, helpful or confusing, outdated, and the like. In those years, the two other training analysts in our study group, as well as the four regular members, also attended Fenichel's seminars and entered the fray whole-heartedly. Fenichel criticized their remarks as freely as those of the candidates and sometimes pointed out, in no uncertain terms, that the older analysts' views were wrong, in his opinion, and the candidate was right. Those evenings were so stimulating that we would never go directly home at the close of the seminar. Usually, several of us continued the debate until well after midnight—on the sidewalk in front of Fenichel's house. The "Three Essays" seminar took a full academic year, but with Fenichel's remarkable fund of psychoanalytic knowledge at his fingertips, he brought into the discussion Freud's other works and the related contribution of countless others. By the time that seminar was over we were familiar with authors from Freud to Karl Abraham, Michael Balint, Berta Bornstein, Sándor Ferenczi, Edward Glover, Ruth Mack Brunswick, Hermann Nunberg, Sandor Rado, Wilhelm Reich, J. Sadger, Richard Sterba and others.

Since that time I have attended many seminars and have taught a great many myself. In so doing, one becomes aware of the broad scope and high caliber of Fenichel's writings. Outstanding are the two textbooks on psychoanalysis, *The Outline of Clinical Psychoanalysis*

(1934), and *The Psychoanalytic Theory of Neurosis* (1945), which actually started out as a revision and extension of the earlier work. Every analyst knows how hard it is to communicate his ideas to his fellow analysts in a concise and comprehensible form. If you try to write a short paper with a few theoretical formulations about a circumscribed clinical problem, it almost always becomes complicated because one clinical problem is so interwoven with another that isolating it seems to violate the material. Furthermore it is so difficult to give the "feel" of a case without going into myriads of details. Yet Fenichel managed to write a systematic, comprehensive, detailed study of every major form of neurosis from a psychoanalytic point of view, separating each clinical entity from the others and yet retaining the essential clinical genuineness of each variety. The theoretical formulations are painstakingly worked out along with old and new, accepted and controversial points of view. Freud's thinking is followed historically on each issue, along with the major contributions of Abraham, Ferenczi, and Ernest Jones. In addition, there is an encyclopedic bibliography containing more than 1600 bibliographic items, each noted in the appropriate place in the text.

This is not only evidence of an enormous fund of knowledge and a fabulously retentive memory; the clarity is a testimony to the rigorousness of Fenichel's thinking and the independence of his intellect. Fenichel was no worshiper of Freud or anyone else. He was a man of deep convictions based on great clinical experience and excellent theoretical thinking. He was essentially a Freudian psychoanalyst because he believed Freud's basic concepts to be correct and necessary for understanding man's behavior. He was a scientist dedicated to uncovering what he considered the closest approximation to the truth; as a consequence, he had no hesitation in strongly and openly criticizing Freud's theory of the death instinct, since he considered it to be in contradiction to the psychoanalytic concept of instinctual drives.

It is also of great importance that, along with being the clarifier of Freud and psychoanalysis, Fenichel was the catalyst who increased the value of the later and lesser contributions by connecting them with Freud. I cannot imagine a serious contemporary psychoanalyst venturing to write a psychoanalytic paper on any subject without referring to Fenichel's textbook. An extraordinary quality of that textbook is that it serves as a stimulus and provocation for new psychoanalytic ideas.

In addition to the two textbooks on psychoanalysis, Fenichel has written a short monograph on psychoanalytic technique (1939). In my biased opinion, apart from the Freud papers, it is the best description of problems of technique. True, it suffers from excessive condensation and is less clearly systematized than his textbooks, but it grapples successfully with the basic technical problems. Fenichel also published some sixty-one papers on special problems of psychoanalysis, touching every aspect of the field. The two volumes of his collected papers cover his writings between the years 1922 and 1946. Some of these contributions have become classics in their field; for example: "The Economic Function of Screen Memories," "On Isolation," "The Psychology of Transvestitism," "Respiratory Introjection," "On the Psychology of Boredom," "The Scoptophilic Instinct and Identification," "The Symbolic Equation Girl-Phallus," "The Drive to Amass Wealth," "The Counterphobic Attitude," "Psychoanalysis of Character," "The Ego and the Affects," "The Misapprehended Oracle," "Neurotic Acting Out," and "Elements of a Psychoanalytic Theory of Anti-Semitism." In addition, some of his book reviews are masterpieces, particularly his reviews of the works of Karen Horney and Erich Fromm. Here one watches a rigorous and knowledgeable mind dissect and separate the correct from the faulty, the new from the old, the progressive from the regressive elements.

At scientific meetings he also revealed the unique blend of man and scientist that was typical of Fenichel. First of all, he had an unusual way of listening: his face and gestures registered his emotional reactions throughout. Fenichel would be nodding his head happily in agreement, or shaking his head sadly or angrily in disagreement, with the speaker. Or his eyebrows would be raised in amazement or wrinkled in puzzlement. Then out would come his little vest-pocket notebook; with his spectacles raised above his eyes he would cock his head to one side and, with one eye open, scribble a few words on the tiny pad. This would happen several times during the course of a presentation, very briefly, so as not to interfere with his listening. When the paper was finished, Fenichel preferred to be the last discussant, giving the younger or more timid members a chance to express their views independently of his.

However, for those of us who were familiar with Fenichel's style of discussing a paper, everyone else's remarks were a mere prelude, a divertissement. In fact, sometimes the original presentation became the secondary feature of the evening. Fenichel omitted all the usual social amenities when he discussed a paper; he made no fluffy introductory remarks, nor did he try to start off with some harmless compliment as a means of softening or diluting his opinion of the material under discussion. He usually began by summarizing what the speaker had just said. It was remarkable how much detail he could recall with only an occasional one-eyed squint at his tiny notebook. He not only condensed the essentials of what the speaker had reported, he also clarified its meaning. Sometimes it was Fenichel's summary that would make an obscure and complicated paper understandable for the first time to the audience. (I have seen Anna Freud display the same gift at some of the meetings of the International.) After the summary, Fenichel would correct what he considered to be the errors and make suggestions for additions or deletions. All these remarks would be backed by precise references to the psychoanalytic literature on the subject. Sometimes he would indicate how a presentation might be changed to make it a worth-while contribution.

But Fenichel was not content with merely discussing the presentation; he also felt obliged, as a teacher of psychoanalysis, to comment on the remarks of the previous discussants, expressing opinions and explaining what he agreed with, what he felt was wrong, or what was valuable or obscure. His manner of speaking was simple, direct, and concise; there was no ornamentation and no attempt to consider convention or etiquette. He would be more restrained in his critical evaluation of a candidate's work, but never to the point of falsifying his opinion. He was outspoken about everyone's contributions, despite the heterogeneity of the audience—training analysts, members, candidates, people in analysis with others in the group. Fenichel was often thought tactless by those he criticized, and their number was legion. I recall an evening in which a paper of his was up for discussion and one of the supposedly more experienced members asked a few vague and innocuous questions—the kind of questions one asks just to show the audience that one is present. Fenichel was no man for small talk of any kind. He said to the disscussant, "If you had been paying attention you would not have to ask such questions, and if you have not been paying attention you shouldn't ask any questions at all." This remark was followed by a thunderous silence. The member in question did not return to a scientific meeting for several years.

Some psychoanalysts felt that Fenichel was opinionated and rigid in his criticisms. There was no doubt that he was a man of strong opinions who did not hesitate to explain and defend his position fiercely. But

Fenichel worked hard to arrive at a point of view, and he had a passion for clarity and systematization because he loved to teach and felt it was his duty. He attacked what he considered wrong or obscure or pretentious, and he did this with considerable emotion. However, I always felt that, since he attacked friend or foe alike, this was not a matter of personal animosity but his way of defending the young science of psychoanalysis. I have seen similar traits in some of the analysts he has analyzed; these may indicate unanalyzed transference identifications, but are perhaps good for the science of psychoanalysis.

Fenichel was so highly thought of as a teacher that in 1933, when he was thirty-five years old, he was asked to go to Norway to head the training school. He did the same in Prague in 1935, and he carried the load of the training program in Los Angeles from 1938 until his death at the age of forty-eight.

Since we had only three training analysts in our Los Angeles study group, I began to present a case to Fenichel for supervision as soon as my personal analysis was interrupted. He refused to charge for this service since I could ill afford it; besides, he enjoyed doing supervision, and we had few candidates. Incidentally, this was also the attitude of Ernst Simmel and Frances Deri, the other supervisors.

I must digress at this point to describe Fenichel's attitude about money and fees. When I began to work with him in 1938, he told me he had already filled up all his five-dollar hours and he would have to charge me eight dollars per hour unless I wanted to wait. I preferred not to wait and began at the higher fee for six days a week. As my analysis progressed, my estimation of my ability as a therapist decreased; so did my practice. I spent most of my day reading in the library; this increased my knowledge but not my bank account. Incidentally, in those days we candidates could boast of our debts; it was taken for granted that we were all broke. However, there came a time when I could no longer borrow money to pay for my analysis, and I had to inform Fenichel of this. His answer was that we would continue to work as long as the transference resistance due to the money problem seemed amenable to analysis. For more than a year and a half, I paid Fenichel whatever I could afford, which meant that I usually paid him less than half of each month's fee, and owed him the balance. I never detected any change whatever in his attitude toward me or toward the analysis. After a few months he announced that he had some good news for both of us: he could now afford to reduce the fee I was *not* paying him from eight dollars to five dollars an hour. In this way my debt would be smaller and he would have less money outstanding!

To return to Fenichel as a supervisor. It was a pleasure to report to him, since he so obviously enjoyed the work vicariously. He paid meticulous attention to all details and got to know my patient almost as if she had been his. Years later when he visited me he would amaze me by recalling some detail about my control case. Fenichel paid particular attention to the danger of my analyzing in his way, on the basis of an unresolved identification. He would say, "It's better to be an original Greenson than an imitation Fenichel."

I was also struck by his humility. Once, after I had described the patient's production in an hour and told him what had occurred to me and how I had intervened, he said that he admired my ability to use empathy and intuition. He usually had to use his intellect and memory to arrive at the most likely interpretation, and he felt my way of working was often better. Imagine a man of Fenichel's stature telling that to a young candidate! This was not said as idle praise but as a clinical fact. Yet he did not hesitate to point out the instances in which he felt I was wrong and he would have done something differently. Or he would say that I seemed to be lost or, sometimes, that we both seemed lost. Throughout our work together, in supervision Fenichel's democratic and scientific spirit was easily discernible. There was no false equality; he was clearly the expert and more experienced, but he deferred to my direct contact with the patient. He not only indicated my weak points but also made me aware of my strengths. He encouraged me to stand up for my point of view when the material was nebulous and would readily admit he had been in error when later material so indicated. The combination of diligence, eagerness, and enjoyment made an indelible impression on me. It seemed that each supervisory hour was another opportunity for exploring, learning, and teaching, and he relished it all.

I was also struck by Fenichel's humanitarian concern for the patient. I recall his reminding me several times of a clinic patient in Europe who continually dreamed of food because he was starving. He was wary of clever interpretations because he felt they usually benefited the analyst more than the patient. Although he was a great one for systematizing and theorizing, he insisted that the clinical material of the patient must have priority over all other considerations. His book, *Problems of Psychoanalytic Technique* (1939), was the result of a seminar he conducted in 1939 with the candidates and members of our Los Angeles study group on a questionnaire Edward Glover had distributed to the British psychoanalysts. Fenichel was constantly critical of answers given out of some mechanical or memorized system of technique rather than derived from the unique clinical material of the particular patient at a particular time.

I learned more and different things about Otto Fenichel on the few occasions he visited me and my family during my service in the Air Force in World War II. In 1943, he and his wife Hanna spent a few days with us in Yuma, Arizona. He was not only interested in learning everything he could about the practice of psychiatry on an Air Force Base, but he was equally fascinated by the methods of the training school for gunners and pilots. Here, too, I became aware of his love for nature and his curiosity and knowledge about the desert. This was our first intimate social visit, and I was struck by Fenichel's naturalness and imperturbability.

I said earlier that Fenichel could not make small talk; however, he could talk easily and well to little ones. He was delighted and at home with my six-year-old son and three-year-old daughter. His approach was fresh and open with them, and very soon they were involved in animated conversation. I shall never forget the sight of big, burly Otto Fenichel holding my little girl's hand as they walked to look at the beautiful setting sun in the desert. This was only a partial vacation for Fenichel since he was hard at work on his second textbook, *The Psychoanalytic Theory of Neurosis* (1945). For a part of every day, before it got too hot, he was driven to a tiny park and left with a card table loaded with pages of the manuscript held down by large rocks gathered nearby. Those rocks were still in his car when I drove with his wife Hanna after he had died. They had been kept as a memento of a joyous occasion.

Early in 1945, the Fenichels visited us in Denver, where I was chief of the Combat Fatigue Section of an Air Force Rehabilitation Hospital at Fort Logan, Colorado. We had a huge psychiatric training program in progress, teaching psychiatrists, general practitioners, social workers, and chaplains—all under the direction of the psychoanalyst, Colonel John Murray. There Fenichel had the opportunity to hear men with acute combat neuroses relive their traumatic experiences under Sodium Pentothal. The terror and anguish of the patients made a deep impression on Fenichel, who wondered how even we therapists could endure the emotional bombardment produced by the treatment. He was full of compassion for the soldiers and learned everything he could about our method of treatment and our methods of training. He attended some of our classes, and in one evening seminar he contributed a brilliant, short improvised paper on the dynamics of depression in combat soldiers. Fenichel had had little experience in the briefer psychotherapies, and he was fascinated by how much could be done for the acute war neurosis, and with personnel with little training. Enthusiastic about our program, he suggested that some day we write a book together on the war neuroses.

However, that book would have to wait because he had decided first to take a year of internship in order to become eligible to take the State Board and obtain an American M.D. degree. The idea seemed preposterous to me. Otto Fenichel, the famous psychoanalyst and teacher, was going to give up his practice and his teaching and spend a year as an intern. Not only did he seem too big a man for so small a job, too much of an expert for so menial a task; he was also almost forty-eight years old, big and heavy, and in no physical condition for night duty and emergency calls. But Fenichel was adamant. He felt that the fate of psychoanalysis in America was precarious. He had grave misgivings about attempts to dilute and confuse psychoanalysis with other forms of psychotherapy. In his opinion, his influence would be limited by the lack of an American medical degree; he might have difficulty in reaching the councils of the American Psychoanalytic Association, as well as psychiatrists in general. A man of courage and a fighter for those things he believed in, Fenichel would not spare himself in the defense of his great love, psychoanalysis.

I last saw Otto Fenichel when I was on leave and he was an intern at the Cedars of Lebanon Hospital in Los Angeles, in the winter of 1945. The first sight of big Otto Fenichel in that tight, ill-fitting, white uniform almost brought tears to my eyes. But he was quick to reassure me. With his usual enthusiasm he breathlessly told me that the work was interesting, he remembered much more medicine than he had imagined, he was excused from some of the strenuous chores, and he was permitted to do some work in the psychiatric clinic. He saw a few psychiatric patients once a week, and he was amazed at how one could help even when seeing a patient only once a week. He proudly showed me a few of the charts he had worked up on patients. They were something to behold. In typical Fenichel manner there was a carefully documented, detailed description of a patient's present complaints, physical examination, recent history, past history, all written with the same painstaking care he gave to a published paper. Above all, I was again impressed by his eagerness, his willingness to work, and his innocence. This was not the attitude of a cynical, disgruntled, middle-aged man, as one might have expected under the circumstances. No, he approached this task as he did everything else, wholeheartedly and in good faith. We were discussing some of his meticulous progress notes on a psychiatric case he was following when he was called away to see a medical emergency. That was the last time I saw him.

Otto Fenichel died suddenly on January 22, 1946, at the age of forty-eight, while he was still in his internship. His writings and his teachings are a lasting monument to his own creativity and to his extraordinary ability to assemble and systematize the ponderous volumes of psychoanalytic knowledge, bringing all of psychoanalysis into a cohesive and living body of scientific data. Those of us who knew the man will always remember him as one who worked hard, loved it, and was happy to share the fruits of his labor with his fellow man.

REFERENCES

Fenichel, O. *Outline of clinical psychoanalysis.* New York: Psychoanalytic Quarterly Press & W. W. Norton, 1934.

Fenichel, O. *Problems of psychoanalytic technique.* Albany, New York: Psychoanalytic Quarterly Press, 1939.

Fenichel, O. *The Psychoanalytic theory of neurosis.* New York: W. W. Norton, 1945.

Fenichel, O. *Collected papers of Otto Fenichel.* New York: W. W. Norton & Co., 1953, 1954. 2 vols.

Karen Horney

1885–1952

THE CULTURAL EMPHASIS

*

JOSEPH M. NATTERSON

The psychoanalytic career of Karen Horney spanned more than three decades. The first phase included her psychoanalytic work in Berlin, from 1919 to 1932; the second phase extended from her arrival in America in 1932 to 1941, when she resigned from the American Psychoanalytic Association. The final phase began in 1941, when she was the leading founder of the American Institute for Psychoanalysis, and ended with her death in 1952.

Horney's work of the final period has been repeatedly and exhaustively discussed in the literature. Her books became best-sellers, and her ideas were well known and widely discussed.

By contrast, the earlier phases of Horney's life and career are less well known. This report deals with Horney prior to 1941. Horney's earliest translated papers indicate her dissatisfaction with prevailing psychoanalytic theory and demonstrate her intense interest in cultural determinants of personality development. Thus the direction of her future thinking is strongly suggested in her early work, and her later concepts represent the logical continuation of these ideas.

Although several brief biographical sketches have been written, including Norman Kelman's memorial (1954), there is only sparse information about Horney's early life. Her daughter, in a gracious letter to me,[1] has written: "My mother's early personal life was difficult and complex. School and the theater were her early territories of pleasure

[1] Eckardt, M. Personal communication, 1964.

and passion. Always an intense student, she pursued her professional development with a remarkable sureness of aim. She knew early in her medical studies that she would study psychoanalysis. What influences led her to such an early decision, I do not know. Her work was her life. Her keen sense of the drama of human existence provided the material for her ever ongoing pursuit of a theoretical system for neurotic development."

Karen Horney was born September 16, 1885, in Hamburg, Germany, to Berndt and Clotilde (von Ronzelen) Danielsen. Herr Danielsen was a Norwegian sea captain, and his wife was of Dutch descent. Horney has told of sea voyages with her father, as a child. There are suggestions that her shipmaster father was a strict and authoritarian parent. For example, Franz Alexander[2] remembered her remark, "I can still recall the frightening gaze of my father's blue eyes." Alexander added that he learned nothing more of her childhood from Horney during the years of association with her.

While a medical student in 1909, at the age of 24, she married Oscar Horney, a Berlin attorney. The Horneys had three daughters. Later they were divorced. She received her M.D. from the University of Berlin in 1913, and she took further psychiatric training at Berlin-Lankwitz, from 1914 through 1918.

Horney was analyzed during the years of World War I by Karl Abraham and Hanns Sachs. In 1919, she began the private practice of psychoanalysis, and at about the same time she became a faculty member of the Berlin Psychoanalytic Institute.

Horney's first publication (1917) deals with psychoanalytic technique, reflecting her early concern with the technical problems of analytic therapy. In discussing this paper, F. Weiss (1954) and H. Kelman (1964) both indicate that it contains the beginnings of Horney's later concepts. Numerous articles appeared in the ensuing fifteen years. Most of them are discourses on problems of feminine psychology. In essence, she has challenged the view that penis envy is of basic importance in the psychological development of the girl: ". . . an assertion that one-half of the human race is discontented with the sex assigned to it and can overcome this discontent only in favorable circumstances—is decidedly unsatisfying, not only to feminine narcissism but also to biological science." She acknowledges that penis envy exists in little girls as a normal phenomenon but holds that it becomes significant in neu-

[2] Alexander, F. Personal communication, 1964.

rotics only because, "as an actual fact," little girls are unfairly treated and are not permitted the same degree of gratification of pregenital instinct components as are little boys. This actual frustration then causes a heightened evaluation of the penis and is the first root of the feminine castration complex. She contends that rape fantasies and hypochondriacal trends in women are based less on penis envy than on the feeling of being "geschlagen" (struck down) by the father; that is, there is a "basic fantasy of having suffered castration through the love-relation with the father." Horney regards this Oedipal fantasy as "the second root of the whole castration complex in women."

Horney contends that feminine psychology is not understood because of prevailing masculine bias in psychoanalysis, as in other fields. The most serious consequence is the tendency to overlook the importance of basic vaginal urges. She challenges the primacy accorded the concept that feminine sexuality arises from a wish to have a penis, which forces the woman first to want a baby as a penis substitute and then to want a man who will provide a baby. She marshals theoretical arguments and clinical data to support an alternative thesis: There are basic sensations and instinctual urges in the vagina of the female (analogous to phallic ones in the male) that provide the basic motive power for such feminine sexual longings as the wish for a baby and the wish for coitus and orgasm. She believes basic vaginal sensations and fantasies are often repressed because of guilt and fear originating in the Oedipal situation.

In another paper (1932a) Horney develops similar ideas to explain the widespread male dread of women. She challenges Freud's contention that it comes from the absence of a penis in women. Instead, she insists, it comes from a basic dread of the vagina, which is concealed behind the dread of the father, or, in unconscious terms, dread of the father's penis in the woman's vagina. The man's endeavor to find the penis in the woman is an attempt to deny the "sinister female genital." She questions Freud's thesis that in childhood the vagina remains undiscovered. Rather, the boy feels his penis is too small for his mother's vagina, and this initiates his inadequacy feelings and vaginal dread. This later intensifies his phallic narcissism and he represses his prior knowledge of the vagina. Man's craving for love is exceeded by the need to prove masculinity, to conquer and debase women. So they marry infantile, nonmaternal, and hysterical women, thereby making a cultural reality of the myth of man's superiority to women and defending themselves against the inadequacy feelings related to the vagina.

Horney participated in the well-known panel discussion of lay analysis (1927). First, she acknowledges that qualified lay persons should be trained in psychoanalysis when it is necessary for their scientific purposes. The basic question is whether philosophical or medical training is the better preparation for psychoanalysts. She asserts unqualifiedly that medical training is her choice. This opinion is based on the general attitude engendered by medicine's emphasis on the study of the living, suffering person. A medical training is essential in the attendant development of special observational skills, a feeling of responsibility to sick people, and the will to heal. She implies that the will to heal has been, unfortunately, ". . . relegated to a humble position" by analysts. Medical knowledge aids the analyst in sensing the presence of organic illness, and psychiatric training is necessary for obvious reasons. Finally, she suggests that if in the future analysis develops in the direction of merging with organic fields, medical training will be important for the analyst.

In an impressive paper (1928) on monogamous marriage, Horney indicates how such marriage is inescapably based on unconscious Oedipal needs. Consequently, the love is always accompanied by rage. Additionally, unconscious conflicts from all sources become involved in marriage. Hence marriage is always difficult. Since the unconscious drive is so great, Horney sees no alternative to monogamous marriage as a way of dealing with universal needs. Analysis can be helpful in dealing with the unconscious conflicts and can prevent dissolution of marriage.

Franz Alexander knew Horney well in Berlin. He was deeply impressed by the outstanding clarity of her thought and by her characteristic way of always beginning her theoretical approach from her clinical observations. She was, he has said, one of the most independent, skeptical, and questioning thinkers in the Berlin group, yet she was at the same time a "full-fledged Freudian." In 1932, Alexander needed a senior analyst as associate director of the Chicago Institute for Psychoanalysis. He made a transatlantic call to Horney in Berlin, and she accepted. However, the association was neither productive nor congenial, and in 1934 Horney went to New York to continue her work. Alexander found three major contributions in Horney's work: (1) her emphasis that general needs lead to the importance of the erogenous zones, rather than the reverse; (2) that ego development does not stop at the sixth year of age; and (3) her emphasis on the present situation.

In New York, Horney continued as a training analyst and writer. Her concern with cultural forces is indicated by her having become a lecturer at the New School for Social Research, in 1935.

Horney's writings continued to show changes consonant with the basic trends in her theoretical development. For example, in that same year she focused on feminine masochism (1935), disputing the view that it is the inevitable consequence of the anatomical-psychic characteristics of the woman. Instead, feminine masochism ". . . must be considered as importantly conditioned by the culture-complex or social organization in which the particular masochistic woman has developed." She has obviously moved further away from libido theory, as is evident in her sparse use of classical analytic terms. Also, she tentatively denies the universality of the Oedipus complex, saying, ". . . ethnological studies have shown it probable that the peculiar configuration denoted by the term Oedipus complex, is nonexistent under widely different cultural conditions."

Papers such as this one were important in preparing the way for Horney's later works. They must also have helped set the stage for the bitterness that attended her later departure from the American Psychoanalytic Association. A comparison of two book reviews demonstrates how marked the change in Horney's position had become. In the first, Horney (1932b) reviews a new book by Rank. The book, she says, is a retrogressive attempt to return to pre-Freudian concepts about the development and education of children; furthermore, ". . . nowhere in the book can one find any solid basis for, or clearly conceived formulations of, the author's contentions." The second review, by Ernest Jones (1940), deals with Horney's first book, which was published in 1937. Jones is severely critical. Stating that basically she depreciates infantile sexuality, he then quotes from the book: "A great part of what appears as sexuality has in reality very little to do with it, but is an expression of the desire for reassurance. If this is not taken into consideration, one is bound to overestimate the role of sexuality." In language rarely used in public discussion of another analyst, Jones describes the above quotation as a "dangerous half-truth."

In the succeeding years, Horney's stand became increasingly explicit, and the conflict of her ideas with the dominant views in the New York

Psychoanalytic Institute became increasingly sharp. The breaking point was reached in 1941, when the New York Psychoanalytic Institute disqualified Horney as a training analyst and an instructor. According to *Current Biography* (1941, pp. 409–410), no official reason was offered and it was estimated that almost 50 per cent of the members present refrained from voting. Horney then resigned and, with a group of colleagues, sent an explanatory letter (Ephron, 1941) to all members of the American Psychoanalytic Association. The events of following years are well known and have been chronicled elsewhere.

Karen Horney's psychoanalytic career germinated in a classical milieu, in which she throve during her early years. This training may have been an important catalyst for her later development. By the early 1920's, she was questioning the etiological primacy of instinctual forces. This questioning evolved into definite repudiation in slightly more than a decade. Had Horney been less strong, independent, and expressive, the outcome might have been different. As it was, however, her convictions about the human situation, and particularly the condition of women, as functions of culture required the most definite assertion; as a creative, self-confident person, she was well prepared for the consequences.

"There seems little doubt that Horney retained a strong devotion to Freud's procedure of a thoroughgoing investigation of psychic conflict and did not sacrifice conscientious work with patients to rapid or superficial methods." These words are part of C. P. Oberndorf's final tribute (1953) to Karen Horney shortly after her death of cancer of the lung in 1952.

REFERENCES

Ephron, H. S., Karen Horney, Sarah Kelman, B. Robbins, & Clara Thompson. Letter from resigning members of American Psychoanalytic Association. *Am. J. Psychoanal.*, 1941, **1**, 9–10.

Horney, Karen. Die Technik der psychoanalytischen Therapie. *Z. Sexualwiss.*, 1917, **4**.

Horney, Karen. Discussion on lay analysis (panel). *Int. J. Psycho-Anal.*, 1927, **8**, 255–259.

Horney, Karen. The problem of the monogamous ideal. *Int. J. Psycho-Anal.*, 1928, **9**, 318–331.

Horney, Karen. The dread of woman. *Int. J. Psycho-Anal.*, 1932, **13**, 348–360. (a)

Horney, Karen. Review of Otto Rank's

Modern education: a critique of its fundamental ideas. Psychoanal. Quart., 1932, **1**, 349–350. (b)

Horney, Karen. The problem of feminine masochism. *Psychoanal. Rev.*, 1935, **22**, 241–257.

Current biography 1941. New York: H. W. Wilson Co., 1941.

Jones, E. Review of Karen Horney's *Neurotic personality of our time. Int. J. Psycho-Anal.*, 1940, **21**, 240–241.

Kelman, H. (Ed.) *Advances in psychoanalysis*. New York: W. W. Norton & Co., 1964.

Kelman, H. In memoriam, Karen Horney, M.D. *Amer. J. Psychoanal.*, 1954, **14** (1), 5–7.

Oberndorf, C. P. Obituary of Karen Horney. *Int. J. Psycho-Anal.*, 1953, **34**.

Weiss, F. A. Karen Horney—her early papers. *Amer. J. Psychoanal.*, 1954, **14**.

BIBLIOGRAPHY

Horney, Karen. On the genesis of the castration complex in women. *Int. J. Psycho-Anal.*, 1924, **5**, 50–65.

Horney, Karen. The flight from womanhood: the masculinity complex in women, as viewed by men and by women. *Int. J. Psycho-Anal.*, 1926, **7**, 324–339.

Horney, Karen. The denial of the vagina. *Int. J. Psycho-Anal.*, 1933, **14**, 57–70.

Webster's biographical dictionary. Springfield, Mass.: G & C Merriam Co., 1962.

Who's who in America, 1950–1951. Vol. 26. Chicago: A. N. Marquis Co., 1950.

Doctors Franz Alexander, Martin Grotjahn, and Harold Kelman have given helpful suggestions for this paper—J. M. N.

Paul Ferdinand Schilder

1886–1940

PSYCHOANALYSIS AND PSYCHIATRY

*

ISIDORE ZIFERSTEIN

When Schilder came to the United States at the age of forty-two, he was already an acknowledged leader in European psychiatry. He had achieved international recognition as a neurologist, by his description, when he was twenty-seven, of encephalitis periaxialis diffusa (Schilder's disease). His researches in philosophy had led to publication of a comprehensive discussion of his philosophical convictions in the book *Gedanken zur Naturphilosophie*. His pioneering efforts at a psychoanalytic interpretation of the symptomatology of organic disorders, such as general paresis and Korsakoff's syndrome, and of psychoses, such as schizophrenia and manic-depressive psychosis, were published in *Entwurf zu einer Psychiatrie auf Psychoanalytischer Grundlage* (Plan for a Psychiatry on a Psychoanalytic Basis). His explorations of the common frontiers of neurology, psychiatry, and psychology had been published in *Medizinische Psychologie*, a book that David Rapaport, in his foreword to the English edition, declared "represents the sweep of the most catholic thinker in the history of psychiatry." This European psychiatrist then became Americanized. In the United States, Schilder gained a deeper appreciation of the social problems of psychiatry, finding that American psychiatry was in closer contact with social realities than was European psychiatry.

Paul Ferdinand Schilder was born in Vienna on February 15, 1886. Although he later wrote that he had few recollections of his father, a silk merchant who died when Paul was three or four years old, "his early memories point to some sort of rebellion." In his vita, written in the third person, Schilder said of himself that "he has never bowed to authority willingly."

His mother, Bertha Fuerth Schilder, gave him a feeling of security and self-confidence, "which never left him, even in the most difficult circumstances." Paul Schilder had one brother, but apparently his mother favored Paul.

"To be in closer relation to human beings" was a desire that prompted the choice of medicine for his life's work. Also, the counsel and guidance of his mother directed him toward medicine, and the combination of this interest with a continuing involvement in philosophical problems brought him to psychiatry, through which "he felt he might help approach the fundamentals of human life." In his student days, he occasionally attended Freud's lectures, but was later to write of this period that he had been "refractory" to Freud's ideas.

In 1909, the year of his graduation from the University of Vienna, four of the twenty-three-year-old Schilder's papers were published, all on neuropathological subjects. As he engaged in deeper psychological study, Schilder found himself concerned with expanding the horizons from which a problem is approached while, at the same time, moving closer to Freud's ideas. In 1914, his study of symbolism in schizophrenia added to his belief in the validity of some of Freud's formulations.

Schilder combined Carl Wernicke's concept of the somatopsyche, Sir Henry Head's postural model of the body, and Freud's idea that the ego is primarily a body ego, to arrive at his own formulation of the fundamental role of the body image in man's relation to himself, to his fellow human beings, and to the world around him. Over the years, Schilder wrote a number of papers developing these formulations, culminating in his book *The Image and Appearance of the Human Body*, published in 1935, which he esteemed highest among his later works.

Along with his increasing interest in psychological problems, and particularly psychoanalysis, Schilder maintained his deep interest in neuropathology, and in 1913 he published his classic description of encephalitis periaxialis diffusa. This interweaving of interest in the organic and in the psychological was to characterize Schilder's work for the rest of his life.

Schilder's researches were interrupted by the outbreak of World War I. He volunteered for military service and spent the war years of 1914 to 1918 serving at the front or at base hospitals. As there were no opportunities for psychological or neuropathological investigation, Schilder's insatiable appetite for intensive intellectual effort took the form of intensive study of philosophy, sometimes under heavy gunfire, culminating in his receiving the degree of Doctor of Philosophy *in absentia* from the University of Vienna. This period of study was of decisive significance in the further development of Schilder's scientific life. In his prewar publication *Selbstbewusstsein und Persönlichkeitsbewusstsein*, Schilder had applied the principles of Edmund Husserl's phenomenology to the psychiatric problem of depersonalization. His wartime philosophical studies deepened his conviction of the need to apply the philosophy of Husserl to the study of the human psyche.

At the end of the war, Schilder returned to Vienna as a member of the staff and faculty of the Clinic of the University of Vienna, where he worked until 1929 under the directorship of Julius von Wagner-Jauregg. During this same period, Schilder came into closer contact with Freud, who invited him to become a member of the Vienna Psychoanalytic Society, although he had not been analyzed and had had no formal psychoanalytic training. In March 1920, he delivered his first paper, "Identification" before the Vienna Psychoanalytic Society.

Later, Heinz Hartmann was to write that Schilder did more for the propagation of analytic findings among European psychiatrists than any other psychoanalyst, apart from Freud himself.

Always a prolific writer, during his years at the university clinic Schilder published his contributions on the psychological and psychogenic aspects of general paresis, Korsakoff's syndrome, epilepsy, encephalitis, and various lesions of the cerebral cortex, as well as agnosia and agraphia. This work led to his formulation of the "principle of the double path," which holds that any behavioral phenomenon may result from either a physiological or a psychological process. Thus, a parapraxis may occur as a result of psychodynamics that can be elicited psychoanalytically, or the same type of parapraxis may come about as a result of fatigue or brain injury, which may be observed more readily by physiological methods.

Schilder never allowed his continuing, deepening interest in psychoanalysis to interfere with his close inspection of the physiological bases of disorders. To his final years, Schilder was always the doctor, and he always believed in the need to carry out a thorough physical examination of his patients before beginning psychotherapy. In 1925, he wrote his *Entwurf zu einer Psychiatrie auf Psychoanalytischer Grundlage* (*Plan for a Psychiatry on a Psychoanalytic Basis*), in which he stated his views of the interrelationship of the organic and the psychogenic.

In 1928, Schilder accepted the invitation of Adolf Meyer to come to the United States to work and teach for three months at the Henry Phipps Psychiatric Clinic. The invitation was prompted by the desire to introduce into the Johns Hopkins environment a many-sided representative of the European tradition.

Maintaining the emphasis that had marked his work in Vienna, in 1931 Schilder published his lectures in *Brain and Personality*, a book designed to fill the gap between the organic and the functional.

Following his tenure as visiting lecturer at the Phipps Psychiatric Clinic, in 1930 Schilder was appointed Clinical Director of the Psychiatric Division of Bellevue Hospital, and Research Professor of Psychiatry at New York University College of Medicine. He continued to work in these capacities until his untimely death in 1940 as the result of an automobile accident.

Schilder is remembered by his students and co-workers as an outstanding teacher and clinician. He was able to give them his ideas without impairing their independent research. He could learn without being enslaved, and he could teach without enslaving. A true scholar, he is best remembered at the New York University College of Medicine for his great interest in the students and his stimulating effect on them.

Schilder's ability to put the patient completely at ease during interviews before large classes of students is recalled with awe by one pupil. In this setting, Schilder was able, for example, to question an inhibited Jewish woman of the lower middle class about the most intimate details of her life without encountering any resistance or producing any discomfort. As Heinz Hartmann has stated, the brilliant manner in which Schilder was able to converse in living contact with psychotic patients can hardly be described. Schilder often listened more attentively to schizophrenic patients than to healthy persons; he probably thought it more worth while.

These ten years of teaching and working also marked a continuation of Schilder's intensive investigative work, carried out in collaboration with various co-workers—especially with Lauretta Bender, M.D., whom he married in 1937. During his years in the United States, Schilder extended his researches into sociology, culture, and ideology. This led him to initiate psychotherapy in groups, and he was a pioneer in the field of psychoanalytically oriented group psychotherapy. In his last years, he became interested in research work on child psychology and psychopathology.

His wide and diverse interests found their natural resolution in psychoanalysis, which Schilder discovered early to be the science that could encompass his theories of man's relation to himself, his fellow human beings, and the world around him.

Schilder's prodigious scientific work did not hinder him from leading a full life aside from his academic career. He was keenly interested in classical and current literature, music, the theatre, and the arts, displaying a particular interest in Chinese art. He enjoyed attending and giving parties.

On December 7, 1940, Dr. Schilder had just left the Doctors' Hospital, where he had visited his wife and newborn daughter, when he was struck by an automobile and sustained serious injuries. He died several hours later, in the early hours of the morning, without recovering consciousness.

One often reads statements about the universality of Schilder's interests. A listing of the titles of Schilder's nearly 300 publications presents a broad range of seemingly unrelated topics. To cite a few examples: "The Psychology of Geometry," "Hypnotic Phenomena in Schizophrenics," "Psychoanalysis and Conditioned Reflexes," "The Illusion of the Oblique Intercept," "On Rotting," "Psychoanalysis and Economics," "A Specific Motility Psychosis in Negro Alcoholics," "Results and Problems of Group Psychotherapy in Severe Neurosis," "The Psychoanalysis of Space," "Language and the Constructive Energies of the Psyche," "The Image of the Body and Social Psychology," "Psychopathology of Time," "The Japanese Illusion and the Postural Model of the Body," "The Motive of Dismemberment," "The Schematic Body Image in the Elevator," "Yellow and Blue," "Psychoanalysis and Biology," "Psychoanalysis and Philosophy," "Notes on the Psychopathology of Pain in Neuroses and Psychoses," "The Body Image in Dreams."

This array of wide-ranging subjects gives an impression of scattering, of a diffusion of energy, of a lack of concentration, but this is not so. Almost from the beginning of his career as a psychiatrist, Schilder had in mind a well-defined goal that motivated and directed all his investigations and writings. This goal was set out in the foreword of his posthumously published *Goals and Desires of Man,* in which Schilder re-ferred to "the vast enterprise which tries to circle the psychological horizon." His goal was a synthesis of the various fields of knowledge about man's relationship to himself, to other human beings, and to the world around him.

Thus, when Schilder studied patients who had lost the capacity to localize their bodies in space because of lesions in the occipitoparietal area of the cortex, this investigation was directly related to his fundamental concept of the body image as a biological, psychological, and social phenomenon. Similarly, his studies of hypnotism, or the psychological effects of benzedrine, or children's ideas about death, all mesh into the over-all scheme of "circling the psychological horizon." This prodigious amount of work is all based on meticulously studied clinical, experimental, or histopathological material.

Schilder shows the profound influence of the phenomenological philosophy of Edmund Husserl (1859–1938), a philosophy that uses as its point of departure the total direct experience, taken naïvely and at face value. This approach runs as a continuous thread throughout the widespread field of Schilder's scientific interests and gives a sense of unity to what seems at first glance a bewilderingly diffuse and scattered array of disconnected ideas. The paradigm for this approach may be observed in Schilder's many studies of perception, wherein, for example, he carried out numerous experimental studies of visual perception in an attempt to learn the characteristics of the earliest, most primitive visual percepts. In these studies, he used such techniques as tachistoscopy, the study of afterimages, visual imagination, eidetic imagery, perceptions in states of intoxication, and perceptions in persons with brain injury. Schilder found that the earliest, most primitive optic percepts often consist of whole configurations, although these configurations may be quite vague. At other times, however, the primitive percept may consist of only a part of the perceived object. Thus, optic experience has two principles at hand: piecemeal construction and destruction, and organization in definite configurations that may mature from primitive to higher stages of development.

Schilder also observed that even in the earliest, most primitive optic experiences, optic perception cannot be isolated from perceptions by the other senses. Even the most primitive optic percept contains within itself elements of perceptions by the other senses, as well as contributions from motility and the vegetative system.

This led Schilder to conclude that it is incorrect to divide the human experience into such elements as sensations, perceptions, motility, memory, and learning. He felt that an artificial division of the human experience into separate elements for purposes of study serves to fragment knowledge and to distort reality. Therefore, his goal was to reunite these various elements of our knowledge of human experience into the whole, inasmuch as only this whole can make the human experience really intelligible. It was inevitable that, from the very beginning of his scientific career, Schilder would set himself the goal—perhaps we should say the impossible goal—of encompassing the whole horizon of man's knowledge about man. This goal constitutes the greatest strength and also the greatest weakness of Schilder's scientific work.

If we keep Schilder's goal in mind, it becomes clear why he stressed again and again that the contrast between organic and psychogenic has been overemphasized and that every condition of the human being must be approached simultaneously from psychological and somatic viewpoints—whether a matter of so-called psychic health or disease, or somatic health or disease. Schilder maintained that so-called functional cases may contain some organic changes that we cannot find with our present anatomical and physiological methods, and that so-called organic cases may not be as independent of psychic processes as they appear at first sight.

Schilder persistently pointed out that sensations are not primitive units out of which more complicated experiences are developed but, rather, are artificial abstractions. Every sensation has a motor aspect as a necessary part of the experience. Perception is not passive; it involves movement and activity on the part of the organism, in the sensory organ, in the nerve fibers that transmit the sensation, and in the brain center that registers the sensation. Perception also has a vegetative aspect, and therefore it is necessary to talk about a sensory-motor-vegetative unit. Even this formulation is incomplete, insofar as the sensory-motor-vegetative unit has meaning only in the specific total situation of which the personality is a part. Whatever we may experience as individuals, we live in actions; and action has its basis in the world we perceive.

Schilder conceived of motility as the intersensory element common to all senses. This motility is an expression of the fact that objects are not merely perceived passively by the individual but are subject to a continuous process of construction and reconstruction. This is a continuous process of reality testing, of trial and error, by which our perception of objects is constantly modified, corrected, and rebuilt. The individual takes parts of the object, assembles them, rejects other parts, molds, and remolds the object. This remolding, reconstructing, and rebuilding is based on a continuous interplay between sensory and motor functions.

Central among the objects and images that the human being constructs and reconstructs is his own body image, the picture of his own body that he forms in his mind, the way in which the body appears to himself. The body image is built up from a combination of visual, tactile, thermal, and pain impressions, as well as sensations from the vestibular apparatus, from the muscles, and from the viscera. It has very close and complex interrelationships with libidinous drives and also with the environmental, social experiences of the individual. In addition to all this is the immediate, direct experience of the individual of the unity of the body.

The first immediate experience of the body is incomplete and far from distinct. Even for this very primitive postural model, the contact with external reality is indispensable. Even the most primitive body image we can picture is one that has already been modified by experience. But experience is not accepted in a passive way; parts of it are taken, parts are rejected. The image of the body is constructed, and, as in every construction, there is continual testing to find out which parts fit the plan and fit the whole. The individual will try to get more and more impressions because he wants to achieve definite formations.

Knowledge about one's body is a dynamic rather than a static process. The static picture we have of our bodies is vague, indefinite, and unclear. If we wish to gain better control of, and additional knowledge concerning, our own bodies, we must build up our knowledge in differential processes that take place only when we are in touch with reality and receive changing impressions by vision, touch, movement.

For this construction and organization, present as well as past experiences are used, and the function of memory is to have material ready for new organization. Memory, learning, and experience are based on the fundamental psychological fact that past experiences do not disappear from our minds and can therefore be utilized for new organization.

Schilder's concepts of the construction of objects and of the body image are closely related to those of the *Gestalt* psychologist. However, he was critical of their static approach and pointed out that—unlike *Gestalt* psychology—psychoanalysis has not overlooked the fact that *Gestalten* are subject to developments that are determined by concrete experiences in life, and that memory and learning are basic for the possibility of organization.

The concept of the body image is a central one in Schilder's psychological theories. If the body image is impaired as, for example, by certain lesions in the parieto-occipital area or in certain states, such as depersonalization, a disorientation results in all of the individual's relations to himself, to other persons, and to the world around him. Social relations are formulated by Schilder as being essentially relations between body images.

Schilder described his own approach to the world as one of naïve realism, and he ascribed the same views to almost all modern psychologists, such as Freud, Jung, and Adler. He formulated this approach as follows. There is a world in which we live and which we perceive. Although this knowledge and perception of the world is incomplete and although we see only phases of the reality, there is no reason to believe that our approach to the world is unreliable. Schilder chided Freud and other analysts because he felt that in their writings the bona fide acknowledgment of reality is impaired by the tendency to put too great emphasis on the projection mechanism.

Schilder also took issue with Freud's basic assumption that desires tend to establish a state of rest. On the contrary, Schilder asserted, drives and desires go beyond mere satisfaction. They do not tend simply to bring the individual back to a state of rest; they thrust outward toward the world. Drives do not have regressive tendencies alone. A constructive effort toward the world is already present in the perception and the creation of objects. Schilder reiterated in many forms this positive constructive attitude of the individual toward the world. He stated that Freud's conception that the child is primarily interested in his body and has no genuine interest in the world has led to serious weakness in the structure of his psychology.

Accordingly, the psychoanalytic concept of primary narcissism as love merely given to one's own body needs revision. Individuals are not only interested in their own existence and self-preservation; they have a full interest in the outside world and its preservation. Forced by his own assumption of the regressive nature of drives, Freud characterized the death instinct as a tendency to one's own death, and overlooked not only one's primitive pleasure in his own existence but also one's pleasure in existence generally. Destructive tendencies exist; they are a necessity in every construction. Nevertheless, and contrary to Freud's belief, the existence of independent destructive tendencies must be denied. Activity and aggressiveness are primarily constructive and are an expression of an interest in the object. Schilder added further that there is no room for any specific death instinct.

Schilder's theories about thought processes are consistent with his theories about perception, "object construction," and the like. He believed that thoughts begin as vague "germs of thought" of which we are aware but which we are as yet unable to formulate and verbalize; these evolve through various stages, until they become logical, well-formulated ideas. He agreed with Freud that, in these early phases, thinking follows the laws of the primary process that characterize the system unconsciously, but he maintained that psychic experiences always have the quality of awareness, although this is a particular type of consciousness.

Experiences of the so-called unconscious type Schilder called experiences of the "sphere." The term "sphere" is borrowed from Carl Buehler, who first used it in connection with experiments on thinking. We are very often aware of thoughts before we can formulate them correctly. Although these germs of thought cannot be formulated in words and differ from fully developed thought, they are in the consciousness. The sphere is the living background of our well-formulated thought; it seems chaotic, but here thinking is created, directed by the energies of the instinctual drives. There are general schemes that thinking utilizes in order to come to new formulations and to bring all the new experiences again and again in relation to each other. These psychic operations, which test and try over and over again new combinations and their value for actions in the outside world, are in the background of the consciousness and are real psychic experiences with the specific qualities of awareness. Past experiences remain in the background of the consciousness. Not only do we know about them when we want to, they are always present. Personality is always a total personality that creates out of the wealth of its total experiences. The concept is different from Freud's approach only insofar as it attributes the quality of awareness to all psychic experiences.

This formulation is entirely consistent with Schilder's holistic approach and his tendency of avoiding statements about dichotomies and opposites. Fire, Schilder asserted, is not the opposite of water; the whole theory of opposites must be changed if one wishes to approach objects in their variety. Thinking in opposites is a primitive way of thinking; it implies that one accepts or rejects a thought or an object without having fully investigated that thought or object. Instead of thinking in opposites, Schilder's thinking is fluid and is in terms of a continuum of gradations. In this connection, David Rapaport writes:

> Schilder having recognized the fluid transition between the primary and secondary process, the multiple layering of synthetic and controlling energy distributions—which Hartmann, Kris, and Loewenstein described as the progressive neutralization or binding of drive cathexes—proceeded to create a conception of the thought process in keeping with the conception of autonomous means-layers or, as recent psychoanalytic ego psychology would put it, in keeping with the conception of autonomous ego apparatuses.

And Heinz Hartmann states, "In my opinion, Schilder's conception of the psychical apparatus is very close to ideas which have been developed in recent years in another field, in the psychoanalytic-psychology of the ego."

Schilder differed sharply with Freud on the question of sex differences, stating that there are no "primary" psychic sex differences outside of feminine and masculine actions in connection with sex anatomy, sex function, and sex behavior. Beyond these, observed differences between male and female psychology arise from social factors.

Schilder's writings are a treasure-trove of original, creative questions, hypotheses, formulations, and conclusions. Some of his pioneering hypotheses, which seemed unorthodox when first enunciated, may sound familiar and even trite to the present-day reader, because they have long since been accepted and incorporated into such various disciplines as psychoanalytic ego psychology, studies in the development of thought, the investigation of image-formation, and group psychotherapy. Others remain to be investigated further and developed, and could provide stimulation for a great deal of productive research.

An overview of Schilder's lifework leaves one amazed at the vast area that his knowledge and investigation encompassed, albeit with an unsatisfied feeling of incompleteness. One might conjecture that, if Schilder had lived out his full span of life, he might have achieved a more complete systematization of the array of data and hypotheses he amassed in a lifetime of restless searching, creative observation, experimentation, and hypothesizing. But it is more likely that he would not have done so, that instead he would have continued broadening the area of investigation. For hand in hand with Schilder's effort "to encompass the whole horizon of psychology" went his warning "not to systematize or crystallize prematurely." Perhaps this, too, is an expression of Schilder's conviction that the organism is constantly seeking closure in the psychological sphere, that is, the creation of *Gestalten* out of incomplete configurations, but that premature closure leads to stagnation, sterility, and neurosis. According to Schilder, the secret of life seems to be the constant seeking after but never quite achieving closure.

Heinz Hartmann

b. 1894

PSYCHOLOGY OF THE EGO

*

RUDOLPH M. LOEWENSTEIN

With the exception of Sigmund Freud, whose extraordinary intellectual vitality made him a pioneer until the end of his life, one may speak of two generations of pioneers in psychoanalysis. The end of World War I roughly divides the two groups. Despite a gradual change in attitude toward Freud's discoveries and ideas, in the third decade of this century psychoanalysis was still regarded with deep suspicion by the general public, by the medical profession, and by academic psychiatry and psychology. Since the first generation of analysts has been relatively few in number, various pioneering functions have been performed by many of the second generation. By virtue of his contributions to psychoanalytic theory, Heinz Hartmann has a particular claim to be considered an outstanding member of this second generation.

A brief sketch of Hartmann's family background may help place his personality, interests, and achievements in proper perspective. His paternal grandfather, Moritz Hartmann, a writer, had been active politically during the 1848 revolution in Germany. After the overthrow of the democratic provisional government, Moritz Hartmann fled to Geneva, where he settled, married, and became a citizen, Heinz Hartmann's father was a renowned historian and a leader in adult education for the working class. After World War I, he served for a time as the Austrian Republic's Ambassador to Germany. Heinz's mother, a highly gifted woman artistically, was a sculptress and an accomplished pianist.

Heinz's maternal grandfather, Dr. Chrobak, professor of gynecology at Vienna University, was described by Freud in 1914 as "perhaps the most eminent of all our Viennese physicians," in "On the History of the Psychoanalytic Movement."

Heinz Hartmann was born in Vienna in 1894. He obtained his medical degree in 1920 from the University of Vienna. During his undergraduate years, his first interest was pharmacology, but he soon decided to specialize in psychiatry. With the exception of one year at the Berlin Institute continuing the analytic training he had begun in Vienna, Hartmann worked at the Psychiatric and Neurologic Institute of Vienna University from 1920 until 1934. Following this period, he was teacher and training analyst, first at the Vienna Psychoanalytic Institute, and then at the Paris Psychoanalytic Institute. Since 1941, he has served in both capacities on the faculty of the New York Psychoanalytic Institute. He was editor of the *Internationale Zeitschrift für Psychoanalyse* from 1932 until 1941. Since its inception in 1945, he has been one of the managing editors of *The Psychoanalytic Study of the Child,* which he founded with Anna Freud and Ernst Kris. In 1948, he was appointed medical director of the Treatment Center of the New York Psychoanalytic Institute, a post he held until 1951. He was president of the New York Psychoanalytic Society from 1952 to 1954, president of the International Psycho-Analytical Association from 1951 to 1957, and has been honorary president of the International Psycho-Analytical Association since 1959.

Although Hartmann and I both became analysts during the 1920s, our paths did not cross until much later, when we met at some international congresses in the mid-thirties. I had followed most of his publications and had great respect for his work. When Hartmann moved to Paris after the Nazi occupation of Austria in 1938, our personal relations were very cordial. In the last summer before World War II, we spent time with our families at the same place on the shore of Brittany. The impending political events, as well as the fears and hopes we shared, brought us much closer together. Shortly afterward, I joined the French army. Hartmann moved to Switzerland and then, in 1941, to America. We renewed our friendship when I arrived in New York in 1942.

I have known Hartmann well for twenty-five years. He and I have had close intellectual interchanges during our many years of collaborative work with Ernst Kris and since Kris's death. Undoubtedly our professional and scientific association—our common interest in psychoanalysis—has been a major bond between us, but our personal friendship, too, has withstood the test of prolonged professional collaboration. No doubt some lack of objectivity is present in this profile, but this drawback may be counterbalanced by an intimate knowledge of the man portrayed.

Despite his friendliness and easy contact with a host of friends and acquaintanaces, I believe Hartmann is reserved and basically a lonely person. He has a fine sense of humor. Although generous and very understanding toward others, he rarely speaks about himself. His usual restraint and self-discipline cause him to maintain a perceptible distance from all but his very intimate friends. This may stem from shyness or pride, probably both. Hartmann's worldly manners and urbanity are qualified by a sharp dislike of banality and pompousness. His ease in communicating with people of diverse intellectual or artistic interests is based primarily on the exceptional breadth of his knowledge in various fields of science and art.

Hartmann studied medicine at a time when a gifted and intelligent student could devote part of his time to extracurricular interests; consequently, he also took nonmedical courses at the University of Vienna. Max Weber's lectures on sociology, for example, made a deep impression on him and influenced his later thinking. However, he did not confine his learning to his university years; he has never ceased to read and study—not in psychoanalysis alone, but in the multitudinous fields of his interest. Aided by an excellent memory, he has acquired an extraordinary fund of learning.

During the years of our scientific collaboration, I have been impressed by Hartmann's remarkable clinical acumen. Nevertheless, in his writings clinical data are usually neglected or only alluded to. This is in accord with his belief that clinical observations per se are of secondary significance, that they acquire primary importance only as a part of a conceptual framework or by illustrating a general theory. This approach rests on the rare ability to formulate general concepts without ever losing the implicit tie to observable data.

Hartmann's publications can be divided roughly into three groups. The first encompasses numerous clinical papers written between 1922 and 1935. The most noteworthy deal with the personality and character of identical twins, on the basis of psychoanalytic concepts. From the standpoint of methodology, Hartmann's papers have become models for subsequent psychiatric and psychoanalytic studies of twins.

An early important book, *Die Grundlagen der Psychoanalyse* (1927), systematically covers a wide range of problems of psychoanalytic theory and methodology. His general position was that of Freud, namely, that psychoanalysis is a natural science (*Naturwissenschaft*) with a scientific methodology adapted to its subject matter, the central problems of the human personality. Hartmann's special interest in comparing and confronting psychoanalytic concepts with those of other schools of psychology was already dominant in this work. Having limited himself to the discussion of German psychological thinking, he believed that the book did not lend itself to translation into other languages. This is regrettable, since his presentation of the psychoanalytic theory and method is remarkably coherent and penetrating. Moreover, his confrontation of psychoanalytic thought with that of other schools is as relevant today as it was in 1927.

Of particular importance is a chapter contrasting psychoanalysis with Karl Jaspers' *Verstehende Psychologie*, in which the approach to psychological phenomena centers exclusively on what can be emphatically understood.[1] In contrast, the psychoanalytic methodology is designed to uncover causal connections between psychological phenomena beyond the reach of empathic understanding; this was made possible by Freud's introduction of the method of free association and through the use of a conceptual framework having an explanatory character.

Two papers mark the beginning of a third phase in his writings. In "Psychoanalysis and the Concept of Health" (1939b), Hartmann avers that one must recognize the existence of a variety of forms of mental health in the same way that one can distinguish different orders of psychopathological formations. In addition, Hartmann aptly discriminates "adaptive processes" from the narrow and often misleading concept of "adjustment to reality."

"Ego Psychology and the Problem of Adaptation" (1939a), which appeared only in German at the time, is an expanded version of a paper he presented in 1927 before the Vienna Psychoanalytic Society. In some respects this essay represents an important departure from exist-

[1] This chapter has been published in English translation under the title "Understanding and Explanation" in *Essays on Ego Psychology* (1964).

ing psychoanalytic theories; it exerted such marked influence on the development of psychoanalysis that further discussion must be prefaced by a few remarks on the history of psychoanalytic ego psychology.

Excellent and exhaustive surveys of the subject have been published by Hartmann (1956b), Kris (1951), and Rapaport (1958). As is well known, Freud's early formulations concerning defense neuropsychoses were followed by a period in which the study of the ego was relatively neglected. His interest in the ego again became evident in "Group Psychology and the Analysis of the Ego," published in 1921, "The Ego and the Id," in 1923, and "Inhibitions, Symptoms and Anxiety," in 1926.

Although Freud's discovery of psychoanalysis was the work of a therapist and clinician, it was apparent from the first that he intended to go beyond the pathological, to use psychoanalysis to discover factors common to all human beings, sick or normal. His aim was to make psychoanalysis the basis of a general theory of personality. He could show, for example, that infant sexuality is not pathological but ubiquitous and normal. Even the psychological processes upon which neurotic symptom formation is based are not products of a disordered mind but identical with those found in dream formation. Likewise, the stages of libidinal development and of the typical conflicts arising therefrom, such as the Oedipal conflicts, proved ever present, even though discovered mostly in pathological manifestations. Freud found not only that neurotic symptoms are based on pathogenic conflicts, but also that conflicts are the essential core of the normal human personality.

He realized that intrinsic conflicts exist between the instinctual drives (the developmental characteristics of which he had described in detail) and the ego (which remained ill defined for a long time). In the main, Freud believed that the ego is formed out of the drives, or, using later terminology, that the ego is a modified cortical layer of the id, formed under the impact of external reality. However, he maintained that the forces involved in the intrapsychic conflict are not merely opposing forms of drives but represent the pitting of instinctual against noninstinctual (ego) forces.

The problem of the independence of ego processes versus drives implicates the role of external reality. To be sure, Freud always took external reality into consideration when referring to objects of drives and to conflicts centered around them, for example, conflicts of the Oedipal period. However, objects were described mainly in terms of drive arousal, gratification, and frustration. This obviously is too limited a concept of reality.

The close relationship of the ego functions with outside reality and their relative independence from instinctual drives were first adumbrated in Freud's study of phenomena of group psychology. This was followed by reformulations of his previous basic theoretical assumptions in "The Ego and the Id" and "Inhibitions, Symptoms and Anxiety," both decisive steps toward the understanding of ego functions.

Even for purely clinical and therapeutic purposes a precise conceptualization of ego functions had become necessary. Time and again, Freud had stressed the importance of analysis of the resistances during treatment, but the lack of clear formulations had left this part of the analyst's work haphazard and uncertain. In 1923, Freud described the unconscious nature of the ego's defensive forces, as well as the unconscious nature of moral demands and self-punitive tendencies (the superego). He thereby provided a valuable conceptual framework for clinical procedure. The subsequent work of such authors as Franz Alexander, Paul Federn, and Wilhelm Reich, is the outcome of this new approach.

Freud's reformulation of his anxiety theory in 1926 had far-reaching consequences. The unifying concept of anxiety as reaction to external or internal danger eliminated the artificial barrier between neurotic and realistic anxiety that had marked his former (toxic) theory of anxiety. He also formulated more precisely the methods used by the ego in dealing with various dangers, that is, the defensive mechanisms of the ego. From being merely a psychopathological theory of anxiety, this became an integral part of a general theory of mental functioning.

In "Inhibitions, Symptoms and Anxiety," Freud further established a sequence of situations that the ego perceives as dangers and to which it reacts with anxiety: fear of losing the object, fear of losing its love, castration anxiety, and superego anxiety. Here we note that, although the various situations to which the ego reacts appear in conflicts, the development of the ego, which accounts for its reaction with anxiety to particular situations, does not result from conflict. The chronological sequence of these danger situations in childhood is thus based largely on what Hartmann later called the "autonomous development of the ego." In "Analysis, Terminable and Interminable" of 1937, Freud stated explicitly that one must assume individual, inherited variations in the functioning and development of the ego.

Anna Freud's "The Ego and the Mechanisms of Defense," published in 1936, is an extremely fruitful and original development of Freud's ideas. With great precision and in great detail, she has described a variety of defense mechanisms directed against drives and affects as well as external dangers. The ego is conceived of as a relatively independent organization, in complex interaction with the external world and with the instinctual demands of the child and the adolescent. For example, she stresses that the parents are not only gratifying or frustrating objects, they are also helpers in the child's inner struggle against his instinctual demands.

It seems important to me to present Hartmann's theoretical contributions against the background of these preceding developments. He himself is profoundly versed in Freud's thought and, unlike some other analytic authors, has always been careful to place his new formulations and concepts in the over-all framework of psychoanalytic theory. His works since 1939 consistently reveal his aim to fulfill Freud's hope of creating a general psychoanalytic psychology. To achieve this end, psychoanalytic theories had to prove valid for both the normal and the pathological in mental life. Freud's theories of the instinctual drives had reached that stage; the theories of the ego and ego development had not. Moreover, at that time, concepts of the ego's functions were not yet designed to account for the individual's interactions with social and biological reality, as well as for the demands of defenses and drives.

In "Ego Psychology and the Problem of Adaptation" (1939a), Hartmann has laid the foundations for the solution of these problems. He notes that what distinguishes psychoanalytic investigation "is not its subject matter but the scientific methodology, and the structure of the concepts it uses," and that the "salient characteristics" of psychoanalysis are "its biological orientation, its genetic, dynamic, economic and topographic points of view, and the explanatory nature of its concepts." To realize its potential of becoming a general theory of personality and development, psychoanalysis must also encompass psychological phenomena that have been the subject matter of psychology but not, thus far, of psychoanalysis. According to Hartmann, psychoanalytic ego psychology differs from "surface psychologies" in the cohesive organization of its propositions.

Hartmann begins the study of ego functions by noting that, although the ego grows as a result of conflict, this is not the only root of its development. He distinguishes two groups of ego functions, those specifically involved in conflict and those that develop outside of conflict, such as perception, thinking, recall phenomena, language, object comprehension, motor development, walking, and learning processes. In the formation and unfolding of these functions, one must draw a distinction—as Freud did in the libidinal development—between maturation (autonomous growth) and development. Development results from environmental influences and consequently also from conflict. Hartmann introduces the concept of a " 'conflict-free ego sphere' for that ensemble of functions which at any given time exert their effects outside the region of mental conflicts."

Hartmann's essential idea is that these functions of the conflict-free sphere possess characteristics of ego functions from birth, or soon thereafter, that is, they are not the result of drive modification. Their independence from drives is also characterized by their autonomous development. (For these reasons, Hartmann later decided to call them "primary autonomous functions of the ego.") Moreover, since these functions—memory, thinking, and language—possess a "formedness," it is plausible to conceive of them as being based on specific "apparatuses" of the ego.

When referring either to development or to functions of the ego, the term "autonomous" implies the notion of independence from instinctual drives, as well as from outside reality. This independence is only relative, for one cannot think of an ego in isolation, without the stimulating influence of drives, superego, and external reality. In contradistinction to the instinctual drives, the autonomous functions of the ego have a particularly close relation to external reality. They are of foremost importance in the adaptation of the individual to his environment.

In accord with Freud, Hartmann conceived of this environment as follows: "In his prolonged helplessness the human child is dependent on the family, that is, on a social structure which fulfills here—as elsewhere—'biological' functions also. . . . The processes of adaptation are influenced both by constitution and external environment."

In describing the processes of adaptation in "Ego Psychology and the Problem of Adaptation," Hartmann has presented some new formulations of great significance. One is that "strictly speaking, the normal newborn human and his average expectable environment are adapted to each other from the very first moment." This formulation contains several propositions. First, it suggests that at birth man is adapted to an average "expectable" environment, that "a state of adaptedness exists before the intentional processes of adaptation begin." Second, it states that man's initial adaptedness and the subsequent adaptation processes imply an interrelationship with biological and social reality.

All these propositions and formulations deal explicitly and implicitly with problems of man's self-preservation and survival, namely, with the question of whether instinctual drives have a survival value, an adaptive function, for the individual. Freud came to the conclusion that man's self-preservative functions are to be ascribed to the ego.[2] Hartmann envisages these in the following way:

> No instinctual drive in man guarantees adaptation in and of itself, yet on the average the whole ensemble of instinctual drives, ego functions, ego apparatuses, and the principles of regulation, as they meet the average expectable environmental conditions, do have survival value. Of these elements, the function of the ego apparatuses . . . is "objectively" the most purposive (1939a).

In a later paper, "Comments on the Psychoanalytic Theory of Instinctual Drives" (1948), Hartmann emphasized the thesis that in animals, particularly in lower animals, instinct guarantees survival. In man —with his characteristic separation between instinctual drives, on the one hand, and ego functions, on the other—adaptedness, the processes of adaptation, and the functions of self-preservation are in the main prerogatives of the ego.

A thought that Hartmann had already expressed in the 1939 paper on the ego and adaptation is elaborated in "Comments on the Formation of Psychic Structure" (1946, pp. 11–38), which he wrote with Kris and myself.[3] As the ego does not develop out of the id, and since the newborn possesses apparatuses that are the roots of the autonomous ego functions, one must assume an undifferentiated early phase of development in which the subsequent ego functions and instinctual drives are not yet differentiated from each other. Or, to put it differently, the ego and the id differentiate gradually from a common matrix in the course of maturation and development. In "Comments on the Formation of Psychic Structure," an attempt is made at a more or less systematic

[2] However, man has preserved some survival functions of his animal ancestors in his id. As any other animal, man can survive only by destroying other living organisms. Man's aggressive drive unquestionably is part of the id (Loewenstein, 1940).

[3] Because the influence of Hartmann's original ideas on our collaborative writings was considerable, I feel justified in drawing from these papers as integral parts of Hartmann's work.

presentation of the development of psychic structure during the first few years of life. This development is viewed as the result of the complicated interaction between instinctual drives, ego defenses, and autonomous ego functions—as a gradual unfolding of the psychic structure under the impact of processes of differentiation and integration. The central problem of early object relations is envisaged mainly from the vantage point of ego development. With the understanding of the complexity of the mental apparatus and its organization, it has become obsolete to speak of the ego simply as an entity or even to equate the ego merely with its defenses.

In the 1939 discussion of adaptability and the process of adaptation, Hartmann had emphasized that one must consider not only earliest childhood but also man's ability to maintain his adaptation in later life. In the life of the individual, the ego's autonomous functions are not limited to those present in early infancy. During his socialization in childhood and his complex later adaptations to the exigencies of society, man forms various behavior patterns, character structures, ego apparatuses, and tendencies. Psychoanalytic investigation has shown, for instance, how character structure reflects unconscious drive derivatives and defenses against them. The connection between these unconscious factors and character structure, a genetic one, is observable only under conditions of partial regression: in pathological states, in dreams, or under the influence of the psychoanalytic process. Under normal conditions, such connections are not apparent.

These ego structures have secondarily become part of the conflict-free sphere by way of a "change of function":

> An attitude which arose originally in the service of defense against an instinctual drive may, in the course of time, become an independent structure, in which case the instinctual drive merely triggers this automatized apparatus . . . but, as long as the automatization is not controverted, does not determine the details of its action. Such an apparatus may, as a relatively independent structure, come to serve other functions (adaptation, synthesis, etc.); it may also—and this is genetically of even broader significance—through a change of function turn from a means into a goal in its own right (1939a).

Some secondary structures, such as motor apparatuses or the various aspects of the function of memory, are formed by means of automatization: "Exercise automatizes methods of problem-solving just as it does walking, speaking, or writing" (1939a).

At a later period, Hartmann has further developed his concept of autonomy (1950b, pp. 74–96; 1952, pp. 9–30). He distinguishes "primary autonomous ego functions," that is, those present at birth or soon after, from "secondary autonomous ego functions," which mature subsequently as a result of change of function. The best known examples of secondary autonomy are the various types of character. Psychoanalytic investigation permits us to trace the formation of certain character traits to conflicts between defense and drive, for example, between reaction formation and anal-sadistic drive derivatives. In normal cases, such character traits as punctiliousness and thriftiness have lost their functional dependence on their genetic instinctual antecedents, whereas in character neuroses such connections have never been completely lost, or have been regressively reactivated.

The stability of such a secondary autonomy can be measured by its "resistivity to regression."

> What started in a situation of conflict, may through . . . a "change of function" become secondarily part of the conflict-free sphere. . . . Many aims, attitudes, interests, structures of the ego, have originated in this way. . . . What developed as an outcome of defense against an instinctual drive may grow into a more or less structured function (1950b, pp. 74–96).

These considerations are extremely important for the understanding of defenses in pathological, as well as normal, development. Through a change of function, a mechanism built on an instinctual model and originally dealing with the outside world may be put into the service of ego defense; in turn, this mechanism may become a means of adaptation and a secondary autonomous function. It may thereby acquire new functions and new goals, and establish new motivations.

In our genetic considerations, the concept of change of function is essential, for example, to the understanding of superego formation (Hartmann and Loewenstein, 1962, pp. 42–81). Disregard of this concept leads to the genetic fallacy. Concerning the superego, the genetic fallacy would be to believe that any inner tendency opposing drive gratification in earlier childhood is due to the superego. There may indeed be some genetic connection between such an early inhibiting tendency and the later superego, but a clear distinction between the two is necessary.

Freud's grasp of psychic phenomena reached beyond the mere descriptive level to an appreciation of the underlying interplay of psychic forces. This dynamic approach is characteristic of psychonanalysis. Many psychologists, psychiatrists, and even psychoanalysts fail to follow Freud's further conclusions, despite their ready acceptance of the concept of psychic dynamics. The various peculiarities of psychic forces require a superordinated concept of psychic energy. The diverse manifestations of instinctual forces can be explained by assuming two distinct drive energies, libido and aggression. The energy of the ego forces is far more difficult to conceptualize; since the ego is regarded as a separate system, one must conceive of it as endowed with a psychic energy of its own. In 1923, Freud described this in terms of a desexualized, sublimated energy at the disposal of the ego.

Hartmann has used the term "neutralization" to describe sublimation with respect to the sexual drive (either libido or aggression) (Hartmann, 1948; Hartmann, Kris, Loewenstein, 1949, pp. 9–36). The neutralized energy thus put at the disposal of the ego may account for the secondary autonomy of some of its functions. For its primary autonomous functions, Hartmann has introduced the concept of a primary ego energy (1955, pp. 9–29). The theory of neutralization of drive energy has two aspects, the use of neutralized energy by the ego and the ability of the ego to neutralize drive energy. These explanatory concepts appear necessary to account for the ego's ability to guarantee its autonomy from the drives. This theory also accounts for the adaptational characteristics of some ego functions, that is, their relation to reality.

These considerations refer, in addition, to two types of psychic functioning that Freud described as "primary process" and "secondary process." Under the sway of the primary process are those psychic phenomena that are chiefly bent on immediate discharge of instinctual energy, on immediate need gratification. Secondary-process phenomena are those having energies that are bound, that is, their discharge is contingent on the exigencies of reality. This "bound" character is a further peculiarity of neutralized psychic energy (1955, pp. 9–29).

The whole concept of the ego as an "organ of adaptation" required further clarification of the concept of reality and even of the reality principle. Ferenczi had described two ways of adaptation, the alloplastic and the autoplastic: man either changing the outside reality to suit himself or changing himself to comply with demands of reality. Hartmann (1939a) then described a third form of adaptation (known from biology): man searching for an environment—for an outside reality—

that best suits his psychological potentials. He also distinguished two uses of the term "reality principle." One refers to a scientific concept, the other to the experience of what is real and what is not. In addition, he has insisted that at some stages of development the pleasure and reality principles do not always oppose each other—that what satisfies the reality principle can also be pleasurable (1956a, pp. 31–53).

Examining the problem of reality in the specific context of adaptedness and adaptation to a given social structure, he emphasized the fitting together of individual and society. If, on the one hand, man's psychic peculiarities enable him to comply with the social order, on the other hand there exists a "social compliance" with the individual, based on the fact that previous generations have molded society in a particular way (1947; 1950a).

Regarding the individual's relationship to the culture in which he lives, a distinction must be made between the "institutionalized" behavior of the individual, which is strongly influenced by the culture, and the part of the personality relatively independent of culture and in which the universal characteristics of human beings are more pronounced (1951).

Hartmann is well aware that the problem of reality, whether external or internal, cannot be understood without taking into account the reality of moral values as well. In *Psychoanalysis and Moral Values* (1960), he has clearly distinguished values, qua values, from psychological processes of valuation and their place in human behavior, convincingly confirming Freud's viewpoint that psychoanalysis as such does not claim to introduce any specific moral values. In this respect it does not differ from any other scientific endeavor. However, since psychoanalysis must recognize and investigate the powerful impact of conscious and unconscious moral forces on human behavior, in its practical, therapeutic application it cannot limit itself to the narrow view of "health ethics."

Nearly all of Hartmann's writings contain methodological considerations and refer to the position of psychoanalysis as a scientific theory. In addition, his views on these aspects of psychoanalysis are specifically set forth in his early volume, *Die Grundlagen der Psychoanalyse* (1927); in "The Genetic Approach in Psychoanalysis," written with Kris (1945, pp. 11–30); in "The Function of Theory in Psychoanalysis," written with Kris and Loewenstein (1953); and, most exhaustively, in "Psychoanalysis as a Scientific Theory" (1959).

Although Hartmann's contributions, as here presented, may seem limited to highly theoretical problems, their bearing on clinical and therapeutic matters is considerable. Hartmann has influenced these areas both directly and indirectly. His paper on schizophrenia (1953, pp. 177–198) has opened new vistas on the relationship between defects in the autonomous functions of the ego and the breakdown of defensive mechanisms so characteristic of psychotic processes. Indirectly, his concept of change of function has advanced our insight into the complexities of adaptive and defensive characteristics of psychopathological phenomena. The recent investigations of disturbances in object relations in borderline cases, for example, have been greatly enhanced by Hartmann's contributions to ego psychology. He has widened our understanding of the theory of psychoanalytic technique, particularly by clarifying the effects of psychoanalytic interpretations (1951).

An innovator in psychoanalytic theory, Hartmann has remained in the main stream of psychoanalysis. His work will continue to have profound influence on the development of psychoanalysis and, consequently, of general psychology.

REFERENCES

Hartmann, H. *Die Grundlagen der Psychoanalyse.* Leipzig: Thieme, 1927.

Hartmann, H. Zur Charakterologie erbgleicher Zwillinge. *Jb. Psychiat. Neurol.,* 1935, **52,** 57–120.

Hartmann, H. Ego psychology and the problem of adaptation. D. Rapaport, (Trans.) *Amer. Psychoanal. Ass. Monogr.,* 1939, No. 1. (a)

Hartmann, H. Psychoanalysis and the concept of health. *Int. J. Psycho-Anal.,* 1939, **20,** 308–321. (b)

Hartmann, H. On rational and irrational action. *Psychoanalysis and the Social Sciences,* 1947, **1,** 359–392.

Hartmann, H. Comments on the psychoanalytic theory of instinctual drives. *Psychoanal. Quart.,* 1948, **17,** 368–388.

Hartmann, H. The application of psychoanalytic concepts to social science. *Psychoanal. Quart.,* 1950, **19,** 385–392. (a)

Hartmann, H. Comments on the psychoanalytic theory of the ego. In *The Psychoanalytic Study of the Child,* Vol. 5. New York: International Universities Press, 1950. (b)

Hartmann, H. Technical implications of ego psychology. *Psychoanal. Quart.,* 1951, **20,** 31–43.

Hartmann, H. The mutual influences in the development of ego and id. In *The Psychoanalytic Study of the Child,* Vol. 7. New York: International Universities Press, 1952.

Hartmann, H. Contribution to the metapsychology of schizophrenia. In *The Psychoanalytic Study of the Child,* Vol. 8. New York: International Universities Press, 1953.

Hartmann, H. Notes on the theory of sublimation. In *The Psychoanalytic Study of the Child,* Vol. 10. New York: International Universities Press, 1955.

Hartmann, H. Notes on the reality principle. In *The Psychoanalytic Study of the Child*, Vol. 11. New York: International Universities Press, 1956. (a)

Hartmann, H. The development of the ego concept in Freud's work. *Int. J. Psycho-Anal.*, 1956, **37**, 425–438. (b)

Hartmann, H. Psychoanalysis as a scientific theory. In S. Hook (Ed.), *Psychoanalysis, scientific method, and philosophy*. New York: New York Univer. Press, 1959.

Hartmann, H. *Psychoanalysis and moral values.* New York: International Universities Press, 1960.

Hartmann, H. *Essays on ego psychology*. New York: International Universities Press, 1964.

Hartmann, H., & Kris, E. The genetic approach in psychoanalysis. In *The Psychoanalytic Study of the Child*, Vol. 1. New York: International Universities Press, 1945.

Hartmann, H., Kris, E., & Loewenstein, R. M. Comments on the formation of psychic structure. In *The Psychoanalytic Study of the Child*, Vol. 2. New York: International Universities Press, 1946.

Hartmann, H., Kris, E., & Loewenstein, R. M. Notes on the theory of aggression. In *The Psychoanalytic Study of the Child*, Vols. 3 & 4. New York: International Universities Press, 1949.

Hartmann, H., Kris, E., & Loewenstein, R. M. Comments on "Culture and personality." In G. B. Wilbur & W. Muensterberger (Eds.), *Psychoanalysis and culture*. New York: International Universities Press, 1951.

Hartmann, H., Kris, E., & Loewenstein, R. M. The function of theory in psychoanalysis. In R. M. Loewenstein (Ed.), *Drives, affects, behavior*. New York: International Universities Press, 1953.

Hartmann, H., & Loewenstein, R. M. Notes on the superego. In *The Psychoanalytic Study of the Child*, Vol. 17. New York: International Universities Press, 1962.

Kris, E. The development of ego psychology. *Samiksa*, 1951, **5**, 153–168.

Loewenstein, R. M. The vital and somatic instincts. *Int. J. Psycho-Anal.*, 1940, **21**, 377–400.

Rapaport, D. A historical survey of psychoanalytic ego psychology. *Bull. Phila. Ass. Psychoanal.*, 1958, 8, 105–120.

Ernst Kris

1900–1957

TWENTIETH-CENTURY *UOMO UNIVERSALE*

*

SAMUEL RITVO

AND

LUCILLE B. RITVO

> "For here was a man who came closer to the ideal of *uomo universale*, than is given to most in this age of specialization."
>
> —E. H. Gombrich

Ernst Kris's words on the occasion of the Freud centennial celebration apply equally to Kris himself.

> There was the drive to reach the fundamental and the general and there was the perseverance of an observer who had been trained early to focus on minute details and who later trained himself to the particular elasticity of a double purpose: he learned to follow in his clinical work the guidance of his theoretical thinking, and in his generalizations to follow the lead of his observations (Kris, 1956).

What Kris saw clearly about Freud had become his own characteristic way of working. The scholarly and intellectual gifts that manifested themselves early, fired by the indefatigable energy with which Ernst Kris always worked, made possible within a short lifetime the achievement of eminence in two careers, art history and psychoanalysis.

His early work in art history had trained his ability to focus on details and to reconstruct the past by historical methods that are essential also to psychoanalysis. His work in psychoanalysis started with a substantial period of years as a member of a group that had a close working relationship with Freud at a time when important new concepts in psychoanalytic ego psychology were being assimilated. In his writings and teaching, Kris not only made valuable contributions to the theory and knowledge of psychoanalysis, he also indicated untouched areas worthy of future study and research.

He had a unique awareness of the historical position of the youngest of the sciences that made him responsive to its institutional needs. At Freud's request, he gave up medical studies in 1933 to take over the editorship of *Imago*. During the war he conceived the idea of a psychoanalytic periodical devoted to child psychology that would help link the workers in the field, who had been dispersed by the war; in 1945, he became one of the founders and managing editors of *The Psychoanalytic Study of the Child*. In the years between his first coronary attack in 1950 and his death on February 27, 1957, Ernst Kris established and directed the Postgraduate Study Group of the New York Psychoanalytic Institute and two group research projects, the Longitudinal Study at the Yale University Child Study Center in New Haven and the Gifted Adolescent Research Project at the New York Psychoanalytic Institute. But "the least conspicuous of his activities," his devotion in his final years of most of his clinical work to training analyses, "may have been among the most important of his contributions to psychoanalysis" because of "the quality of those who benefited from his unique abilities as an analyst" (Loewenstein, 1957, p. 743).

§ The Life

Ernst Kris was born in Vienna on April 26, 1900. The family consisted of Leopold Kris, a lawyer, his wife Rosa, and their seven-year-old son Paul. The older brother, now a resident of Brazil, studied law. Ernst early exhibited an interest in art; this was stimulated and encouraged by an older cousin and her lawyer husband Paul Kurth, who were knowledgeable in art and art history.

At eight, his motor activities were severely restricted for more than a year because of juvenile rheumatism, which affected his heart and which his pediatrician told the family would be fatal.[1] By seventeen, with his typical intensity, he took advantage of unusual wartime circumstances (Gombrich, 1964)[2] to "gate-crash" the graduate seminars in art history at the University of Vienna. Kris's keen participation in the seminar discussions and his outstanding knowledge aroused the lasting interest of Julius von Schlosser, who later, after Kris had become a bona fide Ph.D. candidate, referred to him always as "mein Urschueler" (my arch- or original pupil).[3]

Schlosser, like his friend Benedetto Croce, "was suspicious of the relevance of psychology for aesthetics . . . but he had an extraordinary degree of empathy or what historians call a 'feel for the past' " (Gombrich, 1964), a quality he must have recognized and cultivated in the young Kris, who showed a keen historical sense throughout his life. Also among his first teachers at the university was Emanuel Loewy, the great classical archaeologist and friend of Sigmund Freud (Jones, 1955, Vol. 2, p. 384).[4]

However, it was not through Loewy that Kris met Freud, but through a young medical student, Marianne Rie,[5] whom he was courting and whom he married in 1927. Marianne's father, Oskar Rie, had been an assistant to Freud in an outpatient neurological clinic for children and had written a paper with Freud on "Infantile Cerebral Paralysis and Infantile Poliomyelitis" (Freud & Rie, 1891); he was the Freud family pediatrician and one of Freud's intimate group of Saturday night card players. It was while walking his friend Oskar Rie home

[1] Possibly related to these childhood restrictions on his own activity was the pilot study in 1951 or 1952, which Kris undertook with some of his associates at the Yale Child Study Center, on the psychological reactions of children with rheumatic heart disease to imposed motor restriction.

[2] Fuel shortages in 1917 forced his school to work in shifts; the war also reduced the number of students able to enroll in university classes.

[3] The authors are deeply indebted to Professor Gombrich of London and Dr. Marianne Kris of New York City for their generous help in providing unpublished information about Ernst Kris's early life.

[4] According to Gombrich,[3] "a man of great learning and many psychological interests, Loewy had written a classical paper on the 'Rendering of Nature in Greek Art' based on the psychological notions of ca. 1900 (when the paper came out) and was much interested, later in his life, in the links between magic and art, notably the origins of primitive ornaments in apotropaeic spells against the evil eye, etc."

[5] Marianne Kris, M.D., b. Vienna, 1900; University of Vienna Medical School, 1925; Faculty member, The New York Psychoanalytic Institute and the Western New England Psychoanalytic Institute; Research Consultant in Psychiatry, Yale University Child Study Center.

after a card game one windy Saturday night in 1921 or 1922 that Freud encountered the young couple, and the two men were introduced.

At twenty-two, Ernst Kris received his doctorate in art history[6] and was appointed assistant curator and junior keeper of the Department for Sculpture and Applied Art (*Plastik and Kunstgewerbe*) of the Vienna Kunsthistorisches Museum, one of the great treasure houses of Europe, filled with the collections of Hapsburg emperors and princes during half a millennium. The senior keeper, Leo Planiscig, was a leading expert on Italian bronzes of the Renaissance; Kris, therefore, concentrated on the remainder of the collection, cut glass, gems, intaglios, and goldsmith work. Familiarizing himself with the craftsmen and artists who designed these objects, Kris soon became the leading specialist in this rather neglected field and was in demand as a consultant by museums and private collectors on both sides of the Atlantic. When, in 1924, Freud sought help with his collection of cameos and intaglios, Marianne Rie was able to introduce her friend as the expert. Thus began a personal relationship between Ernst Kris and Sigmund Freud that lasted until Freud's death in 1939 (Jones, 1957, Vol. 3, pp. 207f.).[7]

That same year, the young couple announced their intention to marry. Freud pointed out that difficulties arise in marriages when the wife is an analyst and the husband is not, although they do not seem to be fostered when the reverse is true. Marianne Rie had determined on a career as a psychoanalyst and went to Berlin to be analyzed. Ernst Kris entered analysis in 1924, with Helene Deutsch. By 1927, the year in which he married, Kris was an associate member in the Vienna Institute of Psychoanalysis.

At that time, he thought of himself as a research worker in art history rather than as a future clinician and teacher of psychoanalysis.

He worked in archives and he wrote catalogues; on the whole his papers ranged from discussions of individual pieces of German sculpture of the Gothic period to matters concerning late Renaissance craftsmen. Two prin-

[6] Erroneously listed in the eighth edition of Jaques Cattell, *American Men of Science 1949*, and elsewhere as a Ph.D. in psychology.

[7] Jones records a letter from Freud, March 3, 1936, in which Freud mentions Kris with Anna and Martin Freud. With regard to Jones's inquiry about a report by Stefan Zweig that Freud was writing a work on religion, Freud replied, "I am not inclined to submit it to the easy criticism of opponents. . . . Only a few people, Anna, Martin, Kris, have read the thing." When Freud could not read himself, he liked to have his new writings read to him, which Ernst Kris did during his Sunday visits.

cipal books were the fruit of these researches, his standard work *Die Steinschneidekunst*,[8] on the art of cutting stone, dealing with Renaissance gems, intaglios, and also vessels made of precious or semiprecious stones, one of the favourite objects of princely luxury; the other is the *Catalogue of Goldsmithworks in the Vienna Museum* (Gombrich, 1964).

Shortly before the economic crash in 1929, the Metropolitan Museum of Art in New York obtained the services of Europe's leading expert on cameos and intaglios to catalogue their newly acquired Milton Weil Collection. The venerable European authority, Dr. Ernst Kris, whose incoming boat Milton Weil met, came down the gangplank, a vigorous young man still in his twenties. And in that same year Kris saw the publication of his two-volume *Meister und Meisterwerke der Steinschneidekunst in der Italienischen Renaissance*, which is still the standard work in the field.

From 1930 to 1938, Kris was both assistant curator at the Vienna Kunsthistorische Museum and a lecturer and instructor at the Psychoanalytic Institute of Vienna. In 1933, he studied medicine for six months. While showing certain busts by the Austrian sculptor Messerschmidt to his wife, Kris had been struck by her intuitive remark that the artist must have been psychotic. Checking into the biography, he found that Messerschmidt had indeed been psychotic. His 1933 paper on Messerschmidt, "A Psychotic Sculptor of the Eighteenth Century," was his first important analytic writing and the first of a series of papers in which he applied psychoanalysis to the study of the creative process. Kris wanted to study medicine and do hospital work in order to make his own observations directly on the broad spectrum of clinical psychopathology, including psychosis.

He sacrificed this ambition after one semester of medical courses, when Freud requested him to edit *Imago*. Unlike Freud, he always valued medical education very highly as one of the qualifications of a psychoanalyst. He connected medical studies with an ethical attitude and a deeply ingrained sense of clinical responsibility. To the end of his life, even when he had been made a lecturer at two medical schools[9] and an honorary member of two professional organizations requiring a medi-

[8] For a complete list of Kris's writings, see "The Writings of Ernst Kris" in *The Psychoanalytic Study of the Child* (1958, Vol. 13, pp. 562–573).

[9] Harvard Medical School, Hanns Sachs Lecturer in Psychoanalysis, 1948; Yale Medical School, Child Study Center, Lecturer 1949–51, Clinical Professor of Psychology 1951–53, Clinical Professor of Psychiatry, 1953–57.

cal degree and medical licensure,[10] Kris always counseled those who wished to become psychoanalysts to make every effort to attend medical school. He read deeply in biology, medicine, and physiology and thus acquired a knowledge of these subjects for himself. In 1933, however, when he decided to edit *Imago,* he was attending medical courses, analyzing patients, teaching at the Vienna Psychoanalytic Institute, and working on the Museum Collection.

> Ernst's greatest contribution to the collection was probably his rearrangement of the whole department which he did jointly with Planiscig in 1934–35. I was in close touch with him then, and often visited him in the collection and I know how incredibly hard and devotedly he worked and with what interest and passion he thought about the arrangement of every showcase to display everything to its best advantage. Planiscig and he had completely rejected the earlier arrangement according to media and techniques and had worked out an historical sequence centered on individual monarchs and collectors. The collection thus reflected the changing taste and changing ambient of the successive generations of patrons and also its own history. As you know Ernst did this immensely exacting work at a time when he was already active as an analyst and as an editor of *Imago.* It was a fabulous achievement. Yet he rarely seemed hurried; there were always long chats with Planiscig (who liked long chats) and also with me who was at that time his assistant for the work he planned on caricature. I used to come nearly every day after his supper and we worked together, fortified with black coffee, till late at night. He was no less intense in that work than in his two or three other full-time occupations (Gombrich, 1964).

In 1938, the Krises and their two children[11] followed Freud to England, where, until 1940, Kris was a lecturer and training analyst at the London Institute of Psychoanalysis. From 1939 to 1940, he was also a senior research officer for the British Broadcasting Corporation and organized a special British government department for the analysis of enemy broadcasts. In 1940, he was sent to Canada to start a similar analytic service there, and then to the United States to perform an analogous task.[12] Gifted in language and verbal facility and already fluent in

[10] The American Psychoanalytic Association in 1954, and the New York Psychoanalytic Institute and Society in 1943.

[11] Anna Wolff, M.D., b. Vienna, Nov. 18, 1931; Harvard Medical School, 1957, and Anton Kris, M.D., b. Vienna, July 26, 1934; Harvard Medical School, 1959.

[12] Gombrich reports: "One passage in a Roosevelt speech was due to his work—a pledge that U.S. transmitters would not tell different things to different peoples as the Nazi radio did. I also know of his failure to make Lord Halifax make a pre-arranged impromptu remark that appeasement never pays" (1964).

Italian and French, Kris perfected his English while with the British Broadcasting Corporation. He already had strong links with French culture through friendship with the French novelist Roger Martin du Gard and attendance at several of the meetings of leaders of thought at Pontigny. He had been given some (minor) grade of the Legion d'Honneur for his share in organizing a Daumier exhibition in Vienna.

In September 1940, the Kris family settled permanently in New York City and Kris became a visiting professor at the New School for Social Research, where in April 1941, he initiated and directed with Hans Speier the Research Project on Totalitarian Communication (Kris & Speier, 1944).[13] In 1943, he became a lecturer at the New York Psychoanalytic Institute and taught for a year at the College of the City of New York. In 1946, he became a naturalized citizen of the United States and resumed his visiting professorship at the College of the City of New York. He became a fellow of the American Orthopsychiatric Association and an associate of the American Psychological Association.

> I believe he continued sometimes to be consulted by the Metropolitan Museum, but on the whole he disliked being reminded of his art-historical past. When the Vienna Collection toured the States and *Life* had enormous photographs of the famous salt cellar by Cellini, he remarked how people would be surprised if they knew that it was he who had had these photographs taken in his time. But somehow he preferred their not knowing—he enjoyed having become a different person (Gombrich, 1964).

By the time he settled in America, the psychological aspect of Kris's career had become so important that even the *American Men of Science* lists his Ph.D. degree as in psychology rather than in art history.

But his early interests and experiences in art history continued to play a very important, if less conspicuous, role in his psychoanalytic pioneering. For his doctoral thesis in 1922, Kris had chosen " 'Der Stil "rustique" ' [1936], the current of late sixteenth-century art connected with the potter Palissy[14] and with the new interests in science, nature

[13] The authors report the rich findings of a fruitful collaboration with five graduate students.

[14] The Huguenot potter Palissy used casts taken over actual insects and animals. He concerned himself with the controversial problem of fossil formation, the solution of which eventually led to the discovery by another potter's grandson, Charles Darwin, of the theory of evolution, which strongly influenced Freud.

study and empiricism. . . . In his art-historical interests Kris remained for a long time wedded to the period between 1400 and 1600" (Gombrich, 1964).

When he encountered the young science of psychoanalysis, Kris was steeped in the early history of the natural sciences, which had by now become mature sciences and forgotten many of the gropings, brilliant insights, and efforts of their early pioneers. Thus Kris had a unique contribution to make to psychoanalysis. He applied his historical sense not only to the history of the individual but also to the actual science of psychoanalysis. Through his art studies, he had learned the way in which young sciences grow, by careful, painstaking observation coupled with brilliant insights and hypotheses. In time, they outgrow the ability of the individual scientist working alone and require organizations and journals for the pooling and dissemination of knowledge. Their continued growth eventually requires the coordinating of efforts in group study and research. Unlike many analysts who prefer to work alone on the model of a lonely Freud, Kris recognized even in his art work that studies can benefit from collaboration.[15] In 1933 he asked Robert Waelder[16] to be joint editor of *Imago*. The preface to his wartime collaboration with Hans Speier on *German Radio Propaganda* expressed his feeling that group work, "with its stimulation and mutual criticism, has its salutary effects, when dealing with an intricate subject matter likely to arouse emotional reactions" (1944, p. vi). It is not surprising that Ernst Kris should have been one of the pioneers in establishing group research in psychoanalysis.[17]

The initial step was a three-man collaboration after the war, which was so successful and rich in its contributions that the names of Hartmann, Kris, and Loewenstein are forever linked in the annals of psychoanalysis. Although each of these was well known for his contributions before the collaboration and "it is a healthy sign of the working arrangements among these three men, that after they had done the spade-work, each of them pursued the kind of task which appealed to them individually" (Hoffer, 1957, p. 361), it is impossible to mention

[15] See *Die Legende vom Kuenstler* with Otto Kurz and *Caricature* with E. H. Gombrich.

[16] February 20, 1900; Ph.D. in physics, Vienna, 1922; Professor of Psychiatry (psychoanalysis), Jefferson Medical College, Philadelphia.

[17] Another pioneer in recognizing the need for and establishing group research in psychoanalysis was Anna Freud, at the Hampstead Clinic in England.

any one of the names without evoking thoughts of the other two members of "this memorable alliance" (Hoffer, 1957, p. 361).

The next move was a giant step for psychoanalysis into an ambitious interdisciplinary study in a university setting. It was a longitudinal study of early childhood development carried out by a team of pediatricians, child psychologists, nursery school teachers, psychiatric social workers, and psychoanalysts, at the Yale University Child Study Center under the aegis of Milton J. E. Senn, professor of pediatrics and psychiatry and director of the Yale Child Study Center. In addition to Marianne Kris, Senn and Ernst Kris brought in as collaborators younger people whom Kris felt he could count on to continue the work after he was gone. Already faced in 1950 with the precariousness of his life, Ernst Kris often calmly pointed out to his associates what they might look for in the years ahead when "I may not be here to see it."

Stimulated by observations of creative activities of children in the nursery school of the Yale Child Study Center, Ernst Kris organized a study in the New York Psychoanalytic Institute known as the Gifted Adolescent Research Project. Again he selected younger colleagues who fulfilled his expectations by continuing the Gifted Adolescent Research Project for five years after his death on February 27, 1957. Individual articles have already appeared with some of the findings of the groups that Kris started. The research activities on the Longitudinal Study were completed in 1958, and the monumental task of writing up the massive data and its implications is now in process.

§ The Work

Ernst Kris's training and research in art history and his impressive scholarship provided him with the broad cultural background in the humanities that Freud regarded as desirable for the psychoanalyst. The rigorous historical method he had mastered has many parallels in psychoanalytic technique and methodology; the meticulous attention to detail and the careful reconstruction of the past are essential to both. His first psychoanalytic writings applied the concepts of his new field to problems of art and creativity. In the early 1930s, at a time when his extensive studies included attendance at medical courses, a new development began in his work, which was also something new in the history of psychoanalysis. With the publication of such papers as "A Psychotic Sculptor of the Eighteenth Century," "The Psychology of Caricature," "A Psychological Study of the Role of Tradition in Ancient Biographies," "Ego Development and the Comic," and "Laughter as an Expressive Process" (1952), Kris had come into his own. Analysis had released in him the ardent desire and the capacity to try a new approach in dealing with art and its history. In these and later papers, his authority as an expert and the sure judgment that his professional training as an art historian had given him signaled a new development in applied psychoanalysis. He was also the first to bring to this work the new ideas in psychoanalytic ego psychology that were being elaborated at that time. These papers, with their expression of a highly complex, multidimensional thinking and their greater fastidiousness in scientific methodology than previous work in this area, exerted a strong influence on psychoanalytic thinking and literature (Hartmann, pp. 10f.). Kris had a great love for literature, and his interest in art and the artist included the world created by the poet and writer and the character and personality of the men who created this world. In "Prince Hal's Conflict" (1948), a favorite paper among his own writings, he achieved for a literary creation what he had earlier done with painting and sculpture; he wrote a psychological analysis of an artistic creation that took into consideration the influence of the historical and cultural setting in which the artist worked, acknowledged the artist's own conflicts as determinants, and analyzed the character Shakespeare had created from a genetic as well as a dynamic standpoint.

In the immediate postwar years, the fruitful collaboration with Hartmann and Loewenstein produced the series of classical papers that extended and integrated the newer developments of psychoanalytic theory. In the discussions that led to these writings, his extraordinarily intense curiosity, his patience for detail, his fresh and provocative way of looking at old and new problems were fruitful and stimulating. He was primarily concerned with relating theoretical points to clinical observation and always thought a problem through from the standpoint of how it would be observable. As he excelled at putting ideas into words, he was usually the member of the team to do the writing.[18]

In the group of papers on theoretical subjects and methodological problems published in the late 1940s and early 1950s, Kris was mapping out the ideas and preparing the conceptual tools he would be using

[18] Loewenstein, R. Personal communication.

in the later research in child development and psychoanalytic child psychology. In 1950, Kris wrote his introduction to Freud's *On the Origins of Psychoanalysis* (1950a) and his paper, "The Significance of Freud's Earliest Discoveries" (1950c). For this work he was ideally suited and prepared, both by his gifts and training as a historian and by his familiarity with the principals. Hoffer wrote of these:

> Only a very few of his contemporaries could have lived up to the occasion offered by those exciting documents, the Fliess letters of Sigmund Freud. Sensitivity to historical events is a rare gift. Many aim at too great objectivity; others achieve too little when interpreting intentions read into the past. The task was best entrusted to one who, in addition to his familiarity with the persons concerned, had acquired in an allied field some of the skill and responsibility needed for the appreciation of objects of historical significance. Had Ernst Kris contributed nothing else to psycho-analysis, his Introduction to the *Origins* has caused him to deserve our admiration and thanks for all time (Hoffer, 1957, p. 361).

The problems of art and the creative process continued to be an important interest in Kris's work to the end of his life. He studied these problems for the contribution they could make to psychoanalytic psychology and reciprocally used the growing clinical and theoretical insights of psychoanalysis to elucidate some aspects of the creative process. In the preface and the revised introductory essay to his important book, *Psychoanalytic Explorations in Art* (1952), in which Kris collected papers published over a period of twenty years, he reviewed the development of his thinking about these problems. Originally the work had been undertaken with a double purpose: first, to apply psychoanalytic ego psychology to the problems traditionally treated by the humanities in which he had originally been trained and, second, to study art and creative processes in the broadest meaning of the terms in order to facilitate contributions to psychoanalytic psychology and to crystallize certain impressions gained in clinical work.

Over the years, the first purpose lost some of its urgency because of the rapid development of new types of interdisciplinary co-operation between psychoanalysis and the social sciences; the focus shifted to the second purpose. Kris deplored the tendency to simplify or abbreviate psychoanalytic thinking in discussions of psychoanalysis and art. His approach rested on the assumptions that the complete system of psychoanalysis offers the best chances for understanding and predicting human behavior and that the potential contribution of psychoanalysis to the study of art could only be assessed if one takes advantage of the differentiated tools psychoanalysis has to offer. Kris also saw the study of art as part of the study of communication. The artist was the sender of a message, and the audience were the receivers. He stressed that psychoanalysis in its heroic period had studied certain universal themes in artistic creations. He thought that the development of psychoanalytic ego psychology should sharpen our eyes for the specific within the general, should make it possible for us to see how traditional themes have been varied under specific socioeconomic and cultural conditions. Although we do not have the tools that would permit us to investigate the roots of talent or genius, psychoanalytic material has enabled us to point to the interaction of factors that play a part in the choice of artistic endeavor. In a passage that illustrates how Kris's later interests in child development were related to his interests in art, he wrote:

> We are about to study ego development not only in relation to typical conflicts, but also as far as the ego's capacities and functions emerge from conflict involvement and acquire autonomy. In this connection the endowment of the personality, its innate equipment, plays a significant role. We had been used to view it in terms of potentialities of the individual which might be favored or smothered by life experience, stimulated or suppressed by some of the numerous factors on which maturation and development depend. We are about to appreciate complementary aspects, that is, the influence which endowment may exercise on life experience, and particularly the role endowment may play in facilitating the detachment of certain ego functions from conflict, in establishing autonomy in certain activities. These views prove not only useful in organizing clinical impressions, but particularly stimulating in observing child development (1952, p. 21).

One of the areas from the study of art that he found relevant to observations on child development was the vicissitudes of regression. In his study of caricature, Kris had formulated the concept of "regression in the service of the ego"; many years later he focused on the control of regression in young children as one of the problems in ego development that could be approached in a longitudinal study.

Kris carried the ideas from his art studies into the several research projects he was directing at the time of his death. In the Gifted Adolescent Project, sponsored jointly by the New York Psychoanalytic Institute and Yale University, a group of young people with creative gifts and in need of analysis were being psychoanalyzed. In this way, Kris put into action his deep conviction that the psychoanalytic methodology and the full range of psychoanalytic concepts and propositions should be employed in these problems. Kris was also convinced that this way of pooling the experience and material of psychoanalysts for cases having common problems was a fruitful research approach at this stage in the history of psychoanalysis. He saw this approach as one way of overcoming the handicap of the limited experience any one analyst could have with a particular problem in the course of his professional career.

His views about psychological conflict as an essential ingredient and incentive to personality development and the influence that endowment may exert on life experience figured importantly in the longitudinal study of child development that he organized in 1950 with Milton J. E. Senn at the Yale Child Study Center. His studies of mass communication during World War II, which resulted in his writing the comprehensive and impressive volume, *German War Propaganda*, in 1944, carried his attempt to apply psychoanalytic insights into still another area. Because of this work, carried on by an interdisciplinary group, Kris was not a novice at interdisciplinary work when he led such a group at the Yale Child Study Center.

In "Notes on the Development and Some Current Problems of Psychoanalytic Child Psychology" (1950b, pp. 24–46), Kris formulated some of the ideas underlying the longitudinal study project. In the early 1920s, he had distinguished two phases in the development of psychoanalytic child psychology with a chronological dividing line. The second phase was marked by a number of important developments in psychoanalytic thinking, namely, the formulations on psychic structure, the emphasis on aggressive impulses, and the elaboration of a psychoanalytic ego psychology. He emphasized the relevance of this division into two phases for the relationship between the two main sets of data on which current psychoanalytic child psychology is based—the data gained by reconstruction and the data of direct observation. He pointed out that, whereas in the first phase the data of direct observation were of marginal interest only, in the second phase they could be integrated increasingly with data derived from reconstruction in the psychoanalysis of adults and children. The study he undertook with his co-workers at Yale provided for the organized, longitudinal observation of the development of a selected number of individual children, checked wherever possible and indicated by clinical psychoanalytic investigation. As a research worker, Kris did not cease to be a clinician.

The study was planned as an action research in which service-centered contacts were used for investigative purposes and the investigation was geared to the growth of the child. Thus the children were given sick- and well-baby care and entered the nursery school as early in life as was appropriate. As a clinician and therapist, Kris also expected that studies combining the predictive with the retrospective approach would aid early diagnosis and prevention of mental illness by refining our knowledge of the variations of mental health and pathology.

Since many of the cases in the last decade of his practice were reanalyses, they offered opportunities to study variations and differences in the technique of psychoanalysts. Out of their experience arose his recognition of the need for an historical study of changes in psychoanalytic technique. In his last papers, he began to formulate and explicate some of his ideas on the theory of technique, an aspect of psychoanalysis to which he certainly would have made further contributions had he lived.

The papers he published in the last four years of his life attest to the range and versatility of his mature gifts. They contained the first fruits of his direct observation of children (Kris, Coleman, & Provence, 1953, pp. 20–47; Kris, 1955). In the papers dealing with problems of psychoanalytic technique (1956b; 1956c), Kris demonstrated his superb ability to link theory with observation and to use clinical material in a masterly way to support or verify a hypothesis. The last paper in his bibliography, "The Recovery of Childhood Memories in Psychoanalysis" (1956, pp. 54–88), was his first publication in a new field of interest, the psychoanalytic study of memory, which he had recently embarked on with his characteristic vigor when he was already engaged in enough work to have overwhelmed several lesser men.

§ The Man

Kris was a man of great personal warmth, charm, and graciousness in his relations with people. He possessed a versatility and range of expression and a sense of contact and appropriateness with people that made him an effective and vibrant communicator in a wide range of settings, in talking even more than in writing. The rich quality of his voice, his clarity and lucidity as a thinker, his grasp of clinical and theoretical psychoanalysis, his historical sense and perspective, and his verbal skill made him particularly effective in large groups, such as the panels of the American Psychoanalytic Association, the memorable Arden House Conference in 1954, and the meetings of the New York Psychoanalytic Society. On these occasions, for which he prepared painstakingly, his articulateness and fluency and his unusual capacity for formulating ideas on all levels of abstraction made him especially effective as an explorer and expositor of psychoanalytic concepts and propositions.

His discussions of scientific papers at meetings of the New York Psychoanalytic Society were exciting and spellbinding occasions, in which his power to distill and integrate ideas shone brilliantly. He was frequently able to see more in a colleague's paper than the author himself. His ability to place a new idea or a reformulation accurately in the complex framework of psychoanalytic propositions always added immensely to the value and interest of a paper. His discussions were a postgraduate psychoanalytic education in themselves.

In smaller groups, such as seminars at the Institute, the study groups that he organized among the recent graduates, or the research meetings at the Yale Child Study Center and the Gifted Adolescent Project, the lesser formality and the smaller size of the groups permitted exchanges with individuals that were mutually stimulating. To these settings he brought a grace and charm that put younger colleagues and students at ease and brought out the very best in them, frequently beyond what they thought they had to contribute. In discussions in an informal setting, he had a way of making an intuitive leap based on an observation, then with a broad grin letting one know he was aware of the size of the leap, and the gap in the available information, by saying in mock seriousness, "If you quote me, I shall deny I ever said it."

He had an uncanny power of concentration that made it possible for him to engage in two or three full-time occupations most of his adult life; he also had a corresponding capacity for enjoying relaxation and fun when in a good mood. He might surprise strangers, but not those who knew him well, by leaving a lively conversation with adults to join their children playing on the floor. He had a genuine and deep-seated love of beautiful things and a tremendous talent for arranging them. He told Professor Gombrich, the art historian, that "the garden for him represented the Museum, and that he needed this outlet" (Gombrich, 1964).

Although his contributions to psychoanalysis are preserved in his writings, it was in the spoken word that his passion for psychoanalysis became contagious. His gift for summoning the image, the abstract idea, in a felicitous phrase while holding the student directly in his gaze made him a peerless psychoanalytic teacher. His inventiveness in posing problems of theory or technique never permitted a course to be given the same way twice. What contributed so much to his influence as a teacher was his devotion and unflagging interest in the development of the student or young colleague as a psychoanalyst. Particularly in the last years of his life, after his first attack of coronary thrombosis, the interest in younger colleagues seemed to some to be an attempt not only to insure the fruition of his own ideas and projects, but also an effort to find, encourage, and help young analysts who would contribute to psychoanalysis as a vigorous and viable science.

Firmly convinced that isolation was deadly for the psychoanalyst, he proposed and instituted new ways in which analysts could work together in the study groups and collaborative research projects he organized. In these settings, in his writings, and in individual contacts as a supervisor, he contributed many ideas that he encouraged colleagues and students to investigate and study. He gave lavishly of himself at a time when everyone felt he should have been conserving his strength. Gombrich (1964) tells that on his last visit to Kris, when he urged him to cut down on his work, Kris replied "that he would not learn enough in a day if he did and that was all he cared for. There was not the slightest element of pose in his remark; he was really completely dedicated to the search for truth."

REFERENCES

Freud, S., & O. Rie. Cerebrale Kinderlähmung und Poliomyelitis infantilis. *Klinische Studie über die halbseitige Cerebrallähmung der Kinder.* 1891.

Gombrich, E. H. Personal communication, Feb. 23, 1964.

Gombrich, E. H. A mind of distinction. London *Times,* March 23, 1957.

Hartmann, H. Ernst Kris (1900–1957). In *The psychoanalytic study of the child.* Vol. 12. New York: International Universities Press, 1957.

Hoffer, W. Obituary: Ernst Kris (1900–1957). *Int. J. Psycho-Anal.,* 1957, 38, 359–62.

Jones, E. *The life and work of Sigmund Freud.* New York: Basic Books, 1953–1957. 3 vols.

Kris, E. Der Stil "rustique." *Jahrbuch der kunsthistorischen Sammlungen in Wien,* 1936, 1, 137–208.

Kris, E. Prince Hal's conflict. *Psychoanal. Quart.,* 1948, 17, 487–506. (Also in *Psychoanalytic Explorations in Art.*

New York: International Universities Press, 1952. Ch. 12.)

Kris, E. *Aus den anfängen der Psychoanalyse.* London: Imago Pub. Co., 1950. (English edition: *On the origins of psychoanalysis.* New York: Basic Books, 1953.) (a)

Kris, E. Notes on the development and on some current problems of psychoanalytic child psychology. In *The psychoanalytic study of the child.* Vol. 5. New York: International Universities Press, 1950. (b)

Kris, E. The significance of Freud's earliest discoveries. *Int. J. Psycho-Anal.,* 1950, **31**, 108–116. (Also published in *Yearbook of Psychoanalysis,* 1950, **7**, 31–46.) (c)

Kris, E. *Psychoanalytic explorations in art.* New York: International Universities Press, 1952.

Kris, E. Neutralization and sublimation: observations on young children. In *The psychoanalytic study of the child.* Vol. 10. New York: International Universities Press, 1955.

Kris, E. Freud in the history of science. *The Listener,* 1956, **5** (1416), 631–633. (a)

Kris, E. On some vicissitudes of insight in psychoanalysis. *Int. J. Psycho-Anal.,* 1956, **37**, 445–455. (b)

Kris, E. The personal myth: a problem in psychoanalytic technique. *J. Amer. Psychoanal. Ass.,* 1956, **4**, 653–681. (c)

Kris, E. The recovery of childhood memories in psychoanalysis. In *The psychoanalytic study of the child.* Vol. 11. New York: International Universities Press, 1956. (d)

Kris, E. The writings of. . . . In *The psychoanalytic study of the child.* Vol. 13. New York: International Universities Press, 1958.

Kris, E., Rose Coleman, & Sally Provence. The study of variations of early parental attitudes. In *The psychoanalytic study of the child.* Vol. 8. New York: International Universities Press, 1953.

Kris, E., & H. Speier. *German radio propaganda: report on home broadcasts during the war.* New York: Oxford University Press, 1944.

Loewenstein, R. In memoriam: Ernst Kris, Ph.D., 1900–1957. *J. Amer. Psychoanal. Ass.,* 1957, **5** (4), 741–743.

BIBLIOGRAPHY

Cattell, J. *American men of science.* (8th ed.) Lancaster, Pa.: Science Press, 1949.

Cattell, J. *American men of science.* (10th ed.) Tempe, Ariz.: Jacques Cattell Press, Inc., 1962.

Kris, E. Introduction. In Marie Bonaparte, Anna Freud, & E. Kris (Eds.), *The origins of psychoanalysis: letters to Wilhelm Fliess, drafts and notes, 1887–1902, by Sigmund Freud.* New York: Basic Books, 1954.

Edward Glover

b. 1888

THEORY OF TECHNIQUE

*

CHARLES WILLIAM WAHL

Edward Glover was born on January 13, 1888, in Lesmahagow, Scotland, a small rural community approximately twenty-five miles from Glasgow. He was the third and youngest son of a country schoolmaster who, for reasons of health, had given up a scholastic career in a university center and settled his family in the more intimate and healthy atmosphere of a rural village. His mother had been raised by her uncle, a minister of the Reformed Presbyterian Church, a rigid and demanding sect that maintained that even to use musical instruments in divine service or to whistle on Sunday are egregious sins. She was privately educated, primarily in the domestic arts and in the religious observances of the sect and, as Glover himself has added, "in the current arcana of superstition that prevailed during her childhood and adolescence." She married at what was then regarded as the late age of twenty-eight, but by the time of Edward's birth, through contact with her scholarly and intellectually curious husband, she had lost much of her naïveté and was a competent wife and housekeeper and a restrained but doting mother.

As had many schoolmasters of the period, Edward's father had mastered a wide curriculum and could teach a group of pupils with equal ease in Greek, Latin, Hebrew, French, and English; he also possessed considerable competence in mathematics, natural philosophy, and the technique of water color painting. The elder Glover had an outstanding intellectual capacity and breadth of scholarship which, considering that he had been brought up in somewhat straightened circumstances, indicated the great tenacity of purpose that continued to govern both his private and public life.

Glover remembers himself as a "reluctant, rebellious, contumacious, and obstinate schoolboy," partly as a reaction to the stultifying rigidities of the teaching methods of the day. From the age of three-and-one-half to eleven, he learned little except to abominate religious instruction and the commercial forms of arithmetic that were a part of the lower school curriculum. At the age of eleven, he entered senior school under his father's direction; being treated for the first time like a gentleman, he responded and became an avid and retentive learner.

It was tradition that "sons of the manse or schoolhouse" would pursue either clinical, legal, academic, or medical careers, or prepare themselves for civil or foreign service. As his father was a Darwinian agnostic, the church was out of the question. This left only pedagogy, law, or medicine. At the age of sixteen, after passing the equivalent of both medical and arts matriculation, Edward Glover was undecided whether he should take up teaching (a field to which he was strongly drawn because of identification with his father), or medicine (to which he was also powerfully attracted, since his idolized older brother James had already chosen medicine as a career). Glover states, "In the long run, an identification with my eldest brother, James, prevailed, or shall we say the need of the young brother to copy and surpass his older sibling rival." This was a decision of which his father heartily approved, although he had earlier implied that in comparison with James, Edward was intellectually inferior and would need to be cosseted and supported lest he disgrace the family. The elder Glover suggested that Edward might be able to distinguish himself in research. Perhaps as a result of not fully resolving this vocational conflict, Edward Glover achieved considerable success in all these areas, being actively involved in pedagogy and medical practice, and, in addition, making salient contributions to scholarly research.

He remembers the university years as the happiest in his life. He soon found that he could master the academic requirements with ease, permitting ample time for congenial contracts with his nonmedical colleagues and for enjoyment of the full spectrum of undergraduate life—reading, thinking, enjoying, and reveling. These years were also spent in "rubbing off my Presbyterian edges against more tolerant spirits, and at the same time amplifying the academic influences to which I had been subjected in childhood."

At the age of twenty-one, he received the M.D. and Ch.B. degrees with distinction. He had not yet chosen a field of specialization, but he realized that lack of financial means would bar him from the usual staircase to professional success—staff appointment to a hospital and thence to a university chair, a process then requiring about twelve years. Fortunately, at this time he was offered a position as house physician with Professor John Cowan of the Royal Infirmary of Glasgow. He accepted the post and remained there for several years. Cowan, a noted cardiologist of his day, was a careful scientist who taught his young colleague not only the finer points of examining patients but also how to conduct research and how to control observation. The result was an excellent training in the application of scientific methods to clinical problems and the publication of a number of papers on diseases of the chest, which still have merit.

Further experience in London and Birmingham broadened his medical knowledge and research capacity and brought to his attention the clash between the strictly organic approach to medicine and the scope of actual clinical experience. This contrast increasingly claimed his attention and aroused his curiosity and wonder, but probably what most influenced the young physician to study and take up psychological medicine was a renewed relationship with his brother James. It was James who introduced Edward to the new psychologists, and for the first time Edward began to read Freudian literature. Meanwhile, James moved to London and became associated with Doctors Murray and Turner at the Brunswick Square Psychological Clinic, where he established a psychiatric practice, and was subsequently analyzed by Karl Abraham. Edward had already taken tentative steps in a similar direction when James, returning from The Hague, strongly urged him to abandon organic medicine, undergo analysis, and take up analytic work in London. His decision (at the age of thirty-two years) was prompt and effortless; by Christmas, 1920, he was settled in the Grunewald of Berlin, within a stone's throw of Abraham's residence. Here he underwent what he now recalls as "an apprenticeship rather than a training analysis, with a roving commission to pick up as much psychiatry from the Berlin hospital system as it afforded." He became intimate not only with the English group—his brother, Ella Sharpe, and Mary Chadwick —but also with Ernst Simmel, Karen Horney, Hanns Sachs, Franz Alexander, Harwick, Robert M. Loewenstein, and later, Melanie Klein.

Of these days he says, "flushed with a new enthusiasm I was ready, despite a training in independent thinking dating from my school and undergraduate days, almost to swallow, 'hook, line, and sinker' any undisciplined extravagance in ideology and method." The range extended from the solid clinical and theoretical cast of Abraham's mind to the more metaphysical cast of Sachs's mind. Was psychoanalysis science, art, or religion—or a special compound of the three? "The Berlin experience was largely instrumental in shaping my future interests. What seemed essential to correct extravagances was a common ground of asserted theory with the controlled system of technique."

Glover finished his training in Berlin and returned to London. Shortly thereafter, he became an associate member of the British Psycho-Analytic Society and, in the following year, a full member, as did James.

It is an unusual thing in psychoanalysis for brothers to train and work together and subsequently to share intellectual and professional interests in a meaningful way. All who remember this period were struck by the absence of incapacitating sibling rivalry between the brothers Glover and the admirable way each acted as foil for the mind of the other. Both had active theoretical minds. According to Edward, James was "the genius of the family" but was the more unstable in resolve. It was often difficult to get James to the point of publication, and on two occasions Edward operated as a *vis a tergo*. The Glovers were the first to criticize Rank's birth trauma theory, which had been accepted rather too easily by analysts in general. In this period, James also wrote an early paper on suicide. Their collaboration was brought to an untimely end by James's death from diabetes.

Edward Glover's first marriage, in 1918, lasted only eighteen months, ending with the death of his wife from septicemia. In 1924, he married again. The second Mrs. Glover is the daughter of a provincial lawyer and archaeologist. Their only offspring is a daughter, born in 1926, who from birth was mentally defective. Mrs. Glover has been seriously ill for the past year and has been confined to bed. Glover's life has not been without personal misfortune, but this has not prevented him from enjoying a rich, active, and vigorous life.

His professional life has been active. He was one of the founders of the British Society, director of research at the Institute, and assistant director of the Clinic under Ernest Jones. He later became director, and eventually chairman, of the Training Committee. He held these posts until 1944, when, because of a growing concern over training standards that have been described elsewhere in this volume, he resigned from them as well as from membership in the British Psycho-Analytic Society. Shortly afterward, he was granted an honorary membership in the American Psychoanalytical Association and the Swiss Society, memberships he still maintains. He has also been active in the field of criminology and has been co-editor of the *British Journal of Criminology*.

Edward Glover has been most productive professionally. He is the author of five books and more than 200 professional papers. These span almost the entire field of psychoanalysis, but two large areas of inquiry and interest are outstanding, the early development of man and the technique of psychoanalysis. The first, a *terra incognita* that can still absorb the lifework of a legion of scholars, comprises the development of man from birth to the age when analytic techniques can be used. When asked how he so unerringly perceived this subject to be the major blank spot in the knowledge of human personality, he replied:

> To this day, work on this subject—even when based on the direct observation of infants—is highly speculative and leaves the door open to hypotheses, many of which merely reflect the fantasies of their sponsors. This factor of inaccessibility to direct analysis has inevitably had two consequences, and these are similar to those obtained in the study of the psychoses: the first is that the clinical findings are fragmentary and not easily subject to corroboration; secondly, the theory of mental development derived therefrom is even more haphazard than the observations.

To this end, his early work in this area proceeded in two directions, first, to organize and extend such clinical observations and information on early mental life as seemed psychoanalytically plausible and then to organize the theory of development of mentation that held sway at the time. These ideas were published in 1932 in "A Psycho-Analytical Approach to the Classification of Mental Disorders," in which he has described the clinical manifestation and steps in the development of mental illness, contrasting and comparing these with childhood development—both within the hypothetical reconstitution of the phases of ego development. In this paper Glover also developed his concept of the nuclear theory of ego function, at which he had first hinted two years earlier in "Grades of Ego Differentiation."

This useful formulation developed as a logical extension of Freud's concept of instinctual polymorphous infantile sexuality and as a reflection of Glover's own increasing discontent and recoil from Melanie Klein's more mystical stage-oriented concept of early childhood development. In brief, Glover feels that early types of experience during the oral period produce multiple, part loculi or nuclei within the developing primitive ego. It is, therefore, inappropriate to view stage differentiation of the ego as being synthesized *ab initio;* rather, Glover conceives of the primary ego as being polymorphonuclear, a complex part of ego functions formed by the nature and characteristics of the infant's success or lack of it in achieving instinctual gratification. It is the cohesion of these developing nuclei in the ego that determine ego strength. Hence, to speak of a fixation at the oral stage of development is to be simplistic and imprecise. A fuller expression of these views can be found in "The Concept of Dissociation," published in 1943.

Glover's other professional interests were the study of crime and war. He published *The Roots of Crime*, a book for lay readers, and *War, Sadism, and Pacifism*, still a classic on the subject.

Glover's major contribution is his classic work, *The Technique of Psychoanalysis*, an area that has received insufficient attention from most psychoanalytic writers. His interest in this field antedates most contributions by almost two decades. From the beginning of his psychiatric experience, he was struck by the observation that, even within a given psychoanalytic society, technical practices vary in a most striking manner. He noted among practitioners of analysis a general absence of agreement on technique and a paucity of contributions to the literature in this area—in contrast to the burgeoning number of theoretical papers. Perhaps, as he says, this is because few analysts care to "penetrate the curtain of uncommunicativeness behind which psychoanalysts are only too prone to conceal their theoretical anxieties, insecurities, and guilts." An additional reason might be difficulty in subordinating the art of psychoanalysis to the science.

The Technique of Psychoanalysis actually originated in an offer that Glover made to Ernest Jones when, after James Glover's death, Edward fell heir to the posts for which James had been earmarked. Edward Glover wrote Jones, offering to give a course of lectures on the subject. Acceptance of his offer forced him to think over the skeletal framework of the subject and solve some of the problems that presented themselves. These lectures, first published as a journal supplement in 1928, formed the outline of the later work. Rare is the young psychoanalyst who has not spent considerable time in careful perusal of this helpful book.

In many ways this book typifies Edward Glover's unique series of contributions to psychoanalysis. He realized early that the methods of psychoanalysis differ in many essential respects from those of natural science. He developed an early abhorrence to undisciplined speculation and, throughout his long and productive life, has addressed himself to the fulcrum rather than to the periphery of the technical and theoretical questions that beset his science. He has pursued these interests without sacrificing independence of thought, with a steadfast adherence to the methods and values of science. His capacity to ignore group approval is best exemplified by his resignation in 1944 from the British Psycho-Analytical Society, when these standards were, in his opinion, ignored and infringed upon.

Kate Friedländer

1903–1949

PREVENTION OF JUVENILE DELINQUENCY

*

BARBARA LANTOS

In February, 1962, Anna Freud's well-known and greatly admired Hampstead Child Therapy Clinic celebrated its tenth anniversary. Few persons are aware that this clinic is the fruition of Kate Friedländer's magnificent dream, realized in 1947, when she convinced Anna Freud to organize an analytic training course for child therapists. To Kate, this was the greatest achievement of her life; she took immense pleasure in it, but her joy was short-lived. She fell ill in October, 1948, and died in February, 1949, at the age of forty-six.

Kate and I met comparatively late in life, in our thirties. We came from different countries and first made each other's acquaintance in Berlin when she was undergoing her training there. Just as she finished training, I emigrated to Paris where, in 1934, I met her again, much more intimately. We discovered a number of curious similarities in our family affairs—concerning our children and, in particular, our mothers—and we felt drawn together on the basis of so many joys and sorrows that we seemed to have in common.

At that time, Kate asked me most urgently to come to England and join the London group. Her reasons for this became clear to me after I had settled there, in 1935.

After my arrival in London, we jointly solved the problems created by our aging mothers. In this way, something like a family relationship was established between us. This helped me understand Kate and see in a different light certain of her character traits, which had alienated a number of people from her. She was considered ambitious and aloof and was reputed to use people for her own ends. Within her family, she was the most warm-hearted and self-sacrificing person imaginable. She was a devoted wife, a loving mother, and a dutiful daughter. She took a justifiable pride in her happy home life, wherein she managed to combine the peaceful and quiet atmosphere needed for her work and a gay and generous hospitality.

Outside the family circle, people interested her primarily (and perhaps exclusively) on the basis of a common interest in work. Her extraordinary charm captivated people; after periods of intensive cooperation with her on some project, they felt that a human bond, a real friendship, had developed. These co-workers were often hurt and even shocked when the relationship was abruptly brought to an end, once the work had been completed.

I repeatedly experienced puzzlement and frustration when, after we had worked together on some project with utter concentration and in happy companionship, she disappeared and I did not see her for weeks on end. Then she would suddenly turn up to see her mother, who lived in my house, and pour out her heart to me about family and scientific matters. Because of my dual capacity as colleague and participant in family relationships, we never drifted apart completely; the insight I derived from this double role enabled me to accept her and go on loving her as she was, knowing that this fault in her libido economy might at any time make her fickle, especially if she was following some new line of thought.

It is hardly possible to assess the loss that the psychoanalytic movement suffered through Kate's death. What she achieved in the short span of her professional life gives only an inkling of the vast potential that was just beginning to be realized.

She was a woman of boundless energy and high spirits. Tall and handsome, she derived great pleasure from smart, feminine clothes, which she designed and made out of scraps of material during the bleak war years. She would show me her "finds" with almost child-like delight, and I showed her mine, although my talents in this respect fell far short of hers. Perhaps this was one of the reasons I admired her enthusiasm so much. There was hardly anything she could not be enthusiastic about; she responded to everything that life had to offer. She was as keen on dancing as on mountaineering, on tennis as on swimming and skating. In England she added riding and gardening to her hobbies. In the war years gardening developed into more than just a hobby. Her favorite recreations were artistic and intellectual—music, the theater, and literature. In various of her publications, we see applications of her knowledge of literature to psychoanalytic work.

Kate Friedländer, nee Fränkl, was born in 1902, at Innsbruck, in the most beautiful, albeit the most anti-Semitic, part of Austria. The daughter of middle-class Jewish parents, she had two brothers, both of whom died early in life, and one younger sister, a vivacious and gifted girl whose great abilities and artistic skill Kate warmly admired. Her parents were quite progressive; they eventually sent Kate to study medicine at the University—something which at that time and in that part of the world was unusual. But the narrow-mindedness and racial intolerance that she continually encountered were difficult for her to endure and, once she had obtained her medical degree at Innsbruck (in 1926), she used it as a passport to a better world.

During the years of the Weimar Republic, Berlin had a magnetic attraction for persons who were broad-minded and progressive in outlook, despite the very bad economic conditions and, especially, the widespread and increasing unemployment in Germany. At this time, Berlin offered scope for everything new and progressive in art, science, and the social sciences.

Relying entirely on her own resources, Kate moved to Berlin, where, although not yet accepted by official medicine, psychoanalysis enjoyed recognition and popularity with the educated public. Kate found a job as assistant in Karl Bonhoeffer's psychiatric university clinic (The Charité). Many of the young doctors working at the clinic were interested in psychoanalysis and were in training at the Berlin Psychoanalytic Society and Institute. Bonhoeffer himself, less openly antianalytic than many other leading psychiatrists, tolerated the movement.

In 1930, Kate obtained her second medical degree in Berlin. With her quick grasp of things and her excellent memory, learning presented no difficulty whatsoever. It was child's play; sitting for examinations was great fun. She took a third medical degree in Edinburgh in 1936, and later, the Diploma of Psychological Medicine (D.P.M.) in London, in 1943. Throughout, she demonstrated the same ease and blitheness, as if the passing of examinations were just a hobby. Added to her other duties were the interesting studies in neurology that led to the publication, in 1932, of "A Clinical Entity to Be Separated from Multiple Sclerosis." In the same year, she published "The Social Integration of Malaria-Treated Paralytics," which shows the emphasis on the social aspects that marks her psychiatric work. A new opportunity arose to combine her interest in social welfare with psychiatric work when she was appointed part-time psychiatrist at the Juvenile Court in Berlin. The psychoanalytic approach to the problem of juvenile delinquency became the very center of her professional interest, into which she channeled all her extensive knowledge and varied experience in psychiatry.

The pleasure of all these achievements was soon to be overshadowed by political developments in Germany. Again Kate Friedländer had to leave the place of her activities and seek freedom to live and work in another country. With her first husband and her two-year-old daughter Sybil (now a lecturer in philosophy and sociology at Oxford) she emigrated to London. With the great loyalty she had always shown in family relationships, she tried hard to save her marriage with a husband who was suffering from grave neurotic disturbances. But all her patience and loyalty could not prevail. When I met her in London in 1935, she was involved in difficult divorce proceedings and was greatly concerned about the welfare of her child.

Because my little boy and her small daughter had been born on the same day we shared a birthday celebration, and with Kate's mother coming to live in my household, a kind of joint family unit was established. Later, when we both remarried, almost on the same day, a sisterly friendship was established, with all its pleasures and no disturbing commitments. But the basis of our friendship was—and remained throughout—the common interest in our professional work. It took me some time to understand what was happening inside the psychoanalytic movement in London; then it became clear to me why Kate had derived such enormous pleasure from my settling here.

I had come to England with great expectations. The reception given us by the whole British Psycho-Analytical Society under the leadership of Ernest Jones and Edward Glover was heartwarming. They succeeded in obtaining work permits, which, for all their friendly feelings and goodwill, the French Society had not been able to achieve for us. This was why I had left Paris for London. I again met many distinguished senior colleagues in the British Society whom I had known in Berlin in the twenties when they had had their own training analyses there with Karl Abraham and Hanns Sachs.

I expressed concern about my poor English, which I thought prevented me all too often from understanding problems read and discussed in meetings. Kate remarked that although her English seemed good enough, she frequently experienced the same difficulty. "They *do* speak a different language," she said, "a different analytic language." This was why she had urged me to come to London, to have someone near her with whom she could speak in the analytic language we had learned in our training.

Melanie Klein, who created this different analytic language, was well known to me from my Berlin days. I was all the more surprised to find that she reacted with cool reservation to the naïve pleasure I showed when meeting her again. For a long time, supported by Ernest Jones, she had exercised undisputed leadership in the British Society; most of the members were not aware that her psychoanalytic language, her theories, and the content of her interpretations differed in many ways from the opinions generally held elsewhere. When, in 1936, R. Waelder came to London to discuss the divergencies, few of the members took notice of his comments. The bulk of the British Society remained firmly convinced that they held the true Freudian views.

Kate was neither prejudiced nor narrow-minded. Together, we examined the Kleinian concepts, trying to find justifications for them. However, we ended by refusing to accept the thesis that each healthy baby, thriving and glowing with vitality and happily smiling at his mother, should at the same time harbor terrifying cannibalistic fantasies of devouring and destroying her. In this connection, Kate returned time and again to the problem of regression, which had been overlooked by the Kleinian theory. Kate believed that the oral-cannibalistic fantasies of the four-year-old child are not evidence of their having originated during the first months of life but are, rather, a regressive expression of the child's present conflicts. Apart from Waelder's discussion, which I have already mentioned, there was little wish for an investigation of these problems in the British Psycho-Analytical Society. We were allowed to work with our patients and to give our papers, but we were described *urbi et orbi* as "old-fashioned continental analysts." Personally, we were treated with unchanging friendliness.

I can remember the small private seminars we held with those of our colleagues who did not give in to the Kleinian views. But our position as guests made us reticent and anxious not to cause trouble through recurrent criticism.

This situation, accepted by most of the analyst refugees with some resignation, made Kate acutely unhappy. Nevertheless, she went on with her work and was very productive within the Society. Her great knowledge and clarity earned respect, and she was asked to take part in the training at the Institute. At the Paris Congress in 1938, she read a paper, "On the Longing to Die." The basic motive for this paper was to clarify her own ideas on the death instinct. It dealt with a patient whose suicidal attempts were motivated not by forces of self-destruction but by libidinal forces directed toward early objects to which the patient had remained fixated.

In a paper on Charlotte Brontë, "A Study of a Masochistic Character," written in 1941, she used her great knowledge of literature to understand the author and her heroine from the analytic point of view.

The 1941 paper, "Children's Books and Their Function in Latency and Pre-puberty," also applies the analytic approach to a problem of literature. She proves with many examples that, until the age of fifteen, children rarely read to acquire knowledge; they read to obtain the gratification of fantasies appropriate to their ages. This explains the difference in tastes of boys and girls and the preferences of children of different ages.

Kate continued to feel an outsider in the Society, longing for a more congenial atmosphere. The remedy for this discontent was provided by a historic event. When Freud, his daughter Anna, and his most outstanding followers arrived in London in June, 1938, Kate was overwhelmed with happiness. It is true that we received a slight rebuff from them when we described the situation in the Society; they said it must be our fault if we could not come to terms with these kind, understanding, and generous people in the British Society. Perhaps we did not possess the necessary skill in discussing controversial points. We readily agreed that our English colleagues were generous and hospitable and could not be kinder. The rest we left to the Viennese group to find out by themselves.

We were soon vindicated. The main problem for the refugee group was how to respond with gratitude to the obvious friendliness we were shown, without giving up our scientific convictions. Anna Freud's motto was and has remained, "We are guests in this country and were not brought here to create trouble." Kate accepted this attitude, although by nature she would have preferred a scientific clarification. Anyway, Freud's death and the outbreak of the war kept these problems dormant for a time. Very much on Kate's initiative, we started seminars and discussion groups within our enlarged circle, and this provided Kate with ample compensation. Soon our work became centered in Hampstead, where Anna Freud's war nurseries were opened, and we were allowed to take part in her work and to reap the benefit of listening to her lectures.

The Society continued its work on a reduced scale, leaving us plenty of time for other pursuits. Apart from nursery meetings, a weekly evening meeting was arranged under the chairmanship of Anna Freud at her home in Maresfield Gardens. We brought our case material and our theoretical and technical problems to these meetings and were delighted by her clear, illuminating comments. Once, while we were sadly strolling together through the deserted streets of wartime London, Kate said thoughtfully, "It is terrible what we have had to go through and are *still* going through, but isn't it a gift from heaven that by this very misfortune we have gained the opportunity to work in the same place as Anna Freud?"

And so, under wartime conditions, our analytic work went on peacefully. We regularly attended meetings of the Society. Anna Freud and other colleagues, Kate included, participated in the teaching and business activities. It was rather frustrating to give students this heterogeneous training, but it was Anna Freud's wish to avoid controversy, while giving our students as much as they were willing to accept. This was respected by all of us.

In an attempt to take the personal element out of the controversy within the Society, Anna Freud made the following suggestion: The controversial issues—discussed so far in only a haphazard and highly emotional manner—should be subjected to systematic discussions with well-prepared papers, in which the one group could formulate its concepts and the other group answer the various points. This suggestion, made in 1942, was quickly adopted. Various papers about the controversial issues were circulated and discussed during meetings. For many months, these discussions continued in a satisfactory scientific atmosphere until finally, in June 1946, an agreement was reached to the effect that the two groups representing the divergent views prevailing in the Society be introduced for teaching purposes. In my many "private sessions" with Kate, we contemplated the merits of the compromise. Kate maintained that the opposing group had achieved its purpose. Anna Freud did her teaching within the framework of the Institute of Psycho-Analysis. But what was the gain for the psychoanalytic movement? Was this really the best solution? This remains a moot question to this day.

Work with her patients, the papers she presented and published, and her participation in the administrative work of the Society were not enough to exhaust Kate's abundant energies, nor did they provide sufficient gratification for all her scientific interests. In London, she extended these activities by joining as honorary psychiatrist the Institute for the Scientific Treatment of Delinquency.

The problems of juvenile delinquency became more and more the center of her scientific interest, stimulating her ideas about the role of psychoanalysis. Prevention, rather than cure, appears to be the analyst's main task. To achieve this successfully, one must investigate the many factors and conditions that make for maladjustment, resulting in either neurosis or delinquency. The Institute for the Scientific Treatment of Delinquency gave Kate ample scope to study these complex problems. Under Glover's leadership, it took a tolerant and generous attitude toward the various branches of research, as long as they concerned themselves basically with the psychoanalytic approach. Kate thrived in this atmosphere of friendly animated discussions, about which she reported to me in our "private sessions." Again and again she returned to the question, "What can be the role of psychoanalysis in this vast field?" In certain instances (but not in all), she maintained that psychoanalysis might be the method of choice. However, she believed that the most important contribution psychoanalysis could make to the problem of delinquency is its unique value as the only reliable research method; any ancillary methods of treatment, such as psychotherapy, management, aftercare, and the like, should be based on the findings of psychoanalytic research. Although admitting the usefulness of these other methods of treatment, she remained adamant on one point: the term psychoanalysis should be reserved for Freudian analysis in its original form; no other method, however helpful, should be called psychoanalysis.

The gratification Kate gained from this work compensated her for the frustrations that every analyst encounters in the therapeutic results of his work. Nevertheless, her self-critical and searching mind made her ask again and again, "Am I really a good enough analyst? What can I do to be of greater help to my patients?" Kate knew that the answer to her doubts lay in more and more research. She stressed particularly the need for more knowledge about the interrelationships between the child and his environment in the early years. She believed that the study of the great variety of family constellations and of the situations resulting from their interaction would make the recognition of clinical entities easier.

Kate thought that emphasis on ego psychology rather than exclusive interest in unconscious content was the key to further research. The whole psychoanalytic avant garde of the time was in full agreement with her and working along the same lines. "Isn't it extraordinary," Kate often said, "that they call us 'orthodox' although we are moving all the time, while they stick to the unconscious phantasies of the new-born babes and their terrifying effects?"

But Kate forgot her discontent in happy and exciting occupation with her work, as is well documented in a long sequence of papers, some published in the United States in *The Psychoanalytic Study of the Child,* and some in England, as well as in such popular magazines *Nursing Mirror* and *New Era.*

Kate then embarked on a new venture that, for once, absorbed all her energies. This was the creation of the West Sussex Child Guidance Service. In this great undertaking, she could put into practice all the vast knowledge acquired during her participation in the work at Anna Freud's war-time nurseries. The war was drawing to an end. The Hampstead Nurseries were gradually closing. But to army psychiatrists, as well as to the general public, had come growing appreciation of what psychoanalysis could offer where other methods failed, and they turned to us for help. Kate had an extraordinary skill for making contact with all kinds of people who might become interested in psychoanalysis in connection with the work they were doing. Teachers and educators were attracted by her charm and became impressed by her patient, untiring efforts to explain what psychoanalysis might do for the child population. She succeeded even in getting the very conservative-minded Country Squires interested in her ideas: these people may wield considerable educational authority in rural communities. Lady E., whose first reaction was one of great skepticism, later became the main sponsor of Kate's new scheme, which she called "education of the community."

Kate's most ambitious project, the establishment of the West Sussex Child Guidance Service, was organized in a rural area with a conservative population. In the autum of 1946, three clinics were opened, which, from the start, were enthusiastically supported by the community.

In this undertaking two of Kate's favorite ideas were realized, the education of the community and working with a highly trained staff, without which a service of this kind would be impossible. Out of her experiences in the West Sussex Child Guidance Clinics grew her plan for training skilled workers under Anna Freud's guidance.

After some initial hesitation, Anna Freud entered into this plan and established a clinic for trainees, The Hampstead Child Therapy Course. The candidates who took the training had to undergo a personal analysis and complete a very full curriculum of theoretical and practical lectures and seminars.

The high standards of these child therapists has been acknowledged in the United States. Many of the early trainees went to the United States to practice and have become estabished there. Students from all parts of the world now come to London to participate in the Hampstead Child Therapy courses. As she had only one year in which to enjoy the realization of her hopes, we can only imagine what Kate might have contributed to this work. Nevertheless, it was Kate Friedländer's great vision that led to the organization and establishment of this great training scheme for child therapists.

In the meantime, Kate added still another dimension to her efforts. As an aftermath of the war, a sudden and widespread increase in delinquency had occurred, presenting a major problem to psychologists, psychiatrists, sociologists, and legal authorities. With her long-standing interest and vast experience in this field, Kate could speak with authority on this problem's various aspects. Based on her work at the Institute for the Scientific Treatment of Delinquency, she wrote in 1947 *The Psycho-Analytical Approach to Juvenile Delinquency*, in which she set out the relevant psychoanalytic findings, co-ordinating them with psychiatric and sociological aspects, and pleading for co-operation among the various sciences that have a bearing on the problems of delinquency. Her admirably balanced account is of equal value to research workers in all these fields.

After the completion of her book, Kate visited the United States. Returning from her lengthy trip full of enthusiasm, she summed up what had impressed her most: that in America the sudden postwar realization of the importance of psychoanalysis was even more impressive and widespread than in England; that she, personally, had felt very happy about the warm-hearted reception she had been given by institutions and individuals alike; and that a variety of jobs had been offered to her. She had felt sorely tempted to remain in the United States, but her family ties and her devotion to the work she had built up in England prevailed in the end; she felt she could not abandon these.

In 1947, Kate went on a lecture tour in Switzerland, together with Anna Freud, August Aichhorn, and a number of Swiss professors.

In September 1948, the first Mental Health Congress in London gave her another opportunity for making new contacts with people from all over the world and inspiring them with her enthusiasm. But these weeks were overshadowed by the first signs of her fatal illness: headaches and coughing fits plagued her; a long series of diagnostic tests in the hospital followed. Her spirit still unbroken, she confided to me her secret plan "to let the nurses go on fussing till the child therapy course starts. Then I'll just get out of bed and start working." Two days later found her in distress, and she turned away from me and did not respond. I learned that in getting up she had had a fall, and she realized for the first time that her eyesight was failing. She knew then the diagnosis and the final verdict. The day before her death, her husband, a well-known radiologist, discovered the primary focus of the brain tumor in the lung.

In a note to the editors that accompanied this chapter, Dr. Lantos said that she had been seriously ill but had made the effort to finish the chapter on her friend and colleague Kate Friedländer. A few days later we received the sad news that Dr. Barbara Lantos had died. This paper was her last scientific work.

Anna Freud

b. 1895

and Erik H. Erikson

b. 1902

CONTRIBUTIONS TO THE THEORY AND PRACTICE OF PSYCHOANALYSIS AND PSYCHOTHERAPY

*

EUGENE PUMPIAN-MINDLIN

Anna Freud and Erik Erikson have worked extensively in the areas of childhood and adolescence. Their foci of interest and frames of reference complement each other, but do not overlap in the formal sense, at least at the present time.

§ Anna Freud

Anna Freud's most significant theoretical contribution was *The Ego and the Mechanisms of Defence* (1937). This book is so well known and has been so completely incorporated in the body of psychoanalysis that it is hardly necessary to recapitulate it here. It stems from and is an extension of Sigmund Freud's 1926 work, "Inhibitions, Symptoms, and Anxiety" (1959) in which Freud reintroduced the central role of reality and emphasized the significance of the ego by reformulating his concept of anxiety as a signal function of ego in relation to external and internal reality. This concept of the signal function of anxiety implied the concept of adaptation of reality; it formed the basis of Anna Freud's book and was the precursor of Hartmann's and Erikson's contributions.

In her book, Anna Freud has elaborated on the concept of defense in relation to reality and on the role of specific defenses, as well as the role of affects. She has also devoted two chapters to the ego in puberty and adolescence. She emphasizes the role of the ego as the "seat of observation," discusses the various mechanisms of defense, and describes the avoidance of reality by denial and restriction of the ego. As specific examples of types of defense "identification with the aggressor" and "a form of altruism" are delineated. In her conclusions, parallels are set up between defenses against such inner and outer dangers as repression and denial, reaction-formation and reversal by fantasy, and inhibition and ego restriction.

Since the appearance of this book, most of Anna Freud's writings have been more clinical and practical than theoretical. Most of her work has been devoted to maintaining the distinctiveness of the psychoanalytic approach consistent with advances in ego psychology and modified by her own and her collaborators' work in child psychoanalysis.

Perhaps her most significant contribution over the years lies in the organization and development of the Hampstead Child Therapy Clinic in London (A. Freud, 1959, pp. 122-134; Sandler, 1962), in which she has directed various projects concerned with children and adolescents. Numerous publications produced by both Anna Freud and her collaborators (many of which are listed in the bibliography to this chapter have resulted from these. An excellent résumé of the clinic and the various research projects appeared in the *Proceedings of the Royal Society of Medicine* in 1958 under the title, "Clinical Studies in Psychoanalysis" (A. Freud, Burlingham, & de Monchaux, 1958). In all of this work there is a constant emphasis on direct observation of children and the effect of this observational material on aspects of classical psychoanalytic theory.

Since 1951, the Hampstead Child Therapy Clinic has been engaged in both treatment of children and research in problems of normal and abnormal childhood development. With regard to the latter, the clinic has attempted to attack the basic problem of research in psychoanalysis, the fact that the nature of analytic practice makes difficult a planned systematic approach to any specific problem. The clinic has attempted to solve this difficulty by two methods, first, by pooling the clinical material of a group of analysts, and second, by a planned selection of cases. The pooling of material is illustrated by a project inquiring into the analytic treatment of adolescents, in which a number of analysts are treating various adolescent patients. These analysts meet weekly to present their material and discuss the handling of specific problems. Two particular aspects are being studied intensively, the initial session with such patients and the adolescents' distrust of their therapists.

Another area of research being carried on in the clinic has to do with "experimental situations which are provided by nature and fate." This includes studies of the significance of visual impressions in psychic development and the compensatory processes utilized by children who are born blind (Burlingham, 1961, pp. 121–145) with respect to object relations, language development, and the like. Studies of a similar nature on congenitally deaf children are also planned. Another study in the same category has to do with institutionalized children who were orphaned early in life. This is a continuation of the wartime work of Anna Freud and Dorothy Burlingham, which was published in the books, *War and Children* (1943b), and *Infants without Families* (1943a). This work was done at the Hampstead Nursery, which was the precursor of the Hampstead Child Therapy Clinic.

A further research study being carried on deals with a comparison of observational material with analytic data. This involves the analysis of older children in whom observational data relating to the first two years of life is available. Dorothy Burlingham's research on identical twins (1946) has also been carried on for many years under the auspices of the Hampstead Clinic.

Anna Freud and her co-workers in the clinic have in recent years been more and more concerned with problems of diagnostic evaluation of children. Aside from such purely clinical questions as the practical handling of interviews with children and the use of interventions, Anna Freud has developed the concept of the assessment of pathology (and normality) along developmental lines. She finds that the criteria for assessment of pathology in adults are of no help in children. Symptoms present themselves in chaotic, disorderly fashion. Pathology in children manifests itself in an arrest in development. In order to determine such arrests, one must know something of the lines of development of the child, not merely the level of development of the drives and of the ego functions. Anna Freud speaks of three main categories of developmental lines (1962): (1) maturation—of drives as well as ego functions; (2) adaptation—both to the environment and to the building of object relations; and (3) organization—both integration and conflicts within the structure.

Specifically, she refers to an estimate of what one would expect at any particular age of a child both in terms of accomplishments and in terms of conflicts and difficulties. Although this concept of lines of development is not new or original, it has been applied by Anna Freud more systematically than is usually done, with a fuller and more adequate appreciation of the progressive and regressive swings in the development of the child. Pathology in children is no longer assessed simply on the basis of the presence or absence of a particular symptom or difficulty but, rather, on the evaluation of the relative degree of harmony or disharmony along the various developmental lines in relation to the forces of both ego and id. This results in a far more plastic and flexible evaluation of child development at different stages and a more accurate, if more complex, evaluation of pathological manifestations, the main emphasis being synchrony along the three main lines of development. What results from this reasoning is a far greater tolerance for individual variation within the limits of normality and for progressive and regressive swings within the individual.

One further important aspect of the work of the Hampstead Clinic Group is the Hampstead Index (A. Freud et al., 1958; Sandler, 1960, pp. 128–162; 1961, pp. 121–145). Very early in the course of this joint undertaking, the problem of indexing the case material in usable form arose. The indexing project was proposed originally by Dorothy Burlingham. Although this seemed simple at first, it quickly developed into "a methodological study in its own right" (A. Freud, Burlingham, & de Monchaux, 1958).

Perhaps both the clinical and research significance of the Index and its uses can best be described by quoting from Joseph Sandler's article "Research on Psychoanalysis," which appeared in the *International Journal of Psycho-Analysis:*

The interaction of the clinical observations and the theoretical framework was much more extensive than had been anticipated, and when it was found necessary to modify or amplify the accepted definition of, say, a mechanism of defense, it was equally necessary to give more precise definitions in order to avoid confusion. Much of the work of the Index committees has been taken up with theoretical discussion, discussion which was always related to an actual set of indexed observations. This has led to a number of new formulations, for those which were available in the literature were at times inadequate, imprecise, or contradictory. Such new formulations are, for example, certain of the definitions of the defenses, with special reference to the distinction between defense mechanisms and other defensive measures; or the definitions relating to superego functioning, formulated after it was found that certain distinctions generally accepted in the past did not enable us to categorize the actual observations of the therapists at all precisely—distinctions between such concepts as ego and superego identification. Research groups, stimulated by the problems which have arisen in indexing, are examining such topics as the mechanisms for self-esteem regulation, and the problem of regression (Sandler, 1962, p. 288).

Sandler further distinguishes three stages in the construction of the Index. The first deals with the conceptualization and categorization of the case material by the therapists in terms of "their own impression of psychoanalytic therapy." The second involves the refinement of psychoanalytic concepts to accord more precisely with the clinical observations; the third involves the re-evaluation of the analytic observational material in terms of the revised theoretical formulations. Those working on the project believe that this continuous interchange between clinical observation and theoretical formulation results in more precise scientific observation and conceptualization and reveals problem areas in the theoretical structure of psychoanalysis. This has already led to a number of scientific contributions and the resolution of obscurities in psychoanalytic theoretical formulations.

I have presented the work of Anna Freud interwoven with the work of the Hampstead Child Therapy Clinic and her numerous collaborators because it is literally impossible to separate them. She has been its guiding light since its inception, and much of her contribution lies in this role. The careful and meticulous attempt to systematize and organize psychoanalytic research and to correlate and examine the observational data, which she has inspired, points to her integrity as an investigator and a scientist in our most difficult field.

Many of the fruits of this labor still lie in the future and may well lead to significant scientific contributions both theoretical and clinical. The careful attention to the methodology of psychoanalytic research that characterizes the approach of the Hampstead group under Anna Freud and the insistence upon systematic observation of data, as well as its constant interaction with existing theoretical formulations, are a most significant scientific contribution.

§ Erik H. Erikson

The work of Erik Erikson has profoundly influenced psychoanalytic thinking, particularly in the last decade. Although he began to elaborate his concept of psychosocial development in the late thirties and early forties (1937; 1939; 1940, pp. 557–671; 1942; 1945, pp. 319–350; 1946, pp. 359–396) these culminated in the publication of *Childhood and Society* (1950), which is in its way as classic as Anna Freud's *The Ego and the Mechanisms of Defence*, although by no means as incorporated into the body of classical psychoanalysis as the latter. Unfortunately, his projected book, *Life Cycle and Ethics* has not appeared at this writing, although one chapter (1962b) has been published. This new book promises to synthesize much of Erikson's most recent work and correlate and elaborate on his more recent ideas concerning "values" and "virtues" in relation to his psychosocial theory.

Erikson's psychosocial theory of development rests upon his utilization of the biological theory of epigenesis, a concept borrowed from embryology. Epigenetic development is characterized schematically by the sequential development of organ systems in the fetus, each of which is dominant at a particular stage. These stages must be present in an orderly sequence and in a definite rhythm of growth and development to enable the organism to adapt itself properly to extrauterine life. With this embryological concept as a basis, Erikson extends this idea into the psychological sphere, conceptualizing an orderly sequence of phases in the epigenetic development of the ego, covering the whole of the life cycle. This epigenesis is correlated with a theory of reality relations and of the role and significance of social reality. Erikson's concept of sequential ego developmental phases is the first psychoanalytic theory to encompass the total life cycle, going beyond libido theory to adolescence, adulthood, maturity, and senescence.

In Erikson's conceptualization, each phase of the life cycle is characterized by a specific developmental task that must be resolved in some way before the individual proceeds to the next level. It should be noted that these tasks are never completely resolved but are worked out further in successive stages, each depending on the preceeding stages. Erikson has formulated these in terms of psychological polarities that represent the hypothetical extremes of successful and unsuccessful resolution. The actual outcome, of course, is always somewhere between the polar extremes of the eight polarities he has delineated: (1) basic trust versus mistrust—infancy; (2) autonomy versus shame and doubt—two years; (3) initiative versus guilt—three–five years; (4) industry versus inferiority—latency; (5) identity versus identity diffusion—adolescence and youth; (6) intimacy and solidarity versus isolation—young adulthood; (7) generativity versus self-absorption—parenthood; (8) integrity versus despair—older age.

These phases of development are correlated with the social environment by his concept of mutuality, whereby a co-ordination ("cogwheeling") exists between the significant adult and the developing child, both of whom interact mutually. The representatives of society and the societal institutions transmit to the individual, at each phase of development, the various aspects of social reality (actuality) that are specific to the particular phase. In Erikson's concept, the psychological polarities of the epigenetic phases are universal, but each society presents its own particular resolutions of each phase. Erikson's concept, then, assumes a basic epigenetic social character that interacts with the social norms. Each society thus integrates its members by influencing the way in which each member resolves the specific task of each epigenetic phase.

The mechanism by which society influences the resolution of these phases is related to Erikson's concept of organ modes. The various modes, such as inceptive, retentive, and intrusive, are originally related to the organs and zones of the body, but as development proceeds they become separated from their organ origin and develop into such behavioral modalities in the individual as receiving, giving, taking, and letting go. The libidinal stages of psychosexual development are incorporated into Erikson's epigenetic schema through his concept of organ modes but include much more than is encompassed in these various stages.

Erikson has not attempted to formulate a well-rounded metapsychological theory or to refine his theoretical concepts. However, he believes that three basic aspects enter into any psychological phenomena.

These are (1) the biological substrate, (2) the psychological phase, (for example, the specific developmental polarity), and (3) the societal (psychosocial) environment in which the individual lives. Corresponding to each developmental phase are the significant individuals as representatives of the social institutions, or the societal institutions themselves, which interact with the individual in accord with the principle of mutuality.

In *Childhood and Society* (1950), Erikson formulated his epigenetic ground plan, incorporating the total life span of an individual and its various interacting relationships. Since the publication of this book, he has elaborated particularly in relation to its clinical aspects, on only one specific developmental phase, namely, adolescence, in which the psychological polarity is conceptualized as identity versus identity diffusion. This he did in "The Problem of Ego Identity" (1956; 1959). This was further elaborated with respect to a specific historical individual in *Young Man Luther* (1958). He has written further on the problem of identity in relation to delinquency (1957) and in relation to youth in general (1963).

More recently, Erikson has developed his concept of "Basic Virtues" (1962a), by which he means "implicit human values." These he has correlated with the epigenetic development of the various phases of the life cycle. He characterizes the childhood virtues at the various stages outlined above as hope, will, purpose, and skill; in the adolescent the virtue is fidelity; and in the adult phase the virtues are love, care, and wisdom. His concern with these basic virtues, which are intimately related to the various psychosocial polarities, is correlated with the successful resolution of these polarities in terms of what is generally called "ego strength." Aside from fidelity in adolescence, he has not elaborated in much detail on these virtues. This will, hopefully, be discussed in greater detail in his forthcoming book.

One significant aspect of Erikson's work is that he has been interested more in the elaboration of the normal or normative than of the pathological. Many of his ideas originated in his anthropological work in the study of the Sioux and Yurok Indians, as well as in his studies on play and play configurations in childhood (1937; 1939; 1940; 1942; 1945; 1946). His primary focus has been more upon "the ego's total task of synthesis and adaptation" (1962b, p. 457) than upon the fragmentation of the ego and the pathological manifestations thereof. In addition, he has utilized the technique of psychoanalytic historiography or biography to a considerable extent, as evidenced by his book on Luther, by his discussion of George Bernard Shaw in "The Problem of Ego Identity" (1959), and by his discussion of Freud's "Irma Dream" in "The Dream Specimen of Psychoanalysis" (1954), as well as of Freud's analysis of Dora, in "Reality and Actuality" (1962a). In all of these he utilizes his tripartite schema of biological base, psychological epigenesis, and psychosocial actuality to illustrate and elaborate on his basic theoretical position.

Although he has developed his epigenetic schema in broad outline, his main clinical elaboration of it, as noted above, has been in relation to adolescence, more particularly late adolescence, with its crucial conflict in relation to identity and its polarity-identity diffusion. Erikson elaborated in detail on his concept of identity in his article, "The Problem of Ego Identity" (1956; 1959), although he had utilized the term in a number of papers during the previous decade. He had developed the concept as a result of "the expansion of his clinical awareness to other fields (social anthropology and comparative education) and through the expectation that such expansion would in turn profit clinical work" (1959, p. 101). He further states, "The question before us is whether the concept of identity is essentially a psychosocial one, or deserves to be considered as a legitimate part of the psychoanalytic theory of the ego" (1959, p. 101).

He delineates four different connotations of the term: (1) "a conscious sense of individual identity"; (2) "an unconscious striving for a continuity of personal character"; (3) "a criterion for the silent doings of ego synthesis"; and (4) "a maintenance of an inner solidarity with a group's ideals and identity" (1959). After differentiating between identification and identity, he describes the "identity crises" of adolescence as one of a series of "normative crises" that characterize each psychosocial phase of development. He differentiates sharply between normative crises on the one hand and neurotic and psychotic crises on the other:

> Adolescence is not an affliction but a normative crisis, i.e., a normal phase of increased conflict characterized by a seeming fluctuation in ego strength, and yet also by a high growth potential. Neurotic and psychotic crises are defined by a certain self-perpetuating propensity, by an increasing waste of defensive energy, and by a deepened psychosocial isolation; while normative crises are relatively more reversible, or better, traversable, and are characterized by an abundance of available energy which, to be sure, revives dormant anxiety and arouses new conflict, but also supports new and expanded ego

functions in the searching and playful engagement of new opportunities and associations. What under prejudiced scrutiny may appear to be the onset of a neurosis is often but an aggravated crisis which might prove to be self-liquidating and, in fact, contributive to the process of identity formation (1959, p. 116).

Erikson then delineates the clinical picture of "acute identity diffusion" in young people, the only detailed application of his psychosocial schema to psychopathology. He relates the picture "to a combination of experiences which demand his simultaneous commitment to physical intimacy (not by any means always overtly sexual), to decisive occupational choice, to energetic competition, and to psychosocial self-definition" (1959, p. 123). The clinical picture involves isolation, avoidance of choices, loss of sense of inner continuity, a diffusion of time perspective, inability to work or concentrate, the choice of a negative identity, and the like. In short, Erikson describes what is generally considered an acute psychotic episode, but from his own psychosocial perspective rather than the conventional classical position. He then discusses the therapeutic problems and techniques and the family structure often seen in such cases. Erikson further elaborates on the problem of ideologies and of the concept of the self. He concludes with a summary statement in which he attempts to demonstrate that the concept of identity is a valid and necessary one from both genetic and dynamic points of view, and therefore a valid psychoanalytic concept.

Since this publication in 1956, the concept of identity has been very much in vogue. As Erikson himself stated in "Reality and Actuality":

> . . . this subject matter has had a varied fate in our own ranks, not to speak of the ubiquitous and sometimes faddish use of the term in other fields. Colleagues, in otherwise important contributions, have relegated identity as formulated by me either to oblivion or to a sociological borderland; others have elevated their version of identity to sit right next to the great triad of inner institutions, id, ego, and superego, or to act with the two great principles of mental functioning, pleasure and reality. I am, of course, unwilling to accept for my definition of identity the status of a peripheral concept, but neither would I impose on the hospitality of established theory. Conceptual twosomes and threesomes are logical configurations which cannot, to my mind, be forced to accommodate newcomers. It is important, however, that we all agree that the need for identity has emerged with the evolution of man as an animal with an intricate interdependence of individual development and social organization; and that it evolves

with each man's ego-development as a psychosocial necessity crowning all of childhood (1962b, pp. 461–462).

Unfortunately, the further integration of Erikson's concepts, which will undoubtedly be contained in his forthcoming book, *Life Cycle and Ethics*, is not yet available. Erikson's writings up to the present indicate the great significance of his work in the field of psychoanalysis in its broadest sense.

§ Comments

If we compare the work of the two contributors to psychoanalysis who are the subject of this presentation, we are immediately struck by their divergence.

Anna Freud has continued over the years to remain close to the original sources of psychoanalysis with respect to her clinical orientation and concern with pathological deviations from the norm. Her recent excursions into a discussion of normality derive from and are based on her clinical studies of pathology. They represent, in the main, efforts to extrapolate some criteria as guidelines for her evaluation of what the limits are, particularly in children, that may be accepted as "normal variations" and at what point we must consider a phenomenon sufficiently deviant to require psychoanalytic or psychotherapeutic intervention. She remains fundamentally a clinical observer and practical psychoanalyst, as well as psychoanalytic diagnostician and therapist, rather than a theorist; she is certainly far removed from being a psychoanalytic system-builder or philosopher. Her concern with theory remains secondary to her preoccupation with clinical data and the correlation of these data with the classical theoretical structure of psychoanalysis. Her principal interest for many years has been primarily children and child analysis, and the effects of the direct observation of children on analytic technique and analytic theory. Her principal theoretical concerns lie in the area of modifying aspects of theory as a result of careful clinical observation.

Erikson, on the other hand, has from the beginning been more interested in the application of the theory of psychoanalysis to social and anthropological data and the utilization of analytically based or analytically derived methods of observation in broader areas of human functioning. In his studies, he has focused on the ego and ego functioning to a greater extent and more broadly and encompassingly than has anyone else in psychoanalysis.

His early published work was essentially in the field of the application of psychoanalysis to anthropology and education. Relatively little of his work is related to the study of clinical pathology, the classical area of psychoanalysis. His observational data have been principally related to the synthesizing function of the ego, even more to the relation of the self, that is, the total psychic structure of the individual to the specific sociohistorical environment rather than to the fragmentation of the psychic structure and its resultant pathological manifestations. One sees this perhaps most clearly in his analyses of Shaw and Luther, in which the focus is upon their integration, in constructive synthesizing ways, of what would generally be regarded as pathogenic events.

His focus of interest has been more on the social than on the individual psychological aspects of his psychosocial epigenetic schema, and for this reason the question repeatedly raised has been of his relation to the mainstream of classical psychoanalysis. However, Rapaport has repeatedly affirmed his view that Erikson's concepts fit broadly into the conceptual framework of psychoanalysis and furnish "for the first time a theory and an epigenetic ground plan of ego development" (1960, p. 136).

REFERENCES

Burlingham, Dorothy. *Twins: a study of three pairs of identical twins.* New York: International Universities Press, 1946.

Burlingham, Dorothy. Some notes on development of the blind. *The psychoanalytic study of the child.* Vol. 16. New York: International Universities Press, 1961.

Erikson, E. Configurations in play—clinical notes. *Psychoanal. Quart.*, 1937, 6, 139–214.

Erikson, E. Observations on Sioux education. *J. Psychol.*, 1939, 7, 101–156.

Erikson, E. Studies in the interpretation of play: 1. Clinical observation of play disruption in young children. *Genet. Psychol. Monogr.*, 1940, **22.**

Erikson, E. Hitler's imagery and German youth. *Psychiatry*, 1942, 5, 475–493.

Erikson, E. Childhood and tradition in two American Indian tribes. In *The psychoanalytic study of the child.* Vol. 1. New York: International Universities Press, 1945.

Erikson, E. Ego development and historical change—clinical notes. In *The psychoanalytic study of the child.* Vol. 2. New York: International Universities Press, 1946.

Erikson, E. *Childhood and society.* New York: Norton, 1950.

Erikson, E. The dream specimen of psychoanalysis. *J. Amer. Psychoanal. Ass.*, 1954, **2**, 5–56. (Also in R. P. Knight, & C. R. Friedman [Eds.], *Psychoanalytic psychiatry and psychology, clinical and theoretical papers*, 1954, **1**, 131–170.)

Erikson, E. The problem of ego identity. *J. Amer. Psychoanal. Ass.*, 1956, **4**, 56–121.

Erikson, E. *Young man Luther, a study in psychoanalysis and history.* New York: Norton, 1958.

Erikson, E. Identity and the life cycle. *Psychol. Issues*, 1959, **1**, 1.

Erikson, E. Reality and actuality. *J. Amer. Psychoanal. Ass.*, 1962, **10** (3), 451–474. (a)

Erikson, E. Youth: fidelity and diversity. *Daedalus*, Winter, 1962, pp. 5–26. (b)

Erikson, E. The golden rule and the cycle of life—G. W. Gay lecture, Harvard Medical School, May 4, 1962. *Harvard Bull.*, 1963.

Erikson, E., & Erikson, K. T. The confirmation of the delinquent. *Chicago Rev.*, 1957, **10**, 15–23.

Freud, Anna. *The Ego and the mechanisms of defence.* London: Hogarth Press, 1937.

Freud, Anna. Clinical studies in psychoanalysis: research project of the Hampstead Child Therapy Clinic. In *The psychoanalytic study of the child.* Vol. 14. New York: International Universities Press, 1959.

Freud, Anna. Assessment of childhood disturbances. In *The psychoanalytic study of the child.* Vol. 17. New York: International Universities Press, 1962.

Freud, Anna, & Dorothy Burlingham. *Infants without families.* New York: International Universities Press, 1943. (a)

Freud, Anna, & Dorothy Burlingham. *War and children.* New York: Medical War Books, 1943. (b)

Freud, Anna, Dorothy Burlingham, & C. deMonchaux L. Frankl. Clinical studies in psychoanalysis. *Proc. R. Soc. Med.*, 1958, **51**, 938–47.

Freud, S. Inhibitions, symptoms, and anxiety. In *The complete psychological works of. . . .* Vol. 20. (standard ed.) London: Hogarth Press, 1959.

Rapaport, D. Structure of psychoanalytic theory: a systematizing attempt. Psychol. Issues, 1960, Vol. 2, No. 2, Monogr. No. 6. (International Universities Press)

Sandler, J. On the concept of the superego. In *The psychoanalytic study of the child.* Vol. 15. New York: International Universities Press, 1960.

Sandler, J. Research in psychoanalysis: the Hampstead Index as an instrument of psychoanalytic research. *Int. J. Psycho-Anal.*, 1962, **43**, 4–5; 287–91.

BIBLIOGRAPHY

Burlingham, Dorothy. Present trends in handling mother–child relationships during the therapeutic process. In *The psychoanalytic study of the child.* Vol. 6. New York: International Universities Press, 1951. 31–37.

Erikson, E. Growth and crises of the "healthy personality." In M. J. E. Senn (Ed.), *Symposium on the healthy personality, supplement II; problems of infancy and childhood, transactions of fourth conference.* New York: Josiah Macy, Jr., Foundation, 1950.

Erikson, E. *On the sense of our inner identity—in health and human relations.* New York: Josiah Macy, Jr., Foundation, 1953. (Also in R. P.

Knight, & C. R. Friedman [Eds.], *Psa. Psychiat. Psychol.* [Austen Riggs Center], 1954, 1, 351–364.)

Erikson, E. Freud's "The origins of psychoanalysis." *Int. J. Psycho-Anal.*, 1955, 36 (1), 1–15.

Erikson, E. The psychosocial development of children. In J. M. Tanner, & B. Inhelder (Eds.), *Discussion on child development.* (Proceedings of the WHO Study Group on Psychological Development of the Child. [Vol. 3, pp. 169–188.]) Geneva, N.Y.: International Universities Press, 1955, 1958.

Erikson, E. The syndrome of identity diffusion in adolescents and young adults. In J. M. Tanner, & B. Inhelder (Eds.), *Discussion on child development,* 1955, 1958, 3, 133–154. (Proceedings of the WHO Study Group on Psychological Development of the Child. [Vol. 3, pp. 133–154.]) Geneva, N.Y.: International Universities Press, 1955, 1958.

Erikson, E. Ego identity and the psychological moratorium. In H. L. Witmer, & R. Kosinsky (Eds.), *New Perspectives for research in juvenile delinquency,* 1956, No. 356, 1–23. (U. S. Children's Bureau.)

Erikson, E. The first psychoanalyst. *Yale Rev.*, Autumn, 1956, 40–62.

Erikson, E. The nature of clinical evidence. *Daedalus,* 1958, 87, 65–87. (Also in *Evidence and inference, the first Hayden Colloquium.* Cambridge: Technology Press of M.I.T., 1958.)

Erikson, E. The roots of virtue. In J. Huxley (Ed.), *Humanist frame.* London: George Allen & Unwin, 1961. Pp. 145–165.

Frankl, L. Some observations on the development and disturbances of integration in childhood. In *The psychoanalytic study of the child.* Vol. 16. New York: International Universities Press, 1961. Pp. 146–163.

Freud, Anna. Indications for child analysis. In *The psychoanalytic study of the child.* Vol. 1. New York: International Universities Press, 1945. Pp. 127–150.

Freud, Anna. Psychoanalytic study of infantile feeding disturbances. In *The psychoanalytic study of the child.* Vol. 2. New York: International Universities Press, 1946. Pp. 119–131.

Freud, Anna. Aggression in relation to emotional development: normal and pathological. In *The psychoanalytic study of the child.* Vols. 3 & 4. New York: International Universities Press, 1949. Pp. 37–42.

Freud, Anna. Observation on child development. In *The psychoanalytic study of the child.* Vol. 6. New York: International Universities Press, 1951. Pp. 18–30.

Freud, Anna. Mutual influences in the development of ego and id: introduction to discussion. In *The psychoanalytic study of the child.* Vol. 7. New York: International Universities Press, 1952. Pp. 42–50.

Freud, Anna. Role of bodily illness in the mental life of children. In *The psychoanalytic study of the child.* Vol. 7. New York: International Universities Press, 1952. Pp. 69–81.

Freud, Anna. Some remarks on infant observation. In *The psychoanalytic study of the child.* Vol. 8. New York: International Universities Press, 1953. Pp. 9–19.

Freud, Anna. Discussion: problems of infantile neurosis. In *The psychoanalytic study of the child.* Vol. 9. New York: International Universities Press, 1954. Pp. 25–31, 40–43, 68–71.

Freud, Anna. Problems of technique in adult analysis. *Bull. Phila. Ass. Psychoanal.*, 1954, 4 (3), 44–69.

Freud, Anna. Psychoanalysis and education. In *The psychoanalytic study of the child.* Vol. 9. New York: International Universities Press, 1954. Pp. 9–15.

Freud, Anna. Adolescence. In *The psychoanalytic study of the child.* Vol. 13. New York: International Universities Press, 1958. Pp. 255–278.

Freud, Anna. Child observation and prediction of development: memorial lecture in honor of Ernst Kris. In *The psychoanalytic study of the child.* Vol. 13. New York: International Universities Press, 1958. Pp. 92–117.

Freud, Anna. Clinical studies in psychoanalysis (research project of the Hampstead Child Therapy Clinic). *Proc. R. Soc. Med.*, 1958, **51**, 938–974.

Freud, Anna. Discussion of Dr. J. Bowlby's paper, "Grief and mourning in infancy." In *The psychoanalytic study of the child.* Vol. 15. New York: International Unversities Press, 1960. Pp. 53–62.

Freud, Anna, & Sophie Dann. An experiment in group upbringing. In *The psychoanalytic study of the child.* Vol. 6. New York: International Universities Press, 1951. Pp. 127–168.

This chapter was presented as a paper at the meeting of The Academy of Psychoanalysis on May 3, 1963, in St. Louis, Missouri, and published in the Proceedings of the Academy.

PSYCHOANALYSIS IN ENGLAND

*

EDWARD GLOVER

In studying the pioneering phases of psychoanalysis, one is impressed by the many identities between the biography of an individual and the life of a scientific group. Groups manifest very clearly the influence of family organization and reaction; also, during their earliest phases, small scientific groups reproduce those stages in individual development at which various introjections and identifications shape the mental apparatus and determine the expansion or, alternatively, the contraction (progression or regression) of their subsequent activities.

In psychoanalytic societies, this structural aspect is reinforced by a dynamic factor, namely, the conflict aroused by the ideational content the groups ostensibly set out to sustain and advance. The social historian would, no doubt, be content to express all this by saying that the life history of a scientific group involves a study of its leading personalities and the part each plays in advancing (or retarding) certain scientific aims and theories. Although this is the most labor-saving approach, it tends to overemphasize individual leadership at the expense of specifically group interactions, particularly those unconscious interactions that modify the growth of any society.

The history of psychoanalysis has been marked by repeated dissensions and schisms. Since the end of Freud's leadership, these have become sufficiently manifest for the coining of the term "neo-Freudian," which suggests that psychoanalysis has changed considerably since the days of Freud. The early psychoanalytic groups came into existence following what might be called an "act of participation," a sort of "primary identification" with Freud by his original and closest adherents. To this extent their growth had much in common. But to understand the specific characteristics of each group, one must trace the complicated interplay of group factors—both constructive and disintegrative—that followed the development of independent group function, that is, the birth of the group.

Pursuing this approach in a logical order, the first step toward understanding the course of psychoanalysis in England is to familiarize oneself with the professional life of its first adherent, Ernest Jones. Following his return to London from Canada in the latter part of 1913, he was the founder, leader, and for many years the backbone of the British movement. His approach to psychoanalysis between 1905 and his return to London in 1913, when he proceeded forthwith to establish the London Psycho-Analytical Society, is an essential part of this story. The story is told at various points of Jones's biography of Freud and in his autobiography, *Free Associations* (Jones, 1960).

The situation in London was not identical with that in Freud's Vienna; whereas Freud had worked for almost ten years alone and unsupported, for some time before the formation of the London Society a small number of British psychiatrists and psychologists had evinced a growing interest in the "new psychology," as it was sometimes called. It is difficult to say whether David Eder, David Forsyth, or Bernard Hart exercised the most powerful influence in support of Freudian theory during the period when Ernest Jones was in Canada. Eder was the most enthusiastic and indefatigable of the three (he gave the first clinical lecture on psychoanalysis in 1911, at the annual meeting of the British Medical Association in Edinburgh). Bernard Hart had the most acute mind; despite a certain amount of native caution, he did more than the others to introduce psychoanalysis to intelligent readers and to the psychiatric faculty at large. Forsyth carried the greatest weight among the consultants of Harley Street and Wimpole Street. In England, psychiatry has never played the active role in the development of psychoanalysis that it has in the United States. On the other hand, the influence of cultural groups has been far greater in England; by the early twenties, few Cambridge undergraduates having any pretensions to advanced thought failed to profess an interest in Freudian psychology.

But this is to anticipate. The history of the first London group was significantly brief and inglorious and provides an apt illustration of the ambivalent forces stirred by the new science. Writing of the disappointing impression he first formed of the quality of the early Viennese group, Ernest Jones remarked that under the existing conditions of opposition to psychoanalysis, Freud more or less had to accept whomever he could get as members. The same could be said of the beginnings of the London Society. The original group consisted of nine members, only four of whom—Jones, Eder, Clement Bryan, and Forsyth—practiced analysis. Bernard Hart, another early member, confined himself to psychiatric practice. Two members lived in India, one in Ireland, one in Canada, and one in Syria, bringing the early total to fourteen.

Jones soon had cause to regret his precipitancy in forming the London Society. In his autobiography, he has spoken of the jealousies that weakened the group and in particular of Secretary Eder's habit of introducing members who, doubting the validity of Freudian theory, became ardent Jungians. Constance Long and Maurice Nicol were among these. After a year or two, Eder himself began openly to display Jungian sympathies. (It was not until 1920 that, dissatisfied with Jungian theory and following an analysis with Ferenczi, Eder resumed his Freudian allegiance.) In short, the society became a hotbed of dissension, and after the first two years meetings were suspended—most of the members being on war service anyway.

The next step was taken by Jones in February, 1919. At his invitation, the following met at his rooms at 69 Great Portland Street: Doctors Bryan, Henry Devine, Forsyth, Stanford Read, W. H. B. Stoddart, Mr. Eric Hiller, and Barbara Low. They decided to bring the London Psycho-Analytical Society to a close and to form in its place the British Psycho-Analytical Society, to be affiliated with the International Psycho-Analytical Association. Ernest Jones was elected president, Bryan, secretary, and Stoddart, treasurer. As a precautionary measure, a limited membership was decided upon. At the start, the membership included those present at that first meeting, plus Professor J. C. Flugel. To this list were soon added, among others, Doctor O. Berkeley-Hill, Cyril Burt (now Sir Cyril Burt), Doctor R. M. Riggall, and Joan Riviere. A group of associate members included Doctors W. A. Brend and Bernard Hart, Professor Percy Nunn, Doctor T. W. Mitchell, and Doctor W. H. R. Rivers. By the middle of the summer term, regular meetings were held at which a variety of rather minor psychoanalytic topics were discussed.

This formative period of the society lasted until the end of 1922. Among those granted membership or associate membership during this period were Doctors Maurice Wright, Millais Culpin, John Rickman, James Glover, Miss Ella Sharpe, Mrs. Susan Isaacs, Doctor Edward Glover, Doctor Sylvia Payne, and James and Alix Strachey. By the end of 1922, the society consisted of seventeen members and thirty associate members; the average attendance rose from ten in the first year to seventeen in 1922.

All in all, the British Psycho-Analytical Society was held together by the dialectic skill of Ernest Jones, who was quite clearly master of the situation and determined to retain full control. J. C. Flugel, who was, next to Jones, the most thoroughly oriented member of the society, gave the first full-dress paper, "On the Character and Married Life of Henry VIII" (1920). In retrospect, Flugel confessed that his main concern was not to be found guilty of any outrageous psychoanalytic *gaffe*. And this was the watchword of the group throughout the period. Most of the meetings were concerned with minor points in clinical practice and with reviews of the more recent of Freud's published works.

In 1922, the problem of organizing a scientific program was considered by a subcommittee; from this time, the British Society may be said to have achieved a more solid scientific status. Two other factors reinforced this development in the years immediately following. From the scientific point of view, the impact of Freud's paper on the concept of the id (delivered at the Berlin Congress in 1922), together with his earlier essay on group psychology, afforded the society an opportunity to "catch up" with the current trend of ego psychology and so diminish the British group's feeling of inferiority regarding the original work produced in Vienna, Berlin, and Budapest. Second, preparations were set afoot to organize an Institute of Psycho-Analysis, together with the London Clinic of Psycho-Analysis. Articles of Association were signed in 1924. This plan had originally been put forward in 1920 by Barbara Low, and the actual opening provided an incentive that, together with growing membership, was responsible for an increase in the scientific work and scope of the society. (The foundation of the institute and clinic was made possible through the generosity of Dr. Prynce Hopkins, now of Santa Barbara, California, who gave substantial donations toward this end.) Not long after the Institute was founded a committee set up by the British Medical Association published its 1929 report on psychoanalysis. The committee's deliberations had extended over the best part of three years, and the lion's share of the task of representing psychoanalysis had been contributed by Ernest Jones, whom I assisted on some points. Officially, it was decided that the term psychoanalyst should be applied only to those professing Freudian theories and practices and recognized in the country by the British Society. With this official recognition, the pioneering phase of psychoanalysis in Britain may be said to have come to an end.

During this period and for a few years thereafter, the work of the British Society—although greatly extended—was still most conservative. The Training Committee, set up at about the same time as the Institute, had not yet reached the stage of producing fully trained candidates. Members and associates still acquired their status through an apprentice system; they were recognized on the recommendation of the training analyst, who normally took a supervising interest in their reading and sponsored their early casework. It was perhaps partly a result of the residual transferences engendered under this system that the society was relatively free from dissension, either scientific or personal, a unity that was greatly fostered by the firm direction exercised by Ernest Jones. This may at times have cramped discussion a little, for Jones instilled intellectual fear as well as respect; on the other hand, in the course of time it served to raise the quality of contributions from the floor. Needless to add, the policies of the society in both internal and external affairs were at first exclusively, and later for the greatest part, determined by Jones. In fact, he operated as the leading superego of the group, holding it together by *force majeure*.

It is of some historical interest that the seeds of scientific dissension in the society were in the field of child analysis. Before 1925, only a few analysts were specializing in child analysis, among whom Mary Chadwick, a pupil of Hanns Sachs, was the most prolific. Between 1925 and 1927, two sets of lectures on the subject were given by Melanie Klein, then a child analyst in Berlin. When, in 1926, Melanie Klein transferred to London, the foundations of a child analysis group were laid.

In *The Psycho-Analysis of Children* of 1932, Melanie Klein advanced a number of theoretical and clinical propositions regarding mental development during the first and subsequent infantile years. Some of these constituted genuine advances in the reconstruction of mental development. Others were to provide a focus of active criticism, explicitly expressed from 1934 on when, in the second phase of her theorizing and reconstruction, Mrs. Klein advanced further propositions on depressive and paranoid "positions" and "manic defenses" centering around an Oedipal situation presumed to date from the third month of life. Edward Glover made a critique of the Kleinian system at that time (1945, pp. 75–119).

The earlier formulations of Melanie Klein were welcomed by many members of the British Society, for three reasons: first, because the group as a whole suffered from a sense of inferiority regarding its stereotyped contributions to psychoanalysis; second, because Mrs. Klein's views were strongly supported by Ernest Jones; and third, because her views included a number of original suggestions that illuminated some problems of early mental development. However, the acceptance was guarded; the more enthusiastic of Mrs. Klein's followers came to constitute an unofficial subgroup, whose members were inclined to look down their noses at therapists who clung to the more classical Freudian positions regarding mental development. In short, there were two opposing subgroups within the society, a Kleinian subgroup and one made up of those in active opposition to her later theories.

During the next few years, from 1933 to 1939, this dissension gradually increased; indeed, it was sharpened by the arrival in England of a substantial number of analysts from Vienna and other mid-European centers. Although their arrival partially checked the speculative exuberance of the Kleinian subgroup, the total number of subgroups increased. In direct opposition to the Kleinian subgroup on most points stood the classical subgroup, and intermediate was a subgroup whose members had absorbed some Kleinian ideas and strove to compound them with the more classical teachings.

Inevitably, this division into three subgroups was reflected in the constitution and policies of the Training Committee. Because whoever controls the Training Committee is in a position to influence decisively the scientific orientation of any psychoanalytic society, it seemed that the scientific fortunes of the British Society would depend on the balance of power in that committee, and on the number of candidates trained or influenced by the respective subgroups.

In the years before World War II, dissensions became more apparent. With the outbreak of war, a peaceful period ensued that ended in

1943, when members in the service or who had been evacuated from the city returned to London. At that time it was decided to hold a series of discussions on the Klein controversy. These lasted for over eighteen months, well into 1944. The outcome was inconclusive; neither of the contending groups was prepared to give way, and the middle group signalized its position by "sitting on the fence."

An attempt was made to arrive at a compromise in training. Two groups were formed, the "A Group" (Kleinian) and the "B Group" (Freudian). On admission, candidates for training could indicate their preference for one course or the other, or were influenced in the their choice by the training analysts they had chosen. When no preference was indicated, training analysis was by a member of the middle group.[1] During the first year, candidates attended courses in general Freudian psychology; in the last year, they took part in lectures and seminars conducted by members of all three groups. Although candidates in training with analysts of the middle group were free to attend courses of the Freudians, their main curricular courses were Kleinian in approach. As a result, despite eclectic precautions, a thoroughly unhealthy situation resulted: candidates outside the B Group became ever more Kleinian in their thinking, and the A and B groups became more sharply opposed than ever.

One factor until then unfamiliar in British psychoanalysis is worthy of note. Some psychiatrists who had seen war service had been impressed by the analytic approach and now sought analytic training. As has already been suggested psychiatrists had played little or no part in psychoanalysis in Britain (excepting W. H. B. Stoddart and Bernard Hart, who were a source of support during the earliest pioneering phase). But this postwar infusion of psychiatric blood introduced a more eclectic, if not quite empirical, factor in psychoanalytic development. Writing (1949) on the then current situation, I suggested that the British Society was divisible into four subgroups, (1) an orthodox Freudian subgroup, (2) a Kleinian subgroup, (3) an embryo psychiatric subgroup, and (4) the remnants of the old middle subgroup.

It is chastening to record the trend of my own speculations at that time regarding the future of psychoanalytic movements in Britain. Although I hoped that the standard positions of the Freudian subgroup would maintain strength, I feared the Klein subgroup would prevail. In

[1] Incidentally, it was this provision that in time greatly increased the strength of the otherwise feeble and almost anonymous middle group.

my opinion, the middle subgroup was a timid and unproductive formation that would probably lose influence. For these reasons among others, in 1944 I decided to resign my various offices in the Institute, Clinic, and Training Committee, together with my membership in the British Society. In particular, I had been seriously dissatisfied for many years with the *modus operandi* of the Training Committee, which more than any other body determines the fate of psychoanalysis in any one branch and which, in many important respects, seemed increasingly unscientific in tendency. At the time I saw no prospect of improvement for many years to come—an assessment to which I still hold.

I had underestimated the British love of compromise and trimming and had overestimated the solidarity and political acumen of subgoups. Reviewing the situation in 1961, after the lapse of twelve years, it would appear that, whereas the Freudian and Kleinian subgroups are gradually dwindling, the middle groupers—for whom the expedient term "Independents" is now suggested—have greatly increased their strength and have also acquired strategic administrative power. Further analysis of this new middle subgroup indicates its heterogenous nature, comprising as it does remnants of the original middle group, seceders from the A Group (Kleinian), such ambitious members of the B Group (Freudian) as vary in their allegiance to it (running sometimes with the hares and sometimes with the hounds), together with a number of younger psychiatrists (mostly middle group trainees who, having no historical traditions to guide them, are less prone to be fettered by what they consider to be "dated" allegiances). All this, of course, continues to be subject to the overriding consideration that, like their elders, the younger members are influenced in one direction or another by their training analyst's views and teachings. Although the number of members and associates of psychiatric origin and the complement of lay analysts has greatly increased, the percentage of child analysts is still relatively small.

Two extramural extensions of psychoanalytic activities are worthy of note. The once eclectic Tavistock Clinic, increasingly staffed by analysts after World War II, has developed a twin organization, an Institute of Human Relations, comprised of (1) an investigative branch, concerned mainly with research into a variety of ancillary aspects of social psychoanalysis, and (2) a clinical organization, divided into an adult department, a department for children and parents, and an adolescent unit. In addition, separate organizations have been set up or supported by the Tavistock Clinic, the object of which is to study and handle, for example, family and marital problems. The therapeutic resources of the Tavistock Clinic are directed mainly to "analytic group therapy" and in part to some types of short therapy. More important, in both research and the training of the staff, to say nothing of courses for general practitioners, emphasis is on the application of psychoanalytic viewpoints, which vary in accordance with the group allegiances of the members. A considerable proportion belong to the middle group.

The second and more exclusively psychoanalytic extramural organization, the Hampstead Child Therapy Clinic and Training Center, was promoted by Anna Freud, following the pioneer planning of the late Dr. Kate Friedländer. In the five weekly sessions, children are analyzed either by child therapists in training and working under control analysts or by members and associates of the British Psycho-Analytical Society undergoing training courses in child analysis. A few "mother guidance" cases are dealt with on the basis of one or two sessions a week. In addition, there are some concurrent analyses of parents and children. The training course lasts four years. Lectures and seminars are given by medical and lay analysts, assisted by members of the staff. An important part of the Hampstead Center's activities consists of research work by trained units. Projects include some multidimensional investigations of the work done at the Hampstead Clinic, including syntheses of findings and methods and the testing of psychoanalytic concepts. Whereas the analytic orientation of the Tavistock staff varies, that of the Hampstead Center is classically Freudian.

Before attempting to appraise the scientific as distinct from the political impact of this conglomeration of subgroups, it is essential to assess the factors that have guided their inter-reactions within the British Society. These can be divided into personal factors and factors inseparable from the psychoanalytic approach.

Of the first or personal type, a few examples must suffice. Certainly, one factor was the lack of scientific direction, a result of the failing health and ultimate death of Freud. Nevertheless, even during Freud's lifetime, two mutually opposing reactions to his scientific leadership existed within the psychoanalytic groups. The more obvious reaction was one of strict, almost filial conformity; less manifest but equally powerful was a kind of selective nonconformity. For many years, strict conformity to Freud's views was strongly reinforced by the authority of Ernest Jones. However, Jones found himself in opposition to Freud concerning the nature of infantile sexual development in the boy and the girl. This occurred around the time that Melanie Klein appeared on the English horizon, and Jones seemed to find support for his point of view in her presentations. From that time on, he was a consistent champion of Klein's teachings. In this way, scientific discipline was relaxed, and an increasingly speculative trend has manifested itself in the proceedings of the Society. Melanie Klein was something of a matriarch who gave the impression that those who were not with her were against her. In consequence, discussion at the scientific meetings frequently degenerated into the registration of allegiances rather than a period of objective criticism.

A third factor influencing the subgroups within the society was the exodus to the United States of a number of ex-European stalwarts, some of the most skilled dialecticians among them. Although at that time they were a little too rigidly orthodox, the European psychoanalysts had had a thorough training in the methods and theory of psychoanalysis, and their continued presence in the British Society would have provided an effective check on psychoanalytic thinking in Britain.

As for the more impersonal factors activated by psychoanalytic preoccupations, in principle these are of the same nature as the resistance manifested by patients in analysis. They owe some of their concealed strength to residual training transferences and are consequently exacerbated by the existence of subgroups in the society. These factors can be divided into anxiety reactions, guilt reactions, and ambivalent reactions, then subdivided, according to their manifestations, into positive and negative (reactive) forms. Attention has already been drawn to the inferiority reactions that characterized the British Society in its earlier years. However, the term "English School" began to gain currency, both at home and abroad, giving no clue to the dissensions that existed in the society.

An undercurrent of ambivalence to Freudian theory was of greater importance, contributing in no small measure to the sharpness of opposition among the subgroups. Only the middle groupers were able to achieve an uneasy eclectic compromise, which greatly inhibited their freedom of thought and consequently the value of their contributions. On the surface, the issues were regarded as purely scientific, but on examining the bones of contention, it is not difficult to single out the factor that, more than any other, has caused friction in the British Society: it can best be described as a quasi-scientific manifestation of the battle of the sexes. In its most sublimated form, it consisted of criticism of Freud's views on the mental development of women. There was, however, a good deal of emotional loading of this essentially bisexual controversy; perhaps it is sufficient to quote the privately expressed opinion of a senior member of the feminist group, namely, that only a woman analyst can effectively analyze either male or female patients. To be sure, these various reactions are not peculiar to the British Society, but certainly they have inhibited the free progress of psychoanalytic science in England.

Taking these considerations into account, it is obviously an increasingly difficult task to disentangle subjective emotional factors from the more scientific influences operative in the British Society. And the more subgroups or splinter groups, the more difficult the task. One preliminary consideration is prerequisite to making such an assessment. Examination of Jung's works demonstrates that there are two favorite ways of discounting psychoanalytic principles. One is to displace the focus of interest from dynamic unconscious to more preconscious and immediately interpersonal levels (the "here and now"); the other is to give free rein to speculative reconstructions of phases alleged to exist at a time when it is impossible to check any conclusions by direct analysis. The latter leads either to an overemphasis of constitutional factors or to an attribution of ego (structural) characteristics to the id. As for the more superficial psychologies of individuation and interpersonal relations, the danger is clear. In my opinion, some recent psychoanalytic thinking (to say nothing of methods of treatment) exemplifies the tendencies described.

It can, and no doubt will, be argued by those in favor of the present system that the multiplication of subgroups, particularly the waxing of the middle subgroup, will lead in the long run to a more balanced and disciplined teaching of psychoanalysis. It may be maintained that a series of subgroups constitutes a spectrum of the total British Society, each band representing a different depth of psychoanalytic approach, from the id to perceptual consciousness, and from the subject to the object world. It even may be asserted that there is room in psychoanalysis for every variety of speculation, ranging from biology, ethology, embryology, or neurology to the most superficial aspects of "person-to-person" psychology. This is, after all, a matter of opinion. What cannot be denied is the urgent need to ensure that speculative exercises in reconstruction do not bypass any fundamental Freudian tenets in favor of allegedly "deeper insights," the evidence for which so far remains largely personal predilection and plausibility—not very reliable criteria, for both depend in part on the enthusiasm of the observer or theoretician. Psychoanalysis is subject to peculiar difficulties in these respects. Training transferences themselves permit the continuation of unsound theories and inexact interpretations.

Looking back over the development of the British Society, it appears that psychoanalysis in Britain was potentially in a sounder position during its timid formative years than it is now. And, despite various suggestions that we are now witnessing "modern advances," there is little in current "neo-Freudian" psychology that extends our knowledge and much that would retard it. We may, however, take comfort from the clinical observation that both *doyens* and neophytes in psychoanalysis tend to rediscover Freud throughout their professional lives. It is to be hoped that this tendency may yet stem both undisciplined speculation and adulterization.

REFERENCES

Flugel, J. C. On the character and married life of Henry VIII. *Int. J. Psycho-Anal.*, 1920, 1, 24–55.

Glover, E. An examination of the Klein system of child psychology. In *The psychoanalytic study of the child.* Vol. 1. New York: International Universities Press, 1945. (Reprinted, London: H. K. Lewis, 1950.)

Glover, E. The position of psychoanalysis in Britain. *Brit. Med. Bull.*, 1949, 6, 27–31. (Reprinted in *On the early development of mind.* London: Imago Publishing Co., 1956.)

Jones, E. *Free association.* London: Hogarth Press, 1960.

PSYCHOANALYSIS IN THE UNITED STATES

*

JOHN A. P. MILLET

Psychoanalysis may be likened to an enzyme. As a conceptual system, it is unique in structure; as a dynamism it has been responsible for activating in the tissues of culture both catalytic and anabolic processes that would otherwise not have been set in motion. It seems no accident that the *Interpretation of Dreams* was published in the evening of the reign of Queen Victoria. The impact of Sigmund Freud's early discoveries on nineteenth-century morality was such that the reverberations still echo through the corridors of fundamentalism and Academe. Had two world wars not rocked the foundations of civilization to their depths, it is hard to say what influence the new insights provided by psychoanalytic investigations might have had in penetrating the fabric of a less disrupted society. Certainly the ever more urgent need to understand the nature of man and of his strangely contradictory urges, individual and collective, opened the door wide to its pronouncements.

The North American continent, which has imported and preserved the religious and political forms of Western Europe, became the natural haven for most European psychoanalysts who had been disinherited and exiled by the Nazis. Even before World War I, a small group of American psychiatrists had visited Zurich and Vienna and returned to the United States full of enthusiasm for the new approach that Freud's work seemed to promise for the understanding and treatment of mental disturbances. The truly remarkable development of psychoanalysis in the United States is largely the result of the indefatigable efforts and unwavering conviction of these pioneers. It is the purpose of this essay to trace this development through its most significant phases and to interpret its significance in strengthening or modifying certain familiar aspects of our culture.

The course of psychoanalytic development in this country was temporarily checked and profoundly influenced by the violent disruptions of society occasioned by two world wars. The first three decades of the twentieth century saw the introduction of psychoanalytic ideas and literature into the United States and the beginnings of professional organizations devoted to study and application of the methods developed by Freud and his European colleagues.

The next three decades saw the full flowering of the psychoanalytic movement here and the wide extension of its influence on medicine, education, theology, and the social sciences. This period also encompassed the great migration of European psychoanalysts to the United States, the death of Sigmund Freud, and a rapid increase in the ranks of native-born psychoanalysts. As we enter the seventh decade, new features on the psychoanalytic scene suggest a gradual setting of new patterns, for both theory and the future of psychoanalysis among other behavioral sciences. This period evinces a maturational process in which the tares of outworn assumptions may be winnowed out and the fruitful discoveries harvested.

§ The Years of Discovery

The first half of the twentieth century will be remembered as years in which the acceleration of events surpassed the bounds of credibility, leaving the human race gasping in wonder at its magical powers and aghast at their catastrophic potential. It was the half-century of social revolution, of cataclysmic warfare, of the conquest of space, and of the omnipotence of the atom. In the midst of all this change was heard the rumor—at first barely audible, later swelling to a mighty resonance—of yet another revolution, a revolution in the ways of investigating the hidden secrets of man's mental processes. This was the half-century in which new insights into human motivations and their protean manifestations in health and in disease were revealed through the genius and industry of Sigmund Freud and the patient labors of his enthusiastic disciples. Born in the academic atmosphere of a hostile Vienna, psychoanalysis was to become an outcast from its native shores and to take refuge in a country where, until the second quarter of the century was well under way, it had been accorded a none too friendly reception.

It would be foolish to attempt an evaluation of the development of psychoanalysis in its new habitat without taking full account of the historical events that led to its expatriation and of the forces brought into play in determining its future place within the culture of its new community. A detailed chronicle of the events that preceded the establishment of psychoanalysis here has already been given in such volumes as *A History of Psychoanalysis in America* by Clarence P. Oberndorf (1953), and *Facts and Theories of Psychoanalysis* by Ives Hendrick (1958), as well as in such books as Ernest Jones's biography of Sigmund Freud (1953–7).

Although ten years have elapsed since the completion of Oberndorf's work, certain of his emphases help us understand the directions taken in the advance of the psychoanalytic movement on North America. The first advocates and exponents of the new theories were native-born American physicians who had had a thorough grounding in medicine and neurology and had achieved recognition as competent specialists in diseases of the nervous system. Foremost among these was James Putnam of Boston, a member of a long-respected conservative family and a past president of the American Neurological Association. Nothing seems less likely or harder to conceive than that, in the early twentieth century, a proper Bostonian should espouse the cause of a strange foreigner proclaiming the existence of sexual pleasure in infants and children. Nor was Putnam alone among neurologists of the day in looking to the new insights of Freud for additional understanding of nervous disorders. Oberndorf and A. A. Brill were both excellent neurologists, and even stern, admirable old Frederick Peterson gave cautious credit to Freud in allowing that about 50 per cent of neurotic illnesses are traceable to disturbances in sexual function.

Ives Hendrick (1958, p. 348) reminds us that Peterson was responsible for Brill's going to Zurich to visit E. Bleuler and C. G. Jung in November, 1907. Here Brill met Ernest Jones, whom he later accompanied to the first Psychoanalytic Congress at Salzburg. Subsequently, Brill collaborated with Peterson in translating Jung's classical monograph, *The Psychology of Dementia Praecox* (1909). As we shall see, this meeting of Brill and Jones was highly significant in setting the stage for future developments in North America and England.

Oberndorf suggests that the history of psychoanalysis in North America falls more or less naturally into decades. The first decade of the century might be described as that of the preliminary advance; ushered in by the publication of Freud's classic, *The Interpretation of Dreams,* it ended in 1909 with G. Stanley Hall's invitation to Freud and Jung to present their views at Clark University in Worcester, Massachusetts, of which Hall was then president. In the meantime, Brill had spent two years studying with Bleuler at the Burghölzli in Zurich and with Freud in Vienna. Possibly the first article on psychoanalysis in any American professional journal was that written by Morton Peabody Prince, another Boston "blue-blood," in the *Journal of Abnormal Psychology* (1906). Three years later, Frederick Peterson wrote an article in the *New York Medical Journal* (1909) on Freud and Jung's ideas of free association.

The meeting of William Alanson White and Smith Ely Jelliffe at Binghamton was the start of a long and distinguished editorial partnership. They were an interesting contrast. White was a very thoughtful, rather quiet, modest person, whereas Jelliffe was gifted with facile and expressive speech, was always ready to talk, and had a reputation as an orator. I called on him one day at his summer home on the east shore of Lake George. His study was a sight one could never forget: lined with books, of course, and with a large worktable on which were spread in apparently casual confusion all sorts of material—manuscripts, reprints, page proofs, letters, and the like. It was clearly the workshop of a dedicated scholar and intellectual—no real disorder but the assemblage of documents that would in due course be given a hearing. I deeply regretted that I had so planned my day that I could not accept Mrs. Jelliffe's cordial invitation to stay for lunch.

The most significant event of the decade for later trends in psychoanalytic theory was Freud's move from his original view of psychoanalysis as a method and theory, on which is based a medical procedure for the relief of symptoms, to increasing preoccupation with his newly conceived system of metaphysical psychology. This change is indirectly responsible for most so-called deviations from psychoanalytic theory during the later years in the United States. Heralded by the publication in 1905 of Freud's *Three Essays on the Theory of Sexuality*

(1962), a new stone was laid in the structure of psychoanalytic theory before any formal organizational structure had been built in North America.

The first steps were taken in the next decade. In 1908, Brill had returned from his studies in Zurich and Vienna to begin the practice of psychoanalysis. He soon became known as an indefatigable champion of Freudian theories and method. Scarcely a meeting of the Section on Neurology and Psychiatry at the Academy of Medicine was not enlivened by the acerbities of ideological disputes between Brill and Bernard Sachs. Strong support was often lent to the opposition by Israel Straus and by Foster Kennedy, who on one occasion appeared late at one of these meetings in full evening dress and, during a favorable pause in the exchange, pontificated in his best manner, "It seems to me that while neurologists believe *in facta, non verba,* psychiatrists believe *in verba, non facta!*" Having secured the anticipated effect, he took his leave. These were the days when the Section on Neurology and Psychiatry was dominated by neurologists and the miscegenated group known as neuropsychiatrists. The meetings were well attended, and Brill took full advantage of his membership to plead for the new insights from Vienna. The fledgling science of psychodynamics was given an occasional but reluctant hearing in papers presented at the section meetings.

At the same time, a new voice from across the border began to be heard with increasing frequency and growing assurance, the voice of the dynamic Welshman Ernest Jones, who proclaimed himself the second English-speaking contestant in what manifestly was becoming not only an ideological war but also a tournament in which the champions were out for blood. In 1909, Oberndorf returned from his psychoanalytic studies in Europe to join the fray. In the same year, Jones addressed the American Therapeutic Congress in New Haven, where he received a most unsympathetic response. There was a growing feeling that the time was ripe for forming a new professional organization that could offer the opportunity for scientific exchange among colleagues and begin to offer some instruction to those eager to learn more about Freud's ideas and method of therapy. The main interest of American physicians in psychoanalysis was in its therapeutic possibilities. I shall attempt to show how this original orientation of American physicians has been one of the strongest influences in the development of psychoanalysis in the United States.

We now leave the first decade, the decade in which cells of the new revolutionary fraternity were quietly formed; lectures and seminars or talks to informal gatherings of colleagues were given by Adolf Meyer and August Hoch at Manhattan State Hospital, by Brill at the Vanderbilt Clinic, and by William Alanson White at St. Elizabeth's Hospital. In Boston, Putnam was still somewhat of a lone wolf, although there, too, men like George Waterman and Willis Taylor were greatly influenced by Freud's ideas.

The year 1910 brought further important progress in psychoanalysis. The second meeting of the International Psycho-Analytical Association was held in Nuremberg. In that same year, Adolf Meyer moved to Johns Hopkins, where, as chief of the Phipps Clinic, he began to develop his ideas within the framework that he called psychobiology. Also in that year, some psychiatrists who were dissatisfied with parts of the Freudian teachings estabished the American Psychopathological Association.

On February 11, 1911, Brill invited a few colleagues to his home and, with their consent and help, established the New York Psychoanalytic Society. He was elected president, H. W. Frink, secretary, and B. Onuf, vice president. C. P. Oberndorf was also present. The group was strengthened in its professional competence by the addition in 1915 of Adolf Stern, who left four years later for additional training in Vienna. It soon became the desirable goal for every therapist to go to Vienna for analysis with Freud.

Three months after Brill had established the New York Society, Ernest Jones, with the assistance of Putnam and colleagues from other cities, established the American Psychoanalytic Association, an organization designed to include all persons in the United States and Canada interested in psychoanalysis. It was Ernest Jones's hope that this group would be the sole authoritative body on the North American continent, with powers delegated to it by the International Psycho-Analytical Association.

However, when the outbreak of World War I led to the disintegration of the International Psycho-Analytical Association, the newly formed American Psychoanalytic Association declared itself independent of international control and set up its own board of professional standards, under the presidency of Putnam. Differences began to develop between the New York Society and the American Psychoanalytic Association with respect to controls over training standards, and with America's entry into the war, things became rather unsettled. After Putnam's death in 1918, it looked as though the American Psychoanalytic Association might be dissolved, but in 1919 Meyer brought his influence to bear, pointing out that with the growing interest in psychoanalysis in America there was a definite need for a national organization to serve as a center for education and scientific exchange. Its continued relationship to the parent discipline of psychiatry was assured.

This decade was also noteworthy as that in which Jung broke with Freud, subsequently resigning his membership in the International Psycho-Analytical Association. The New York Society aligned itself with complete unanimity on the side of Freud. Nevertheless, by this time, Freud was becoming highly dissatisfied with the developments in psychoanalytic organization in the United States. He felt that the "pure gold" of analysis was being alloyed by the imperfect adherence of some early enthusiasts to the totality of his conceptual system and method of treatment. This second decade of psychoanalytic advance was finally submerged in the tidal wave of global war. As soon as peace was declared, however, the American group—whose teachings had shown the way to a better understanding of the effects of stress on the individual—was again on the march.

The return of Oberndorf in 1922 and Frink in 1923 from their work with Freud was soon followed by some serious differences within the New York Society. Nominated by Freud to restore order in the councils of the Society and to purify it of deviant thinking, Frink became the self-declared leader of the Educational Committee. However, the differences at this time foreshadowed the serious breakdown that later terminated Frink's "reign" and restored harmony. The disturbance initiated by the publication of Freud's paper "The Ego and the Id" (1962, Vol. 19, pp. 13–66) clearly presaged a shift in Freud's interest from his earlier preoccupation with the peregrinations and involvements of the libido. The general unrest in the Society that resulted from these disputes led Brill to resume the presidency, and he held this post from 1925 until 1936. Throughout these early years, he had always been recognized as the first proconsul in the psychoanalytic movement in the United States. It was he who had been the first authorized to translate Freud's writings into English; it was he who carried the ball when the opposing team had to be smashed through. His inimitable language, ready wit, quickness in repartee, and genuine humanity made him a natural leader.

By 1925, the hegemony of the International Psycho-Analytic Association had been quite fully restored. At its congress in Bad Homburg, five European societies and the New York Psychoanalytic Society were admitted to the International Training Committee. Differences arose concerning the admission of laymen to training in the recognized institutes. It had long been Freud's policy to accept gifted laymen for training, with a view to their becoming therapists. This view ran counter to the deep-seated prejudice of the Americans. Here, once more, the influence of the original American conception came into play—therapy of any kind is the function of the physician, and the chief value of psychoanalysis for the physician must be its usefulness as a therapeutic device. Psychoanalysis, then, for these pioneers, was always to be considered a branch of psychiatry.

By 1927, this controversy had reached its peak in the councils of the New York Society and the American Psychoanalytic Association. Laymen had been going to Europe for analysis by Freud and his colleagues and had assumed that on their return they would be welcome in the psychoanalytic fellowship. When this proved not to be so, there was "hell to pay." Freud was furious, Brill adamant. Paul Schilder's trenchant comment reflected the feelings of those who had first brought psychoanalysis into favor in this country, "It seems to me that unquestionably the treatment of the sick is a matter for the physician.

This third decade witnessed increasing interest in the publications of the European analysts and the begining migration of some of them to this country. In 1926, Sandor Lorand arrived; after teaching psychoanalytic principles at the Central Neurological Hospital on Welfare Island for a year, he joined the staff of the Mount Sinai Mental Hygiene Clinic, where Abram Kardiner, Oberndorf, and Monroe Meyer were already at work. In 1927, the New School for Social Research invited Sándor Ferenczi to give a four-month lecture course. Two years later, a similar invitation was sent to Fritz Wittels, who stayed to become one of the stalwarts of the faculty of the New York Psychoanalytic Institute.

Also during these years, Adolf Stern, in 1920, Leonard Blumgart and Kardiner, in 1929, Clarence Oberndorf, in 1922, Monroe Meyer, George Fink, and George Daniels, in 1923, and Albert Polon, in 1927

—all returned from Europe where they had undergone personal analyses in Vienna or Berlin.

It is important to recall that when the New York Society wished to establish a clinic, the application was denied—despite appeals by such nationally known leaders as Thomas W. Salmon, Floyd Haviland, and George H. Kirby—on the ground that the New York institute had no connection with a medical school or hospital. This same criticism is being leveled today at some institutes.

In the meantime, Otto Rank had come to the United States, where his imaginative constructions and literary gifts had brought him considerable fame. Nevertheless, his influence on the main stream of psychoanalytic developments in this country was not great. His views on the purposive handling of conflicts were enthusiastically adopted by social workers in Philadelphia and, under the leadership of Frederick Allen and Jessie Taft, were consistently applied in the planning and supervision of social casework in the community.

Eventually Brill made peace with Freud over the question of lay analysts. Under the terms of the compromise, no lay person would be accepted for "training analysis" by Freud and his associates unless first cleared by the profession in the United States. The American insistence on keeping psychoanalysis within the family of medical sciences was continued.

§ Problems of Adolescence

In 1929, the ruling had been definitely established for the first time in the New York Society that membership was open only to physicians who had undergone a training analysis. This provision, now long recognized as fundamental to any educational program designed to develop psychoanalysts as therapists, had not previously been formally adopted as an essential first step in psychoanalytic training in this country. Nineteen-thirty was a red-letter year in the history of psychoanalysis in the United States. Three significantly relevant events signalized the opening of a new era. The first of these was the First International Congress on Mental Hygiene—organized by Clifford Beers, with the help of distinguished American and foreign psychiatrists. It was held in Washington, D. C., in May; the second was the organization of the Boston and Chicago Psychoanalytic Societies; and the third was the invitation from the University of Chicago to Franz Alexander (who was soon to work on problems of delinquency and crime with William Healy at the Judge Baker Foundation in Boston) to become the first professor of psychoanalysis appointed in the United States. Subsequently, in 1932, a similar honor was to be bestowed on Hanns Sachs by Harvard, a unique instance of a layman invited to lecture at the Harvard Medical School.

The year 1930 also marked Gregory Zilboorg's return to this country from his induction into psychoanalysis at the Berlin Institute. An individual of rare intellectual gifts, his presence on the stage of American psychoanalysis, indeed on any stage, was sure to arrest the attention and interest of his audience. He will perhaps be best remembered for his contribution to the *History of Medical Psychology* (Zilboorg & Henry, 1941) and his work in editing the volume *One Hundred Years of American Psychiatry* (Zilboorg, Hill, & Baker, 1944), which was published at the time of the centenary celebration of the founding of the American Psychiatric Association in Philadelphia. His contribution to the study of suicide and his work in the field of criminology are also worthy of mention. He was brilliant as a teacher, absorbingly interesting as a speaker, and he had a remarkable gift for language. Arriving penniless from Russia in flight from the Bolsheviks, he had attracted the notice of Thomas Salmon, through whose influence he was given advanced standing in the College of Physicians and Surgeons and thereby enabled to go on into his chosen speciality of psychiatry.

For me, also, the year 1930 was a year of decision. After seven years of psychotherapeutic experience at Stockbridge, Massachusetts, with Austen Fox Riggs, whose early studies of Freud's work had left him a severe critic of psychoanalytic practice, I had decided to inform myself more fully on the subject. When I returned to New York, I was invited by Ramsay Hunt to participate in a group discussion of current views on the etiology and treatment of the neuroses. These meetings, held weekly for a time at the Neurological Institute, were attended by junior staff members and such persons as Paul Schilder. The orientation with which I was most familiar at the time—that developed at Stockbridge by Austen Fox Riggs—was held in high esteem by the leading New York neurologists of the day, whose psychotherapeutic efforts were founded largely on a combination of clinical intuition and the authoritative posture, but these men were at least ready to discuss psychoanalysis. By this time psychoanalysis was regarded in ever widening circles as so new and vitalizing a force that die-hards among the leading neurologists were beginning to feel the shadow of an approaching eclipse of their priority as the only true specialists in the field of nervous disorders.

An opportunity presented itself within a year of my arrival. On September 15, 1931, the New York Psychoanalytic Institute opened its newly acquired quarters. Brill and his colleagues had invited Sandor Rado to come over from Berlin as educational director of the Institute. The following autumn I became a student at the Institute, from which I graduated in the fall of 1935, after presenting the required scientific paper. At this time, fellowship in the Institute automatically led to membership in the American Psychoanalytic Association and in the International Psycho-Analytical Association. Besides Rado and Bertram Lewin, other gifted teachers were Kardiner, who gave us an idea of the meaning of cultural anthropology and its areas of contact with psychoanalysis, and Zilboorg, who drilled into us his newly found enthusiasm for the libido theory, the successive stages of libidinal organization, the Oedipus complex, repression, and the theory of instincts.

Within two years, three additional formal centers of psychoanalytic education and training had been founded. In 1930, the Boston Institute, under the leadership of Ives Hendrick, M. Ralph Kaufman, and John M. Murray, was given formal recognition, and the Washington-Baltimore Institute was organized. In 1932, the Chicago Institute was established under the direction of Franz Alexander.

By 1934, American psychoanalysts were receiving a more considerate hearing in the councils of the International Psycho-Analytical Association; at the Lucerne meeting, requirements for admission to training were amended to suit American requirements. The American Psychoanalytic Association began to take on more clearly defined outlines, beginning with the drawing up of a new constitution and bylaws, which were ratified in 1935. The four established societies (New York, Boston, Washington-Baltimore, and Chicago) became members of a federation, with no centralized authoritarian controls. This first effort at forming a national organization was well suited to the democratic forms that have always been held so important in the United States.

With the gradual disintegration of the International Training Committee, as a result of strictures imposed on psychoanalysts by Hitler and the increasing tide of emigrating analysts, it became clear that new developments in psychoanalytic organization were inevitable. In the interest of facilitating the necessary changes, Ernest Jones suggested in 1936 that the American Psychoanalytic Association be divorced from all control by the committee. The center of psychoanalytic organization was shifting rapidly from Europe to the United States. The American Psychoanalytic Association began publishing a bulletin reporting the proceedings of the meetings regularly, along with special articles. Karen Horney had joined Alexander in Chicago; she later moved to New York, where she began active teaching at the New York Institute. Under the increasing threat of persecution and imprisonment many Austrian and German psychoanalysts began to seek asylum in England and North America. By far the largest group headed for New York, which had the strongest concentration of psychoanalytic forces and where Rado was in charge of the educational program at the New York Psychoanalytic Institute. In 1938, a committee of the American Psychoanalytic Association was set up to assist these exiles in their personal and professional adjustment to the new environment.

The ranks of American psychoanalysts, progressively thinned by calls to military service, were rapidly swelled by refugees from Nazi tyranny. The European analysts soon made their influence felt in the councils of the local societies and the national organization. Many were regarded with sincere affection and found a ready place in the social life of their colleagues. Those with facility in English took pains to obtain licenses to practice medicine, without which they could not be accepted as members of either the local or the national association. Discovery of this handicap caused deep distress to some of the older men, long distinguished for their contributions in analysis. Before the end of the decade, two new societies had been formed, soon to be added to the roster of the American Psychoanalytic Association, Philadelphia, in 1937, and Topeka, in 1938. In 1939, came the outbreak of war. By this time German-speaking analysts were so numerous at the meetings of the New York Society that one heard far more German spoken than English, although the papers were presented and discussed in English. Regular attendants at these meetings included Bela Mittelmann, Ludwig Jekels, Paul Federn, and Hermann Nunberg.

The thirties might well be considered the period of early maturation of the American Psychoanalytic Association. Toward the end of the decade, the reunion of the recently arrived European analysts and their former pupils set in motion forces that tended toward the development of a close-knit inner circle of teachers; their influence set the pattern for later developments in the organizational structure and in policies of the local and national associations and the emerging institutes.

If the thirties were the years of early maturity, the forties should be classified as the "roaring forties." The political world was engaged in a life and death struggle that had minor reflections in increasing dissonances within educational committees of the local institutes and in the councils of the American Psychoanalytic Association. In an earlier essay I described the emergence of these new forces as follows:

> As more and more of the refugee analysts became qualified as members of local societies and joined the faculties of the training centers, the influence of their authoritarian approach to training became more and more apparent. Regulations as to qualifications for training analysts, minimum duration of training analyses, frequency of analytic sessions, number and frequency of supervisory sessions, etc., became more numerous, more exacting, and spread over more areas of the training process. By the time the United States entered the war a new pattern of administrative policies was emerging in which the influence of the European group and their American pupils was paramount. The number of analysts whose training had been secured in a local institute was too small for them to pit their experience and ideas successfully against the strength, both in numbers, reputation and experience, of their elders. The accolade of knighthood in the order of traditional conceptualists had already been given to a handful of American leaders either in Vienna or in Berlin. Their acceptance of the authority vested in Freud and handed down through the International Association was sustained, fortified, and crystallized through reunion with their exiled colleagues.
>
> It should not be forgotten that in 1939 the American Psychoanalytic Association declared its independence of the International Psycho-Analytical Association and made it very clear that actions of the American would no longer be subject to approval by the International. The above account, however, makes it plain that, despite this decision, control over the policies of the American Psychoanalytic Association was re-established by the European group and their analysands, thus reconstituting in fact, though not in principle, the authoritarian control of the original Viennese group.
>
> It would be more accurate to say that the American analysts who had received their training in Europe had found it both advisable and easy to adhere to the strict discipline imposed by their teachers, and found through this renewed fellowship renewed strength in their struggle to gain recognition. As so often happens in a hierarchical fellowship those most recently inducted are apt to be the most vehement in defending the authority from which their position derives its sanction (1962, p. 127).

Whether or not this analysis of the situation is correct, one fact is incontrovertible. Teachers who felt unduly restricted by the regulations and teaching schedules of the New York Psychoanalytic Society's Educational Committee became increasingly restive. Those who were present have not forgotten the drama of the evening when Karen Horney and a group of her supporters walked out of the meeting and, abandoning all fealty to "the establishment," prepared to organize the Association for the Advancement of Psychoanalysis. Shortly afterwards, a dozen or so members decided to form an informal group for monthy scientific exchange, the members taking turns in providing the evening's program. This group, which chose Carl Binger as its presiding officer, included Sandor Rado, George Daniels, George Goldman, Richard Frank, Bela Mittelman, Abram Kardiner, Viola Bernard, Emil Oberholzer, and me. We met in the apartment of David Levy, whose gracious hospitality provided a most auspicious setting for cultivated discussions. This group was the nucleus of what, in 1945, became the Association for Psychoanalytic and Psychosomatic Medicine and, one year later, was reorganized and renamed the Association for Psychoanalytic Medicine.

The establishment of this new association and its acceptance by the American Psychoanalytic Association as an affiliate was accompanied by the establishment of a new institute under the Department of Psychiatry of the College of Physicians and Surgeons, Columbia University. This was made possible through the good offices of Nolan Lewis, then head of the Department of Psychiatry at Columbia and director of the Psychiatric Institute. Sandor Rado was appointed director of the Clinic; the other full professors were David Levy, George Daniels, and Abram Kardiner.

The founding of the new society and the new type of institute, established two precedents. Until this time, it had not been considered proper for more than one society and institute to be approved in any one city. Furthermore, with the exception of the training program established two years previously at the Flower-Fifth Avenue Medical School (which had not sought the sanction of the American Psychoanalytic Association), no institute had ever been started within the framework of a department of psychiatry in an established medical school. Most influential persons in the American Psychoanalytic Association regarded this new arrangement as a threat, inasmuch as some question might arise as to which institution should have final approval of the curriculum. Consequently, it took some very active leg work to organize a group of voters sympathetic to the loosening of old, outworn, and constricting regulations.

However, these changes have made possible similar arrangements in other communities, as will appear later. It took quite a few years to persuade those most disturbed by these new arrangements to accept the Columbia clinic completely; as recently as 1960, the term "that Columbia problem" was occasionally heard during discussions in the American Psychoanalytic Association. Undoubtedly, the fact that Rado was engaged in a thorough re-examination of the original Freudian hypotheses was felt by the old guard to be most threatening. This influential group sought safeguards against any possible loss of autonomy.

Six new societies were founded in this decade: Detroit, 1940, San Francisco, 1941, the Association for Psychoanalytic Medicine, 1945, the Los Angeles Psychoanalytic Society, 1946, and the Baltimore Psychoanalytic Society, 1946. The split of the Washington-Baltimore Psychoanalytic Society into two separate societies met with fierce opposition for a time; the rationale of this opposition is hard to understand except in terms of a power struggle. Finally, in 1949, the Philadelphia Association for Psychoanalysis was given its charter.

In the meantime, our European colleagues, whose professional activities had been completely disrupted under the grinding tyranny of the Hitler regime, exerted growing pressure for the re-establishment of the International Psycho-Analytical Association. Ernest Jones was the prime mover in this undertaking, representing as he did the rapidly thinning ranks of the old guard in Europe. After considerable discussion of plans for a meeting between him and representatives of the American Psychoanalytic Association, a committee was appointed by the president of the American Association to review the constitution and bylaws of the International Psycho-Analytical Association and to arrange a meeting with Jones in London to consider what changes should be made to bring these up to date. I was the chairman of the committee. Since the center of psychoanalytic organization was in the United States, it was expected that the views of the American committee, which included Max Gitelson and Edward and Grete Bibring, would be given full consideration. I was warned by some of my colleagues that Jones might be difficult to deal with; he did not like Americans and was resentful that the center of the movement was no longer in Europe or even in London, where Anna Freud and some of her friends and colleagues had settled.

Jones invited the committee to dine with him at a well-known restaurant, an unusually hospitable gesture at a time when meat, sugar, and other food products were still strictly rationed in England. He could not have been a more genial and interesting host. He advised us that during our after-dinner deliberations we were to be the guests of Anna Freud. After dinner, therefore, in a sort of reverential anticipation, we repaired to her house, where Freud had spent his last days. We all felt greatly honored to be there. As soon as the introductions had been made and the committee assembled, Jones opened the discussion in the friendliest manner conceivable. Our committee believed that we did not need a lengthy document with the constitutional aims bolstered and defended by a long list of bylaws. To my great surprise, Jones concurred. After the incorporation of a few minor changes suggested by him, we found no difficulty in achieving consensus on the various points in the draft, which became the proposal for a new constitution of the International Psycho-Analytical Association, which was to be submitted to the national associations for consideration and approval. That evening's experience in August, 1948, is unforgettable. The ready friendliness of our British hosts carried with it none of the authoritarian flavor so familiar in the councils of our national association.

Since that time, the International Psycho-Analytical Association has been gradually restored in some degree to its position as arbiter of the fitness for full accreditation of newly organized psychoanalytic societies. A certain aura of authority still clings to its name. Most new groups eager for recognition outside their national boundaries seek its accreditation. It still publishes its official organ, the *International Journal of Psycho-Analysis*, and the international psychoanalytic congresses are held every second year under its auspices. The roster of its presidents includes several Americans, both native-born and naturalized; however, it no longer exercises any control over the educational programs of the various psychoanalytic institutes, whose graduates belong to their national associations.

Before moving from the "roaring forties" to the "precipitate fifties," we should look at the personalities responsible for the recent additions to psychoanalysis. The large gap between the educational background and cultural breadth of most American-born analysts and their European colleagues is a matter of some embarrassment and explains the exiles' great influence in developing the training programs of the new institutes. I remember well my impression, of instance, of Otto Fenichel, on the one occasion when I had the pleasure of meeting him. We met after the Minneapolis meeting of the Association in 1932, while I was a student at the New York Institute. Fenichel had the ordered type of mind that makes such a textbook as his *Outline of Clinical Psychoanalysis* (1934) required reading for psychoanalysts of current and future generations. He and Ernst Simmel were among the westward pioneering advance guard; after staying awhile with the Menningers, he moved on to help found the new institutes in San Francisco and Los Angeles.

It is interesting to consider the ratio of American-born analysts to those educated and trained abroad among the founding members of the various societies. In societies established before 1940 the number of foreign-trained founding members was negligible. From 1940 on, however, as the wave of pioneers moved westward, the proportions began to change. In Detroit, Richard and Editha Sterba, husband and wife, formed the educational nucleus of the association, although, during its early years before the stresses developed that led to temporary cancellation of the institute program, Leo Bartemeier and several other well-known American analysts were active in the Detroit Society and in the training program. In San Francisco, the core of experienced analysts was of foreign extraction—Bernhard Berliner, Fenichel, George Gero, Bernhard Kamm, Simmel, and Emanuel Windholz. Four of the founding members came directly from the Menninger Clinic, which already had a "colonizing" status. The Los Angeles Psychoanalytic Society was less richly seeded with experienced analysts from abroad, but Ernst Simmel and Ernst Lewy are good examples of men thoroughly competent in their field. The American-born members had received their training in Topeka, Chicago, and New York. In contrast, the new Baltimore Society included only two foreign analysts in its organizing group. The evidence of western migration is clear. The San Francisco Society soon included the distinguished scholar, writer, and teacher, Erik H. Erikson, who served one term as president and later, with Anna Freud, was honored by election to honorary membership.

I have termed the next decade the "precipitate fifties" because of the rush of applications for enrollment of new psychoanalytic associations under the national banner of the American Psychoanalytic Association.

In chronological order of establishment: The Society for Psychoanalytic Medicine of Southern California, 1950; the Western New England Psychoanalytic Society, with headquarters in the Austen Riggs Center at Stockbridge, Massachusetts, 1951; the New Orleans Psychoanalytic Society, 1953; the Psychoanalytic Association of New York and the Michigan Psychoanalytic Association, 1955; the Western New York Psychoanalytic Society, 1956; the Cleveland Psychoanalytic Society and the Seattle Psychoanalytic Society, 1957; and, in 1959, the Pittsburgh Psychoanalytic Society and the New Jersey Psychoanalytic Society. Finally, the sixties got off to a good start with the organization of the Westchester Psychoanalytic Society in 1960. Thus, the decade of the fifties marked the flood tide of the psychoanalytic invasion.

During World War I, the medical profession began to realize that a large percentage of the disorders encountered in civilian life are caused or complicated by conflicts and emotional stress. This discovery played a large part in promoting interest in the study and treatment of the psychoneuroses. During the twenty-one-year interval between the two world wars, psychoanalysis had begun to attract the attention of advanced thinkers in the fields of education, social science, and religion, attention sometimes favorable, sometimes hostile. World War II left waves of dissatisfaction with the old, traditional organization and procedures of American psychiatry. Many who carried the heaviest responsibility for planning and directing psychiatric services in the armed forces were psychoanalysts. The "old guard," comprised largely of administrators of mental hospitals, had shown neither initiative nor leadership in preparing for the inevitable. Not until William Menninger was appointed director of psychiatric services in the office of the chief surgeon did things begin to move. His rare gift for organization and selfless devotion to his job marked him as the natural leader of the group that, after the war, formed the shock troops of the revisionist revolution in American psychiatry.

This group, known to the general profession as GAP (The Group for the Advancement of Psychiatry), was a self-appointed group of psychiatrists—many of the leaders were psychoanalysts—who had been disillusioned by the failure of organized psychiatry to realize the significance of the advances made by the emerging science of psychodynamics, or to appreciate the changes in the concepts of care for the mentally ill that war experiences had helped develop. The work of Roy Grinker on battle fatigue and the leadership of John M. Murray in the

Air Force and of Uno Helgesson in Navy psychiatry helped create a wholly new understanding of the intricate responses of the human organism to small and great stresses. Here we see again the characteristic capability of American-born and American-trained psychoanalysts for putting the new insights of psychoanalysis to work on the battlefield, as well as on the civilian front.

In this connection I should mention the Committee on Morale of the American Psychoanalytic Association, of which I had the honor of serving as chairman and which included such brilliant members as Ernst Kris, David Levy, and Robert Waelder. During several intellectually stimulating exchanges of ideas, meetings with Kris introduced us to much of his thinking and experience in the areas of mass communication and propaganda. An effort was made to effect a useful contact with the Office of Facts and Figures, at that time under the direction of General William ("Wild Bill") Donovan. Meetings were arranged and various individuals interviewed. It soon became apparent that most key positions in the areas concerned were already firmly held by psychologists; although everyone was courteous and ready to listen, nobody in authority could see any special need for giving consultative status to a self-appointed committee of psychoanalysts. Times have changed since those days; many government departments have since found it advisable to have psychoanalysts as consultants for special or continuing assignments. I have referred to the important work by Roy Grinker in the handling of "battle fatigue"; notable work was done in the Merchant Marine service by Daniel Blain and Robert Heath, and on the civilian front by such distinguished psychoanalysts as David Levy, Jules Masserman, and Bela Mittelmann. Abram Kardiner has reported his studies of traumatic neuroses of war (1941). It was becoming clear that all psychoanalysts are not long-haired, mysterious personages who never emerge from their burrows and are proper subjects for facetious stories and caricatures.

I cannot leave this topic, the initiative of psychoanalysts in taking measures to remove obstacles to progress, without mention of a special occasion on which such initiative succeeded in a most unexpected way. The occasion was the annual meeting of the American Psychiatric Association in May, 1948. Harry Stack Sullivan remarked to several of us that it might be possible to nominate a candidate from the floor, in accordance with the time-honored democratic process, and thus to break through the hierarchical methods of determining succession to the presidency of the Association. We all agreed that, if possible, this would be a highly desirable accomplishment. The name of George S. Stevenson was proposed, after which the group scattered to lobby among friends and acquaintances. Evidently, many had hoped for some time that something could be done to break the ranks of the embattled hierarchy, for the strategy was successful. Charles Burlingame, the hierarchy's candidate, was (most unexpectedly, to me) roundly defeated by George Stevenson. This event marked the transformation of the American Psychiatric Association from a static debating society into a dynamic force for improving the care of the mentally ill and for involving the interest of the general public in the "new look" of dynamic psychiatry.

To return to the story of psychoanalysis in its newly established homes, the breakthrough that the Columbia group had achieved in setting up a second psychoanalytic society within the geographical limits of a city, and a new institute within the framework of a university medical college, was responsible not only for the abolition of outworn regulations but also for the increasing reluctance of the members to take on faith many of the traditional assumptions on which psychoanalytic teaching had been based. Certain institutes that held firmly to the traditional theories and techniques of treatment came to be known as "orthodox" or "conservative," whereas others in which the questioning voices predominated were labeled "liberal" institutes. The semantic parallels to divisions existing in political and religious organizations is very striking. The procedures laid down by the Board on Professional Standards as criteria for membership in the Psychoanalytic Association and for the acceptability of new institutes—especially with relation to rules governing frequency and length of therapeutic and supervisory sessions—led to many heated arguments at the Board meetings, which came to be the authoritative nucleus of the Association and which laid down the rules and strove to maintain maximum conformity in their execution.

Informal meetings of three or four of the more liberal members eventually developed considerable momentum. In December, 1951, several members who had expressed concern over these matters were invited to meet under the chairmanship of George Mohr on the morning preceding the annual business meeting. I was requested to present a motion that the Executive Council of the American, appoint a special committee to investigate the procedures and functions of the Board on

Professional Standards and to recommend such modifications as they considered desirable. In advance of the meeting, Robert P. Knight, president of the Association, was informed of the plan in detail. The motion was promptly seconded. Knight spoke from the chair in support of the motion, which was passed with one lone dissenting "nay" from the back of the hall. The Task Committee, as it was called, was under the chairmanship of M. Ralph Kaufman. Its recommendations included a very minor change in the time requirements, permitting slight flexibility. One recommendation that caused great commotion in the Board on Professional Standards was that, when election of candidates was deferred by the membership committee, the president might appoint a special three-member committee—one member from the faculty of the candidate's own institute—to review the findings and report directly to the Board. When the chairman of the membership committee protested that this recommendation would undo the hard work of his committee, he was ruled out of order by the Board chairman, whereupon he and three or four of his loyal adherents made a dramatic exit—a gesture reminiscent of the dramatic revolt of Karen Horney and her pupils.

At the meeting in May 1952, Dr. Leroy Maeder, then secretary of the executive council, reported that a standing operating committee on the theory and practice of psychoanalytic training had been established under the chairmanship of Dr. Leon Saul. Following his resignation, I became the chairman. This committee made two fundamental recommendations: first, that qualifications for membership in the Association should in all essentials be determined by competence and integrity as observed at the local level rather than only after exhaustive inspection of the details of the candidate's record by the membership committee, whose members might have no personal acquaintance with the candidate. Second, that regular rotation should be established between institutes in the composition of the membership committee. Objections to these "double blind" bases for evaluation gave rise to recurrent suggestions that a board for certification in psychoanalysis be established.

After many energetic discussions of such innovations, including objections to these further refinements of methods for assessing a candidate's fitness, there was sufficient doubt, in the minds of all but a few, to defeat the proposal. The new committee was found to be an unnecessary addition to those entrusted with the preservation of the essentials in psychoanalytic training and, under the pretext that the committee had been unable to come up with a working definition of psychoanalysis, it was abolished by the council in 1956. Evidently the thought of critical re-examination of assumptions was too threatening to the authoritarian structure of the Association at that time. A surviving small, informal part of the original group established the practice of holding a Friday luncheon at the meetings of the Association. Gradually, new members were added to this group, which soon afforded a rather pleasant and rewarding opportunity for the informal exchange of opinions on problems of training—discussions being sparked by some member's report on development of a new training facility. In this group, the ideal of progress through friendly exchange and discussion continued to provide the chief inducement for meeting and a pleasant contrast to the struggles for status and the maintenance of traditional regulations that had become salient features of the proceedings of the Board on Professional Standards.

Complications arose because of distance between the new and expanded training centers and the nearest established institutes. To keep training in the hands of approved training analysts, heroic measures were necessary; whereas previously it had been the custom for a new group desiring recognition as a study group or training center to be "proposed" by some mother institute, the plan was modified. If a new training facility were proposed only to be blackballed by the Board on Professional Standards, the action could be—and on at least one occasion had been—construed as a slap in the face for the would-be foster mother.

Under the new plan, with the establishment of a committee on new training facilities, the reins were held more closely by the central authoritative nucleus of the Association. Inspection, consultation, and advice were used to determine fitness. Under this new regulation and the so-called geographic rule, every teacher at the new facility had to be approved by the Board. The net result has been that each proposed institute has had to send its candidates, often over great distances, to the mother institute of its choice, or has arranged for approved teachers to fly in at regular intervals to give courses of lectures, seminars, and supervisory sessions. The clumsiness of such an arrangement seems hard to justify if some other solution can be found. It represents another attempt to keep a tight rein on the controls, as opposed to a serious effort to help new centers develop their own initiative and to submit programs for examination and consultation.

As recently as May, 1962, at the Toronto meeting, the chairman of a department of psychiatry that includes psychoanalysts previously approved as training analysts told me that, despite the fact that he had a ready-made psychoanalytic faculty and that he would welcome the addition of psychoanalytic training to his postgraduate facilities, no potential training analyst on his staff would dare collaborate in such a venture because he might endanger his status in the institute where he did his teaching! Such unnecessary obstacles to the expansion of established programs have aroused questions in the minds of many of our foremost educators in psychiatry and psychoanalysis as to the justifiability of such a pyramid of restrictive regulations.

There can be little doubt that these restrictions have needlessly delayed the development of psychoanalytic training in university medical schools, where most recently appointed heads of departments are fully qualified psychoanalysts. Thanks to this preference for psychoanalysts as heads of departments of psychiatry, the recognition of psychoanalysis as one of the medical sciences seems on the way to general acceptance. Its continued membership in this ancient and distinguished family, however, will depend on the determination of these leaders to hew to the line of scientific method in their teaching and research. No more tangible proof is possible that psychoanalytic training is now considered an essential requirement for all psychiatrists who aspire leadership in organization, research, and teaching in their chosen specialty.

In his historical survey, Oberndorf expressed the opinion that the rapid diffusion of interest in psychoanalysis among social scientists and educators in the United States resulted from their early recognition of the practical uses to which the new insights could be put in furthering the cause of their respective disciplines. The fact that Freud sponsored the acceptance of gifted men and women into his circle of trainees served to promote these hopes.

Perhaps the influence of psychoanalysis on the thinking of anthropologists is first perceptible in the work of Géza Róheim, who was invited to lecture at the New York Psychoanalytic Institute in the thirties. More recently, the rapid development of cultural anthropology has required of all its adherents a thorough understanding of psychoanalysis. The work of such outstanding individuals as Ruth Benedict, Cora du Bois, Gregory Bateson, Margaret Mead, and Clyde and Florence Kluckhohn clearly illustrates the interpenetration of the two disciplines. Nor has this been a one-sided affair; from the early days of the

New York Psychoanalytic Institute, the significance of research in the field of cultural anthropology had been stressed by Abram Kardiner, whose teaching at that Institute and, in later years, at the Columbia Psychoanalytic Clinic has been one of the highlights of the curriculum.

More resistance to the contributions of psychoanalysis has been met among sociologists. Recently, however, with the better understanding of intergroup tensions and racial prejudice, the role played by individual and group motivation in favoring or disrupting such programs as improvement in housing, resettlement of immigrant populations, and combating crime has brought about a marked change in attitude. Even as psychoanalysis has become an integral part of the educational equipment of the heads of psychiatric departments and of those engaged in psychiatric research, those who are planning programs of research and action in the sociological field must take into consideration those elements of human motivation and control that have been clarified through psychoanalytic research. Nevertheless, practicing psychoanalysts are rarely selected as consultants for such projects; the consultative posts are usually given to psychologists who have had some psychoanalytic training, often including a personal analysis.

Clinical psychologists play an increasingly significant role in our culture as private practitioners, advisers to industry, consultants to government agencies, and members of interdisciplinary groups in a variety of community agencies and in hospital settings. Taking advantage of the obvious shortage of psychiatrists, the relatively short period of training required for a doctorate in philosophy, and the ease of obtaining a personal analysis from a previously analyzed colleague, they have taken an increasingly firm stand on their right to do therapy—including formal psychoanalytic therapy—without benefit of medical supervision or consultation. In fact, some educational institutions grant certificates implying full competence as psychotherapists. Needless to say, this new influx of nonmedical psychotherapists poses a considerable problem, both for the future of psychoanalytic practice and for the place of psychoanalysis in the minds of the medical profession. In the last analysis, only the psychiatrist has the legal right to diagnose a patient's condition, to decide whether involuntary admission to the hospital is necessary, or to give the "green light" for discharge. The psychiatrist does hold the final responsibility, but he may be consulted only when the psychologist fears that his patient is getting out of hand. The psychiatrist alone has the legal right to prescribe drugs for the nervous patient or the psychotic whose illness is in remission. Because of this fact, and in the light of the rapidly increasing knowledge of the interrelationship between complex psychic states and specific physiological functions of the brain, it seems proper from the medical standpoint and for public safety that psychotherapy conducted in individual and group settings be under the supervision of experienced psychiatrists. Since most nonmedical psychotherapy worthy of the name comes under the heading of lay analysis, such a requirement means supervision by an experienced medical psychoanalyst.

This judgment is not intended to imply that no psychologist can be considered a competent psychotherapist or able to conduct a formal psychoanalytic treatment; it does mean, however, that it should be the responsibility of an experienced psychiatrist, or medical psychoanalyst, as the case may be, to delegate the task, to be kept informed of progress as frequently as he considers necessary, and to be consulted if drugs are considered desirable.

These considerations were at first given high priority in the councils of the American Psychoanalytic Association and its affiliated institutes. In recent years, however, when some specially gifted and creative worker who has no medical degree is needed in a given setting, ways have been found to smuggle him into the training program, and some institutes, both those approved and those not approved by the American Psychoanalytic Association, are giving courses of instruction to nonmedical personnel who have had personal analyses, with the express purpose of training them to become research workers or to do therapy under supervision.

The law of supply and demand seems to provide part of the answer to this phenomenon. Once the tidal wave of psychoanalytic interest swept the country and the word got around that psychoanalysts were "coining money," the academic gates were besieged by bright young persons who saw fame, fortune, and status lying under the mortar board of the Doctor of Philosophy. This wave of interest is now showing signs of recession, even along the shores of psychiatric territory.

The theoretical constructions of Freud and his followers have taken such a hold on the sophisticated public that terms and concepts once familiar only to students and practitioners of psychoanalysis are to be heard at cocktail parties, over the radio, or even from the mouths of taxi drivers. In certain circles, psychoanalysis is "the rage." Everyone has his analyst. It has almost become a status symbol. No copy of some well-known magazines is complete without a joke about the psychoanalyst; no theater season is complete without a play about a psychoanalyst, whether as villain or hero.

The year 1956 saw the birth of an entirely new development, the organization in Chicago of the Academy of Psychoanalysis. The feeling had grown that there was need for a free forum for scientific discussions to keep alive the spirit of scientific inquiry, good fellowship, and exchange of views with scientists from allied disciplines.

The establishment of the Academy of Psychoanalysis signaled the confluence of several streams of dissatisfaction with the increasingly exclusive regulations by which the Board on Professional Standards sought to maintain its authority over all organized teaching of psychoanalytic theory and practice. By 1956, several legally established centers of postgraduate education in the field had long-established programs of instruction and training under the leadership of experienced and dedicated psychoanalysts who had established, with the help of sympathetic colleagues, independent centers of psychoanalytic education and training.

Already in 1941, due to what they felt was a lack of academic freedom, Karen Horney, Clara Thompson, William Silverberg, and others left the New York Institute and organized themselves into the Association for the Advancement of Psycho-Analysis, with its teaching branch, the American Institute for Psychoanalysis. Harry Stack Sullivan and Erich Fromm gave support to this new group. However, new tensions developed in this splinter group due to resistance on the part of Karen Horney to nonmedical personnel participating in the training of students. Again on grounds of lack of academic freedom another group led by Clara Thompson, Erich Fromm, and Harry Stack Sullivan withdrew from this new Association and in 1942–1943 formed what is now known as the William Alanson White Institute. In 1944 Stephen Jewett suggested that Horney's Association for the Advancement of Psycho-Analysis join the Psychiatric Department of the New York Medical College. On her refusal to do so a group led by Bernard Robbins, Jewett, Silverberg, and Judd Marmor withdrew from the Association and organized the first medical-school-affiliated psychoanalytic training institute in the New York Medical College, Flower-Fifth Avenue Center.

During the 1940s, it was the custom for an affiliated institute to propose newly established training centers for acceptance in the American Psychoanalytic Association. Although Columbia favored the admission of the William Alanson White Institute, the American Psychoanalytic Association turned down the application, on the grounds that professional training was being given to psychologists, social workers, and other nonmedical personnel. The continuing divergence of opinion concerning this question created tensions within the William Alanson White Institute. Although the influence of Erich Fromm, Clara Thompson, Rollo May, and others has survived these differences, no clear-cut resolution has been achieved. Some who have felt that the essentials of Sullivan's teaching were not receiving the respect they deserved have broken away and established a small training group for teaching Sullivan's theories and methods without adulteration. For the William Alanson White Institute to restrict its acceptance to medically trained candidates at this time would only run counter to its founder's traditions; the Institute now has a professional responsibility to an increasing number of nonmedical graduates, and their interests would be adversely affected if it should discontinue its certification of lay personnel and thus disinherit its graduates.

The most recent independent center of psychoanalytic education and training has been established at Tulane University in the Medical School's Department of Psychiatry and Neurology, under the leadership of Robert G. Heath. This undertaking was sponsored informally by the Columbia University Psychoanalytic Clinic for Training and Research. Several of the senior faculty members at Columbia, Sandor Rado, David Levy, Nathan Ackerman, and I among them, have made annual trips to Tulane to give lectures and hold seminars. Heath took with him three assistant professors, all graduates of the Columbia clinic. His application for membership in the American Psychoanalytic Association was rejected, first on one ground, then on another; the application of one of his colleagues, Russell Monroe, was also rejected.

This story is not among the brightest recorded in the official archives. Here, then, was established a new facility for psychoanalytic training within the structure of a university medical school, integrated with residency training in psychiatry and neurology. When Heath decided to develop his department without reference to the American Psychoanalytic Association, he became the second department head to ignore the American Psychoanalytic Association's claims to exclusive authority over all psychoanalytic training. However, all subsequent attempts to set up integrated programs of postgraduate psychiatric and psychoanalytic training have been planned under the supervision of (and therefore subject to the approval of) the Committee on New Training Facilities of the American Psychoanalytic Association. This remarkable trend toward conformity, as opposed to independent enterprise, is perhaps accounted for partly by the conformist trend in American culture; but above all, it signifies the power still wielded by the Board on Professional Standards.

Still further removed from the original source of psychoanalytic traditions are the institutes established by disciples of C. G. Jung and Alfred Adler and by such free-wheeling individualists as Theodor Reik and Wilhelm Reich.

Emergence of young and dynamic psychiatrists into leading positions during the war began to create an altered public image of the psychoanalyst, at least among medical men. As they returned to civilian life and resumed their posts and their practices, these young psychiatrists spearheaded movements for reform in the parent organization, the American Psychiatric Association, and in their own psychoanalytic societies and institutes. It is a curious fact that, whereas they were successful in establishing GAP (Group for the Advancement of Psychiatry) and upsetting the old hierarchical succession to the office of president, in the psychoanalytic societies they accepted authoritarian control over training that had been affected through the co-operative efforts of the refugee analysts and the older, European-trained American analysts. Revolts against these restraints had been headed by two of the three most gifted older European analysts, Horney and Rado; Franz Alexander, the third, soon began to arouse the hostility and suspicion of some of his colleagues, who accused him of modifications in theory and practice that made him a traitor to the cause.

By this time, clearly drawn lines were becoming apparent between therapists opposed to any but the most minor changes in the techniques of classical psychoanalysis and those seeking ways to test the old theories, to try new and more flexible techniques, and to attempt scientific validation of results. Nevertheless, it would be false to say that the classical tradition was maintained only through the influence and activities of the European analysts, and that the new approaches were created by American-born analysts. It is, rather, like the situation in our political parties: there are nominal Republicans and nominal Democrats, but some Republicans act like Democrats and vice versa.

National specialty boards had been established in most fields of medicine. It was no longer sufficient for a surgeon to belong to the American College of Surgeons or for an internist to belong to the American College of Physicians. Any physician who sought leadership in his profession, whether in surgery or medicine, was obliged to take specialty board examinations. In medical psychoanalysis, the same exclusiveness was made possible by the assignment of power (under the new bylaws of the Association) to the Board on Professional Standards and its membership committee. The American Psychoanalytic Association ceased to be a federation of American psychoanalytic societies and became a membership corporation; for many years its policy was to insist on centralized control of teaching and of membership certification, rather than to encourage experimentation, research, and critical testing of traditional theories and techniques. This encapsulated philosophy served further to foster dissension and to maintain the doubts of other scientists as to the validity of psychoanalytic theory and the rationale of methods used in therapy.

As these dissensions became known to the more sophisticated public, they increased the anxiety of many persons who might well have benefited from contact with an analyst but who exploited these doubts to avoid such confrontation. Increasingly, patients tended to ask the analyst, "What school do you belong to?" or other such anxiety-laden questions. However, despite these byproducts of intramural strife, which at times took on a quasi-religious intensity, the demand for psychoanalytic training continued to increase. Gradually the word therapy became a symbol around which battles for professional status were waged among all the behavioral disciplines. At the conclusion of Ernest Jones's address at the Centennial Celebration of Freud's birth in 1956, his last words were an admonition to the American Psychoanalytic Association to reverse its position on the question of medical training as a prerequisite for membership. With such authority to back the claims of nonmedical personnel, it is hard to maintain a united front in the battle to keep psychoanalytic training and practice within medical science. This Centennial Celebration was remarkable not only for the numerous special lectures throughout the land memorializing the achievements of the Master, but also for the assembling of a vast exhibit of memorabilia from Freud's personal and professional activities. Credit for their assembly must go to the committee of the Association charged with the task.

Having briefly reviewed the story of the so-called neo-Freudian and non-Freudian developments in the training of psychoanalysts in the

United States, I must turn back to the story of the Chicago Academy of Psychoanalysis and its impact on the officers and members of the American Psychoanalytic Association. It soon became clear that persons at the helm of the Association believed that the Academy was trying to establish a rival organization that would challenge their claim to sole control over training. As evidence for this assumption, they noted that the meetings of the Academy were planned at first to coincide with those of the Association. The purposes of the Academy, as clearly stated in its constitution and bylaws, were given little heed. Immediately an effort was made to establish a subspecialty board in psychoanalysis under the parent American Board of Psychiatry and Neurology. On meeting no direct opposition to this plan, the Association tried to arrange for the examining board to be appointed by the president of the American Psychoanalytic Association. When this was firmly opposed and it became apparent that all duly chartered psychoanalytic institutes would have to be represented on such a board, enthusiasm for the project waned and the final vote of the constituent societies was negative. For the moment, there is no plan for establishing such a board.

In the meantime, the Academy has continued its regular programs. A joint meeting with the American Association for the Advancement of Science was held in Philadelphia in December 1962. During the summer of 1962, the Academy cosponsored an open psychoanalytic forum in Amsterdam with groups of German, Dutch, and French psychoanalysts who were not satisfied with the attempts of the International Psycho-Analytical Association to re-establish controls over training on the Continent. Furthermore, there is an increasing impatience with the repetitive programs given at the international meetings, in which many papers seem to be trying to determine how many angels can dance on the head of a needle or to discover some new variation on classical themes that, although satisfying to the author, bring no new scientific enlightenment.

The speed and intensity with which new institutes were launched after World War II evinced a need for conformity and for membership in a mystical inner circle or ruling clique. The younger men's hunger for more thorough training in dynamic psychiatry and for exposure to psychoanalytic training was universal. In many instances, absence during service had brought a new and extensive revaluation of previous concepts of the etiology and treatment of emotional and mental disorders. The returning enthusiast in the specialty of psychiatry had to begin his career or attempt to re-establish the practice and institutional connections from which he had been cut off so unexpectedly and hurriedly. If he found acceptance in an established and fully recognized institute, he felt as high school graduates of today feel when they are accepted by an Ivy League college. Although not generally regarded as essential for leadership and success in psychiatry before the war, psychoanalysis had become the *sine qua non* in the planning of most ambitious and inevitably anxious young veterans. The fires of enthusiasm for psychodynamics kindled in time of national emergency spread like wildfire. Gradually, at first almost insensibly, a widespread conviction arose that only psychiatrists who were qualified to practice psychoanalysis could aspire to the highest rank in teaching and in private practice. This conviction has not subsided entirely, although most institutes complain that the volume and quality of candidates for training have fallen off. Many young residents exhibit no anxiety to conform to the fashion of the day; some say they think they might benefit from a personal analysis and may undertake it when financially able, but that they very much doubt the need to go through the expense, time, and inconvenience of psychoanalytic training. Whereas after World War II there was an oversupply of desirable candidates and only one out of every three or four applicants was accepted, today a greater proportion of candidates are unsuitable and there are fewer suitable candidates.

The establishment of the Academy of Psychoanalysis may have been partly responsible for the decision of the Executive Council of the American Psychoanalytic Association to recommend a thorough survey of the functioning of the institutes. Bertram Lewin and Helen Ross, who were entrusted with the task, spent four years conducting an exhaustive survey. The published volume of their findings (1960) is written in a style and with a humor all too rare in the writings of psychoanalysts. Despite the tiresome necessity of trying to evaluate the statistics, it is a delight to read. However, two criticisms seem appropriate. First, any critical survey of institutions by persons who have had a considerable part in determining their characteristic patterns of function may be considered prejudiced or incomplete by persons not directly associated with that institution. Second, no attempt was made to include in the survey institutes not under the aegis of the American Psychoanalytic Association. It is likely that an impartial survey of all institutes chartered to teach psychoanalysis would disclose a large area of agreement on the basic requirements of psychoanalytic education, and that the differences in course offerings and requirements is no greater between the duly accredited and the independent institutes than it is between units of the inner circle of approved institutes.

In addition to the new scientific knowledge made available, one of the few fortunate results of the last war was the emergence of trained psychoanalysts as capable administrators and promoters of research. The appointment of William Menninger as chief of psychiatry in the surgeon general's office signaled very important improvements in Army psychiatry. His opposite number in the Navy was also a psychoanalyst. Increasingly, key appointments carrying large responsibilities were given to psychoanalysts, who responded enthusiastically to their new responsibilities—John ("Jock") Murray in the Air Force; M. Ralph ("Mo") Kaufman, Henry ("Hank") Brosin, and Roy Grinker in the Army; Howard Rome in the Navy; and Daniel Blain in the Merchant Marine. Others who, for reasons of age or indispensability, were not in uniform were active in Selective Service as planners, examiners, and consultants, or they advised persons in charge of Civilian Defense on such matters as the handling of panic, building morale, training air raid wardens, giving lectures to citizens' groups and Red Cross workers. For example, in Chicago, Jules Masserman became Special Consultant in Civilian Defense; in New York City, an Emergency Committee of Neurological and Psychiatric Societies was formed under psychoanalytic leadership, to advise on all matters pertaining to psychiatric training.

These experienced psychoanalysts were not only successful as organizers and administrators; through their understanding of the effects of stress on immature or unstable individuals, they helped immeasurably to prevent the return to duty of persons who had suffered acute shock during the height of combat.

As the century passed the halfway mark, the surge of fledgling psychoanalysts neared its peak, yet the need for additional psychoanalysts as members of psychiatric faculties, on the staffs of community clinics, and as clinicians in private and hospital practice seemed inexhaustible. The work of the pioneers had gone far beyond expectations, and those who planned programs of psychoanalytic education found it very difficult to meet the demand. The cost of training became even more exorbitant, the competition for admission to the most highly regarded institutes even keener.

In looking back over forty years in psychiatric practice, thirty-two devoted to the specialty of psychoanalysis, I am amazed at the revolution that has taken place in the thinking of educated people about the complex sources of human behavior and patterns of culture. The new enlightenment in the field of individual motivation that has come into being since Freud published *The Interpretation of Dreams* has played a significant part in contributing to this change.

This necessarily brief survey of the history of the psychoanalytic movement in the United States cannot do justice to the many who have labored faithfully and long to extend their knowledge and to make use of psychoanalysis for the benefit of the community. Quite arbitrarily, I selected about forty men and women who seem to be doing genuine pioneering work in the field, in the hope that they might give me a brief summary of what they consider most valuable in what they have sought to accomplish or in what they have added to the body of theory or the techniques of therapy. I wrote these good people a circular letter, begging them to send me a two-page critique of their own contributions to the theory and practice of psychoanalysis. Surprisingly enough, out of this number sixty per cent have answered; most of them succinctly, some all too briefly, some with undue modesty, some with a long list of their publications. My special thanks go to them for their helpfulness. A special article is planned that will attempt to do justice to the very interesting replies and to place them in context with the main theme of this essay. Industry, tough thinking, creative artistry, imaginative power, organizational zeal, administrative excellence, pedagogic brilliance, clinical acumen, literary style—above all, a sort of evangelistic dedication—all these and other gifts of the human spirit are there for all to see, in their writings, their organizations, and their community activities. Perhaps most outstanding in the personalities and publications of these forty-odd pioneers is the scope of their interests and the diversity of their talents. In many instances, it is hard to evaluate any one in terms of one special contribution; each major contribution has represented more than can be catalogued and described under a single heading such as "theoretical brilliance" or "teaching ability." Most of the group (and many others not mentioned in this essay) are multidimensional in their endowments, having served long as teachers, organizers, clinicians, and publicists. Who, for instance, would feel competent to evaluate priorities in the abilities and activities of a Bertram Lewin, a Karl Menninger, a Franz Alexander, an Ernst Simmel, a Lawrence Kubie, or an Ernst Kris?

On the other hand, certain group characteristics seem recognizable in the centers where the influence of such men dominates the approaches to teaching and practice. For instance, from the very beginning of the interest in psychoanalysis, Boston has been a center of orthodoxy, in both the theory and the techniques of training and practice, and continues to be a true representative of the old tradition. Teaching begun by Isador Coriat and continued by such dynamic neophytes as "Jock" Murray and "Mo" Kaufman—later bolstered by the addition of such well-known Europeans as the Bibrings and Helene and Felix Deutsch—has continued closely along traditional lines. The New York Psychoanalytic Society has long played a dominant role in setting the style for the governing bodies of the American Psychoanalytic Association; perhaps it also has been the main force in preserving the traditional approach to training, technique, and research along lines considered essential by Freud and his early disciples. Many young psychiatrists in the New York area prefer the shelter of such an authoritarian institute to the freer climate of the Columbia clinic or the unaligned institutes. The presence of such distinguished scholars and dedicated theoreticians as Ernst Kris, Heinz Hartmann, and Rudolph Loewenstein on the New York Institute faculty has brought a special and well-deserved atmosphere of scholarship and breadth of culture to the teaching program.

Despite Freud's many complaints against its independent attitude in the early days, the New York Psychoanalytic Society has always been the chief source of efforts to maintain contact with the European analysts. It is also distinguished for the important role played in its organization and teaching by such unusually gifted women as Phyllis Greenacre, Margaret Mahler, Marion Kenworthy, and Edith Jacobson. Insofar as length of the personal analysis is concerned, the training program is notorious for the long time required for the average analysis to be considered complete. Figures in the Lewin and Ross report (1960) tell the story. Until recently, the New York Society also claimed among its members René Spitz, whose epoch-making observations on the behavior of infants separated from their mothers has added a new challenge to our understanding of depressive behavior.

Finally, in the New York area there is yet another citadel of traditional psychoanalysis, the institute affiliated with the Downstate Medical College in Brooklyn. Sandor Lorand, as first director of training, represented the school of European analysts influenced most strongly by Ferenczi. The general tendency in training, however, now adheres closely to the standards set by the Board on Professional Standards.

The other two of the four original institutes comprising the American Psychoanalytic Association have undergone considerable change. In the days when Columbia was beginning its training program, both the Washington School of Psychiatry and the Washington Psychoanalytic Institute favored the idea that more than one institute and society should be approved in a given metropolis. Members of the Institute's present faculty represent quite divergent views of the validity of certain theoretical assumptions and of rigid technical requirements in training and therapy. With the death of Harry Stack Sullivan and the departure of William Silverberg, Ralph Crowley, and Clara Thompson to New York, the complexion of the faculty was considerably changed. With the death of Frieda Fromm-Reichmann, a most dedicated and liberal spirit was lost to the Institute, although Dexter Bullard (who was responsible for bringing Frieda Fromm-Reichmann to Chestnut Lodge) and Leon Salzman have continued to manifest that openness to experimentation and to less constricted contact with the patient that marks the confident physician as opposed to the regimented technician. Edith Weigert, with her serene humanity and sensitive perception, reflects all that is most desirable in a female psychoanalyst. It is interesting that the Baltimore Society, whose separation from its twin in Washington was successfully achieved with the help of representatives of the liberal institutes, is now recognized as one adhering most closely to the classical traditions.

As founding Fellows of the Academy of Psychoanalysis, Frieda Fromm-Reichmann, Leon Salzman, and Edith Weigert were among the first to see the need for a new organization to promote communication and exchange of views. The featured speaker at the organizational meeting of the Academy back in 1956 was Jurgens Ruesch, whose important study of the processes of communication made him the obvious choice.

Finally, we come to the last of the four original societies, the Chicago Psychoanalytic Society, which was free from any connection with an institute. The Chicago Psychoanalytic Society has been a way station through which great numbers of analysts, both foreign-trained and native, have passed enroute to new centers of psychoanalytic organization. The untimely death of Lionel Blitzsten took one of the most dedicated teachers of psychoanalysis in Chicago. Despite the difficulties and antagonisms generated by the appointment of Franz Alexander as professor of psychoanalysis at the University, he was successful in organizing an independent institute; an influential board of trustees drawn from among the civic leaders in the community gave him all necessary support. Alexander's leadership generated a new emphasis on research among the entire staff, and a vast amount of collaborative work was undertaken by staff and students. Chicago became one of the great centers of clinical research in psychosomatic medicine. The work of Alexander and Catherine Bacon on peptic ulcer, and of Thomas French on bronchial asthma laid the groundwork for theoretical formulations of the sources and nature of emotional influences on disease that have profoundly influenced both teaching and treatment of these and other illnesses. From the Chicago Institute came leaders of psychiatric and psychoanalytic organization such as Karl Menninger, Robert Knight, and Leo Bartemeier, gifted research workers such as Arthur Mirsky, and distinguished clinicians and teachers such as Maurice Levine, Leon Saul, and Catherine Bacon.

In addition to launching this co-ordinated program of research, the Institute organized three national conferences on the exploration of results obtained by briefer forms of therapy based on psychoanalytic insights. Sponsored by the Albert and Mary Lasker Foundation, this enterprise was the first serious effort to encourage revision of the therapeutic postulates on which psychoanalytic therapy had been based. Alexander, his colleagues, and sympathizers with Alexander's views in other centers became the target of much controversy. The very citadel of psychoanalytic dogma was under siege. The terms "psychoanalytic psychotherapy" and "psychoanalytically oriented psychotherapy" began to appear in the literature.

In this effort, Alexander showed the primacy of interest in therapy that is the hallmark of the true physician. It is not surprising that his leadership in this direction found such a sympathetic response among the growing numbers of young psychoanalysts who shared his interest in therapeutic progress. In this undertaking as well as in their researches in psychosomatic medicine, Alexander and his colleagues revived the therapeutic optimism that had led the first American pioneers to establish a psychoanalytic beachhead in the United States. When, at a later date, Rado and his co-workers established the Columbia clinic in New

York, direct supervised experience in treating patients with psychosomatic illnesses and other disorders with psychoanalytic psychotherapy became part of the required curriculum for student analysts; Rado has termed this modified form of treatment "reparative therapy." As experience in teaching this method grows, it becomes increasingly difficult to define exactly where psychoanalytically oriented psychotherapy ends and psychoanalytic therapy begins.

In 1945, when the Columbia clinic was arguing its claim to separate existence and recognition, the Chicago group provided the strongest support. When a delegation of Rado, Daniels, Binger, and I went to Chicago to argue our case, we found genuine support. Alexander, George Mohr, and Martin Grotjahn were there at the time, as well as Helen McLean, Roy Grinker, Jules Masserman, and others. Chicago became one of the earliest battlefields on which the forces of traditionalism were deployed to meet the onslaught of champions of the new approach—an approach that spelled re-examination of old hypotheses and experimentation with modifications of old therapeutic techniques. There was cleavage in the Chicago Society on these grounds. Many of the more adventurous graduates of the Chicago Institute moved to other cities to start new training centers, although some stalwarts on both sides remained to continue the struggle. Max Gitelson became the most influential member of the Chicago Institute staff; Masserman and Grinker went ahead with their plans of organization, teaching of residents, and research.

As I have mentioned previously, at this time the Menninger Clinic was expanding rapidly. Here again the classical tradition was basic to the programs of psychoanalytic training and practice, although (as the plans of organization reached maturity) a close relationship grew up between that clinic's management and the clinical services of the Kansas State Hospital and the Veterans Administration facility in Topeka. While completing their psychiatric residencies, candidates for psychoanalytic training had the opportunity for excellent psychiatric education under the auspices of the Menninger Clinic.

A rapid increase in the number of psychoanalytic societies has occurred during the last twelve years, the most recently organized being the Denver Psychoanalytic Society. The westward movement skipped some of the principal centers of medical education. The new "forty-niners" were recruited from the ranks of European analysts and from Americans trained in Chicago and Topeka. The first two presidents of the San Francisco Society, Ernst Simmel and Emanuel Windholz, were Europeans; Simmel later became the first president of the Los Angeles Psychoanalytic Society, for the year 1946–47. When The Society for Psychoanalytic Medicine of Southern California was formed in 1950, the first two presidents Milton Miller and May E. Romm were American-born analysts. Martin Grotjahn, the third president, is the only foreign-born and foreign-trained analyst on the list. It is perhaps significant that, as in New York and Philadelphia, the divergent views on theory and practice created a natural cleavage in the ranks of the local California profession, leaving the door open for the organization of two societies, within the ranks of which there was a greater mutuality of interest and of personal cordiality. It is interesting that in Philadelphia the more tradition-oriented members broke away from the original society, whereas in Los Angeles the opposite occurred. In New York, there is a considerable overlap in membership between the New York Psychoanalytic Society and the Psychoanalytic Association of New York; in both institutes the techniques of training follow the orthodox tradition. The newer societies in the neighborhood of New York City (Westchester and New Jersey) have a very mixed membership from the standpoint of past training. Most of their members belong also to the American Psychoanalytic Association.

The Western New England Society developed under the leadership of Robert Knight and Lawrence Kubie, after Knight left his position at the Menninger Clinic to take over the reorganization of the Austen Fox Riggs Center for the treatment of the psychoneuroses. Since its acceptance as an affiliate society by the American Psychoanalytic Association in 1952, The Western New England Society has been fortunate in having for a few years the services of such a distinguished theorist and teacher as Erik Erikson and of David Rapaport, whose untimely death was a severe loss to psychoanalysis.

In the meantime, there have been somewhat belated extensions of psychoanalytic training in the Midwest. The Detroit Society, which was organized in 1940 under the leadership of Leo Bartemeier and the Richard Sterbas, ran into some difficulty when the institute was obliged to undergo reorganization. It is once again beginning to function under the wing of the Chicago Institute. The fledgeling Cleveland Institute, however, has been "raised" under the absentee parentage of the New York Institute, whereas in Cincinnati and in Ann Arbor the problems of establishing properly accredited training programs remain unsolved.

Finally, in the extreme southeast and northwest corners of our country, psychoanalysis has also taken firm hold. The New Orleans Society has had to depend on Washington for qualified teachers to staff their local institute. Meanwhile, at Tulane, Robert Heath has organized a well-integrated program of residency training in psychiatry, including (for residents considered suitable) a complete psychoanalytic course. This well-established curriculum, within the framework of a university medical school, is another instance of independent enterprise undertaken without the authorization or approval of the American Psychoanalytic Association.*

I hope that this outline of recent developments in the field has given some idea of the extraordinary growth of interest in the establishment of psychoanalytic training. Most of the newly established centers have some connection with a well-known medical school and include faculty members who teach undergraduate medical students; this indicates a generally accepted belief that psychoanalysis is best taught in a setting wherein its theoretical assumptions and therapeutic techniques become an essential part of postgraduate education for the specialty of psychiatry and are considered to have a proper place in the family of medical sciences.

As pointed out earlier, psychoanalysis was first viewed by its sponsors in the United States as an additional tool for the study and treatment of mental disorders. We seem to have come full circle. The old type of sequestered institute, giving classes by gaslight at the close of a hard day's work and with no associated clinical facilities, is giving way to the establishment of psychoanalytic training as part of the basic curriculum in postgraduate psychiatric education.

Psychoanalysts have from the start contributed greatly to the study and treatment of psychosomatic disorders. The establishment of the American Psychosomatic Society coincided approximately with the establishment of the New York Psychoanalytic Institute. Among the founders was Flanders Dunbar, whose monumental volume, *Emotions and Bodily Changes,* now in its fourth edition (1954), was planned under the aegis of a joint committee of psychiatrists and clergy under the auspices of the Academy of Medicine in New York, with Mrs. Sherman Hoyt as chairman. When the Psychosomatic Society decided

* The New Orleans Psychoanalytic Society was organized in 1953 and was accepted as a Constituent Society by the American Psychoanalytic Association in 1955 (Editors).

to publish its journal, *Psychosomatic Medicine,* Dunbar became the chief editor. Under her editorship and especially under the editorship of Carl Binger, which lasted for fifteen years (from 1947 until 1962), this journal has attained a well deserved reputation, both national and international. Centers of psychosomatic research were formed in New York, where Dunbar, Daniels, Mittelman, Binger, Ackerman, and others were working; in Chicago where Alexander, Thomas French, Helen McLean, Milton Miller, Grinker, Masserman, Mohr, and Bacon did their well-known research; in Boston, under the leadership of Stanley Cobb and Jacob Finesinger (at the Massachusetts General Hospital); in Cincinnati under Maurice Levine and his associates; and in Philadelphia under Spurgeon English, Gerald Pearson, Leon Saul, Lauren Smith, and Kenneth Appel.

Developments in Cleveland are of special interest in view of the close tie of teaching with a department of psychiatry under the energetic leadership of Douglas Bond. The price paid for early accreditation of the new institute was the requirement that the development of psychoanalytic training be supervised by an established institute. Weekly, multiple air flights from Cleveland to New York insured that all proper steps were completed in accord with the requirements of the Board on Professional Standards.

Perhaps the best test of this system is now supplied by the coexistence of two psychoanalytic training centers in New Orleans: one, under the leadership of Robert Heath, built into the residency training program at Tulane University Medical School, the other, the New Orleans Psychoanalytic Institute, nurtured by the Washington Institute. In most instances, the graduates of both training facilities are on excellent social terms but are battling "to the death" in their claims for professional superiority. Time will tell which group contributes most to science and to the community and produces the best clinicians. There is some visiting back and forth between the professional associations.

§ Approach to Maturity

It is time to say a few words about the other outstanding contributions of psychoanalysis, contributions that belong more to science than to the quest for organizational absolutism. For the most part, the scientific papers presented at the regular meetings of the American Psychoanalytic and the International Psycho-Analytical Associations concern either involved and often repetitious interpretations of clinical observations in the traditional language of Freudian metapsychology or the finding of an appropriate quotation from Freud in support of the speaker's thesis. A quotation from Phyllis Greenacre (1962) calls attention to a theoretical Rubicon, which divides psychoanalysis in the United States into two major contending communities: one has as its main interest the pursuit and elaboration of Freud's theories and therapeutic techniques, which they interpret as the sole proper role of the psychoanalyst; the other looks upon the discoveries of Freud and his early followers as offering new scientific data that may be brought into dynamic relationship with the data of other sciences and so be made an effective tool of collaborative research into more comprehensive techniques of therapy. Dr. Greenacre writes:

> The significance and importance of the consideration of the biologically determined concerns of early infancy for psychoanalysts and for psychoanalytic theory may be a moot question. There may be a wish to exclude them from our consideration as not belonging to metapsychology and therefore outside the field of psychoanalysis.

Here is the very nub of the problem. All who dwell in the metaphysical region of psychoanalysis have little concern with or respect for those who dwell across the Rubicon. Amusing although tragic is the fact that Freud has written so much and (as any true investigator must) has modified his ideas so frequently that almost any approach to the interpretation of psychoanalytic observations can be supported by some corroborating phrase in Freud's writings. The original interest of the American psychoanalysts was in the new light that Freud's work threw on the causes of mental illness and in the improvement in therapy that might result therefrom. Although these interests still motivate both groups of psychoanalysts, the metaphysicians and the scientists, the American physician is likely to think in pragmatic terms when treating patients and to be impatient with restrictions imposed on his freedom to experiment and to find his own way of handling the tools he has learned to use.

Freud had hoped that one day neurosis would be found to have an organic root that could be remedied; such a discovery seems far from realization, despite the enthusiasm of the drug companies and some biological chemists. With the work of the geneticists, on the one hand, and such elaborate neurophysiological researches as those conducted at Tulane by Heath and his colleagues, on the other, some long-neglected approaches to the understanding of mental illness have been attempted. These exemplify the complexity of the issues involved in basic research designed to test old assumptions or new theories.

The American psychoanalyst of today is rarely content to limit his activities to sitting behind the heads of a dozen patients every day, trying to piece together the complex patterns of intrapsychic traffic problems. If not a teacher, or an administrator, or both, he is likely to be involved in collaborative efforts to promote the integration of health services or in research in some biological or social science area. American psychoanalysts are best classified as a group within the family of behavioral scientists, a group whose members have detailed acquaintance and a sensitive familiarity with the sources, complexity, and puzzles of human motivation and with the relationship between emotional stress and behavior. Psychoanalysts trained exclusively in the United States are now required to have a thorough grounding in the basic sciences, in clinical medicine, and in general psychiatry; at least theoretically, this should insure that they do not lose sight of their primary identification as physicians. Those of us who have had the responsibility and the opportunity to teach undergraduate medical students as well as psychiatric residents are not likely to lose touch with our scientific alma mater.

Limitations of space prevent any attempt at classifying and enumerating the community agencies that seek consultation or active participation in programs by experienced psychoanalysts. The cross-fertilization of psychoanalysis with clinical psychology, social work, and the social sciences has already been mentioned. Psychoanalysts have contributed to the study and maintenance of student mental health—from the nursery school through the graduate schools of great universities—as well as to the selection and training of ministers of religion and personnel of rehabilitation centers of all kinds. There is increasing interest by government agencies, both national and international, in involving psychoanalysts as participants and consultants in the selection and management of their personnel.

The proportion of women to men in the membership of psychoanalytic associations and on the faculties of the institutes may be somewhat greater than in other branches of clinical medicine; their contributions to the field have equalled and in many instances surpassed those of all but the most brilliant men. As might have been anticipated, they have been particularly active in pursuing inquiries into the developmental sequences and conflicts that characterize their own sex. The work of Helene Deutsch in Boston, Therese Benedek and Helen McLean in Chicago, Clara Thompson and Phyllis Greenacre in New York, and Edith Weigert and Frieda Fromm-Reichmann in Washington is especially worthy of mention. These women and others have been untiring in their efforts to maintain existing organizational practices, in addition to carrying heavy teaching schedules and private psychoanalytic practices. The dedication of such people as Henrietta Klein, Charlotte Babcock, May Romm, Mabel Cohen, Edith Jacobson, Hilde Bruch, Catherine Bacon, and Eleanor and Sarah Tower qualifies them at least for "honorable mention" among the pioneers in the field during the past twenty-five years. It is noteworthy that three women have held the presidency of national psychoanalytic groups, Marion Kenworthy and Grete Bibring in the American Psychoanalytic Association and Frances Arkin in the Academy.

Foremost among women educators is Marion Kenworthy, whose inexhaustible energy found new opportunities for creative effort after her long years of service as professor at the New York School of Social Work had come to an end. Consultant to the armed forces, chairman of the Group for the Advancement of Psychoanalysis (GAP), and finally president of the American Psychoanalytic Association, she has always shown a devotion to physicians' ideals and the goals of effective teamwork that has won her the affection and respect of her colleagues in a measure rarely accorded to a member of her sex.

Outstanding contributions to theory and technique in therapy of the psychoses were made by Frieda Fromm-Reichmann during her later years in Chestnut Lodge. Her book, *The Principles of Intensive Psychotherapy*, is among the best on the topic. Psychoanalysis in America owes much of its humanity and some of its technical advances to the work of the distaff members of the local and national associations. Some of the leading organizers, a few of the more original teachers, and many of the most thorough clinicians and scholars are women. Not a few have expanded their activities beyond the routine boundaries and have participated actively in community activities of one sort or another, often in programs that were definitively pioneering; Marianne Kris has been active in leading child analytic seminars and longitudinal studies of the mother-child relationship during the first five years of life. In Rockland

County, New York, Margaret Lawrence has for three years pioneered a project designed to provide comprehensive interdisciplinary consultation to the professional staffs of the public schools. In Chicago, Helen McLean is as well known for her collaborative studies in the field of social psychiatry as for her teaching and contributions to the literature of psychoanalysis. Margaret Mahler early became interested in thinking beyond the " 'ivory tower' of analytic practice," and after pioneering the teaching of the Rorschach method in Vienna, became known in this country for her studies of symbiotic child psychosis and other serious psychiatric syndromes in early life.

Basic studies of the mother-child relationship and of infantile psychopathology, such as those just mentioned, and the researches of David Levy and René Spitz represent the type of excellent direct observational work that has been so badly needed to provide proof or refutation of the theoretical retrospective reconstructions of emotional development on which the structure of Freudian psychoanalysis has been erected. Psychoanalysis is under continuing attack from biological scientists and social scientists for making absolute claims that cannot be verified and that they believe add little to the understanding of man. To meet such criticisms, we must insist on a multidisciplinary orientation in the teaching programs, and we must bring human ingenuity (aided by the specialized competence of the electronic computer) to the longitudinal study of individual and collective behavior of various groups. We must study the nature and impact of the "intercom" system between therapist and object(s) of therapy, and pursue psychological studies that will add ever more reproducible data to what already has been assembled in the study of body–mind relationships.

Theoretical advances attributable to the efforts of leading psychoanalysts in the United States have been minimal. However, the generation of younger psychoanalysts is better trained in clinical work, and certain trends hold promise for the future. Interest in "pure psychoanalysis" has centered on ego psychology; such terms as "ego strength" and "ego defense" have become familiar. Some psychoanalysts have lost interest in teaching the libido theory, and some emphasize environmental and cultural imperatives as sources of behavior. The increasing interest in communication has helped us realize that the psychoanalytic experience has been insufficiently studied. From the Weinstock study and other studies we have learned that the psychoanalytic experience holds no special magic. Nevertheless, probably none of us would say that our experience in undergoing personal analysis and psychoanalytic training has neither benefited us enormously nor facilitated our understanding of emotional disorders.

Under the fragmented conditions of civilization that have existed since the end of World War II, it is not surprising that interest should be directed toward understanding and using the patient's total personal resources, rather than in increased delving into the dark recesses of a largely forgotten past. Erik Erikson has turned the brilliant light of his intellect to the study of forces that aid or hinder the sense of identity, of the self that we need to develop and rely upon. Sandor Rado has redirected our attention to the original view of psychoanalysis as a science rooted in new discoveries in the motivational system of the human organism, and to the point that human behavior cannot be understood if the biological problems of adaptation are not central to the study of man: hence his systematized conception of the human organism as destined by its nature to be guided by hedonic self-regulation for the fullest and freest use of its powers, with the maximum tolerance for frustration, and the speediest exercise of talents for repair when adaptive responses have met with an unexpected setback. In other words, Rado would stem the tide of metaphysical speculation and return the thinking of his colleagues and students to the concept of man as a unitary being with a co-ordinating nervous apparatus through whose properly integrated activities alone this goal of hedonic self-regulation can be achieved. His views have been fully set forth in two volumes of his collected papers (Rado, 1956–1962).

Direct observation of an infant with a gastric fistula, by George Engel and his associates (Engel, Reichman & Segal, 1956), has verified many research findings in child development and the psychopathology of childhood. The ramifications of emotional disturbance in a family, resulting from what, at first, may appear to be a breakdown in integration of one child's adaptive resources, led naturally to the idea that since each individual in a family lives in an intimate social environment, wherein the interactional processes of emotional exchange involve each member of the group in some way or other, it would be far more enlightening to study the processes of interaction in the entire family group. One of the early books foreshadowing this branch of psychoanalytic research is the report of a collaborative study at the Cornell Medical School by Henry B. Richardson in *Patients Have Families* (1948). In his book, *Psychoanalysis and the Family Neurosis* (1960),

Martin Grotjahn presents a viewpoint that may well presage a certain trend in future psychoanalysis. More recent enthusiasts in launching these studies have been Nathan Ackerman (1959) in New York, John Spiegel (1959) in Boston, and Donald Jackson (1959) in Palo Alto. Their researches have shed much new light on the problems arising in families when a crack develops in the integration of emotional forces in one or more members of the group. This type of study has an almost unlimited horizon as far as research into maladjusted patterns of family life is concerned. As John Spiegel has demonstrated, most problems that arise in such a situation are not solely determined by some biological inadequacy; there are also elements derived from cultural patterning within groups of diverse racial origins and socioeconomic standing.

It has often been said that our culture is child-centered. Certainly, at times it seems to us oldsters that the adolescent society lives by its own rules and tends to ride herd on the parent generation. With the development of the child guidance movement, under the leadership of William Healy and Augusta Brunner, the close partnership of psychoanalysis and clinical psychology was recognized as especially desirable in the study and treatment of children's disorders. Within a year of the establishment of the Judge Baker Foundation in Boston, Elmer Southard's ideas led to the founding of the Smith School of Social Work. Two years later, Marion Kenworthy, a pupil of Southard and Healy, joined Bernard Glueck, Sr., in inaugurating a two-year program of instruction at the New York School of Social Work. Within a year or so after the inauguration of this curriculum, child guidance clinics began to spring up in many cities. The now familiar pattern of the interdisciplinary team, psychiatrist, psychologist, and social worker, was the natural product of these early collaborative enterprises.

In 1927, Lawson Lowrey and David Levy established The New York Institute for Child Guidance, for some years the showpiece of child therapy. After the establishment of the New York Psychiatric Institute, an increasing number of child psychiatrists sought psychoanalytic training. Many of the early specialists in this field were women: Margaret Ribble and Margaret Fries in New York, Marian Putnam (daughter of the first American psychoanalyst, James Putnam) and Edith Jackson in New Haven, Eleanor Pavenstedt in Boston, and Sibylle K. Escalona, a psychologist, in Topeka. Later years saw child analysis develop into one of the most important of all subspecialties, although as the years go by there seems a tendency for seasoned psychonanalysts to leave it to the clinical psychologists and the younger members of the specialty. Play therapy with unruly twelve-year-olds is not an easy job for any but the most dedicated and athletic.

From the time that Freud turned his interest to the development of an ego psychology, this subject became the concern of the principal centers of psychoanalytic training in this country. Gradually, however, interest in the animistically created substance of the ego as studied *in vacuo* has begun to yield to study of a more generally understandable abstraction, the self, an abstraction that subsumes the integration of all vital forces, organic and psychic, into a unitary being, the human person.

Studies have been made of the individual who has been exposed to varying sorts of stress, from infancy to adult life. Efforts are under way to conduct extensive studies of individual development throughout the life cycle, with special reference to the factors that seem responsible for variations in response to stimuli and for the hierarchy of motivational impulses. Efforts to correlate physiological changes with emotional responses continue to occupy the interest of many investigators.

Recognition of the importance of interactional processes set in motion by the complex dynamics of human relationships has led to the development of psychoanalytic therapy applied to groups and to the attempt to study the interactional processes of whole families by direct observation. More recently, this type of study has led to attempts to structure methods of family therapy. This area of investigation offers an excellent opportunity to test the dynamic bases of communication within the original biosocial group.

So rapid has been the advance in the new science of microbiology that we may be nearing the goal that Freud hoped his professional heirs would some day reach, the discovery of the underlying causes of neurosis and other forms of mental illness. It seems apparent that any hope of achieving new insights into these conditions through isolation of psychoanalytic teaching from the biological sciences would be futile.

In brief, all signs indicate that psychoanalysis must be regarded as one of the essential scientific disciplines, whose discoveries have had profound effects on the direction of thought and the development of new cultural traditions in the Western world, and also one that has now embarked on a serious effort, in collaboration with other scientific disciplines, to find ways for applying its discoveries to increasingly fruitful research into the complex problems of individual and group adaptations in this troubled world. Perhaps we are returning at last to first principles, the need for increasingly exact observations before launching new theories into the areas where verification of hypotheses is impossible.

§ Epilogue and Forecast

During the past quarter-century, psychoanalysis has spread its influence over every branch of culture in the United States, with the force and speed of a forest fire. What began in its country of origin as a revolutionary set of hypotheses, stoutly resisted by the professional community and deemed subversive by the guardians of morals, has achieved recognition as offering the one substantial foundation on which to erect a modern science of psychodynamics. It is somewhat ironic that the genius who dared to open Pandora's box (as well as those who suffered temporary martyrdom with him) should live to see the fruits of his labors harvested in a foreign land in which he never felt at home. That his daughter, who above everyone symbolizes total unquestioning allegiance to the entire conceptual framework that Freud deeded to his professional heirs, should be loaded with honors in this strange environment, provides the surest proof of the esteem with which she is held in the highest academic circles and is some small compensation for Freud's not having been similarly honored during the evening of his life.

Certain features in our culture and tradition have served to entomb Freud's theoretical assumptions within an authoritarian organization; these include a passion for organization, an uneasy preference for conformity, and the tendency to "ride a novelty to death," whether it be moral rearmament, canasta, or the twist. The need to grab and try out something new is perhaps another evidence of our immaturity and of the lack of any crystalline culture. We have some redeeming features, which play a part in our eagerness to experiment; these are ingenuity, inventiveness, a passion for individual freedom, and a special aptitude for making things work. This last quality is responsible for the initial interest in psychoanalysis in this country. Would psychoanalysis help the physician do a better job in treating his patient? Unfortunately, partly because of the two world cataclysms that have shattered so many hopes and created such uncertainty for the future, those tendencies in our culture that represent the uncertain and insecure side of an emerging civilization—the need to hold to the old and eschew the new, the need to join together and consolidate forces, the need to cry "traitor" if someone questions an assumption—these seemingly adolescent trends have for a long time dominated the development of psychoanalytic organization and education. With the gradual passing or aging of the older generation, who inevitably have an intense loyalty to the old order, the other elements in our culture—the ingenuity, the readiness to question authority (the "show me" attitude), the venturesomeness of the pioneer—these and other more promising trends have emerged. As new centers of postgraduate training in psychiatry develop, the old order of centrally located authoritarian edicts governing the selection, training, and accreditation of psychoanalysts will be resisted even more strongly. Already there are centers of psychoanalytic training in medical schools. This pattern must certainly become more acceptable; as the younger analyst becomes integrated with his community, his view of his specialty will undoubtedly become less myopic. Even the danger that the promise of financial reward may continue as the chief desideratum in psychoanalytic training will lessen, unless clinical psychologists and social workers who have been analyzed or graduated from some training facility are enjoined from independent practice.

The tie of psychoanalysis to medicine is gradually being strengthened as psychoanalysts continue to work as respected members of university and hospital staffs, teaching undergraduate medical students and undertaking fundamental research. I profoundly hope that the trend toward integration of psychoanalytic training with psychiatric residency programs will become the preferred, and eventually the sole, pattern for the education and certification of psychoanalysts, and that the present structure of the American Psychoanalytic Association will be reviewed with the aim of decentralizing authority and returning to the system of federated societies and training centers. Let the term "institute" die a slow but painless death. For one who has participated in discussions leading to the present mode of organizational practices, both in the United States and on the international scene, this pious hope expresses a part of his *apologia pro vita sua*.

The future influence of psychoanalysis depends on an ever increasing assimilation of the insights developed by the science of communication. It is to the everlasting glory of the founder of our discipline that psychoanalysis has been able to develop and, to some extent, understand effective communication between physician and patient at levels hitherto unknown. Through improving the techniques of this new form of human exchange, psychoanalysts should be able to contribute significantly to the science of communication and perhaps to the solution of hitherto insoluble blocks to understanding and co-operation between groups with divergent or antagonistic viewpoints. Psychoanalysis must attempt to meet this challenge if it is to merit continuing recognition and full partnership in the great company of the behavioral sciences.

REFERENCES

Ackerman, N. The psychoanalytic approach to the family; individual and family dynamics. In J. Masserman (Ed.), *Science and psychoanalysis.* Vol. 2. New York: Grune & Stratton, 1959.

Bertine, Eleanor. *Human relationships.* New York: Longmans, Green, 1958.

Dunbar, Helen Flanders. *Emotions and bodily changes.* (4th ed.) New York: Columbia Univer. Press, 1954.

Engel, G. L., F. Reichsman, & H. L. Segal. A study of an infant with a gastric fistula. *Psychosomat. Med.*, 1956, 18, 374–398.

Fenichel, O. *Outline of psychoanalysis.* New York: W. W. Norton, 1934.

Freud, S. *Complete psychological works of Sigmund Freud.* (Standard ed.) Vols. 7 & 19. London: Hogarth Press, 1953–.

Greenacre, Phyllis. The theory of the parent-infant relationship. *Int. J. Psycho-Anal.*, 1962, 43, 235–237.

Grotjahn, M. *Psychoanalysis and the family neurosis.* New York: W. W. Norton, 1960.

Harding, Esther. *Woman's mysteries.* New York: Longmans, Green, 1935.

Harding, Esther. *The way of all women.* New York: Longmans, Green, 1937.

Hendrick, I. *Facts and theories of psychoanalysis.* (3rd ed.) New York: Knopf, 1958.

Hinkle, Beatrice. *The re-creating of the individual.* New York: Harcourt, Brace, 1923.

Jackson, D. Family interaction, family homeostasis, and some implications for conjoint family psychotherapy. In J. Masserman (Ed.), *Science and psychoanalysis.* Vol. 2. New York: Grune & Stratton, 1959.

Jones, E. *The life and work of Sigmund Freud.* New York: Basic Books, 1953–1957. 3 vols.

Jung, C. G. The psychology of dementia praecox. A. A. Brill, & F. Peterson (Trans.). *Ment. Nerv. Dis. Monogr.*, 1909, No. 3.

Kardiner, A. *The traumatic neuroses of war.* New York: P. Hoeber, 1941.

Lewin, B. D., & Helen Ross. *Psychoanalytic education in the United States.* New York: W. W. Norton, 1960.

Millet, J. A. P. Changing faces of psychoanalytic training. In L. Salzman, & J. H. Masserman (Eds.), *Modern concepts of Psychoanalysis.* New York: Philosophical Library, 1962. Pp. 127–139.

Oberndorf, C. P. *A history of psychoanalysis in America.* New York: Grune & Stratton, 1953.

Peterson, F. Some new fields and methods in psychology. *N.Y. Med. J.*, 1909, 90, 945–948.

Prince, M. P. The psychology of sudden religious conversion. *J. Abnorm. Psychol.*, 1906, **1**, 42–54.

Psychosomat. Med., 1962, **24** (1).

Rado, S. *The psychoanalysis of behavior.* New York: Grune & Stratton, 1956–1962. 2 vols.

Richardson, H. B. *Patients have families.* New York: Commonwealth Fund, 1948.

Spiegel, J. Some cultural aspects of transference and countertransference. In J. Masserman (Ed.), *Science and psychoanalysis.* Vol. 2. New York: Grune & Stratton, 1959.

Wickes, Frances. *The inner world of childhood.* New York: Appleton-Century, 1940.

Zilboorg, G., & G. M. Henry. *A history of medical psychology.* New York: W. W. Norton, 1941.

Zilboorg, G., J. R. Hill, & A. Baker. *One hundred years of American psychiatry.* New York: Columbia Univer. Press, 1944.

I wish to express warm thanks and deep appreciation to Miss Anna T. Clark of the Social Work Staff, Metropolitan Hospital, for her tireless energy and accuracy in looking up endless details for me, and to my secretary and friend of many years standing, Miss Grace Nicotra, without whose patience and untiring zeal this manuscript could never have been completed—J. A. P. M.

Name Index

Abraham, Hilda, 2
Abraham, Karl, 1–12, 43, 46, 52–56, 67, 69, 103, 181, 187, 190–191, 200, 212, 243, 262, 274, 276, 285, 361, 374–375, 392, 403, 433, 441, 451, 503, 512
Ackerman, Nathan, 572, 585, 591
Adler, Alexandra, 84 n.
Adler, Alfred, 38, 73, 78–86, 92, 145, 150, 166, 187, 339, 465, 573
Adler, Kurt, 84 n.
Adler, Nelly, 84 n.
Adler, Vali, 84 n.
Aichhorn, August, 148, 348–358, 518
Alexander, Bernard, 385, 397
Alexander, Franz, 20, 43, 75, 215, 240–248, 286, 305, 375, 384–398, 433, 451, 453, 456 n., 474, 504, 555-557, 573, 581–582, 585
Allen, Frederick, 554
Amenhotep IV, 9
Amsden, George, 431
Andreas-Salomé, Lou, 39 n., 235–236, 238–239, 319, 324, 412
André-Thomas, 231
Anton, Gabriel, 230
Appel, Kenneth, 585

Babcock, Charlotte, 588
Bacon, Catherine, 581, 585, 588
Baker, A., 555
Balint, Michael, 14, 32, 55, 113–114, 441
Balzac, Honoré de, 298
Bartemeier, Leo, 562, 581, 583
Bateson, Gregory, 568
Bauer, Wilma (Mrs. Paul Federn), 144
Becker, Philip L., 160–168
Beer-Hofmann, Richard 250–251, 263
Beers, Clifford, 554
Behn-Eschenburg, Hans, 170
Bender, Lauretta, 460
Benedek, Therese, 588
Benedict, Ruth, 568
Bennet, E. A., 63, 74-75
Bergler, Edmund, 164
Berkeley-Hill, O., 536
Bernard, Claude, 79
Bernard, Viola, 559
Bernays, Minna, 412
Bernfeld, Anne, 417
Bernfeld, Siegfried, 300, 415-429
Bernfeld, Suzanne Cassirer, 426-427
Bibring, Edward, 287, 560
Bibring, Grete, 154, 287, 560
Biedermanns, A. E., 174
Bier, August, 339
Bing, Robert, 230
Binger, Carl, 391, 559, 582
Binswanger, Ludwig, 66, 73
Bircher-Benner, 335
Bismarck, Otto von, 193, 308
Blain, Daniel, 564, 577
Blane, François, 401
Blanton, Smiley, 431
Bleuler, Eugen, 2, 10, 51, 64–66, 68, 161, 170, 212–213, 230, 343, 346, 398, 548
Blitzsten, Lionel, 581
Blumgart, Leonard, 29, 553
Boas, Franz, 275

Bobach, Frieda, 158
Boehm, Felix, 3
Bolk, Louis, 278
Bonaparte, Lucien, 401
Bonaparte, Marie, 399–414
Bonaparte, Napoleon *see* Napoleon Bonaparte
Bonaparte, Pierre, 401
Bonaparte, Roland, 401
Bond, Douglas, 585
Bonhoeffer, Karl, 2, 230, 510
Bornstein, Berta, 441
Bosch, Robert, 339
Boss, M., 318
Boswell, James, 163, 166
Bottome, Phyllis, 82
Brahms, Johannes, 162, 164
Brend, W. A., 536
Brett, George, 75
Breuer, Joseph, 240, 390
Briehl, Marie H., 282–298
Briehl, Walter, 430–438
Brierley, Marjorie, 267
Brill, A. A., 26, 29, 48, 64, 166, 210–222, 229, 548–552, 554, 556
Brill, Edmund, 219
Brill, Gioia, 219
Brill, Rose Owen, 219
Brontë, Charlotte, 513
Brosin, Henry, 577
Bruch, Hilde, 588
Brunner, Augusta, 591
Brunswick, David, 375, 383
Brunswick, Ruth Mack, 431, 441
Bryan, Clement, 5, 536
Buber, Martin, 417
Buehler, Carl, 466
Buerger, Leo, 300
Bullard, Dexter, 580
Bunzlfedern, Rabbi, 143
Burlingame, Charles, 565
Burlingham, Dorothy, 521–522
Burt, Ceril, 536

Caesar, Julius, 197
Caligula, Gaius Caesar, 196
Cannon, W. B., 79
Cattell, Jacques, 487 n.
Céline, Louis Ferdinand, 412
Chadwick, Mary, 504
Charcot, Jean Martin, 301
Charlemagne, 122
Chessman, Caryl, 412
Claparède, Edouard, 171
Clark, Anna T., 596
Cobb, Stanley, 391, 585
Cohen, Hermann, 52
Cohen, Mabel, 588
Colby, K. M., 82 n.
Coleman, Rose, 497
Colette, Sidonie Gabrielle, 298
Cooper, James Fenimore, 352
Coriat, Isador, 27, 579
Cowan, John, 503
Croce, Benedetto, 486
Crowley, Ralph, 580
Culpin, Millais, 537

Daniels, George, 553, 559, 582, 585
Denielsen, Berndt, 451
Darwin, Charles, 37, 103, 230, 274, 490 n.
Dauthenday, Max, 163
David, I. I., 145
Deri, Frances, 375, 383, 427, 445
Deutsch, Felix, 3, 184, 284, 288–289, 299–306, 579
Deutsch, Helene, 282–298, 301, 405, 487, 579, 588
Devereux, George, 275–276
Devine, Henry, 536
Dobson, Bee, 224
Donovan, Gen. William, 564
Dostoevski, Fëdor M., 37, 42, 162, 184, 263
Dreyfuss, D. K., 60–62
Dreyfuss, George, 230
du Bois, Cora, 568
du Gard, Roger Martin, 490
Dunbar, Flanders, 391

Eckardt, M., 450 n.
Eckermann, Johann Peter, 163–164
Eckstein, Emma, 412
Eckstein, Fritz, 149
Eder, David, 535-536
Eisenstein, Samuel, 36–49
Eissler, K. R., 358
Eitingon, Max 2, 51–62, 181, 183, 191, 201, 373
Eitingon, Mira, 60
Ekstein, Rudolf, 415–429

Ellis, Havelock, 216
Engel, George, 590
English, Spurgeon, 585
Eppinger, Hans, 230
Epstein, Raissa Timofeyewna, 78
Erikson, Erik H., 291, 524–530, 562, 583, 590
Escalona, Sibylle K., 591
Evans, Elida, 229
Evans, Margaret, 372

Federn, Annie, 144
Federn, Ernst, 40, 155–156
Federn, Paul, 19, 142–159, 167, 286, 337–339, 350, 430, 474, 557
Federn, Salomon, 143
Federn, Walter, 144, 147, 158
Federn, Wilma Bauer, 144-145
Feigenbaum, Dorian, 27 n., 147
Feitelberg, Sergei, 424, 426
Fenichel, Hanna, 447
Fenichel, Otto, 22, 257, 375, 427, 439–449, 562
Ferenczi, Sándor, 2–3, 6, 14–34, 41, 43, 48, 53, 57, 69, 92–93, 101, 140, 187, 191, 241–242, 273–274, 276, 311, 315, 318, 332, 361, 363, 375, 426, 431, 480, 536
Figner, Vera, 283
Finesinger, Jacob, 585
Fink, George, 553
Flagg, Glenn W., 299–306
Flaubert, Gustave, 251, 253
Flechsig, Paul, 230
Fliess, Robert, 236
Fliess, Wilhelm, 3, 403, 411
Flugel, J. C., 536–537
Foerster, Gottfried, 230
Forel, August Henri, 212, 301, 336
Förster-Nietzsche, Elizabeth, 187
Forsyth, David, 535–536
France, Anatol, 251, 263
Fränkl, Kate, *see* Friedländer, Kate
Frank, Richard, 559
French, T., 247, 581, 585
Freud, Anna, 28, 55, 61, 80, 94, 150, 154–155, 157–158, 196, 301, 312, 317, 350, 356, 360, 411, 413, 444, 470, 475, 487 n. 491 n., 508, 513–514, 517, 519–530, 561
Freud, Ernst L., 51, 53, 57, 58 n. 399
Freud, Martin, 299, 487 n.
Freud, Sigmund, 2–3, 6–7, 9–12, 14–15, 17–18, 24, 26, 28, 30, 32–33, 38–39, 41–43, 45–47, 49, 51–52, 54 n., 55 n., 56–60, 64–70, 72–83, 90–91, 94–97, 99, 103–107, 110–113, 116–117, 119–127, 131, 136, 138, 145–146, 148–151, 153, 155, 157, 160–162, 165–167, 169–170, 175–177, 180, 184–185, 188, 191, 195–196, 205–206, 208, 213–215, 217, 222, 226–228, 230, 235–237, 239–240, 242–244, 250, 253, 255–256, 259, 274, 285–287, 293, 299, 301, 309–310, 312, 316, 319, 323, 326, 329–333, 341, 343, 345–346, 351, 356, 362–363, 369, 374, 379, 385–386, 390, 392–394, 398–399, 402, 404, 408, 410–412, 418–421, 425, 427, 434–435, 441–443, 459, 465–467, 469, 472–473, 475–476, 479, 481, 484–488, 491–492, 494, 513–514, 516, 520, 527, 534–535, 542, 544, 546–548, 552, 561, 574, 578–579, 586, 592–593
Freund, Anton von, 53, 56
Friedemann, Adolf, 333–347
Friedländer, Kate, 508–518, 542
Fries, Margaret, 591
Frink, H. W., 27, 551–552
Frobel, Friedrich, 347
Fromm, Erich, 75, 120, 340, 443, 571–572
Fromm-Reichmann, Frieda, 311, 315, 318, 340, 580, 588
Frumkes, George, 383
Fuchs, G., 418

Gabe, Sigmund, 372
Gandhi, Mohandes K., 165
George, Prince, 407
Gero, George, 562
Gerstmann, Joseph, 231
Gillespie, W. H., 91, 95, 125
Gitelson, Max, 560, 582
Glauber, I. Peter, 155
Glover, Edward, 22, 114, 433, 441, 447, 501–507, 511, 515, 534–544
Glover, James, 266, 502–503, 506, 537
Glueck, Bernard, Sr., 591
Goebbels, Joseph, 420
Goethe, Johann Wolfgang von, 42, 109, 162, 164, 167, 189, 251, 261, 316–317, 341
Golan, S., 202
Goldenweiser, Alexander, 275

Goldman, G., 559
Goldwyn, Samuel, 11
Gombrich, E. H., 484, 486, 488–490, 498–499
Göring, Hermann, 75
Göring, M. H., 75
Gorky, Maxim, 298
Gosselin, R., 184–185
Graves, R., 128
Greenacre, Phyllis, 579, 586, 588
Greenson, Ralph R., 439–449
Grillparzer, Franz, 152
Grinker, Roy R., 301, 563–564, 577, 582, 585
Grinstein, A., 282, 309
Groddeck, Emmy, 309, 311
Groddeck, Georg, 301, 308–319
Groddeck, Karl, 308
Groddeck, Lina, 308–309
Gross, Otto, 101
Grotjahn, Martin, 1–12, 43, 235–239, 262, 308–319, 341 n., 347 n., 372, 384–398, 456 n., 582, 591
Guilbert, Yvette, 147
Gumbel, E., 52, 60
Gustin, 252

Haeckel, Ernst Heinrich, 230
Haenel, Joachim, 383
Hall, G. Stanley, 549
Hampshire, S., 103
Hamsun, Knut, 163
Hannibal, 420
Hansen, Howard, 357
Harms, Ernest, 75
Hart, Bernard, 535–536, 540
Hartmann, Heinz, 459–460, 467, 469–482, 493, 520, 579
Hartmann, Moritz, 469
Harwick, 504
Haviland, Floyd, 554
Head, Henry, 458
Healy, William, 591
Heath, Robert G., 564, 572, 584–585, 587
Heidegger, Martin, 395
Heine, Heinrich, 261
Heisenberg, Werner, 394
Helgesson, Uno, 564
Helmholtz, Hermann, 427
Hendrick, Ives, 548, 556
Henry, G. M., 555
Herskovits, Melville J., 275–276
Hill, J. R., 555
Hiller, Eric, 536, 560
Hirschfeld, Magnus, 339
Hitler, Adolf, 52, 58, 130, 181, 286, 318, 423, 436, 556
Hitschmann, Edward, 160–168, 230, 286, 301, 430
Hitschmann, Hedwig, 160
Hitschmann, Margaret, 160
Hoch, August, 551
Hoelderlin, Friedrich, 337
Hoffer, Willi, 157, 418, 491–492, 494
Hoffmann, E. T., 42
Hollós, Stefan, 31
Hopkins, Prynce, 537–538
Horace (Quintus Horatius Flaccus), 12
Horkheimer, Max, 340
Horney, Karen, 3, 86, 131, 286, 311, 314, 403–404, 443, 450–455, 504, 557, 566, 571, 573
Horney, Oscar, 451
Howard, Diana, 383
Hoyt, Mrs. Sherman, 584
Huber, Hans, 341
Hug-Hellmuth, Helma von, 285, 301
Hunt, Ramsay, 555
Hurwitz, Rosetta, 419
Husserl, Edmund, 459, 462

Ibsen, Henrik, 37, 298
Idelson, D., 58
Ignotus, Hugo, 31
Illing, Hans, 235–239
Isaacs, Susan, 262, 537

Jackson, Donald, 591
Jackson, Edith, 591
Jacob, Hans, 230
Jacobson, Edith, 579, 588
Jacques, Eliot, 372
Jaffe, Ruth, 200–208
James, William, 163, 165
Janet, Pierre, 64, 79, 93, 119
Jaspers, Karl, 472
Jauregg, Julius Wagner von, *see* Wagner-Jauregg, Julius von
Jekels, Ludwig, 127, 557
Jelliffe, Bee Dobson, 224
Jelliffe, Helena, 224
Jelliffe, Smith Ely, 147, 213, 224–233, 549

Jelliffe, William, 224
Jesus Christ, 144, 175, 380
Jewett, Stephen, 571
Jodl, Friedrich, 250
Johnson, A. M., 356
Johnson, Samuel, 163, 165–166
Jolly, Julius, 200
Jolyffe, Thomas, 224
Jones, Ernest, 2–6, 10, 12, 19, 22, 25–26, 29, 32–33, 41–43, 46, 51–54, 57, 59, 69, 87–141, 180, 185, 187, 213–214, 230, 269, 312, 361, 375, 392, 402–403, 412–413, 442, 454, 486–487, 505–506, 511–512, 535–539, 543, 548–551, 557, 560–561, 574
Jones, Mervyn, 89, 91, 94–95
Jones, Thomas, 98
Juliusburger, Otto, 200
Jung, Carl Gustav, 2, 10, 63–77, 91–92, 212, 225, 230–231, 343, 465, 548, 573

Kahane, Heinrich, 78
Kahn, Lee, 412
Kamm, Bernhard, 562
Kant, Immanuel, 63
Kardiner, Abram, 431, 553, 556, 559, 564, 569
Karpf, F. B., 46
Kauf, Emil, 302
Kaufman, M. Ralph, 301, 556, 566, 577, 579
Keller, Gottfried, 163
Kelman, Harold, 451, 456 n.
Kelman, Norman, 450
Kennedy, Foster, 233, 550
Kenworthy, Marion, 579, 588, 591
Kestenberg, Judith, 139 n.
Kipling, Rudyard, 186, 188
Kirby, George H., 554
Klein, Arthur, 360–361
Klein, Emanuel, 27 n.
Klein, Eric, 360, 362, 372
Klein, Hans, 360
Klein, Henrietta, 588
Klein, Melanie, 3, 6, 94, 99, 108, 124–125, 141, 319, 360–372, 403–404, 504, 506, 512, 538–539, 543
Klein, Melitta, *see* Schmideberg, Melitta
Kleist, Heinrich von, 109, 141
Klemperer, Paul, 157
Kluckhohn, Clyde, 568
Kluckhohn, Florence, 568
Knight, Robert P., 566, 581, 583
Kohn, Erwin, 418
Kovács, Vilma, 31, 274
Kraepelin, Emil, 64–66, 212, 230, 284
Krafft-Ebing, Richard von, 64, 78
Kramer, August, 230
Kris, Anton, 489 n.
Kris, Ernst, 411, 467, 470, 473, 477, 480–481, 484–499, 564, 579
Kris, Leopold, 485
Kris, Marianne, 486, 492, 588
Kris, Rosa, 485
Kroeber, Alfred L., 275
Kubie, Lawrence S., 579, 583
Kurth, Paul, 485

La Barre, Weston, 272–281
La Fontaine, Jean de, 411
Lagerlöf, Selma, 163
Lampl de Groot, Jeanne, 293
Landauer, Karl, 337, 340
Lantos, Barbara, 508–518
Lawrence, Margaret, 589
Leavy, Stanley A., 238–239
Lemming, Helena Dewey, 224
Levine, Maurice, 581, 585
Levy, David, 559, 564, 572, 589, 591
Lewandowsky, Felix, 230
Lewin, Bertram, 55, 166, 386, 556, 576, 578–579
Lewis, Nolan D. C., 224–233, 559
Lewy, Ernst, 562
Liebermann, Hans, 3
Liepmann, Hugo, 230
Lindon, John Arnold, 360–372
Loe, 98
Loewenstein, R. M., 187, 412, 414, 467, 469–482, 485, 491, 493, 504, 579
Loewy, Emanuel, 486
Long, Constance, 536
Lorand, Sandor, 13–34, 553, 580
Low, Barbara, 536
Lowie, Robert H., 275
Lowrey, Lawson, 591

McLean, Helen, 582, 585, 588–589
Maeder, Leroy 231, 566
Magnes, J. L., 60
Mahler, Gustav, 251, 263
Mahler, Margaret, 579, 589
Malinowski, Bronislaw, 275, 410

Mann, Thomas, 293
Marburg, Otto, 230
Margolin, Sydney, 160
Marie, Pierre, 212
Marmor, Judd, 571
Masserman, Jules H., 564, 577, 582, 585
May, Karl, 352
May, Rollo, 572
Mead, Margaret, 275–277, 568
Mendel, K., 200
Meng, Heinrich, 149, 172, 175, 177, 333-341
Menninger, Karl, 579, 581
Menninger, William, 563, 577
Merzbacher, Ludwig, 230
Meyer, Adolf, 211, 232, 460, 551–552
Meyer, Monroe, 431, 553
Michelangelo Buonarotti, 263, 313
Miller, Milton, 583, 585
Millet, John A. P., 546–595
Mingazzini, Giovanni, 230
Mirsky, Arthur, 581
Mitchell, T. W., 536
Mittelmann, Bela, 557, 559, 564, 585
Möbius, Paul Julius, 161
Moellenhoff, Fritz, 180–199
Mohr, George J., 348–358, 359 n., 565, 582, 585
Molnar, Ferenc, 251
Monakoff, Constantin von, 230
Monchaux, C. de, 522
Monroe, Russell, 572
Moore, Ann, 182, 184
Moore, Merrill, 182, 184
Moreno, Jacob, 319
Moroni, Giambattista, 60
Morphy, Paul Charles, 110–111, 132–133, 140–141
Moses, 127–128, 162, 174, 193, 262
Mozart, Walfgang Amadeus, 44
Munroe, Ruth, 86 n.
Murray, Jesse, 266
Murray, Col. John M., 447, 556, 563, 577, 579

Napoleon Bonaparte, 37, 401
Natterson, Joseph M., 249–263, 450–455
Nemon, Olen, 222
Neumann, Liesl, 423
Nicol, Maurice, 536
Nicotra, Grace, 596
Nietzsche, Friedrich, 37–38, 84, 263
Nissl, Franz, 336
Nonne, Max, 230
Nothnagel, Herman, 144–145
Nunberg, Hermann, 40, 54–56, 287, 430, 441, 557
Nunn, Percy, 536

Oberholzer, Emil, 170, 559
Oberndorf, Clarence P., 26–28, 146, 431, 548, 550–553, 568
Oedipus, 8, 41, 263, 401
Olden, Rudolf, 425
Onuf, B., 551
Oppenheimer, Heinrich, 230
Orwell, George, 420
Owen, Rose K., 219

Pabst, G. W., 190
Palissy, Bernard, 490
Paret, Suzanne Cassirer, 426–427
Pavenstedt, Eleanor, 591
Pavlov, Ivan, 392
Payne, Sylvia, 537
Pearson, Gerald, 585
Pearson, Karl, 127
Peck, John S., 373–383
Pestalozzi, Johann Heinrich, 422
Peterson, Frederick, 548–549
Pfister, Erica Wunderli, 175
Pfister, Oskar, 169–179, 230, 312, 343–344
Piaget, Jean, 171
Planck, Max, 394
Planiscig, Leo, 487, 489
Poe, Edgar Allan, 331, 406–410
Polon, Albert, 553
Pomer, Sidney L., 51–62
Pötzl, Otto, 151, 230, 339
Prometheus, 8
Provence, Sally, 497
Pumpian-Mindlin, Eugene, 519–530
Putnam, James J., 103, 213, 548, 551–552, 591
Putnam, Marian, 591

Rabelais, François, 312
Rado, Sandor, 31, 191, 240–248, 287, 441, 556–557, 559, 572, 581–582, 590
Rank, Beata, 42, 48
Rank, Otto, 2, 8, 10–11, 20, 36–49, 69,

92, 146, 161, 180, 186–187, 191, 193, 230–231, 252, 311, 454, 554
Rapaport, David, 457, 467, 473, 530, 583
Read, Grantly Dick, 319
Read, Stanford, 536
Reich, Wilhelm, 257, 287, 423, 430–438, 441, 474, 573
Reichenbach, Hans, 424
Reichsman, F., 590
Reik, Arthur, 250, 258, 261
Reik, Caroline, 249
Reik, Ella, 250, 253–254, 258
Reik, Marija, 250
Reik, Max, 249
Reik, Miriam, 261
Reik, Theodor, 3, 8, 167, 191, 249–263, 274, 573
Reik, Theodora, 250, 261
Reitler, Rudolf, 78, 145
Ribble, Margaret, 591
Richardson, Henry B., 590
Rickman, John, 537
Rie, Marianne (Mrs. Ernst Kris), 486
Rie, Oskar, 486
Riggall, R. M., 536
Riggs, Austen Fox, 555
Riklin, Franz, 69, 274
Ritvo, Lucille B., 484–499
Ritvo, Samuel, 484–499
Rivers, W. H. R., 536
Riviere, Joan, 412, 536
Roback, A. A., 198
Robbins, Bernard, 571
Róheim, Géza, 114, 272–281, 319, 410, 568
Róheim, Ilonka, 280
Rokitansky, Karl von, 143
Rome, Howard, 577
Romm, May E., 210–222, 375, 583, 588
Rorschach, Hermann, 170, 344
Roscher, Wilhelm, 279
Rosen, John, 319
Rosenfeld, Otto, *see* Rank, Otto
Ross, Helen, 55, 576, 579
Rüdin, Ernst, 230
Ruesch, Jurgens, 580

Sachs, Bernard, 218
Sachs, Hanns, 2–3, 41–42, 44–45, 49, 146, 180–199, 236, 252, 266, 287, 338, 375, 386, 418, 426, 451, 504, 512, 538, 558
Sachs, Max, 182
Sachs, Olga, 182
Sadger, J., 162, 441
Salmon, Thomas W., 554–555
Salomon, Anne, 417
Salzman, Leon, 580
Sandler, J., 522–523
Sapir, Edward, 275
Sarasin, Philipp, 170
Sarto, Andrea del, 109, 140
Saul, Leon, 581, 585
Schalith, 201
Schilder, Bertha Fuerth, 458
Schilder, Paul, 231, 339, 430, 457–468, 555
Schiller, Johann Christoph von, 194
Schlesinger, Therese Eckstein, 149
Schlick, Moritz, 424
Schlosser, Julius von, 486
Schmideberg, Melitta, 360–361, 372
Schmidt, Vera, 201
Schneider, Ernst, 171, 340, 343
Schnitzler, Arthur, 251, 253, 263
Schopenhauer, Arthur, 37–38, 63, 163
Schreber, Daniel Paul, 6, 69, 71, 76, 155, 161, 236
Schubert, Franz, 163, 166
Schur, Max, 157, 412
Schuster, Paul, 230, 339
Schwabe, Benno, 341
Schweitzer, Albert, 165
Schweninger, Ernst, 308, 310, 314
Schwing, Gertrud, 154
Sechehaye, M. A., 319
Segal, H. L., 590
Segantini, Giovanni, 8
Selesnick, Sheldon T., 63–86
Senn, Milton J. E., 492, 494, 496
Shakespeare, William, 78, 107, 121, 140, 182, 195–196, 251, 261, 265, 268, 313, 385, 493
Sharpe, Ella Freeman, 118, 265–270, 504, 537
Shaw, George Bernard, 527
Siegfried, 316
Silberer, Hans, 230
Silverberg, William, 571, 580
Simmel, Ernst, 3, 6, 53–55, 201, 311–312, 373–383, 427, 445, 504, 562, 579, 583
Simon, Ellen, 61
Smith, Lauren, 585

Sokolnicka, Mme., 400
Sophocles, 314
Southard, Elmer, 591
Spanjaard, Jacob, 321–332
Specht, Gustav, 230
Speier, Hans, 490–491
Spiegel, John, 591
Spielmeyer, Walther, 230
Spinoza, Baruch, 263
Spitz, René, 6, 278, 291, 319, 579, 589
Spitzer, Ernestine, 143
Stärcke, August, 321–332
Stärcke, Johan, 322
Staub, Hugo, 386
Steinach, Eugen, 339
Steiner, G., 146
Stein-Monod, Claude, 399–414
Stekel, Wilhelm, 78, 81, 92, 145, 162, 230, 339
Stendhal (Henri Beyle), 183
Sterba, Editha, 562
Sterba, Richard, 441, 562, 583
Stern, Adolf, 27, 551
Stevenson, George S., 564
Stevenson, Robert Louis, 42
Stoddart, W. H. B., 536, 540
Strachey, Alix, 537
Strachey, James, 537
Strumpell, Ernst, 230
Sullivan, Harry Stack, 27, 86, 564, 571, 580
Swedenborg, Emanuel, 163
Szurek, S., 356

Taft, Jessie, 38, 47–49, 554
Tandler, Hans, 230
Tarachow, S., 22
Tausk, Victor, 40, 146, 235–239
Taylor, Willis, 551
Thompson, Clara M., 571–572, 580, 588
Tidd, Charles, 375
Tolstoy, Leo, 298
Tower, Eleanor, 588
Tower, Sarah, 588
Trotter, Wilfrid, 93, 127

Urfer, Martha, 344

Vaihinger, Hans, 84
Veszy-Wagner, Lilla, 43, 87–141
Victoria, Queen, 546
Vogt, Oskar, 339
Vinci, Leonardo da, 162
Vogel, Paul, 230

Waelder, Robert, 428, 491, 512, 564
Wagner-Jauregg, Julius von, 151, 231, 339, 430, 459
Wagner-Jauregg Clinic, 284
Wahl, Charles William, 265–270, 501–508
Wallace, Alfred R., 275
Waterman, George, 551
Watson, J. B., 25
Weber, Max, 471
Wedekind, Frank, 37
Weigert, Edith, 580, 588
Weil, Milton, 488
Weininger, Otto, 37, 323
Weinstock, 589
Weiss, Edoardo, 142–159, 393
Weiss, Frederick, 451
Werfel, Franz, 162, 165
Wernicke, Carl, 458
Wertheim-Salomonson, Johannes, 322
Weygandt, Wilhelm, 230
White, William A., 225–226, 231, 551
Wilde, Oscar, 42
Williams, Frankwood, 25
Wilson, S. A. K., 230
Wimmer, August, 230
Windholz, Emanuel, 562, 583
Winkler, Cornelis, 322
Winnicott, D. W., 90–91, 101
Wittels, Fritz, 553
Wolff, Anna, 489 n.
Woolf, Moshe, 200–208
Wright, Maurice, 537
Wunderli, Erica, 175

Ziehnen, Theodor, 200, 230
Ziferstein, Isidore, 457–468
Zilboorg, Gregory, 293, 555–556
Zulliger, Hans, 169–179, 340, 342–347
Zulliger, Martha, 344
Zuppinger-Urner, Martha, 176
Zweig, Stefan, 487 n.

Subject Index

abreaction, 376
Academy of Medicine, New York, 584
Academy of Psychoanalysis, Chicago, 453, 571, 575–576, 580
acting out, 22, 256, 378
"active imagination" method, 74
activity therapy, 19-22
actuality, 528–529
adaptation, 476–478
adaptational therapy, 240–248
Affectivity, Suggestibility, and Paranoia (Hitschmann), 161
aggression, 79–80, 85–86, 254, 353–354, 366, 393, 434, 466, 480, 520
agoraphobia, 290
A la Mémoire des Disparus (Bonaparte), 406
Albert and Mary Lasker Foundation, 581
Alcoholics Anonymous, 380
alcoholism, 245, 336, 375, 380
alienation, 394
alienist, 101
American culture, woman in, 262
American Educational Committee, 30, 55 n.
American Institute for Psychoanalysis, 450, 571
American Men of Science 1949 (Cattell), 487 n.
American Neurological Association, 548
American Orthopsychiatric Association, 490
American Psychiatric Association, 222, 565
American Psychoanalytic Association, 26–29, 59, 217, 244, 288, 450, 455, 489–490, 498, 551, 553, 556–560, 564–568, 570–594
American Therapeutic Congress, 88, 550
amnesia, 329
Anake, 123
anal character, 433
anal drives, 165
anal eroticism, 17, 117, 138
analysis, "fractured," 256; trial, 191; *see also* psychoanalysis
Analysis of the Total Personality (Alexander), 386
analyst, lay, 28–29, 41, 170, 227, 337, 453; love from, 23; teaching and training of, 25, 51–62, 388; transference of libido to, 213, 246
anamnesis, associative, 301, 304, 306
anguish, development and, 323
anorexia nervosa, 205
anthropology, cultural, 556; psychoanalysis and, 272–281
anti-Semitism, 11, 75, 127, 130–131, 253, 283, 299, 318, 380–381, 421
Anti-Semitism, A Social Disease (Simmel), 380
antisocial behavior, 348
anxiety, in child, 364; creative, 314; greed and, 369; knowledge and, 333; libido and, 326; primal, 47; separation, 47, 206, 371; superego and, 474
anxiety hysteria, 290
anxiety theory, reformulation of, 474

anus, symbol for, 113; versus vagina, 139
aphanisis, 137, 139
Applied Psychoanalysis (F. Deutsch), 304
archaeology, 427
archetypes, 74
Army psychiatry, 563, 577
art, creativity and, 494; psychoanalysis and, 109; socializing aspects of, 194
arthritis, 393
artist, ideology and, 49; psychic conflict, in, 39; unconscious and, 317
Artist, The (Rank), 38–39
Artzlich Volksbuch, Das (Federn), 149
"as if" personality, 291
Association for Psychoanalytic Medicine, 559
Association for the Advancement of Psychoanalysis, 559, 571
associative anamnesis, 301, 304, 306
autoerotism, 10
autosuggestion, 136

Bad Homburg Congress, 56
Baltimore Psychoanalytic Society, 560 580
Basel, University of, 63, 73
Basic Principles of Psychoanalysis (Brill), 219
Basic Writings of Sigmund Freud (Brill), 213
bedwetting, 203
Behn-Rorschach Test, 344, 346
Bellevue Hospital, New York, 460
Berlin, University of, 451
Berlin Neuropsychiatric Society, 200
Berlin Psychoanalytic Institute and Society, 2, 9, 52 n., 54–55, 60, 243, 286, 314, 373–374, 385, 510, 515, 537
Berne, University of, 345
Beyond the Pleasure Principle (Freud), 72, 330
Bezalel Art Institute, 59
Bible, 174, 251, 402
Biel Institute for Mental Hygiene, 345
bioanalysis, 18
biography, analytic, 162
biology, 18–19, 211
"biones," 436–437
birth trauma, 45, 47, 296, 419
bisexuality, 81, 403–405
Black Mountain College, 182
body ego, 195
body image, 464–465
body organs, erogeneith of, 21
Book of the It, The (Groddeck), 312
Boston Psychoanalytic Institute, 165, 181, 195, 288, 301, 306, 554
Boston University Medical School, 306
Brain and Personality (Schilder), 460
brain injury, 65
British Journal of Criminology, 505
British Medical Association, 94, 538
British Psycho-Analytical Society, 32, 88, 266–267, 504, 507, 511, 536–537
Brooklyn Polytechnic Institute, 224
Bücher des Werdenden (Meng), 341
Budapest, University of, 24, 241, 273, 385
Budapest Medical Association, 15–16
Budapest Psychoanalytic Congress, 19, 54, 273, 361

Cambridge University, 89
cancer, fear of, 125
castration, of father, 40; symbolism of, 108
castration complex or fear, 81, 113, 115, 131, 137, 164, 170, 203, 206, 314, 321–332, 400–404, 474; in girls or women, 164, 245, 404, 452
cathexis, 152–153
Center for Advanced Study in Behavioral Science, 394
Central Islip State Hospital, 211
Cerebellar Functions (André-Thomas), 231
character analysis, 430–437
Character Analysis (Reich), 432
character armor, 433
Character Formation and the Phobias of Childhood (Reich), 435
character resistance, 434
character types, 433
chess, psychology of, 133, 210
Chicago, University of, 387, 557
Chicago Academy of Psychoanalysis, 453, 571, 575–576, 580
Chicago Institute for Psychoanalysis, 387, 393–394, 453, 554, 582–583

child, acting out in, 378; psychoanalysis of, 178, 343, 363–365
child behavior, 363–372
child development, 522, 590
childbirth, natural, 313, 319
Childhood and Society (Erikson), 524, 526
childhood disappointments, 291
child-parent relationships, 246–247; *see also* father; mother
child psychology, 363–365, 461, 496
children's books, 513
Christian ethos, 169
Christianity and Fear (Pfister), 176
circumcision, 254, 279
Civilisation and Its Discontents (Freud), 131
clairvoyance, 126
Clark University, 16
Cleveland Psychoanalytic Institute, 583
Clinical Interview, The (F. Deutsch & Murphy), 305
clinical psychologist, role of, 569
clitoris, 161, 400, 404
coitus, 17–18, 296, 405, 452
colitis, 393
collective unconscious, 74–75
Colorado, University of, 160
Columbia University College of Physicians and Surgeons, 211, 218, 224, 559
Columbia University Psychoanalytic Institute, 243, 572, 581–582
Communist party, 202
complex, 65, 75; inferiority, 78–86
compulsion, 6, 298
conscience, 328
constipation, psychic, 207
constitutional factors, 6
coprophilia, 141
Cornell Medical School, 590
countertransference, 86, 338, 388–389
counterwish, 148
Creation of Woman, The (Reik), 259
Creative Unconscious, The (Sachs), 194
creativity, 162–164, 195, 494
Criminal, The Judge and the Public, The (Alexander), 386
Cro-Magnon man, 323
cultural anthropology, 556
culture, personality and, 276–278
Curiosities of the Self (Reik), 262 n.
current conflict, 246

daydreaming, 96, 162, 194
death, love and, 315, 317
death penalty, 412
death wish or instinct, 125, 153, 195, 317, 330, 381, 435, 465, 513
defense mechanisms, 475, 519-522
delerium tremens, 238
delinquency and delinquents, 348–358; latent, 349; prevention of, 508–518; scientific treatment of, 515
delivery, masochistic pleasure in, 296
delusions, 154, 324, 332
dementia praecox, 64, 70, 73, 76, 373; *see also* paranoia; schizophrenia
denial, 215, 292
depersonalization, 152–155, 238, 459
depression, 6, 165, 244, 289
derealization, 154
Detroit Psychoanalytic Society, 583
deuterophallic phase, 140
development, law of, 323
Development of Psychoanalysis (Ferenczi & Rank), 20, 43
Devil, God and, 165
Diaries of Youth (Bernfeld), 422
diphtheria, 173
dogmatism, 389
Don Giovanni (Mozart & Da Ponte), 44
Doppelgänger, Der (Rank), 42
double path, principle of, 459
dream and dreamwork, 74, 105, 146, 148, 155, 192, 315
Dream Analysis (Sharpe), 269
Dreams and Myths (Abraham), 8
drive energy, neutralization of, 480
drives, Adler's theory of, 79–80
drug addiction, 6, 245
Dutch Psychoanalytic Society, 321–322

eating, as sexual perversion, 204
education, boundaries of, 415–429; psychoanalysis and, 169, 342–347
ego, autonomous development of, 474; dreaming, 155; epigenetic development of, 524; Jones' definition of, 136; manic, 205; military, 376; narcisstic, 154 (*see also* narcissism); and organic defect, 304; psychoanalytic theory of, 527; psychotic, 155–156,

ego *(cont'd)*
380; reality and, 473; real versus ideal, 136; schizophrenic, 154; structural hypothesis of, 324 (*see also* ego structure)
ego-alien affects, 219
ego analysis, 244
Ego and the Id, The (Freud), 43, 46, 311, 552
Ego and the Mechanisms of Defence, The (A. Freud), 80, 519–520, 524
ego boundaries, 155
ego cathexis, 152, 155
ego defense, 292, 474, 589
"ego diseases," 155
ego dynamics, 292
ego feeling, 152, 207
ego function, 23, 152–153, 433, 473–478
ego ideal, 21, 355
ego identity, 385, 397
ego instincts, 79, 260, 325–326
ego psychology, 17, 21, 153, 157–158, 323, 467–482, 494–496, 516, 589
Ego Psychology and Psychoses (Federn), 158–159
ego regression, 17
ego resistance, 434
ego states, 153
ego strength, 589
ego structure, 303, 366, 433, 478
Eighth International Association Congress, 431
Ein Weg zur Seele des Geistekranken (Schering), 154
ejaculatio praecox, 7, 16, 238
ellipsis, 328
Emotions and Bodily Changes (Dunbar), 584
empathy, 265–270, 356
encephalitis periaxialis diffusa, 457
England, psychoanalysis in, 534–545; *see also* British Psycho-Analytical Society
environment, response to, 73
envy, love and, 167
Envy and Gratitude (Klein), 362
epigenetic development, 524–527
"epileptic" stage, 326
Eros, 330
Essays in Applied Psycho-Analysis (Jones), 106
estrangement, 152, 155, 238
euphoria, 204
exhibitionism, 118
existential despair, 394
extrasensory perception, 147
extroversion, 73

Facts and Theories of Psychoanalysis (Hendrick), 548
faith, 169–178
famous persons, psychoanalytic studies of, 162
fanaticism, guilt and, 166
fantasy, cannibalistic, 512; "end of world," 70; euphoria and, 205; fellatio, 108; infantile, 7, 369; sexual, 409; unconscious, 367
fatalism, 74
father and father figure, 68, 119, 404; castration of, 40, 134, 295; as ego ideal, 296; God as, 116; homosexuality and, 206; killing and eating of, 105 n.; memory and, 165; as sexual object, 297
father–daughter relationships, 295–297
father-penis identification, 139
father–son relationships, 111, 254
Faust (Goethe), 316
fear, 129, 137
feces, and castration complex, 324; scybalum and, 324, 331
feeling stimulus, 303
fellatio fantasy, 108
female sexuality, 138–139, 164, 399–414
Female Sexuality (Bonaparte), 403–405
femininity, as "weakness," 81
fetishism, 7, 203
fictional goal, 86
Fifth International Psycho-Analytic Congess, 25
First International Congress on Mental Hygiene, 554
First International Psychoanalytical Congress, 68
Flower-Fifth Avenue Medical School, 559, 571
fore-displeasure, 258
Fragment of a Great Confession (Reik), 259, 261
Frankfurt, University of, 340
free association, 23, 102, 260, 363

Free Associations (Jones), 96, 116, 535
Freud, Master and Friend (Sachs), 184
Freud Prize, 410
Freud Society, 68
Freud's Contribution to Psychiatry (Brill), 214
Freud's Theories of the Neuroses (Hitschmann), 162
frigidity, 400
Frigidity in Women (Hitschmann), 164
From the Unconscious Mental Life of Our Youth (Zulliger), 172, 344, 346
From Thirty Years with Freud (Reik), 259–260
frustration, 365
function, three levels of, 232
Fundamental Concepts of Psycho-Analysis (Brill), 214
Further Contributions to the Theory and Technique of Psychoanalysis (Ferenczi), 21–22

Gedanken zur Naturphilosophie (Schilder), 457
Geisterseher, Der (Schiller), 194
general paresis, 459
General Paresis (Kraepelin), 231
genetic research, 586–587
genital ego character, 433
genius, nature of, 110–111
German War Propaganda (Kris), 496
Geschlecht und Charakter (Weininger), 323
Gestalt psychology, 464–465
Gifted Adolescent Project, 492, 495, 498
glial proliferation, 65
Goals and Desires in Man (Schilder), 462
God, 116, 119; as collective superego, 381; Devil and, 165
Goethe Prize, 317
grandfather figure, 118
Great Depression, 57
Great Men (Hitschmann), 167
Great Mother cult, 8
Group for the Advancement of Psychoanalysis, 563, 573, 588
group psychology, 131, 467
group psychotherapy, 467
Grundlagen der Psychoanalyse, Der (Hartmann), 481
guilt, 137–138, 254, 292, 371, 376–377, 406; infantile, 101, 370; masochism and, 297; regression and, 165

hallucinations, 154, 163, 205, 216, 237
Hamlet and Oedipus (Jones), 106–109, 140
Hampstead Child Therapy Clinic, 508, 517, 520–523, 542
happiness, 291
Harvard Medical School, 181, 489 n., 555
Hashomer Hatzair, 202
hate, 138, 330, 367–368
Haunting Melody, The (Reik), 259–261
health, illness and, 303
Hebrew University, 59–60
Henry Phipps Psychiatric Clinic, 460
herd instinct, 127
hermaphrodite, psychological, 81
"hexing," 216
Hippocratic oath, 218
Hippokrates (pub.), 339
historical figures, studies of, 196–197
History of Medical Psychology (Zilboorg & Henry), 555
History of Psychoanalysis in America (Oberndorf), 26, 147, 548
History of the Psychoanalytic Movement, The (Jung), 67, 73
hole anxiety, 401–402, 409
homeostasis, 79
homosexuality, 6, 16, 81, 107–109, 129, 141, 205–206, 254, 260; determinants of, 206; female, 8, 293; hallucinations of, 163; hate and, 140; New York law on, 221; paranoia and, 16–17
Hungarian Ethnological Society, 273
Hungarian Psychoanalytic Society, 241, 243, 357
hyperinsulism, 393
hypnosis, 26, 212, 376, 462
hypochondria, 32, 238
hysteria, 21, 65, 101, 205, 212, 289

id, ego and, 477, 522; origin of term, 309
ideal ego, 136
idealism, 419
idealized image, 86
ideal (nonneurotic) man, 37
identification, 215
identity, meaning of, 527–528

Illinois, University of, 388
illness, psychosis as, 325; trauma and, 309
illusions, in hysterical attack, 205
Image and Appearance of the Human Body, The (Schilder), 458
Imago (pub.), 41, 161, 180, 190, 243, 254, 485, 488–489, 491
incest, 41, 161, 254, 296
Incest Motif in Poetry and Saga, The (Rank), 41
Index of Psychoanalytical Writings (Grinstein), 282
infancy, striving toward, 317; unconscious and, 365–372
infant, anxiety in, 290; ego identity and, 397; guilt in, 101; sexuality in, 67, 170
Infants without Families (A. Freud & Burlingham), 521
inferiority, will to power and, 84
inferiority complex, 78–86, 130
"influencing machine," Tausk's, 236–238
inhibition, 148
Innsbruck Congress, 56–57
insight, in children, 363; cognitive, 389; unconscious, 215
instincts, 152, 301, 477
Institute for Scientific Treatment of Delinquency, 515
Institute of Psycho-Analysis, *see* Berlin Psychoanalytic Institute and Society
insurance medicine, 300
International Board of Mental Hygiene, 149
International Congress of Psychiatry and Neurology, 225
International Congress of Psychic Hygiene, 288
Internationale Zeitschrift für Psychoanalyse, 41, 149, 229, 240, 243, 470
International Journal of Psycho-Analysis, 19, 24, 27, 92, 257, 522, 561
International Psychoanalytic Association, 11, 52 n., 57, 59, 73, 91–93, 170, 187, 241, 243, 411, 470, 551–553, 556, 560–561
International Training Commission, 55, 59 n., 241, 287, 556
Interpretation of Dreams, The (Freud), 42, 46, 64–65, 112, 122, 145, 184, 250, 284–285, 310, 408, 546, 549, 578
intrapsychic phenomena, 86
Introduction to Psychoanalysis (Freud), 400
introjection, 366–367
introversion, 73, 75
intuition, 242, 260
Israel, psychoanalysis in, 200–208
"It," concept of, 309, 312–315, 317, 319

Jewish humor, 262
Jewish Wit (Reik), 259, 262
Jews, in Germany and Austria, 92, 130, 181, 252, 412; Jung's views on, 75–76; projection and paranoia in, 380–381; religion and culture of, 255; role of in psychoanalysis, 67; self-justification of, 130
Journal for Psychoanalytic Education, 340
Journal of Abnormal Psychology, 549
Journal of Nervous and Mental Disease, 225, 231
Judge Baker Foundation, 591
juvenile delinquency, *see* delinquency

kibbutz movement, 202
Kinderheim Baumgarten (Bernfeld), 417–418
kingship, idea of, 128–129
Korsakoff's syndrome, 459

Lasker Foundation, 581
latent delinquency, 349
lay analysis, 28–29, 41, 170, 227, 337, 453
Lectures on Psychoanalytic Psychiatry (Brill), 215
libido, 67, 74–75, 82, 326, 434–436, 441, 480; as death instinct, 330; displacement of, 146; fear and, 137; hypochondria and, 238; rejection of theory concerning, 260; transference of, 213
lies and dissimulation, 327
Life and Work of Sigmund Freud, The (Jones), 117–127
Life Cycle and Ethics (Erikson), 524
life style, 84
Listening with the Third Ear (Reik), 257, 259–261
literature, psychoanalysis of, 161, 183, 192
London Clinic of Psycho-Analysis, 537

London Institute of Psychoanalysis, 489
London Psychoanalytic Society, 2, 535–536
London School of Clinical Medicine, 101
loneliness, 394
Loosened Chains (Zulliger), 346
Los Angeles Psychoanalytic Society, 560, 583
love, from analyst, 23; being in, 292; death and, 317; "despairing cry for," 244; gratitude and, 370; hate and, 330, 367–368; morality and, 137; primal, 47; Reik's view of, 260; in sex act, 314
love object, 166, 324, 371, 379
lying, 290

magical thinking, 17
Magic and Schizophrenia (Róheim), 278 n.
maladaptation concept, 245–247
Maladies of Civilisation (Jones & Trotter), 127
Manhattan State Hospital, 551
manic-depressive psychosis, 6, 32, 205, 215, 325, 368–369
manipulation, 391
martyr, as masochist, 258
masculine protest, 81-82
masculinity, masochism and, 297
Masks of Love and Life (Sachs), 183
masochism, 11, 146, 166; guilt and, 297; narcissism and, 298; in women, 294, 405, 454
Masochism in Modern Man (Reik), 251, 257–258, 260–261
mass psychology, 421
mastery, masochism and, 258
masturbation, 146, 202, 290, 313–314, 405; castration anxiety and, 206; clitoral, 161; homosexuality and, 206
mater dolorosa attitude, 297
Measure for Measure (Shakespeare), 196
Medizinische Psychologie (Schilder), 457
melancholia, 6, 290
memory, 464, 497
Menninger Clinic, 582
Mensch als Symbol, Der (Groddeck), 317
menstruation, fear of, 207
Mental Health Congress, London, 518
mental hygiene, 331–341
metaphor, 112
metaphrenia, 325
military neuroses, 6, 284, 373–377
Minutes of the Vienna Psychoanalytic Society, v
miracles, belief in, 174
mistrust, 291
monarchy, 128–129
monogamy, 453
morality, love and, 137
Moscow, University of, 201
mother, body contact with, 24; fixation on, 404; incest with, 161; love–hate relationship with, 366–368
mother–child relationships, 296–298, 313, 365
motherhood, fear of, 404
mother love, 313–314
mother's nipple, castration complex and, 324
mother substitute, 293
motility, 463–464
motion pictures, psychology of, 190
Mount Sinai Hospital, 29, 395
murder, war and, 133
My Dream (Hitschmann), 166
Mystery on the Mountain (Reik), 259
mysticism, 112
myth, 8, 40, 74, 193, 219
Myth and Guilt (Reik), 259
Myth of the Birth of the Hero, The (Rank), 40, 49

nakedness, erotic, 41
narcissism, 6, 10, 17, 71, 117–118, 152, 155, 162, 164, 192, 203, 207, 289, 325, 328, 355, 419; healthy versus diseased, 154; infantile, 203; masochism and, 298; naïve, 195; primary, 136, 465
narcotic elation or superpleasure, 245
Narrative of a Child Analysis (Klein), 362
National Psychological Association for Psychoanalysis, 261
natural childbirth, 313, 319
Nazis and Nazism, 133, 149, 164, 257, 292, 341, 357, 374, 412–413, 435–436, 557
necrophilia, 141, 409

need, development and, 323
Nefesh Hayeled, 201
nervous system, 232
Neues Wiener Tagblatt (pub.), 416
Neurologic Society, 300
neurosis, adaptational, 245–248; character versus symptom, 433–434; hospitalization for, 378; latent, 290; marginal thinking in, 17; psychosis and, 39, 71; transference, 289
Neurotic Constitution, The (Adler), 84
neutralization, 480
New Orleans Psychoanalytic Society, 584
New School for Social Research, 25, 454, 553
New York Academy of Medicine, 584
New York City College, 211
New York Institute for Child Guidance, 591
New York Medical Journal, 549
New York Psychiatric Institute, 591
New York Psychoanalytic Institute, 156–157, 222, 470, 485, 492, 495, 553, 557, 569, 571, 584
New York Psychoanalytic Society, 27, 156, 217, 243, 259, 498, 551, 553, 559, 579, 583
New York School of Psychiatry, 244
New York School of Social Work, 591
New York Society of Neurology and Psychiatry, 217–218
New York University, 211, 460
nightmare, 97, 99, 146
nihilism, 395
Nineteen Eighty-Four (Orwell), 420
Ninth International Psychoanalytic Congress, 289
nipple, castration complex and, 324
nonego ego, 292
nonneurotic (ideal) man, 37
Notes about the Knowledge of Human Beings (Sachs), 197
Nottingham University, 265
Nürnberg Congress, 24

object cathexis, 152, 191
object-libido, 72
object loss, 207, 371
object relationships, 290
obsessional neuroses, 6
odors, significance of, 215–216
Oedipus complex or situation, 41, 45–46, 81, 107, 115, 124, 131, 140, 165, 170, 193, 207, 254–255, 278, 326, 339, 365, 371–372, 386, 405, 410, 454, 473
Oedipus myth, 8, 41, 74
Of Love and Lust (Reik), 259
Old Testament, 174, 251, 402
olfactory hallucinations, 216
omnipotence, 17, 245, 326
One Hundred Years of American Psychiatry (Zilboorg *et al.*), 555
On Love (Stendhal), 183 n.
On Narcissism (Freud), 72
On the Nightmare (Jones), 106–108, 113
On the Origins of Psychoanalysis (Freud), 494
On the Psychology and Pathology of So-Called Occult Phenomena (Jung), 64
optic perception, 462
oral phase, 165, 203, 433
organic dysfunction, 304
organ inferiority, 79, 85, 166
organ modes, 525
orgasm, alimentary, 245; masochism and, 258; wish for, 452
originality, 104, 111
original sin, 314, 370
Origin and Function of Culture, The (Róheim), 276, 278
orthophrenia, 325
Outline of Clinical Psychoanalysis (Fenichel), 439, 441, 562
overadjusted society, 398

paedoanalysis, 178, 343, 363–365
Paget's disease, 233
pain, pleasure and, 136
paleopsychology, 230
Palestine Psychoanalytic Society, 58, 201
Papers on Psycho-Analysis (Jones), 106
paradosis, 328
paranoia, 101, 260, 368; anal eroticism and, 16–17; in child, 364; hate and, 138; homosexuality and, 16–17
paranoia somatica, 238
paranoid delusions, 6
paranoid-schizoid position, 368–369, 371
parapraxis, 329, 459
paresis, 459

Paris Psychoanalytic Institute, 470
parricide, 254
passive-feminine role, 393
Passover laws, 207
"pathographies," 161
pathoneuroses, 21
Patients Have Families (Richardson), 590
pavor nocturnus, 97, 146
peace, war and, 84
Peer Gynt (Ibsen), 316
penal system, 220
penis, feces and, 113; loss of, 207, 403; unconscious meaning of, 204
penis envy, 7–8, 81, 139, 295, 297
People of a Strange Planet, The (Sachs), 197
perfume, 216
persecution complex, 238, 324, 332
perversions, 21
petit mal, 202
phallic phase or stage, 139, 203, 206, 403
phallic symbol, 410
phallus, rejection of, 403
pharmacognosy, 225
pharmacothymia, 245
Philadelphia Association for Psychoanalysis, 560
Philosophy of the "As If," The (Adler), 84
phobias, 32, 125, 289–290
pleasure principle, 136, 195, 240, 319, 326
poetry, artist and, 39; incest motif in, 41; orality and, 165
positivism, 84
postural behavior, 305
power, will to, 84
preconscious, 74
pregnancy, reaction to, 396
premature ejaculation, 7, 16, 238
primal fixation, 47
primal repression, 47
primal scene, 402
primal trauma, 47
primary drives, 79
Principles of Intensive Psychotherapy, The (Fromm-Reichmann), 588
prize fights, identification in, 219
Problems of Anxiety (Freud), 155
Problems of Psychoanalytic Technique (Fenichel), 446
projection, 215, 292, 366–368
pseudologia fantastica, 290
psyche, in coitus and in sleep, 18
Psychiatric Neurological Institute, Moscow, 201
psychiatry, psychoanalysis and, 457–468
psychic conflict, 39
psychic physiognomy, 195
psychic suicide, 216–217
psychic trauma, *see* trauma
psychoanalysis, in art, 494–495; attacks on, 589; body illness and, 303; "cult" of, 117; in education, 342–347; "encyclopedia" of, 439–449; ethical basis of, 341; faith and, 169–178; first instructor in, 101; medicine and, 594; mental hygiene and, 333–341; psychiatry and, 457–468; psychotherapy and, 167; recogition for, 66; sanitarium treatment and, 379; semantic innovations in, 240; "spreading" of, 193; as status symbol, 570–571; teaching of, 577–579; in United States, 546–595; *see also* analysis; paedoanalysis
Psychoanalysis and Moral Values (Hartmann), 481
Psychoanalysis and the Drama (Jelliffe), 233
Psychoanalysis and the Family Neurosis (Grotjahn), 590–591
Psychoanalysis: Its Theory and Application (Brill), 215
Psychoanalysis of Children (Klein), 364, 538
Psychoanalysis of the Neuroses (H. Deutsch), 286, 289, 292 n.
Psychoanalysis Today (Lorand), 30
Psychoanalytic Ambulatorium, 286
Psycho-Analytic Approach to Juvenile Delinquency, The (Friedländer), 517
Psychoanalytic Association of New York, 583
psychoanalytic education, 169–178
Psychoanalytic Experience within the Public Schools (Zulliger), 171
Psychoanalytic Explorations in Art (Kris), 494
Psychoanalytic Institute of Vienna, *see* Vienna Psychoanalytic Society
Psychoanalytic Method, The (Pfister), 175

Psychoanalytic Observations from Public Schools (Zulliger), 346
"psychoanalytic psychotherapy," 581
Psychoanalytic Quarterly, The, 27 n.
Psychoanalytic Reader, The (Fliess), 236
psychoanalytic research, 87–88, 395–396
Psychoanalytic Review, 225
Psychoanalytic Society of Palestine, *see* Palestine Psychoanalytic Society
Psycho-Analytic Studies on Character Development (Abraham), 433
Psychoanalytic Study of the Child, The (pub.), 470, 485, 516
psychoanalytic technique, 260, 501–508
Psychoanalytic Technique (Rank), 48
psychoanalytic theory, foundations of, 339
Psychoanalytic Theory of Neuroses, The (Fenichel), 442, 447
psychoanalytic training, 51–62, 554, 577–579
Psychoanalytic Year Book, 11
Psychoanalytische Volksbuch, Das (Federn), 149, 152
psychodrama, 319
psycho-hygiene, 333
psychology, clinical, 569; medical, 101; "new," 535; person-to-person, 544
Psychology of Dementia Praecox, The (Jung), 64, 66, 213, 231, 548–549
Psychology of Sex Relations, The (Reik), 259–260
Psychology of Women, The (H. Deutsch), 282, 293–294
psychopathology, 16, 101
Psychopathology of Everyday Life, The (Freud), 122, 200, 310
psychosis, psychodynamics of, 7; theory of, 142–159, 325
psychosomatic illness or medicine, 85, 224–239, 300, 302, 308, 391–392
psychotherapy, 167, 581; group, 467
psychotic ego, 155–156, 380
psychotics, 154, 213–214, 324
psychotoxin, 66

Quislingism, 129

rationalization, 136
Raynaud's disease, 301
reaction formation, 166–167
reality and reality theory, 17, 246, 319, 480, 520, 524–525
reality testing, 155, 464
reconciliation, psychology of, 348
regression, 21, 47, 165, 193, 303, 326–327, 330, 389, 478
religion, 114–115, 165–166, 169–178, 219; as delusion, 328–329; myth and, 74; unconscious and, 193
repetition, 326–327
repressions, 82, 301, 327
reproduction, function of, 294–295
research, psychoanalytic, 87–88, 395–396
resistance analysis, 433
retrogenesis, law of, 323, 328
Revue Française de Psychoanalyse, 411
rhythmical repetition, 326
Riddle of the Sphinx, The (Róheim), 276–277
Ring of the Nibelungen, The, 316
Ritual (Reik), 254
role-playing, 391
Roots of Crime, The (Glover), 506
Rorschach Test, 170, 346
Royal Anthropological Institute, 46
Russia, psychoanalysis in, 200–208

sadism, 146, 166, 173, 409–410
salt, symbolism of, 114
San Francisco Psychoanalytic Society, 375, 428
sanitarium treatment, 378–379
Schilder's disease, 457
schizophrenia, 10, 21, 154, 215, 236, 319, 364, 368
schools, Freudian, 105
Schreber Case, The (Freud), 155
scopophilic instinct, 108
scotomata, 324
screen memory, 377
scybalum, 324, 331
sea, as mother, 406
Searchlights on Delinquency (Eissler), 358
Search Within, The (Reik), 259, 261
secondary process, 480
Secret Self, The (Reik), 259, 261
Seelensucher, Der (Groddeck), 310–311
self, unknown, 316
self-esteem, 86

self-hatred, 207
self-preservation, 381–382, 465, 477
self-realization, 74, 398
self-reliance, 128
semantic innovations, 240
semen, sexual significance of, 114
sensations, 462–463
separation anxiety, 47, 206, 371
Sex and Character (Weininger), 37
sex differences, 467
sex fantasy, 409
sex play, 206
sexual instinct, smell and, 216
sexuality, female, 138–139, 164, 399–414; infantile, 67, 170; in war neuroses, 376
sexual process, biology of, 18–19
sickness, neurosis and, 313
Significance of Psychoanalysis for the Mental Sciences, The (Rank), 42, 44, 193
Sisyphus or the Boundaries of Education (Bernfeld), 419
Sketches in Psychosomatic Medicine (Jelliffe), 229
Sleep Walking and Moon Walking (Sadger), 231
slips of the tongue, 214
smell, sense of, 215–216
snake symbolism, 113
Social Aspects of Psychoanalysis (Jones), 131
social compliance, 481
Society for *Free* Psychoanalysis, 83
Society for Individual Psychology, 83
Society of Social Democratic Physicians, 149
sociological problems, 24
somatic defect, 79
son, rebellion of, 40
son–father relationships, 111, 254
"sphere," experiences of, 466–467
sphincter morale, 21
"splitting," in infant, 367–368
sport, psychology of, 292
Sprüche in Reimen (Goethe), 189
Studies on Hysteria (Freud & Breuer), 64
style of life, 84
sublimation, 111–112, 136, 291, 480
suicide, 37, 109, 125, 207, 221, 235–236; psychic, 216–217
superego, 21, 137, 165, 189, 205, 268, 290, 328, 349, 364, 376, 380, 479; female, 193, 296
Surprise and the Psychoanalyst (Reik), 257
Swiss Organization of Psychological Warfare, 345
Swiss Society for Psychoanalysis, 170, 172, 318, 346
symbols and symbolism, 74–75, 108, 112, 136, 317, 319, 401, 410; in Poe's works, 406–410
symptom-complex, 204
symptom neurosis, 433

Tavistock Clinic, 541–542
teaching, *see* training
technique, theory of, 260, 501–508
Technique of Psychoanalysis, The (Glover), 506
teleology, 74, 82
telepathy, 124, 126, 146, 290
Tempest, The (Shakespeare), 195–196
Temptation, The (Reik), 262
Temptation of St. Anthony, The (Flaubert), 253
tension, posture and, 305–306
Textbook of Psychiatry (Bleuler), 213
Thalassa: A Theory of Genitality (Ferenczi), 18
therapeutic situation, 388–391
Therapeutic Values in Play Activities (Zulliger), 346
therapy, active, 19–22
Three Essays on the Theory of Sexuality (Freud), 18, 231, 549–550
tics, 7, 21, 165
tonic stages, 326
Totem and Taboo (Freud), 69, 76, 105 n., 131, 274–275
totemism, 69
toxin, 66
tragedy, poetry and, 39
training, psychoanalytic, 51–62, 554, 577–579
Training Committee, 56, 538–539, 541
transference, 86, 155, 213, 246, 293–294, 314, 327, 338, 349–350, 352, 355–356, 378, 389–390, 434
transference neurosis, 289

trauma, birth, 45, 419; cultural, 277; illness and, 309
Trauma of Birth, The (Rank), 11, 36, 44–45
traveling, symbolism of, 113
truth, 329
Tulane University, 572, 584

unconscious, 17–18, 74, 466; archaic, 69; artist and, 317; civilized life and, 193; collective, 74–75; infancy and, 365–372; language of, 313
United States, new psychoanalytic associations in, 562–563; psychiatry in the Services, 563, 577; psychoanalysis in, 546–595
universal man, 484–499
University Hospital, Berlin, 200
University of London Board of Studies for Comparative Philology, 128
Unknown Self, The (Groddeck), 316
urine, sexual significance of, 114

vagina, versus anus, 139; "awakening" of, 404, 452; cathexis of, 295; as ego, 295; prehistory of, 404; symbolism for, 113, 406–410
values, psychology of, 84
vector analysis, 392
vegetotherapy, 436
Verlag (publishing firm), 56, 58
Verstehende Psychologie (Jaspers), 472
Verwahrloste Jugend (Aichhorn), 350, 358
Vienna, University of, 41, 151, 160, 243, 249, 284, 360, 458–459, 470
Vienna General Hospital, 144
Vienna Neuropsychiatric Institute, 430
Vienna Psychoanalytic Clinic, 164, 180
Vienna Psychoanalytic Society, 33, 40, 81, 83, 145, 149, 154, 160–161, 202, 250, 253, 285–286, 350, 357, 430, 459, 470, 472, 489
Voices from the Inaudible (Reik), 262 n.

Wandlungen und Symbole du Libido (Freud), 69–71
war, "aggressive" versus "quarrel" types, 132; chess and, 133; peace and, 84; sublimation and, 132
War, Sadism, and Pacifism (Glover), 506
War and Children (A. Freud & Burlingham), 521
war neuroses, 6, 373–377
war orphans, 417
Washington-Baltimore Psychoanalytic Society, 556, 560
Wayward Youth (Aichhorn), 350, 358
Weltanschauung, religious, 165–166
Western Mind in Transition, The (Alexander), 395, 397
West Sussex Child Guidance Center, 516
will, Schopenhauer's idea of, 163
Willem Arntz Foundation, 322
William Alanson White Institute, 571–572
Winter Veteran's Hospital, 156
wish-fulfillment, 74, 237
Wish Fulfillment and Symbolism (Maeder), 231
womb, return to, 313, 408–409
women, bisexual constitution of, 81, 403–405; castration complex in, 164, 245, 404, 452; dominance of in American culture, 262; male dread of, 452; masochism in, 294, 405, 454; psychology of, 282–298; three types of, 405
World War I, 31, 42, 53, 93, 133, 147, 235, 250, 266, 278, 309, 341, 376, 379, 385, 422, 451, 469, 551, 563
World War II, 59, 133, 270, 375, 420, 447, 470, 539, 563, 575, 590

Yale University Child Study Center, 275, 485, 492, 496, 498
Young Man Luther (Erikson), 526

Zeitschrift für Psychoanalytische Pädagogik, 152, 205
Zentralblatt für Psychoanalyse, 81, 323
Zionism, 131, 416–418
Z test, 346
Zur Psychoanalyse du Kriegsneuroses (Simmel), 375
Zur Psychologie der Revolution (Federn), 148